U N D E R S T A

C A N A D I A N S

UNDERSTANDING CANADIAN SOCIETY

JAMES CURTIS
Department of Sociology
University of Waterloo

LORNE TEPPERMAN
Department of Sociology
University of Toronto

MCGRAW-HILL RYERSON LIMITED

Toronto Montreal New York Auckland
Bogotá Cairo Caracas Hamburg Lisbon
London Madrid Mexico Milan New Delhi
Panama Paris San Juan São Paulo
Singapore Sydney Tokyo

UNDERSTANDING CANADIAN SOCIETY

ISBN 0-07-549201-6

1 2 3 4 5 6 7 8 9 0 D 7 6 5 4 3 2 1 0 9 8

Technical Illustrations by Deborah Crowle

Printed and bound in Canada

CANADIAN CATALOGUING IN PUBLICATION DATA

Main entry under title:

Understanding Canadian society

ISBN 0-07-549201-6

1. Canada - Social conditions. I. Curtis, James E., date - . II. Tepperman, Lorne, date-

HN103.5.U63 1988 306′.0971
C87-095185-8

This volume is dedicated to the memory of John Porter and Harold Innis, who led the way in "mapping" Canadian society and culture. Their insights are still proving useful even as new generations of scholars revise them to fit a changing terrain.

c o n t r i b u t o r s

PROFESSOR ROD BEAUJOT
Department of Sociology
University of Western Ontario

PROFESSOR RAYMOND BRETON
Department of Sociology
University of Toronto

PROFESSOR WILLIAM CARROLL
Department of Sociology
University of Victoria

PROFESSOR WALLACE CLEMENT
Department of Sociology
Carleton University

PROFESSOR JAMES CURTIS
Department of Sociology
University of Waterloo

PROFESSOR MARGRIT EICHLER
Department of Sociology in Education
Ontario Institute for Studies in Education
University of Toronto

PROFESSOR JOHN HAGAN
Faculty of Law
University of Toronto

PROFESSOR EDWARD B. HARVEY
Department of Sociology
Ontario Institute for Studies in Education
University of Toronto

PROFESSOR JOHN JACKSON
Department of Sociology
Concordia University

PROFESSOR NANCY MANDELL
Department of Sociology
York University

PROFESSOR M. PATRICIA MARCHAK
Department of Anthropology and Sociology
University of British Columbia

PROFESSOR WILLIAM MICHELSON
Department of Sociology
University of Toronto

PROFESSOR MICHAEL ORNSTEIN
Department of Sociology
York University

PROFESSOR ROBERT PIKE
Department of Sociology
Queen's University

PROFESSOR LORNA MARSDEN
Department of Sociology
University of Toronto

PROFESSOR RICK PONTING
Department of Sociology
University of Calgary

PROFESSOR ARNAUD SALES
Department of Sociology
University of Montreal

PROFESSOR JOHN SIMPSON
Department of Sociology
University of Toronto

PROFESSOR PETER R. SINCLAIR
Department of Sociology
Memorial University of Newfoundland

PROFESSOR LORNE TEPPERMAN
Department of Sociology
University of Toronto

PROFESSOR MORTON WEINFELD
Department of Sociology
McGill University

PROFESSOR FRED WIEN
School of Social Work
Dalhousie University

PROFESSOR S.J. WILSON
Department of Sociology and Anthropology
Wilfrid Laurier University

c o n t e n t s

preface

This book is an introduction to the study of Canadian society. We asked twenty-one of Canada's most eminent sociologists to write about their own field of interest and specialization. Each describes the sociological essentials of a particular area of Canada's social life, how it has changed, and how it relates to Canadian society as a whole. They also discuss how Canadian society differs from other societies. The result is a feast of information and interpretations concerning changes in Canadian society and culture. We have enjoyed helping to prepare this feast, and we trust you will enjoy the result.

All the chapters are new and never before published. Moreover, many put forward insights and analyses that will not be found elsewhere. Unlike other textbooks that only discuss the prevailing, mainstream knowledge in a field, this book contains much that is novel, challenging, and even exciting. Unlike other sociology textbooks that present bits and pieces about a variety of societies to illustrate their arguments, this volume paints a complete picture of one society, Canada, showing how the parts fit together, how and why they change, and how the total society is unique.

The first chapter presents both sociological building blocks to get us started — some key concepts and a description of sociology's main goals — and an overview of the prevailing interpretations of Canadian society informing the chapters that follow. The sections of the book are ordered according to the major forces of change discussed in the volume. These are: Canada as demographic processes, Canada as class relations, and Canada as a sociocultural environment. Also included is a section that focuses on how social inequality, in its various forms, and the protests around it are motors of change for the society and culture.

Many individuals deserve our thanks for their help with aspects of this project. First thanks must go, though, to the contributing authors. This is their volume; it could not have come into being without their work. They handled their initial drafts and responses to our suggestions for revisions with energy and creativity, and in a real spirit of co-operation. To a person, our requests for revisions were met with good humour, often under strong deadline pressure.

Beyond this, our support from McGraw-Hill Ryerson was very significant. Fred Chorley, College Editor, provided the resources to bring our contributors together, along with moral encouragement and strong enthusiasm for the project. Pat Banning performed numerous editorial tasks for the book with grace, dispatch, and great effect; and Norma Christenson handled many clerical tasks in the same fashion. Also, Al Wain, a freelance editor, made the volume's prose clearer and more straightforward in many instances; we owe him a heavy debt for his editorial touch. At the University of Waterloo, Lorraine Thompson very ably kept the project moving forward in the mails between Waterloo, Toronto, and authors' locations from coast to coast. Finally, several reviewers provided many valuable suggestions for improvements in individual chapters or for the overall project.

James Curtis
Lorne Tepperman

UNDERSTANDING
CANADIAN SOCIETY

Introduction

The Fathers of Confederation at their Convention in Charlottetown, Prince Edward Island in 1864.
Courtesy of National Archives Canada/C733

> *"The social bonds of Canadians with other Canadians . . . differ from the bonds of Canadians with Americans (and vice versa). We need only consider the strong, shared attachments that Canadians and Americans have to different national symbols . . . to know that we are speaking of two societies."*

c h a p t e r o n e

Studying Change and Continuity in Canadian Society

James Curtis **Lorne Tepperman**

INTRODUCTION

The detailed descriptions of Canadian social and cultural patterns in the following chapters cannot be adequately summarized in a few pages in this introduction; the chapter authors will be allowed to speak for themselves. What we would like to do here, instead, is to (1) explain what is common in the sociological approaches taken by the different chapter authors, (2) define and clarify some basic concepts frequently employed or assumed by the authors, and (3) discuss alternative broad theories put forward to account for many of the social and cultural trends. We also want to place the volume's materials in the context of the history of Canadian **sociology** and sociology in general.

SOCIOLOGY AS THE STUDY OF SOCIETY

What is the sociological approach? ***Sociology*** is the science that constructs theories about the social relations that make up a society. This apparently simple definition includes four important elements.

First, the word **science** means much the same for sociologists as for physicists or biologists: namely, the careful description of the real world and the construction and validation of theories about the real world. A science of social relations is more complex than one concerned with atoms or amoebae. But, in principle, the goals of all sciences are the same.

Theories are, for sociologists as for physicists, tentative explanations of observable reality and the basis for predicting future events. Every theory is judged against competing theories in terms of thoroughness and economy of explanation. A science tests and retests its theories to improve and even discard them in favour of better ones.

Social relations are any relationships in which people's actions have consequences for others. People are bound together by these relationships. Therefore, the subject matter of sociology is also the *social bond*, which connects individuals in groups and societies.

Societies, then, are collections of social relationships. Canadian society is made up of all the families, clubs, groups, and corporations in which its members may participate. Seeing the boundaries of a given society is sometimes difficult, for many social relationships may span international borders, like the one between Canada and the United States. Indeed, some writers have wondered whether Canada and the United States, which are certainly distinct nation-states, should be viewed as distinct societies. Others have wondered whether the two have distinct economies. These questions come up, of course, because of the close ties of economic trade and ownership and the frequent flows of people, as travellers and migrants, between the two societies.

Yet *Canadian* society still is a meaningful entity to sociologists because, as you will see in the pages that follow, the social bonds of Canadians with other Canadians indeed differ from the bonds of Canadians with Americans (and vice versa). We need only consider the strong shared attachments that Canadians and Americans have to *different* national symbols—the one national anthem versus the other anthem, the one national flag versus the other, the Canadian Parliament versus the Congress, Canada's "mechanical arm" in the United States' space shuttle versus the United States' space program — to know that we are speaking of two societies here. Most Canadians share in the strong positive sentiments that the idea of "Canadian society" elicits; few Americans would do so. Moreover, the following pages will also show how Canada and the United States differ.

Kenneth Westhues (1982:18ff) has helped us better understand sociology's approach to society by comparing it with other similar activities. For example, he shows how sociology is different from journalism and history, which describe real events, as does sociology. However, journalism and history only sometimes base their descriptions on a theory or interpretation, and then it is often an implicit theory. Sociology is different. It strives to make its theories explicit in order to test them. Telling a story is important for sociologists, but less so than the interpretation on which the story is based. Sociology may be good preparation for doing history or journalism, but it differs from these disciplines.

Sociology also differs from philosophy. Both are analytical — that is, concerned with testing and refining theory. However, sociology is resolutely *empirical*, or concerned with evidence grasped by the senses, while philosophy is not. Philosophy has no greater concern with the internal logic of its arguments. Sociological theories must stand up logically, but they must also stand up to observable evidence in a way philosophical theories need not. A sociological theory whose predictions are not supported by evidence gathered in an agreed-upon way will not be accepted by sociologists, no matter how logical the theory may be.

Finally, sociology differs from psychology, which is also analytical, empirical, and interpretative. The difference here lies in the *units of analysis*. Psychologists study the behaviour of *individual humans* (or, sometimes, animals), and generally under experimental conditions. Sociology's subject matter is the *social relationship* or *groups of relationships* observed in nature. The family, the educational system, the media, the way work is organized, or the total society are the matters of inquiry. Sociology and psychology come together in a field called social psychology; but even this field is defined differently by sociologists and psychologists.

Sociology is also what people who call themselves "sociologists" do. As a result, the discipline has developed differently in different countries (see, e.g., Curtis and Petras, 1970). In some places, sociology has been more influenced by social psychology (e.g., the United States); in others, by anthropology (e.g., Great Britain); and in other places still by philosophy (e.g., Germany). In Canada, as Donald Whyte and Frank Vallee have shown, all of these disciplines influenced the development of sociology (Whyte and Vallee, 1985; Vallee and Whyte, 1968).

As well, much Canadian sociology was shaped by the study of history and political economy, particularly in French Canada (see, e.g., Vallee and Whyte, 1968: 833–52; Harp and Curtis, 1971:57–70). Whyte and Vallee, 1985). Even in some quarters of English-speaking sociology the connection with history and political economy has been strong for four decades. This approach began with the work of political economist Harold Innis (1894–1952) at the University of Toronto (see, e.g., 1930; 1956). It was then fostered in the work of his protegés, among them sociologist S.D. Clark (see,e.g., 1959; 1976). Through the migration of Innis's students to teaching positions elsewhere, this approach came to influence sociological work all around the country. Thus, it is little wonder that you will see close attention to matters of the political economy in the chapters that follow, starting with William Carroll's broad stocktaking of changes in the political economy, in Chapter 5.

Other important elements entered into the development of Canadian sociology. The British Fabian socialist tradition made itself felt in work by Leonard Marsh (1906–1982) in the 1930s and 1940s and, more importantly, the studies of John Porter (1922–1979) in the 1950s to 1970s (e.g., Marsh, 1940; and Porter, 1965; 1979). This approach set the enduring character of Carleton University's "school" of sociology, for example, and it has helped lead into Marxist-oriented sociology as practised today by Wallace Clement (a student of John Porter's), among others. Clement is among those who will illustrate the Marxist approach in this volume in his analysis of the labour process in Canada (see Chapter 6).

The Marxist approach emphasizes the struggle between social classes as the explanation of the organization of society, and the source of major sociocultural change. Here the political economy approach and the Marxist approach have strong kinship. Both study how the dynamics of the economy affect the way societies operate. A basic difference between the two approaches, however, lies in how much economic and social factors beyond the struggle between social classes enter into explanations of society and social change. The political economy approach is more eclectic in its explanations. Carroll's and Clement's chapters, along with Fred Wein's discussion of theories of regional inequalities in Chapter 4, will elaborate on these theoretical approaches.

At McGill University, Everett Hughes (1897–1983) introduced the "Chicago School's" approach. Instead of economic factors, this perspective emphasized how urbanization and industrialization were changing society's cultural values in a more "modern" direction (see, e.g., Hughes, 1943; compare Guindon, 1960; 1978:280–96). Economic processes were not ignored, but they did not have the central position held in Marxist and political economy studies. Hughes's teaching in Canada, along with that of other American-trained scholars over the years, linked Canadian sociology with this major strand of American research. We shall return to the influence of this approach in our discussion of S.M. Lipset's studies of Canadian cultural values below. Also, William Michelson's analysis of patterns of urbanization and their effects (Chapter 3), Lorna Marsden's chapter on the work world (Chapter 16), and Edward Harvey's chapter on technological change (Chapter 10) will illustrate the "urbanization and industrialization approach."

If sociology were all the specifics of what different sociologists do, it would be hard to identify from one "school of thought" to another and from one nation to another. However, the variation is not really so great when we stand back and look for the common elements listed above. Sociology is a particular inclination toward *studying and theorizing about society with the help of data*. Sociologists around the world can readily understand one another and make use of one another's findings. Without stretching the point, there is probably more unified thinking among the world's sociologists than between the sociologists and economists, or sociologists and psychologists, or sociologists and anthropologists, of any given country.

MACROSOCIOLOGY VERSUS MICROSOCIOLOGY

This book will emphasize a **macrosociological** approach, one which takes a holistic look at social relations. **Macrosociology** is the study of social relations against the broad backdrop of the whole society (see, e.g., Coleman et al., 1970; Clement, 1977). It involves studies of social relations embedded within the society and its history.

Macrosociology also looks at factors in social life that exist independent of any particular group of individuals (such as social change trends), but which may shape people's behaviour nonetheless. An example would be the way in which, currently, the proportion of young people who are completing university degrees is growing, accompanied by smaller increases in the number of new jobs available for university graduates. This means greater difficulties now for graduates seeking employment than in some preceding periods. There will also be more "underemployment" as current graduates settle for lower status jobs than did their counterparts in preceding years.

Microsociology, the other form of sociology that is practised, focuses upon individuals, and their beliefs, perceptions, and interpersonal interactions. It is the sociologist's version of the *social psychological approach* mentioned above. Microsociology looks at social life through the eyes of individuals, while macrosociology looks at life in terms of how society is structured and changing, and how this affects society members. Some have described this difference as the difference between studying social life "from the top down" (macrosociology) versus "from the bottom up" (microsociology).

Both types of sociology should be conducted because they complement each other in the types of information and theories they yield. We have opted for an emphasis on macrosociology in this volume because we want to know about the contours of Canadian society and changes in them. Macrosociology will best generate information on these topics.

Studies focused on individuals or small groups of individuals can tell us little about trends in the overall society. An example will demonstrate this point: since social relations are the core topic of sociology, both macro- and microsociologists have studied families, marriage, and having children. Macrosociologists would pay special attention, though, to such issues as changes in the birth rate in Canada. They would have found the rate has decreased markedly over time. Moreover, they might ask if the birth rate varies by region, and would ask why the birth rate is now lowest in Quebec, of all provinces, where it used to be comparatively high. Microsociologists might study, instead, what couples say about how they decide on the number of children to have. This research might be done through intensive interviews with couples in a local community sample. This micro approach does not allow us to know about historical and regional (let alone cross-societal) trends, except by adding together many repeated replications of the interviews over time and across settings. These replications would be so costly in money and time it would not be possible to conduct them, at least for the full range of aspects of Canadian society that we would like to know about. Without macrosociology we would be unable to learn much about the total society and the way it is changing. Yet without microsociology, we would be less able to understand the interpersonal dynamics producing these changes.

SOCIETY AND CULTURE

There is another side to social life that must be acknowledged at the outset. This is **culture**. An adequate sociological study of society can not go forward without considering culture.

What is culture? A classic definition by social anthropologist Edward Tyler runs as follows: culture is "that complex whole which includes knowledge, belief, art, morals, law, custom, and any other capabilities and habits acquired by man as a member of society" (Tyler, 1871:1). Thus, culture includes *ideas* that are shared by society members. Culture includes *meanings* that people learn from others. It includes **beliefs**, some of which are descriptive (for example, ideas about what "is," or "was," or "will be"), while others are normative (ideas about what "should be," "ought to be"). It also includes **values**, which are general criteria by which we judge people's behaviours. It involves **ideologies**, which are emotionally charged sets of beliefs that explain and justify how society is organized or should be organized. And culture also contains **norms** — rules, regulations, laws, and informal understandings.

Culture and society are intimately linked. They are different sides of the same coin of social reality. Society, as we said above, is made up of sets of social relationships. Culture comprises the ideas that are developed in the social relationships, and are fostered, taught, and learned through social relationships. Culture also helps determine how social relationships take place because these relationships are

THE RELATIONSHIP OF SOCIETY AND CULTURE

Clifford Geertz, a noted social anthropologist (1957:1), once drew the distinction between culture and society in these words:

> Culture is the fabric of meaning in terms of which human beings interpret their experience and guide their actions; social structure is the form that action takes, the actually existing network of social relations. Culture and social structure are then but different abstractions from the same phenomena.

guided by shared norms, values, and so on.

Because culture is shared by people, social relationships and society are made possible. For one thing, people can act predictably with each other when they share culture. Take automobile traffic on Canada's streets and roads, for example. Drivers know what to expect of other drivers, as well as pedestrians, on the basis of commonly understood rules of the road. We can make reasonably accurate predictions about other drivers' behaviours on the basis of what others *should* do according to the rules. Indeed, we routinely stake our lives on these understandings. And the social relationships of traffic run more or less according to plan, day in and day out. Imagine travelling in an automobile across one of our cities if we did not share such understandings!

We can take this conception of culture as *shared* too far though. Not all parts of a culture are shared by all members of the society. Some aspects of culture are learned and known by most of us, but other cultural items are shared by only a choice few. In addition to the rules of traffic, most of us know the meanings of such concepts as "money" (e.g., what a dollar will buy today), "work," "family," or "education." Very few of us, however, are privy to the information shared in the federal Cabinet; only some of us know much about classical music, or jazz, or blue grass music; and very few know how to fly a jet plane, perform a heart transplant, or build a house. In other words, for much of the culture that has been accumulated within a society, there are **subcultures**. These subcultures share some of the common culture with others, but not all of it. Without some shared culture, though, there can be no society because we would no longer have the social relationships that are requisite for society. And without social relationships and society there can be no culture.

The purpose of this volume is to describe major patterns of change and continuity in both society and culture in Canada — *sociocultural trends*. The second purpose is to spell out some sources of the social and cultural patterns.

THE PERSISTENCE OF SOCIETY AND CULTURE

Our society and culture are undergoing major changes, as we shall see, but they are also persistent. Why do society and culture exist and persist over time? Perhaps it is foolish to ask this question. After all, nobody has suggested they are about to disappear, except in observations that the Canadian and American societies and cultures are becoming more similar, and moving toward one culture and one society. Most of us take the survival of Canadian society and culture for granted. Yet it will be useful to pursue the matter briefly, because understanding why society and culture exist helps us to understand what they are.

There are two basic arguments for the necessity of society and culture, one based on a conception of human nature, the other on the problem of human survival. These are listed below.

First, the individual organism is helpless to meet its own needs at birth and for quite a while afterwards. People must protect and sustain it; otherwise it will quickly perish. What is required of the human organism is a complex learning process: to acquire the culture, to learn the things necessary to live. This must come from prolonged association with others, which means at least an elementary form of society.

From this, in turn, there is a derivative point. Through prolonged association with others (and especially after interaction is facilitated by the acquisition of language), the person begins to become attached to interaction itself. The individual is bound more firmly than ever to relations with others. The person comes to need to be loved and to love, to give and receive respect and consideration. We all come to feel it is painful not to be respected and not to have people close to us. Thus, becoming human means sharing in a social and cultural existence that is always more than physical survival.

The second reason for the persistence of society and culture is survival. Human survival in a sometimes capricious, often hostile, environment can only be accomplished if human beings act collectively. Co-operation can accomplish things no one could manage alone. From this perspective, society is a collective adaptation to a natural environment, a process of finding how to live co-operatively to make the natural order yield enough to sustain life. Through co-operative activity among an aggregate of people skills are acquired; knowledge is accumulated; techniques and tools are developed; and all are transmitted to the next generation through the culture.

From this argument come two other observations. For any society to exist, it must organize people; and sustaining organization makes additional demands on people to accept the requirements of a collective existence. Social organization requires co-ordination and control processes; procedures for assigning individuals to roles and tasks; and means to teach the culture, to produce people who can fill the roles well. A society is carried on by the actions of its members; each new member must learn what the necessary actions are.

Human beings, then, cannot even survive physically except through co-operation to produce food, protection, and care. This means *work* is a central human activity. Many sociologists believe this is sufficient reason for concluding the economy is the basic form of organization of any society, from which all else is derivative. The activity necessary to provide the material basis for life is required before anything else can occur in the society.

THE SOCIOLOGIST'S DATA SOURCES

The chapters that follow will quickly show that there is no one main source of data for the macrosociologist. He or she takes relevant information on the society and culture from wherever it can be obtained. All that is required is that the data truly bear upon the aspect of social or cultural life that the researcher wishes to study. The best approach, though, is to use as many different types of information as it is possible to obtain. When one finds evidence supportive of the same theory from different sources, the theory is given more credence because it is not likely that the researcher has inadvertently chosen data that are invalid for his or her purpose.

Macrosociologists work with two types of data, as do most sociologists, and each of these has many specific sources. These are quantitative data and qualitative data. *Quantitative* data are those to which number values can be assigned; *qualitative* data are those to which such values cannot be assigned. Some researchers regard qualitative data as a poor approximation to quantitative data, indicating a low level of understanding of the phenomenon under study. Others, however, regard qualitative data as capturing more fully and accurately the "meaning" of observed phenomena than do numerical measurements, where the latter are forced onto social reality. In fact, the more clearly interpretable data of each type we have, the better we do our jobs as sociologists. Each allows us to understand more fully.

By this last criterion you are in for a treat, an information and interpretation feast, as you move through the chapters that follow. They overflow with important information of both the qualitative and quantitative types and with theoretical interpretations to go with each of them. The data sources range, to name only a few examples, from Roderick Beaujot's (Chapter 2) and William Michelson's (Chapter 3) use of quantitative government statistics on fertility, mortality, and urbanization, respectively; John Hagan's use of crime rate statistics (Chapter 15); and S.J. Wilson's (Chapter 19) data on labour force and education participation by women; to John Jackson's (Chapter 11) qualitative interpretation of materials from the media and the arts; Raymond Breton's (Chapter 20) sweeping analysis of historical materials on French–English relations; and Marchak's (Chapter 17) qualitative interpretations of shifting patterns of ideological beliefs on how power ought to be exercised in the society, for whose interests. Marchak's data are drawn from general observations of what political organizations (and their leadership) have done and said over time. Then there is William Carroll's (Chapter 5) use of public data on who is a director of what corporation and which corporations are owned by which others; Michael Ornstein's (Chapter 7) use of attitudinal and census data on occupational and class differences; Robert Pike's (Chapter 9) use of quantitative data on educational participation rates and quantitative and qualitative measures of shifting elite values around education's role in the country; and Arnaud Sales's, Peter R. Sinclair's, J. Rick Ponting's, and Morton Weinfeld's use of qualitative and quantitative data on patterns of social conflict by, respectively, elites, classes, Native peoples, and ethnic groups.

Any source of information on the society and culture that helps one better understand it is "fair game" for the macrosociologist.

THEORIES OF SOCIOCULTURAL CHANGE

How do societies and cultures change? Robert Brym (1988) has recently reminded us that major writers in the early development of sociology left sociology two different theories on how social behaviours and, by extension, most social and cultural patterns are determined. One theory argues economic factors provide the basis for major continuities and changes in society and culture. The other theory emphasizes that cultural values and ideologies, independent of economic forces, are often the impetus for social and cultural change.

That both economics and values are influential is suggested time and again in the analyses of Canadian society that follow. It should be helpful, then, to describe the origins of these two theories.

Social Class Conflict Creates Sociocultural Change

The *economic* interpretation of social and cultural change is most closely associated with Karl Marx (1818–1883), the German economist. Actually, though, this interpretation considerably antedates Marx (e.g., Marx, 1859; 1964; Marx and Engels, 1848; 1962). Like most sociological theories with strong explanatory power, it has an ancient lineage. Most societies, even in the distant past, have had scholars that addressed sociological problems. For example, Pitirim Sorokin, an early student of sociological theory, found forms of the economic theory of change in the books of the Chinese sages (such as Confucius); in the sacred books of the East; and in the Christian Bible (1928:514ff). One finds it expressed also, and sometimes with great clarity and emphasis, in the writings of the Greek historians and philosophers. For example, Plato, in the *Republic*, said: "For indeed any city, however small, is in fact divided into two, one the city of the poor, the other of the rich; these are at war with one another." This captures one element of Marx's theory.

Unlike earlier theorists, Marx thoroughly analyzed the history of class relations and the consequences of class conflict for social change. He also studied the relationship between ideologies and social organization and change in a systematic way. Other distinctive features of Marx's theory are its clarity and the broad sweep of history and types of societies that it is said to apply to. Also distinctive is the great influence the theory has had upon social scientists and political leaders since Marx's time.

Marx reminded us, first, of the biological truism that one must eat in order to live. Moreover, he emphasized, in all but a minority of cases, one must work in order to eat. Factors involved in the production and distribution of food thus become paramount in human life. From a study of the history of economies, Marx confirmed that many people lack the food they want while some have more than others; there is always an economy of scarcity rather than of abundance, of a poor rather than perfect distribution of food. Marx emphasized that all societies develop ways of handling the production-distribution problems. These ways also get set down in norms, values, and beliefs which almost everyone follows—norms of barter, trade, exchange, and property. In other words, economics are both behavioural and cultural.

Marx believed that any changes in the ways and norms of the economy introduced additional changes throughout the remaining fabric of society. He believed the prime factor in social and cultural changes was the social class relations that people have with one another. Society is said to comprise always economic interest groups pitted against one another for economic advantage; class struggle is inevitable.

The division of society into social classes means, according to Marx, that there will also be sets of ideas—religious, political, ethical—that *reflect* the existing class positions. The ideas will tend to consolidate, or undermine, the power and authority of the dominant class, depending on which class they originate in. Yet the two types of ideas are not equally powerful:

> The ideas of the ruling class are, in every age, the ruling ideas; i.e., the class which is the dominant *material* force in society is at the same time its dominant intellectual force. The class which has the means of production at its disposal has control at the same time over the means of mental productions (Marx, [1845–1846], 1964:78).

However, oppressed classes, too, generate counter-ideologies to promote their interests, when they can perceive these interests. In times of major changes in the class relations, these counter-ideologies may come to prevail, become dominant ideologies. As Marx said:

> The ruling ideas of each age have ever been the ideas of the ruling class. When people speak of ideas that revolutionize society, they do but express the fact that within the old society the elements of a new one have been created, and that the dissolution of the old ideas keeps even pace with the dissolution of the old conditions of existence ([1845–1846] 1962:52).

In saying this, Marx suggested that ideas or culture shared within a subordinate class can affect social conditions, but this influence itself was traceable, he believed, to underlying economic conditions. He saw the ideological influences of any particular time as analogous to a "sieve," which filters economically predetermined social and cultural processes without affecting them appreciably. Ideas were, thus, a **superstructure** which arose from a more important economic **infrastructure.** It is within the conception of a total society that Marx saw class struggles developing and taking place; each class as an economic entity was stirred into consciousness and action by its objective position within the economic arrangements.

Marx also argued that class position determines "ideological advantage" or disadvantage for classes. The class holding the most economic power would have an advantage because communication of ideas flows from them, i.e., "trickles down from them," to the lower classes, and not vice versa. The ruinous controlling effect of the ideology of the ruling class is heightened by the fact that economic and political power go hand in

THE MARXIAN CONCEPT OF SOCIAL CLASS RELATIONS

Here are Marx's basic propositions in his own words:

> In the social production which men carry on, they enter into definite relations that are indispensable and independent of their will; these relations of production correspond to a definite stage of development of their material power of production. The totality of these relations of production constitutes the economic structure of society—the real foundation, on which legal and political superstructures arise and to which definite forms of social consciousness correspond. The mode of production in material life determines the general character of the social, political, and spiritual processes of life. It is not the consciousness of men that determines their being but, on the contrary, their social being determines their consciousness (Marx, [1859] 1964:51).

And in *The Communist Manifesto* we find these famous lines on the class struggle:

> The history of all hitherto existing society is the history of class struggle. Freeman and slave, patrician and plebeian, lord and serf, guildmaster and journeyman, oppressor and oppressed stood in constant opposition to one another, carried on an uninterrupted, now hidden, now open fight, a fight that each time ended either in a revolutionary reconstitution of society at large, or in the common ruin of the contending classes (Marx and Engels, [1848] 1964:200).

hand. To control the ideology of one realm is to control it in the other. Objective superiority in the class structure means also subjective superiority, the power of ideological exploitation. (It is interesting that Marx's own success as an ideologue helps disprove his theories that ideas are secondary, and that they "trickle down"; although, of course, he could not be expected to know how influential his ideas would become.)

In his later writings Marx gave a somewhat different argument, saying that *both* economic forces and cultural factors could affect change, that cultural factors had some autonomy in this regard (see Coser, 1968). Both he and his collaborator, Friedrich Engels, had set aside any simple idea that the economic infrastructure alone determined the course of all of the superstructure of ideas. He emphasized, though, that the economic structure was "ultimately" or "in the final analysis" a causal factor. This position is articulated in the following excerpt from a letter by Engels in 1890:

> According to the materialistic conception of history, the ultimately determinant element in history is the production and reproduction of life. . . . Hence, if someone twists this into saying that the economic element is the only determining one, he transforms that proposition into a meaningless abstract and senseless phrase. The economic situation is the basis, but the various elements of the superstructure . . . also exercise their influence upon the course of the historical struggle and in many cases preponderate in determining their form (1962:488).

In the later writings, Marx acknowledged, for example, that changes in mathematics and the natural sciences and, thus, perhaps many technological inventions were exempt from the direct influence of the economic infrastructure. This qualification took the Marxian view in the direction of the other major theory that we introduce to you.

Values and Ideologies Shape Sociocultural Change

The next theory says that various ideas that people share, and ideas that are not limited to norms of the marketplace, can also be powerful motivating forces in social and cultural change. They can be more important than economic factors, it is argued. Particularly important here are religious values and ideologies, but the theory is not limited to religious ideas.

Once again, we have a rich literature from early sociology which emphasizes this approach. In order to keep our discussion within manageable limits, however, we shall present only one early version of the theory, that developed by German sociologist Max Weber (1864–1920). This is an appropriate choice because Weber developed his theory in response to, and in partial contradiction of, Marx's theory.

In his study of *The Protestant Ethic and the Spirit of Capitalism* ([1904–5], 1958) Weber argued Protestantism had an important influence on the development of the capitalist economy. He thought the theology of certain Protestant sects, and in particular Calvinism, gave rise to a new "worldview" which greatly aided the development of capitalist activity in its formative period. While the theology did not alone produce capitalism, it reinforced its development.

Weber began by presenting findings from analyses of historical data. He pointed out that during the sixteenth and seventeenth centuries districts in Europe that were most highly developed economically were also mainly Protestant. He also noted that Protestants in various countries, regardless of whether they were a majority or minority group, appeared to show a special aptitude for commercial enterprise. The business acumen of Protestants, according to Weber, contrasted sharply with the limited skill and low value placed on economic activities by Catholics. Weber also drew attention to evidence from census data for German cities in the later 1800s that showed the "greater relative participation of Protestants in the ownership of capital, in management, and the upper ranks of labour in great modern industrial and commercial enterprises" ([1904–5], 1958:35). Further, the percentages of Catholic graduates from higher educational institutions, in contrast with Protestants, lagged behind their proportions in the total population. Catholics were also underrepresented in commercial schools; they seemed to prefer humanistic studies which were less appropriate for occupations in an industrially oriented society. For Weber, "the type of education favoured by the religious atmosphere of the home community and the parental home have determined the choice of occupation, and through it the professional career" (1958:39).

To explain the special affinity between Protestantism and capitalistic enterprise, Weber studied religious ideas back in the Pre-Reformation period, when economic activity was governed by what Weber termed "a traditionalistic" approach to the pursuit of economic gain. Business dealings were generally relaxed and highly personal. Usury was scorned. Profit was not actively or rationally (systematically) sought. Work was regarded as a necessary evil with little intrinsic satisfaction of its own. What was generally missing in economic activities was economic rationality. This was the basis of modern capitalism for Weber. In his words: "the rational utilization of capital in a permanent enterprise and the rational capitalistic organization of labour have not yet become dominant forces in the determination of economic activity" ([1904–5]), 1958:58). Weber maintained it was no coincidence that the change from traditional economic practices to capitalistic methods of business closely paralleled the great Protestant movements of the Reformation period.

It was "this worldly" ascetic form of Protestantism dominated by Calvinism and its related branches—Puritanism, Pietism, Methodism, and the Anabaptist sects—that Weber claimed was the seedbed of "the spirit of capitalism." Lutheranism was considered by Weber to have developed along different lines that more closely approximated Catholicism. The spirit of capitalism was defined by Weber as that attitude that seeks profit rationally and systematically with a feeling of obligation toward work and money-making. Weber added that this attitude no longer needed any religious justification, but when it first appeared it was met with a "flood of mistrust, sometimes of hatred, (and) above all of moral indignation" ([1904–5] 1958:69). It was totally out of keeping with the traditional way of life. As Weber said, it would have taken an unusually strong character whose motivation was firmly set by religious or other beliefs to withstand such social censure.

The key elements of Protestant beliefs isolated by Weber as the forces contributing to the development of "the spirit of capitalism" were the doctrine of the calling, the value of asceticism, and predestination. First, the doctrine of the calling was a central belief of all Protestant denominations, although its interpretation differed among them. The calling meant that by the decree of God each individual had been assigned a position in worldly labour. For Calvinists, this was interpreted as a moral obligation to be diligent in work activities for the greater glorification of God, whatever one's job. Since man's position was part of God's divine plan, it was one's religious duty to perform the "task set by God" to the best of one's ability. Work, therefore, became a positive value. For Lutherans, in contrast, work was not regarded as a moral duty reflecting the person's relationship with God; it was rather a fate which one must submit to and make the best of. According to Weber, the value placed on one's worldly work activities was generally missing in the teachings of the Roman Catholic Church, too, whose emphasis was more on earning salvation of the soul.

Second, Weber emphasized that the asceticism of Calvinists, Puritans, Pietists, Methodists, and Anabaptists did not allow the individual to spend freely the money that was accumulated through hard work. Luxury of the flesh was condemned (1958:172). Money could be used only for utilitarian purposes to serve the individual and the community. Therefore, monies in excess of the amount needed for daily life could be accumulated as savings or capital, and were available for reinvestment in business.

Third, Weber argued that predestination, which was most strongly emphasized in Calvinist theology, meant that by the decree of God individuals had been preselected for salvation or damnation. There was nothing the individual could do about this—either he or she was predestined for eternal life in the hereafter or he or she was condemned to everlasting death. Followers of the faith were, of course, anxious to prove to themselves and to others that they were among the elect. Since it seemed likely that God would bestow good things upon those whom He favoured in occupational or business pursuits, success was interpreted as a sign of election. Believers spurred on by their need to prove election were highly motivated to succeed in economic activities. Further, because any departure from the moral teachings would indicate divine rejection, or a sign of nonelection, Calvinists were prompted to systematically organize their lives and shun the more frivolous pleasures of life. According to Weber, the approach to life of ascetic Protestantism eventually developed into a "systematic rational ordering of the moral life as a whole" (1958:126). And this approach eventually permeated business affairs everywhere as economic rationality, Weber argued.

In summary, Weber believed these values and beliefs of the ascetic branches of Protestantism prompted believers to work hard, save their money, avoid self-indulgence, and attain material success to prove they were among the elect. The unceasing drive to acquire wealth as a sign of God's blessing, coupled with the compulsion to save, resulted in the accumulation of capital. As it was luxury, not business acumen, that was scorned, monies were carefully reinvested in business.

Weber pursued his theory further in a monumental set of studies of the world religions. One of his conclusions from this work was that the rationality found in capitalism was only one expression of a quite pervasive rationalism in Western civilization, and was not found in the classical civilizations of India and China. Weber traced its origins to the Hebrew prophet's concern for purposiveness and consistency in life.

Other Interpretations of Sociocultural Change

The works of Weber and Marx, coupled with research by many disciples of each, have made a good case for economic factors and values as sources of social and cultural change in various other sociohistorical contexts. Moreover, Canadian society, past and present, is no exception. The following chapters will add support to both the Marxian and Weberian theories from Canadian studies.

There may well be much more to the sources of social and cultural patterns than economics and cultural values, however. In particular, there are theories of sociocultural change which point to causes that lie in the *population* of the society. One factor often shown to be important is size, and changes in size, of the society. For example, an expanding population in any country brings many changes in the nation's economy in terms of markets and available labour; and a contracting population has effects of a contrary kind. Population pressures, actual or expected, have frequently been cited as the cause of wars. Differential fertility rates across social classes — where the capitalist class does not produce enough sons to fill expanding numbers of class positions — have been cited as a source of changes in the character of the capitalist elite (see, e.g., Tepperman, 1977).

Many other demographic phenomena also influence society and culture. These include, for example, the age distribution, urbanization, regional distribution, ethnic composition, sex ratio, differential mortality and morbidity rates, immigration and emigration, and many others. Changes in some of these factors cause uncertain destabilizing effects, and all of them have *some* demonstrated effects. Therefore they should not be discounted when trying to solve the problem of social and cultural change. The following chapters make this point in many ways.

A great deal of social and cultural change has occurred, too, through the invention and dispersion of new *technologies*. Consider, for example, all the social consequences of the telephone, automobile, or computer. These technologies have radically transformed our work and private lives. Technological change often leads to unanticipated, and sometimes uncontrolled, change. (The same is true of the invention of new "organizational tools," such as bureaucracy, the city, the nation-state, and rule of law.)

Now, technological innovations and demographic processes may involve values and ideologies and economics, too, in the final analysis. After all, some say, most inventions involve ideas put into material form for the purpose of profit-making; and differences in population size also mean differences in market opportunities and sizes of labour forces. These arguments are correct. But the demographic and technological examples mentioned above take us beyond the focus on the class struggle and religious values in Marx and Weber's work, and become themselves potential separate prods to social and cultural change.

THE FORCES OF CHANGE IN CANADIAN SOCIETY

As we have said, the explanations of change emphasized by Marx and Weber are still with us in Canada. This will be made abundantly clear in the twenty-one chapters that follow. Time and again the explanation for a particular social or cultural trend is found in influences flowing from the economic arrangements characterizing Canada, or in the values and ideologies subscribed to by Canadians currently or in the past.

Canadian Society as Economic Forces

Canadian researchers have documented the changes occurring in Canada's class relations and economy over time and leave no doubt that economic factors play a significant role in sociocultural change. All that is at issue is whether these economic forces are the *basic* impetus for change, as Marx argued.

We can ask whether they are basic in

two senses: (1) do economic factors lead to the most consequential changes for Canadian society and culture, and (2) do they ultimately cause *all* change.

A compelling case *cannot* be made for the economic fact as the root of all change. Even if we question the adequacy of contemporary analyses in the tradition of Weber's work (and we will do that in a moment), there are still the exceptions having to do with demographic and technological changes. It is difficult to reduce all of these effects to economic effects.

A persuasive case can be made for the less demanding criterion that economic processes have been the "most consequential" factors in social and cultural change. Consider the following list of social class dynamics and their consequences in Canada from Clement's work (1977:33; cf. 1975, 1977):

1. The implications of external relations for internal development, especially early colonial ties with France and the United Kingdom and current dependence on the United States in many economic, political, and military activities.
2. The persistently active role of the Canadian state in the economy and its fragmented federal-provincial structure.
3. The continued survival of two nations within a single state — the conquered French and the conquering English—and the near demise of the native population.
4. The role of immigration in filling the West during the early stages of development (1879 to 1914) and the urban centres of today (especially Montreal, Toronto, and Vancouver) which serve to build an indigenous labour force and domestic market while creating an ethnically diverse society stratified by class.
5. The persistence of enormous regional differences within the country, especially the underdevelopment of the Atlantic region and the northern sections of the central and western provinces.
6. The constraints imposed by geography, especially the rapids of the St. Lawrence River, the Laurentian Shield, the Rockies, and now the North.
7. The effect of technology and the ownership of that technology, especially patent rights, in shaping the economy and labour force.
8. The tremendous costs of transportation networks from early roads, canals, ports, seaways, and railways, to pipelines for oil and gas and their role in creating a national and continental economy.
9. The dependence on external markets, both as outlets for raw materials (making Canada vulnerable to world conditions) and as capital sources (which ultimately act as drains on capital).
10. The origin of Canadian capitalism in a staple economy, its movement into commercial and financial specialization, and its continued reliance on resource extraction.
11. The persistence of a petty bourgeoisie class as the most powerful class outside the capitalist class until World War II, prior to which Canada was largely rural and agrarian/resource-based.
12. The slower development of an industrial working class, the product of large-scale industrialization, which does not become a dominant force in Canada until well into the twentieth century and continues today to be

> rivalled in importance by the service sector of the labour force, especially the growing number of state workers adding to an already overdeveloped commercial section.

All of these twelve processes have already had profound effects in establishing Canada's social and cultural character.

It is true, of course, that writers in the Marxist and political economy research traditions emphasize different aspects of the phenomena in this list. Each sees things a little differently in terms of how economic change takes place. They all use interpretations rooted in the economic structure, but the details of a theory of change are still being worked out as more and more interpretative materials become available.

The literature shows, for example, that Leo Johnson (1972; 1977), following Marx, sees the relationship of the capitalist class and workers as the primary dynamic in the economic history of the country. Stanley Ryerson (1972, 1975) writes in the same vein, but he believes class dynamics alone cannot explain Canada's history; also important, he thinks, is an additional type of inequality—the "unequal union" between French Canadians and English Canadians.

Harold Innis (1930, 1956) argued "the character of the staples economy," based in extractive raw materials, was central in defining how Canada developed economically in the eighteenth and nineteenth centuries. While they do not disagree completely with Innis's analysis, Donald Creighton (1937), and R.T. Naylor (1972: 1–4; 1975) have emphasized instead the role of commercial capital, working in concert with the state, in facilitating Canadian development. Creighton and Naylor disagree, though, on the specifics of that role. Marchak (1983) emphasizes the staples theory when she studies the role of "green gold" in the British Columbia economy; she finds today the same inherent weakness of the staple economy pointed to by Innis in studying a much earlier time.

In most of the Marxist and political economy literature, the state is said to facilitate and justify the economic changes that occur. This implies a reasonably unified ruling class, comprising economic and political elites, as Clement theorizes in two major studies of Canadian elite members (1975, 1977a). However, this idea was not accepted by sociologist John Porter (1965). In *The Vertical Mosaic*, he denied the unity of the ruling class, and emphasized a plurality of interests within the economy, within the political system, and between the economy, politics, and other social institutions: the media, education, and religion. In a similar vein, Michael Ornstein (1985), beginning from a Marxist perspective, has surveyed recent elite opinion and found considerable differences in ideological views between capitalists and members of the state elite.

It is important to note, however, that Clement, Porter, and Ornstein all believe the most important decisions affecting Canadian society are *economic and political* ones made by *elites*. They are not made by ordinary people, and they are not made in other arenas — households, religion, or the schools. Arnaud Sales's chapter (Chapter 8) on public and private bureaucracies in this volume gives a comprehensive discussion of elite dynamics and their importance in determining Canada's fate.

Still other writers have given greater attention to *external economic influences* upon Canada, and to Canada's economic activity in other countries. For example, Gordon Laxer (1985) has used cross-national data to determine whether Canada had to depend on foreign capital because it industrialized relatively late. Comparing Canada to other equally late

JOHN PORTER ON THE INFLUENCES OF ELITES AND IDEOLOGY

In his monumental study of power elites and social inequality, *The Vertical Mosaic* (1965), John Porter was led to conclude that continuity and change were very much the result of actions, or failures to act, on the part of the *elites*. He saw no room for the average person to effect social change except by working through organizations that might ultimately affect the behaviours of the elites. Thus, organizations, such as unions and other lobby groups for vested interests, were essential weapons if average people were to have any effect on change at all.

Porter also, however, saw a real role for *ideas* in effecting social change, albeit through the elites. In his view, every society's elites work with some ideological understanding having to do with the proper future. These understandings shape the behaviours of the elites, and the masses, both in the present and in the future. In North America, this image of the future includes, for example, the notion that capitalism is for the common good. Porter saw a major difference between Canada and the United States in their images of the future, though. He believed that Canada did not inherit, through its history, an ideology that called for social equality to the same extent that the United States did. He observed that:

> Canada has no resounding charter myth proclaiming a utopia against which periodically progress can be measured. At the most, national goals and dominant values seem to be expressed in geographic terms, such as from "sea to sea" rather than in social terms, such as "all men are created equal" or "liberty, fraternity, and equality." In the United States, there is a utopian image which slowly over time bends intractable social patterns in the direction of equality, but a Canadian counterpart of this image is difficult to find (1965:366).

Since he sought ways of achieving greater equality, Porter would have welcomed the framing of the *Canadian Charter of Rights and Freedoms* in 1981, which he did not live to see occur. The Charter contains, of course, such goals as:

> Everyone has a right to life, liberty and security of the person and the right not to be deprived thereof except in accordance with the principles of fundamental justice (section 7).
>
> Every individual is equal before and under the law and has the right to equal protection and equal benefit of the law without discrimination and, in particular, without discrimination based on race, national, or ethnic origin, colour, religion, sex, age, or mental or physical disability (section 15-1).
>
> This charter shall be interpreted in a manner consistent with the preservation and enhancement of the multicultural heritage of Canadians (section 27).
>
> Notwithstanding anything in this Charter, the rights and freedoms referred to in it are guaranteed equally to male and female persons (section 28).

Porter would have emphasized that such goals reflect, and will reinforce, the multicultural themes in Canadian culture. He would also have been quick to point out, though, that the Charter does *not* contains certain other equality goals that might have been in it if the society's prevailing ideology was different. For example, it does not guarantee equality of opportunity for higher education (the basic avenue to higher incomes in Canada). It does not guarantee free university education for those who wish it but cannot afford it. Nor does the Charter (1) place limitations upon how much wealth one person or group can accumulate to the disadvantage of others, or (2) establish a minimum level of economic well-being and security for the poor. These remain questions of counter-ideology, not dominant ideology.

industrializers convinces him the problem does not lie there, but in the failure to develop strategic industries (especially military industries) and the weakness of anti-elitist agrarian movements in late nineteenth century Canada.

Jorge Niosi (1985) has emphasized that, at the same time that American multinational corporations are increasing their command of the Canadian economy with profits earned in Canada, Canadian-owned multinationals are behaving in the very same ways elsewhere. In his analyses in this volume (Chapter 5) and elsewhere, Carroll (see also 1985 and 1987) extends this perspective to show how Canada is a secondary imperialist region of a complex international capitalist system. His chapter shows the Canadian economy can only be fully understood when placed in an international system of capital accumulation.

Canadian Society as Central Values

Now let's consider how values may have been involved in social and cultural changes in Canada. The most sustained study of this topic has been by Seymour M. Lipset, an American-based sociologist who once lived and taught in Canada (see 1963a; 1963b; 1964; 1965; 1970; 1972; 1985; 1986). Beyond its comprehensiveness, his work provides a focus for our discussion because he explicitly places his analyses in the Weberian tradition of comparative studies of the influence of values (see, e.g., Lipset, 1964:173–74; 1970:37–39; 1986:115–20). If anyone can be said to have applied Weber's theory to Canadian society it is Lipset. We shall also criticize his studies, however, as many others have, because their results are open to alternative interpretations. Lipset's analyses will allow us to illustrate the importance of economic relations, population, and technology as explanations of cultural change.

Lipset argues Canada is low on the values that are most consonant with strong economic development, and certainly when compared with the United States. He concludes Canada may have been slower to develop than the United States because its value structure hindered advancement. From a wide variety of data, he argues "Canada is lower than the United States on . . . equalitarianism, achievement, and universalism" (1963:521) and that "Canada, with its greater stress on elitism and particularism than the United States, should be somewhat more collectively oriented" (1963:530). Lipset defined these values as follows: "A society's value system may emphasize that a person in his orientation to others (1) treats them in terms of their abilities and performances or in terms of inherited qualities" (achievement-ascription); (2) "applies a standard or responds to some personal relationship" (universalism-particularism); . . . (3) understands "that all persons must be respected because they are human beings . . . or emphasize(s) the general superiority of those who hold elite positions" (equalitarianism-elitism); and (4) believes that "a superordinate collectivity has a claim on the individual units within it to conform to the defined interests of the larger group as contrasted to the perceived needs of the unit" (collectively orientation–self-orientation) (Lipset, 1963a: 515–16, 530). Lipset also argued, as had some Canadian commentators before him (e.g., Wrong, 1955; Underhill, 1960; Naegele, 1961: 497–522; and Clark, 1962), that Canadians were more traditional and conservative than Americans. Canadians were said to be slower to experiment with and endorse change in economic, political, and moral affairs, and this was described as related to between-country differences in the other values (cf. Lipset, 1985; 1986).

Lipset goes on to hypothesize that the sociohistorical sources of such cultural differences lie in the respective political and religious origins of the two countries. The value patterns were said to derive from a counter-revolutionary past in Canada as opposed to a revolutionary past in the United States, Canada's need to differentiate itself from its powerful neighbour to the south, and the following for which there were no counterparts in United States history: influence of monarchial institutions, a dominant Anglican religious tradition, and a governmentally controlled expansion of the Canadian frontier. Lipset argued that once such differences in historical experiences "had formed the structure of the two nations, their institutional character was set" (1970:60), and events later tended to reinforce or maintain the differences. Lipset believes the value differences have persisted throughout this century to the present day, although he thinks they are on the wane (see Lipset, 1985; 1986).

This theory has received widespread dissemination and has helped to form Canadian and American sociologists' definitions of United States–Canada differences. Yet Lipset's analyses have also been critically debated, especially among sociologists in Canada. The different elements in Lipset's comparison of Canadian–American value differences have been accepted as accurate by most commentators, so long as they are applied to *historical*, or pre-World War II, differences (see, e.g., Porter, 1965; Chapter 1, 1967; Vallee and Whyte, 1968; Romalis, 1972; Crysdale and Beattie, 1973:9–12, 39–42; I.L. Horowitz, 1973; Clark, 1975; cf. G. Horowitz, 1966; and Truman, 1971), but several authors have explicitly or implicitly questioned the validity of Lipset's comparative observations for *recent periods* (see, e.g., Davis, 1971:6–32; Curtis, 1971; Truman, 1971; Romalis, 1972:211–31; Horowitz, 1973; Clark, 1975; Cuneo and Curtis, 1975; Goldenberg, 1977; Rich, 1976; Shiry, 1976: 3–58; Pineo, 1976; and Brym, 1986). The criticism has occurred largely because the evidence Lipset used has been evaluated as inadequate and imprecise.

Lipset examines evidence from educational, legal, crime, and divorce statistics (e.g., 1964:174ff; 1986:128ff). He notes the following comparisons: (1) proportionately fewer Canadians than Americans are enrolled in colleges and universities for the age cohort twenty to twenty-four; (2) the ratio of police to population is much greater in the United States than in Canada and there are similar differences in the distribution of lawyers; (3) far fewer police officers are killed in criminal action in Canada than the United States; and crime rates for particular offences against person and property are substantially higher in the United States than in Canada; and (4) Canada's divorce rate is significantly lower (see the chapters on education, crime, and the family in this volume). The first observation is given as evidence of greater elitism and lower achievement-orientation in Canada; the second and third points are said to show greater respect for public authority and the law in Canada and, thus, greater elitism and collectivity-orientation; and the last point is said to reflect Canada's greater traditionalism and collectivity-orientation.

Lipset has also compared attitudes to figures of authority, including political leaders, in the two countries. Americans believe in the equality of all people and the dignity of the ordinary individual more than Canadians, he contends. For example, all free men got the right to vote in the United States in 1845; they did not get the same privilege in Canada until 1898. Thus property qualifications (i.e., unequal wealth) limited the number of voters for a half century longer in Canada than in the United States (e.g., 1964:175ff; 1970:44ff; 1986:139ff).

Symbols of the pioneer experience in the two countries also came in for scrutiny. Lipset reports that mythology on the American West was full of rugged individuals—free-spirited, gun-slinging cowboys. Canadians do not imagine such wildness, he argues, when they think about the frontier. The Canadian West was dominated by the red-coated enforcers of the law, the R.C.M.P., says Lipset, and this is reflected in Canada's myths. Indeed, he observes the purpose of the Canadian state, according to the B.N.A. act was to secure the blessing of "Peace, Order, and Good Government," not liberty in the pursuit of happiness (e.g., 1964:183).

Lipset believes even political corruption, which many think is more common in the United States than in Canada, has its sunny side. It shows, for Lipset, the greater strength of the American people's wish to achieve and succeed. So much stress is placed on success that following the rules, which may slow the attainment of success, is comparatively weak (e.g., 1970:49). The same sort of interpretation is applied to explain the higher rates of serious crimes against person and property in the United States (e.g., 1964:176ff; 1986:128ff). Thus, Lipset's value analysis glosses over some of what is worst in American society, and, like the legendary philosopher's stone, turns dross into gold.

At the same time, Lipset portrays Canada as "lacking" on the following counts. Canada's labour legislation, Lipset says, is more restrictive than the United States' because it limits the right to strike to formally organized unions. Canadians are slower to invest in the economy or start a new business. They have less faith in free enterprise. Generally, Canadians are quicker to ask the government for help in achieving their collective goals. "Proposals for medicare, support for large families, government intervention in the economy, and public ownership of major enterprises have encountered much less opposition north of the border than south of it" (1964:178). These examples supposedly show Canadians have less desire to achieve or to realize their personal potential.

Canada's continuing ethnic inequality, the "vertical mosaic," is said to be another built-in restraint to Canadian achievement. This situation compares poorly, in Lipset's eyes, to the "melting pot" approach of the United States. Lipset points out that the Canadian census and, until recently, Canadian passports, have kept track of each person's ethnic origin. Canada's ethnic (and religious and regional) separation has taken its toll, he argues. Politically, for example, the "third parties" that have appeared represent narrow sectional interests, he believes. They have stimulated neither progress nor unity (e.g., 1964:180ff; 1986:142ff).

Many have doubted the merit of Lipset's arguments for recent periods. In some cases, they believe, the opposite conclusions could be drawn from the same data he cites. A few have attacked his way of explaining the observed value differences, arguing these differences can be explained by "cultural lag" if one assumes Canada is similar to the United States, but falls culturally twenty, thirty, or forty years behind it. By this account, one should compare current Canadian data with American data from the 1940s or 1950s to measure the true depth of cultural similarity.

Various plausible alternative interpretations, not necessarily involving recent value differences, have been offered for the behaviour differences. Among these is Horowitz's suggestion that higher U.S. crime rates result from the comparative absence in Canada of large-scale racial strife (1973:34; cf. Truman, 1971; Davis, 1971; Romalis, 1972). Others have attributed the differences to better policing and reporting of crime in the United States (cf. McDonald, 1976). The divorce rate differences of a few years ago and earlier have been described as a result of different laws, the latter based on value differences that held sway in previous periods, but not any more. The large increase in divorce in Canada immediately after liberalization of the divorce laws suggests Canadians' shared values concerning divorce were not well-reflected in the earlier rates or in the laws prior to their change (see this interpretation and the trend data in Pike, 1975; cf. Horowitz, 1973). The educational participation differences may not have been so much an indication of Canada's greater elitism as they were evidence that the country imported more of its training. Canada has had a history of reliance for much of its highly skilled workforce on other more developed educational systems, such as those of the United States and Great Britain (see Truman, 1971; Horowitz, 1973; Goldenberg, 1976). Also, Rich (1976) has argued that there are roughly the same proportions of persons with working-class origins among university students in the two countries. He has argued that some evidence of greater exclusion of the working class from higher education in Canada might be expected if the lower educational participation rates in this country were an appropriate measure of value differences regarding elitism–equalitarianism.

Economic Forces Lead to Values?

Even Lipset's theory on the *historical* differences in values and their sources is, it seems, vulnerable to other theoretical interpretations. If we look more closely at one origin of the value differences pointed to by Lipset—close government control of Western expansion in Canada and not in the United States — we arrive at an economic explanation.

Let's explore this for a moment as a Canadian example of economic forces of change. And let's do this by asking what might be the implications of Harold Innis's political economy theory for the phenomena studied by Lipset. Innis (1930, 1956) argued Canadian society must be understood as one small part of an empire whose control lies elsewhere. Canada was opened up—explored, exploited economically, and settled—in response to foreign demands for staple products: cod, timber, furs, wheat, oil. Thus, the westward march of Canadian settlement reads simultaneously as a history of British and American commercial interest in British North America, then Canada. No serious or successful attempt was ever made to keep out foreign investment or to plan the economy and society independent of foreign commercial demand.

With the growth of demand for a particular staple, the staple-producing region was quickly organized to extract and ship out that commodity. Social organization—including transportation and communication substructures, government-supported agricultural production, and other services — was hurriedly created on demand in company towns. With the decline in demand for that staple, the local economy, almost wholly organized around producing the staple, falls, impoverished, into disarray, and the supporting social structure falls apart. What follows is either deep and seemingly irrecoverable poverty, massive out-migration, or both. As a consequence, Canadian development has been very uneven, speeded up and then slowed down over time, and varying widely in degree from one region to another.

It is easy to see how such a society might spawn "conservative" values and beliefs. The governmental and economic elite were subservient first to British, then to American interests. This situation may have compelled them to be reluctant to take risks, and a dependency upon the government for security. Moreover, the elite would, in this situation, have been unlikely to promote the values of achievement and equality (and lesser respect for elite positions) as strongly as their American counterparts. The explanatory dynamic, in other words, may lie more in economic dependence and its effects on the Canadian elite, and not so much in the effects of political events upon average Canadians' beliefs.

There seems to be little disagreement about Canada's history. Even most Marxist and political economic researchers would agree Canadians have historically tended to lag behind Americans in economic risk-taking and technical innovation, nor would they deny that Canadians depend more on state intervention in the economy than Americans. There is certainly more room, though, for disagreement around the explanations of these differences.

The political economy scholars would also assert that Canadians have always had the psychological potential for change, and have on occasions fought free of enslaving myths and economic constraints. They would agree with Lipset that the value differences reflect realities not of Canadians' choosing and not easily modified. The precise source of the value differences, and whether the value differences continue, and will continue, is in dispute.

Demographic Effects

The Canadian-American value differences might be rooted, too, in demographic processes. We shall use this point to illustrate demographic effects upon Canadian society and culture.

The question "Why is Canada so conservative?" is not the same as asking "Why are Canadians so conservative?" The former implies we must look for an answer in the persistence of social arrangements, while the latter implies the answer resides in the minds and hearts of individual Canadians — that is, that each Canadian is a miniature version of the complete Canadian society and value system. This latter view is, we think, one of Lipset's mistakes. There can be a conservative Canada without conservative Canadians (and perhaps vice versa). Said otherwise, Americans transplanted to Canada might be, and seem, as conservative in their thinking and behaviour as Canadians; and conversely, Canadians transplanted to the United States might be, and seem, as progressive as Americans. The social structure sets limits to how much progressivism can be expressed and in what forms. The fact that so many Canadians have emigrated to the United States and succeeded like Americans suggests Canada does not thwart the thinking of progressive thoughts, only their expression in Canada. What we need, then, is to understand what it is about Canada that tends to conserve tradition.

The answer may lie in the size of Canadian society. In this country, in any given

THE IMPACT OF IMMIGRATION ON CANADIAN CULTURE

Another demographic interpretation of Canadian–American value differences worth considering is the different immigration experiences of the two societies over the past century or so (see Bell and Tepperman, 1979:90ff). Since Confederation, people born elsewhere have constituted 10 to 20 percent of the Canadian population; and since 1910 or so this proportion has been much higher in Canada than in the United States (see Table 1). Except during the Depression, every decade in the twentieth century in Canada has seen a great deal of immigration, with more than a million people migrating to Canada in each. Some decades have witnessed almost equally high rates of emigration to the United States and elsewhere. Such rapid turnover has kept the ratio of immigrants to total population high. If we suppose that it is the native-born population, and not recent immigrants, who are best schooled in the traditional, dominant values of Canadian society, whatever they are, then this would mean that the values should have more consensus around them in the United States.

Table 1

PERCENT OF FOREIGN-BORN POPULATION IN CANADA AND THE U.S., 1871–1981

	Percent Foreign-Born	
Year	*Canada*	*U.S.*
1871	16.9	14.0
1881	13.9	13.3
1891	13.3	14.7
1901	13.0	13.6
1911	22.0	14.6
1921	22.3	13.2
1931	22.2	11.6
1941	17.5	8.8
1951	14.7	6.9
1961	15.6	4.0
1971	15.3	4.7
1981	16.1	6.2

Sources: From various publications based on the censuses of the two countries; years of the U.S. censuses were one year earlier in each instance; i.e., 1870, 1880, and so on.

field of activity—economy, arts, science, or fashion—both the numbers of creators of new products and the buyers for them may be too small to support much novelty. Thus, the traditional standards, the traditional ways of doing things continue to get rewarded. The numbers are too few to support any particular "counter-institution."

Take, first, the numbers of creators. Because eccentricity is not well rewarded, people are less likely to enter creative fields in Canada; or, if entering them, are less likely to find financial and moral support for their efforts. Here, the state (in the form of agencies that give financial aid) is likely to be the greatest supporter of eccentricity. But there are serious limits to how far the state will go in this regard; for ultimately these agencies are answerable in Parliament at the lowest common denominator. For example, the amount of private funding for the arts—by patrons or foundations—is much more limited than in the United States or other countries and, conversely, the role of the state is much greater.

Take then the numbers of buyers. There are people in Canada to buy new products and ideas. But this market is small compared to the U.S. market. With the United States so close at hand, the creative person finds it easy and sensible to simply move across the border for access to a larger audience. (The U.S. audience for Canadian-based cultural products is small; whether this is because of poor distribution across the border or an American disdain for foreign creations is unclear).

The problem of indigenous buyers of Canadian products is complicated by the fragmented character of Canadian society. In Canada, loyalties to region and ethnic or linguistic group are strong. Francophone writers are virtually unknown in English Canada; Anglophone writers are often shunned in Francophone Canada. And while Ontario thinkers may be known in the Maritimes and Prairies, the reverse is rarely true. Thus, we start with a market that is already small, then fragmented by regional and linguistic loyalties. The real number of consumers for some new idea is perhaps a small fraction of all the people in the province in which it is conceived. It is not clear that there is a national audience, as in the United States.

Technology's Effects

We cannot deny, either, that there are technological explanations for the findings on changes in values discussed above (see especially Horowitz, 1973). If Canadian and American values have become similar over time—which even Lipset agrees to—or identical, this is in part a result of the effects of mass communication and travel between the two societies. These exchanges between the two countries have been made very frequent by modern technology.

Let's imagine for a moment that there were no telephones, no television or radio, no airplanes or automobiles. Would we expect highly similar cultures in the two societies? This would not be very likely. The more isolated the society, the more we would expect its people to develop and maintain distinctive ways of doing things. It is the easy movement of messages and people between Canada and the United States that makes it difficult for Canadian culture to remain unique.

These flows of messages and people between the two societies have astonishing magnitudes. One illustration is provided later in this volume in John Jackson's chapter. He shows how English Canadians apparently view much more television programming originating in the United States than in Canada. For French Canadians the pattern is reversed, but there is still a lot of American-origin material in their viewing.

Long distance telephoning shows much interaction between the two societies, as well. In 1985, Canadians made 35 billion telephone calls; about 5 percent of these were toll calls. Only about 7 percent of the toll calls were, in turn, long distance calls to the United States. However, even this small proportion constituted about 128 million calls, which is equal to *five calls for every living Canadian*. And this number ignores calls to Canada originating in the United States. Also not included is the amount of contact by other means of telecommunication. Much of this telephoning may be for business transactions, of course, but it is cultural contact, nonetheless. This type of cross-cultural contact seems to be increasing over time, too. For example, in 1975, there were far fewer calls in total, at about 21 billion, with 4 percent of them toll calls. The calls to the United States were 49 million for 6 percent of all toll calls. This was equivalent to only

THE TELEPHONE IN CANADIAN SOCIAL LIFE

Because we make so much use of the technology, it is easy to take for granted the telephone and its impact upon social interaction in Canada.

The telephone was invented in 1876 by Alexander Graham Bell, who went on to make the first successful long distance telephone call in that year—from Brantford to Paris, Ontario. Use of the technology spread quickly, and by 1886, only ten years later, there were thirteen thousand telephones in operation in Canada (Statistics Canada, 1986a:5).This was only the beginning, however, as the accompanying table shows. The numbers continued to increase until the usage reached sixteen million telephones within the past decade. About 70 percent of these telephones were in residences, with the remainder largely in commercial locations. There were enough telephones overall in the 1980s for over 60 percent of Canadians to each have one of their own.

The number of telephone calls has increased steadily over the years, too, for both local and toll calls. Table 2 shows that the 34.7 billion calls made in 1985 amounted to enough for over two thousand calls per telephone and over one thousand calls for each woman, man, and child in the country.

Table 2

TELEPHONES AND TELEPHONE CALLS: CANADA, 1976–1985

Year	*Telephones (in millions)* Residential	Total	*Telephones per 100 people*
1976	9.8	13.9	60
1978	10.7	15.2	64
1980	11.5	16.5	69
1982	11.8	16.8	68
1984	11.8	16.5	65
1985	11.3	15.9	63

Year	*Telephone Calls (in millions)* Local	Toll	Total	*Calls per telephone*	*Calls per person*
1976	21 301	918	22 219	1600	953
1978	22 987	1083	24 070	1586	1020
1980	25 501	1340	26 841	1674	1114
1982	27 554	1475	29 029	1728	1173
1984	31 205	1641	32 846	1994	1300
1985	32 926	1792	34 718	2173	1361

Source: Adapted from Statistics Canada, 1986a:16.

about two calls per year per Canadian (Statistics Canada, 1986a:16–17).

The number of people crossing the Canada–U.S. border is equally remarkable. In 1985, for example, the figure was 37.4 million person-trips from Canada to the United States and 34.1 million coming to Canada from the United States, according to Statistics Canada (1986b:76). Scheduled air flights only accounted for a small proportion of the 1985 figures, yet they reached 6.8 million person-trips from Canada to the United States. Also, air travel between Canada and the United States was surprisingly high in comparison to air travel between major Canadian cities (11.9 million person-trips in all). For example, there were 1.2 million person-trips between Toronto and Montreal, Canada's busiest between-cities route, while one million flights originated in these two cities and went to New York City (Statistics Canada, 1986b:120–21). Again, the trips involve both business and pleasure, but each brings the cultures into solid contact for influence of the one by the other. Given the much greater economic power and scale of American society, it would be surprising if it did not influence Canadian society more than vice versa (see also William Carroll's chapter for information on the flow of capital between Canada, the United States, and other nations).

The Book's Approach

The contributors to this book employ *each* type of explanation illustrated here: economic, values, technological, and demographic; but economic forces are cited more often than the other factors. And this is probably as it should be, given the results of Marxist and political economy studies in Canada. Imagine, for example, trying to describe the recent history of Canadian society without invoking any of the twelve economic processes listed above. It would be difficult, indeed, to make Canada recognizable to many people.

You will find, too, that many of the authors do not approach their explanations in a uni-causal way. In most instances, both economic and cultural factors are drawn upon, and sometimes all four categories of social change factors are employed. Margrit Eichler's chapter on changes in the organization of the family and family policy, Chapter 13, is a case in point. She begins by showing how trends in fertility, divorce, and marriage are similar across highly industrialized nations, Canada included, suggesting that something in their economic structures or their values caused the changes. Next she points to how culture, in the form of family policy and laws, has lagged so far behind the social organization and demography of the family that it has been inadequate to handle problems resulting from the changes taking place. Then she shows how the new technology around reproduction has the potential for drastically changing the way having children will be handled in the future. She reminds us that the employment of this technology inevitably will be shaped by the values and definitions of family life held by Canadians.

The chapter authors rarely invoke Lipset's theory of the uniqueness of Canadian values in their explanations. Where values enter interpretations, *other* values are employed. Only three authors find Lipset's approach particularly useful: John Hagan finds Lipset's theory helpful in explaining why Canada has more of a "crime control model" of law than the United States; Morton Weinfeld (Chapter 21) subscribes to Lipset's view that Canada is an "ethnic mosaic" compared to the United States; and Robert Pike (Chapter 9) finds the type of equality values discussed by Lipset to be important underpinnings of the organization of U.S. *and* Canadian education. Pike, however, suggests that, in some respects,

Canadian education may be more equalitarian (less elitist) than U.S. education. Nancy Mandell (Chapter 14) is critical of available evidence on Canada–U.S. differences in national identity without explicitly discussing Lipset's arguments on differences in identity. And, Peter Sinclair proposes an alternative to Lipset's values interpretation of Canada–U.S. differences in the growth of unionization.

The limited acceptance today of Lipset's value analysis is surprising, given the extent to which it has informed so many scholars' interpretation of Canadian social history. However, social values in Canada changed a great deal since the period in which the value differences were said to be formed. Though Canadians probably once differed from Americans in the ways suggested by Lipset, this must be much less true now. The decline of the British Commonwealth, expansion of the Canadian economy with increased control from the American economy, and the heavy impact on Canadian culture of the American mass media have all reduced Canadian–American differences in values.

Also, Lipset's research strategy was intended to, and does, "magnify" small differences between the two countries. When it comes to explaining sociocultural changes, our authors have not found these small differences very useful. They find much more utility in major social forces that are similarly affecting Canada, the United States, and other highly industrialized countries.

THE INDIVIDUAL, COLLECTIVE ACTION, AND SOCIOCULTURAL CHANGE

The forces of sociocultural change that we have been discussing probably sound fairly powerful and "deterministic." Even if we are not sure which factor is most influential in shaping a particular aspect of our lives, any of them can seem beyond our individual control. Sad to say, this is generally true. Can an individual, then, have an impact upon the future? The answer, surprisingly, is "yes, one can."

How can this be? There is a two-part answer to the question. Let's begin with the smallest bit of good news. It is an axiom of the sociological approach that we all affect our social environment and history while being shaped by it, however limited the effect may be. This message is contained in the theories of Marx and Weber and those of any sociologist who has built upon their work. C. Wright Mills, a disciple of both theorists, put the issue this way:

> Every individual lives, from one generation to the next, in some society . . . lives out a biography and . . . lives it out within some historical sequence. By the fact of his living, he contributes, however minutely, to the course of its history, even as he is made by society and by its historical push and shove (1959:6).

This set of facts alone will be little consolation, though, for those of us who wish we could substantially shape our destinies. Mills also reminds us of the second part of the answer. He emphasizes that one payoff from the "sociological imagination," from coming to have an informed sociological understanding of society, is that:

> the individual can understand his own experiences and gauge his own fate only by locating himself within his period, that he can know his own chances in life only by becoming aware of those of all individuals in his circumstances. In many ways it is a terrible lesson; in many ways a magnificent one (1959:5).

Mills adds "knowledge is power," if we choose to act upon it. That is to say, when we know what is going on in society, and then act accordingly, we stand some chance of maximizing our opportunities.

ASSESSING COLLECTIVE SOLUTIONS TO UNEQUAL LIFE CHANCES

In our society, a variety of social collectivities—workers' unions, professional associations, ethnic organizations, business conglomerations, and so on—use social organization as a tool for achieving greater advantage for their members. These collectivities can be successful solutions for the short run; they are creative adaptations in the competition for scarce and valued resources of better working conditions, income, wealth, and such. However, they are not successful solutions to the problem of inequality of access to rewards for the society; they do not provide a long-run or thorough solution.

The problem is that they lead to a situation similar to people watching a parade: first a few stand on their toes to see the parade better, then a few more, and so on; when everyone is standing on tiptoes, each one's ability to see the parade is as unequal as it was before, and still the people in the front rows see best.

Long-run and thorough solutions to the problem of unequal opportunity must be truly co-operative ones, involving all segments of the society. Anything else will work only for selected people for a while, and will result in continued economic and political conflict.

There are two broad strategies to be followed in acting upon sociological understanding: *individual-level coping procedures and group-based action*. Under the individual-level response, you act to "work the system" to your benefit. For example, if you learn some sections of the workforce are shrinking while others are expanding, you can consider preparing yourself for a job you would like in one of the expanding sectors.

A recent book by Robert Kennedy, an American demographer, emphasizes that we all have "choices" of this type to make. He says:

> Your power of choice means that while "society" or some mix of "social forces" may constrain your options, they do not entirely determine your life. . . . What the individual chooses to do at certain points in life can make a difference—personal actions have consequences. Opportunities can be exploited or squandered, difficulties can be overcome or compounded (1986:5).

You can also consider getting involved in groups or organizations—there are political parties and interest groups of all sorts. Some of these must have goals for social changes that you would like to see realized. Here, too, knowledge of your society and culture is a prerequisite for making good decisions about which groups and organizations are most appropriate to your interests. Your values and ideologies (which are socially derived, remember) will also determine your choices of goals and organizations.

History is made by people acting in groups and organizations. The chapters that follow will demonstrate this many times over for different areas, especially around recent social policy changes. Consider, for example, Margrit Eichler's discussion of the changes in family law (Chapter 13) that have been forced by reform groups, and those yet to come, by her recognizing.

Be warned, though, that this strategy of "political" action via groups and organizations can be a very slow road. And many of your journeys may be unsuccessful. The sociological approach that we have discussed also suggests that dominant interest groups which oppose social change will not likely give ground easily and, as Marx especially told us, they will have considerable organizational and ideological power. However, political struggles can be won. There are some recent examples from Canada and the United States of successful protest movements by subordinate groups—the civil rights movement in the United States, the "Quiet Revolution" in Quebec (see Raymond Breton's chapter [Chapter 20] in this volume), the women's movement (see S.J. Wilson's chapter [Chapter 19]), and "the revolt of pensioners" that stopped pension changes proposed by the Mulroney government. Also, an important case-in-point is the success of the labour movement in Canada and the United States over the decades in securing better wages and job conditions for the working class (see Peter R. Sinclair's chapter [Chapter 18]). Such developments should give us heart concerning the possibilities of political action. There *has* been some room to move, some room to effect change.

Let's proceed to the chapters, and see what characterizes the terrain in which you will choose to move.

DISCUSSION QUESTIONS

1. How would a macrosociological analysis of the Canadian family differ from a microsociological analysis? Give concrete examples.
2. How do society and culture differ? Define each, and compare them. Give examples from aspects of Canadian society and culture.
3. Defend or criticize Lipset's theory that there are contemporary Canada–U.S. differences in achievement values by mustering what you see as the most compelling evidence.
4. Suppose that Marx and Weber were able to read Lipset's account of Canadian society and culture, and later discussed it. What would each of them emphasize in the discussion?
5. Take any specific element of Canadian society or culture that is changing over time and discuss the extent to which the changes are likely due to economic factors? to cultural values or ideology? to technology? to demographic processes?
6. C.W. Mills argued that "every individual . . . contributes, however minutely, to the course of . . . history." Discuss this proposition.

GLOSSARY

beliefs ideas about what is, was, or will be (descriptive beliefs); or ideas about what should or should not be (normative beliefs)

culture shared symbols and their meaning, which are present in any society; includes all beliefs, norms, values, and ideologies

ideology descriptive and normative beliefs and values that either explain and justify the status quo in how the society is arranged (dominant ideologies) or call for and justify change (counter-ideologies)

infrastructure in Marx's theory, the basic economic relations of the society, which give rise to and shape ideology and other aspects of culture

macrosociology sociology that analyzes and theorizes about social organization or societies, and the ways in which they change and continue over time

microsociology sociology that analyzes and theorizes about individuals, their social psychological characteristics, and patterns of interaction

norms rules indicating how people are expected to behave in a particular situation; they may range from written laws to informal understandings

science the careful description of the real world and the construction and validation of theories about this subject

social relations any relationships in which people's actions have consequences for others

society largest-scale collections of social relations studied by sociologists (save for relationships between societies); includes all groups and organizations

sociology the science that studies and explains the social relations making up a society

subcultures groups of people with shared, more or less distinctive beliefs, norms, ideologies, or values that are shaped by the infrastructure of economic relationships

superstructure culture, including dominant ideology, that arises from the subculture of economic relations

theories tentative explanations of observable reality

values views about what are desirable goals, and what are appropriate standards to live by

BIBLIOGRAPHY

Bell, David and Lorne Tepperman
1979 *The Roots of Disunity*. Toronto: McClelland and Stewart.

Brym, Robert
1986 "Anglo-Canadian Society." *Current Sociology*, 34, 1.

——
1988 "Foundations of Sociological Theory." In Lorne Tepperman and James Curtis, eds. *Readings in Sociology: An Introduction*. Toronto: McGraw-Hill Ryerson.

Carroll, William K.
1985 "Dependence, Imperialism and the Capitalist Class in Canada." In Robert Brym (ed.) *The Structure of the Canadian Capitalist Class*. Toronto: Garamond.

——
1987 *Corporate Power and Canadian Capitalism*. Vancouver: University of British Columbia Press.

Clark, S.D.
1959 *Movements of Political Protest, 1640–1840*. Toronto: University of Toronto Press.

——
1962 *The Canadian Community*. Toronto: University of Toronto Press.

——
1975 "The Post Second World War Canadian Society." *Canadian Review of Sociology*, 12 (February):25–32.

——
1976 *Canadian Society in Historical Perspective*. Toronto: McGraw-Hill Ryerson.

Clement, Wallace
1975 *The Canadian Corporate Elite: An*

Analysis of Economic Power. Toronto: McClelland and Stewart.

——

1977a *Continental Corporate Power: Economic Linkages Between Canada and the United States*. Toronto: McClelland and Stewart.

——

1977b "Macrosociological Approaches Toward a Canadian Sociology." *Alternative Routes: A Critical Review*, 1, 1:1–37.

Coleman, James S., Amitai Etzioni, and John Porter
1970 *Macrosociology: Research and Theory*. Boston: Allyn and Bacon.

Coser, Lewis A.
1968 "The Sociology of Knowledge." In David L. Sills (ed.) International Encyclopedia of the Social Sciences, Vol. 8. New York: Macmillan and Free Press.

Creighton, Donald
1937 *The Empire of the St. Lawrence*. Toronto: Macmillan (1956).

Crysdale, Stewart and Christopher Beattie
1973 *Sociology Canada: An Introductory Text*. Toronto: Butterworths.

Cuneo, Carl J. and James Curtis
1975 "Social Ascription in the Educational and Occupational Status Attainment of Urban Canadians." *Canadian Review of Sociology and Anthropology*, 12 (February):6–24.

Curtis, James
1971 "Voluntary Association Joining: A Cross-National Comparative Note." *American Sociological Review*, 36 (October):872–80.

Curtis, James and John W. Petras
1970 "Introduction." In their *The Sociology of Knowledge*. New York: Praeger.

Davis, Arthur K.
1971 "Canadian Society and History as Hinterland versus Metropolis." In Richard J. Ossenberg (ed.) *Canadian Society: Pluralism, Change and Conflict*. Scarborough, Ontario: Prentice-Hall.

Geertz, Clifford
1957 "Ritual and Social Change: A Javanese Example." *American Anthropologist*, 59, 1 (February):32–54.

Goldenberg, Sheldon
1977 "Canadian Encouragement of Higher Educational Participation: An Empirical Assessment." *International Journal of Comparative Sociology*, 17 (3–4):285–99.

Guindon, Hubert
1960 "The Social Evolution of Quebec Reconsidered." *Canadian Journal of Economics and Political Science*, 26, 4 (November).

——

1978 "The Modernization of Quebec and the Lengthening of the Canadian State." In D. Glenday, H. Guindon, and A. Turowitz (eds.) *Modernization and the Canadian State*. Toronto: Macmillan.

Harp, John and James Curtis
1971 "Linguistic Communities and Sociology." In James E. Gallagher and Ronald D. Lambert (eds.) *Social Process and Institutions*. Toronto: Holt, Rinehart and Winston.

Horowitz, Irving Louis
1973 "The Hemispheric Connection: A Critique and Corrective to the Entrepreneurial Thesis of Development with Special Emphasis on the Canadian Case." *Queen's Quarterly*, 80 (Autumn):327–59.

Hughes, Everett
1943 *French Canada in Transition*. Chicago: University of Chicago Press.

Innis, Harold A.
1930 *The Fur Trade in Canada*. New Haven, Connecticut: Yale University Press.

——

1956 *Essays in Canadian Economic History*. Toronto: University of Toronto Press.

Johnson, Leo
1972 "The Development of Class in Canada in the Twentieth Century." In Gary Teeple, ed. *Capitalism and the National Question*. Toronto: University of Toronto Press.

——

1977 *Poverty in Wealth*. Toronto: New Hogtown Press.

Kennedy, Robert E., Jr.
1986 *Life's Choices: Applying Sociology.* New York: Holt, Rinehart and Winston.

Laxer, Gordon
1985 "The Political Economy of Aborted Development." In Robert Brym, (ed.) *The Structure of the Canadian Capitalist Class*. Toronto: Garamond.

Lipset, Seymour M.
1963a "The Value Patterns of Democracy: A Case Study in Comparative Analysis." *American Sociological Review*, 28 (August):515–31.

——
1963b *The First New Nation: The United States in Historical and Comparative Perspective*. New York: Basic Books.

——
1964 "Canada and the United States: A Comparative View." *Canadian Review of Sociology and Anthropology*, 1 (November):173–85.

——
1965 "Revolution and Counterrevolution: Canada and the United States." In Thomas Ford (ed.) *The Revolutionary Theme in Contemporary America*. Lexington, Kentucky: The University of Kentucky Press.

——
1970 *Revolution and Counterrevolution*. Garden City, New Jersey: Anchor Books, 2nd ed. (Basic Books, 1968, 1st edition).

——
1985 "Canada and the United States: The Cultural Dimension." In Charles F. Doran and John H. Sigler (eds.) *Canada and the United States*. Englewood Cliffs, New Jersey: Prentice-Hall.

——
1986 "Historical Traditions and National Characteristics: A Comparative Analysis of Canada and the United States." *Canadian Journal of Sociology*, 11, 2:113–55.

Marchak, Patricia M.
1983 *Green Gold: The Forest Industry in British Columbia*. Vancouver: University of British Columbia Press.

Marsh, Leonard
1940 *Canadians In and Out of Work: A Survey of Economic Classes and Their Relation to the Labour Market*. Toronto: Oxford University Press.

Marx, Karl
1859 *A Contribution to the Critique of Political Economy*. Moscow: Progress Publishing (1970).

——
1964 *Selected Writings in Sociology and Social Philosophy*. Thomas B. Bottomore, trans. London: McGraw-Hill.

Marx, Karl and Friedrich Engels
1848 *The Communist Manifesto*. With an introduction by A.J.P. Taylor. Harmondsworth: Penguin Books (1967).

——
1845–6 *The German Ideology*. New York: International Publishers (1930).

——
1962 *Selected Works*, 2 vols. Moscow: Foreign Language Publishing.

McDonald, Lynn
1976 *The Sociology of Law and Order*. London: Faber.

Mills, C. Wright
1959 *The Sociological Imagination*. New York: Oxford.

Naegele, Kaspar D.
1961 "Canadian Society: Further Reflections." In Bernard R. Blishen et al. (eds.) *Canadian Society: Sociological Perspectives*. Toronto: Macmillan.

Naylor, Tom
1972 "The Rise and Fall of the Third Commercial Empire of the St. Lawrence." In Gary Teeple (ed.) *Capitalism and the National Question in Canada*. Toronto: University of Toronto Press.

——
1975 *The History of Canadian Business, 1877–1914*, 2 vols. Toronto: James Lorimer.

Niosi, Jorge
1985 *Canadian Multinationals*. Trans. by R. Chodus. Toronto: Garamond.

Ornstein, Michael
1985 "Ideologies of Canadian Capital and the Canadian State." In Robert Brym (ed.) *The Structure of the Canadian Capitalist Class*. Toronto: Garamond.

Pike, Robert M.
1975 "Legal Access and the Incidence of Divorce in Canada: A Socio-historical Analysis." *Canadian Review of Sociology and Anthropology*, 12 (May):115–33.

Pineo, Peter C.
1976 "Social Mobility in Canada: The Current Picture." *Sociological Focus*, 9 (2):109–23.

Porter, John
1965 *The Vertical Mosaic: An Analysis of Social Class and Power in Canada*. Toronto: University of Toronto Press.

———
1967 "Canadian Character in the Twentieth Century." *Annals of the American Academy of Political and Social Science*, 370 (March):48–56.

———
1979 *The Measure of Canadian Society: Education, Equality and Opportunity*. Toronto: Gage.

Rich, Harvey
1976 "The Vertical Mosaic Revisited." *Journal of Canadian Studies*, 10, 1:14–31.

Romalis, Coleman
1972 "A Man of His Time and Place: A Selective Appraisal of Lipset's Comparative Sociology." In Andrew Effrat (ed.) *Perspectives in Political Sociology*. Indianapolis: Bobbs-Merrill.

Ryerson, Stanley
1972 "Quebec: Concepts of Class and Nation." In Gary Teeple (ed.) *Capitalism and the National Question in Canada*. Toronto: University of Toronto Press.

———
1975 *Unequal Union: Roots of Crisis in the Canadas, 1815–1873*. Toronto: Progress Books.

Shiry, John
1976 "Mass Values and System Outputs: A Critique of an Assumption of Socialization Theory." In J.H. Pammett and M.S. Whittington (eds.) *Foundations of Political Culture*. Toronto: Macmillan.

Sorokin, Pitirim A.
1928 *Contemporary Sociological Theories*. New York: Harper and Row.

Statistics Canada
1986a *Telephone Statistics*. Ottawa: Minister of Supply and Services.

———
1986b *Tourism and Recreation: A Statistical Digest*. Ottawa: Minister of Supply and Services.

Tepperman, Lorne
1977 "Effects of the Demographic Transition upon Access to the Toronto Elite." *Canadian Review of Sociology and Anthropology*, 14:285–93.

Truman, Tom
1971 "A Critique of Seymour M. Lipset's Article: Value Differences, Absolute or Relative: The English-Speaking Democracies." *Canadian Journal of Political Science*, 4 (December):497–525.

Tyler, Edward
1871 *Primitive Culture: Researches into the Development of Mythology, Philosophy, Religion, Language, Art and Custom*. London: John Murray.

Vallee, Frank G. and Donald R. Whyte
1968 "Canadian Society: Trends and Perspectives." In Bernard R. Blishen et al. (eds.) *Canadian Society: Sociological Perspectives*, third edition. Toronto: Macmillan.

Weber, Max
1904—5 *The Protestant Ethic and the Spirit of Capitalism*. Trans. by T. Parsons. New York: Charles Scribner and Sons (1958).

Westhues, Kenneth
1982 *First Sociology*. New York: McGraw-Hill.

Whyte, Donald R. and Frank G. Vallee
1985 "The Field of Sociology." In *The New Canadian Encyclopedia*, Vol. III. Edmonton: Hurtig Publishers.

Wrong, Dennis
1955 *American and Canadian Viewpoints*. Washington, D.C.: American Council on Education.

p a r t   o n e

Population and Places

Immigrants arriving in Canada, probably sometime around 1910. *Courtesy of National Archives Canada/PA 48697*

"The period 1895 to 1914 saw the arrival of three million persons.... The recorded arrivals for 1913 exceeded four hundred thousand when the base population was just over seven million. As a proportion, that would be like admitting 1.4 million immigrants in one year into the 1981 population."

c h a p t e r t w o

Canada's Demographic Profile

Roderic Beaujot

INTRODUCTION

Demography is the study of populations, their size, distribution and composition, and the immediate factors causing population change (births, deaths, migration). We are interested in the stock and flow of population. The stock, or the population state, is a picture of a population at one time, including its size, its distribution over geography, and its composition along a variety of characteristics including age, sex, marital status, education, language spoken at home, occupation, income, etc. The flow, or the population processes, changes population from one point in time to another. People are born, move around, and die. Demographically, these processes are called fertility, mortality, and migration.

In trying to understand how a society changes and its situation in comparison to other societies, it is natural to start by describing its demographic profile. For instance, in the 120 years since Confederation, Canada's population has increased more than sevenfold, while in the same period the world population increased less than fourfold. At 3.5 million, the population of Canada was very small in 1867. It was about one-tenth the size of each of the United States, France, or the United Kingdom. While Canada retains this relationship to the United States, it is now closer to half the size of France or the United Kingdom. This rapid population growth may have helped to increase Canada's status in the world community.

The study of population is closely intertwined with the study of society. One looks to the broader society in attempting to understand both the causes and the consequences of demographic phenomena. In addition, the study of population has a practical importance. To plan public services, it is important to know the nature of the population groups subject to these services. How many people are at retirement ages and how will this change in the future? How many single parent families exist? What proportion of the unemployed are secondary wage earners in their families? These are among the host of questions that are important to the structuring of social programs.

Because of these practical issues, the government of Canada regularly gathers demographic data. Censuses are taken every five years; births and deaths are registered in vital statistics. Immigration procedures also produce accurate statistical data. That leaves only **emigration** and illegal immigration to be estimated. In addition, many surveys chart the demographic situation. In 1984, the National Fertility Survey gathered information on childbearing and contraception, and a Family History Survey traced people's experiences in cohabitation, marriage, separation, and divorce. The federal government's Demography Division of Statistics Canada tracks the population's yearly changes. Internationally, the United Nations promotes the collection of demo-

DEMOGRAPHY AND POLITICS

A country's demographic profile also results from its political, social, and economic situation, and it would make sense to put the population chapter last in the study of a given society. For instance, the English–French duality in Canada has had demographic consequences. Writing in 1907, the French historian André Siegfried noted

> But the artificial unity which is the work of the Confederation has not solved the problem of the races. We must return to our study of their struggle. To whom is the country ultimately to belong? To the French, ever growing in magnitude by virtue of their philoprogenitiveness? To the English, increasingly reinforced by armies of immigrants? Rivals in numbers, but rivals also in their customs and ideals. . . . The *tete-â-tete* of Quebec and Ontario cannot continue forever. Whilst the Anglo–French antagonism persists in the East, scarcely modified by the years, a new Canada is being developed in the West (Siegfried, 1907:4–6).

In other words, the political struggle between the two groups had demographic consequences. The English used their dominance on the federal scene to promote **immigration** from the United Kingdom. The French elite, who were often also religious leaders, encouraged childbearing to retain the relative size of their group in Canada (*la revanche des berceaux*). For much of Canadian history, the English–French rivalry had a demographic consequence in terms of high English immigration and high French fertility. Now that the demographic "props" of this rivalry are no longer available, the sensitive questions involve assimilation across linguistic frontiers.

graphic data through censuses and surveys around the world.

MORTALITY

Long-Term Changes in Mortality

The earliest mortality estimates for Canada as a whole date back to 1831, when the **life expectancy** was 38.3 years for men and 39.8 for women (Bourbeau and Légaré, 1982:77). Today, only three countries have life expectancies below forty years: Afghanistan, Gambia, and Sierra Leone. Only over the last 150 years have serious gains in life expectancy been made. Data for Canada in 1981 indicate life expectancies of 71.9 for men and 79.0 for women. International data compiled by the Population Reference Bureau (1986) shows only Japan, Sweden, and Iceland, representing 2.6 percent of the world's population, have life expectancies higher than Canada's.

How did life expectancy in Canada increase from thirty-nine years in 1831 to seventy-six years in 1981? First, we must consider the changes in causes of death, especially the decline in deaths from infectious diseases like tuberculosis, pneumonia, diphtheria, scarlet fever, enteritis, and diarrhea. Even in 1926, when accurate national statistics started to be available, some 25 percent of deaths were due to infectious diseases, compared to 7 percent in 1984. These are diseases that struck at all ages; often the very young were particularly vulnerable. In fact, the biggest contribution to the improvements in life expectancy are because of the drop in infant mortality. Almost one in five children did not survive to age one in 1831, compared to one in one hundred in 1981.

The further analysis of why infectious diseases have declined brings us to consider the standard of living as well as medical knowledge. As a component of the standard of living, improved nutrition played an important role (McKeown et al., 1972). Poor nutrition increases the susceptibility to infection, and increases the likelihood that the infection will be fatal. The medical improvements relevant to infectious diseases have especially involved preventative medicine, including knowledge about the importance of sanitation, improvements in the care and feeding of infants, and the development of effective vaccines. Without going into detail on other causes of death, we can say that improved life expectancy has been a function of economic development and associated scientific advancement.

We turn now to some of the consequences of these long-term changes in mortality conditions. Improvements in life expectancy have reduced an important element of uncertainty in life, allowing people to plan realistically for longer time horizons. For instance, it is now more clearly worthwhile to spend many years on education, knowing this investment will not likely disappear through an early death. One might argue this longer planning horizon has boosted economic development. Thus, not only has development brought about improvements in mortality conditions, but the longer life expectancy has itself contributed to development.

To illustrate how life has changed through reduced mortality, consider the typical life cycle (Beaujot and McQuillan, 1986:59, 63). Falling mortality rates have allowed the vast majority of the population to reach retirement ages. The proportion of persons living to age sixty-five has increased from 32 percent in 1851 to 80 percent in 1981 (Nagnur, 1986:85).

Let us assume that at each year we could look at a "representative village" of one thousand people whose age structure and mortality pattern by age reflected that of the entire country. In 1851, the village of one thousand people would experience a death of a child under age one every month and a half, while in 1981 one such death would occur every seven years. Similarly, at ages one to four, a death occurs every 2.5 months under 1851 conditions but every thirty-three years under the 1981 conditions. Deaths of children aged one to four are now virtually nonexistent. From the perspective of the general practitioner for this village, assuming a professional life of thirty-five years, the doctor would see 465 deaths of children before their fifth birthday in 1851 conditions, but only six such deaths under 1981 conditions. Deaths of older people are now more frequent. In a village of one thousand people there would be a death of a person over age eighty every fifteen months in 1851 but every six months in 1981. The greater frequency of deaths of older people is because there is a higher proportion of older people in the population.

Life expectancy at age twenty reveals the proportion of adult life that might be spent in retirement. In 1851, having reached age twenty, an average person could expect to live another forty years. If retirement starts at after age sixty-five, the average person could not expect to retire. In 1921, people could expect at age twenty to spend 3 percent of their adult life in retirement, while in 1981 it would be 21 percent. Stated differently, in 1921 having reached age twenty, one could expect to work 34.6 years for each year of retirement, but by 1981 it would be 3.8 years of work for each year of retirement.

These demographic changes have had far-reaching effects on the attitudes of Canadians toward a number of issues. The family, perhaps more than any other institution, has been transformed by the decline in mortality. The orphan was a significant figure in much nineteenth century literature, reflecting the frequency of orphans in society. Under conditions of life expectancy similar to those experienced in Canada in 1851, 11 percent of children would have been maternal orphans by age ten, while under 1981 conditions such would be the case for only 1 percent of children (Burch, 1965). More generally, under high mortality conditions, a large amount of chance and variability are injected into human affairs (Ryder, 1975). For instance, in seventeenth century New France, an estimated one-half of couples would have lost a child before their sixth wedding anniversary, while now in only 10 percent of cases would a child die or leave the family by the fifteenth wedding anniversary (Lapierre-Adamcyk et al., 1984). Perhaps the greater role played in the past by relatives outside the nuclear family was in response to the greater likelihood of family disruption due to death. As death rates have fallen, the need for this form of insurance has declined as well.

Other social and psychological consequences of falling mortality rates are harder to measure. For example, our increasing ability to relegate death to the older ages of life has profoundly affected attitudes towards and customs surrounding death. Ariès (1974) traced the evolution of customs associated with death in Western societies and argued that modern societies attempt to banish death from sight to remove the reminder of the inevitability of dying. The increasing predictability of death allows us to handle it in a more businesslike and orderly fashion. Blauner (1966) argues that "the disengagement of the aged in modern societies enhances the continuous functioning of social institutions." That is, companies, bureaucracies, and other institutions can suffer from the sudden disappearance of a given person. By setting old people aside, institutions are less subject to this disruption. The problem, of course, is that while the disengagement of the aged may benefit society, older people themselves bear the social costs of this isolation.

The fall in mortality has also revolutionized relationships between parents and children. Many authors have pointed to the poor quality of care accorded to small children in premodern societies (Shorter, 1975; Stone, 1977). Much of this can be traced to the low standard of living in such societies, but the high infant mortality rates may also have discouraged the development of strong emotional bonds between parents and children. Parents resisted making large emotional investments in their children until they demonstrated their ability to survive. Thus, high infant mortality is a vicious circle: children are valued less because they are less likely to survive, and the lower emotional investment in children reduces their survival chances.

Children's views of parents must also have been transformed by changing death rates. Most children now expect their parents to live until they achieve adult status, and a large proportion can expect to interact with their parents as adults for as long or longer than they did as children. Indeed, for many, at least one parent may be dependent on them for as long as they themselves were dependent during childhood.

Because of the increased length of life, the various parts of the life cycle have become more differentiated and more strictly tied to age. For instance, the boundaries between middle age and old age have sharpened. In addition, new life stages have emerged such as the empty nest period, and for women, typically, a long period of widowhood. The empty nest stage between the marriage of the last child and the death of one's spouse is an important feature of contemporary marriages. By 1981 the average couple could expect to live together for fourteen years beyond the marriage of their last child. Interestingly, research suggests that many couples view this stage as among the happiest in their marital life (Lupri and Frideres, 1981).

The potential length of marital life has been altered considerably. If all marriages are assumed to end in the death of one partner, the average duration of marriage will have increased from twenty-eight years in 1851 to forty-seven years in 1981. In the mid-nineteenth century, only 6 percent of couples would have celebrated their fiftieth wedding anniversary, compared to 39 percent under 1981 conditions. When romantic love was introduced into Western civilization as the basis for marriage, the promise to "love each other for life" had a vastly different time horizon. When young lovers make a lifetime promise, they probably do not realize that it is for almost fifty years. An unhappy marriage is probably more likely to be broken when one faces a long life to "endure." The longer life provides the opportunity for a "new" life, including the possibility of a new spouse. In fact, the longer married life and the sharpening of boundaries between the various life stages may put an additional strain on marriage, as not all couples can adapt to the successive sets of new roles (Stub, 1982).

Recent Trends and Variations

One might think that improvements in life expectancy would end as the possibilities of extending life are exhausted. In fact, from 1961 to 1971, the male gain of life expectancy was only 0.9 years. However, there are two important differences in the trends as observed in 1981. First, the increases in life expectancy have gained momentum, amounting to 2.6 years for men between 1971 and 1981. Second, for the first time, the sex gap in life expect-

TRENDS AND CAUSES OF DEATH

The big killers are no longer infectious diseases but degenerative ones, in particular cardiovascular illnesses and cancer, as well as accidents. Data from the mid-1970s shows 55 percent of Canadians can expect to die from heart disease, 20 percent from cancer, and 6 percent from accidents (Péron and Strohmenger, 1985: 156). The years of life lost due to these causes are 5.4 for heart disease, 2.7 for cancer and 1.7 years for accidents (idem, p. 176). Over the period of 1971 to 1981, death rates due to cardiovascular diseases declined for both sexes and across all age groups. (Dumas, 1984:86). The same cannot be said for cancer fatalities. Despite the efforts to combat this disease, the situation has worsened, especially for people over fifty. Lung cancer is increasingly serious for both sexes. Accidents rank third as a cause of death, but for persons aged five to twenty-nine, accidents are the leading cause of death, accounting for 72 percent of deaths (Statistics Canada, 1986:179). Traffic accidents are the largest component of accidental deaths, and these rates have declined between 1971 and 1981 (Dumas, 1984:89). Several factors are responsible here, especially the greater use of seat belts, lower speed limits, higher costs of gasoline, and improved medical treatment of victims.

ancy has declined slightly between 1976 and 1981. This gap had increased steadily from 2.1 years in 1931 to 7.3 years in 1976, but it has since returned to its 1971 level of 7.1 years. The improved gains overall are a function of many factors, including the care of low birthweight babies, treatment of heart disease, and lower accident rates.

To further interpret the recent dynamics of mortality, it is useful to note differences across various groups by sex, marital status, and social class.

Males are more likely to die before birth, and at very young ages, which means the differences are not simply due to lifestyle or stress on the job. Females are the stronger sex from the point of view of survival. However, the biological advantages of females would probably account for only about half of the seven year difference in life expectancy. Three other factors need to be considered. Men are more likely to engage in unhealthy behaviours such as smoking, drinking, and aggression. Smoking has become more equalized by sex over time, but for people aged sixty-five and over, where death is more likely to occur, 25 percent of women but 71 percent of men have "ever smoked on a regular basis" (Péron and Strohmenger, 1985:137). Tobacco and alcohol use can account for 3.7 years of life lost for men and 2.2 years for women (idem, p. 178). The more aggressive attitude of males especially affects the likelihood of accidental deaths. The probability of a violent death over the lifetime is 7.5 percent for men compared to 4.3 percent for women (idem, p. 156). While some men suffer from more dangerous working conditions, the differential working patterns of men and women do not explain the mortality differences. In most cases driving to and from work is more dangerous than the work itself.

While men exhibit detrimental behaviours, women are socialized to admit discomfort and to solicit assistance. An interesting example of this occurred in the 1978 Canada Health Survey (Péron and Strohmenger, 1985:145). People were asked about their hypertension before the actual level of hypertension was measured. More men had hypertension than thought they did. For women, more thought they had it. Other studies have shown that women are more likely to see doctors, even for diseases where men have the most problems, as measured by mortality. Women are more likely to seek medical attention, and may have the habit of more regular medical visits surrounding pregnancy and children. Women typically take care of their husband's and family's health. Since no one takes care of the wives, they are more likely to turn to the outside help of doctors. For men, the "emphasis on being strong may lead them to interpret signs of illness as signs of weakness and therefore to suppress or to ignore them as long as possible" (Gee and Veevers, 1983:84).

The differences by marital status are equally important. Life expectancy data for 1981 suggests single women die three years sooner, and widowed and divorced women die five years sooner than married women (Adams and Nagnur, 1986). Single men had an eight-year and the widowed and divorced men a nine-year disadvantage compared to married men. The differences are mostly due to lifestyles. For instance, the single and divorced are more likely to suffer from cirrhosis of the liver, a disease related to alcoholism (Beaujot and McQuillan, 1982:46). Some authors have argued that being alone, without social support, is detrimental to health (Lynch, 1977). It is interesting that it is men who profit the most from the "tender loving care" of the marriage relationship.

With advanced medicine and medical insurance, one might expect that social differences in mortality would disappear in highly industrialized countries. That is not what happened. Using five income levels, Wilkins and Adams (1983:98) find those in the highest income class have a three-year life expectancy advantage for women and a six-year advantage for men over the lowest income class. In all likelihood, the environment plays a role in these social class differences; that is, the unequal living and working conditions. However, lifestyle is also important. That is, attitudes and behaviour harmful to health have survived longer in underprivileged groups, especially for men. Even though medicare offers universal insurance, important differences remain in the use of medical facilities. In part, persons of higher status are more capable of making their way through complex medical systems, and medical personnel may respond better to rich people. The higher mortality of lower income classes is partly a function of controllable causes of death, like bronchitis, pneumonia, and cancer of the stomach (Billette, 1977). Pamuk (1985) provides an interesting analysis of social class differences in mortality for England and Wales. In the post-war period, there has been an increase in differentials, in spite of significant increases in overall affluence and in spite of socialized medicine. Pamuk thinks the explanation has to do with available resources and behavioural patterns. For example, education determines not only a person's available resources but also their attitude toward health. This attitude, in turn, determines how effectively the available resources are used to prevent and treat illnesses.

Finally, certain medical advances have benefited women more than men. Deaths in childbirth have been all but eliminated. Also, more progress has been made for breast cancer than for cancer of the prostate. Here again, faster diagnosis may have helped the medical profession to make more progress on diseases that typically affect women. Sex differences in mortality show that sex roles affect the very chances of life and death.

We should note the low life expectancy of the Native population. Estimates for 1981 place the life expectancy of Registered Indians at 62.4 for males and 68.9 for females, a disadvantage of ten years compared to the total Canadian population (Rowe and Norris, 1985:32). Especially striking are the importance of deaths due to accidents, poisonings, and violence, which are in part related to alcohol consumption. The further analysis of these differences would bring into play the marginalization of the Native peoples, including the fact that they often live far from medical services.

It is useful to conclude with some implications for the health care system. We have clearly much on which to congratulate ourselves; life expectancy has progressed steadily and only a handful of countries have better health conditions than Canada. However, when one notices a seven-year difference by sex, seven years by marital status, five years by income levels, and the ten-year disadvantage of the Registered Indian population, there is clearly room for further progress. This analysis does not tend to point to "hard curative medicine" as the important factor that would reduce the differences. It is true that advances in neonatal care of low birthweight babies and in treatment of heart disease and of certain cancers has been important in the recent reductions of mortality. However, it is also clear that "doctors plus hospitals" does not equal health. Equally important are questions of lifestyle, especially smoking, drinking, and driving habits, and also the effective use of the existing health care system. This points to the importance of "preventative medicine," including public education on health questions. While we spend some 7 percent of our G.N.P. on our medical care, it can be argued that this expenditure is excessively aimed at the "doctors plus hospitals" part of the equation for improved longevity.

FERTILITY

The Trend in Fertility

The long-term trend in fertility has also involved radical changes. Measured in terms of the **total fertility rate**,[1] the average births per woman has declined from 7.0 in 1851 to 1.7 in 1985. But fertility patterns have not been uniform over time. In particular, the baby boom of 1946 to 1966 involved a departure from the long-term trend.

The long-term decline is probably best viewed as a consequence of economic development and the spread of new ideas regarding appropriate behaviour. Economic development has radically changed the role of children in the lives of parents. At low levels of development, children have economic roles as family help and apprentices at young ages. Also, children are a form of security against the uncertainties of life, especially those of old age. One might even say that alternative forms of investment were not available and thus people invested in children. With a radically changed economic environment, children no longer have economic roles at young ages. In fact, they pursue long years of schooling before entering the labour force. Thus, children are now a net economic cost to their parents for a longer period of time. Also, because of other forms of social security and investments, parents no longer depend on children as a basic source of security.

While there is much appeal to this "economic" explanation of the long-term trend, it is not complete. Fertility changes have not always coincided with economic changes. Fertility changes seem to spread

CANADA'S FERTILITY IN COMPARATIVE PERSPECTIVE

Canada is now among the "club" of rich, developed countries with levels of fertility significantly below replacement. It takes 2.1 children to replace one generation with the next, that is, one woman or two parents must have 2.1 births on average. In the 1970s, most developed countries started to have fertility levels below replacement. Compared to Canada's high fertility in the postwar period, the recent trends constitute a "baby bust." As of 1986, only eight countries, representing 3.3 percent of the world population, had total fertility rates lower than Canada's level of 1.7: Austria, Belgium, Denmark, Italy, Luxembourg, the Netherlands, Switzerland, and West Germany (Population Reference Bureau, 1986).

through societies much like new modes of behaviour or innovations are diffused, that is, through channels of communication (van de Walle and Knodel, 1980). The idea of limiting births within marriage and the use of contraception are innovations whose legitimacy has spread over time, although cultural barriers have sometimes impeded the spread of these new models of fertility behaviour. In Belgium, for example, lower fertility gained momentum sooner in the French-speaking population than in the Flemish group. And in Canada, French-Canadian fertility for a long time stayed above that of English Canada. For instance, among women aged sixty-five and over at the time of the 1961 census, those of English mother tongue indicated 3.2 births on average compared to 6.4 births for those of French mother tongue (Henripin, 1974: 10). Economic factors alone would certainly not explain this entire difference. Henripin (1975: 133) further estimates that among couples who completed their families between 1880 and 1930, the French mother tongue population had twice as many children as the English. This differential was reduced to 50 percent by 1950 and to 15 percent by 1960. In the 1971 census, French mother tongue women under thirty-five had slightly fewer children than their English counterparts.

Minorities sometimes resist the "penetration" of different forms of behaviour, including the adoption of changed modes of fertility. For instance, until the mid-1960s Native people had fertility levels that corresponded to traditional childbearing behaviour. Over fifteen years, their fertility changed from almost 7 to about 3.5 births per woman (Romaniuc, 1984: 18).

Patterns of Nuptiality and Childbearing

Demographers measure **nuptiality** by the average age at marriage and the proportion of people who ultimately marry. Contrary to popular impression, people married relatively late in the past century. Gee (1982) estimates that before the turn of the century, the average age at first marriage was 29.1 years for men and 26.0 for women. Average ages increased from 1851 to 1891, that is, during the early stages of fertility decline. In part, this was due to emigration of men to the United States, which reduced the availability of mates.

Over the first six decades of this century, marriage was becoming more popular and occurring earlier in people's lives. This was especially true in the post-war "marriage rush." The causes of this trend remain uncertain, but it seems a question of basic attitudes toward marriage and the family wherein people gave greater priority to this aspect of their lives. For instance, the 1950s have been called the "golden age of the family." Life was family centred, the roles of women and men revolved around their family functions, and we laughed at the comic character "Dagwood" for his inability to play these roles properly. For instance, only 11 percent of married women were in the labour force in 1951, compared to 56 percent in 1986. The availability of efficient contraception also made it possible to get married at younger ages, without waiting to be in a financial position to have children. Over the century, people were becoming less constrained by institutional and social pressures, and thus were more free to marry according to their preferences. That is, there was less concern about being "established" before marriage, so picking partners and the timing of marriage became more a matter of individual choice.

Until recently, this preference included marriage, and in fact relatively early marriage. In 1971, the median age at first marriage was 21.3 for brides and 23.5 for grooms (Beaujot, 1986). In fact, 30 percent of first-time brides were less than twenty. The popularity of marriage was at an all-time high in 1971, with only 5 percent still single at age fifty, down from 13 percent at the beginning of the century.

In the next decade the pattern reversed, with the median age at first marriage rising to 23.7 for brides and 25.6 for grooms by 1985. The average age at marriage tends to be a rather stable statistic, yet the figures for 1981 and 1985 demonstrate a year of increase for each sex, a change whose magnitude and direction are unprecedented in the history of Canadian marriage statistics. Not since 1940 has the median age of brides at first marriage been so high, and in 1985 only 10 percent were under twenty.

As in the immediate post-war period, but in the opposite direction, the changes have been general and rapid, affecting all age groups at once. Not only young people are suddenly less likely to marry, but older single people, too. The proportion remaining single to age fifty has changed from 5 percent to 12 percent in one decade; that is, virtually back to its level at the beginning of the century.

There is also an increase in the number of people living in a "post-divorce single" state. Formerly, most divorced people remarried. That, too, is changing. As a consequence, 20 percent of women and 26 percent of men are not "currently married" at ages twenty-five to thirty-four.

Not only are people less likely to enter legal marriages, but they are more likely to abandon them. A useful figure to cite is the extent to which marriages are terminated by death or divorce, since these are the only two ways of ending a marriage. Of the marriages that ended in 1961, 9 percent were dissolved by divorce, while by now 43 percent of dissolutions are voluntary. But we must not exaggerate the predominance of divorce. The 1984 Family History Survey shows that among ever-married persons aged forty to forty-nine, the number who have ever divorced or separated amounts to 19 percent (Burch, 1985:12).

While the interpretation of these trends remains speculative, it seems the greater likelihood of leaving marriage is related to the lesser likelihood of entering it. In both cases, marriage and the family are given less priority in people's lives. The delay of marriage and the lower likelihood of getting married is not because it is harder to get married than it was ten or fifteen years earlier. Mostly, it is because marriage no longer plays such important roles in people's lives, especially for women. Various commentators have spoken of a long-term change involving greater personal choice in many aspects of individual and family life (e.g., Lesthaeghe, 1983). While in the post-war period that choice included marriage, this is less true today. The choice now focuses particularly on the individual's personal fulfillment in a plurality of arrangements, including living single, living together, and living in marriages of less durability. In the past, one was constrained to live by one's choices. But now, if a given choice no longer provides enough fulfillment, it is considered legitimate to change to another.

If marriage can be abandoned, many have come to doubt its necessity in the first place. Of course, there is considerable acceptance of other forms of relationships. According to a 1984 survey, 21 percent of persons aged thirty to thirty-nine have been at one time or other in a nonmarital cohabitation (Burch, 1985:14). Most adults continue to marry and have children in the context of stable relationships, but the numbers who do not fit this pattern are becoming a significant minority.

Trends in fertility can also be read as an increase in individualism and a larger variety of alternate life choices. Fertility was at its post-war peak around 1961 at 3.8 births per woman on average; the sharpest decline was to 2.8 in 1966, but by 1972 the figure was below the replacement level of 2.1, and in 1985 it stands at 1.7 births per woman.

In analyzing the situation further, it is useful to concentrate on married women aged twenty-five to thirty-four, since these are the prime ages for childbearing. In 1961, these women had an average of 2.5 children, but by 1981 they had 1.6 children. In 1961, only 12 percent had no children, but two decades later 22 percent were childless. Thus not only are 20 percent of women aged twenty-five to thirty-four unmarried, but among the married another 22 percent have no children. Clearly, part of what is at stake here is the delay of marriage and childbearing. There has been a slight increase in childbearing at older ages. However, only 6.4 percent of births in 1985 occurred to women aged thirty-five and over.

Having children presents considerable costs, especially for women. No one would be surprised to hear that women who were married or had children early in life would suffer disadvantages, but the same appears true (admittedly to a lesser extent) for women who have children later. Considering women who were aged thirty at the time of the 1981 census, Grindstaff (1985a) found that those faring best in terms of completed education and personal income had no children or had never married.

When voluntary childlessness was first studied, it was seen as questioning fundamental assumptions about adult life: parenthood is inevitable, marital happiness requires children, a family cannot exist without children (Veevers, 1980). Now, childlessness is often seen as a means of devoting energy to other pursuits. By not having children, women have more possibilities for achieving social mobility. In fact, childlessness may be the easiest route to equality. As more and more women realize that childbearing is detrimental to long-range economic outcomes, Grindstaff (1985b) expects as many as 20 percent of married couples may remain childless.

Thus, inasmuch as couples, and women in particular, consider the costs and benefits of children when making childbearing decisions, it is clear that the balance sheet often argues against having children. It is also interesting that couples tend to justify their childbearing decisions in terms of the costs and benefits that children offer.

Thus, individualism reigns supreme with regard to marriage and childbearing. As Kettle (1980) notes, the parents of the baby boom were a "dutiful generation" committed to sacrificing themselves, while their children are a "me generation" brought up to have high expectations of success and personal gratification. But having a child fundamentally goes beyond the individual's gratification. It requires a "letting go" of self-centred considerations. Lux (1983) has argued that having children requires a certain detachment from calculations of how the child will be a cost or benefit for oneself. It requires a certain commitment to some community beyond oneself, be it one's family, kin, social, national, or human group. The fact that individualism is so highly involved in motivations surrounding childbearing implies there will be fewer children.

In one sense it is encouraging to see people making decisions based on their self-interest: it makes for happier people. But it also means people will have fewer children and many will have none. Having a child is a "fateful decision" that stays with you forever. Even if giving birth corresponds with one's interests now, the same may not be true later, for instance, if a marriage ends. It is much safer, according to this calculation, to avoid the risks by having no children.

In concluding this section, we should mention the study of differential fertility across social groups. This also points to the importance of alternative life goals as a key determinant of fertility. Traditionally, there have been important fertility differences across groups, as defined by ascriptive factors such as ethnicity, language, and religion. However, these differences have all but disappeared, so that Romaniuc (1984:13) speaks of an "overall convergence toward a low fertility level." However, the remaining differences are a function of achieved characteristics, such as education and labour force participation (Beaujot and McQuillan, 1982:75). In other words, a woman's role in society rather than her social origins is now the crucial factor affecting her fertility. This again points to the broader issue of sex roles as a key factor in understanding fertility. In the past, childbearing and childrearing were seen as an essential part of a woman's role. As women now give more importance to economic roles, children are a reduced part of the picture, and women who give the greatest priority to their economic roles have fewer children and are the most likely to choose to not have children.

Contraception and Anticipated Childbearing

Couples could always reduce their chances of pregnancy. For instance, fertility was low in the 1930s before modern contraception became available. What has changed is the relative ease of contraception and the efficiency of methods. In that sense, few things have had such a profound impact on married life as the extent and effectiveness of control over fertility. The advent of the birth control pill in the later 1960s was the topic of much public awareness. In the late 1970s, the increasing use of sterilization received much less attention. These modern methods have become so effective that couples often think they have complete control over reproduction. This is unique in human history. By giving women more control over the number and timing of births, contraceptive technology allows them to better plan their labour market activity.

The 1984 National Fertility Survey provides an accurate picture of contraceptive usage (Balakrishnan et al., 1985:211). Among all women aged eighteen to forty-nine, some 68.4 percent were using contraception at the time of the survey. Contraceptive usage is highest among cohabitating never-married women (83.1 percent), but it is still used by 50.8 percent among never-married women who are not cohabitating. For single women who are using contraception, 71.2 percent are using the pill. Among persons using contraception, 59.4 percent of the currently married and 66.0 percent of the previously married are using sterilization. The condom and I.U.D. account for 9.1 percent and 8.3 percent of usage, respectively. Use of other methods is negligible.

Another observation suggested by these data is that contraception remains largely the responsibility of women. Even though the male operation is much simpler, there are 2.3 sterilized wives for every sterilized husband, and there are 2.1 users of the pill, I.U.D., diaphragm, or foam for every user of the condom or withdrawal.

This fertility survey also gathered information on current and anticipated childbearing. Altogether, women aged eighteen to forty-nine had 1.52 children on average and expected another 0.78, for a total of 2.30 children (Balakrishnan, 1986: Table 3.2). In each age group, the total expected exceeded 2.0 children. If these anticipations are correct, the total fertility rate of 1.7 underestimates the ultimate completed fertility. However, not all anticipated births may materialize. For instance, people responding to this question largely assume they will be married and stay married. Comparisons to earlier surveys taken in the Province of Quebec and in Toronto indicate people mostly revise their expected fertility downward. Possibly a more useful indication is the number who "expect no more children." Among women who have two children already, 88.9 percent expect no more children. Even for women with one child, 45.4 percent expect no more children. For all women aged eighteen to forty-nine, some 76.7 percent expect no more children.

Unwanted Fertility and Low Fertility

Having too many or too few children can be a serious problem for individuals and for societies. For individuals, subfecundity can be devastating, but the more common problem is unwanted conceptions and births. The number of officially recorded abortions were 62 000 in 1984; that is, one abortion for every six live births, up from one in thirty-three live births in 1970. We also know that 16.8 percent of births in 1984 were to mothers who were not married. While some of these births were desired, the majority probably represent contraceptive failure. In addition, 6.5 percent of births were to mothers under the age of twenty. While sometimes these births occur within stable relationships, it is usually better for the child, the mother, and others if the birth occurs later. Encouragingly, since 1975 birth rates to teenagers and the proportion of abortions involving teenagers have gone down.

The whole society has a stake in the reproduction of its members and in finding a space for additional people. Childbearing is in a sense too important to be left to individuals alone to decide. All societies and groups try to influence or constrain the choices individuals make in this regard. Sometimes fertility is too high and there are social pressures to reduce it, as in many developing countries today. In Canada, fertility has been below replacement since 1972, and it may be time to think about policies that would sustain childbearing (Beaujot, 1986). In a book provocatively entitled *Le choc demographique: le declin du Québec est-il inévitable?*, Mathews (1984) argues that Quebec needs to do something to sustain fertility. The concern over low fertility has in fact reached the political agenda in Quebec, where the fertility rate was 1.4 in 1984 compared to 1.7 for Canada as a whole (Bureau Statistique du Québec, 1986:53). The Commission de la Culture (1985) reported to the Quebec Assemblée Nationale that it is time to counter demographic trends. It proposed that the cultural,

PRO-NATALIST POLICIES

Some countries have attempted pro-natalist policies, but the assessment of their impact is difficult because many things influence the birth rate besides government action. The most sustained pro-natalist policies in recent years have been in Eastern Europe and France. The fertility rate in Eastern Europe was once comparable to that of Western Europe, but in 1986 the average births per woman were 2.1 in Eastern Europe and 1.5 in Western Europe. The contrast between East and West Germany is striking at 1.8 and 1.3, respectively, a difference of nearly 30 percent. The fertility rate in France has traditionally been among the lowest in the world, but it is now significantly higher than other countries of Western Europe.

Various policy interventions are possible, some of which would be less acceptable on other grounds. One could limit the availability of contraception and abortion, which has actually been done in Romania, but many would have serious reservations about such draconian approaches. The state could "buy babies," for instance, give people a free house if they have two children, but that would be expensive. There could be attempts to move women out of the labour force, which actually occurred in the immediate post-war period as soldiers were returning, but this would go against the liberalizing trend in sex roles that many would want to see continue.

In all likelihood, the more acceptable policies would be in two areas. There could be a higher level of public support for the various services needed by families with young children. These would range from the greater availability of day care and more generous parental leaves, to tax structures that favour parents. It is probably the general support of social programs that is responsible for higher fertility in Eastern Europe, rather than the more draconian pro-natalist interventions. Second, there could be attempts to influence the public consciousness regarding the importance of childbearing. That has happened in France, where there is a large consensus to the effect that higher fertility would be good for the society. In Canada, the state has taken a rather neutral stand. For instance, when he was minister of justice, Trudeau said that "the state has no business in the bedrooms of the nation." One could take a different stance, arguing that by having children parents are making an important contribution to the future of the society. There could follow from this orientation a recognition that children are not only the responsibility of parents, but the entire society has a stake in its reproduction through future generations. This type of public intervention has been helpful in reducing fertility in many developing countries. In part, people have responded to the call of the state for a lower level of population growth. It is not inconceivable that, based on a shared sense of priorities, the state could promote a higher level of births. Along similar lines, there could be attempts to promote the greater involvement of men in childcare, which would put the onus of childbearing less on the shoulders of women.

These are all debatable questions that require further research and discussion. Moreover, the discussion is based on the assumption that sustaining the level of fertility is itself important, which is also a debatable issue.

social, and economic impact of current demographic trends threatens Quebec's future as a distinct society. The insert on pronatalist policies discusses the potential interventions and the likelihood of their success.

INTERNATIONAL MIGRATION

Trends

Immigration has always been important to Canadian population growth. With lower fertility, the demographic contribution of immigration is likely to be even higher in the future. Immigrants do not just constitute an inflow of population; they have various characteristics, such as level of education, and they bring with them various culture and traditions. In some regards, the policies and programs that regulate immigration hold the key to the future of Canadian society. Not surprisingly, then, immigration is hotly debated in policy circles and beyond.

How immigrants are doing in Canada is of more than passing concern. Questions of adaptation and economic integration are of course important to immigrants themselves. In addition, these questions reflect on Canadian society itself, on the extent to which it grants equal opportunity to its newest arrivals. Finally, in a country of immigration like Canada, the very culture and social and economic development are influenced by immigrants.

Figure 1 shows immigration has fluctuated extensively over time. **Net migration** was negative from Confederation to about 1895. This was a period of depressed international trade, during which there was low demand for Canadian raw materials. Industrialization was occurring faster in New England, and many

Figure 1

Annual levels of immigration and emigration, Canada, 1900 to 1986

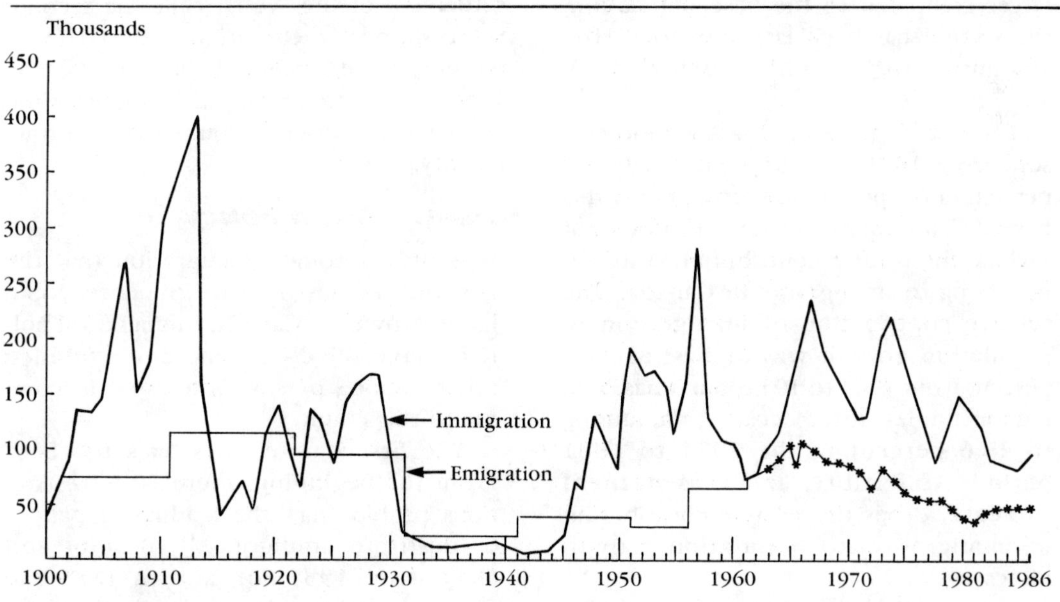

Source: Table 2; Dumas, 1984: 100; Beaujot et al., 1987: Figure 1; and Statistics Canada, Postcensal Annual Estimates, Catalogue No. 91–210, 1987:60.
Adapted by author.

Canadians, especially French Canadians, moved southward (Lavoie, 1972). The picture changed radically at the end of the nineteenth century, as the long depression ended and the Canadian prairies became attractive for settlement. The period 1895 to 1914 saw the arrival of three million persons. The annual intake was particularly high from 1910 to 1913; in fact we have never since seen figures of this magnitude. The recorded arrivals for 1913 exceeded four hundred thousand when the base population was just over seven million. As a proportion, that would be like admitting 1.4 million immigrants in one year into the 1981 population. This first wave of post-Confederation immigration quickly halted with the first world war. The whole period 1914 to 1945, involving two world wars and a major depression, was an interlude in immigration. The arrivals were never above 20,000 per year from 1933 to 1944. In the 1930s the net figures were again negative. The post-war period saw a second immigration wave. While the first wave was larger compared to the base population, the second has been larger in total size, amounting to 5.5 million arrivals from 1946 to 1986.

The **net migration** of 4.0 million persons from 1901 to 1981 comprised 21.2 percent of the population growth over this period. This figure, of course, does not include the further contribution of births occurring to immigrants in Canada. The relative contribution of immigration to population growth was highest at 44.1 percent from 1901 to 1911, but it has been high in the last three decades, amounting to 28.6 percent in the 1971 to 1981 period. As fertility, and thus **natural increase**, drops the relative contribution of immigration to population growth increases.

As measured by the decennial censuses, the proportion of the total Canadian population who were immigrants has been about 15 to 16 percent in the post-war period. According to the 1971 census, another 18.5 percent of the Canadian-born population had one or two foreign-born parents. This means that slightly more than one-third of the population were first or second generation Canadians.

The 1981 figure of 16 percent foreign-born is considerably higher than the 1980 figure for the United States at 6 percent. While figures are higher in Australia (20 percent in 1976) and Israel (45 percent in 1972), Canada is among the few countries where immigrants constitute a significant share of the total population.

The two post-Confederation surges of immigration came when the rate of growth of the native-born labour force had slowed considerably. The first wave made up for the emigration losses of the depressed post-Confederation era, while the second wave compensated for the small proportions of young adults in the 1950s that resulted from the decline of fertility in the 1930s. The first wave contributed to the settlement of the West, while the second wave supported the urban industrial expansion of the 1950s and 1960s. In the late 1980s, some are arguing that immigration should be increased to compensate for low fertility.

Immigration Policy

It is only through immigration that the government has tried to influence population growth in Canada. Immigration policies have selected some and excluded others among persons interested in coming to this country.

The first Statute dates back to 1869. From the beginning, there were restrictions prohibiting "the landing of pauper or destitute immigrants" (Beaujot and McQuillan, 1982:80), and in 1885 the Chinese Immigration Act imposed a "head tax" on prospective Chinese immigrants.

This Act was updated several times and only set aside in 1947. In 1907 and 1908, measures were taken to limit immigration from Japan and India. In effect, until 1962 there were restrictions on immigrants from places outside of Europe and the United States.

Other policies have promoted immigration. There was the Free Grants and Homestead Act of 1868, which was designed to help settle Canada's West. Subsequently, numerous efforts were extended to bring in agriculturalists, including aggressive recruitment in the United Kingdom and Europe. Many arrivals during the first wave of 1895 to 1914 provided unskilled labour for early Canadian industrial development (Avery, 1979).

During the "interlude" between the two waves, various restrictions discouraged immigrants. The Act of 1910 allowed the Governor-in-Council to regulate the volume, ethnic origin, or occupational composition of the immigrant flow. While restrictions were lifted in the 1920s, in 1933 various categories of immigration were deleted, and even British subjects were discouraged from coming. Whenever immigration was favoured, persons from Britain and the United States were the most welcomed, Northern Europeans were relatively well received, other Europeans were accepted if no one else was available, and non-Whites were not welcome (Manpower and Immigration, 1974:17).

After World War II, there was uncertainty regarding the appropriate direction for future immigration. The Quebec Legislative Assembly had indicated in 1944 its opposition to mass immigration. When the war ended, many argued that priorities should concentrate on integrating the returning soldiers. Others were concerned that Canada might return to the economic situation of the 1930s, for which immigration would be inappropriate. Others argued Canada could raise its international stature by helping to rescue displaced persons from the war in Europe. Also, a report to the deputy minister responsible for immigration concluded that a larger population made sense from an economic point of view (Timlin, 1951).

In 1947, Prime Minister Mackenzie King set out the government's immigration policy in a frequently quoted statement that involved a careful compromise between these divergent concerns. King called for immigration as a support for higher population growth, but not in excess of the number that could be advantageously absorbed. While he recognized an obligation to help those in distress, he would not support a massive arrival that would alter the "character of our population." The character of our population could mean various things, but it obviously included "keep it white." An important administrative procedure used to admit immigrants involved the widening of eligible categories of "sponsored relatives." This was an interesting political solution, since those who had argued for restricted entries could hardly oppose the arrival of relatives. It also assured that immigrants would largely be from the traditional "preferred" sources.

The 1953 Immigration Act allowed the Governor-in-Council to prohibit the entry of immigrants for many reasons, including nationality, ethnic group, and "peculiar customs, habits, modes of life, or methods of holding property." In effect, preference was given to persons of British birth and people from France and the United States. Second preference went to Western Europeans. Persons from other countries could not enter unless sponsored by a close relative. A small exception involved an arrangement in force between 1951 and 1962 allowing for selective arrivals from Asian Commonwealth countries. However, very low limits were set: three hundred people per year from all of India, Pakistan, and Sri Lanka (Hawkins, 1972).

Discriminating against certain places of origin concerned the government of John Diefenbaker, which lifted the racial bars to immigration in 1962. In 1967, a "points system" for selecting independent immigrants was established. This reinforced the nondiscriminatory aspect by formulating the "education, training, skills, and other special qualifications" under which immigrants were to be selected. The multiculturalism policy promulgated in 1971 underlined Canada's openness to immigrants from around the world.

Immigration policy was reviewed from 1973 to 1975, culminating in the 1976 Immigration Act, which took effect in 1978. The main change was that the minister was to set a target level for immigration each year, after reviewing the regional demographic needs and labour market conditions, and consulting with the provinces, especially on how immigrants might be helped to adjust to Canadian society. Because of the importance placed on immigration, the Act requires an annual "statement to Parliament" on the government's goals. In other regards, the Act reinforced past practice. It explicitly affirmed the fundamental objectives of Canadian immigration laws, which included family reunification, nondiscrimination, concern for refugees, and the promotion of Canada's demographic, economic, and cultural goals.

Characteristics and Adaptation of Immigrants

As we have seen, the definition of a "desirable" immigrant has changed regarding ethnic preferences and restrictions. Since 1962, the official policy has been one of nondiscrimination, but only slowly have the origins of arriving immigrants come to resemble somewhat the distribution of the world population. Thus, the proportion arriving from countries other than Europe and the United States was 7.9 percent from 1956 to 1962, rising to 59.7 percent from 1977 to 1984 (Beaujot et al., 1987:8). As another example, the arrival from Asian countries amounted to 2.8 percent of the total from 1956 to 1962 but 39.4 percent in the period from 1977 to 1984. At the same time the proportion from Europe declined from 83.8 to 19.5 percent.

While immigrants have constituted a stable proportion of Canada's population, the place of origin of immigrants has become more diversified. The percent of all foreign-born from the United Kingdom has declined from a clear majority (57.9 percent) in 1901 to less than a quarter (22.9 percent) in 1981. The proportion from countries other than Europe and the United States was only 5.1 percent in the 1901 and 4.3 percent in 1961, but reached 25.1 percent in 1981 (idem, p. 10). In absolute numbers, the persons who were born in places other than Europe and the United States amounted to 368 000 in 1971 and 969 000 in 1981, a 260 percent increase in one decade.

Given the diversity among immigrants, it is hard to generalize about their adaptation in Canada, but the most recent arrivals tend to have the most difficulty. From the turn of the century to the 1930s, the "new immigrant groups" from Eastern and Southern Europe, along with Orientals and Blacks, had the most hardships (Avery, 1979). More recently, it is the "new immigrant groups" from Asia, Latin America, and Africa who are more likely to be at a disadvantage.

The study of the adaptation of immigrants is further complicated in that they arrive with a varied profile of characteristics. Because of the selectivity of immigrants, they often start with several advantages. On average, immigrants have higher education and are more likely to be

IMMIGRATION ISSUES

There are continuous debates about the appropriate level of immigration and the composition of the immigrant stream. The prevailing points of view have often changed quickly. A mid-1960s White Paper reflected enthusiasm for the importance of immigration to Canada's continued economic expansion. In the mid-1970s, the Green Paper was much more ambivalent. Many questioned the economic need for immigration, with the arrival of the large and well-educated baby boom generation onto the labour force.

Some think immigration adds to the level of unemployment in Canada. However, studies have failed to confirm this theory (Richmond, 1984). In fact, by increasing the demand for goods and services, immigrants may add more jobs than they take from the Canadian economy (Samuel and Conyers, 1986).

It is important that immigration does not exceed the numbers that can be successfully absorbed. In comparative perspective, societies are rarely open to the arrival of persons with racial or ethnic characteristics different from its own (Weiner, 1985). The movement of people changes the very composition of the population and therefore potentially the sense of national identity, and even domestic policies. In a sense, Canada is trying something unique and needs to ensure that this continues to be a successful experiment.

However, the analysis presented here suggests that immigration has made important contributions to Canadian economic development. That is why the McDonald Commission (1985:668) recommended "Canada should support some increase in immigration flows closer to the historical average of the post-war years." In the early 1980s, immigration levels had been as low as eighty-five thousand per year. Returning to the post-war average would mean levels around one hundred and fifty thousand per year.

in the labour force, more likely to work full time, and more likely to be in large urban centres. All these factors are advantages, at least in economic adaptation.

Using average total income as a measure of economic adaptation, it is interesting that the foreign-born do even better than the Canadian-born. The foreign-born men had an average income 11.9 percent above the Canadian-born average, while women were 6.6 percent above their Canadian-born counterparts (Beaujot et al., 1987:47, 57). However, further analysis controlling for age and education indicates that men arriving after 1960 and women after 1970 have average incomes below the Canadian-born. For the most recent arrivals, those of the period 1975 to 1979, the average income of immigrant men represented 80 percent of that of the Canadian-born. For women, the immigrant average was 85 percent of the Canadian-born group.

POPULATION GROWTH

Having analyzed mortality, fertility, and international migration, the overall picture of population growth can now be presented. Table 1 captures the basic figures over the census intervals from 1851 to 1986. The last column, giving the rate of increase, merits special attention. We see that population growth has varied considerably over Canadian history. There have been three periods when growth was close to 3 percent per year: 1851–1861, 1901–1911, and 1951–1956. These are rapid rates of growth indeed, surpassing the most recent figures for developing countries. By comparison, population growth in the Third World as a whole peaked in 1965 at 2.4 percent per year.

On the other hand, there have been two periods of population growth at or near 1 percent per year: 1881–1901 and 1976–1986. Since 1982, Canada's average annual growth slipped slightly below 1 percent. Yet this figure is higher than that of the total for all developed countries (about 0.6 percent). According to United Nations (1984) estimates, Australia was the only major developed country with a population growth more rapid than Canada from 1980 to 1985.

The higher growth in Canada as compared to most other developed countries is due to immigration and the after-effect of the baby boom. Canada's below replacement fertility has until now been offset by the large numbers of young adults at childbearing ages. Although they are having fewer than two children each, thre are so many couples at childbearing ages that there are more births than deaths in the population. Therefore, in terms of popu-

Table 1
COMPONENTS OF POPULATION GROWTH IN CANADA, 1851–1986

	Change Over Preceding Census					
	Total Population	*Total Population Increase*	*Immigration*	*Emigration*	*Ratio of Net Migration to Total Growth*	*Average Annual Growth Rate*
	(Numbers in thousands)					
1851	2 436					
1861	3 230	793	352	170	23.0	2.9
1871	3 689	460	260	410	−32.6	1.3
1881	4 325	636	350	404	− 8.5	1.6
1891	4 833	508	680	826	−28.7	1.1
1901	5 371	538	250	380	−24.2	1.1
1911	7 207	1 835	1 550	740	44.1	3.0
1921	8 788	1 581	1 400	1 089	19.7	2.0
1931	10 377	1 589	1 200	970	14.5	1.7
1941	11 507	1 130	149	241	−8.1	1.0
1951	14 009	2 141	548	379	7.9	1.7
1956	16 081	2 071	783	185	28.9	2.8
1961	18 238	2 157	760	278	22.3	2.5
1966	20 015	1 777	539	280	14.6	1.9
1971	21 568	1 553	890	427	29.8	1.5
1976	22 993	1 424	841	357	34.0	1.3
1981	24 342	1 349	588	279	22.9	1.1
1986*	25 591	1 249	500	238	20.9	1.0

*Estimates

Source: Beaujot et al., 1987: Table 1; Statistics Canada Catalogue Number 91-210, 1987:50. Adapted by author.

lation growth, we are still living off the baby boom. Once this generation passes beyond childbearing age, a continued low fertility would mean much lower rates of population growth.

Rapid economic and demographic growth have tended to coincide in Canada. The periods of economic and demographic expansion have been, especially, from 1851 to 1861, 1895 to 1914, and 1951 to 1966. These have corresponded to the boom preceding Confederation, the settlement of the West along with early industrialization, and the period of sustained post-war growth. On the other hand, the periods of less rapid growth have been from 1861 to 1895, the 1930s, and 1980s. It is difficult to interpret this coincidence of economic and demographic growth. Certainly, the economic climate has influenced the openness of immigration policy and the extent of interest in migration to Canada. The economic climate was also a factor in the low birth rates of the 1930s and the high rates of the baby boom era.

One also might argue that population growth has influenced the economic climate. Slower population growth can weaken the incentive for long-range business investment, or at least undermine consumer demand, especially the demand for new housing. It is interesting that declining rates of population growth actually preceded the economic decline of the 1930s. Admittedly, it is difficult to be conclusive on the basis of a few time points. However, the evidence suggests population growth and the economic climate have reinforced each other in Canada. This is very different from what is generally concluded for developing countries. Here, poor economic performance is seen as one of the reasons for rapid population growth. Some even claim rapid population growth hinders economic development.

Returning to Canada, it is worth looking at the projections of future population growth. These projections are based on various assumptions for mortality, fertility, and international migration (Statistics Canada, 1985). The results are especially sensitive to the fertility and immigration assumptions. If we assume a fertility level of 1.66 births per woman, that is, close to its present level, the population would peak in 2023 or 2031, depending on whether net immigration is 50 000 or 100 000 per year (Foot, 1984). This peak would be 30.0, or 32.7 million persons, respectively. Over the thirty-five-year period from 1951 to 1986, the population increased by 84 percent. Over the next thirty-five years to 2021, it would increase by 17 percent or 25 percent according to these projections. Population decline would occur after the second or third decade of the next century. The rate of population growth would already be as low as 0.3 percent or 0.5 percent per year from 1996 to 2001 under these two sets of assumptions. If fertility decreased further to 1.4 births per woman, the population would start declining after 2013 if net migration was 50 000 persons per year, and after 2003 if net migration was zero.

The picture of population growth is likely to become very different in the future. While rates of growth were always at or above 1.0 percent per year until 1982, we are not likely to see such rates again. In fact, the population will probably start to decline in absolute numbers early in the next century. Canada will not be alone as a declining population. However, these are very uncharted grounds. Until now there have been very few experiences of population decline in the modern era.

POPULATION DISTRIBUTION AND COMPOSITION

Population Distribution

Up to this point, we have analyzed three population processes (mortality, fertility,

Figure 2
Relative growth of provinces and territories, 1921 to 1986

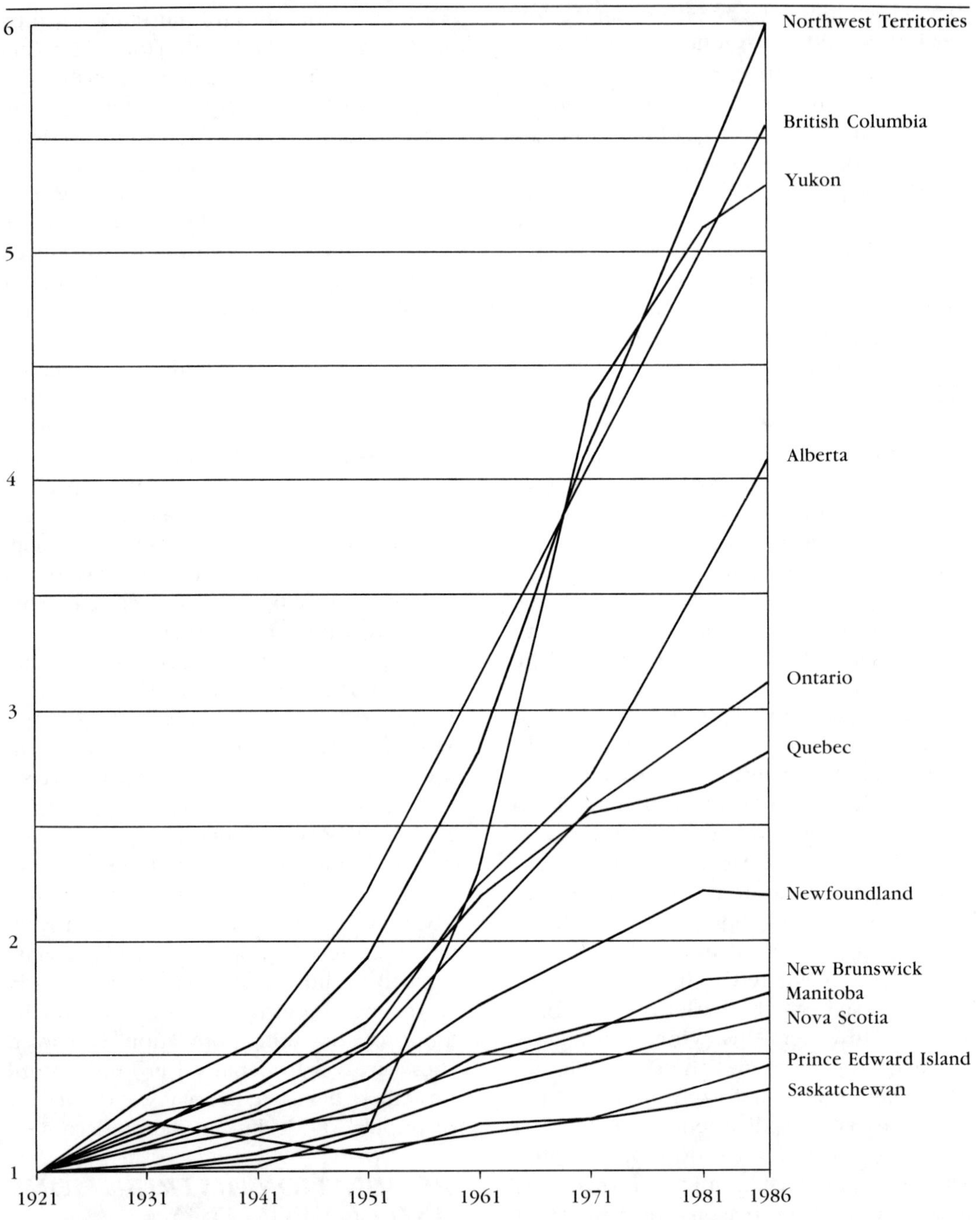

Source: Foot, 1982:12; and Statistics Canada Catalogue No. 91–210, 1986, p. 35.
Adapted by author.

and international migration) and one population state (size). We now turn to two other population states: distribution and composition. The study of the distribution of population over space requires adding another process, that is, migration within the country. The differential growth of the various parts of Canada has somewhat been a function of fertility and mortality, for instance, the higher fertility in Quebec from 1880 to 1960 (Beaujot and McQuillan, 1982:151). However, this differential growth is mostly a function of internal migration and the extent to which immigrants choose to go to various regions. These population shifts tell us important things about the attractiveness of the various parts of the country, and its change over time. In addition, the population distribution affects the regional dynamics of the country.

Around the time of Confederation, Ontario had 43.9 percent of the population, Quebec 32.3 percent, the Maritime provinces had 20.8 percent, and the remaining 3.0 percent was west of Ontario (Beaujot and McQuillan, 1982:147). The major changes in population distribution occurred with the immigration wave of 1895 to 1914. The four western provinces comprised 11.1 percent of the population in 1901, but 23.9 percent in 1911. The change in population distribution since western settlement has been much slower and less profound. In the period 1921 to 1986, the percentages have varied within a narrow range: Ontario has comprised between 33 percent and 36 percent of the total, Quebec has had between 26 percent and 29 percent, the Prairies between 16 percent and 23 percent, the Atlantic provinces between 9 percent and 12 percent, and British Columbia has increased from 6 percent to 11 percent.

From another point of view, the changes since Western settlement remain significant. Even small relative disadvantages have often concerned given provincial governments. Figure 2 shows the relative population growth of the various provinces since 1921. We see the population of British Columbia has increased 5.5 fold in this sixty-five-year period, while Saskatchewan and Prince Edward Island increased by less than 50 percent. The difference between Ontario (3.1 fold increase) and Quebec (2.8 fold) is also noteworthy. In 1921, Ontario's population was 24 percent larger than Quebec's; it is now 39 percent larger. Some of the rank orderings among provinces have even changed. In 1921, Saskatchewan was the third largest province, in 1986 it is the sixth largest. Conversely, British Columbia has moved from sixth to third.

The further analysis of change in distribution involves considering internal migration and the differential settlement patterns of international immigrants. In the first two decades of the century, the Prairie provinces received the largest share of immigrants, but since 1921 Ontario has consistently been the principal destination of immigrants. Table 2 shows how the net inflow of foreign-born were distributed in 1981. For the country as a whole, the foreign-born amount to 16.1 percent of the total. However, these figures range from less than 2 percent foreign-born in Newfoundland and less than 5 percent in the Maritime Provinces to over 23 percent in British Columbia and Ontario.

Table 2 also includes the figures on the net influence of migration of the native-born. In a given five-year period, only about 5 percent of the population changes residence across provincial boundaries. However, once these moves are cumulated over a lifetime, they can have an important impact. In comparing the place of birth and the place of residence for persons born and living in Canada at the time of the 1981 census, only three provinces have net gains. In absolute numbers, the

Table 2
NET INTERPROVINCIAL LIFETIME MIGRATION OF NATIVE-BORN AND INFLOW OF FOREIGN BORN, BY PROVINCE, 1981

	Native-Born	Foreign-Born	Total Migrants
	(In thousands)		
Newfoundland	−108.5	9.8	− 98.7
Prince Edward Island	− 28.7	4.6	− 24.1
New Brunswick	−125.6	41.7	− 83.9
Nova Scotia	−111.5	27.6	− 83.9
Quebec	−231.8	526.0	294.2
Ontario	230.2	2,025.8	2,256.0
Manitoba	−230.1	146.1	− 84.0
Saskatchewan	−409.0	83.7	−325.4
Alberta	339.7	364.8	704.5
British Columbia	662.5	631.6	1,294.1
Yukon	5.0	2.9	7.9
Northwest Territories	7.7	2.8	10.5
	(Rate per 100 population)		
Newfoundland	− 19.2	1.7	− 17.5
Prince Edward Island	− 23.7	3.8	− 19.9
New Brunswick	− 15.0	5.0	− 10.0
Nova Scotia	− 16.2	4.0	− 12.2
Quebec	− 3.6	8.3	4.6
Ontario	2.7	23.7	26.4
Manitoba	− 22.7	14.4	− 8.3
Saskatchewan	− 42.8	8.7	− 34.0
Alberta	15.3	16.5	31.8
British Columbia	24.4	23.3	47.7
Yukon	21.8	12.5	34.3
Northwest Territories	16.9	6.1	23.0

Source: 1981 Census of Canada, Catalogue No. 92-913, Volume 1 — National Series Tables 1A and 1B. Adapted by author.

largest gains are for British Columbia, followed by Alberta and Ontario. Expressed as a percentage of the population, the net gain for British Columbia is overwhelming at 24.4 percent, followed by Alberta at 15.3 percent and Ontario at 2.7 percent. The net losses are highest for Saskatchewan at 42.8 percent, followed by Prince Edward Island and Manitoba at about 23 percent.

Adding the foreign-born and the internal migration of native-born shows only four provinces have made net gains: British Columbia, Alberta, Ontario, and Quebec. This is a striking observation. While Canada is a country of immigration, having received 5.5 million immigrants in the post-war period, the net impact of both international and internal migration is positive for only four provinces. In all other provinces, population movement has been to their net disadvantage.

While we have here concentrated on provinces and regions, there are other ways to analyze population distribution. As late as 1931, over half of the population lived in rural areas and 31.1 percent were "rural farm." By 1981, only 4.3 percent lived in rural farm areas. In 1871, only Montreal had one hundred thousand or more people, and it amounted to only 3 percent of the Canadian population. By 1981, there were 24 census metropolitan areas of this size, housing 56.1 percent of the nation's population. Toronto and Montreal dominate the urban landscape, with populations of 3.0 and 2.8 million, respectively (Statistics Canada, 1984b). These metropolitan populations are larger than the total populations of any province, except, of course, Ontario and Quebec themselves.

We will conclude this section by reflecting on the role of population in the regional dynamics of the country. Regional questions result from geographic, economic, political, and demographic factors.

Geography promotes regionalist distinctions. Canada's population is concentrated in a long, thin ribbon along the border with the United States. Even at that, the ribbon is broken twice, once by the Canadian Shield and once by the Rocky Mountains. The French historian André Siegfried (1937:16) noted that, because of the narrowness of this band of habitation, Canada lacks a point of identification and is always tempted to seek a centre of gravity from outside of itself.

Canada's economic history, especially the importance of the staples economy, has also weakened national unity. The exploitation of natural resources or staples for export has balkanized the nation into economic areas; the focus has been on seeking external markets rather than on national aspirations. The economic heartland of Canada, especially Toronto and Montreal, is closer to the core of the world economy, given its proximity to the United States. This has helped to establish the Windsor–Quebec axis as the centre of Canada, providing both a source of unity in its large population, and of disunity due to resentment from outlying parts of the country. For instance, some argue "the Maritimes were better off before they became a satellite of Upper Canada and lost their potential for local industrialization, urbanization, economic and political independence, and cultural integrity" (Gillis, 1980:53). Other outlying areas, especially the Prairies, fear they might experience similar "backsliding" once their resources are no longer useful.

Regional population diversity is a further barrier to social cohesion. The populations of various regions are diverse. For instance, Newfoundland is 93 percent British origin, while Quebec is 81 percent French origin, and the Prairie provinces are almost half of origins other than British or French. The relative size of the population in various regions remains unbalanced, giving weight especially to the Windsor–Quebec axis. The population movements through internal migration have largely not served to "blend" the peoples of the various regions, and movements rarely cross Ontario going east or west.

Age and Sex Composition

Besides studying the distribution of population over categories of space, we can also consider its composition over the categories of various other factors, such as education, ethnicity, or language. Since age and sex are key variables in demographic studies, we will focus on these factors. The composition by age is a function of births, deaths, and migration. In turn, the age profile affects the demographic processes, as fertility, mortality, and migration vary by age and sex.

Age and sex are important outside of demography. These key ascriptive characteristics affect expectations and behaviour across the whole span of human activities.

Especially evident in Figure 3 is the impact of the baby boom of 1946 to 1966 and the subsequent baby bust. While deaths have some impact on an age structure, they occur over all ages and therefore their impact is not as visible. Now that there is less room for declines in mortality at younger ages, the declines are more concentrated at older ages, which therefore slightly increases the relative weight of the top of the pyramid. International migration is concentrated at young adult ages, and it therefore tends to increase the relative size of this part of the pyramid. But it is especially births, and their change over time, that influences the basic shape of Canada's age pyramid.

The age structure can also be described in terms of the median age and the proportion over age sixty-five. The median age has increased from 17.2 in 1851 to 22.7 in 1901, 27.7 in 1951, and 29.6 in 1981 (Statistics Canada, 1984a:1). The proportion over sixty-five years of age was 2.7 in 1841 and 9.7 in 1981. Population aging will continue, at an even more rapid rate, in the future. By 2006 the median age should be about thirty-nine to forty and about 14 percent of the population will be over sixty-five.

The changing age composition has affected the educational system, is influencing the labour force, and will eventually impact greatly on pension and health care. The story of the movement of the baby

Figure 3
Age pyramid of the population of Canada, June 1, 1961 to 1986

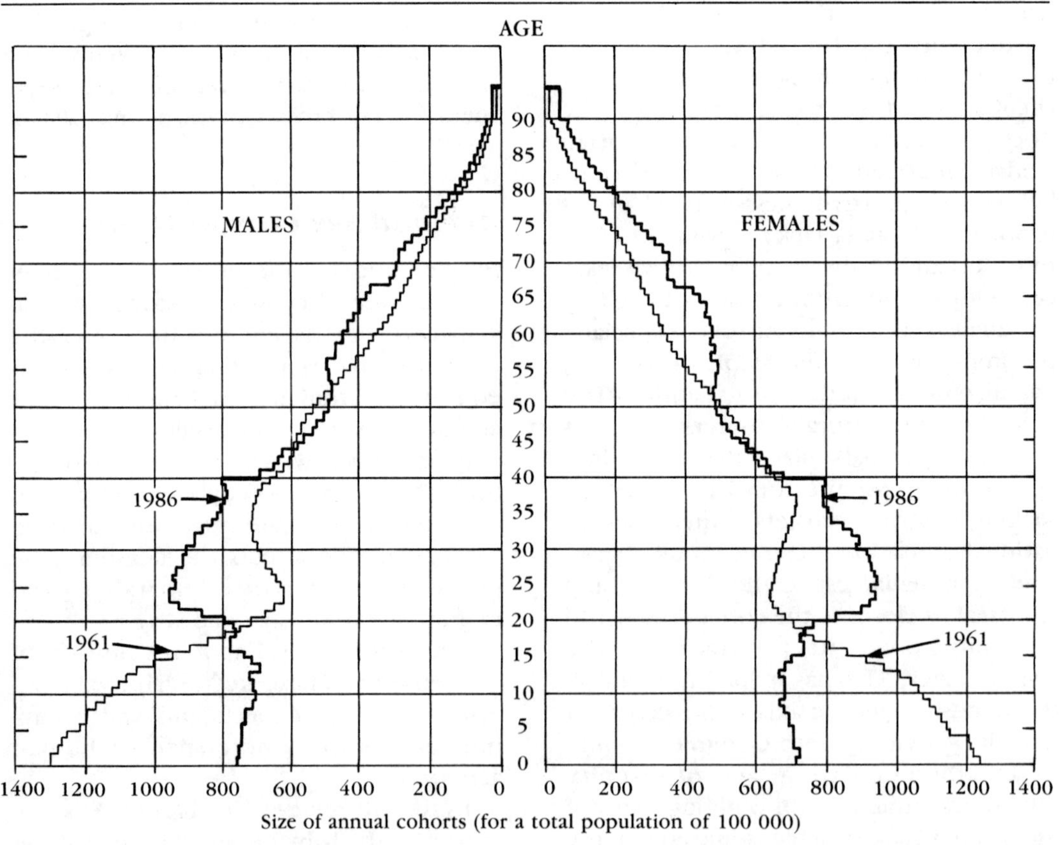

Source: Statistics Canada Catalogue No. 91-210, 1987:23.

boom and baby bust generations through the educational system is now well known. For instance, total elementary school enrolment peaked in 1960 and by 1976 it had declined by 22 percent (Statistics Canada, 1978:35). The labour force grew 3.4 percent per year from 1971 to 1981. After 1991, this growth is likely to be under 1 percent per year (Statistics Canada, 1985:13; Foot, 1982:199). This is likely to exercise a downward pressure on unemployment.

In the second decade of the next century the baby boom will reach old age. That will strain health and pension systems. A significant part of old age is spent in poor health. Estimates based on the 1978 Canada Health Survey indicate men can expect to spend 11.6 years and women 15.5 years in restricted activity, disability, and institutionalization (Wilkins and Adams, 1983:73). As a proportion of G.N.P., health costs are likely to increase from 7.0 percent in 1980 to 9.2 in 2031. Pensions will be affected both by the larger number receiving pensions and the small baby bust generation contributing to pension plans. Pension costs would increase from 3.4 percent of G.N.P. in 1981 to 8.3 percent in 2031 (Denton and Spencer, 1984:42).

Population aging is affecting Canadian society in a variety of ways. For instance, specific segments of the labour force will age differently from the average of the entire population. As an example, many young elementary school teachers were hired in the 1950s when the school system was expanding, and very little new hiring has occurred in recent years. If these trends continue, the largest group of elementary teachers in 2011 could be those aged sixty to sixty-four (Seward, 1987:9). The increased predominance of older people, along with the expectation of younger people that they will some day be part of the older population, is already affecting governmental spending priorities. For instance, the 1985 federal budget had anticipated de-indexing the pension payments to the elderly. There was such a public outcry against this move that the government eventually went back on its decision.

In ending this section, it is worth quoting from a recent book, *Canada's Aging Population*:

> There is no doubt that aging of the Canadian population will create new challenges for policy makers. It is also clear that the capacity exists to meet these challenges. A panic reaction to an alleged crisis of population aging seems unwarranted and ill-advised (McDaniel, 1986:117).

This author observes that population aging is due largely to fertility declines; therefore, it is a by-product of economic success. Also, aging occurs slowly and many developed countries have older populations than Canada. Finally, when we add both older and younger dependants, the period from 1981 to 2011 is one of historic low levels of dependency. Thus "a period of grace has been built into the age structure," allowing us to slowly shift social resources from the young to the old (McDaniel, 1986:114).

CONCLUSION

The demographic point of view gives us insights into Canadian society. The increased life expectancies have reduced uncertainty in life and allowed people to plan realistically for a long life, including several years of retirement.

Differentials in mortality point to lifestyle as a factor responsible for the shorter life spans of men and of non-married persons. Fertility has undergone equally radical changes, to the point that we can raise questions about effective population replacement. The dynamics of fertility indicate that liberalizing sex roles are responsible for recent trends and variations. Immigration is an important component of population growth, which also increases the diversity of the population. As a consequence of these components, our population has increased more than sevenfold since Confederation. However, since the early 1980s growth is under 1 percent per year, and it will likely stop after the second or third decade of the next century. Population gains have been largest for Ontario and British Columbia.

The population dimension gives Canada a certain uniqueness in the world community. Only 2.6 percent of the world population lives in countries with higher life expectancy than ours, and only 3.3 percent in countries with lower fertility than ours. In addition, our relatively high and diversified immigration promotes a "cultural mosaic" in Canada. In other ways, we share in the slower population growth and the consequent population aging that characterizes the more developed countries. Canada is on one side of an important demographic rift that divides these from the rapidly growing and young populations of the Third World. Since Canada receives more than half of its immigrants from Asia, Latin America, and Africa, this may help to ensure that we do not completely lose a common sense of destiny with the other three-quarters of humanity.

Notes

[1]The total fertility rate is the number of births a woman would have over her lifetime if she was subject to the fertility conditions of a given year.

DISCUSSION QUESTIONS

1. How does economic development affect mortality, and how might mortality affect economic development?
2. How does the study of mortality differentials help us to understand the factors underlying mortality in Canada? What does this imply regarding possible interventions to reduce mortality?
3. We interpreted the long-term decline in fertility as a function of economic questions and the adoption of new ideas regarding appropriate behaviour. Can these interpretations be used in understanding the baby boom and the baby bust?
4. How have immigration flows into Canada responded to changes in population growth and in economic growth?
5. Analyze the relative importance of natural increase and net migration in Canada's population growth.
6. Explain how the demographic processes (mortality, fertility, migration) affect the age composition. How does the age composition affect these demographic processes?

GLOSSARY

demography the study of populations, their size, distribution, and composition, and the immediate factors causing population change in births, deaths, and migration.

dependency (demographic) a measure of the proportion of an age distribution that is normally not eligible to be part of the labour force, compared to the population at working ages. The dependency ratio divides the number at ages birth to fourteen, plus those sixty-five and over, by the number at ages fifteen to sixty-four.

emigration the number of people leaving a specific country over a given period of time

immigration the number of people moving into a specific country over a given period of time

internal migration movement of people within a given country. Generally only movement across municipal boundaries is counted as internal migration. Interprovincial migration is a specific case of internal migration.

life expectancy an estimate of the average number of additional years a person can expect to live, based on the age-specific death rates of a given year. Unless otherwise indicated, it refers to life expectancy at birth.

natural increase the difference between the number of births and the number of deaths in a population over a given period. Natural increase can be given in absolute numbers or as a percentage of the mid-year population.

net migration the difference between the number of immigrants and the number of emigrants in a population over a given period. Net migration can also refer to the net balance of internal migration (in-migration minus out-migration to a particular area).

nuptiality the study of the frequency of marriage (proportion of people getting married) and of the timing of marriage (average age at marriage)

population growth the change in population size over a specific period of time. For a given country, population growth is a function of natural increase (birth minus deaths) plus net migration (immigration minus emigration).

total fertility rate the average number of children that would be born to a woman during her lifetime if she were to pass through all her childbearing years conforming to the age-specific fertility rates of a given year. In effect, it is an indicator of the level of childbearing in a population, measured in terms of births per woman.

BIBLIOGRAPHY

Adams, O.B. and D.N. Nagnur
1986 *Marriage, Divorce and Mortality: A Life Table Analysis for Canada and Regions, 1980–1982*. Ottawa: Statistics Canada.

Ariès, Philippe
1974 *Western Attitudes Towards Death*. Baltimore: Johns Hopkins University Press.

Avery, Donald
1979 *Dangerous Foreigners*. Toronto: McClelland and Stewart.

Balakrishnan, T.R.
1986 *Current and Expected Fertility*. Manuscript.

Balakrishnan, T.R., Karol Krotki, and Evelyne Lapierre-Adamcyk
1985 Contraceptive Use in Canada, 1984. *Family Planning Perspectives*, 17:209–15.

Beaujot, Roderic
1986 "Trends in marriage and childbearing." "In *Policy Options*, 7(7):3–7.

Beaujot, Roderic and Kevin McQuillan
1982 *Growth and Dualism*. Toronto: Gage.

——
1986 "The Social Effects of Demographic Change: Canada 1851–1981." *Journal of Canadian Studies*, 21(1):57–69.

Beaujot, R., K.G. Basavarajappa, and R. Verma
1987 *Income of Immigrants, 1980*. Manuscript.

Billette, A.
1977 "Les inégalités sociales de mortalité au Québec." In *Recherches sociographiques*, 18:415–30.

Blauner, Robert
1966 "Death and Social Structure." *Psychiatry*, 29(4):378–94.

Bourbeau, Robert and Jacques Légaré
1982 *Evolution de la Mortalité au Canada et au Québec, 1831–1931*. Montréal: Les Presses de l'Université de Montréal.

Burch, Thomas K.
1965 "Some Social Implications of Varying Mortality." In United Nations, *World Population Conference, Belgrade*.

——
1985 *Family History Survey: Preliminary Findings*. Cat. no. 99-955. Ottawa: Statistics Canada.

Bureau Statistique du Québec
1986 *La Situation démographique au Québec: Edition 1985*. Québec: Bureau Statistique du Québec.

Commission de la Culture
1985 *Etude de l'Impact Culturel, Social et Economique des Tendances Démographiques Actuelles sur l'Avenir du Québec comme Société Distincte*. Québec: Hôtel du Parlement.

Denton, Frank T. and Byron G. Spencer
1984 "Population Aging and the Economy: Some Issues in Resource Allocation." *Quantitative Studies in Economics and Population Research Reports*, no. 105. Hamilton, Ontario: McMaster University, Department of Economics.

Dumas, Jean
1984 *Current Demographic Analysis: Report on the Demographic Situation in Canada, 1983*. Cat. no. 91-209. Ottawa: Statistics Canada.

Foot, David K.
1982 *Canada's Population Outlook*. Toronto: James Lorimer and Company.

——
1984 *Immigration and Future Population*. Ottawa: Employment and Immigration Canada.

Gee, Ellen M. Thomas
1982 "Marriage in Nineteenth-century Canada." *Canadian Review of Sociology and Anthropology*, 19(3):311–25.

Gee, Ellen M. and Jean E. Veevers
1983 "Accelerating Sex Differentials in Mortality: An Analysis of Contributing Factors." *Social Biology*, 30(1): 75–85.

Gillis, A.R.
1980 "Urbanization and Urbanism." In R. Hagedorn (ed.) *Sociology*. Toronto: Holt, Rinehart and Winston.

Grindstaff, Carl F.
1985a "Educational Attainment for Females: The Long Term Consequences of Differential Timing in Marriage and the Onset of Childbearing." Paper presented at the International Population Conference in Florence, Italy, June.

——
1985b "The Baby Bust Revisited: Canada's Continuing Pattern of Low Fertility." *Canadian Studies in Population*, 12:103–10.

Hawkins, F.
1972 *Canada and Immigration: Public Policy and Public Concern*. Montreal: McGill–Queen's University Press.

Henripin, Jacques
1974 *Immigration and Language Imbalance*. Ottawa: Manpower and Immigration.

_____
1975 "L'avenir des francophones au Canada." In *Mémoires de la Société Royale du Canada*, Série IV, Tome XIII:133–39.

Kettle, John
1980 *The Big Generation*. Toronto: McClelland and Stewart.

Lapierre-Adamcyk, Evelyne, et al.
1984 "Le cycle de la vie familiale au Québec: vues comparatives, XVIIe-XXe siècles." *Cahiers Québécois de Démographie*, 13(1):59–77.

Lavoie, Y.
1972 *L'Emigration des Canadiens aux Etats-Unis avant 1930*. Montréal: Les Presses de l'Université de Montréal.

Lesthaeghe, Ron
1983 "A Century of Demographic Change in Western Europe: An Exploration of Underlying Dimensions." *Population and Development Review*, 9(3):411–35.

Lupri, Eugen and James Frideres
1981 "The Quality of Marriage and the Passage of Time: Marital Satisfaction Over the Life Cycle. *Canadian Journal of Sociology*, 6:283–305.

Lux, André
1983 "Un Québec qui vieillit: perspectives pour le XXIe siècle." *Recherches Sociologiques*, 24(3):325–77.

Lynch, James J.
1977 *The Broken Heart: The Medical Consequences of Loneliness*. New York: Basic Books.

Manpower and Immigration
1974 *The Immigration Program*. Ottawa: Information Canada.

Mathews, Georges
1984 *Le Choc Démographique: Le Déclin du Québec est-il Inévitable?* Montréal: Boréal Express.

McDaniel, Susan A.
1986 *Canada's Aging Population*. Toronto: Butterworths.

McDonald Commission
1985 *Royal Commission on the Economic Union and Development Prospects for Canada*. Ottawa: Supply and Services Canada.

McInnis, R.M.
1980 "A Functional View of Canadian Immigration." Paper presented at the annual meetings of the Population Association of America, April, Denver, Colorado.

McKeown, Thomas, R.G. Brown, and R.G. Record
1972 "An Interpretation of the Modern Rise of Population in Europe." *Population Studies*, 26(3):345–82.

Nagnur, Dhruva
1986 "Rectangularization of the Survival Curve and Entropy: The Canadian Experience, 1921–1981." *Canadian Studies in Population*, 13(1): 83–102.

Pamuk, Elsie R.
1985 "Social Class Inequality in Mortality from 1921 to 1972 in England and Wales." *Population Studies*, 39(1):17–31.

Péron, Yves and Claude Strohmenger
1985 *Demographic and Health Indicators: Presentation and Interpretation*. Cat. no. 82-543. Ottawa: Statistics Canada.

Population Reference Bureau
1986 *World Population Data Sheet*. Washington, D.C.: Population Reference Bureau, Inc.

Richmond, Anthony H.
1984 "Immigration and Unemployment in Canada and Australia." *International Journal of Comparative Sociology*, 25:243–55.

Romaniuc, A.
1984 *Current Demographic Analysis: Fertility in Canada*. Cat. no. 91-524. Ottawa: Statistics Canada.

Rowe, G. and M.J. Norris
1985 *Mortality Projections of Registered Indians, 1982 to 1996*. Ottawa: Indian and Northern Affairs Canada.

Ryder, Norman B.
1975 "Reproductive Behaviour and the Family Life Cycle." Vol. III in United Nations, *The Population Debate: Dimensions and Perspectives*. New York: United Nations.

Samuel, John and T. Conyers
1986 "The Employment Effects of Immigration: A Balance Sheet Approach." *Population Working Paper Number 2,* Employment and Immigration.

Seward, Shirley B.
1987 "Demographic Change and the Canadian Economy: An Overview." *Discussion Paper on the Demographic Review*. Ottawa: Institute for Research on Public Policy.

Shorter, Edward
1975 *The Making of the Modern Family*. New York: Basic Books.

Siegfried, André
1907 *The Race Question in Canada*. London: Eveleigh Nash.

——
1937 *Le Canada, puissance internationale*. Paris: Librairie Armand Colin.

Statistics Canada
1978 *Out of School—Into the Labour Force*. Cat. no. 81-570. Ottawa: Statistics Canada.

——
1984a *Highlights: 1981 Census of Canada*. Ottawa: Statistics Canada.

——
1984b *Urban Growth in Canada*. (Cat. no. 99-942). Ottawa: Statistics Canada.

——
1985 *Population Projections for Canada, Provinces and Territories, 1984–2006*. Cat. no. 91-520. Ottawa: Statistics Canada.

——
1986 *Causes of Death, 1984*. Cat. no. 84-803. Ottawa: Statistics Canada.

Stone, Lawrence
1977 *The Family, Sex and Marriage in England 1500–1800*. New York: Harper and Row.

Stub, Holger R.
1982 *The Social Consequences of Long Life*. Springfield: Charles C. Thomas Publisher.

Timlin, M.F.
1951 *Does Canada Need More People?* Toronto: Oxford University Press.

United Nations
1984 *United Nations World Population Data Chart*. New York: United Nations.

van de Walle, Etienne and John Knodel
1980 "Europe's Fertility Transition: New Evidence and Lessons for Today's Developing World." *Population Bulletin*, 34(6).

Veevers, Jean E.
1980 *Childless by Choice*. Toronto: Butterworths.

Weiner, Myron
1985 "International Migration and International Relations." *Population and Development Review*, 11(3):441–55.

Wilkins, Russell and Owen B. Adams
1983 *Healthfulness of Life*. Montreal: Institute for Research on Public Policy.

Urban means concentration of people and automobiles. *Courtesy of Dean Goodwin*

"Everyday commuting has become a fixture of life in industrial cities. Long commutes are surely found elsewhere, but far fewer urbanites in nations like Canada live and work in the same location."

c h a p t e r t h r e e

Urbanization and Urbanism

William Michelson

INTRODUCTION

Canada and the Soviet Union surround the frozen Arctic. While a few nations reach up to touch the North and share some of our geographic features, no others reflect the northern extremities of their continents with such expansive, sparsely populated, and hard-to-exploit east-west land masses. Stark environmental realities present a nation with a context — weather, resources, growing conditions, and the like — but they do not determine where and how people live.

This chapter on urbanization and urbanism addresses precisely these questions. What is the pattern of settlement within Canada? What does this pattern mean for people's lives and activities?

Although such matters might appear highly formalistic, their understanding involves a web of considerations bound to the nature and development of Canadian society, no less than would be true in analyzing the Soviet case, or that of France or India. The structure of a society helps determine whether large portions of its population are urban or rural, and helps specify what kinds of cities are found within its borders. Conversely, at any time settlement patterns provide a context, with opportunities and constraints, that help explain how a given society operates in the lives of its citizens. Societies and cities are thus chickens and eggs. At any point, they are interdependent.

Canadians are typically proud of Canada and its cities. This is no accident. Canada's cities reflect Canadian society. Our cities support aspects of daily life and social structure that, in turn, help perpetuate this society.

Therefore, this chapter will focus both on how societies transform *where* people live and on ways that settlement patterns influence *how* people live. The concept of urbanization addresses the first, while urbanism deals with the second.

The application of these concepts to Canadian urban areas and life becomes much clearer when comparisons are made. One comparison always made is with conditions in the United States. Because of proximity and the assumption of similarity adopted by outsiders, Canadian–American similarities and differences are closely scrutinized. But fixing on this comparison ignores the potential range of differences. For example, Canadians who call their currency strong when it gains a few cents against the American dollar, while losing 20 percent or more to other major world currencies, have a limited comparative view.

Attention will be focused first, therefore, on Canadian urbanization and urbanism in an international perspective. In this regard, Canadian patterns strongly resemble those of the United States. Nonetheless, the two have significant differences.

Finally, variation is not just between societies, but within them. In a nation with the variety and breadth of Canada, it is not surprising to find major differences in where and how people live, by region, economic base, and culture. Such considerations conclude this chapter.

KEY CONCEPTS

Urbanization refers to the percentage of residents of a nation that live in its urban areas. The requirement for a settlement to qualify as urban is not generally high. But the minimum size of 2500 to 5000 persons ensures the resulting area contains a critical mass of persons who are not in the primary occupations of agriculture, hunting, or fishing. Obviously, many urban areas thus classified are much larger. Excluded are farming settlements.

Urbanization thus refers to settlement patterns. Therefore, it is particularly sensitive to the state of a society and its changes.

Urbanism, on the other hand, refers to the ways of living typically found in cities. The unit of analysis for urbanism is thus directed downward in scale from the society to the individual. What the urban dweller typically does, or how he or she typically reacts, are different from similar phenomena among rural counterparts.

Explanation for various traits of urbanism, however, lies at higher levels of aggregation. Presumably, the word urbanism implies there is something about urban areas that *causes* what's found there. A famous journal article called "Urbanism as a Way of Life" (Wirth, 1938), for example, said that the large size, high density, and social heterogeneity of urban areas determined a host of behaviours and social processes from distrust to social mobility. Another study (Simmel, 1950:400–427) traced urban impersonality and the blasé attitude of urbanites to persistent sensory stimuli in cities.

Nonetheless, while city life is in many ways different from life elsewhere, there is disagreement about what explains characteristic urban behaviours. A Canadian task force, for example, differentiated between phenomena "of the city" and those "in the city" (Lithwick, 1970:15). The former refer to behaviour caused by the generic structure of cities, while the latter reflect a variety of societal and subcultural causes, however pronounced their appearance within cities and hence their apparent association with them. This task force implied most urbanism is of the latter type.

If urbanism were "of" cities, one could reasonably expect a common behaviour in cities around the world. Presumably, the similarity of certain kinds of behaviour among societies is then a function of the degree of urbanization (i.e., the percentage of societal population living in cities). If, on the other hand, urbanism were predominantly "in" cities, magnifying nonphysical social conditions among great numbers of city dwellers, then one could reasonably expect variation in the way of life of cities in different societies. Several recent writings suggest that the society and the particular social composition of specific cities both influence the typical behaviours found there but that such effects are made possible by certain characteristics of the cities themselves — a combination of the two perspectives on urbanism (cf. Fischer, 1976).

Thus, the study of Canadian urbanism has to tackle the extent to which it includes certain proportions of universal as well as societal ways of living.

URBANIZATION IN COMPARATIVE PERSPECTIVE

About 75 percent of Canada's population is concentrated in urban areas.[1]

One might argue the bulk of Canadian territory, including the Canadian shield and sub-Arctic and Arctic terrains, is unsuited for agriculture and cloaked with extreme climatic conditions — hostile to extensive settlement. Canada's cities lie largely in more temperate regions, within one hundred miles of the American border, seemingly more attractive surroundings for residence. Nonetheless, Canada's urbanization level is in the same league as countries like the Netherlands, which differ enormously in geography, while differing from the Soviet Union and its guard over the other half of the North. Furthermore, although its geography has remained stable, Canada has not always been highly urbanized.

Urbanization levels reflect the degree of technological development of nations (and regions within large nations). Before the start of the Industrial Revolution in the eighteenth century, all nations were largely rural. The famous old cities were small compared to those of today: none had even a million residents; most cities were much smaller. As water, steam, and coal became harnessed to industrial production, production became focused in increasingly larger settlements; workers moved nearer to the factories that employed them. The industrial process also required persons in other developing sectors of the urban economy. Some were related to industrial products: specialists in finance, middlemen, warehousers, sales personnel, transportation specialists, etc. Others provided material support to other persons: to house them, feed them, clothe them, etc. Eventually the municipalities required great numbers just to provide necessary services: police, fire, health, and the like. The result was the burgeoning of urban populations as more jobs appeared because of industrialization.

But societies with the technology to implement industrial production apply it to agricultural and extractive activities as well (farming, fishing, and mining). Agricultural mechanization in technologically developed societies has permitted fewer persons to cultivate larger tracts of land. Indeed, even more recent use of chemical fertilizers has further increased crop yield, though their long-term impact on soil and water supplies is less positive. Similar increases in the efficiency of mining and fishing have led to lower personnel intensity. Thus, the same societal trends that increase urban populations decrease rural populations.

Canada belongs to a group of technologically developed nations, including Britain, Australia, New Zealand, northwestern European countries, Japan, and the United States, with high levels of urbanization. Exact data for international comparisons are difficult to obtain because of different national definitions of settlement areas and types, as well as varying data availability and quality. But according to Statistics Canada (1984), Belgium has the greatest degree of urban settlement at 87 percent, with Australia next at 86 percent. Most of the above-named nations are clustered in the mid-70 percent range. In this regard, Canada and the United States are less than 1 percent apart.

Far different settlement patterns are observed in less technologically developed areas of the world — which include the bulk of world population. According to what may be the most painstaking international comparison ever made (Davis, 1972), only 38 percent of the world's population lived in urban areas as of 1970, leaving the balance of 62 percent rural. At that time, for example, India had only 18.8 percent of its population living in urban areas; China, 23.5 percent (Davis, 1969, Table C). All of Asia had only 25.4 percent urban, Africa 21.8 percent (Golden, 1981:77). Estimates for 1980 indicated a world increase in urbanization by only 3 percent to 41 percent (Light, 1983:134). Even in today's jet and computer age, Canadian technology is being transformed for application to the vast rural Indian market. Alcan makes streamlined, lightweight oxcarts destined for more than half a million villages and their fleet of fifteen million oxcarts (Elliot, 1987).

Such great societal differences in urbanization levels appear paradoxical in view of well-known, heavily populated cities in less-developed countries. Shanghai, Calcutta, and Bombay, for example, are huge cities. Indeed, twenty of the largest thirty-five cities in the world in 1980 were in the Third World, averaging more than eight million inhabitants each (Light, 1983:137). But at least two factors underlie major differences in Third World settlement patterns from those experienced in nations like Canada. First, without an accompanying technological development in society, a *network* of cities based on power industry did not appear in the less-developed countries. Rural residents flocked to those Third World locations, which nations like England, France, the Netherlands, Spain, and Portugal carved out as their headquarters from which to control local populations and to extract local raw materials. But this migration reflected the hope of betterment rather than any plentitude of jobs accompanying industrialization. And with the importation of selected standards of public health, the traditionally high birth rates yielded a greater percentage of survivors and hence a population that exploded through migration and natural increase. Thus, less-developed nations got some cities with huge populations while remaining predominantly rural.

Even nominally industrial nations like the U.S.S.R. have sizable rural segments belied by the prominence of major cities. Where technology has not been transferred equally well to agriculture, there is a larger rural population component.

A second factor in the paradoxical coincidence of large cities in predominantly rural nations is that rural densities are greater when intensive person-power is needed to till the soil. While the large cities are populous, so also are the interstitial rural areas, which obviously cover vastly more territory. As a rural geographer remarked, just because rural areas fill the "white" areas on maps does not mean that they are unused or uninhabited. For example, the rural areas of India had an estimated 145 persons per square mile, when Denmark, with a high degree of development and land almost entirely suitable for cultivation, had but twenty-three people per square mile in its rural areas (Davis, 1969: Table H). According to the same data, Canada had a rural density of but one person per square mile; the U.S.S.R. with

THE CANADIAN TREND TOWARD URBANIZATION

Insofar as the technology applied to both urban and rural activities was necessary for so many to be urbanites, it is not surprising that Canadian settlement patterns were not always this way.

At Confederation, Canada was overwhelmingly rural. Figure 1 shows urbanization rates increased at very gradual, though steady, rates from just under 20 percent in 1871 to the 1981 figure of 75.5 percent. Half the Canadian population became urban only by 1931, and Canada's level of urbanization has remained steady since the early 1970s.

Figure 1

Estimated percentage of Canada's urban population, 1871 to 1981

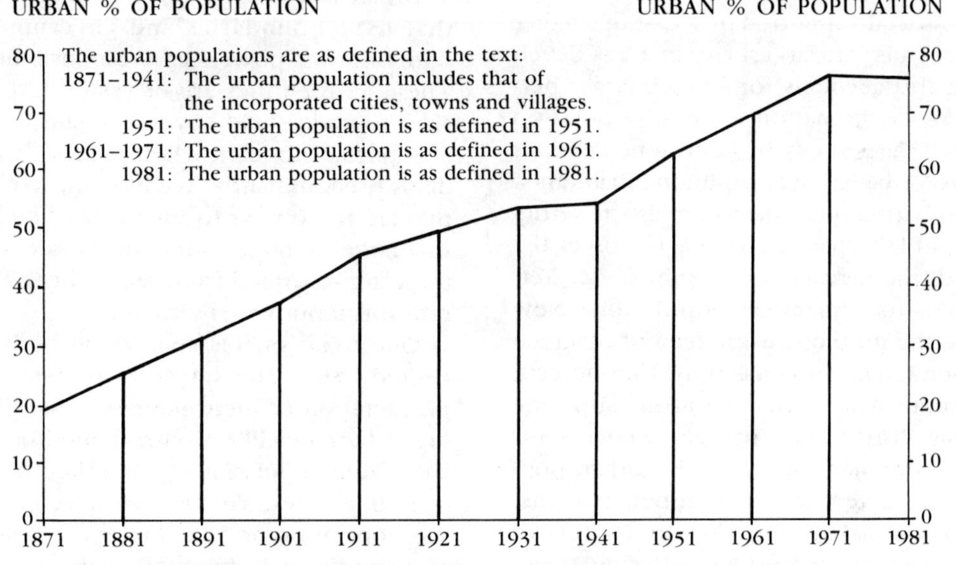

Source: 1971 and 1981 Censuses of Canada.
Reproduced with permission of the Minister of Supply and Services Canada.

Like other countries with Native peoples who fell under the influence of European imperial powers, Canada did not lack urban settlements in its early years. Consistent with contemporary Third World examples, Canada's early cities were based on fur trading/trans-shipment centres (Montreal, Vancouver) and military/naval garrisons (Halifax, Quebec City, Winnipeg, Calgary), with these functions often combined. Nonetheless, despite the rigours and isolation inherent in Canadian geography, the population was overwhelmingly rural in the early days of European settlement—well below the level at Confederation. Land was a meaningful commodity to Europeans who never had their own or who were losing it due to European industrialization, on the one hand, and famine, on the other.

its rough geographic comparability, had four times the rural density. The U.S.A., with a significantly greater percentage of tillable land than Canada and the U.S.S.R., though far less than Denmark, had a rural density of five, very low in world standards, but reflecting the onset of "agribusiness" and its underlying technology.

Given the differing circumstances surrounding the origin and context of cities, it is not surprising that the pattern of cities differs between developed and less-developed areas beyond sheer level of urbanization. The giant cities of the Third World are less well-supported by a cast of smaller cities. Thus, the largest city in a less-developed area accounts for a much larger percentage of its nation's urban population than the largest city in a developed nation. Addis Ababa has over a million inhabitants, but is virtually alone as an urban settlement in Ethiopia. Santiago is ten times the size of the next largest city in Chile. Yet, despite its enormous population, New York (the **metropolitan area** of nineteen million inhabitants) has only 10.5 percent of urban Americans. London, supreme among British cities in size, accounts for only 25 percent of the British urban population. Like other developed nations, Canada's urban population is spread among many centres of differing scale; Toronto, the largest, accounts for only 15 percent, while Montreal is a similar size.

Canada thus has a distinctive pattern of urban settlement shared with relatively few technologically advanced countries, in which about three-quarters of the population is distributed in urban areas of varying size across its territory.

The trend towards urbanization in the United States is similar to Canada's. Nevertheless, the earlier industrialization south of the border, reflecting earlier political autonomy, is reflected in urbanization levels, which ran approximately 5 percent higher than Canadian levels until about 1950 to 1951. Thereafter, these levels have been virtually identical (Palen, 1981:60).

CURRENT CANADIAN TRENDS

Metropolitanization

Given that most Canadians are now urban, living in a variety of areas, our next question is: is urban living in Canada largely metropolitan living or does it predominantly involve self-contained communities scattered across the landscape?

Urban settlements form municipalities that have boundaries and governments with differing powers and responsibilities. These legal entities are of vastly differing size. To understand how Canadians live, it is important to learn whether urban Canadians predominantly live in municipalities that are fitted next to each other like tiles in a larger, more continuous mosaic, or if these are separated from each other by significant nonurban environments.

One trend of this century, in both the United States and Canada, has been the proliferation of metropolitan areas. Existing older cities like Montreal and Toronto have large populations within their historical boundaries. Yet, as they have grown, the population and land-uses that constitute the *de facto* functional city in terms of everyday commuting, markets, servicing, communication, and the like have pushed throughout and beyond the borders of neighbouring, nominally independent municipalities. This has forced authorities to recognize the concept of metropolitan entities in addition to the historically sovereign municipal areas. These contemporary cities are called metropolitan areas.

Both Statistics Canada and the U.S. Bureau of the Census have explicit procedures for identifying metropolitan areas. The definitions for metropolitan areas changed between the two countries over time to reflect existing conditions. Nonetheless, the common pattern is that there should be a central municipality of at least fifty thousand inhabitants and that adjacent municipalities and areas be included if their characteristics indicate nonrural activities, daily commuting to and/or from the central city or other adjacent areas, and the presence of functions vital to the central city (e.g., an airport). The latest Statistics Canada rules require that a Census Metropolitan Area have at least one hundred thousand persons spread among one or more municipalities. Outlying municipalities are included if at least 40 percent of their employed residents work in the central city, or if at least 25 percent of the jobs in this municipality are filled by central city residents (Statistics Canada, 1983:vi).

There are currently twenty-five C.M.A.s in Canada ranging in size from Toronto (3 409 751) to St. John (120 353) (Statistics Canada, Preliminary Count for 1986). Montreal (2 896 684) is nearly the size of Toronto, but Vancouver (1 359 863), third in size, is less than half the previous two. There is then another major jump in size to a half dozen more cities: Ottawa–Hull (809 695), Edmonton (779 663), Calgary (667 005), Quebec City (597 586), Winnipeg (621 143), and Hamilton (554 589). Still another cluster forms between approximately 200 000 to 350 000 in size: St. Catharines/Niagara (340 599), London (339 664), Kitchener (309 710), Halifax (293 160), Victoria (253 000), Windsor (252 510), and Oshawa (202,620). Finally, well under 200 000 but larger than St. John are Regina, St. John's, Saskatoon, Sudbury, Chicoutimi-Jonquière, Trois-Rivières, and Thunder Bay.

In both Canada and the United States, there are internal variations in the structure of metropolitan areas. Predominantly older areas, largely in the Eastern and Central regions, are more likely to contain many municipalities, old and new, while the more recently established cities in the Western regions are more likely to be restricted to a single, growing municipality (or, in any case, fewer entities). The Saskatoon and Calgary Census Metropolitan Areas (C.M.A.s) for example, are identical to the cities by those names.

Figure 2

Division of 1981 population of Canada by residence in metropolitan areas, nonmetropolitan urban areas, and rural areas

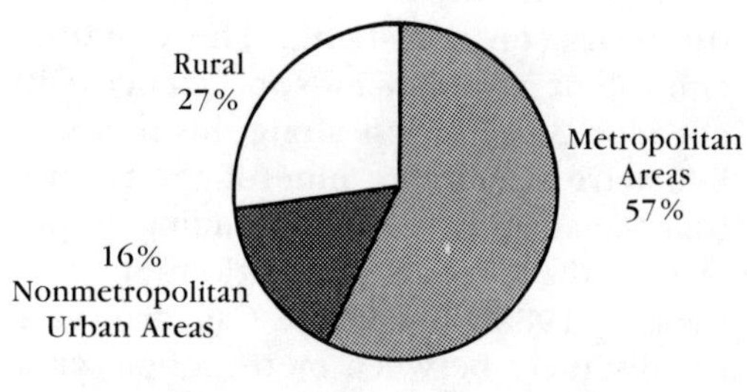

Source: Simmons and Bourne, 1984, p. 24.

In any case, Canada and the United States are virtually identical once again in that the great majority of urbanites are not in isolated settlements. Nearly 75 percent of urban Canadians live in C.M.A.s (Statistics Canada, 1983). As of 1981, 58 percent of *all* Canadians lived in agglomerations of over one hundred thousand persons. Indeed, more than half of these were in areas with a million or more inhabitants. Only 16 percent of Canadians lived in areas of 10 000 to 99 999 in the smaller, self-contained cities (Simmons and Bourne, 1984:24). Figure 2 indicates this breakdown.

The term **megalopolis** was coined with reference to the corridor between just north of Boston to just south of Washington, D.C. (Gottman, 1961). Here, major metropolitan areas are arrayed into a larger, functionally continuous agglomeration. Although the same intensity of urban development is not continuous along the entire length of the axis, nor are individuals expected to commute anywhere except within their own metropolitan areas, a form of economic and transport interdependency is found among the pearls on the string. The Canadian equivalent is the Windsor–Quebec City corridor. More or less along this thousand kilometre stretch are nine of the twenty-four Canadian C.M.A.s, containing 60 percent of the national population (Statistics Canada, 1980). But in the Canadian case, the distances between metropolitan areas are typically greater and the cities smaller. Only in the Oshawa to St. Catharines–Niagara Golden Horsehoe can a case be made for reasonably continuous urban development. The corridor nonetheless justifies high-speed transportation facilities, which further join the areas functionally to each other, and to American markets nearby.

National Urban Growth Patterns

There has been considerable speculation in recent years on the emerging shape of the Canadian urban settlement pattern. For example, in the late 1960s, urbanists thought that Toronto, Montreal, and, to a lesser extent, Vancouver were growing so quickly that they would absorb the overwhelming proportion of the Canadian

Figure 3
Concentration of population in Canadian cities

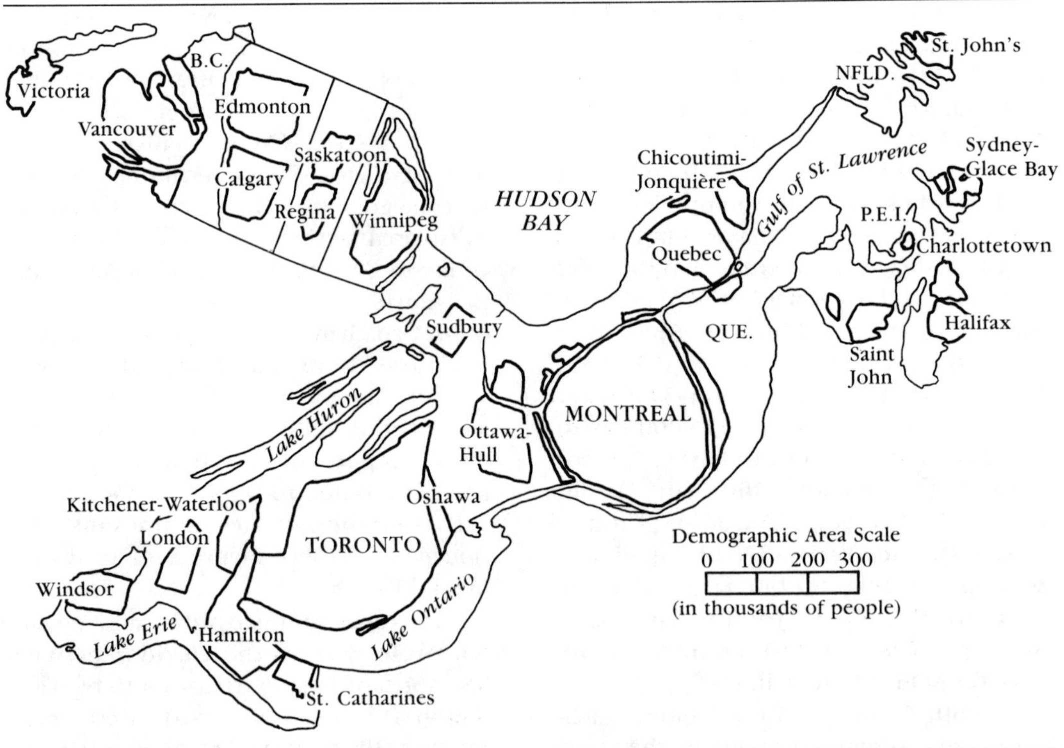

Sources: L. Skoda and C.I. Jackson, "A Mechanical Method of Constructing Equal Population Density Maps." Discussion Paper 8.72.4 (Ottawa Ministry of State for Urban Affairs (MSUA), 1972) and L. Skoda and J.C. Robertson, *Isodemographic Map of Canada*. Department of Environment, Geographical Paper No. 50 (Ottawa Information Canada, 1972). Reproduced by permission of the Minister of Supply and Services Canada.

CONTROLLING URBAN GROWTH PATTERNS

National urban growth paterns are ostensibly open to control by governments. Several countries have tried to control and direct urban growth. Sweden is among the more successful, placing services and facilities such as hospitals and universities and relocating public service jobs so as to bring about a national network of medium-sized cities, curbing the overwhelming influence of Stockholm. Britain had an official new towns policy to channel growth away from London. The U.S.S.R. promotes the growth of Siberian resource cities, while attempting to control Moscow's growth by issuing few residence permits. Brazil built a new capital to focus attention and development away from Rio and São Paulo.

Canada has not taken such active steps. Urban matters are a provincial responsibility; so co-ordinated policies are difficult to achieve. The objectives of the late Ministry of State for Urban Affairs involving co-ordination were largely not achieved. Federal initiatives have been directed to remedying regional economic disparities, but without conspicuous success even without regard to urban impacts (Bourne, 1975).

A contemporary footnote on this potentiality is the designation by the Mulroney government of Montreal and Vancouver as international banking centres, presumably to bolster relative economic weaknesses there. Critics, however, say that the number of jobs thus created would probably be only a few hundreds, not the most incisive demonstration of governmental direction.

population at the expense of smaller urban areas. Projection of then-current trends portrayed in Figure 3 (a map showing territory in size as a function of the population there) alarmed people who saw this as the tail wagging the dog. One outcome was the formation of a Ministry of State for Urban Affairs in Ottawa, an attempt, later abandoned, to stimulate and co-ordinate a federal interest in Canadian urban growth patterns and issues.

This projection, however, did not foresee the oil crisis of the early 1970s, nor the decline in foreign immigration to Canada, nor the effects of Quebec's cultural politics. Between 1971 and 1976, Calgary grew by over 16 percent and Edmonton by 12 percent, compared to 8 percent for Toronto and Vancouver, and not quite 3 percent for Montreal (Statistics Canada, 1980, chart 6). In the following five years, these margins widened. Calgary grew by another 25.7 percent and Edmonton by 16.9 percent, compared to Vancouver's 8.7 percent, Toronto's 7 percent, and Montreal's 0.9 percent (Simmons, 1984:24).

Those who then extrapolated from these figures were wrong again. International oil prices weakened, as did interest in exploiting Alberta's oil sands, sending large numbers of persons elsewhere for employment and causing hardship for investors in these large Alberta cities. The communities that have grown the most in the recent half decade are the smaller ones on the fringes of existing metropolitan areas.

Although following a broad urbanization pattern of developed nations, Canada's exact pattern follows trends unique to its society and the forces acting within it:

Figure 4

Canadian Census Metropolitan Areas maps, indicating tremendously large portions for suburban growth

Source: Statistics Canada, Perspective Canada III, Ottawa: Minister of Supply and Services, 1980. Reproduced with permission of the Minister of Supply and Services Canada.

Figure 4 (continued)

Source: Statistics Canada, Perspective Canada III, Ottawa: Minister of Supply and Services, 1980. Reproduced with permission of the Minister of Supply and Services Canada.

Figure 4 (continued)

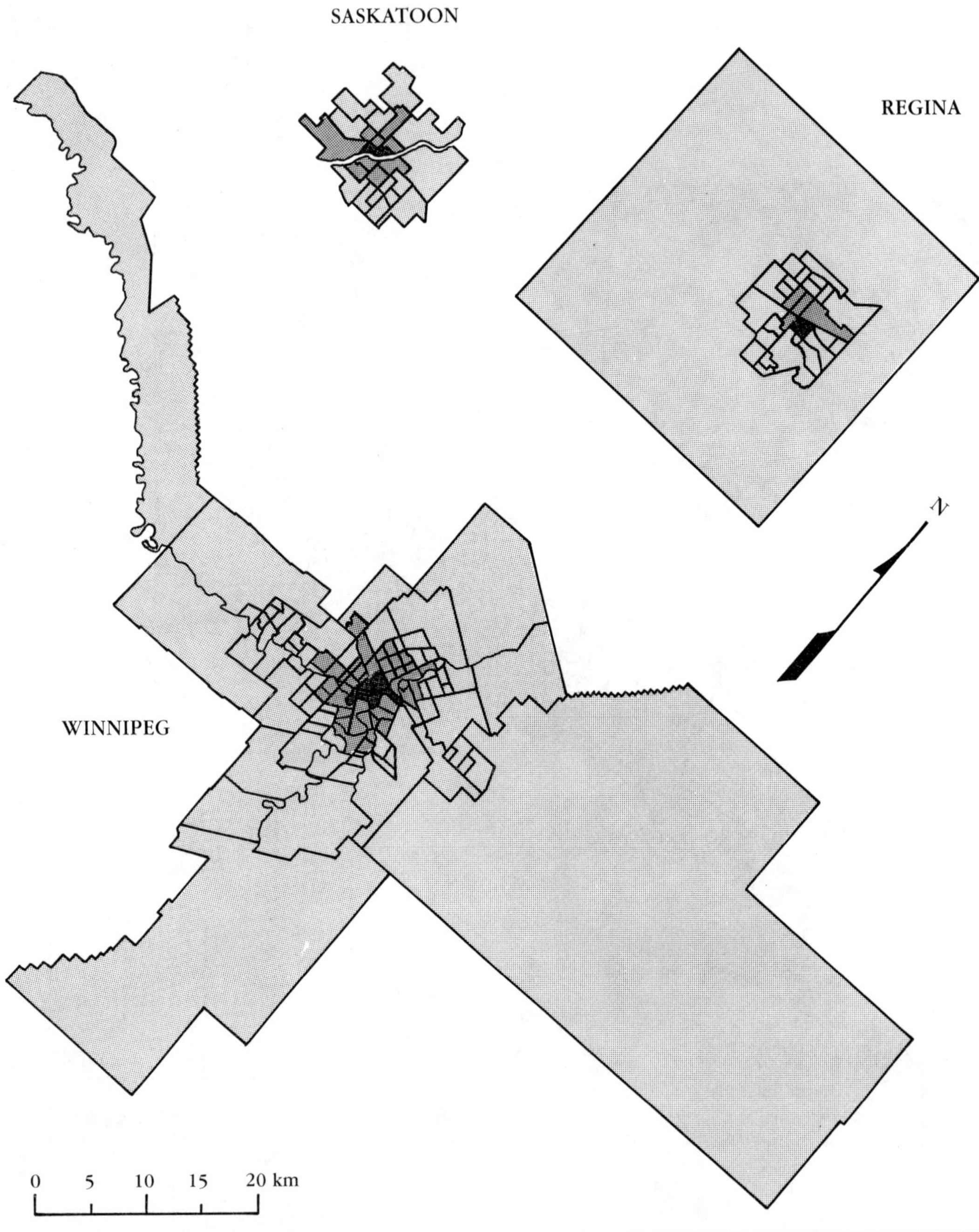

Source: Statistics Canada, Perspective Canada III, Ottawa: Minister of Supply and Services, 1980. Reproduced with permission of the Minister of Supply and Services Canada.

Figure 4 (continued)

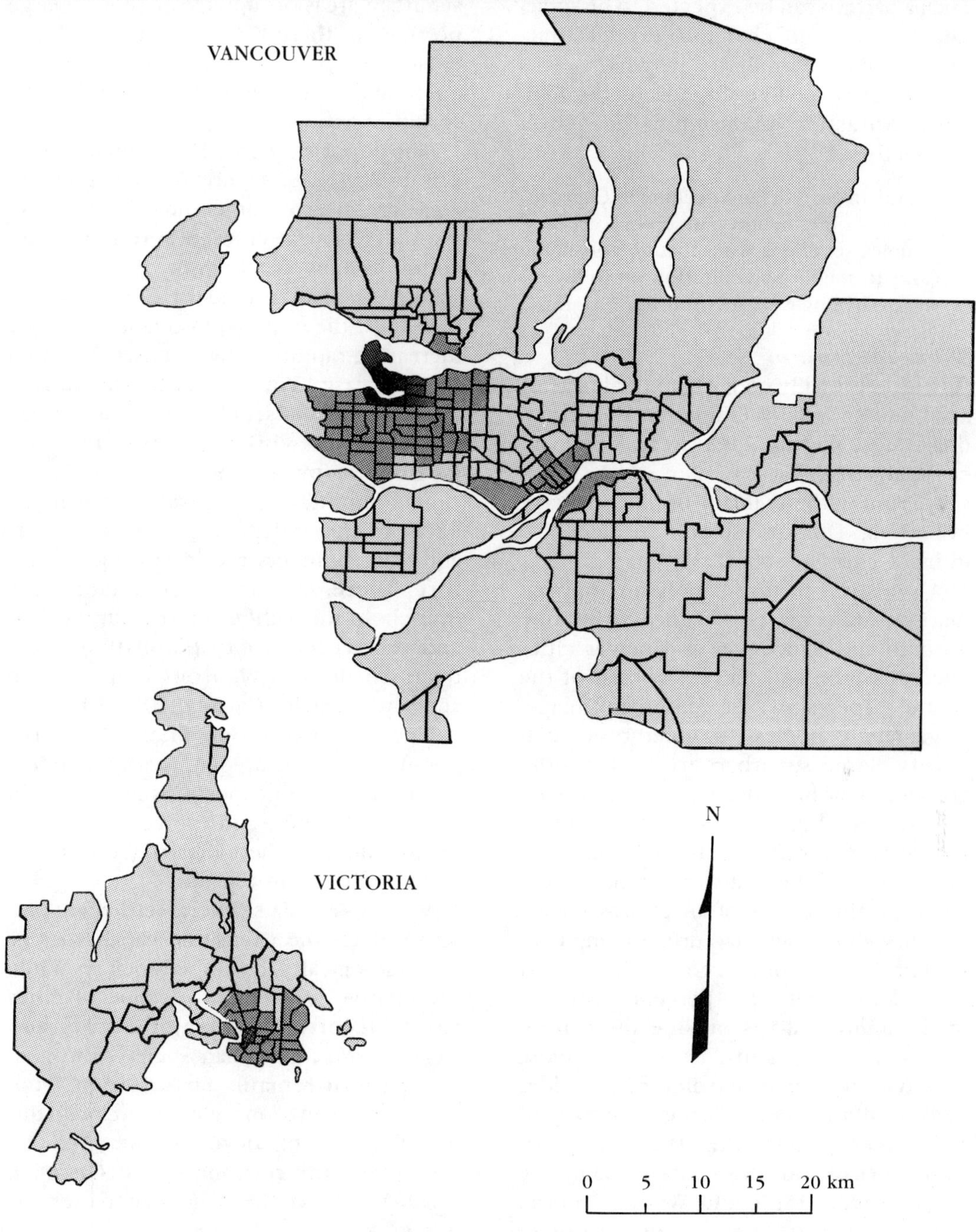

Source: Statistics Canada, Perspective Canada III, Ottawa: Minister of Supply and Services, 1980. Reproduced with permission of the Minister of Supply and Services Canada.

economic, demographic, and cultural. Such a pattern can be expected to be societally unique and changeable over time, despite general similarity to what occurs in nations most like Canada technologically. An astute analyst put the matter succinctly:

> . . . urban growth (and decline) in Canada, or in any other country, involves a very complex set of processes that do not submit easily to simple generalizations or to the search for single causes (Bourne, 1984:1).

Suburbanization

Cities traditionally conjure up the image of aged and/or large buildings in dense settings. Most metropolitan areas, however, contain *suburbs* — newer, with more space, and with the image of more privacy in housing. Do most urban Canadians live in inner cities or suburbs?

A statistical picture is only an approximation. Many parts of older cities like Toronto and Vancouver and newer cities like Edmonton and Calgary consist of the central aspects of the suburban image: single-family homes on quiet residential streets. Some suburban areas of rapidly growing areas like Toronto and Ottawa are replete with high-rise apartments, albeit spaced to allow for fresh air (often very much of it!). The statistics cannot document the fine points of an elusive image. But they show Canadian urban living goes well beyond the older central cities. Most Canadian urbanites (52 percent) now live in the municipalities outside the central cities (Statistics Canada, 1983). This figure is heavily weighted by some of the older metropolitan areas: Toronto, Montreal, Vancouver. If one takes the settings of these suburbs and adds them to the nature of the newer Prairie and Western central cities, Canada is clearly devoted to modern, suburban residential patterning.

Figure 4 illustrates this point with reference to maps of selected Canadian Census Metropolitan Areas. The newer suburban areas occupy tremendously large portions of these C.M.A.s, simultaneously presenting space for large populations and a potential opportunity for living in more spacious settings.

The population growth shown in Figure 4 is indicated in Figure 5. The suburban areas are clearly burgeoning. To the eye, the older central cities, where rental and condominium apartments often replace smaller residential units or nonresidential buildings, the population ought also to be increasing rapidly. This is, however, often not the case. Young people are starting independent households at an earlier age than before, while the birth rate has declined below the point of population replacement. Older persons are more likely to live independently than before, and their numbers are increasing. Therefore, there are far fewer persons per household throughout most central cities, and some central city populations have declined despite vigorous construction activity (Statistics Canada, 1980:196).

The suburbanization of the Canadian population is not unique. Nearly identical urban–suburban proportions are found in the United States, and the suburban population plurality there occurred during the same decade as in Canada.

In sum, Canada's general settlement pattern reflects the needs and capabilities of a technologically developed society. While the relative growth and decline of cities varies according to major events and trends *within* Canadian society, the general pattern remains far different from those of the nations with extremely different levels of development. And by this token, the resemblance of Canadian urbanization to the American pattern is unmistakeable.

Because two teams play on similarly arranged fields does not mean they play the game the same way. How people live

Figure 5
Population by zone and population change, 1961 to 1976

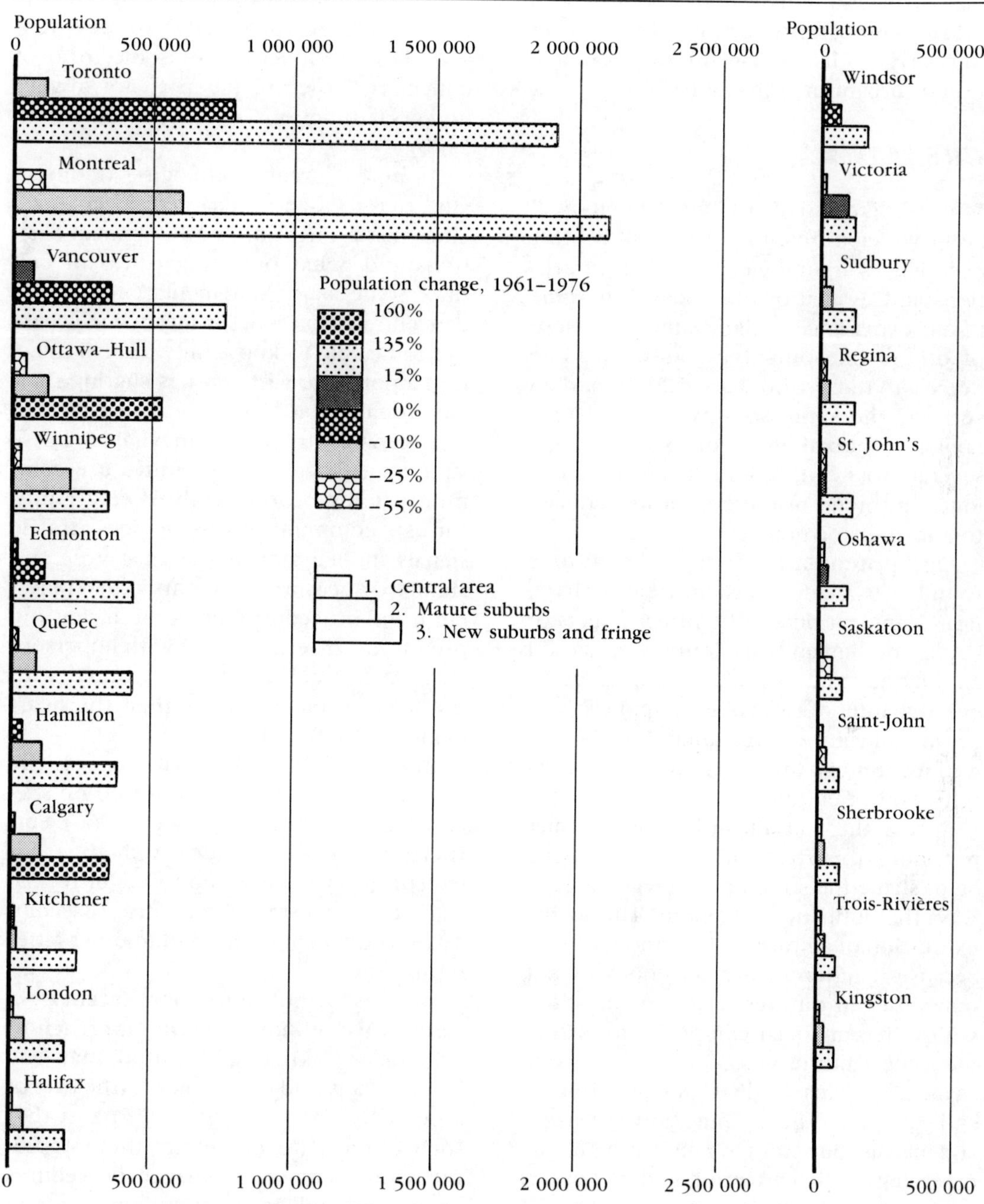

Source: Statistics Canada, Perspective Canada III, Ottawa: Minister of Supply and Services, 1980.

within their urban areas is not determined entirely by urbanization levels, the number, size, and clustering of cities, and urban–suburban proportions. For a closer look at Canadian urban life, an examination of urbanism is necessary.

URBANISM

What it's like to live in a Canadian city will be answered differently by each of us. Our experiences are unique, as are our perceptions and evaluations of them. But some of our experiences will be similar to those of others like ourselves, and, in some degree, to those who share the same urban setting, the same society and culture. Looking at urban life involves considering several cross-cutting influences on behaviour. And none of these is easily reduced to a formula or number.

One potent influence on behaviour found in Canadian urban areas will go nearly unmentioned. The direct effects of culture on human behaviour are powerful and varied. They should be expressed in every chapter of this volume, applicable to urban and rural Canada alike. But there is nothing unique in cities to behavioural reflection of culture.

Where the cultural influence becomes pertinent to urbanism is when culture helps shape the structure of given cities in ways that influence behaviour. The spatial expression of culture is of intrinsic interest because it differentiates the looks of not only cities in different cultures but cities with different social compositions within the same culture. Once local structure is shaped, it helps facilitate some activities and constrain others. Thus, how we shape and manage our cities is a mediating factor deserving explicit attention in this chapter, while culture itself does not.

Urbanism, therefore, does not deal with the explanation of all behaviour found in cities, but rather with that related to some conceptual or concrete aspect of city structure found at a collective level. Urbanism addresses phenomena "in the city" which are "of the city" to the extent that they are functions of some form of collective structure (even if not always universal functions of cities) (Lithwick, 1970).

As noted, urban sociologists traditionally tried to identify characteristics of *all* cities that brought out similar human reactions and behaviours, regardless of culture. Some major statements cited earlier concentrated on what it means for urbanites to be able to know only a small selection among the vast throngs sharing their city, usually at a high enough density that contact with strangers is inevitable. These statements suggested urbanites use commonly understood symbols (e.g., uniforms), communications devices (traffic signals, police whistles, sirens, etc.), and standard measures (weights, currencies, etc.), and procedures (universal hiring and promotion criteria) to deal with impersonality. As Simmel put it, one worked with the head in cities, rather than the heart (Simmel, 1950:400–27).

But although many writers took the same direction, they never agreed on specific traits of urbanism (Dewey, 1960). Furthermore, studies uncovered apparent exceptions to these supposed universal traits of urbanism: whole cities (Bascom, 1955) and communities within other cities (Gans, 1962).

But this did not stop a more recent U.S.-based wave of interest in this approach to urbanism. Taking for granted that one lived in "a world of strangers" (the title of a book by Lyn Lofland, 1973) and that some of them are *dangerous*, these studies focus on common avoidance procedures people use and on showing how clothing styles and residential stratification provide legitimation for necessary contacts (see also Karp, Stone, and Yoels, 1977).

Although the behaviour discussed in this regard is no doubt recognizable to most readers, this emphasis and the priority given to it applies mainly to the American urban context.

The study of urbanism in Canadian society benefits less from accepting or rejecting the universalism of selected characteristics derived largely from the United States and more from asking what conditions pertain in given Canadian settings, and with what behavioural implications. Are these similar or different from those found in American cities?

Fischer (1976) argued against across-the-board determination of urbanism as a function of the nature of cities, noting a slew of studies showing how population subgroups influence behaviour. But rather than stick with this compositional explanation of behaviour alone, he juxtaposed the latter with the macro deterministic school of thought. Cities in general, because of their size, allow particular subgroups to become sufficiently large and thus have strong effects internally on behaviour. Such subgroups attain *critical mass* in cities. A few people whose background or interests are unusual in a small town (and hence not supported or reinforced) can find themselves in a compatible subculture in the right city. Furthermore, the fundamental characteristics of a given city — its economic base, location, climate, existing culture, housing stock, etc. — selectively attract new residents, contributing to a particular nature or combination of subcultures there. Common urban behaviours, according to this view, are a function of the characteristics of general urban scale, the fundamental characteristics of given cities, and the subcultures attracted to them.

We now turn to some aspects of Canadian society with implications for urban structure and, hence, for behaviour.

Canada's high level of technology has certain aspects of urbanism in common with similar nations. Home and work became separated during the rise of factories long ago (Sjoberg, 1960). Cottage industries and residential districts of craft specialists gave way to specialized production centres. Workers lived close by when they had to walk to work, but farther away as transportation services improved. Everyday commuting has become a fixture of life in industrial cities. Long commutes are surely found elsewhere, but far fewer urbanites in nations like Canada live and work in the same location.

The latest wrinkles in communications technology enable decentralized operations. Indeed, the computer makes possible some form of return to cottage industry, insofar as some employees can work at home without apparent loss of communication. These innovations facilitate the division of company operations, with the suburbanization of many of them, lessening the single-minded development of an undisputed city centre. It has also diffused commuting patterns away from that traditional central target. But it has not as yet done away with widespread commuting.

A second aspect of technology is the imposition of standards to safeguard health, welfare, and safety. Increasingly elaborate laws now specify how development should occur in cities. These include the level of water, sewage, roads, and other aspects of physical infrastructure. They also deal with which land-uses are permitted in juxtaposition with other ones. Such land-use regulations try to keep the proverbial glue factories away from where people live, and these have until recently increased the separation of different activities — and especially residential areas from commerce and industry — adding to the need for daily travel.

Furthermore, laws now regulate the size of buildings and the spaces between and

DOWNTOWN REVITALIZATION IN CANADA AND THE UNITED STATES

The issue of how to revitalize downtown areas highlights a major Canadian–American difference. The aura of central city desertion except for work, coupled with an ever-present spectre of crime, led to the perception that the modernization and change of land-use in and around American central cities could not occur except by governmental direction. Thus, publicly financed urban renewal came into being. Much centrally situated land was cleared and consolidated; considerably less new commercial and residential development ensued. Although specific cities and projects can be cited with pride (e.g., Baltimore; Boston's Faneuil Hall, and government centre area), American downtowns have experienced no renaissance to this point. Although Canada has had the legislative tools for renewal projects, the lion's share of the extremely effective revitalization sweeping the downtowns of its major cities has been from private developmental interests. There is far less fear of crime and other obstacles to development, and the appreciation of land value in the central cities in Canada have caused many private interests to invest in projects whose cumulative effects have been considerable.

Rapoport (1984:50–75) explores the impact of culture on urban structure. He notes "to understand [urban structure], . . . one needs to understand the cultural context of that particular urban order." City centres have always focused on buildings that were symbols of their cultural priorities. The cathedrals of medieval cities were early examples. Railway stations and city halls became North American symbols of civic pride. These stars have faded. The great Canadian symbol is the bank tower, a reinforcement of central-city private investment. Corporate symbols like the C.N. and Husky Towers are similar. Although some American cities have parallel symbolism (e.g., Chicago's Sears Tower and the John Hancock Building), more typical recent American symbols are self-contained sports stadia, complex freeway networks and interchanges, and vacant lots — all symbolizing ambivalence towards central city revitalization. (Much disenchantment with Toronto's Sky Dome reflects disagreement with the priorities in urban development symbolized by this particular use of centrally situated land.)

around them. Although workplaces, offices in particular, have been allowed to grow spectacularly in size, and high-rise residential buildings have been permitted to sprout in many districts, the size and spacing legislation has lowered residential densities and spread residential areas across greater expanses of territory. Travel, once again, is made a compelling aspect of everyday life.

The increasing separation of home and work tends to make the typical city in developed nations have a downtown centre devoid of people after working hours, nights, and weekends. The City of London, England, for example, is empty after hours. American cities have typically had centrally located entertainment centres; but increased crime has played chicken and egg with persons on the downtown streets at night, "killing" the central city even more. Toronto's downtown, by contrast, partly due to low crime rates and a later decentralization of non-residential land-uses, is still lively after dark. Capitalizing on this "vestigial" advantage, just as increasing numbers of restaurants and places of entertainment are accompanying the suburban development of commercial and residential land-uses throughout Metro Toronto, City of Toronto regulations require major developers of the central area to provide new housing units downtown to keep people *on* the streets. The result has been new districts of housing units catering to relatively affluent populations, with new cycles of restaurants, night clubs, cinemas (no longer just movies!), art galleries, theatres, and similar land-uses that enhance the area's liveliness.

Having the eyes and ears of ordinary people in sufficient numbers on the street at night seems to deter crime. People go out for recreation when they feel safe, and they close their shutters around them at home when they feel threatened. The demise of movie theatres and the ascent of pay television and V.C.R.s in the United States are not coincidental. The urban lives people lead are heavily influenced by how societal trends interact with urban structure.

Transportation and Society

How to reconstruct central city vitality is a specific concern within the more general phenomenon of the increasing level of daily travel brought on by wide-scale suburbanization. How the different societies address these problems shows how urban structures are created, with subsequent influences on urban life. In this case, how do societal values square with increasingly extensive and complex transportation needs?

David Popenoe wrote a thoughtful and provocative book called *Private Pleasure, Public Plight* (1985). The title indicates Popenoe's view that city structures reflect the problematic choice between public and private amenity. He argues that a growing emphasis on private consumption, found at its extreme in and around American cities, has led to bigger homes on larger lots, incorporating recreation and entertainment in or near home, and a focus on automobile transportation. He thinks it is difficult if not impossible to create collective solutions to common problems like transportation when both public and private spending is focused on roads and vehicles as a solution reflecting the values of private amenity. This becomes problematic insofar as the poor, children, the aged, and the handicapped do not typically own automobiles.

Although Popenoe thinks most advanced societies favour private pleasure, he describes how Sweden invested in superior public transportation in its urban areas at the cost of higher taxes, fewer freeways, and more control over residential development. This last-named control has led to a greater clustering of new urban developments, in contrast to sprawl, enabling more efficient planning and utilization of public transit, by rail and road. While Swedes have no monopoly on public transit, their priorities towards public amenity in travel have resulted in most persons using public transit for workday commuting, even if they use a car for commercial and recreational use. The Swedish system also serves a greater range of persons.

Canadian cities have recently put more priority on collective solutions to travel needs than have American cities. This does not mean public transportation is unknown in the United States. Major streetcar, subway, and bus systems were developed and used for years in most large American cities; but when post-war suburbanization blossomed, collective adaptations were secondary to personal transportation investments. It is probably no coincidence that the public transportation systems cracked simultaneously with the lowering of residential proximity among different population subgroups. Residential areas were increasingly at arm's length, and persons of different backgrounds no longer rubbed shoulders on buses and trains. Motor vehicle manufacturers accelerated the switch to an emphasis on road transportation by lobbying and by buying up and deactivating streetcar systems (Yago, 1984). Public programs then financed expressway construction, which cemented the emerging patterns of travel. Some cities (e.g., Washington, Atlanta, San Francisco Bay Area) *have* built new subway systems in the same recent period that saw new rail systems appear in Toronto, Montreal, Edmonton, Calgary, and, in 1986, Vancouver. But the over-all pattern is one of much more support for and use of public transit, whether bus or rail, within Canada.

In a thoroughgoing comparison of urban development in Canada and the United States, Goldberg and Mercer (1986:153, 252) found 85 percent of American commuters use automotive transportation compared to 66 percent of Canadian commuters. A quarter of the Canadians use public transit, compared to an eighth of the Americans — twice as many. The typical American urban area has four times as many lanes of freeways, and Americans own and operate 50 percent more automobiles per capita. This difference reflects, in part, notable societal differences regarding private amenity, insofar as loan interest on consumer purchases like automobiles has been tax deductible in the United States (until 1987) but not in Canada, with a significant impact on the presence or absence of second cars within households.

Because of societal processes that place more of families' transportation resources at the disposal of husbands, women have become more dependent than men on public transportation. This has been widely documented throughout the United States (Rosenbloom, 1978) and in Canadian cities (Chumak and Braaksma, 1981; Michelson, 1985). Thus, transportation especially benefits women as well as other subsectors of the population who don't own automobiles.

Ethnicity and Urban Structure

The pattern of settlement of different segments of the urban population is an age-old question. It can run from complete mixture of persons (i.e., total integration) to rigorous clusterings of subgroups apart from each other (i.e., segregation or even apartheid). A perspective that views the relative location of population groups (and also land-uses) *vis à vis* each other within cities is called "ecological," even though the scientific term of ecology applies to many other phenomena (Michelson, 1976).

The ecology of population groups is pertinent to urban life because clusters of homogeneous persons can immediately, spontaneously, and tangibly reinforce whatever a critical mass within the population might have in common. Some common forms of local homogeneity are socioeconomic status, ethnicity or race, stage in the life cycle, and religion.

In Western Europe, where royalty and its attendant culture were situated in city centres, wealthier persons often lived in prime central locations near their occupational, social, and cultural institutions. Less wealthy persons lived around them. This situation is also found in the less-developed nations with imperial ties, where the nonlocal interests established elaborate, centrally located quarters, while native residents lived at varying distances according to economic capacity. Such a pattern is graphically visible in cities like Canton and Shanghai, where the former European colonies still stand in stark contrast to the rest of the city as a result of their traditional Northern European architecture. Another typical fixture of cities in less-developed nations is the makeshift settlements beyond the formally developed areas of the cities, occupied by great numbers of economically marginal migrants, attracted by the possibility of urban jobs. Such areas are called shanty towns, favelas, bustees, and bidonvilles.

When American researchers first looked into residential patterns, they also found the influence of socioeconomic status to be strong, but in the inverse direction. The city centres of the older American cities contained railroads, factories, and warehouses because these were coming into ascendancy when city structures were becoming set. Living near these land-uses, along with the usual stores, offices, hotels, and restaurants, were the city's poor. Such central residential areas were considered a poor environment and subject to incursions from future growth from the central business district. Population affluence *increased* with distance away from the centre, reflecting the greater ability to pay for higher-speed transportation to city-centre jobs (Burgess, 1925) and the greater site amenities (Warner, 1969). Chicago was advanced as a model for this presumed North American type, however inaccurate it turned out to be.

American cities developed a racial dimension in residential patterning with the flow of Blacks in mid-twentieth century out of the rural south and into urban settlements throughout the nation. Insofar as discriminatory actions locked in an initial settlement pattern based on low socioeconomic level, Blacks lived predominantly in segregated, central-city locations. As their numbers increased and real estate practices confined them to adjacent central areas with engineering turnovers of homes from White occupants to Black, the Black population became marked in central city areas. The politically autonomous suburban municipalities became the loci and instruments of the White population (e.g., in institutional matters like schooling). Although in recent years Blacks have joined in suburbanization, there is still marked racial segregation within American metropolitan areas (and even between suburban municipalities). Insofar as racial segregation means different living conditions and differential exposure to subcultural values, occupational opportunities, infrastructural supports (e.g., good schools, recreational facilities, fast transportation), and crime, this has been a highly salient, even dominant, aspect of American urban life. Goldberg and Mercer (1986:46), for example, cite a major American survey in which 90 percent of White respondents felt they lived in predominantly White neighbourhoods, while about the same percentage of Blacks claimed residence in neighbourhoods that are all or mostly minority districts or racially balanced (which for Americans usually means on the way to becoming Black neighbourhoods).

The presence of Black segregated communities in central cities has diverted much private American capital away from central city revitalization and towards suburban expansion. American research has also identified family structure (familism) as a basis for residential patterning (Shevky and Bell, 1955; Schmid, 1950). Studies have found areas are often divided into ones mainly housing families with children (traditionally, with a nonemployed housewife), or areas mostly housing singles or childless couples engaged in the labour force.

One major Canadian departure from American urban patterns is the near absence of the Black/White ecological and social polarity, with its undertones and implications. But residential differentiation also occurs within Canadian metropolitan areas.

During the period of greatest Black migration to American cities, foreign immigration was (in historical terms) relatively limited. The thirty years following World War II was a period of great immigration to Canada from Europe and Asia in particular, with most persons arriving in Canada's cities. There had already been in many cities Chinatowns, cabbagetowns, Jewish communities, and more, but the degree of differentiation increased dramatically, with Italian, Portuguese, East and West Indian, Greek, Ukrainian, and many other communities joining earlier immigrant groups and native Canadians.

Ethnic ecological proliferation was well known from earlier periods in American cities and in some cases continuing parallel to racial differentiation. New York's Lower East Side, Chicago's Milwaukee and Archer, Boston's North End, and San Francisco's Grant Avenue convey popular images. Los Angeles, among others, has a Hispanic "ghetto," while a colony of Vietnamese has emerged in suburban Orange County. Yet the American society has adopted the image of a melting pot, in which identities other than national allegiance are assumed to melt away. Residential differentiation along ethnic lines is frowned upon, even though it is forced upon certain minorities. Thus, while allowing little recent large-scale immigration (except during international incidents in which American foreign policy has created or defined new categories of acute refugees) and with an ethos denying the salience of ethnic identity, the relative importance of the ethnic dimension in American residential patterning (apart from race) has declined.

At the same time, Canadian society's image of a mosaic has had considerable implications for urban structure.

Studies comparable to those of American cities show residential differentiation occurs according to the same dimensions, except that the predominantly racial dimension becomes ethnic (Schwirian and Matre, 1974). Furthermore, within Canada such differentiation has linguistic dimensions in cities like Montreal and Winnipeg (St. Boniface).

The largest cities present more opportunity for critical masses of persons from a given ethnic background to be present and hence to form residential communities. Not surprisingly, Toronto and Montreal are well above the Canadian urban mean on a standard measure of ethnic segregation, the latter uniquely high. In contrast, Vancouver, though next in size, is well below average. Winnipeg and Ottawa/Hull are also above average, while Halifax, St. John, Victoria, and Thunder Bay have the least ethnic segregation (McGahan, 1986:167).

Despite the ethnicity in Canadian residential patterning and the clear vitality of many ethnic neighbourhoods with the *support* of the societal ethos, Canadian cities do not sort most persons into ghettos by ethnic background. A colleague's story of being begrudged housing in a certain neighbourhood and urged to seek his own true area, because of his elicited identity as a "lapsed Mennonite," is only part of the complex web of residential process. Ethnic groups are part of spatially proximate communities only selectively. Some groups such as Jews and Italians live in relatively strong enclaves voluntarily to maintain supportive commercial, religious, and social institutions in close proximity to their homes, creating what Breton has called "institutional completeness" (1964). Toronto, for example, has many such areas, centred around not only these two groups but at least half a dozen others.

SUBCULTURAL COMMUNITIES NEED NOT HAVE A SPATIAL DIMENSION

Where subcultural communities take on spatial dimensions, neighbourhood and community are identical, the former representing territorial identity and the latter interpersonal interaction. Nonetheless, research by Wellman and his colleagues in Toronto illustrates how the expression of community can vary in the contemporary Canadian city (1987). The spatially proximate ethnic community is but one option. Modern communications and transportation technologies enable people to be in touch without living close by. One may gain "community without proximity" (Webber, 1963:23–54). Thus, some ethnic groups whose members are relatively affluent have not formed enclaves, but maintain their ties (e.g.,Germans, Scandinavians).

On the other hand, segregation may represent, as in the historical American case of Blacks, an involuntary action by the group itself, reflecting its poverty or discrimination against them. Native Canadians are highly segregated in Canadian cities on the former ground (with Winnipeg as a clear example), while the original Vancouver Chinatown illustrates the latter process (cf. McGahan, 1986).

Although ethnic differentiation in Canadian cities is a vibrant reality, it isn't the only determinant of residential ecology. There is considerable differentiation by socioeconomic status and by what Shevky and Bell (1955) called familism, as discussed earlier. Although many cities follow a pie-shaped, sectoral pattern regarding socioeconomic status rather than concentric zones (e.g., Toronto—Murdie, 1969), there are too many exceptions (e.g., Winnipeg and Regina — McGahan, 1986) for any single pattern to apply to all Canadian cities. Familism, however, has been generally found distributed in a concentric zone pattern, with greater fertility at increasing distances from the city centres. Nonetheless, living in a self-contained dwelling and women participating in the labour force are less closely associated with family size than in the American case (Schwirian and Matre, 1974), even though the pattern of distribution of children strengthens over time (Balakrishnan and Jarvis, 1979). Some Canadian central cities have had considerable social and legal controversy over the desirability of adult-only apartments. Indeed, the attitudes underlying adult-only proposals have extended into debates about support for institutional and infrastructural aspects of central cities like schools and recreation. The general aging of the electorate is magnified by residential differentiation by age, producing critical masses of persons with different interests than the young in some urban areas.

Municipal Multiplicity and Urban Structure

Canadian and American metropolitan areas typically cover many governmental jurisdictions as population growth extends to suburban areas. Houston, with the unusual legal right to regularly annex surrounding areas as necessary, and Saskatoon, with a municipal land-bank for future growth, are exceptions that prove the rule.

The challenge facing citizens in most metropolitan areas is how to achieve the benefits of co-ordination throughout the *de facto* city made up of many municipalities. There are many such benefits. First, the duplication of administering bureaucracies, side by side, each organizing the same function in a different municipality, is unnecessarily costly. Second, area-wide services like public transportation are more appropriate when provided by a jurisdiction of equal size, rather than by component jurisdictions with conflicting interests. Third, insofar as money and population subgroups are not evenly distributed throughout a metropolitan area, special needs and the money to respond to them are often not found in the same local areas; redistribution of funds usually involves crossing municipal borders. Fourth, where the resources to address a common need (e.g., hospitals, parks, sewage disposal sites, etc.) are found in only specific municipalities, a format for common usage and shared costs is desirable. Fifth, where people do so many things in such proximity, uniformity of standards and licensing practices helps them all.

Canada has been reasonably progressive in overcoming the disadvantages of municipal multiplicity. Municipalities are formally creatures of the provinces. Therefore, it is not surprising that different methods have been implemented across the country. Yet, more progress in this regard is found in Canada than in the United States.

Metropolitan Toronto is a textbook solution to urban fractionation. The Province of Ontario created "Metro" in 1953 in the face of financial inequalities among the City of Toronto and its old and new suburbs. Money was needed for infrastructural development in specific rapidly growing areas and for co-ordination among the parts of the metropolis. Although no single municipality wanted "Metro," Ontario imposed it for the common good. The province decided which functions of urban government should most efficiently be conducted at the level of the whole area; these would subsequently be run by single bureaucracies at the Metro level, under the jurisdiction of a council made up of members of local municipal councils and a full-time executive selected by them. Funding for Metro services would come from assessment by standardized methods across the metropolis. Furthermore, the division of functions between the existing municipalities and Metro, making a two-tiered system, could be changed after periodic reviews. In fact, the number of functions done at the Metro level has increased regularly in its roughly thirty-five years of operation.

The success of Metropolitan Toronto led Ontario to create a series of regional municipalities, including Hamilton-Wentworth, Peel, Durham, Thunder Bay, the last a total amalgamation of Port Arthur and Fort William, and more. The Ottawa–Hull National Capital Area is a special case, involving federal considerations but similar principles. The irony is that the more recent regional government creations around Toronto now stand in the way of recognition that the scale of the Toronto metropolitan area (and hence its future planning and finance) has grown to include them all.

Montreal has also a metropolitan "community," but the balance in size of the municipalities involved is not as equal as in Toronto and far fewer services are performed at this level. In Vancouver, a Greater Vancouver Regional District coordinates functions linking the City of Vancouver with its many suburbs; its level of activity reflects varying commitments by changing provincial governments.

Manitoba, on the other hand, transformed local government into metropolitan government with the inception of Unicity Winnipeg. Because many people believe the best government is the one "closest to home," councils in which local citizens can formally advise their Unicity councillor were institutionalized within districts. This was intended to provide the benefits of both metropolitan-wide co-ordination and local networking.

Ironically, despite the clear successes of these attempts at co-ordinating urban functioning, there is no guarantee that metropolitan councillors will banish their parochial interests from unified chambers. Hence, on more socially oriented issues, on councils with a suburban majority, suburban interests dominate to the detriment of the centre city population (Rose, 1972). In Toronto, for example, suburban interests made symbolic war on city interests in attempting to remove an unconventional community from winterized cottages on one of the Toronto Islands to make way for expanded metropolitan park lands, while turning a blind eye to several yacht clubs occupying even more of the sparsely used land (Gibson, 1984).

When municipal restructuring based on the logical growth of urban areas has not occurred, some limited goals can be achieved by special districts or agencies. These organizations handle specific area-wide tasks, such as running transit and providing water. Experience shows such organizations are extremely *ad hoc*, with ambiguity as to whom they really serve, how they are to be financed, and how they relate to other aspects of local government. Yet, these special solutions fill a vacuum when more comprehensive steps cannot be taken.

American cities rarely have an upper tier or metropolitan level of government. In most states, residents in all the municipalities involved in a new government have to approve its formation. Given the ecological differentiation which has occurred and the racial undertones accenting suburban migration by Whites and subsequent city–suburb political dialogue, metropolitan governments almost never win the suburban vote. Therefore, special districts and agencies proliferate, but without the same responsibility for accountability to municipal political bodies or electorates. County governments sometimes provide more co-ordinated planning and finance. But these don't cross county lines and do not build in municipality interests as in two-tiered governments.

Federal governments sometimes play a more important role in American cities because they can provide direct aid, rather than leaving most implementive policies to the states, as Canada does with the provinces. Thus, many federal solutions to American urban problems (e.g., renewal, freeway building) put a relatively uniform stamp on the cities where they are implemented, reflecting explicit regulations and costing formulas. Goldberg and Mercer (1986) note how, in contrast, Canadian cities find unique innovative solutions due to separate provincial–municipal dialogues. Furthermore, American cities face the periodic drying up of federal support, since some federal administrations are reluctant to address local urban problems.

Thus, although there are clear variations throughout Canada, Canadian metroplitan areas suffer fewer of the glaring contrasts in welfare, infrastructure, and supportive services differentiating American central cities and suburbs. Canadian cities usually provide more co-ordinated services and facilities throughout their metropolitan areas.

All these factors increase the quality of urban life, particularly for those who cannot purchase privately what is publicly unavailable in their communities (''Let them drive a Rolls . . .'').

CANADIAN VARIATIONS

While placing Canadian urbanization in world perspective, one treats this phenomenon holistically. When comparing

Canadian urbanism to its American counterpart, one treats general tendencies and features of urban life in the two nations; disclaimers of uniformity are easily disregarded. But Canada is diverse as a society, and so are its cities. Several aspects are worth noting.

Regional Disparities and Urbanization

The high level of urbanization in Canada is not distributed evenly across the land. One highly concentrated Windsor–Quebec City axis — or even just the Golden Horseshoe—has the effect that, by process of elimination, vast areas of the country will be sparsely populated and its cities smaller. Indeed, the Toronto and Montreal Census Metropolitan Areas each have larger populations than every province outside Ontario and Quebec except British Columbia (c.f. Kennedy, 1983:85–86).

There are different plateaus of urbanization within Canada. Ontario is highest, with a level of 81 percent urban residents, followed by British Columbia at 78 percent, Quebec at 77.6 percent, Alberta at 77.2 percent, and Manitoba at 71.2 percent. There is then a jump to the range of 50 to 58 percent for all remaining provinces but Prince Edward Island, which has a level of only 36.3 percent, (Statistics Canada, 1984).

Given the population sizes in the respective provinces and the lower urbanization levels in the lesser-populated provinces, it does not take a mathematical genius to understand that the number and size of cities in the Atlantic provinces and Saskatchewan must be extremely restricted.

Functional Specialization of Cities

Fischer's subcultural theory of urbanism (1976) stated that the critical masses in a city are attracted differentially by the unique characteristics of that city. One major characteristic of a city is its economic base. Cities that specialize in one or more economic activity have populations which vary by proportions of gender, socioeconomic status, and age. The population mix can produce cities with different typical ways of life.

No cities are completely devoted to only one occupation. Some mix of activities is necessary for everybody's survival. But the relative balance is telling. For example, a provincial capital like Victoria attracts bureaucrats and clerical workers with decent levels of education and usually more women than men. Regina may resemble Victoria on that account but differs because the former is also an agricultural service centre, with predominantly male occupations, while the latter, due to its climate, is settled by many retirees, an elderly and increasingly female population. Hamilton and London are close in geography and size, but the former has an economic base reflecting two major steel mills, while the latter is an insurance and finance centre. These two attract different gender and socioeconomic mixes. The recreational and spending demands of residents thus differ greatly.

One group of urban areas with a very unusual position is the single-industry town, usually resource-based. These cities, typically located in remote locations with extreme climates, reflect the precise site where a mineral (gold, uranium) or ore (iron, nickel) is found or where power is produced. These settlements are not founded for the attractions of the site for residents but for the economics of extraction or production there.

Because Canadian workers have been reluctant to remain in extreme locations, companies have tried to create agreeable residential areas and to recruit widely. Yet the lives people lead there differ from lives in other urban settlements. First, these are typically small settlements without immediate access to additional urban amenities. They are largely self-dependent for recreation and servicing, though the company providing the economic base is ultimately at the heart of most decisions about these matters as well. Mining or industrial jobs that bring males to such towns may not have similar job opportunities for their wives. With relatively few recent exceptions, the site planning has reflected what persons in Canada's "southern" cities find attractive; yet people have to live most of the year in bitterly cold, windy weather suitable for much more compact, sheltering architecture. Finally, people are tremendously vulnerable to the single industry for their livelihood and any investments they make in the area. This is a very different feeling than people have in larger areas with more diversified economic bases (c.f. Lucas, 1971).

According to a recent account, there are fifty-six single-industry towns in Northern Ontario alone. Insofar as most of them "have seen better days" and many are dying, major unemployment and abandonment of homes and businesses occurs. "If you want to find work, you've got to leave town" (Reguly, 1987). Even the major recreation centres, the taverns, are closing. But while this crisis is difficult, one of the main characteristics of the single-industry town is the threat that this can always happen. Elliott Lake, for example, has always waxed and waned according to the world demand for uranium, its economic base.

CONCLUSION

It is easier to predict what will not happen than what will happen. There is little likelihood that Canada will return to a low state of technology. This would be economic suicide, so Canada will likely retain its high level of urbanization.

But how many and which cities will thrive—to what degree and for the benefit of whom — is unknowable. Events with great impact occur with little or no notice: wars, currency fluctuations, technological innovations, and changes in resource availability and pricing. Our federal government is currently discussing free trade with the United States. Yet nobody knows what the range of implications of this may be for Canada. Under the economic terms agreed upon, will Canadian cities become more like those to the south? At the extreme, might their economic bases collapse? Or will those built on some economic bases thrive and others decline?

If mystery creates suspense, Canada's urban future will be at least as interesting as its past!

Notes

[1]Judith Kjellberg of the Centre for Urban and Community Studies, University of Toronto, contributed extremely helpful statistical documentation.

DISCUSSION QUESTIONS

1. Discuss the statement that societies and cities are interdependent. How is this so?
2. Compare and contrast urbanization and urbanism.

3. What is the role of technology in the development of cities?
4. Compare the urbanization patterns in Canada and Third World countries.
5. What are the differences in urbanization in Canada and the United States?
6. How have Canadian and American approaches to transportation needs and ethnic structures in cities differed?

GLOSSARY

metropolitan area a central municipality of at least 50 000 inhabitants and adjacent municipalities and areas where their characteristics indicate nonrural activities

megalopolis major metropolitan area arranged into a larger, functionally continuous conglomeration

suburbs municipalities of largely single homes and apartment residences around central cities

urbanism the ways of living typically found in cities

urbanization the percentage of a nation that lives in urban areas

BIBLIOGRAPHY

Balakrishnan, T.R. and George K. Jarvis
1979 "Changing Patterns of Spatial Differentiation in Urban Canada, 1961–1971." *Canadian Review of Sociology and Anthropology*, 16: 218–27.

Bascom, William
1955 "Urbanization Among the Yoruba." *American Journal of Sociology*, 60: 446–54.

Bourne, L.S.
1975 *Urban Systems: Strategies for Regulation*. Oxford: Oxford University Press.

——
1984 "Canadian Perspectives on Urban Growth and Decline." In *Urbanization: Canadian Perspectives on Urban Growth and Decline*. Vancouver: Centre for Human Settlements, University of British Columbia.

Breton, Raymond
1964 "Institutional Completeness of Ethnic Communities and the Personal Relations of Immigrants." *American Journal of Sociology*, 70: 193–205.

Burgess, Ernest
1925 "The Growth of the City." In Robert E. Park and Ernest Burgess (eds.) *The City*. Chicago: University of Chicago Press.

Chumak, A. and J.P. Braaksma
1981 "Implications of the Travel-Time Budget for Urban Transportation Modeling in Canada." *Transportation Research Record*, 784: 9–27.

Davis, Kingsley
1969 *World Urbanization*, vol. I. Population Monograph Series, No. 4. Berkeley: University of California.

——
1972 *World Urbanization*, vol. II. Institute of International Studies. Berkeley: University of California.

Dewey, Richard
1960 "The Rural-Urban Continuum: Real But Relatively Unimportant." *American Journal of Sociology*, 66: 60–66.

Elliot, John
1987 "High-tech Fine, But How Will Bullock Feel?" Toronto: *The Globe and Mail*, February 17: B19.

Fischer, Claude S.
1976 *The Urban Experience*. New York: Harcourt Brace Jovanovich.

Gans, Herbert J.
1962 *The Urban Villagers*. New York: The Free Press.

Gibson, Sarah
1984 *More Than an Island*. Toronto: Clark Irwin.

Goldberg, Michael and John Mercer
1986 *The Myth of the North American City*. Vancouver: University of British Columbia Press.

Golden, Hilda H.
1981 *Urbanization and Cities*. Toronto: D.C. Heath.

Gottman, Jean
1961 *Megalopolis*. New York: Twentieth Century Fund.

Karp, David, Gregory P. Stone, and William C. Yoels
1977 *Being Urban*. Toronto: D.C. Heath.

Kennedy, Lesley W.
1983 *The Urban Kaleidoscope: Canadian Perspectives*. Toronto: McGraw-Hill Ryerson.

Light, Ivan
1983 *Cities in World Perspective*. New York: Macmillan.

Lithwick, N.H.
1970 *Urban Canada: Problems and Prospects*. Ottawa: Central Mortgage and Housing Corporation.

Lofland, Lyn
1973 *A World of Strangers*. New York: Basic Books.

London, Bruce
1987 "Structural Determinants of Third World Urban Change." *American Sociological Review*, 52, 28–43.

Lucas, Rex
1971 *Milltown, Minetown, Railtown*. Toronto: University of Toronto Press.

McGahan, Peter
1986 *Urban Sociology in Canada*, 2nd edition. Toronto: Butterworths.

Michelson, William
1976 *Man and His Urban Environment: A Sociological Approach*. rev. ed. New York: Random House.

——
1985 *From Sun to Sun: Daily Obligations and Community Structure in the Lives of Employed Women and Their Families*. Totowa, New Jersey: Rowman and Allanheld.

Murdie, Robert
1969 *Factorial Ecology of Metropolitan Toronto*. Department of Geography Research Paper No. 116. Chicago: University of Chicago.

Palen, John
1981 *The Urban World*, 2nd ed. Toronto: McGraw-Hill Ryerson.

Popenoe, David
1985 *Private Pleasure-Public Plight*. New Brunswick, New Jersey: Trans-Action Books.

Rapoport, Amos
1984 "Culture and the Urban Order." In John Agnew, John Mercer, and David Sopher (eds.) *The City in Cultural Context*. Boston: Allen and Unwin.

Reguly, Eric
1987 "The Other Ontario." Toronto: *The Financial Post*, March 2: 17.

Rose, Albert
1972 *Governing Metropolitan Toronto: A Social and Political Analysis 1953–1971*. Berkeley: University of California Press.

Rosenbloom, Sandra, ed.
1978 *Women's Travel Patterns: Research Needs and Priorities*. Washington, D.C.: U.S. Department of Transportation.

Schmid, Calvin
1950 "Generalizations Concerning the

Ecology of the American City." *American Sociological Review*, 15: 264–281.

Schwirian, Kent P. and Marc Matre
1974 "The Ecological Structure of Canadian Cities." In Kent P. Schwirian (ed.) *Comparative Urban Structure*. Toronto: D.C. Heath.

Shevky, Eshref and Wendell Bell
1955 *Social Area Analysis*. Stanford: Stanford University Press.

Simmel, Georg
1950 "The Metropolis and Mental Life." In Kurt Wolff, ed. *The Sociology of Georg Simmel*. New York: The Free Press.

Simmons, James W.
1984 "Key Processes in Canadian Settlement Trends." In *Urbanization: Canadian Perspectives on Urban Growth and Decline*. Vancouver: Centre for Human Settlements, University of British Columbia.

Simmons, James W. and L.S. Bourne
1984 "Recent Trends and Patterns in Canadian Settlement, 1976–1981." Toronto: Centre for Urban and Community Studies, University of Toronto, Major Report No. 23.

Sjoberg, Gideon
1960 *The Preindustrial City*. New York: The Free Press.

Statistics Canada
1980 *Perspectives Canada III*. Ottawa: Minister of Supply and Services.

———
1983 *1981 Census of Canada, Census Metropolitan Areas with Components*, vol. 3 (Profile Series B). Ottawa: Minister of Supply and Services.

———
1984 *Urban Growth in Canada*. Ottawa: Minister of Supply and Services.

Warner, W.L.
1969 *Yankee City* (abridged edition). New Haven, Connecticut: Yale University Press.

Webber, Melvin
1963 "Order in Diversity: Community Without Propinquity." In L. Wingo (ed.) *Cities and Space*. Baltimore: The Johns Hopkins University Press.

Wellman, Barry, Peter Carrington, and Alan Hall
1987 "Networks and Personal Communities." In S.D. Berkowitz and Barry Wellman (eds.) *Structural Sociology*. New York: Cambridge University Press.

Wirth, Louis
1938 "Urbanism as a Way of Life." *American Journal of Sociology*, 44: 1–24.

Yago, Glenn
1984 *The Decline of Transit*. New York: Cambridge University Press.

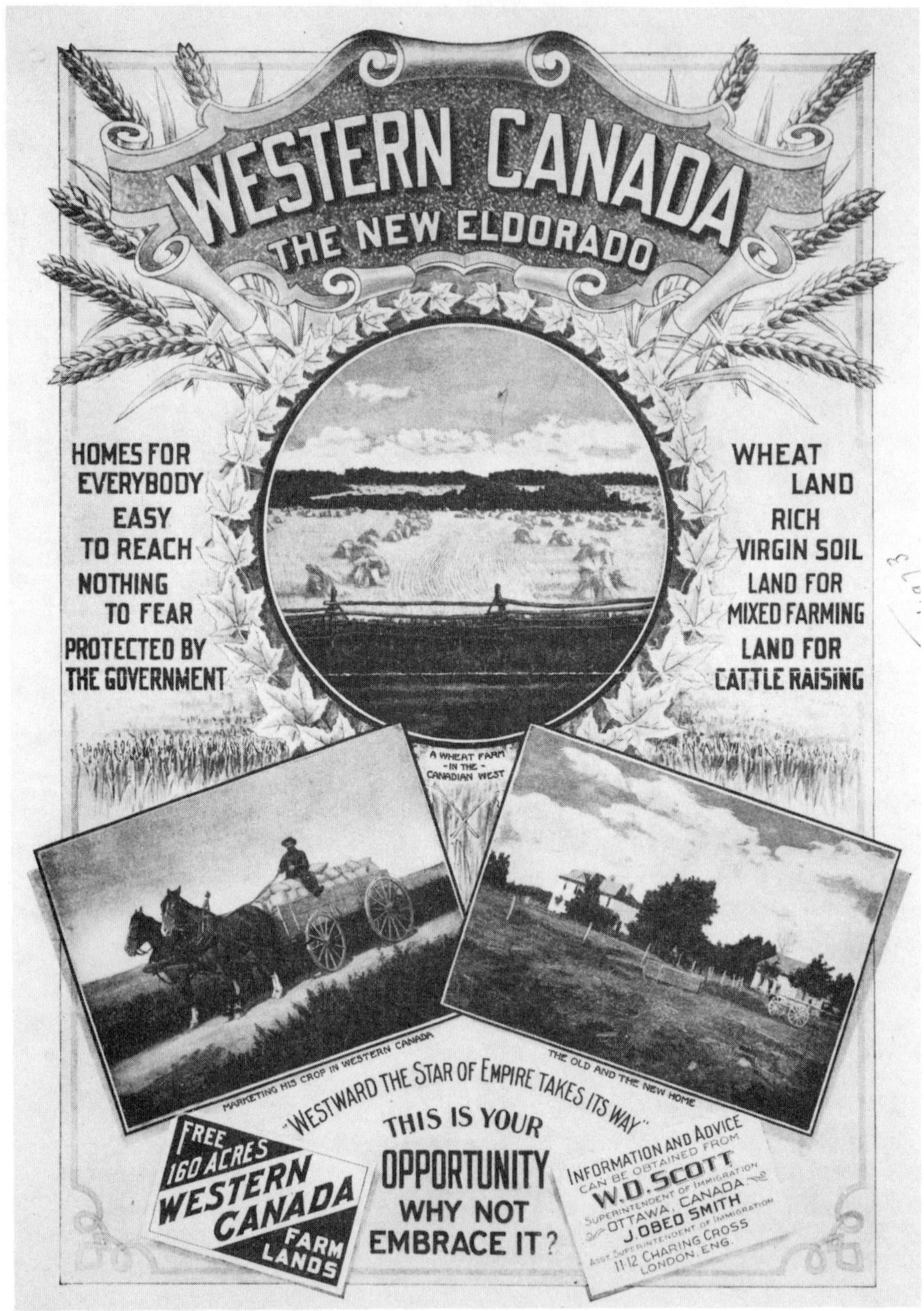

A poster encouraging migration to farm lands in Western Canada. *Courtesy National Archives of Canada/C85854*

> *"The key issue is . . . how to bring about self-sustaining, indigenous economic development in the disadvantaged regions. How should or can a region overcome locational disadvantages, resource shortcomings, or external dependencies?"*

c h a p t e r f o u r

Canada's Regions

Fred Wien

INTRODUCTION

One distinctive feature of being Canadian and living so close to the elephant next door is the continuing puzzle of what makes Canada different from the United States. The significance and severity of regional **inequalities** is part of the answer. A leading student of regional development planning in North America, Benjamin Higgins, says ". . . there is probably no advanced country where regional disparities play so great a role, economically, socially, and politically, as they do in Canada." He adds "regional disparities are a pressing problem in Canada; the proportion of the populations of lagging regions living in genuine **poverty** is higher and the regions designated as retarded much larger than those of the United States" (Higgins, 1986: 132, 160).

This is perhaps not surprising. Canada is vast; there are significant natural and social barriers separating one **region** from another, and considerable differences in population, resources, and industrial structure as one goes from east to west and north to south. In addition, the overwhelming importance of our links to the United States through trade and investment ties may have different implications for different regions.

While regional disparities are important, they do not always occupy a central stage in Canada's political concerns. In times of economic expansion, when all regions are registering economic growth, one is likely to hear less about the problem, and this is also the case when important national issues (such as mobilization for World War II and national reconstruction thereafter) dominate the political agenda. Even in the post-war period, the report of the 1957 Royal Commission on Canada's Economic Prospects said little about regional inequalities. At a press conference to mark the release of the report, the chairman suggested the rather innovative policy of converting the country's distressed areas into national parks.

Since then, however, governments have taken a more aggressive and informed approach to the problem. In particular, they have sought to alleviate the hardship faced by the unemployed and the poor, and to create conditions of **socioeconomic development** on a regionally equitable basis. In the 1960s and 1970s, many optimists hoped these long-standing problems could be resolved by government intervention.

The climate of the 1980s is considerably more subdued. After extensive efforts to reduce regional disparities in Canada, the stubborn problem is still not easily amenable to policy solution. Much has been learned, especially about what not to do and how ineffective many policy options have been. Those interested in regional development are undertaking a sober assessment of what has been accomplished and are searching for new solutions. New issues, such as the free trade negotiations with the United States, the rapid movement to a technology-based post-industrial society, and the changing patterns of the ownership and investment of capital in the world economy, pose new challenges whose implications for regional inequalities are not yet clear.

In this chapter, we review the debate on regional inequality in Canada, with appropriate comparisons to the United States. In particular, we will examine: what is the extent of regional inequality in Canada? How do social science theorists explain it? What have governments, especially national ones, tried to do about the problem? How successful have these measures been? And what lessons can be drawn from this experience as we look ahead to new issues in this perplexing field?

The study of regional inequality is interdisciplinary. Sociologists have contributed to broad explanatory theories of development and underdevelopment, criticized prevailing approaches, conducted empirical research in the field, and participated in applied development projects. While sociologists are actively searching for explanations and solutions, their role is overshadowed by economists, geographers, urban and regional planners, and policy analysts from political science and public administration, who dominate the study of regional inequality in Canada.

THE DIMENSIONS OF REGIONAL INEQUALITY

While there is agreement on the importance of regionalism and regional inequality in Canada (Matthews, 1980), the definition of a region remains an important problem. It is an issue for measuring inequality and changes over time — what unit of analysis should be used — and for implementing policy. As we shall see later, successive governments have, in the last three decades, taken quite different interpretations of what constitutes a disadvantaged region for purposes of targeting various policy initiatives; they make their decisions as much on political grounds as on the basis of a rational analysis of pertinent social and economic characteristics.

The issue is this. The larger the area encompassed by the term "region," the more likely it is that it will include significant internal variations or disparities. For example, the Western region (Manitoba, Saskatchewan, Alberta and British Columbia) has some characteristics in common, but also enormous diversities. Similarly, the Atlantic provinces are often lumped together, but the provinces differ considerably in their potential for the development of agriculture, forestry, manufacturing, or energy, for example. On the other hand, if a small, localized area is targeted (for example, a census district or a disadvantaged area within a province), policy solutions may be handicapped because the underlying conditions contributing to the problem may require consideration of a broader geographic area. Can the problems of Cape Breton be resolved in isolation from the mainland of Nova Scotia? Can the stagnation of Eastern Ontario be considered outside of the context of the developments centred around Toronto, Ottawa, or Montreal?

In practice, the province is most often used as the unit defining a region because data are most readily available at the provincial level, and less so for municipalities and other units. This is also occasioned by Canada's federal nature and the political and legal/constitutional significance of provincial governments. The province, however, is not always the ideal unit for defining a region, since it may contain significant internal diversity or it may be too small for the effective application of regional development policies.

In any event, what are some indicators of regional inequality in Canada, using provincial-level data? Typically, economic measures are used and, among these, per capita income and unemployment rates are most prevalent. Other economic measures often cited reveal the productive capacity of the province (e.g., provincial gross domestic product per person which measures the value of goods and services produced) and rates of poverty. Other social indicators describe the educational level of the labour force, the health of the population (e.g., infant mortality rates), or living standards (e.g., a crowding index with respect to housing). Some contemporary data measuring regional inequality are found in Table 1.

Table 1

MEASURES OF REGIONAL INEQUALITY IN CANADA, BY PROVINCE, RECENT YEARS

Province	Personal Income per Capita (1983)	Unemployment Rate (1986)	Provincial GDP (1981)	Poverty Rate (Families) (1984)	Poverty Rate (Individuals) (1984)
Newfoundland	67.6	208	52.0	23.0	45.1
Prince Edward Island	74.3	140	50.5	12.4	48.3
Nova Scotia	80.4	140	61.3	16.0	39.5
New Brunswick	74.2	150	63.1	18.9	46.1
Quebec	92.5	115	86.0	17.2	46.8
Ontario	109.2	73	106.5	11.8	34.7
Manitoba	93.0	80	88.1	14.6	36.7
Saskatchewan	93.7	80	108.8	17.0	35.5
Alberta	108.4	102	146.0	16.3	31.0
British Columbia	106.0	131	109.4	15.5	36.4
Canada	100.0	100.0	100.0	15.0	38.4
Disparity ratio (Highest to lowest ratio)	1.62	2.85	2.89	1.95	1.56

Source: 1. Columns 1 and 3: Statistics Canada, Provincial Economic Accounts.
2. Column 2: Statistics Canada Catalogue 71-001, December 1986.
3. Columns 4 and 5: National Council of Welfare, *Poverty Profile 1985*. Ottawa: Supply and Services Canada.

The figures from Table 1 show substantial inequalities on all the measures. Per capita income in Newfoundland is only 62 percent of what it is in Ontario. The unemployment rate is more than four times as much, and the likelihood of having families or unattached individuals in poverty also varies sharply between the provinces.

From these and other figures, it is obvious that social and economic outcomes of individual and family well-being differ significantly by region. Just as it makes a difference into what family one is born, so it makes a difference where the family is located by region.

EXPLANATIONS OF REGIONAL INEQUALITY

The next logical question is why do regional inequalities exist and how are they maintained? If these questions could be clearly answered, we would be well on the road to understanding how inequalities might be reduced—to the extent policy measures can address the underlying conditions. We will examine policy issues in the following section.

There are some reasonably clear theoretical interpretations of regional inequality available. Each explains why inequalities exist and each suggests what policies might remedy the situation. The difficulty is that *competing* explanations suggest strategies that are incompatible with each other, and there is no agreement on which framework is the most appropriate. Many analysts feel none gives a complete explanation, and they pragmatically suggest some wisdom is found in most, if not all, the alternatives. Others argue some explanations are better at explaining the origin of disparities in previous decades, while others are better under contemporary conditions.

Because of this uncertainty, and because of the lack of agreement on the definition of a region, Savoie (1986) suggests that there is more room than usual for politicans to use regional development programs for short-term political considerations, rather than as part of a sustained, well-informed attack on regional inequality.

One can identify close to a dozen theoretical perspectives, but to describe each would be tedious and unnecessary. We will outline three approaches, one of which groups several similar theories together. These perspectives have dominated the debate on regional disparity for the last decade and, in some instances, for much longer.

The Staples Approach

Staples are "raw or semi-processed materials extracted or grown primarily for export markets and dominating the regional or national economies" (Marchak, 1985: 674). In view of Canada's historical reliance on staple production and export, it is not surprising that Canadian social scientists would emphasize this factor when explaining regional inequality and national development. The roots of a staples approach trace back to the writings of Mackintosh (1923), Innis (1930; 1940; 1956), and others who examined successive staples, such as furs, cod, square timbers, and wheat, their social, political, and economic impact, and the factors that shaped their development. More contemporary interpretations that attempt to specify the theory more clearly and to delimit its applicability are found in Watkins (1977) and Scott (1978). Watkins, in particular, suggests staples theory as elaborated in the earlier writings only has explanatory value if applied to "new" countries such as Australia, New Zealand, or Canada. These countries historically have had few people in relation to their land and other resources, and few inhibiting traditions.

In this context, it is argued, a region's prosperity depends on the availability and marketability of its natural resources, and the region's success in using the production or extraction of the staple (and the proceeds derived from this) in developing the rest of its economy. In other words, a region will prosper if it has a valued resource that can be profitably marketed abroad, and if it can extend appropriate linkages to other economic sectors (manufacturing, services, etc.) so that they receive a stimulus from the export sector.

There are many conditions under which a given staple can become the engine of economic growth. Simply discovering a valued resource may be the key; changes in technology or transportation may make it economical to produce a staple that has already been discovered, but not exploited. Alternatively, the demand (and price) for a resource may increase, depending on levels of need in importing countries and its availability from other suppliers. In any case, if the conditions are favourable, capital and labour would likely flow into the region to develop and export the staple.

As noted above, whether the exploitation of the staple will lead to significant spread effects to benefit the economy of the region as a whole depends on the linkages established. For example, if a lot of equipment is required to extract or produce the staple, and if that equipment can be locally manufactured, then the manufacturing sector will be stimulated. If the natural resource can be processed locally rather than being exported in a raw state, then the regional economy will gain jobs and income. If labour is attracted to the export sector and receives high wages, then a local demand for consumer goods will be created. The region's long-term economic development, therefore, depends on the extent to which the stimulus provided by the exploitation of the staple can be generalized to diversify the economy.

Unfortunately, it is in the nature of staple production that the demand for a given staple, and therefore its price, may eventually decline. Consumer preferences may change, new synthetic alternatives may be found, the resource may be exhausted, production costs may increase, or other regions or countries may take over an established market. If the region has diversified its economy, the decline in the staple exporting sector is less of a problem. Labour and capital freed up in the declining sector can be redeployed to other productive uses. Some migration outside the region can also be expected, depending on factors such as government policy and opportunities elsewhere. It is more likely, however, that dependence on the staple product continues and that there will be a reluctance to adjust to the situation by encouraging economic adjustments. Attempts may be made to subsidize and protect the declining industry, rather than encouraging a search for alternative sources of economic growth. Governments may also seek to retain their population base, rather than encouraging migration from the region. Unless a new staple can be found and developed, the region may stagnate and decline.

There are perhaps two additional, important features of staple theory as it has been developed by Canadian political economists. First, the importance of staple production for a region or country is not restricted to its narrowly economic implications. Each staple, including the way its production is organized, leaves its imprint politically, socially, and culturally on the region. The transition in Alberta from an economy dominated by farming, for example, to one dominated by energy production and export sped up the urbanization trend in the province, encouraged the development of a large managerial/entre-

IS THE STAPLES APPROACH DATED?

Critics of a staples approach often suggest the perspective provided important insights historically, when regional economies centred around the fur trade, the cod fishery, or wheat growing. They suggest, however, that staple production has receded in importance over time; Buckley (1958) in fact dates the decline of the utility of the approach as early as 1820. The Economic Council of Canada (1977:8) concludes ". . . . the maturing Canadian economy has reached the point where resources and transportation are no longer, as in the past, the only important determinants of regional variations in the well-being of Canadians, and we now have productive processes that are more complex and utilize natural resources somewhat differently."

Others disagree and continue to use the staples approach when analyzing the impact that staple development has on economies such as Alberta's (Mansell, 1986), British Columbia's (Marchak, 1983), Newfoundland's (Royal Commission, 1986) or Canada's North (Berger, 1977).

preneurial class, and replaced a populist-agrarian political regime with one responsive to the new urban elite (Mansell, 1986). Second, writers, such as Innis and, more recently, Watkins (1977), Drache (1976), and a host of others, have emphasized the negative implications of a staple economy — notably, the dependence on a foreign industrial centre through market and trade relations that are exploitative and constraining, the periodic crises and boom/bust periods, and the distortions induced in the economy and society of an area that lacks a diversified, self-reliant, and self-regulated economic base. We will return to this theme when we discuss **dependency** theory in a later section.

The Economic Council's approach to explaining regional inequality emphasizes the presence or absence of productivity factors in the region. We turn now to this approach.

Perspectives Emphasizing Regional Deficiencies

Students studying the **underdevelopment** of Third World countries in the 1950s and 1960s became acquainted with the modernization, or development, model. It suggested important characteristics of the traditional sector in a given country needed to be overcome if development were to proceed. The source of change, and the model for development, was the modern, urban, industrial sector of the country. Characterized by technologies based on machine production in large factories, the modernization approach suggested the relationships, culture, political institutions, and social structures appropriate to modern industrial society would spread from the (modern) centre to the (traditional) periphery. This spread was to be effected primarily by the competition mechanism of the free market, which would destroy or transform the backward enterprises and the traditional characteristics of the groups working in them. Increased mobility of individuals between country and city, mass communications and transportation, formal education and the development of a modern state, would all serve to disseminate rational, income-maximizing behaviours that would eventually be common to all members of the society.

The development perspective was also applied to explain regional underdevelopment in advanced industrial societies. It was not transferred without modification, however. For example, it was recognized that the economic structure differed significantly. While it is difficult to speak of development in Latin American countries without dealing with the overwhelming significance of the agricultural sector and the need for land reform, such is not the case in Canada. The debate in Canada also does not dwell particularly on differences in progressive or traditional attitudes, values, and social structures between one part of the country and another.

It is argued, however, that some regions of Canada are underdeveloped because their deficiencies stand in the way of their improving their situation in employment and income terms relative to other regions. Several factors have been identified: location in relation to markets and therefore the burden of transportation costs; lower rates of capital investment; shortcomings in infrastructure, such as roads, railways, harbours, sewers, schools, and hospitals; lower levels of investment in education and training of the work force (human capital); inferior managerial quality; and lower levels of investment in new productive technology. Most of these factors contribute to the productivity of industry and thus to income and employment levels in the region.

Analysts proceeding from different theoretical perspectives identify other deficiencies. Keynesian economists, for example, suggest the demand for goods and services in a region may be too low and should be stimulated by government policy. Regional scientists look at the distribution of people in areas. They argue, for example, that growth in income and employment has occurred more rapidly in urban areas than in small town or rural areas; hence, some regions may be too sparsely populated. Growth centres or development poles need to be encouraged so industries can be located next to each other in an industrial complex and take advantage of complementarities and of a large urban market for goods and services.

Running through much of the mainstream, orthodox approach to regional disparities is a faith in the operation of the free market, characteristic of neoclassical economic perspectives. Here, the deficiencies highlighted are the rigidities and other forms of interference with the market which maintain and exacerbate regional inequalities. As Courchene puts it, regional disparities are to some extent a problem of economic adjustment, a problem of interference with the natural adjustment mechanisms of the economy. According to this view, disparities in unemployment rates, for example, could be reduced if wages were flexible, i.e., if employers could offer wages to those currently unemployed at a level low enough to make it attractive for firms to hire new staff. For several reasons, however, wage rates may be rigid rather than flexible — the power of unions may raise or maintain them artificially, governments and national corporations may deliberately pay the same wage rate across the country, or government minimum wage rates may set an irreducible floor. Thus, the natural adjustment mechanism of the market, which would dictate that wage demands be reduced in circumstances of excess labour, cannot function as it should, and unemployment remains higher in one part of the country than another.

If one were focusing on interregional differences in incomes, the neoclassical approach would assume that, under free market conditions, workers would move from a low income to a high income area of the country as they seek to improve their economic condition. Again, however, artificial impediments prevent this "natural" equalization from occurring. If in the poorer region minimum wage rates are higher than they should be, or if U.I.C. payments are more generous in the amount paid and its duration, then the incentive to leave the region is correspondingly reduced. As these examples illustrate, the deficiency identified by neoclassical economists is not limited to the disadvantaged area, but is also built into the policies and practices of national governments, unions, or corporations in interaction with the poorer region. Courchene concludes that because the natural adjustment mechanisms of the market are not free to work as they should, provincial governments increasingly depend on federal transfers to sustain themselves, which exacerbates the problem. He suggests the various problems interact — if wages are inflexible in a poor province, then unemployment remains high. This triggers an influx of federal funds (e.g., for unemployment insurance). But the more money that flows in, the less incentive there is for the province or region to worry about the adequacy of wage adjustment and factor (labour, capital) mobility. "This is a vicious circle, and it is imperative that it is broken" (Courchene, 1986:35).

Perspectives Emphasizing Exploitation and Dependence

The reference to Courchene has introduced the idea of dependence as a problem to be overcome in the context of a neoclassical framework. In the last major theoretical framework to be reviewed here, dependence of a disadvantaged region on other regions or countries, and exploitation by the latter, becomes the focal point of the analysis. While modernization and development theory prevailed in the 1950s and 1960s, perspectives emphasizing dependence and exploitation were most popular in intellectual circles in the 1970s and early 1980s.

Dependency theory first appeared in the late 1960s and generated considerable intellectual excitement because it directly challenged the main tenets of modernization theory (Frank, 1972). Articulated primarily by Latin American intellectuals, the approach contains three main arguments.

First, dependency theory suggests underdevelopment is caused by exploitation by capitalist metropolitan centres. Far from being models of modernity to be emulated, the "developed" areas prosper at the expense of the "traditional" societies. Further, the exploitative relationship between, for example, the United States and Latin America is reproduced within both developed and underdeveloped countries — thus accounting for regional inequality. One early application of the dependency perspective to Canada by A.K. Davis (1971) divided the country into metropolitan (e.g., the urban industrial core) and satellite (e.g., the North, the West, and Atlantic Canada) areas. Davis argued the **metropolis** continuously dominates and exploits the hinterland, but the hinterland groups and interests tend to fight back against their metropolitan exploiters.

Second, underdevelopment occurs when resources are drained from peripheral to central areas. The latter control the terms of trade for products. Thus, raw materials are exported from **satellite** regions at prices below their true value, and manufactured goods from the central area are sold at exorbitant prices. Banks headquartered in core areas drain the regions of their savings and invest them outside these areas, and labour is attracted to the core when needed, but sent back to the periphery when not. Often, the multinational corporation is regarded as the chief agent of exploitation, and the relationship between core and periphery is seen as uniformly negative. In other versions, multinationals in a peripheral area and producing goods for a local market can be acknowledged as a source of growth and dynamism, since they need to create some internal prosperity in order to sell their consumer goods. However, while some local wealth is generated, substantial losses of capital resources from the area occur through profit remittances, interest payments, and royalties. If the result is not uniform underdevelopment in the peripheral region, it is at best uneven development or dependent development (Cardoso, 1972).

Numerous Canadian studies in the dependency tradition emphasize this theme—for example, examinations of the deindustrialization of the Maritimes from 1890 to 1920 and its continuing underdevelopment in the interim (Archibald, 1971; Acheson, 1977; Forbes, 1977; Matthews, 1977; House, 1981). A similar perspective has been used in studies of agriculture and oil development on the Prairies (Fowke 1957, 1968; Pratt, 1976; Knuttila and McCrorie, 1980) and in examinations of Native–White interactions in

DEPENDENCY THEORY AND ITS CRITICS

Dependency theory as an explanation for regional inequality in Canada has numerous critics. Some question the applicability of a model articulated initially to explain underdevelopment in the Third World to the Canadian context, where neither low returns for labour (i.e., low wages), nor low returns for the exported resource product, nor a large traditional population sector have obtained (Marchak, 1985). Others have questioned whether the theory has much to add to what has already been articulated, perhaps more appropriately for Canada, by staple theorists such as Innis and Watkins. In many ways, the debate has moved on to larger questions and broader perspectives due to dissatisfaction with the rather simplistic dyadic relationships of dependency theory (Friedman and Wayne, 1977). In particular, more attention has been paid in recent years to encapsulating dependency theory (and also staples theory) within the broader Marxist paradigm. This has shifted the debate in several ways. For example, the thrust in early dependency theory on relations between geographic areas is replaced by a focus on the relations between social classes (located in different regions, to be sure) defined in Marxist terms. Rather than focusing on the exchange of raw materials between regions or countries, and the terms of trade governing that exchange, attention has shifted back to the classical Marxist concern about relations of production, ownership of the means of production, the extraction of surplus labour, and how the resulting benefits and costs are distributed in regional terms. Other Marxist concepts—the theory of imperialism, the reserve army of labour, the nature of class-based resistance movements—are also prominent in the literature, as are debates about the nature of the capitalist class in Canada and its regions (Veltmeyer, 1979; Naylor, 1975; Clement, 1975, 1977; Niosi, 1978 and 1981). As Brym and Sacouman put it with reference to Atlantic Canada, "underdevelopment . . . is a result neither of the natural or human resource deficiencies of the region, nor of the unfair treatment accorded the eastern-most provinces by the more powerful central and western ones, but of capitalist development itself" (Brym and Sacouman, 1979).

the context of resource development in the Canadian North (Watkins, 1977; Kellough, 1980; Elias, 1975).

If development is externally controlled and exploitative, economic and social distortions will arise in the dependent area. In economic terms, development usually focuses on extracting raw materials according to a timetable dictated by the external interests. The development of an integrated, balanced economy in which local resources are harnessed by local entrepreneurs to meet local needs is hampered by external decision making and the co-optation of social resources. Here, the dependency theory argument is similar to the more pessimistic version of the staple theory, which suggests the backward, forward, and final demand linkages that would stimulate the development of a balanced economy do not, in fact, materialize.

In social terms, dependency theory focuses on the class structure of the metropolitan and satellite areas. While different analysts of particular regions or countries will identify various kinds of social class constellations, all analyses identify dominant elites and subordinate labourers in both centre and periphery. Parts of the dominant periphery elite are linked to the centre elite and serve as its agent in the satellite area (Matthews, 1980; Dos Santos, 1971; Stavenhagen, 1974). In the Canadian context, for example, Clement argues a portion of the economic elite of Canada's peripheral regions has been bought out by Central Canadian and American business interests, and serves those interests in the region (Clement, 1983).

PUBLIC POLICY MEASURES

While regional issues are of ongoing importance in Canada, perhaps the earliest policies explicitly directed to alleviating regional disparities were the measures undertaken to counter the drought and Depression experienced by the Prairies in the 1930s. World War II intervened and shifted attention to the need for mobilization in support of the war effort and to national reconstruction when the war ended. Economic prosperity lasting until the mid-1950s kept regional inequalities off the national agenda.

In the last thirty years, however, regional disparities have been a more important consideration in government policy. In part, this results from less favourable economic circumstances; in part, because of a more interventionist approach by governments in resolving social and economic problems. Perceptions of the issue also changed with the growing recognition that the relative gap between regions was the important consideration, not their absolute level of poverty or well-being, nor their current rates of economic growth or stagnation.

In examining the policies pursued, one is struck by the variety of measures implemented and by the frequent changes in approach. There are a myriad of policies designed to promote regional development or reduce disparities, and all three levels of government are active in the field. And while some policies are clearly and explicitly directed at the problem, others have only indirect implications, while still others, not directed to the problem at all, end up frustrating the intent and effect of the more explicit approaches.

There is considerable and frequent change in policies in part because regional development policies are important for voter support. Thus, each successive government wants to put its stamp on regional development efforts. The approaches change as well because conditions change — policies appropriate during economic growth may be inappropriate in a period of decline. When the growth of most sectors of the economy and regions of the country are turning down, as they did in the post-1973 period, governments may wish to emphasize national development and support the more advanced regions, rather than the weaker ones, in an effort to stimulate economic activity in the country. Sometimes the policy changes and the attendant administrative reorganizations are so rapid that the particular approaches do not receive a fair chance to work.

What is the source of regional development policy? One source is the theoretical perspectives outlined in the previous section, each suggesting certain policies consistent with the analysis presented. In general, however, governments are less dogmatic than academics. Thus, in any given period, public policy makers usually employ a range of measures chosen (deliberately or not) from several analytical frameworks and applied pragmatically. The Liberal and Conservative federal governments of the post-war period have at various times employed policies consistent with staple theory (at least in its more benign version) and other policies rooted more in a regional deficit perspective, including theory related to growth poles. Leftist dependency theory has had much less influence on policy pertaining to *regional* development, although measures such as the National Energy Program and the Foreign Investment Review Agency reflect that perspective's view of Canada's national development and relationship to the United States.

In addition to the theoretical and pragmatic considerations, political concerns also influence regional policy. A good example is the 1970s shift in resources and attention designed to counteract separatist sentiment in Quebec.

The major kinds of initiatives that have been undertaken by the federal government — sometimes in co-operation with the provinces and sometimes unilaterally — are:

1. Investments in infrastructure such as roads, harbours, schools, hospitals, wharves, and railroads.

2. Human capital investments and personal adjustment. Here the emphasis is on providing education, training, and mobility grants for the unemployed who wish to change careers or move to an area that offers better opportunities.

3. Policies of industrial assistance. These have included tax exemptions, tax credits, loan guarantees, or cash grants to individual firms to encourage them to locate in a depressed area. The same measures have been used to help new firms get started or existing ones to expand, diversify, or export more of its products. Much debate has taken place about the effectiveness of industrial assistance policies. They have been criticized for supporting capital intensive (rather than employment-intensive) establishments, and for attracting "footloose" industries to a region — that is, firms with few backward and forward linkages and with little commitment to their new location.

4. Policies directed to resource and sectoral development. The federal government, under its Department of Regional Economic Expansion in the latter 1970s and more recently under other auspices, has signed general development agreements with the provinces. The agreements have provided federal financial support for the development of forestry, agriculture, or tourism. In the early 1980s, brief attention was given to stimulating the economy through investments in energy-sector mega projects such as the extraction of coal in British Columbia and oil in Alberta. Declining oil prices forced several large projects to be put on hold, however.

5. Compensatory and transfer policies. By far the greatest amount of federal money in support of the provinces and their residents is spent not for explicit development policies, but as cash transfers to the provinces and to individual citizens or families. Equalization grants, funds for hospitals, medicare and post-secondary education, payments for unemployment insurance, family allowances, and similar grants make up the bulk of these transfers. They greatly overshadow the budgets of the explicit regional development programs mentioned above (Lithwick, 1986). The grants to the provinces have made the provincial governments of the poorer regions very dependent on federal transfer for their total spending budget. Some 56 percent of P.E.I.'s provincial revenues came from federal sources in 1980/1981, for example, and the figure is only slightly less for the other Atlantic provinces. At the other extreme, only 12 percent of Alberta's revenues come from the federal treasury. The dependence of individuals on personal transfer income is also substantial in the poorer provinces and is growing over time. In 1981, 27.7 percent of the personal income of Newfoundlanders came from government transfers as compared with 9.1 percent in Alberta. Twenty years earlier, the comparable percentages were 17.6 percent and 8.8 percent, respectively (Savoie, 1986).

The policies designed to stimulate regional development have been pursued within several organizational frameworks. In the late 1950s and for much of the 1960s, discrete policies, such as the Federal Fund for Rural Economic Development, were administered by a variety of departments. The Trudeau administration, beginning in 1969, tried to consolidate all relevant programs under the newly created Department of Regional Economic Expansion. DREE was disbanded in 1982, however, in favour of an approach that provides for a federal co-ordinator's office in each region and the consideration of regional implications by Cabinet for all economic policies, not just those explicitly directed to regional development. Many DREE programs were allocated to other departments in the 1982 reorganization. Most recently, the Mulroney government has begun to establish regional development agencies in Atlantic Canada and the West.

Different target areas have also been used — whole provinces, disadvantaged areas within and/or across provinces, focused growth poles and their hinterlands, and so forth.

One wonders, then, what has been the result of this diversified three-decade onslaught on regional disparities. This is the focus of the following section.

THE PERSISTENCE OF REGIONAL DISPARITIES

There is widespread agreement among experts in regional development on the main conclusions to be drawn.

First, in per capita income, one main measure usually employed to measure regional inequality, the gap between the richest and poorest provinces, has decreased over time. Table 2 shows the poorest provinces improved their relative per capita incomes from approximately 55 to 70 percent of the national average in the period 1956 to 1983. The richer provinces, Ontario and British Columbia, have moved closer to the national average over time. One can also observe sharp fluctuations around the average, particularly on the part of Saskatchewan, which is very

Table 2

PERSONAL INCOME PER CAPITA, BY PROVINCE, 1926–1983
(RELATIVE TO THE NATIONAL AVERAGE, CANADA = 100)

Province	1926	1931	1936	1941	1946	1951	1956	1961	1966	1971	1976	1980	1983
Newfoundland	—	—	—	—	—	48.2	53.5	58.2	59.9	63.6	68.5	64.0	67.6
Prince Edward Island	56.1	51.4	55.6	46.9	58.2	54.4	58.7	58.8	60.1	63.7	68.6	71.0	74.3
Nova Scotia	67.8	75.9	79.6	77.1	85.9	69.1	71.9	77.5	74.8	77.4	78.8	79.1	80.4
New Brunswick	64.8	67.2	67.4	63.9	75.2	67.0	65.9	67.8	68.9	72.2	75.6	71.1	74.2
Quebec	84.6	94.9	92.1	86.6	81.5	83.9	86.1	90.1	89.0	88.8	93.0	94.5	92.5
Ontario	114.4	127.9	125.5	129.4	115.7	118.3	117.8	118.3	116.9	117.0	109.0	107.0	109.2
Manitoba	108.4	90.7	92.4	92.8	102.9	100.8	96.9	94.3	91.9	94.0	93.7	89.5	93.0
Saskatchewan	101.8	44.9	58.0	59.3	96.1	107.1	93.5	70.8	92.9	80.3	99.6	91.0	93.7
Alberta	113.7	77.9	76.3	80.0	107.8	111.0	104.6	100.0	100.0	98.9	102.6	111.6	108.4
British Columbia	112.1	129.9	131.9	120.9	114.9	119.2	121.1	114.9	115.9	109.0	109.1	111.3	106.0
Canada	100.0	100.0	100.0	100.0	100.0	100.0	100.0	100.0	100.0	100.0	100.0	100.0	100.0
Disparity gap (Highest to low ratio)	2.18	2.53	2.37	2.58	1.99	2.47	2.26	2.03	1.95	1.84	1.59	1.74	1.62

Source: Statistics Canada, Provincial Economic Accounts, adapted from Polese (1987).

dependent on the vagaries of production and prices in the agricultural sector. Overall, however, there has been considerable improvement in relative per capita incomes over the period when policy intervention has been most intense, and this was not the case before 1960 (Economic Council, 1977).

Second, Table 3 shows almost all the improvement can be attributed to transfer payments, such as U.I.C., family allowances, old age security, payments under the Canada Assistance Plan, and so forth. If these kinds of compensatory transfers to individuals and families are excluded from per capita income, as they are in Table 3, the improvement in relative per capita incomes has been very small. Put another way, the attack on regional inequality has resulted in greater equity in the country as a result of transfers from the richer provinces to the poorer ones (via the federal treasury), but it has not improved the productive capacity of the poorer regions, i.e., their capacity to generate higher earned incomes relative to the national average on the basis of their own productive resources.

Similarly discouraging data is provided by Table 4, which gives the results for unemployment rates, another common measure of regional disparity. We see improvement in the disparity between 1961 and 1971, largely because Newfoundland's rate improves significantly in this period. The trend, however, is for increasing disparity again between 1971 and 1981, with the 1981 disparity not far removed from what it was in 1966.

We began this chapter by suggesting regional inequality was a substantial and persisting problem in Canada, which made it unique among advanced industrial (or post-industrial) societies. We are, perhaps, in a somewhat better position now to pursue the comparison with the United States' experience to gain a comparative perspective on the problem.

Geography's influence is important. While Canada has significant natural resources, the United States has the added advantage of a wide dispersion of good

Table 3

EARNED INCOME PER CAPITA, BY PROVINCE, 1961–1981
(RELATION TO THE NATIONAL AVERAGE, CANADA = 100)

Province	**1961**	**1966**	**1971**	**1976**	**1981**
Newfoundland	53.2	52.5	54.8	56.1	53.4
Prince Edward Island	53.5	53.6	57.0	60.2	59.0
Nova Scotia	75.0	71.5	74.2	74.2	73.4
New Brunswick	64.1	65.1	68.1	69.0	64.9
Quebec	89.5	89.2	87.8	90.4	89.9
Ontario	121.1	118.3	119.2	112.5	110.6
Manitoba	93.5	91.0	93.7	93.9	92.9
Saskatchewan	67.2	92.3	78.7	99.5	98.9
Alberta	100.3	99.0	98.6	105.0	114.4
British Columbia	113.7	111.0	109.5	109.5	109.7
Canada	100.0	100.0	100.0	100.0	100.0
Disparity gap (Highest to lowest ratio)	2.27	2.25	2.17	2.00	2.14

Source: Statistics Canada, Provincial Economic Accounts.

Table 4
PROVINCIAL UNEMPLOYMENT RATE, 1961–1981, BY PROVINCE
(RELATION TO NATIONAL AVERAGE, CANADA = 100)

Province	1961	1966	1971	1976	1981	1986
Newfoundland	275	171	135	189	186	208
Prince Edward Island	—	—	—	135	150	140
Nova Scotia	114	138	113	134	134	140
New Brunswick	148	156	98	155	154	150
Quebec	130	121	118	123	137	115
Ontario	77	76	87	87	87	73
Manitoba	70	82	92	66	79	80
Saskatchewan	58	44	56	55	61	80
Alberta	66	74	92	56	50	102
British Columbia	120	135	116	121	88	131
Canada	100	100	100	100	100	100
Disparity gap	4.74	3.88	2.41	3.43	3.72	2.85

Source: Statistics Canada, The Labour Force.

agricultural land, mineral resources, and forests. Its people are also more evenly distributed and its urban centres are more balanced in size and location at various points along the coast and in the interior. By contrast, much of the Canadian population is concentrated in the Toronto–Montreal area, as is the preponderance of its manufacturing capacity and financial institutions. The greater concentration in Canada is explained not only by the advantages of a central location to serve the more peripheral areas of the country, but also because most foreign (i.e., American) investment is located in southern Ontario, close to the major U.S. markets and to American head offices. Thus, the overwhelming importance of the United States in trade and investment exerts its influence on the regional distribution of productive resources and population in Canada (Semple, 1987). The United States, has no similar relationship to a foreign power. Many different centres relate to a number of international contexts—Boston/New York on the Atlantic relating to Europe, Miami in the south oriented to Latin America, Los Angeles and San Francisco on the Pacific, and so forth. In addition, regional centres in the interior provide urban focal points for their surrounding areas—St. Louis, Minneapolis–St. Paul, Chicago, to name a few.

Canada is also much more dependent on resource exports and is therefore more subject than the United States to the distortions, uncertainties, and pitfalls that this kind of economic development brings, as the staple and dependency theorists have described.

Another significant difference between Canada and the United States is the cultural make-up and distribution of the two populations. In Canada, the large concentration of the French-speaking population in Quebec and adjacent areas overlaps with regional disparities. In the United States the significant ethnic and racial minorities are not concentrated in one area. Higgins (1986) argues that the United States has had an extraordinary mobility of labour and capital, and that this has helped to even out regional disparities. The attachment of Canadians to their cultural

PUBLIC POLICY AND THE TREND IN REGIONAL INEQUALITY

In a recent article, Polese states:

> The regional structure of the Canadian economy and the income disparities which accompany it show a high degree of stability in the long run. The broad regional patterns and trends are well-defined. Perhaps most striking, over seventy-five years, is the consistent weight of the Ontario and Quebec economies and the persistent income disparity between the Atlantic provinces and the rest of Canada. Major shifts occur only under exceptional circumstances, such as the Great Depression and the 1973 oil crisis. . . .
>
> The obvious conclusion to be drawn from these results is that there are definite limits to the capacity of public policy to alter long-run patterns. Location does matter; geography cannot be legislated away. The locational advantages and disadvantages which accrue to the various regions of Canada, including the externalities built up over many decades, are in large measure the reflection of now well-established (often man-made) patterns and geographic realities. Crudely put, given the spatial structure of the North American economy, Newfoundland and Saskatchewan are simply not very profitable locations for the production of most goods and services (unless destined for local markets). The locational differences between regions, in terms of economic costs, are such that it is unreasonable to assume that they can be totally subsidized away, unless society is willing to devote truly impressive sums of money to the cause of "balanced" regional development, however defined (Polese, 1987).

communities is said to have reduced mobility.

As a result of these factors, regional disparities are less significant in the United States, and less entrenched. Significant reductions in regional disparities have taken place over the long term, and in the short run some regions are declining (e.g., the New England area in the 1970s), while others are growing rapidly (e.g., the sunbelt of the south). The intractable problems of localized underdevelopment seem more associated with problems of the decay, neglect, and exploitation of core areas within large urban centres than with large geographic regions. In the urban context, however, racial/ethnic divisions often overlap with areas of underdevelopment.

CONCLUSION

As noted above, the stability of regional inequality patterns in Canada is impressive, more so than the changes caused by thirty years of concerted effort. This is not to say that the policy measures undertaken have failed, since the situation could have worsened without these measures.

Also, much has been learned in the process. For example, it is now clear that transferring funds to provincial governments and to families and individuals reduces inequalities in region per capita incomes, and is defensible on equity grounds. The debate on whether they have a negative effect on the economic development of the region, by interfering with the adaptive process, as Courchene maintains, continues. There is a tendency, however to regard this as only a side issue, although the search for transfer policies designed to minimize interference with the adjustment mechanisms of the economy continues.

The key issue is clearer now than it was before: how to bring about self-sustaining, indigenous economic development in the disadvantaged regions. How should or can a region overcome locational disadvantages, resource shortages, or external dependencies? A good deal of searching and experimenting is taking place. In the Atlantic region for example, there is considerable interest in community-based economic development — setting up nonprofit community development agencies that rely on local initiative and external support to promote economic and social development (MacLeod, 1986). Provincial governments are charting plans for the economic development of their provinces: in Nova Scotia through a policy of "building competitiveness," in Newfoundland through "building on our strengths" (Report of the Royal Commission on Employment and Unemployment, 1986). And significant changes are taking place in the private sector as the trend toward consolidation of ownership in the hands of a few local families continues in provinces such as New Brunswick and Nova Scotia, where some large, internationally competitive companies are being established.

The growing emphasis on regional initiative is due in part to the apparent retreat of foreign capital to other parts of the world, where wages and regulations are less demanding. There is evidence of a decline in foreign investment in Canada's manufacturing sector, and thus a greater need to rely on domestic resources (Marchak, 1985; Bonin and Verrault, 1987). In addition, the federal government has retreated from regional development issues—in budget terms because of federal deficits, in ideological terms as renewed faith is placed in the workings of the market, and in priority terms as national issues such as free trade dominate the agenda.

The future of Canada's disadvantaged regions will also be shaped by events and trends impinging on the regions from outside. The free trade negotiations are a case in point; while there is agreement that the disadvantaged regions will gain as consumers (in that prices are likely to be lower as trade barriers with the United States are reduced), it is not clear what the differential impact of free trade would be on the productive capacity of the regions (Watson, 1987; Pinchin, 1986). The shift to an information-based economy, signalled by the continued growth of the service sector and the increased significance of knowledge-based industries, also holds out opportunities and problems. The trend is potentially positive for disadvantaged regions in that the new technology could overcome some locational and natural resource disadvantages (Macrae, 1986). There are questions, however, about the speed of adoption of new technology in disadvantaged regions, and about limitations in the size of markets and urban centres, among other considerations (Lesser, 1987).

The study of regional inequality is therefore at a turning point in that the perspectives and policies prevalent for many years are increasingly being questioned — with respect to their results and usefulness in dealing with present and future issues. In this time of reassessment, it is comforting to know that those of us who live in Canada's disadvantaged areas have a fallback position to rely on. As the chairman of the 1957 Royal Commission suggested, the poorer regions of the country can always be converted into national parks!

DISCUSSION QUESTIONS

1. Has regional inequality decreased in the last three decades or remained at about the same level? Explain in what sense both answers may be correct.
2. What, in your opinion, is the best explanation for the causes of regional inequality in Canada? Why do you think it is the best explanation?
3. Is the problem of regional disparities more or less severe in Canada compared to the United States? Explain the reasons for the difference.
4. If you were the Minister for Regional Industrial Expansion, what would you do to reduce inequalities in Canada?
5. To what theoretical explanation of regional inequality is your strategy most closely allied?

GLOSSARY

dependency the term in its political context denotes a country or province subject to the control of another of which it does not form an integral part. The term is also applied to relations between individuals and groups.

inequality a condition of inequality obtains when valued resources such as wealth, power, or status are distributed so that some have more than others. The term refers to relative differences between individuals, groups, or regions.

metropolis the largest city of an area having economic and social dominance over the area. Writers in the dependency tradition extend the term to whole regions or countries that exercise relations of dominance over other regions or countries.

poverty individual or family insufficiency of assets, income and public services.

region the term "region" denotes a geographical area which either possesses certain homogeneous characteristics that distinguish it from adjacent areas or other regions, or which serves as a unit of government or administration.

satellite this term refers to the city, region, or country that is dominated by the metropolis.

socioeconomic development increase in social and economic complexity.

staples raw or semi-processed materials extracted or grown primarily for export markets and dominating the regional or national economies.

underdevelopment condition of a low level of socioeconomic development, or a suboptimum utilization of natural and human resources. The term is sometimes used to refer to the process whereby an area or group of people become impoverished as a result of exploitation.

BIBLIOGRAPHY

Acheson, T.W.
1977 "The Maritimes and 'Empire Canada.' " In D.J. Bercuson (ed.) *Canada and The Burden of Unity*. Toronto: Macmillan.

Archibald, Bruce
1971 "Atlantic Regional Underdevelopment and Socialism." In L. LaPierre et al. (eds.) *Essays on the Left*. Toronto: McClelland and Stewart.

Berger, Justice Thomas R.
1977 *Northern Frontier, Northern Homeland: The Report of the Mackenzie Valley Pipeline Inquiry*. Ottawa: Supply and Services.

Bonin, Bernard and Roger Verrault.
1987 "The Multinational Firm and Regional Development." In William J. Coffey and Mario Polese (eds.) *Still Living Together: Recent Trends and Future Directions in Canadian Regional Development*. Montreal: The Institute for Research on Public Policy.

Boudeville, J.R.
1968 *Problems of Regional Economic Planning*. Edinburgh: Edinburgh University Press.

Brym, Robert and James Sacouman (eds.)
1979 *Underdevelopment and Social Movements in Atlantic Canada*. Toronto: New Hogtown Press.

Buckley, Kenneth
1958 "The Role of the Staple Industries in Canada's Economic Development." *Journal of Economic History*, 18 (December): 439–50.

Cardoso, Fernando
1972 "Dependency and Development in Latin America." *New Left Review*, 74 (14) (July–August): 83–95.

Clement, Wallace
1975 *The Canadian Corporate Elite*. Toronto: McClelland and Stewart.

———
1983 *Class, Power and Property: Essays on Canadian Society*. Toronto: Methuen.

Courchene, Thomas
1986 "Avenues of Adjustment: The Transfer System and Regional Disparities." In Roger Savoie (ed.) *The Canadian Economy: A Regional Perspective*. Toronto: Methuen.

Davis, A.K.
1971 "Canadian Society and History as Hinterland Versus Metropolis." In R.J. Ossenberg (ed.) *Canadian Society: Pluralism, Change and Conflict*. Scarborough, Ontario: Prentice-Hall.

Department of Development
1984 *Building Competitiveness: The White Paper on Economic Development in Nova Scotia*. Halifax: Government of Nova Scotia.

Dos Santos, Theotonio
1971 "The Structure of Dependence." In K.T. Fann and D.C. Hodges (eds.) *Readings in U.S. Imperialism*. Boston: Porter Sargent.

Drache, Daniel
1976 "Rediscovering Canadian Political Economy." *Journal of Canadian Studies*, 11 (3) (August): 3–18.

Economic Council of Canada
1977 *Living Together: A Study of Regional Disparities*. Ottawa: Supply and Services Canada.

Elias, Peter
1975 *Metropolis and Hinterland in Northern Manitoba*. Winnipeg: The Manitoba Museum of Man and Nature.

Forbes, Ernest
1977 "Misguided Symmetry: The Destruction of Regional Transportation Policy for the Maritimes." In D.J. Bercuson (ed.) *Canada and the Burden of Unity*. Toronto: Macmillan.

Fowke, Vernon
1957 *The National Policy and the Wheat Economy*. Toronto: University of Toronto Press.

———
1968 "Political Economy and the Canadian Wheat Grower." In Norman Ward and Duff Spafford (eds.) *Politics in Saskatchewan*. Toronto: Longmans Canada.

Frank, Andre Gunder
1972 "Sociology of Development and Underdevelopment of Sociology." In James Cockcroft et al. (eds.) *Dependence and Underdevelopment: Latin America's Political Economy*. New York: Doubleday.

Friedman, Harriet and Jack Wayne
1977 "Dependency Theory: A Critique." *Canadian Journal of Sociology*, 2 (4) (Winter): 399–416.

Higgins, Benjamin
1959 *Economic Development: Principles, Problems, and Policies*. New York: W.W. Norton.

———
1986 "Regional Development Planning: The State of the Art in North America." In Donald Savoie (ed.) *The Canadian Economy: A Regional Perspective*. Toronto: Methuen.

House, Douglas
1981 "Big Oil and Small Communities in Coastal Labrador: The Local Dynamics of Dependency." *Canadian Review of Sociology and Anthropology* 18 (4) (November): 433–52.

Innis, Harold
1930 *The Fur Trade in Canada*. Toronto: University of Toronto Press.

———
1940 *The Cod Fisheries*. Toronto: University of Toronto Press.

———
1956 *Essays in Canadian Economic History*. Edited by Mary Q. Innis. Toronto: University of Toronto Press.

Isard, Walter
1975 *Introduction to Regional Science*. Englewood Cliffs, New Jersey: Prentice-Hall.

Kellough, Gail
1980 "From Colonialism to Economic Imperialism." In J. Harp and J. Hofley (eds.) *Structured Inequality in Canada*. Scarborough, Ontario: Prentice-Hall.

Knuttila, K.M. and J.N. McCrorie
1980 "National Policy and Prairie Agrarian Development: A Reassessment." *Canadian Review of Sociology and Anthropology*, 17 (3) (August): 263–72.

Lesser, Barry
1987 "Regional Development: Some Thoughts Arising From a Review of Research Sponsored by the Institute for Research on Public Policy." In William Coffey and Mario Polese (eds.) *Still Living Together: Recent Trends and Future Directions in Canadian Regional Development*. Montreal: Institute for Research on Public Policy.

Lithwick, Harvey (ed.)
1978 *Regional Economic Policy: The Canadian Experience*. Toronto: McGraw-Hill Ryerson.

———
1986 "Regional Policy: The Embodiment of Contradictions." In Donald Savoie (ed.) *The Canadian Economy: A Regional Perspective*. Toronto: Methuen.

Mackintosh, W.A.
1923 "Economic Factors in Canadian History." *Canadian Historical Review*. IV (1) (March): 12–25.

MacLeod, Greg
1986 *New Age Business: Community Corporations That Work*. Ottawa: The Canadian Council on Social Development.

Macrae, Norman
1986 "A Forecast of What the Knowledge-Based Society Will Bring." Presentation to the Symposium on the Revolution in Knowledge: Atlantic Canada's Future in the Information Economy. Halifax: Dalhousie University.

Mansell, Robert
1986 "Energy Policy, Prices and Rents: Implications for Regional Growth and Development." In William Coffey and Mario Polese (eds.) *Still Living Together: Recent Trends and Future Directions in Canadian Regional Development*. Montreal: Institute for Research on Public Policy.

Marchak, Patricia
1983 *Green Gold: The Forest Industry in British Columbia*. Vancouver:

University of British Columbia Press.

——

1985 "Canadian Political Economy." *Canadian Review of Sociology and Anthropology*, 22 (5) (December): 673–709.

Matthews, Ralph

1977 "Canadian Regional Development Strategy: A Dependency Theory Perspective." *Plan Canada*, 17 (2): 131–43.

——

1980 "The Significance and Explanation of Regional Differences in Canada: Towards a Canadian Sociology." *Journal of Canadian Studies*, 15 (2): 43–61.

Meier, Gerald M.

1984 *Leading Issues in Economic Development*, (Fourth Edition). New York: Oxford University Press.

Naylor, Tom

1975 *The History of Canadian Business* (2 volumes). Toronto: Lorimer.

Ness, Gayl (ed.)

1970 *The Sociology of Economic Development: A Reader*. New York: Harper and Row.

Niosi, Jorge

1978 *The Economy of Canada*. Montreal: Black Rose Books.

——

1981 *Canadian Capitalism*. (Trans. by Robert Chodos). Toronto: James Lorimer.

Pinchin, Hugh

1986 "A Framework for Assessing the Impact of Free Trade in North America." In W. Shipman (ed.) *Trade and Investment Across the Northeast Boundary: Quebec, the Atlantic Provinces and New England*. Montreal: Institute for Research on Public Policy.

Polese, Mario

1987 "Patterns of Regional Economic Development in Canada: Long Term Trends and Issues." In William Coffey and Mario Polese (eds.) *Still Living Together: Recent Trends and Future Directions in Canadian Regional Development*. Montreal: Institute for Research on Public Policy.

Pratt, Larry

1976 *The Tar Sands*. Edmonton: Hurtig Publishers.

Ross, David and Peter Usher

1986 *From the Roots Up: Economic Development as if Community Mattered*. Croton-on-Hudson, New York: Bootstrap Press.

Royal Commission on Employment and Unemployment

1986 *Building on Our Strengths*. St. John's: Queen's Printer.

Savoie, Donald

1986a "Introduction: Regional Development in Canada." In *The Canadian Economy: A Regional Perspective*. Toronto: Methuen.

——

1986b "Defining Regional Disparities." In *The Canadian Economy: A Regional Perspective*. Toronto: Methuen.

——

1986c *Regional Economic Development: Canada's Search for Solutions*. Toronto: University of Toronto Press.

Scott, A.D.

1978 "Policy for Declining Regions: A Theoretical Approach." In H. Lithwick (ed.) *Regional Economic Policy: The Canadian Experience*. Toronto: McGraw-Hill Ryerson.

Semple, R. Keith

1987 "Regional Analysis of Corporate Decision Making Within the Canadian Economy." In William Coffey and Mario Polese (eds.) *Still Living Together: Recent Trends and Future Directions in Canadian Regional Development*. Montreal: Institute for Research on Public Policy.

Stavenhagen, Rodolfo

1974 "The Future of Latin America: Between Underdevelopment and Revolution." *Latin American Perspectives* 9 (1) (Spring): 124–48.

Veltmeyer, Henry

1979 "The Capitalist Underdevelopment of

Atlantic Canada.'' In R.J. Brym and R.J. Sacouman (eds.) *Underdevelopment and Social Movements in Atlantic Canada*. Toronto: New Hogtown Press.

Watkins, Mel

1963 ''A Staple Theory of Economic Growth.'' *Canadian Journal of Economics and Political Science*, 29 (May): 141–58.

——

1977a ''The Staple Theory Revisited.'' *Journal of Canadian Studies*, 12 (Winter):83–95.

——

1977b *Dene Nation—The Colony Within*. Toronto: University of Toronto Press.

Watson, William

1987 ''The Regional Consequences of Free(r) Trade With the United States.'' In William J. Coffey and Mario Polese (eds.) *Still Living Together: Recent Trends and Future Directions in Canadian Regional Development*. Montreal: Institute for Research on Public Policy.

p a r t t w o

The Base in Political Economy

Scene from a Toronto rally in opposition to the free trade talks, 1986. *Courtesy of the Ontario Federation of Labour*

> *"To Canadian finance capitalists . . . a continentalist business strategy makes sense in an era of crisis, instability, and contraction in the world market. To Canadian labour, however, free trade carries different ramifications."*

c h a p t e r f i v e

The Political Economy of Canada

William K. Carroll

INTRODUCTION

Political economy has a double meaning in Canadian social science. On the one hand, it refers to a *topical area of study*, namely, the ways economics and politics have been intertwined in Canada. On the other, it refers to an interdisciplinary and historical *style of social analysis*, which draws upon economics, political science, and sociology in attempting to understand power in modern market societies. In both respects, political economy transcends the traditional disciplinary boundaries that often fragment knowledge of the social world into separate compartments and invites us to develop a unified understanding of societies.

By focusing on power and social dominance, political economy links social analysis to critique. As Patricia Marchak has observed, political economy involves "the study of power derived from or contingent on a system of property rights; the historical development of power relationships; and the cultural and social embodiments of them" (1985:673). Political economists hold that the confluence of power and property relates to the "way of life" that predominates in a given society and the lifestyles and life chances of groups within a society. In exploring how prevailing social structures serve the interests of dominant groups, political economists often expose the *systemic* nature of inequality, and highlight the need for basic structural change in economic and political arrangements. Thus, in contemporary Canadian sociology, political economy provides a critical, even radical, perspective informed by interdisciplinary, historical analysis.

This broad approach has been fruitfully applied to such phenomena as gender inequality (Armstrong and Armstrong, 1984; Maroney and Luxton, 1987), regionalism

(Brym, 1986b) and crime (MacLean, 1986), but in this chapter we shall concentrate on political-economic perspectives on Canadian society *as a whole.*[1] Since the resurgence of Canadian political economy in the late 1960s, the field has been dominated by two distinctive and somewhat opposed theoretical frameworks: dependency theory and Marxism (Brym, 1985:1–20). These perspectives both emphasize the relation between economic and other forms of domination and the need for concrete historical analysis to reveal Canada's *specficity*. They also agree that Canadian society must be understood in relation to other elements in the world capitalist system, and that these international relations are imbued with power.

The perspectives differ, however, in many particulars and provide different images of Canadian society. The major differences can be highlighted by examining each perspective in terms of three issues: (1) what is the basis of economic power?; (2) how is economic power translated into political power?; and (3) what is Canada's specific location in the world system?

CANADA AS A RICH DEPENDENCY

The Dependency Approach

Dependency theory developed in the 1950s and 1960s as Third World scholars studied the problems faced by less-developed countries (LDCs) as a consequence of their disadvantageous location in the world capitalist system (Frank, 1979). The striking parallels between Canada and many LDCs led social scientists to use the dependency formulation to understand Canada's place in the same system.

In this formulation, economic power is embodied in the metropolis–hinterland relation between a dominant country or region and a subordinate jurisdiction, whose economic backwardness contributes to the relative affluence of the metropole. As Marchak puts it,

> Economic **imperialism** means deliberate **exploitation** of one country's resources for the benefit of nationals in another country, ultimately backed by the potential use of force. The "centre" or "metropolitan" region exploits resources on the "periphery" or in the "hinterland" region for its own benefit, and such exploitation eventually culminates not only in underdevelopment of the hinterland but in a reversal of such development as has already taken place. The hinterland becomes incapable of reversing the exploitation, and inevitably becomes poorer and less powerful (Marchak, 1979:100).

The Staples Thesis

The dependency approach gained many adherents in the 1970s as two long-standing traditions of social analysis were synthesized to focus on the dangers of continued American domination. The first tradition was the **staples thesis**, an interpretation of Canadian economic history pioneered in the 1920s and 1930s by Harold Innis (1970) and W.A. MacIntosh (1923). The staples approach viewed **hinterland** development as shaped by the pattern of demand and level of technology in the metropole and by the geography and resources of the hinterland, which trades its raw material staples for manufactured goods from the metropole (Laxer, 1985a:313). Such an international division of labour could produce a **staples trap**—with the hinterland perpetually exporting raw materials and failing to develop its own independent industries (Watkins, 1963). Since most economic initiatives arose from the changing economic demand, cultural tastes, and industrial techniques in the metropole, the hinterland's development was attributable to the economic power of the metropole, as it constrained activities in the hinterland (Laxer, 1985a:313).

Contemporary Canada was thus viewed as the product of a succession of metropolis–hinterland relations, beginning with French colonization of New France, continuing through British colonization of British North America, and culminating in this century with American neocolonization. As economic and cultural conditions in the metropolitan countries changed, so did their demand for particular raw materials. The result is a Canadian economy developed around a succession of export-oriented staple industries. "The history of Canada . . . is the history of its great staple trades: the fur trade, the cod fisheries, square timber and lumber, wheat, and the new staples of this century — pulp and paper, minerals, oil and gas" (Watkins, 1973:116; see also Easterbrook and Aitken, 1956; Drache, 1977).

The Study of Elites

The second tradition that contributed to the dependency perspective was the systematic analysis of elites, first pursued in Canada by John Porter in *The Vertical Mosaic* (1965). Porter viewed power as concentrated in the hands of individuals who controlled major social institutions. Thus, economic power was held by an economic elite — the directors and executives of the largest corporations — while political power was held by a political elite of politicians, judges, and senior state bureaucrats.

LEVITT'S "SILENT SURRENDER"

The most influential modern statement of the metropolis-hinterland interpretation was made by Kari Levitt in *Silent Surrender* (1970). Despite a brief era of independent national development during the National Policy of 1879 to 1929, and despite institutional changes in the metropolis–hinterland relation, Levitt held that the trajectory of twentieth century Canada is toward recolonization and underdevelopment. In place of the great mercantilist monopolies such as the Hudson's Bay Company, which organized the staples trade under British colonialism, Canada is now dominated by U.S.-based multinational corporations, which have reorganized the staples trade into a "neomercantilist" system (Levitt, 1970:24–5). Levitt pointed to the dramatic increases between 1948 and 1963 in U.S. control of Canadian industry as evidence of Canadian business's silent surrender to the stronger American bourgeoisie, as the former traded independent entrepreneurship for the secure but subordinate status of branch-plant managers and coupon clippers (1970:39–40). In consequence, the Canadian economy lacks the innovative force of successful entrepreneurship. Levitt concluded "to the degree that Canadian business has opted to exchange its entrepreneurial role for a managerial and rentier status, Canada has regressed to a rich hinterland with an emasculated, if comfortable, business elite" (1970:77). In the contemporary Canadian political economy, foreign control perpetuates the staples trap by denying Canadians the means of independent economic development. Canada has become "the world's richest underdeveloped country" (Levitt, 1970:25).

In the 1970s, Tom Naylor (1972:1–41, 1975) and Wallace Clement (1975, 1977a) employed elite analysis in elaborating on Levitt's account of Canadian business's role in perpetuating Canada's hinterland status. They argued Canada's business elite developed as a mercantile class, a mediating agent of foreign colonial powers. In the nineteenth century, leading Canadian capitalists made their fortunes not through industrial entrepreneurship but by providing the financial, commercial, and transportation services necessary to the staples trade. The same commercial elite denied financial support to the small-scale industrialists of southwestern Ontario and allied themselves with American industry, whose expansion into Canada was partly financed by Canadian bankers and encouraged by the protective tariff of the National Policy (Naylor op.cit. 1972).

In *The Canadian Corporate Elite* (1975), Wallace Clement argued this long-standing alliance is evident in the composition and structure of Canada's economic elite. Compared to other industrialized liberal democracies, Clement held that the structure of economic power in Canada was *distorted* in two respects. First, the dominance in industrial Canada of U.S.-controlled branch plants meant much economic activity was ultimately controlled not by Canadians but by the executives and directors of foreign parent firms, acting through the managers of their Canadian subsidiaries, who formed a **comprador elite**. Second, Canada's business leaders had specialized in unproductive, commercial activities, such as finance and transportation — stifling the development of indigenously based industry. Clement concluded that "the Canadian bourgeoisie is primarily a commercial one, engaged in circulation rather than production, while in other nations the bourgeoisie is typically both industrial and financial" (1975:355).

Now for the second question of how economic power is translated into political power. In the staples approach, government activities were usually traced to economic factors originating in the metropole. Thus, for instance, Confederation in 1867 was attributed to the need for railway finance so the staples of the late nineteenth century could be efficiently transported to market. In the elite approach, political power relations are similarly simple: the economic elite is said to exert direct influence over state policy (Laxer, 1985a:313–15). In Panitch's (1977:11) view, the Canadian state's "close personal ties to the bourgeoisie" also demonstrate Canada's distinctiveness among the industrialized liberal democracies. Panitch describes these ties, from Confederation onward, as " 'a confraternity of power' of such dimensions as to permit the clear employment of the term 'ruling class' in the political as well as the economic sense in the Canadian case" (1977:13). This reasoning underlay Naylor's (1972:19) claim that the protective tariffs of the National Policy were implemented at the behest of the powerful commercial elite to expand the scale of the economy, and thus the volume of their commercial activities, by enticing American entrepreneurs to set up branch plants within the protected Canadian market. Clement's (1977b) study of the interpenetration of the corporate elite within the political elite in contemporary Canada reinforced this view by showing that 46 percent of the corporate elite had direct or indirect (kinship) positions in the state apparatus.

Elite analysis views political power as a direct reflection of economic power: the Canadian state is considered the *political instrument* of the economic elite. By implication, Canadian politics have been shaped by the peculiar composition of the economic elite. Thus, Canada's movement

THE CONTINENTAL ALLIANCE

Clement elaborated on a thesis in his comparative study of the American and Canadian political economies (1977a), where he argued that the structure of economic power in Canada is arrayed along a continental axis—an alliance of leading Canadian commercial capitalists and leading American industrial capitalists. This alliance is particularly evident in the pattern of interlocking directorships between dominant American and Canadian companies, which "because of the particular historical development of each nation, occur in such a way that they are mainly from Canadian finance to U.S. manufacturing and from U.S. manufacturing to Canadian finance—from strength to strength" (1977a:179). The result is an unusual situation in which "the financial–industrial axis is continental for Canada, but national within the United States" (Clement, 1977a:179).

Clement's study was a landmark in Canadian political economy, portraying the continental economy as a system within which the metropolis–hinterland power relation was sustained by an alliance of economic elites. Canada's status as a dependency within the American empire was marked not just by the staples trap, but by a definite structure of economic power. Not only had metropolitan demand for staples determined the pattern of development in the Canadian hinterland, but the dependence of Canada's merchants and bankers on the economic surpluses generated by U.S.-controlled industry meant their power was subordinate to the economic decisions of American multinationals.

into the orbit of the American empire has not only changed the composition of the economic elite, it has altered the locus of political power. In its strongest form, the dependency approach asserts "the Canadian state is now in the control of the dominant section of the ruling class in Canada —the U.S. corporations" (Hutcheson, 1978:174). Stated less boldly, to the extent Canadian capitalists have entered into a dependent alliance with stronger American multinationals, the Canadian **state** has also assumed "a relatively dependent position within the system of U.S. hegemony" (Clement, 1983:84)

What, then, of the third key issue in Canadian political economy: how does the dependency approach describe Canada's location in the world capitalist system? From Levitt forward, scholars in this tradition have argued that Canada occupies an intermediate position "at one and the same time, in a metropolitan relation to some countries and in a hinterland relation to others" (1970:103). Although Canada's manufacturing and resource industries are foreign-dominated, Canadian capitalists—notably, financial institutions—have also expanded into areas of the world that are even more peripheral than Canada, such as the Caribbean. Even so, Canadian investments abroad do not represent an independent expansion of Canadian capitalism, but constitute "branch plant quasi-imperialism": they are either centred around the commercial sectors that the Canadian bourgeoisie still controls or are ultimately controlled by the U.S. parents of Canadian subsidiaries (Naylor, 1972:34; Clement, 1977:115).

As applied to Canada, the dependency approach has yielded a thesis of *excep-*

tionalism, presenting Canada as unique in the world system. Canada is neither a fully developed, metropolitan capitalist society, nor merely a hinterland on the periphery. Rather, the external relations with Britain and the United States, which defined Canada as a new settler society within the prosperous North Atlantic Triangle, and the indigenous commercial elite which grew up within that context, have produced the anomaly that is Canada: a rich dependency.

PROBLEMS IN THE DEPENDENCY THEORY

The dependency formulation has been criticized by many Canadian social scientists. The theoretical difficulties in the dependency approach are beyond the scope of this discussion (see, however, Carroll, 1986: chap. 2). Instead, let us focus on four specific problems.

Several recent studies have cast doubt on the notion that Canada's economic elite has had an exceptionally commercial orientation. Investigations of corporate interlocking in the early twentieth century (Piedalue, 1976; Richardson, 1982) and in the post-World War II period (Park and Park, 1973; Carroll, 1984, 1986) failed to find a cleavage between industrial and financial–commercial sectors. Researchers have found a dense network of interlocks between Canadian industrial corporations and financial institutions, similar to the structure of corporate capital found throughout the advanced capitalist world (Scott, 1985). The claim that Canada's commercial capitalists are aligned with U.S. multinationals has also been questioned. Throughout the 1946 to 1976 period, leading Canadian financial institutions were approximately three times more likely to share multiple directors with Canadian-controlled industrial corporations than with U.S.-controlled industrial firms (Carroll, 1982). The capitalists at the centre of Canada's corporate network are not bankers and merchants, nor mere industrialists, but *finance capitalists*, meaning that they maintain strong involvements in *both industry and banking/commerce*. And Canadian finance capitalists have only weak ties to American branch plants (Carroll, 1984).

The exceptionality of the continental interlocks linking Canadian and American corporate elites is also questioned. In a study of the international network of interlocks among large corporations from twelve countries, including Canada, Fennema (1982) found one large network of European and North American companies and a smaller network of Japanese corporations. The existence of a Euro–North American network puts the "continental elite" into a broader, comparative perspective as a segment of a larger, international structure: an "Atlantic ruling class" (Van der Pijl, 1984). As such, continental connections may speak less of a peculiar metropolis–hinterland relation and more of the extent to which capital has become internationalized since World War II.

This alternative raises a second problem in the dependency interpretation. The singular focus on U.S.–Canada relations as a means of highlighting Canada's distinctiveness in the twentieth century is methodologically inadequate in two respects. In the dependency formulation America's development is tacitly assumed to be "normal" for an advanced capitalist, metropolitan power, thus providing a compelling contrast with supposedly exceptional trends in Canada. Concomitantly, however, dependency analysts have tended to ignore similarities between Canada and industrialized liberal democracies of comparable size. Their narrow focus on Canada's relationship with the United States has obscured two crucial

SOME ECONOMIC AND SOCIAL COSTS OF DEPENDENCY

More than exceptional, dependency analysis has viewed Canada's position as unviable in the long term. The cumulative effects of dependent development bring a host of distortions and deficiencies to the Canadian economic and social structure. Instead of a balanced, diversified industrial structure, the economy consists of a truncated, branch plant manufacturing sector whose small size limits international competitiveness, and an overextended raw materials sector precariously based in nonrenewable resources and vulnerable to fluctuations in world markets (Watkins, 1973, 1977; Drache, 1977; Hutcheson, 1978; Clement, 1983). Concomitantly, the essentially permanent nature of foreign direct investment dampens the prospects for economic growth. Multinational corporations drain capital from Canadian subsidiaries in the form of patriated dividends and artificially low transfer prices; they perpetuate Canada's technological dependency by locating research in the head office; they adopt employment priorities that favour American workers over Canadians — all of which leads in Canada to economic stagnation, high unemployment, and even de-industrialization (Levitt, 1970; Watkins, 1970: Laxer and Jantzi, 1973; Clement, 1977, 1983; Drache, 1977, Marchak, 1979).

The economic costs of dependency are great, but the social price may be even steeper. Levitt (1970) argues deepening north-south linkages with the American metropole are breaking the east-west axis that has been the basis of our national existence, while American multinationals diffuse metropolitan values and tastes among Canadian consumers. Prolonged economic dependency thus brings political balkanization, cultural homogenization, and, as noted earlier, the regression of the Canadian state to a dependency of the American empire.

comparisons: the *similarities* between Canada and other parts of the advanced capitalist world and the *differences* between the United States and all other advanced capitalist democracies, differences which mark the United States as an exceptional case (Therborn, 1977; Davis, 1986).

The metropolis–hinterland framework also tends to view international differences in purely qualitative terms. Once Canada has been identified as a hinterland — albeit a rich one — it becomes difficult to view the differences between Canadian capitalism and other advanced capitalist regions as matters of degree. Yet in many respects the historical trends support such an interpretation. This is so, for instance, regarding foreign direct investment. Although the extent of U.S. control in sectors such as automobiles, petroleum, and electrical equipment has been especially great, all of the advanced capitalist economies have experienced increased foreign control, particularly since World War II (Szymanski, 1981:502). In this sense, Canada simply presents the first case of a general trend in the internationalization of industrial capital (Schmidt, 1981:92); hence its exceptionality is dubious.

As a fourth inadequacy in the dependency perspective, we can note its insensitivity to major changes in international capitalist relations. The metropolis–

hinterland relation suggests cumulative development in the metropolis at the expense of the hinterland. However, dramatic changes in the relative positions of nation-states contradict this model.

Consider the position of the American metropole. From the end of World War II through the 1960s, the United States was the hegemonic power, providing unrivalled economic and political leadership to enhance the unity of the world system (Camilleri, 1981:141). In this period, U.S. transnationals reigned supreme, investing in Canada and Western Europe as well as in select Third World economies. At the peak of its hegemony, the United States accounted for over 60 percent of the output of O.E.C.D. member countries and controlled over half of all foreign investments among major capital-exporting countries (Currie, 1983:83; Moore and Wells, 1975:22). This was why Levitt (1970:92) predicted that 80 percent of world production would be under American control by 1990.

But it was not to be. Instead, the relations of international dominance that grew up under the wing of American hegemony ultimately eroded the U.S. position. The United States' direct investment brought state-of-the-art industrial production to other capitalist economies, improving their competitiveness *vis-à-vis* American capital (Camilleri, 1981:141). Indeed, the massive expansion of U.S. multinationals in the 1950s and 1960s led to a relative *stagnation* of U.S. production, as the foreign operations of U.S. transnationals effectively competed with domestic American enterprises (Friedman, 1978:134, 138–39; Castells, 1980:109). Contrary to dependency theory, U.S. direct investment abroad led to de-industrialization in the American metropole, as the northeastern states earned the unenviable title "the rust belt" (Portes and Walton, 1981:154–61; Bluestone and Harrison, 1982). The decline of the United States from unrivalled hegemony can be seen in the shrinking U.S. share of steel and machine-tool production (Barnet, 1980:273–75), the decreasing number of the world's largest companies based in the United States (Droucopoulas, 1981), and the declining U.S. share in world capital exports (Szymanski, 1981:504). By the mid-1980s, the

Table 1
GROWTH IN REAL GROSS DOMESTIC PRODUCT FOR SEVEN MAJOR CAPITALIST COUNTRIES, 1966–1984

Country	Average 1966–1973	Average 1974–1979	1980	1981	1982	1983	1984	1985	1986*
					Percent				
Canada	5.5	3.2	1.1	3.3	−4.4	3.3	4.7	3.9	3.0
United States	3.9	2.8	−0.3	2.5	−2.1	3.7	6.8	2.9	2.8
Japan	9.9	3.7	4.8	4.0	3.3	3.0	5.8	4.5	2.2
Germany	4.1	2.4	1.9	−0.2	−1.1	1.3	2.5	2.6	2.8
France	5.4	3.1	1.1	0.2	2.0	0.7	1.8	1.1	2.0
United Kingdom	3.2	1.4	−2.1	−1.1	1.9	3.3	2.0	3.7	2.2
Italy	5.4	2.7	3.9	0.2	−0.4	−1.2	3.0	2.3	2.5
Seven major countries	5.4	2.8	1.2	1.9	−0.5	2.8	5.0	3.0	2.5

*Provisional figures.

Source: Canada, Department of Finance *Economic Review* (April, 1985), O.E.C.D. *Main Economic Indicators* (February–April, 1987).

United States was saddled with a massive trade deficit and the world's largest foreign debt. Although its enormous military machine and home market give the United States a pre-eminent status among the advanced capitalist countries, American hegemony has ended.

In the meantime, smaller capitalist powers, such as Canada, had improved their relative standing in the world economy. As Table 1 shows, between 1966 and 1979 most major capitalist economies—including Canada—grew faster than the American economy, although in 1983 and 1984 the United States regained some of the ground it lost to Japan, Western Europe, and Canada in the 1970s. Contrary to dependency theory, the massive U.S. presence in Canada has not brought economic stagnation. With the exception of the deep recession of 1982, the Canadian economy has expanded at or above the rate of the seven major countries throughout the period.

Moreover, the extent of that U.S. presence in Canada has significantly decreased since the early 1970s. With the weakening of American dominance, Canadian capitalism entered into a "renaissance of economic nationalism" (Niosi, 1981:31–34) characterized by the decline of the **comprador** bourgeoisie and the rapid expansion of Canadian investment abroad (Niosi, 1985b). Table 2 shows indigenous Canadian capitalists have not silently surrendered to foreign multinationals; they have greatly increased their control of domestic mining and manufacturing capital, while retaining control of other sectors. Between 1970 and 1983, foreign control of Canadian mining fell from 69.40 percent to 35.35 percent, and foreign control

Table 2

FOREIGN AND CANADIAN CONTROL OF NONFINANCIAL CORPORATE ASSETS BY ECONOMIC SECTOR, 1970–1983

		Control		
Sector*	*Year*	*Foreign*	*Canadian*	*Total*
Mining	1970	69.40	30.60	100
	1976	55.21	44.79	100
	1983	35.35	64.65	100
Manufacturing	1970	59.63	40.37	100
	1976	54.51	45.49	100
	1983	44.52	55.48	100
Utilities	1970	7.86	92.14	100
	1976	7.47	92.53	100
	1983	3.53	96.47	100
Wholesale and retail trade	1970	27.25	72.75	100
	1976	24.19	25.81	100
	1983	18.04	81.96	100
All nonfinancial corporations	1970	37.90	62.10	100
	1976	32.32	67.68	100
	1983	24.30	75.70	100

*Mining includes petroleum and natural gas; utilities include transportation, communications, storage, and public utilities; total includes the sectors listed plus construction and services. Very small corporations are excluded as are nonprofit organizations; most Crown corporations are included.

Source: Canada, Corporations and Labour Unions Returns Act, *Report, Part 1: Corporations* (various years).

of manufacturing fell from 59.63 to 44.52 percent.

In the same period, Canadian capitalists continued exporting capital in the form of foreign direct investment. As we saw earlier, dependency analysts have viewed Canadian capital exports as a manifestation of Canada's intermediate status in the world economy — as hinterland to some countries and metropolis to others. Niosi, however, in his study of Canadian multinationals, identifies Canada as a major exporter of capital throughout this century, ranking seventh as a source of foreign direct investments in 1976 (1985a:445). Since the late 1960s, Canadian direct investment abroad has grown at a faster rate than its American counterpart, and has been directed into a wide range of less-developed countries. Canadian foreign investments, which were highly concentrated in the United States after World War II, are "now spread all over the globe" (Niosi, 1985a:44).

If these dramatic changes in the international flow of capital cast doubt upon the notion of Canada as a rich dependency, what can we say of the other symptoms of Canadian dependency? This is a large question, which we can only address in passing. One oft-cited symptom of dependency is Canada's relatively small manufacturing sector, which has been described as "truncated" (Ehrensaft and Armstrong, 1981:99–155), "arrested" (Williams, 1983), "aborted" (Laxer, 1985b:67–102), and undergoing "de-industrialization" (Laxer and Jantzi, 1973). As Table 3 indicates, in 1980 32 percent of Canada's exports and 59 percent of imports were finished manufactures. Although the former percentage represents nearly a threefold increase from twenty-five years earlier, Canada's trade

Table 3

FINISHED MANUFACTURED GOODS AS A PROPORTION OF TRADE, SELECT INDUSTRIALIZED AND LESS-DEVELOPED COUNTRIES (PERCENT OF TOTAL TRADE)

	Exports				Imports
Industrialized Countries	*1913*	*1929*	*1955*	*1980*	*1980*
Japan	31	43	64	71	11
Italy	31	41	47	61	28
Germany	46	54	65	60	34
Sweden	23	26	33	53	45
United States	21	37	48	52	38
Great Britain	58	49	62	50	39
France	44	47	38	50	35
Canada	5	14	11	32	59
Less-Developed Countries					
India	13	19	31.0	23*	27*
Brazil	—	—	0.4	22**	29**
Argentina	—	—	0.4	14*	49*
Turkey	—	—	0.4	7**	39**
Egypt	—	—	3.0	4.0	35
Zaire	—	—	0.8	0.6*	48

*1978.
**1979.

Source: From *Not for Export: Toward a Political Economy of Canada's Arrested Industrialization*, by Glen Williams. Used by permission of the Canadian Publishers, McClelland and Stewart, Toronto.

situation still differs from that of other industrialized countries, where a majority of exports but a minority of imports are comprised of finished manufactures. Indeed, Canada seems midway between this group and the semi-industrialized countries, where exports tend to be raw materials and semi-processed goods and imports tend to be finished manufactures.

Williams (1983) has explained this by using a variant of the dependency interpretation. He describes Canada not as a hinterland, but as a centre economy. In the formative period of Canadian capitalism, prior to World War I, however, Canada's position within the British Empire encouraged a more passive industrial strategy than is typical in a centre country. While economic development was directed toward building a staples economy based on the production and export of western wheat, Canadian manufacturers *positioned* themselves in a domestic market protected against foreign competition by the National Policy tariffs. Unlike capitalists in other industrial nations, who aggressively competed for shares of the world market, Canadian manufacturers adopted an "extreme home market orientation" (Williams, 1983:79).

The growth of American branch plants exacerbated this problem, further undermining the international competitiveness of Canadian manufacturing. Williams argues Canada's branch plant economy raises administrative and technological barriers to the full development of manufacturing. Administratively, branch plants are set up by M.N.C.s to service the home market of the host country, not to compete in the world market with the head office (1983:105). The result is a manufacturing sector limited to short production runs and unable to compete internationally. Technologically, M.N.C.s concentrate their research activities in their home countries, thus denying their branch plants the capacity to create exportable innovations (Williams, 1983:110).

Williams (1983:151) emphasizes that the 1980s have brought changes to the world economy that may transform the limited home market orientation of Canadian manufacturing. Movement since the

Table 4

AVERAGE ANNUAL GROWTH RATES IN MANUFACTURING OUTPUT AT CONSTANT PRICES FOR TEN INDUSTRIALIZED CAPITALIST COUNTRIES, 1965–1984

Country	1965–1973 (percent)	1973–1984 (percent)
Canada	5.4	1.1
United States	2.9	1.4*
Japan	14.4	7.2*
Germany, Federal Republic	5.3	1.9
France	7.7	1.7
United Kingdom	2.6	−1.7
Belgium	7.4	1.3
Sweden	4.1	−0.1*
Norway	4.6	0.0
Australia	4.9	1.0*

*Figures are for 1973–1983.

Source: The World Bank, *World Development Report 1986*, p. 183.

1960s toward freer trade among the industrial capitalist countries should threaten manufacturers whose viability rests on protective tariffs. Although he discusses options for the adjustment of Canadian manufacturing to the challenge of more direct international competition, Williams suggests that in the contemporary period "the industrial sector as a whole appears to be in decline" (1983:154). Like the issue of foreign direct investment, this claim requires careful comparative analysis. Table 4 indicates the Canadian manufacturing sector has actually been growing since 1965 at a rate similar to that of most other advanced capitalist countries, although much more slowly than Japan's. From 1973 to 1984 manufacturing output in Canada grew more slowly than German, French, U.S., and Belgian manufacturing, but more quickly than Australian, Norwegian, Swedish, and British manufacturing.

Nonetheless, Canadian manufacturing may still have exceptionally poor prospects, compared with its advanced capitalist rivals. Under capitalism, a country's industrial prospects hinge not merely on increased output, but on the capacity to compete in an increasingly open world market. In this respect, manufacturing productivity is crucial. Other conditions assumed equal, countries with strong productivity gains will produce at lower relative costs, and therefore improve their competitive position. Table 5 compares manufacturing output per hour worked among twelve leading capitalist countries from 1960 to 1984. The general trend is toward slower productivity gains in the 1970s and 1980s, as the world capitalist economy stagnated. Japan records the strongest gains from 1960 through 1973, an annual growth rate of 10.6 percent—nearly four times that of the United States, which shows the weakest productivity increases. Canada's productivity growth rate is similar to Norway's and Britain's, although lower than those of the other European countries. In the 1973 to 1980

Table 5
ANNUAL PERCENT CHANGES IN MANUFACTURING PRODUCTIVITY, TWELVE INDUSTRIALIZED CAPITALIST COUNTRIES, 1960–1984

	Output per hour						
Country	**1960–1984**	**1960–1973**	**1973–1980**	**1981**	**1982**	**1983**	**1984**
Canada	3.4	4.5	2.0	2.0	−2.8	6.4	3.7
United States	2.4	2.8	1.7	2.2	2.2	6.6	4.9
Japan	8.3	10.6	5.9	3.7	6.1	5.4	7.0
Germany	4.9	5.9	3.9	2.1	1.6	6.1	4.6
France	5.7	6.7	4.9	3.9	6.1	4.2	5.7
United Kingdom	3.5	4.4	1.2	6.2	4.5	7.3	4.7
Italy	5.5	6.9	3.5	3.5	2.0	2.4	6.6
Sweden	4.7	6.6	2.2	0.4	3.0	7.7	5.7
Norway	3.6	4.5	2.0	0.4	2.7	5.6	2.0
Netherlands	6.6	7.6	5.2	2.7	2.4	5.3	10.5
Denmark	5.6	6.4	4.5	1.6	−0.7	3.5	0.8
Belgium	7.1	7.0	6.4	6.9	4.7	6.8	4.6

Source: Edwin Dean et al., "Productivity and labor costs trends in manufacturing, 12 countries." *Monthly Labor Review* 109(3), 1986, p. 4.

period, increases in U.S. manufacturing productivity remained sluggish, but British performance was even poorer. Japan, Belgium, and the Netherlands experienced relatively rapid productivity increases. Canada's record is comparable to Norway's and Sweden's, but poorer than France's, Germany's, Italy's, or Denmark's. The Canadian economy was hit particularly hard by the international recession of 1982; however, in the following two years its productivity gains were similar to those of other advanced capitalist countries.

It is difficult to make these statistics show a progressive deterioration in Canada's position as a manufacturing economy. Clearly, Canada is not in the league of Japanese manufacturing, but neither is it experiencing de-industrialization *relative to the other major economies.*[2] The reasons for this are complex, and they take us beyond the interpretation of Canada as a rich dependency. We can do no more here than point to a few of them.

Consider, first, the changing character of foreign-controlled manufacturing. If such firms produced only for the Canadian market, they would be unable to reap the economies of scale necessary for substantial productivity increases. However, as Williams (1983:155) notes, the most important branch plant sector, the automobile industry, has since the signing of the Auto Pact in 1965 been organized on a continent-wide basis. Motor vehicle plants in Canada have specialized in producing products for both the U.S. and domestic market. In other industries, Canadian subsidiaries of U.S. multinationals have been granted world product mandates as the exclusive manufacturers of specialized products for the international market (Atkinson, 1985:125–44). Such mandates allow access to the world market, reduce the requirement of buying components from or through the parent, and develop independent Canadian research and development and international marketing capacities (Williams, 1983:155).

Second, although foreign control of industry means that Canada devotes a relatively small proportion of its Gross Domestic Product to research and development (Williams, 1983:112), the importance of technology in international competition lies not so much in what innovations a country produces, but in its ability to *master* new technologies, whatever their origins (Niosi, 1983). According to Niosi (1985a:170–72) major Canadian corporations have done just that, acquiring foreign technologies and adapting them to the Canadian context. Thus, Canadian capitalists have taken advantage of their location with the international structure of capital: "Canada's geographical, cultural and commercial closeness to the United States and Britain allows Canadian companies to absorb technology a short time after it is introduced in these highly advanced industrialized countries" (Niosi, 1985a:166).

A third reason for the resilience of Canadian manufacturing concerns the actions of the Canadian state. In industries like textiles, which face strong competition from newly industrializing countries, the state has helped restructure capital toward improved competitiveness. An example is the creation in 1981 of the Canadian Industrial Renewal Board, "empowered to offer lower interest on loans for mergers and acquisitions, grants covering up to 80 percent of the costs of consultants' fees, and grants up to 25 percent (now 50 percent) of the capital costs of approved modernization projects" (Mahon, 1984:145). The same Canadian state that is committed to trade liberalization has been attempting to bolster Canadian manufacturing's competitiveness in a freer trade environment (Mahon, 1985:235–36).

Finally, it is important to reiterate that a great deal of Canadian manufacturing is not carried out by foreign-controlled companies but by Canadian-controlled firms, the largest of which are increasingly oriented to the world market. In the textile sector — which Levitt (1970) dismissed as destined to die a slow death from its inherent uncompetitiveness — leading companies like DomTex have modernized their operations and become transnational corporations, and have specialized domestic production (Mahon, 1984:120). In other industries, Canadian capitalists have had a competitive, multinational presence for some time, including steel, aluminum, liquor, forest products, agricultural implements, and telecommunications equipment (Niosi, 1985a).

These trends in Canadian manufacturing have counterparts elsewhere in the advanced capitalist world as states and economies adjust to what has been termed the "new international division of labour" (Cameron, 1985). The flow of capital has led to de-industrialization in sectors of advanced countries (such as the U.S. steel industry) and to selective industrialization in parts of the Third World. This internationalization of capital has increased economic uncertainty and competition and decreased the ability of states to manage national economies. The political and economic problems that this changing order poses are formidable to other advanced capitalist countries. The serious challenges facing Canadians in the waning years of the twentieth century primarily stem not from the failures of Canadian capitalism, but from the profound crisis that is transforming the entire system of world capitalism.

CANADA AND THE THEORY OF CAPITALIST DEVELOPMENT

Karl Marx, in introducing *Capital*, observed "the wealth of those societies in which the capitalist mode of production prevails, presents itself as 'an immense accumulation of commodities'. . ." (1954:43). According to Marx, to understand economic and political power in such societies, it is necessary to understand the specific mode of production that causes this accumulation. Likewise, to understand Canada as a capitalist society one must examine how this mode of production and related aspects of modern capitalism have arisen within Canada's distinctive historical context. As a comparative perspective, Marxism emphasizes the complex historical processes that have shaped specific capitalist societies. It offers a means of appreciating Canada's distinctiveness without assuming Canada is an exceptional case.

Several useful contrasts can be drawn between Marxism and dependency theory as perspectives on Canada.[3] The latter, as we have seen, views economic power as concentrated in the hands of an elite and wielded within a system of metropolis-hinterland relations that favour the metropole. Marxism views economic power as embodied in the capitalist mode of production, an economic structure founded upon two principles: class exploitation and competition. With respect to the former, participants in the capitalist production occupy two opposed class positions, determined by their relationship to the **means of production**: the economic resources such as machinery and raw materials used in goods and services. Members of the **capitalist class**, or bourgeoisie, own the means of production and employ members of the **working class** to produce commodities in order to reap a profit. Aside from their personal effects, workers own only their **labour-power**—the physical and mental ability to work—which they sell to capitalists for a wage. The purchase and sale of labour-power is the basis of the great power differential between capitalist and working classes:

> Because the bourgeoisie owns the means of production, it has the power to determine what is produced and who is to receive what proportion of the benefits from production. Because the working class does not own the means of production, it is excluded from this kind of power (Cuneo, 1980a:238).

The working class must purchase commodities, such as food, clothing, and shelter, which replenish the capacity to work. Thus, the capital-labour relation at the heart of capitalist production continuously reproduces a capitalist class, which collectively exercises a monopoly over the means of production, and a working class, whose labour produces commodities of three sorts: wage goods consumed by workers, luxury goods consumed by capitalists, and capital goods used in further production processes.

These two classes are inherently interdependent under capitalism: the capitalist class cannot exist without the working class, since the latter is the source of capitalist wealth; the working class needs the capitalist class, since workers must earn a wage to support themselves (Cuneo, 1983:69). As is explained in the next chapter [The Labour Process], however, the new wealth created under capitalist control in the labour process exceeds the value of wages paid to workers in exchange for their labour-power. The difference between these quantities is **surplus value**, the basis of capitalists' profit. Underlying the capitalist's profit motive, then, is a social relation of class exploitation. Moreover, where workers resist this exploitation, there is a *class struggle*. To maximize their profits, capitalists attempt to minimize wage costs by lowering wages or limiting wage increases, intensifying the work process, and displacing workers with more cost-effective technologies. To defend or enhance their standard of living and the quality of their working lives, workers press for higher wages and for control over working conditions and technological change. Within the mode of production, class struggle takes the form of conflict between unions and employers, but it also occurs in the broader society—as in the conflict between liberal or conservative parties that advocate private ownership of the means of production and socialist parties that advocate public ownership under democratic control (Brodie and Jenson, 1980).

The class conflict between labour and capital is not the only social relation in the capitalist mode of production. The capitalist class is fragmented into separate, competing units, namely, capitalist firms. The surplus value appropriated by each capitalist is only realized as profit when the capitalist's commodities are sold in the market. Capitalists compete over rates of profit, which express the share of total surplus value individual capitalists receive. This compels each capitalist to cheapen production costs so commodities can be sold at relatively high profits. The penalty for being uncompetitive is severe: in the long term, uncompetitive firms go bankrupt or are absorbed by more competitive firms.

Just as the capital-labour struggle has important historical implications (leading, for instance, to the development of class-based organizations, such as unions, business associations, and political parties), intercapitalist competition has been a major dynamic force. Class struggle and competition operate in tandem, since the need to remain competitive—not any personal malice toward workers — moves capitalists to exploit their workforces with maximal efficiency. By the same token, the development of unions in the nineteenth century limited the extent to which capitalists could increase surplus value through lowering wages and lengthening the work day. In mature capitalism, business strategies are focused around continual improvements in the productivity of labour: production costs are lowered by introducing sophisticated technologies and techniques, such as the assembly line or robotics. Thus, intercapitalist competition is waged chiefly through reinvesting profits in expanding, retooling, and revolutionizing the means of production. The result is an economy in which ceaseless technological innovation supports increases in the general standard of living, even as class exploitation and struggle continue.

Three other implications of intercapitalist competition are worth mentioning. First, capitalists constantly search for new markets, making capitalism a *highly expansive* mode of production. Capitalism has drawn once isolated societies — the "New World," the "Third World"—into an increasingly integrated world market. In the industrialized world capital has penetrated deeply into the cultural realm, replacing community-based activities with the commercialized entertainment of the mass cultural industries. Capitalism has thus drawn most of the world's population and a vast range of human practices into its orbit.

Second, as an economic system organized around many competing units, capitalism entails *uneven development*, both in space and time. Lacking any comprehensive economic plan, capitalism develops in cycles of booms and busts, which relates to the changing profit prospects facing capitalists as a class. Since the Great Depression and World War II, for instance, the world capitalist system has moved from unprecedented economic expansion in the 1940s, 1950s, and 1960s to serious recessions interrupted by weak recoveries (Wolfe, 1983). Similarly, the unplanned character of capitalist economies results in uneven regional development, as capital flows toward areas and industries offering relatively high profit rates. The upshot is that certain regions within countries (e.g., Newfoundland, the Canadian Prairies, and British Columbia), and even whole countries (e.g., much of Latin America), become highly specialized in certain lines of commodity production. By the same token, dramatic swings in the profit prospects for key industries can quickly transform economically specialized regions from prosperity to despair, as in Alberta's oil economy in the 1980s. Within Marxist political economy, the metropolis–hinterland dichotomy is seen as a consequence of the uneven capitalist accumulation process (Walker, 1978).

Third, and in combination with the two implications just noted, intercapitalist competition brings a long-term process of capital concentration and centralization, resulting in corporate, or **monopoly capitalism**. Capital becomes concentrated as firms reinvest their profits to stay competitive by expanding their operations; it becomes centralized as larger, more competitive firms take over smaller companies, particularly during recessions. The result, in the twentieth century, is an economy dominated by a relatively few large corporations and financial institutions, which are controlled by a financial-industrial elite of leading capitalists. Through a complex network of interlocking directorates, intercorporate ownership, creditor-debtor relations, and familial ties, large corporations and financial institutions are integrated into a structure of **finance capital**, within which groups of monopoly capitalists compete for shares of surplus value (Overbeek, 1980:102–3). In the advanced economies finance capitalists form the dominant fraction of the capitalist class. Moreover, control of enormous quantities of capital and of sophisticated technologies permits them to *internationalize* their investments by establishing multinational corporations and transnational banks. Thus, the world market is further extended and integrated, not simply in

INTERLOCKS BETWEEN CORPORATIONS AND THE STATE

The Canadian state's relative autonomy from direct capitalist control is evident in the pattern of overlapping memberships between corporate boards of directors and high-level state organizations. In their study of these relations between 1946 and 1977, Fox and Ornstein (1986) find levels of interlocking between corporations and the state far lower than levels of interlocking among corporations. They also report most career switching occurs not from the corporate boardrooms to the state (as would happen if corporations controlled the state), but from the state to the private sector, a pattern that "suggests corporate efforts to understand and influence a state not under corporate domination" (Fox and Ornstein, 1986:502). The Canadian state's relative autonomy from capitalist control is also evident in the political positions state elites take. For instance, the political attitudes of Canadian bureaucrats and senior civil servants are substantially to the left of leading business executives, although they resemble business attitudes more closely than the attitudes of labour leaders (Ornstein, 1985:142).

terms of trade but in terms of capital exports, i.e., foreign investment. The process of capitalist expansion, however, is an uneven one, punctuated by crises, regional disparities, and the concentration of economic power in fewer hands.

Particularly since World War II, the internationalization of capital has brought two important changes to world capitalism. First, the export of industrial capital to certain Third World countries has engendered capitalist relations of production — and capital-labour conflict — in those societies (Portes and Walton, 1981; Szymanski, 1981). Second, the enhanced international mobility of capital has increased the class power of capitalists relative to workers. Finance capitalists control investments that span national borders, enabling them to maximize profits on an international scale, but workers are organized into unions and political parties on a national basis. Thus, if a union strikes against the local branch of a multinational corporation, the company can weather the disruption if it can step up production in other countries. Ultimately, the multinational corporation can meet labour militancy with a "strike" of its own: it can withdraw capital (and thus jobs) from the offending workforce, transferring its operations to a more convivial environment.

This discussion of economic power raises the question of how capitalists' economic power is translated into political power.[4] Contemporary Marxist political economy grants that sometimes particular capitalists or capitalist groups can direct influence over political policy through close ties to senior state officials and politicians (Coleman, 1986:151). Generally, however, the connection between economic and political power in capitalist societies is impersonal and highly *mediated*, precisely because the economic process of capital accumulation is institutionally detached from the political process. Overall, the state is viewed as an ensemble of organizations — legislatures, bureaucracies, the judiciary, the armed forces, and police — with *relative auton-*

omy from direct influence by particular capitalists.

This detachment from direct capitalist control, however, does not render the state an ''impartial umpire'' capable of fairly representing all interests in capitalist societies (Craven, 1980). Ultimately, the state rests upon the material basis of the capitalist mode of production, which constrains political policy to be consistent with the requirements for continued capital accumulation. By meeting these requirements the state helps maintain capitalist class dominance.

The most obvious example is the structural dependence of the state upon revenues generated within the capitalist economy. To mount a political program, governments must raise funds that derive from workers' wages (e.g., most income tax) and capitalists' profits (e.g., corporation tax). This gives sitting governments a profound interest in the continued buoyancy of the private sector. Because that sector is dominated by capitalists, state policies will tend to be consistent with capitalist class interests. Policies that seriously contradict these interests will be met with the sanction of capital withdrawal, as investors invest in jurisdictions offering better profit prospects (Offe, 1984:244). Such capital flight erodes the state's own budgetary base and undermines the government's popularity, since lowered investment means slower economic growth and fewer jobs. Politicians therefore avoid policies that may threaten capital accumulation. In this sense, the ongoing internationalization of capital has increased capitalists' power, not just *vis-à-vis* workers but *vis-à-vis* states, whose political projects now depend upon the good graces of international investors.

At the same time, however, the modern state has an interest in regulating capital-labour conflict. Obviously, extreme conflicts, such as general strikes, interfere with the capitalist mode of production by rupturing the accumulation process. Less obviously, perhaps, the mobilization of the working class in unions and political parties has in the twentieth century brought reforms, which have transformed the state while securing working-class consent to continued capitalist dominance. In Canada, for instance, unemployment insurance had its origins in working-class protest in the 1930s (Cuneo, 1980b), while collective bargaining rights were granted to labour to buy industrial peace during World War II (Palmer, 1983). Other components of the Canadian welfare state, such as Medicare, were assembled during the post-war boom, partly in response to the initiatives of the labour-oriented N.D.P. (formerly C.C.F.) (Swartz, 1977). Here again, Canadian trends are consistent with those in other advanced capitalist democracies.

These, then, are some key features of the advanced capitalist democracies: an industrialized economy organized in terms of the capitalist mode of production and dominated by finance capitalists, whose control of major industrial and financial enterprises spans national borders; an interventionist, liberal-democratic state whose social and economic policies regulate capital-labour struggle while promoting capital accumulation. Within the world capitalist system, such nation-states occupy a dominant or *imperialist position* as centres of capitalist class power. Although relations between advanced capitalist states have often been pierced with conflict and rivalry, since World War II the major states have achieved remarkable co-operation in facilitating the free flow of capital and commodities, and therefore in maintaining capitalist class power in an increasingly internationalized world system. As noted earlier, working-class mobilization within unions and parties enabled workers in the advanced countries to share in the material benefits from the rising productivity and growing markets that marked the post-war boom. In the more recent period of deepening economic crisis, working-class organizations in the advanced capitalist countries have resisted the demands of profit-oriented capitalists and restraint-minded governments for such concessions as wage rollbacks, labour-code changes, and social service cutbacks.

In much of the Third World, however, the free flow of capital and commodities has carried different implications. There, finance capital controlled in the imperialist centres and oriented toward the world market has penetrated into largely pre-capitalist economies, often organized around feudal relations of production (Laclau, 1971). As these societies have been drawn into the world market, the peasantry has been pressured off the increasingly commercial agricultural lands. Enormous numbers of landless peasants have gravitated to the urban areas, forming a vast reserve of labour. The shantytowns around such Third World cities as Bombay, Manila, Lagos, and Mexico City are grim testimony to the human costs of capitalist internationalization (Castells, 1983). Moreover, in concert with authoritarian states that limit working-class organization, the chronic oversupply of available labour has kept the wages of Third World workers very low (Amin, 1974). This abundant supply of cheap labour has attracted multinational corporations, which have increasingly incorporated state-of-the-art technologies into their Third World subsidiaries. The productivity of labour in countries such as South Korean is often comparable to productivity levels in the advanced capitalist economies, yet South Korean workers are paid only a fraction of what workers in North America or Western Europe receive (Barone, 1983).

This super-exploitation of Third World workers has exerted downward pressure on wages in the advanced countries, as low-priced imports compete with domestic manufactures. Throughout the advanced capitalist world, "fractions of the working class compete with each other to retain capital's 'allegiance'" (Burawoy, 1985:264). This illustrates an important difference between Marxism and dependency theory as perspectives on world capitalism. Marxists view the world political economy not as a set of metropolis–hinterland relations, but as a system of class relations that crisscross a network of unevenly developed nation-states. Our question is, what is Canada's location within this network?

CANADA AS AN ADVANCED CAPITALIST MIDDLE POWER

The evidence supports an interpretation of Canada as an advanced capitalist middle power. The capitalist mode of production developed in Canada later than in Britain and the United States, which have been the major capitalist states in the nineteenth and twentieth centuries. As in other "late follower" countries, such as Germany and Italy, Canada's industrial revolution began in the mid-nineteenth century, and coincided with nation-building (Laxer, 1985a, 1985b). Confederation in 1867 and the adoption of the National Policy twelve years later created the political means for consolidating capitalism in Canada.

The National Policy encouraged the full establishment of a capitalist production in Canada. Thousands of European immigrants were recruited to stock the developing labour market, and the Prairies were opened up for settlement. In the 1890s, as the wheat economy came of age, so did a state-subsidized railway system to move commodities to markets and a tariff-protected manufacturing sector to process the wheat, to supply farmers with agricultural implements, and to produce other goods for domestic consumption and export. With the factories and industrial projects (particularly railroad construction) came a class of mainly immigrant, propertyless wage-workers and a national bourgeoisie of industrialists, bankers, and merchants in control of the expanding home market (Ryerson, 1973; Craven and Traves, 1979; Pentland, 1981).

Social historians have documented how Canadian workers resisted capitalist domination, whether in the initial period of industrialization (Kealey, 1982) or in the twentieth century (Palmer, 1983). Concurrently, the capitalist class was transformed, as capital concentrated and centralized into ever larger units. By the 1920s, close ties had developed among the leading corporations and financial institutions; the dominant fraction of the capitalist class became organized as a financial-industrial elite (Carroll, 1986:51–4). Canadian finance capitalists also expanded abroad into banking and life insurance in the Caribbean and transportation and electrical utilities in Latin America (Park and Park, 1973:122–61). Since World War II, Canadian-based multinational corporations and banks have come of age, establishing subsidiaries in both advanced capitalist and less-developed countries (Niosi, 1985a; Kaufman, 1985). Meanwhile an extensive welfare state was constructed, both as a concession to working-class pressure from below and in order to promote capital accumulation by maintaining a well-educated, healthy, and compliant labour force.

In all these respects, Canada resembles other advanced capitalist democracies, where capital-labour struggle and inter-capitalist competition have spawned similar social structures. It is equally important, however, to examine how class struggle and capital accumulation have, in the Canadian context, generated distinctive patterns of social development (Marchak, 1985:683).

Unlike the major advanced capitalist states, the Canadian state played a subordinate role in the scramble for the control of territory which characterized international capitalism up to World War II. Canada never acquired colonies or spheres of influence, within which its capitalists could exploit subject populations, nor did Canada adopt the militaristic foreign policies that were part of colonial domination. Instead, Canadian capital internationalized within the British Commonwealth and within the U.S. sphere in North and South America. In this sense, Canada has been no more than a *secondary* imperialist power: while its finance capitalists have exerted economic power over workers in various countries, they have relied on other strong states (Britain and the United States) to safeguard their investments (Moore and Wells, 1975). The same is true of other "dominion capitalist" countries, such as Australia and New Zealand (Ehrensaft and Armstrong, 1981), and of the smaller nation-states of Western Europe; Switzerland, Belgium, and the Scandinavian countries.

Since World War II, this difference between Canada and the major imperialist powers has diminished. In the era of U.S. hegemony, pre-war colonial empires were replaced by a system of open trade and investment. The transformation from an imperialist system organized around bilateral relations of colonial domination (spheres of influence) to a multinational network in which capital and commodities move freely gave Canadian capitalists greater latitude in internationalizing their investments. More recently, with the decline of American hegemony, much of the political locus of imperialist dominance has shifted from the American state to supranational organizations, such as the International Monetary Fund (I.M.F.),

PROFILING THE I.M.F.

Introduction

Created as part of the 1944 Bretton Woods Agreement, the International Monetary Fund (I.M.F.) was conceived as a means of promoting world commerce by providing short-term financing to countries with balance of payments difficulties. Its membership includes most of the world's capitalist countries; however, voting rights are assigned according to the relative economic size of member countries, ensuring that the advanced capitalist powers dominate I.M.F. decisions:

> At the beginning of 1984, the voting shares of various country groupings were as follows: 1. industrial capitalist countries, 60.4 percent, of which the United States held 19.2 percent; 2. major oil exporters, 11.4 percent; 3. all other countries, 28.1 percent.
>
> Because major decisions require either 70 percent or 85 percent of the total votes, the United States, together with a few of its Western allies, e.g., Canada, can veto any attempt to change the basic rules and procedures of the I.M.F. (Gatt–Fly, 1985:24).

As the international debt crisis has deepened, the I.M.F. has come to play a direct political role, imposing austerity programs on debtor countries as a condition for further financing. Such progams shift the balance of class forces in favour of capitalists, but they also tend to provoke working-class resistance, as was evident in the 1977 case of Peru:

> The medicine [the I.M.F.] prescribed is a classic example of the conditions that the I.M.F. attaches to most of its loans:
>
> —harsh spending cuts in all public enterprises,
> —an increase in petroleum prices,
> —a sharp cut in purchases of machinery for public sector investment,
> —elimination of all import quotas,
> —a 30 percent devaluation of the currency,
> —wage controls that would keep wage increases below the rate of inflation.

Popular resistance to the program of the banks and the I.M.F. took the form of a general strike in June of 1977. Police and army units moved to crush the strike, killing ten workers. Hundreds were arrested, and factory owners were allowed to dismiss some six thousand strikers from their jobs (ibid.:21).

From the perspective of Canadian finance capital, the virtues of I.M.F. austerity programs have been summarized by the vice-president for international operations of the Royal Bank: ''There certainly is a need for [the I.M.F.] to be in there as a lender and as a disciplinarian and that's the thing all of us like about the I.M.F. They, perhaps like no one else, can make conditions on loans, which ensures some tightening of the belt'' (ibid.). In Phillips's (1983:79) estimation, the I.M.F. has emerged as a ''global cop'' attempting to enforce capitalist discipline within particular nation-states while guiding the world economy in order to foster global accumulation. It is for this reason that the I.M.F. can be described as an agency of collective imperialism, relatively autonomous from the interests of particular countries or capitalists, and thus able to view the capitalist system from a global vantage point. However, this detachment also limits the I.M.F.'s capacity to enforce its demands upon unwilling governments, as recent refusals by Brazil and Peru to accept I.M.F. strictures make clear. Phillips concludes,

> Because the political institutions of capitalism are still primarily on a national basis, the I.M.F. lacks the political power to impose its own will. Whether the I.M.F. can, in fact, gain this political power, i.e., if national sovereignty is lost to an international power, is the key question for the future of the international monetary system and global capitalism (ibid.:80).

which dictate political policies to a growing number of heavily indebted Third World countries (Cameron, 1983). Contemporary imperialism is primarily organized not around U.S. hegemony, but around the collective organizations of the major capitalist powers: the I.M.F., World Bank, Organization for Economic Cooperation and Development, and the "G-7" (namely, the United States, Japan, Germany, Britain, France, Canada, and Italy). Canada's active role in such organizations of **collective imperialism** and the extensive international investments of Canada's major capitalists distinguish Canada as an advanced capitalist middle power. The deep interests in maintaining world capitalism are also reflected in Canada's international alliances, most notably the North Atlantic Treaty Organization (Moore and Wells, 1975:31–3).

The notion of Canada as an advanced capitalist middle power provides a basis for an alternative analysis of the role of U.S. direct investment in Canada. In dependency theory, this foreign investment is seen as a symptom of our dependent hinterland status. Within Marxist political economy, the establishment and growth of U.S. branch plants in Canada is seen as the first case of a general internationalization of capital. Canada is distinctive in that monopoly capitalism in Canada emerged on the basis of both *domestic* concentration and centralization of capital and *international* concentration and centralization through U.S. direct investment (McNally, 1981:55). Why was investment in Canada more attractive to American capitalists than ventures elsewhere, and why didn't Canadian capitalists gain and maintain a strong presence in the industries that fell to American control? The answer lies in the specific way capital-labour conflict and intercapitalist competition combined to create an advanced capitalist regime in Canada.

As they began to internationalize their investments around the turn of the century, the largest U.S. corporations were attracted to Canada for many reasons. Canada was a high-growth economy in its own right and a member of the Commonwealth trading bloc (Williams, 1983). Canada offered access to a large expanding market. On the other hand, for American capitalists investment opportunities in other capitalist economies were not as promising. The enormous advances in transportation and communication that would make full-fledged transcontinental production feasible after World War II had not occurred (Cypher, 1979). Canada thus was a favoured outlet for the enormous surplus of capital which the American economy began to generate in the late nineteenth century.

At the same time, the specific conditions of class struggle in Canada limited the Canadian capitalists' ability to directly compete with U.S. branch plants. Given Canada's later start toward industrialization and its smaller domestic market, Canadian firms tended to be smaller and less technologically advanced than their American counterparts (McNally, 1981: 55). To compete with the expanding American multinationals, Canadian capitalists would have had to pay their workers substantially less than U.S. firms. But the balance of class forces at the time ruled out this option.

In the nineteenth century, the Canadian working class developed as a *high-wage proletariat*, not only relative to the Third World, but relative to Europe. The reasons for this include (1) Canada's character as a settler society based in the level of civilization achieved by Western Europe and reliant on attracting skilled (and relatively expensive) labour from Europe; (2) the availability to Canadian workers of western agricultural land, which meant industrial wages could not fall too far below returns to western wheat farmers (3) Canada's promixity to the relatively open American labour market, which meant wage rates in Canada would move toward those in the United States; and (4) the unionization of skilled workers in Canada and the United States and their militant collective struggles over wages and working conditions (Panitch, 1981:16–19). According to this analysis, "American capital came to dominate Canadian industry because, given the balance of class forces in a continental capital and labour market which the National Policy could not alter even if it had wanted to, American industry was more profitable than Canadian in a great many cases" (Panitch, 1981:21). In short, the combination of labour-capital struggle and inter-capitalist competition in North America—not the stultifying impact of a commercial elite dependent on the staples trade — led to the relatively high levels of U.S. control.

CONCLUSION

We have seen the dynamics of world capitalism and the subtleties of Canada's place within the world system cannot be adequately grasped by depicting economic and political power as a metropolis-hinterland relation. Canada is best described as an advanced capitalist middle power with a distinctive history. Nevertheless, the dependency approach has left an important legacy by pointing out how Canadian capitalist development has been profoundly shaped by being adjacent to the dominant capitalist nation-state.

This legacy can be appreciated in the current debates around the prospects for a Canada–U.S. free trade agreement. Throughout the twentieth century, but particularly since the formation of the European Economic Community in 1957, Canadian capitalists have shifted their trading relations away from Europe and toward the United States. Canada's strong trade surplus with the United States in recent years and the growing direct investment of Canadian capitalists there testify to the competitiveness of Canadian capital in the American market (Niosi, 1983, 1985b). However, this competitiveness — which Canadian capitalists share with their European and Japanese counterparts—has threatened the profits of some American capitalists and the jobs of mainly American workers. In recent years, the U.S. trade union movement and sections of the American bourgeoisie have pressured the state to impose protectionist barriers. Given the high volume of Canada–U.S. trade, American protectionism is a serious threat to the Canadian economy and state. Canadian overtures toward freer trade with the United States are an attempt to secure for Canadian capitalists unimpeded access to the world's largest and most politically stable market. To Canadian finance capitalists, such a continentalist business strategy makes sense in an era of crisis, instability, and contraction in the world market.

To Canadian labour, however, free trade carries different ramifications. Most obviously, there is no guarantee where jobs will be located under free trade, nor how economic gains will be distributed (Watkins, 1985:9). These questions point up a crucial Canada–U.S. difference that has great relevance to the political economy of free trade. Among the advanced capitalist democracies, the American working class has an exceptionally low level of mobilization (Therborn, 1977; Davis, 1986). Compared to the working classes of Western Europe, Canada, and Australia, U.S. workers now have the weakest economic and political organizations — the lowest levels of unionization and no mass-based socialist political parties (Brym, 1986a:236). This has meant the gains made elsewhere through working-class mobilization were only partially implemented in the United States. The American welfare state, for instance, is noteworthy for its minimalist character; and the anti-welfare backlash of neo-conservatism has been most effective in the United States (Esping-Anderson, 1985:245).

By integrating the American and Canadian economies, a free trade agreement would shift the balance of class forces in Canada in favour of capitalists. In a continental economy, the larger and organizationally weaker American working class would set the standards for wages and working conditions in Canada, as capital would flow to the cheapest and most compliant workforces.

Moreover, to implement free trade it would be necessary to *harmonize* the economic and social policies of participants in the agreement, so no country had a competitive advantage outside of the market itself. Since the Canadian state has been more interventionist than the American state, harmonization would curtail the Canadian government's capacity to formulate independent policies. For instance, the Canadian government's marketing boards and assistance to farmers, regional development grants, Crown corporations, and environmental laws have all been cited as areas for policy harmonization (Turk, 1985:37). As Watkins (1986:15) puts it, "for a medium-sized and politically moderate Canada, harmonization *with* a large and politically reactionary United States is harmonization *into*; our policies, which are at the heart of what makes Canada distinct from the United States, could be obliterated to conform to its free-market deregulated world." At the time of writing, the prospects for a free trade agreement are uncertain. What is clear, however, is that Canadian sovereignty itself is a question near the surface of the free trade debate. Ironically, the drift toward a continental economy may result in the worst of both worlds: the eclipse of Canada as an independent state (the central political issue in dependency theory) and the erosion of the Canadian working class's capacity to struggle for better lives (the central political issue in Marxism).

Notes

[1]For a wide-ranging bibliography of Canadian political economy, see Drache and Clement (1985).

[2]Indeed, between 1963 and 1984 employment in Canadian manufacturing grew by 26.8 percent, compared with a growth of 23.5 percent in the United States and decreases of 21.8 percent in Japan, 9.1 percent in France, 22.2 percent in West Germany; 35.0 percent in Britain, 14.1 percent in Italy, 16.0 percent in Sweden, and 4.8 percent in Australia (International Labour Office, 1978:315–33, 1985:301–44).

[3]For a more extensive introduction to Marxist political economy, see Fine (1984).

[4]The following account of the capitalist state is necessarily brief. For fuller discussion, see Knutilla (1987).

DISCUSSION QUESTIONS

1. What does it mean to claim that Canada has become "the world's richest underdeveloped country"?
2. Compare the view of the Canadian state as a *political instrument* of the economic elite with the view of the state as *relatively autonomous* from specific classes and groups in Canadian society.
3. Assess the evidence for and against the theory of Canada as a rich dependency.
4. What does it mean to claim that Canada is an "advanced capitalist middle power"?
5. Compare the metropolis–hinterland conception of economic power with Marx's theory of capitalist development.
6. How might a dependency theorist and a Marxist interpret the political-economic implications of a Canada–U.S. free trade agreement?

GLOSSARY

capitalist class the class of employers and major investors that owns the means of production, controls investment decisions, and employs wage and salary earners in order to extract surplus value which is realized as profit when commodities are sold

collective imperialism under monopoly capitalism, an arrangement of international relations in which the major capitalist powers co-operate in attempting to maintain the conditions for global capital accumulation

comprador elite directors of dominant Canadian corporations under foreign control

exploitation the extraction by a dominant class of surplus labour from a subordinate class, enabling the former to enjoy a high standard of living and to play a leading role in economic, political, and cultural affairs

finance capital under monopoly capitalism, capital that is formed by the close integration of financial capital and industrial capital, through intercorporate ownership, creditor-debtor relations, and interlocking directorates

hinterland an underdeveloped region or country from which an economically developed metropole extracts resources

imperialism in the era of monopoly capitalism, the process of capitalist accumulation on a world scale involving both the internationalism of capital and relations between capitalist states

labour power the capacity of workers to play an active role in the production or circulation of commodities

means of production the raw materials, tools, and machinery used in producing goods and services. Under capitalism most of the means of production are organized within firms owned by capitalists

monopoly capitalism the stage of capitalist development in which capital has become concentrated, centralized, and internationalized under the control of an elite of finance capitalists

staples raw materials or semi-processed goods, such as fur, fish, lumber, wheat, oil, and minerals, which are produced within hinterland economies mainly for export

staples trap an economic vicious circle in which a hinterland's specialization in staple exports perpetuates its dependence on imported manufactured goods

state the system of organizations that has a monopoly over the legitimate use of force within a specific territory. In contemporary Canada, the state includes the armed forces and police, Parliament, and subcentral governments, the judiciary, and the civil service.

surplus value the specific form that surplus labour takes under capitalism: the difference between the value of the product the working class produces and the value of the means of production and labour power expanded in the production process

working class the class of employees that does not own the means of production and that sells its labour power to capitalists in exchange for a wage or salary

BIBLIOGRAPHY

Amin, Samir
1974 *Accumulation on a World Scale*. New York: Monthly Review Press.

Armstrong, Pat and Hugh Armstrong
1984 *The Double Ghetto*, revised edition. Toronto: McClelland and Stewart.

Atkinson, Michael M.
1985 "If You Can't Beat Them: World Product Mandating and Canadian Industrial Policy." In Duncan Cameron and Francois Houle (eds.) *Canada and the New International Division of Labour*. Ottawa: University of Ottawa Press.

Barnet, Richard J.
1980 *The Lean Years*. New York: Simon and Schuster.

Barone, Charles A.
1983 "Dependency, Marxist Theory, and Salvaging the Idea of Capitalism in South Korea." *Review of Radical and Political Economics*, 15, no. 1:41–70.

Bluestone, B. and B. Harrison
1982 *The Deindustrialization of America*. New York: Basic Books.

Brodie, M. Janine and Jane Jenson
1980 *Crisis, Challenge and Change: Party*

and Class in Canada. Toronto: Methuen.

Brym, Robert J. (ed.)

1985 "The Canadian Capitalist Class, 1965–1985." In *The Structure of the Canadian Capitalist Class*. Toronto: Garamond Press.

——

1986a "Incorporation versus Power Models of Working Class Radicalism with Special Reference to North America." *Canadian Journal of Sociology*, 11:227–252.

—— (ed.)

1986b *Regionalism in Canada*. Toronto: Irwin.

Burawoy, Michael

1985 *The Politics of Production: Factory Regimes under Capitalism and Socialism*. London: NLB.

Cameron, Duncan

1983 "Order and Disorder in the World Economy." *Studies in Political Economy* 11:105–26.

——

1985 "Canada in the Emerging World Economy." In Duncan Cameron and Francois Houle (eds.) *Canada and the New International Division of Labour*. Ottawa: University of Ottawa Press.

Camilleri, Joseph

1981 "The Advanced Capitalist State and the Contemporary World Crisis." *Science and Society*, 45:130–58.

Carroll, William K.

1982 "The Canadian Corporate Elite: Financiers or Finance Capitalists?" *Studies in Political Economy* 8:89–114.

——

1984 "The Individual, Class, and Corporate Power in Canada." *Canadian Journal of Sociology* 9, no. 3.

——

1986 *Corporate Power and Canadian Capitalism*. Vancouver: University of British Columbia Press.

Castells, Manuel

1980 *The Economic Crisis and American Society*. Princeton: Princeton University Press.

——

1983 *The City and the Grassroots*. Berkeley: University of California Press.

Clement, Wallace

1975 *The Canadian Corporate Elite*. Toronto: McClelland and Stewart.

——

1977a *Continental Corporate Power*. Toronto: McClelland and Stewart.

——

1977b "The Corporate Elite, the Capitalist Class, and the Canadian State." In Leo Panitch (ed.) *The Canadian State: Political Economy and Political Power*. Toronto: University of Toronto Press.

——

1983 *Class, Power and Property*. Toronto: Methuen.

Coleman, William

1986 "The Capitalist Class and the State: Changing Roles of Business Interest Associations." *Studies in Political Economy* 20:135–59.

Craven, Paul

1980 *"An Impartial Umpire": Industrial Relations and the Canadian State, 1900–1911*. Toronto: University of Toronto Press.

Craven, Paul and Tom Traves

1979 "The Class Politics of the National Policy 1872–1933." *Journal of Canadian Studies*, 14, 3:14–38.

Cuneo, Carl J.

1980a "Class, Stratification and Mobility." In Robert Hagedorn (ed.) *Sociology*. Toronto: Holt, Rinehart and Winston of Canada.

——

1980b "State Mediation of Contradictions in Canadian Unemployment Insurance, 1930–1935." *Studies in Political Economy* 3:37–65.

——

1983 "A Classical Marxist Perspective." In J.P. Grayson (ed.) *Introduction to Sociology*. Toronto: Gage.

Currie, David

1983 "World Capitalism in Recession." In Stuart Hall and Martin Jacques (eds.) *The Politics of Thatcherism*. London: Lawrence and Wishart.

Cypher, James M.
1979 "The Transnational Challenge to the Corporate State." *Journal of Economic Issues*. 13:513–42.

Davis, Mike
1986 *Prisoners of the American Dream: Politics and Economy in the History of the U.S. Working Class*. London: Verso.

Drache, Daniel
1970 "The Canadian Bourgeoisie and Its National Consciousness." In Ian Lumsden (ed.) *Close the 49th Parallel, etc., The Americanization of Canada*. Toronto: University of Toronto Press.

——
1977 "Staple-ization: A Theory of Canadian Capitalist Development." In Craig Heron (ed.) *Imperialism, Nationalism, and Canada*. Toronto: New Hogtown Press and Between the Lines.

Drache, Daniel and Wallace Clement (eds.)
1985 *The New Practical Guide to Canadian Political Economy*. Toronto: James Lorimer.

Droucopoulos, Vassilis
1981 "The Non-American Challenge: A Report on the Size and Growth of the World's Largest Firms." *Capital and Class*, 14:36–46.

Easterbrook, W.T. and H.G.J. Aitken
1956 *Canadian Economic History*. Toronto: Macmillan.

Ehrensaft, P. and W. Armstrong
1981 "The Formation of Dominion Capitalism: Economic Truncation and Class Structure." In A. Moscovitch and G. Dover (eds.) *Inequality: Essays on the Political Economy of Social Welfare*. Toronto: University of Toronto Press.

Esping-Anderson, Gosta
1985 "Power and Distributional Regimes." *Politics and Society*, 14:223–56.

Fennema, Meindert
1982 *International Networks of Banks and Industries*. Boston: Martin Nijhoff.

Fine, Ben
1984 *Marx's Capital*, second edition. London: Macmillan.

Fox, John and Michael Ornstein
1986 "The Canadian State and Corporate Elites in the Post-War Period." *Canadian Review of Sociology and Anthropology*. 23: 481–506.

Frank, Andre Gunder
1979 *Dependent Accumulation and Underdevelopment*. New York: Monthly Review Press.

Friedman, Jonathan
1978 "Crises in Theory and Transformations of the World Economy." *Review* 2:131–46.

Gatt-Fly
1985 *Debt Bondage or Self-Reliance: A Popular Perspective on the Global Debt Crisis*. Toronto: Gatt-Fly.

Hutcheson, John
1978 *Dominance and Dependency*. Toronto: McClelland and Stewart.

Innis, Harold A.
1970 *The Fur Trade in Canada*, rev. ed. Toronto: University of Toronto Press.

International Labor Office.
1978 *Yearbook of Labour Statistics*.
1985 Geneva: United Nations.

Kaufman, Michael
1985 "The Internationalization of Canadian Bank Capital (With a Look at Bank Activity in the Caribbean and Central America)." *Journal of Canadian Studies*, 19, 4:61–81.

Kealey, Gregory S.
1982 "Toronto's Industrial Revolution, 1850–1892." In Michael S. Cross and Gregory S. Kealey (eds.) *Canada's Age of Industry, 1849–1896*. Toronto: McClelland and Stewart.

Knutilla, Marray
1987 *State Theories: From Liberalism to the Challenge of Feminism*. Toronto: Garamond Press.

Laxer, Gordon
1985a "Foreign Ownership and Myths About Canadian Development." *Canadian Review of Sociology and Anthropology* 22:311–345.

——
1985b "The Political Economy of Aborted Development: The Canadian Case." In Robert J. Brym (ed.) *The Structure*

of the Canadian Capitalist Class. Toronto: Garamond Press.

Laxer, Jim and Doris Jantzi
1973 "The De-industrialization of Ontario." In Robert Laxer (ed.) *(Canada) Ltd., The Political Economy of Dependency*. Toronto: McClelland and Stewart.

Levitt, Kari
1970 *Silent Surrender*. Toronto: Macmillan of Canada.

MacIntosh, W.A.
1923 "Economic Factors in Canadian History." *Canadian Historical Review*, 4 (1):12–25.

MacLean, Brian (ed.)
1986 *The Political Economy of Crime.* Toronto: Prentice-Hall.

McNally, David
1981 "Staple Theory as Commodity Fetishism: Marx, Innis and Canadian Political Economy." *Studies in Political Economy*, 6:35–63.

Mahon, Rianne
1984 *The Politics of Industrial Restructuring: Canadian Textiles.* Toronto: University of Toronto Press.

——
1985 "The Canadian State's Response to the New International Division of Labour: Textiles." In Duncan Cameron and Francois Houle (eds.) *Canada and the New International Division of Labour*. Ottawa: University of Ottawa Press.

Marchak, Patricia
1979 *In Whose Interests?* Toronto: McClelland and Stewart.

——
1985 "Canadian Political Economy." *Canadian Review of Sociology and Anthropology* 22:673–709.

Maroney, H.J. and M. Luxton (eds.)
1987 *Feminism and Political Economy.* Toronto: Methuen.

Marx, Karl
1954 *Capital*, vol. 1. Moscow: Progress Publishers.

Moore, Steve and Debi Wells
1975 *Imperialism and the National Question in Canada*. Toronto: privately published.

Naylor, R.T.
1972 "The Rise and Fall of the Third Commercial Empire of the St. Lawrence." In Gary Teeple (ed.) *Capitalism and the National Question in Canada*. Toronto: University of Toronto Press.

——
1975 *The History of Canadian Business 1867–1914*, 2 vols. Toronto: James Lorimer.

Niosi, Jorge
1981 *Canadian Capitalism*. Toronto: James Lorimer.

——
1983 "The Canadian Bourgeoisie: Towards a Synthetical Approach." *Canadian Journal of Political and Social Theory* 7, 3:128–49.

——
1985a *Canadian Multinationals*. Toronto: Garamond Press.

——
1985b "Continental Nationalism: the Strategy of the Canadian Bourgeoisie." In Robert J. Brym (ed.) *The Structure of the Canadian Capitalist Class*. Toronto: Garamond Press.

Offe, Claus
1984 *Contradictions of the Welfare State.* Cambridge, Massachusetts: MIT Press.

Ornstein, Michael D.
1985 "Canadian Capital and the Canadian State: Ideology in an Era of Crisis." In Robert J. Brym (ed.) *The Structure of the Canadian Capitalist Class.* Toronto: Garamond Press.

Overbeek, Henk
1980 "Finance Capital and the Crisis in Britain." *Capital and Class* 2:99–120.

Palmer, Bryan D.
1983 *Working-Class Experience*. Toronto: Butterworths.

Panitch, Leo
1977 "The Role and Nature of the Canadian State." In Leo Panitch (ed.) *The Canadian State: Political Economy and Political Power*. Toronto: University of Toronto Press.

——
1981 "Dependency and Class in Canadian Political Economy." *Studies in Political Economy* 6:7–33.

Park, Libbie and Frank Park
1973 *Anatomy of Big Business.* [1962] Toronto: James Lewis and Samuel.

Pentland, H.C.
1981 *Labour and Capital in Canada 1650–1860.* Toronto: James Lorimer.

Phillips, Ron
1983 "The Role of the International Monetary Fund in the Post-Bretton Woods Era." *Review of Radical Political Economics* 15(2):59–81.

Piedalue, Gilles
1976 "Les groupes financiers au Canada 1900–1930." *Revue d'Histoire de l'Amérique Française* 30, 1:3–34.

Porter, John
1965 *The Vertical Mosaic*. Toronto: University of Toronto Press.

Portes, Alejandro and John Walton
1981 *Labour, Class, and the International System*. Toronto: Academic Press.

Richardson, R.J.
1982 "Merchants Against Industry: An Empirical Study." *Canadian Journal of Sociology* 7:279–96.

Ryerson, Stanley B.
1973 *Unequal Union*. Toronto: Progress Books.

Schmidt, Ray
1981 "Canadian Political Economy: A Critique." *Studies in Political Economy* 6:65–92.

Scott, John
1985 *Corporations, Classes and Capitalism*. London: Hutcheson.

Swartz, Donald
1977 "The Politics of Reform: Conflict and Accommodation in Canadian Health Policy." In Leo Panitch (ed.) *The Canadian State: Political Economy and Political Power*. Toronto: University of Toronto Press.

Szymanski, Albert
1981 *The Logic of Imperialism*. New York: Praeger.

Therborn, Goran
1977 "The Rule of Capital and the Rise of Democracy." *New Left Review* 103:3–41.

Turk, Jim
1985 "Free Trade with the United States: The Implications for Canada." *Canadian Dimension* 19(4):13–15, 37–38.

United Nations
1983 *Transnational Corporations in World Development, Third Survey*. New York: United Nations.

Van der Pijl, Kees
1984 *The Making of an Atlantic Ruling Class*. London: Verso.

Walker, Richard A.
1978 "Two Sources of Uneven Development under Advanced Capitalism: Spatial Differentiation and Capital Mobility." *Review of Radical Political Economics* 10 (3):28–38.

Watkins, Mel H.
1963 "A Staple Theory of Economic Growth." *Canadian Journal of Economics and Political Science*. 29:141–58.

——
1973 "Resources and Underdevelopment." In Robert Laxer (ed.) *(Canada) Ltd.: The Political Economy of Dependency*. Toronto: McClelland and Stewart.

——
1977 "The Staple Theory Revisited." *Journal of Canadian Studies* 12:83–95.

——
1985 "From the Heretic's Mouth: A Political Economist Exposes the Menace of Free Trade." *Canadian Forum* (August/September): 7–11.

——
1986 "Ten Good Reasons to Oppose Free Trade." *This Magazine* (April/May): 13–16.

Williams, Glen
1983 *Not for Export: Toward a Political Economy of Canada's Arrested Industrialization*. Toronto: McClelland and Stewart.

Wolfe, David
1983 "The Crisis in Advanced Capitalism: An Introduction." *Studies in Political Economy* 11:7–26.

A salmon canning plant in British Columbia. *Courtesy of Wallace Clement*

"Work is a social activity involving relations of power. For management, the classic problem has been how to translate the labour time they purchase from workers into effort."

c h a p t e r s i x

The Labour Process

Wallace Clement

INTRODUCTION

This chapter is about work, how it is organized, and the changes it has undergone. The "labour process" is a set of factors that combine when work occurs. It is part of a chain involving the transformation of goods and/or services whereby labour is applied. Labour, of course, is the exertion of physical or mental effort toward some conscious end. The conditions and characteristics of labouring, however, are complex, varied, and not always obvious. It is easy to see that working in an office or factory for wages is labour, as are working the fields or seas to obtain agricultural or fish products for sale as commodities. Less obvious is **domestic labour** because it is not done directly for payment; yet it, too, is part of the overall labour process, as well as having its own immediate labour process.

While the labour process can be abstracted from the broader society for analytical purposes, it should be situated in the context of other forces and relations. As mentioned, for example, production for payment needs to be related to reproduction of labour both in the immediate sense of supporting paid workers, but also ensuring future generations of workers. In another sense, the structure of control within the workplace is related to factors outside work, such as the gender division of labour or the place of ethnicity in segmenting work. While originating outside the immediate labour process, these divisions can be used and reinforced at work as part of the structure of domination that controls how labour is used.

In several senses, the labour process is always political. To be political means to involve relations of power. Those power relations can refer to the relationship between the labour process and the labour movement, such as the undercutting of craft unions or rise of industrial unions that accompanied transformations in the organization of factory work. Similarly, there has been the recent rise of large "white collar" unions for state employees within bureaucratic organizations and widespread expansion of clerical and service jobs. Another level involves relations between nations influenced by the international division of labour and its impact on the relative trading power of nations. Microchip **automation** and the electronics revolution have altered production. Multinational corporations have sought cheap, plentiful labour in Asia to perform detailed work previously done in advanced capitalist countries, thereby initiating a restructuring of labour forces with worldwide implications. Thus, the labour process is both an immediate and concrete phenomenon that has consequences in sweeping and abstract ways.

This chapter will introduce various ways of understanding the labour process by outlining several approaches and drawing upon illustrations from a variety of work sectors, such as clerical work, domestic labour, resource industries, factories, and work in fast-food **franchises**. It will also address several issues, such as automation, **skill** levels of workers, utilization of various control structures at work, and the resistance by workers to these processes.

The labour process is itself a perspective for understanding how society is organized. It locates the way work occurs in the context of developments in technology and the specific organization of work. Work is set within the context of how a society's resources are mobilized and controlled. Consequently, the labour process is at the heart of class analysis. At the personal level, the labour process poses issues concerning how people organize their work and preparation time, co-operate with others, and "make a living." Thus, work is not only a system of production, but a source of identity and a basis upon which people are evaluated (and assess themselves). The social psychology of work involves not only "worker motivation," but also consciousness and how people form their understandings about their places in the world.

A POLITICAL ECONOMY OF THE LABOUR PROCESS

In this chapter, a political economy approach will be used. Classical political economy begins with the writings of Adam Smith and David Ricardo on how society's production is organized. This liberal tradition was the foundation upon which Karl Marx constructed his *A Contribution to the Critique of Political Economy*, where he outlined the genre of historical materialism upon which current studies of the labour process rely so heavily. In his famous Preface to that document, he argued:

> In either the social production of their existence, men [sic] inevitably enter into definite relations, which are independent of their will, namely, relations of production appropriate to a given stage in the development of the material forces of production. The totality of these relations of production constitutes the economic structure of society, the real foundation, on which arises a legal and political superstructure and to which correspond definite forms of social consciousness. The mode of production of material life conditions the general process of social, political, and intellectual life. It is not the consciousness of men that determines their

existence, but their social existence that determines their consciousness ([1859] 1970, 20–21).

In **historical materialism**, the central principle is the process of production to satisfy the material needs basic to the way societies are organized. Such processes involve constant change through internal tensions and contradictions, which are the motor force of history. Obvious from the quotation are the social/cultural dimensions of ideology alongside the political and economic. (Marx's references to "men," meaning people, are indicative of the sexist language commonly used before the women's movement altered how the control of work is discussed and understood.)

For now, attention will be focused on the revolutionary change wrought by Marx's historical materialist analysis of the process. Marx is central to writings about the labour process, both as the guide for many contemporary researchers and as a foil for most critics. He set the agenda for debate and chronicled the emergence and transformation of capitalism as a mode of production.

In *Capital* ([1867] 1967:178) Marx argued the basic elements of the labour process are (1) purposeful activity, that is, work itself, (2) the subject of that work and, (3) the instruments of work. The first element is called *living labour*, meaning the actual person who is working. Second is the *material of labour*, or the raw materials worked upon, and, finally, the *means of labour*, which include the fixed capital and equipment used in work. These elements combine to make a *labour process*. ([1867] 1967:178). How the labour process is organized, that is, the social relations of production, distinguish historical epochs (simple co-operation, manufacture, and industry) and modes of production (feudalism, capitalism, or socialism).

Human labour is distinctive because the final result exists in the mind of the labourer before it occurs. The means of labour are combined with the material of labour by the living labourer. Labour is incorporated into the subject and transforms it. The labour process creates value. This is the crux of the **labour theory of value** developed by Ricardo and used by Marx. In Marx's theory, "the value of labour-power [daily cost of maintenance] and the value which that labour-power creates in the labour-process [daily expenditure in work] are two entirely different magnitudes; and this difference of the two values was what the capitalist had in view when he was purchasing the labour-power."[1] Appropriating value from the workers who produce it is the basis for exploitation in Marx's analysis.

Surplus value (that value above the cost of reproducing the workers) gets expanded two ways: absolutely, by lengthening and intensifying the working day or, relatively, by changing the technical and social conditions of the labour process, thereby increasing the productiveness of labour. This process decreases the part of the day devoted to reproducing the necessary daily cost of maintaining the worker and makes available greater surplus value to be struggled over. A central conflict within capitalism is over surplus value, with capitalists seeking to realize as much as possible and labour seeking to acquire a share. This contest is a key to Marx's notion of class struggle. As labour gains in strength through unionization, for example, it can command an increased part of surplus value.

Marx thought "the value of a commodity is determined, not only by the quantity of labour which the labourer directly bestows upon that commodity, but also by the labour contained in the means of production" (ibid.:315).[2] In other words, both the material of labour and the means of labour are themselves the products of earlier labour processes and repositories of "dead" labour "stored" in those processes to be "surrendered" at another stage of the labour process. The labour from all these sources then becomes embodied in the transformed product. If a labourer makes a piece of furniture, for example, the labour embodied in that piece includes direct labour plus part of the labour surrendered from the tools, and the building used during manufacture, plus the value already contained in the lumber and hardware.

According to Marx, "capitalist production only then really begins . . . when each individual capitalist employs simultaneously a comparatively large number of labourers; when consequently the labour-process is carried on on an extensive scale and yields, relatively, large quantities of products" (ibid.:322). The initial difference with handicraft production is one of scale, but "even without an alternation in the system of working, the simultaneous employment of a large number of labourers effects a revolution in the material conditions of the labour-process," since the buildings and tools become consumed in common and the necessary conditions for social labour based upon co-operation are created (ibid.:324). Furniture makers, in the example, no longer work in individual shops but under "one roof," using techniques of simple co-operation. The workers produce products in their traditional manner, but the products are owned by the capitalist who pays the workers. Initially "the subjection of labour to capital was only a formal result of the fact that the labourer, instead of working for himself, works for and consequently under the capitalist." Out of this combination of labour emerges the requirement of "a directing authority, in order to secure the harmonious working of the individual activities" (ibid.:330).

At this point the transition becomes critical as "the work of directing, superintending, and adjusting becomes one of the functions of capital from the moment that the labour under the control of capital becomes co-operative." The relationship between capital and labour, however, is not unidirectional. There is also a transformation in the character of labour. "As the number of the co-operating labourers increases, so too does their resistance to the domination of capital, and with it, the necessity for capital to overcome their resistance by counterpressure" (ibid.:331). This new social labour process engenders antagonisms to which capital must respond. The capitalist "hands over the work of direct and constant supervision of the individual workmen, and groups of workmen," such that a special category of supervisors is created to "command in the name of the capitalist" (ibid.:332).

Marx contextualizes these transformations in the shift from simple co-operation to manufacture to industry. The first shift is based upon a new division of labour with co-operation where, "instead of each man being allowed to perform all the various operations in succession, these operations are changed into disconnected, isolated ones, carried on side by side; each is assigned to a different artificer, and the whole of them together are performed simultaneously by the co-operating workmen" (ibid.:337). Handicraft is decomposed into its components, yet it "retains the character of a handicraft, and is therefore dependent on the strength, skill, quickness, and sureness, of the individual workman in handling his tools" (ibid.: 338). Making of furniture, following the example, becomes disaggregated into the component parts whereby some people make only legs, others only drawers, others only finishing, etc. The **detailed division of labour** results in specialization, not only of the worker but the tools. The instruments of labour become adapted

Figure 1
Marx's periodization of the labour process

	SIMPLE CO-OPERATION	MANUFACTURE	INDUSTRY
CHARACTERISTICS			
Technology	handicraft	specialized tools	machinery
Division of Labour	low	detailed	even more detailed
Skill	craft	skilled and unskilled	semiskilled
Control System	personal/ tradition	supervisors	technical subordination
Ownership	producers	capitalists	joint stock
Site	workshop	"one-roof"	factory
Organization of Work	individual/ group	collective	simplified
Focal Point of Period	guilds	division of labour	machinery
	tradition	separates conception & execution	technical subordination
TENDENCIES			
Subordination of labour	"formal" →	"real"	
Surplus value	"absolute" →	"relative"	
Technique	skill →	science	
Technical basis	conservative →	revolutionary	
Processes	decomposition →	de-skilling	
Capital	variable →	constant	

Source: Based on Karl Marx, *Capital*, chaps. 14, 15, and 16. This is merely a schematic of very complex processes and relationships.

to specialized actions, thus creating "at the same time one of the material conditions for the existence of machinery" (ibid.:341–42).

The detailed division of labour is the hallmark of manufacture and, in class terms, manufacture produced "unskilled labourers." Unlike simple co-operation, "manufacture thoroughly revolutionizes it, and seizes labour-power by its very roots" (ibid.:360). Manufacture also features the employer's "complaint of the want of discipline among the workmen" (ibid.:367).

The following period is characterized primarily by the shift from tools to machines. "In manufacture, the revolution in the mode of production begins with the labour-power, in modern industry it begins with the instruments of labour" (ibid.:371). There develops a "real machine system," which combines "detail

> **MARX ON THE TREND TOWARD MACHINE MINDING**
>
> Writing in 1867, Marx made some prescient observations about "an organized system of machines, to which motion is communicated by the transmitting mechanism from a central automation" (ibid.:381). Marx noted a **de-skilling** tendency, whereby workers are levelled to machine minders (ibid.:420) and begin to experience the means of labour as "dead labour" in a form of "technical subordination" (ibid.:423). Workers often confused the domination by the instruments of labour with that of capital. "It took both time and experience before the workpeople learnt to distinguish between machinery and its employment by capital, and to direct their attacks, not against the material instruments of production, but against the mode in which they are used" (ibid.:429).[4]

machines" with the operator merely attending the "automatic system of machines," which are "susceptible of constant improvement in its details" (ibid.:374–81).[3] Again, using the furniture example, the worker becomes a machine minder, watching as legs and other parts are mass produced by specialized equipment designed specifically for that task.

The periodization of the labour process identifies major tendencies and directions of change characteristic of particular epochs. Within the era of modern industry, processes organized on the principles of manufacture and even pockets of simple co-operation still exist. Marx's genius was his ability to identify emergent qualities and possibilities around the fundamental principles of organizing the labour process. But he was also writing well over a century ago, and many changes have occurred, only some of which he anticipated.

OTHER THEORIES

Weber on Bureaucracy

Another major contributor to the labour process tradition was Max Weber, whose influences were especially strong until the mid-1970s, when Marx's approach experienced a revival in this field. As Clegg, Boreham, and Dow argue, "While Marx focuses on control of the *means* of production, Weber also insists that we consider differential control of the *methods* of production" (1986:56). Whereas Marx focused upon the labour process of the factory and its control systems, Weber's concerns were on the office and state **bureaucracies**. For Weber, bureaucracy was a cancer which could spread and choke humanity ("the iron cage"), whereas for Marx the oppression of the factory was the breeding ground for liberation ("the dialectic"), whereby workers respond to their oppression and seek to change conditions.

Undoubtedly, Weber's notion of bureaucracy, with its order by rules, files, and staff of officials, is a system of social control, which he called the "means of administration." For Weber, "the principles of office hierarchy and of levels of graded authority mean a firmly ordered system of super- and subordination in which there is a supervision of the lower offices by the higher ones." (Weber, 1946:197). Bureaucracies are instruments of power, and in Weber's analysis "the bureaucratic structure goes hand in hand with the concentration of the material means of management in the hands of the master. This concentration occurs, for instance, in a well-known and typical fashion in the development of big capitalist enterprises, which find their essential characteristics in this process. A corresponding process occurs in public organizations'' (ibid.:221). Given the rise of administrative apparatuses in the twentieth century, the Weberian approach to bureaucracy came into favour among analysts of work and organizations.

Blauner on Technology

Besides bureaucracy, the other feature most often used to characterize the organization of work in the twentieth century has been technology. It has been argued by some analysts, such as Robert Blauner in *Alienation and Freedom*, that the technological organization of the labour process is the crucial feature accounting for the experience of work (Blauner, 1964:vii). He argues the shifts from craft to machine to line to process technologies and their associated divisions of labour determine the experience and response to work. Most notable, as will be discussed later, has been the reaction to automation by analysts as either a liberating or repressive force. Historical materialists, however, do not see technology as an independent force. Rather, ''technological development reflects the present social relations of production'' and different social relations would change technological development (Noble, 1978:315).[5] There is no technological imperative. It is rather a social process both in its development and utilization.

A TREND TOWARD DEGRADATION OF LABOUR

Braverman's Theory

Labour process research underwent a revitalization in the mid-1970s with the publication of Harry Braverman's *Labor and Monopoly Capital: The Degradation of Work in the Twentieth Century* and the outpouring of responses his views stimulated.[6] Braverman crystallized developments already under way in the field. James Rinehart, for example, published *The Tyranny of Work* about the same time as Braverman's book, focusing on ''who determines the way work is organized and the purposes for which work is undertaken'' (1975:1).[7] Unlike Braverman, however, Rinehart dealt with the subjective side of work (alienation), resistance (union struggles) and, to some extent, women's work. But Braverman's book serves as the focal point.

Braverman's central paradox is: Why, with the increasing automation, education, training, wages, and ''mental'' work, is there also mounting worker dissatisfaction in production and administrative workplaces? His answer is contained in his analysis of the ''degradation of work'' resulting from the de-skilling of most work and, related to this, an intensification of control over the workplace by capitalists and their managers. He argues that capital dominates labour and uses technology and the organization of work to reinforce this control to facilitate capital accumulation. In the labour force, this is manifest in the actual labour process and the allocation of workers to different occupations and economic sectors.

According to Braverman (1974:14), the major transformations in capitalism since the industrial revolution have resulted in a rapid introduction of technology, increasing labour productivity, and a rise in consumption by the working class. These successfully undermined the labour movement and ''revolutionary impetus,'' turning workers toward economic issues and unions into business unions. Since the 1960s, however, labour's dissatisfaction turned ''not so much on capitalism's inability to provide work, as on the work it provides, not on the collapse of its productive process, but on the appalling effects of these processes at their most "successful." These are issues the expansion of capital and wealth cannot resolve, since they are caused by this very expansion, and are exhibited in high turnover rates, absenteeism, sabotage, work slowdowns, wildcat walkouts and strikes, in spite of higher wages.

With the introduction of capitalist industrial production, labour power is transformed into selling a worker's time to capitalists for the purpose of expanding capital. Therefore, labour is no longer simply a means of transforming an object or providing a service; it is a means of expanding someone else's capital in return for wages or salaries. Technology becomes an instrument of the capitalist to expand the productivity of the labour power (workers' time) and an instrument to control the labourer. There are problems of co-ordination for management, which has to provide a workplace, order the processes, supply materials, schedule work, keep records, organize sales, and finance the operation. Most basic, however, is capital's need for a disciplined labour force.

Control of Labour

Control, Braverman argues, is facilitated by the division of labour, which he calls "the fundamental principle of industrial organization" (ibid.:70). By this he does not mean societal divisions of labour such as those based on gender or age; rather, he means the "detailed division of labour" introduced in the factory and administrative structures which result from the breaking down of tasks through planning and control and assigning workers repetitive parts of the process, turning workers into "detail workers." Thus most labour becomes separated from "special knowledge and training and reduced to simple labour" (ibid.:82). The parallel with Marx is obvious.

But Braverman goes beyond Marx by investigating the principles and application of Taylorism. **Scientific management** (or Taylorism), Braverman contended, was a conscious attempt by capitalists to control workers by adapting them to capital's demands. Seeking to squeeze the most productivity out of the labour power they have purchased, capitalists dictate each detail of the labour process. Here Braverman identifies the three basic operating principles of Taylorism:

> 1. Dissociation of the labour process from the skills of the workers . . .
>
> 2. Separation of conception from execution . . .
>
> 3. Monopoly over knowledge to control each step of the labour process and its mode of execution (ibid.:113–14, 119).

Scientific management separates the "mental" and "manual" aspects of labour so work becomes executed in the plant and planned or conceptualized in the administration, whereby production is separated from functions such as "design, planning, calculation, and recordkeeping" (ibid.:124). It is not technology per se that causes this separation, but the dominating relation of capital over labour that strives to maximize productivity.

Whereas Frederick Taylor was concerned about the detailed technical subdivision of work, later focus shifted to the social organization of work and the psychology of group interaction by workers. The most noted proponent of this approach was Elton Mayo, who used social engineering to provide work conditions that would foster productivity. This resulted in a flourishing of personnel and labour relations departments and an interest in the work process by academics from disciplines such as psychology, sociology, and commerce. As Braverman describes it, the issue for labour relations analysts "is not that of the degradation of men and women, but the difficulties raised by the reactions, conscious and unconscious, to that degradation" (ibid.:141). Thus social engineering added another level of control to scientific management.

Aside from control through management techniques, Braverman also examines the mechanization and control of workers through technology. He thinks that there has been a "transformation of labour from a basis of skill to a basis of science" (ibid.:155). Besides the effect of technology on the labour force as a whole (and not simply a small scientific stratum estimated at about 3 percent—architects, chemists, designers, scientists, and technical engineers), Braverman notes the implications of technology (specifically coal-petroleum, electricity, internal combustion engines, and steel) for the centralization and concentration of capital. Since large capital controls research and development, science becomes a commodity purchased by capital to dominate rivals and extend its domain.

Braverman notes the result of using new technology "is not the *elimination* of labour, but its *displacement* to other occupations and industries" (ibid.:172). Hence, the increasing productivity as a result of technology "frees up" a larger part of the working class to engage in other types of labour. For Braverman the key distinction is whether the machinery is controlled by the worker or whether it makes the worker a "machine-tender." Since those who control the machinery determine its operation, the direction of change has been toward using machinery to control workers and the pace of work.

Clerical Work

The final part of Braverman's analysis examines changes under way for clerical workers and occupations in service and retail trade. He distinguishes between clerical workers of the nineteenth century and those of today, with the earlier ones "the ancestors of modern professional management" and today's as "virtually a new stratum" (ibid.:293). The earliest clerical workers were highly paid, often close to the capitalist, and male. Three basic changes have occurred in the clerical stratum: the relative pay has declined to less than that for industrial workers, most of the workers are now female, and the tasks have become segmented into detailed labour.

The growth in clerical workers resulted from changes within factory offices and a growth of "clerical industries." The first process is reflected in the proportion of administrative and office workers in Canadian manufacturing, increasing from one in ten in 1917 to two in ten by 1940 and three in ten by 1982. Second, the rise of "paper empires" in the commercial sector like banks, trust companies, life insurance, real estate, etc., are primarily clerical, including recordkeeping involving accounts, stocks, and payrolls.

Braverman contends office work has become its own labour process, which is controlled through office management. Paralleling Taylorism in the factory, practitioners like William H. Leffingwell and Lee Galloway began to systematize office routines. This was easiest with activities such as typing and production records, but soon spread. By applying scientific management principles, the first "solution" was found in the technical division of labour and then in mechanization, both involving fragmentation of work into a process that readily followed the application of numerical and mathematical controls.

As a result, the distinction between mental and manual labour has been destroyed. Once the office has been rationalized, the distinction between production

DOMESTIC LABOUR

Debates in the labour process literature since the mid-1970s have typically begun with an evaluation of Braverman's position. One major critique has focused on his failure to acknowledge domestic labour in his analysis, particularly the relationship between paid and unpaid labour. This is obviously a gender issue, since women do most of the domestic labour in our society. Since Braverman ignored patriarchy (systems of power based on gender), he was silent on such issues. Canadian literature in this field, however, has been particularly rich. *Hidden in the Household: Women's Domestic Labour Under Capitalism*, edited by Bonnie Fox (1980), is a theoretically sophisticated analysis, while Meg Luxton's *More Than a Labour of Love: Three Generations of Women's Work in the Home* (1980) is a detailed investigation based upon an ethnography of Flin Flon, Manitoba. Luxton has extended her analysis in a collection of papers with Harriet Rosenberg called *Through the Kitchen Window: The Politics of Home and Family* (1986). Also of interest is Charlene Gannagé's *Double Day, Double Bind: Women Garment Workers* (1986) because it concentrates on the relationship between paid labour and the domestic situation, a theme explored in broader terms by Pat and Hugh Armstrong in *The Double Ghetto: Canadian Women and Their Segregated Work* (1984).

In an interesting paper, Veronica Strong-Boag has claimed "women in the home make up the largest single group of Canadian workers" and goes on to offer a valuable categorization of "five essential work processes" associated with domestic labour. First is "housework" as typically associated with domestic labour, followed by "reproduction and care of dependent children," then "care of working adults." Each of these is commonly understood as domestic labour, but she identifies a further two: "care of dependent adults" and "paid work within the home" (1986:124, 126–27). Each work process merits detailed exploration. One process involves internal transformations within the home, where the trend appears to be from production-based activities to consumption-based ones, accompanied by changes in household equipment. The most important changes involve the structure of living units from the traditional family to a much more complex variety of structures than commonly assumed. Meriting special attention is the relationship between developments in domestic labour and their implications for working outside the home, both for paid and unpaid workers. Production separated from reproduction blinds labour process analysis to important sources of explanation about the making of a labour force. There is a dynamic relation, for example, between the struggle for child care facilities and women's labour force participation. Childcare both makes possible and is made necessary by the increasing demand for women to work for pay.

and conceptualization loses significance because "thought and planning become concentrated in an ever smaller group within the office, and for the mass of those employed there the office became just as much a site of manual labor as the factory floor" (ibid.:316).

Office mechanization has proceeded

most rapidly in handling information, especially through the use of computers. What was a "craft" in the early days of computerization has changed into "detail" labour today. Work with computers today involves a small stratum of systems analysts and programmers, while the remaining (mainly women) workers have labour-intensive tasks such as coding, keypunching, verifying, and word-processing.

Rosemary Crompton and Stuart Reid's work confirms many of Braverman's observations concerning clerical work in the United States. They argue de-skilling for clerical workers is a double-edged process which "involves both the process of fragmentation, simplification and standardization of work tasks and the diminution of the clerical worker's role as an "intermediary" between management and the mass of routine workers." Their investigations confirm the view that clerical workers have lost the "total view" of the process while at the same time losing the delegated authority from management (1985:175).

In Canada, Graham Lowe has examined clerical and adminstrative work in detail, including its mechanization through the introduction of typewriters that shaped the sequence and pace of work, new systems of work organizations like pools and standardized procedures, or even punch and computer operations resembling assembly lines. Lowe argues that these new machines and the new organization of work created a clerical stratum, but the intersection of class and patriarchal factors explain why women received the low-valued jobs.

SKILL AND DE-SKILLING

Braverman has also been criticized for the fairly loose way he deals with skill, even though it is a master concept in his argument about the degradation of work. When combined with the gender issue, the notion of skill becomes particularly germane, as Mercedes Steedman discovered in her analysis of their relationship in Canada's clothing industry. She argues "skill is intricately tied to the gender of the worker, and the notion of skill in the clothing industry often has less to do with the job itself than with the sex and the bargaining position of the worker in the production process." Steedman clearly connects her analysis with the earlier points concerning domestic labour when she observes "the basis of women's work in the clothing industry lay in the social view that their ultimate destiny as wives and mothers made them peripheral to the paid work world" (1986:152).

Cynthia Cockburn has identified at least three dimensions of skill worth noting:

> There is the skill that resides in the man himself [sic], accumulated over time, each new experience adding something to a total ability. There is the skill demanded by the job—which may or may not match the skill in the worker. And there is the political definition of skill: that which a group of workers or a trade union can successfully defend against the challenge of employers and of other groups of workers (1985:133).[8]

What is important in terms of the labour process is less the "technical" skills of the worker than the control over production that they exert; that is, the "politics" of skill are far-reaching in terms of exclusionary practices through training, apprenticeships, or certification. They are also important in terms of the organization of skills that will influence the degree of autonomy workers can exercise. Most fundamental to this view of skill is that the politics is not a simple process designed by "capital," but the outcome of a relationship. Obviously, this has important implications for fractions within the working class based upon divisions around skill, but it is also significant for gender. Cockburn reminds her readers that skill involves more than the politics of class; it is also "a sex/gender weapon. Skill as a political concept is more far-reaching than the class relations of capitalism—it plays an important part in the power relations between men and women. The sexual division of labour in society is of great antiquity: men and women tend to do different work. Over very long periods of patriarchal time, women's particular abilities and work processes have been arbitrarily valued lower than those of men" (ibid.:136).

The politics of de-skilling require more careful analysis than Braverman provided. He focused mainly on the displacement of craft workers by machinery and the fragmentation of tasks. These are common processes, but their effects are by no means identical. As Paul Thompson has pointed out, "Homogenization is a weak link in the chain of argument on skills and the labour process. There is a great difference between all work being subject tendentially to the same *trends* with respect to skills, and saying all work is the *same*. As the starting points of occupations are different, experiences and consequences will vary correspondingly" (1983:119).

The way de-skilling takes place has significant effects for the way it is received by the workers. De-skilling the "job" does not necessarily mean de-skilling the "person," as the following argument using Canada's mining industry will illustrate. Massive amounts of equipment have been introduced into the underground operations of Canada's mines since the mid-1970s, displacing a traditional bastion of craft-like production where miners performed a complete cycle of work, had very little direct supervision and were highly skilled in their tasks (Clement, 1981). The mechanization of the drilling, hauling, and development work in the mines occurred unevenly, since one mine at a time tended to be "brought-on-stream," while others were closed in Inco's network of about fifteen mines located around Thompson and Sudbury. Existing mines have a limited capacity to accept the diesel equipment, whereas the new mines were adapted from their original engineering to the requirements of ventilation, ramps to move the equipment, and areas for maintenance. Each new mine essentially creates a new labour force, where the new recruits tend to be young people who are quickly trained to operate the new equipment. The machines require less training, the process is less physically demanding and, although the miners on the machines earn less, it also takes them less time to attain a level of proficiency where they gain some bonus income. The new process does not *directly* displace workers, especially skilled workers who remain in demand in older operations. Displacement within mining is accomplished through periodic booms and busts, with layoffs characteristic of the industry and not attributed to the use of new labour processes. Clearly the aggregate effects mean fewer workers are required to produce as much as before and overall the number of skilled jobs is reduced. Inco, Canada's largest mining company, has shrunk its labour force from 21 000 to 13 200 since 1982, but its metal output has increased by 70 percent. Three out of five jobs at Inco have disappeared since 1980 (*The Globe and Mail*, 1985:B6;B20). Bulk mining techniques using extensive mechanization have increased from less than a third of production in 1982 to over half by 1983, with two-thirds projected for 1985. A mining engineer reports vertical crater retreat mining means "no skilled labour is required and a two- or three-man crew is sufficient for drilling, measuring, plugging and charging the holes" (ibid.:1983:B13).

Parallel, yet distinct, processes have been identified by Ian Radforth in pulpwood logging in northern Ontario. Radforth reveals important changes in the demands for labour and the labour process influenced by natural conditions, such as topography, weather, and the trees themselves. Most revealing, however, is his finding of the lack of mechanization in logging prior to the 1950s (in spite of mechanization in other phases of the forest industry), since there was an abundant and cheap supply of labour. Production was seasonal and men were recruited from agriculture and construction during the winter. It was a crisis in this labour market along with pressures for cost reductions because of market competition from the southern United States) that explained mechanization. Particularly acute was the decline of available agricultural labour with the reduction of the agriculture sector; some 60 percent to 70 percent of timber had been cut by agriculturalists. Alongside a decreasing supply of labour was an increasing demand for higher wages by the woods-workers' unions.

Given these pressures, a long-term strategy of making logging capital-intensive was in initiated, but it ran into technical difficulties. A combination of "bull-work" and skill were replaced by machine operations and new skills. The traditional organization of production was around a piecework system, which rewarded skill and maximized workers' independence. With the introduction of equipment like fellers, bucker/pliers and slusher/loaders, independence decreased since this division of labour had to be co-ordinated, thus introducing for the first time industrial-like production schedules, including shiftwork, an end to piecework, increased supervision, and management-controlled training. The new machine operators have become skilled at maintaining and operating machines. Their geographical isolation has meant they have not been subject to as intense a de-skilling and division of labour as is possible in a factory setting (1986).

There are some contrasts with mining. Mechanization tended to produced teamwork in logging, unlike the traditional individual organization of work. Whereas in mining, exactly the opposite need occurred. The machine operators in logging need to be more skilled than in mining since, Radforth contends, they do some maintenance work as well as operating the equipment. In mining, these are separate activities. Otherwise the effects have been quite similar: a movement from piecework to an incentive system; decreased bull-work; increased supervision; increased shiftwork; and increased managerial control over training. The broad tendencies are similar, but the specific effects differ, since the original labour processes are themselves not identical. The de-skilling process involves much more subtlety and complexity than Braverman portrayed.

FACTORY AUTOMATION

There are two basic expressions of automation on the shop floor. Numerical control involves the programming of machines to perform detailed metal work. It has had its greatest impact on skilled workers (machinists and millwrights) who have been de-skilled, since they have less discretion and require less training to operate the machine. Robotics, on the other hand, have been applied to assembly line operations (usually welding and painting), typically performed by low-skilled workers who are actually displaced through automation. Unclear is the total effect on maintenance, a skilled task, for either numerical control or robotics. But initially a good deal of skill is required in setting up the equipment and addressing technical flaws.

In Canada, the impact for both types of

automation has been limited, yet each is growing. From 500 numerically controlled machines in 1974, the number rose to 3500 by 1984. While this may appear substantial, in 1983 numerical control accounted for only 4.4 percent of machines on shop floors in Canadian manufacturing, compared to 8 percent in the United Kingdom, 13 percent in the United States, and a staggering 38 percent in Japan (Ontario Ministry of Industry, Trade and Technology, 1985:9). For robots, the numbers have risen from fewer than 20 in 1975 to 1032 in 1985. Of these, 70 percent are in the automobile industry. This accounts for the concentration of robots in U.S. branch plants (74 percent) compared to Canadian-owned companies (26 percent). For robot technology, Canada depends entirely on imports: 18 percent from Europe, 20 percent from Japan, and 61 percent from the United States (ibid.: 27,28,29).

CONTROL RECONSIDERED

Work is a social activity involving relations of power. For management, the classic problem has been how to translate the labour time they purchase from workers into effort. Their answers have involved a variety of control systems. Whereas Brav-

ROBOTICS IN CANADA AND OTHER NATIONS

Table 1

ROBOTS PER 10 000 EMPLOYED IN MANUFACTURING, 1984

Japan	32.1	Belgium	5.9
Sweden	20.1	United States	4.7
West Germany	7.2	Italy	3.9
Czechoslovakia	7.2	Canada	3.7
France	6.9	United Kingdom	3.1

Source: Ibid., p. 9.

As Table 1 illustrates, Canada is considerably behind most advanced industrial nations in use of robotics. Sweden is a particularly interesting case in this respect. Around 1980 there were about four thousand numerical control machines and one thousand industrial robots in the engineering industry. The key to their acceptance by unions has been the industrial relations system and labour market practices in Sweden, whereby unemployment has been kept low and workers are guaranteed reasonable treatment by employers because of strong unions (Goranzon et al., 1982:7). When fear for their jobs is removed, workers usually welcome the relief from much tedious and difficult work now accomplished by automation. With justification, the Canadian labour movement fears automatic technology because workers have little protection against its adverse effects, whereas in Sweden many unionists believe they share in the benefits and do not have to worry about being thrown out on the streets. In Japan, where such machinery has also gained widespread acceptance, workers in central firms are protected against arbitrary layoffs because of technological change by a system of paternalism (Littler, 1987).

erman places great weight on the practices of Taylorism, others have sought a more dynamic understanding of control, involving both resistance and the production of consent. Littler and Salaman argue "*all* forms of control contain, in different degree, two dimensions of control: the specification of levels of performance (and this may vary from highly specified to highly autonomous) and some effort to develop some level of consent or acceptance of the legitimacy of the employment relationship" (Littler and Salaman 1984: 57). Control is a more complex subject than Braverman allowed. The requirement for domination must, at times, be balanced with obtaining creativity and initiative on the part of workers.

Under capitalist relations of production, labour is a commodity, but a commodity with consciousness and capacity to disrupt the transformation from labour time into labour power. Andrew Friedman has stressed the need by capital to capture the creative qualities of some labourers, hence the development of alternatives to the type of control stressed by Braverman.

Braverman's analysis is challenged by Friedman for failing to analyze class consciousness and workers' resistance. There is not one managerial strategy, namely Taylorism, but several; moreover, Friedman suggests Taylorism's applicability was mainly to the first decade of the twentieth century, and even then was much less widespread than Braverman suggests. Friedman argues that since workers have independent wills and are alienated by the work process, they organize to resist managerial power. When workers resist this power, it is not necessarily the "best strategy" for managers to separate the conception and execution of work, as Braverman contends. Rather, "if the costs of scientific management in terms of worker resistance or lost flexibility are too great, alternative strategies will be tried" through the organization of work, particularly if technical changes in work occur frequently (Friedman, 1977:82).

Friedman discusses various forms of worker resistance, such as individual or collective sabotage, absenteeism, quitting, and work-to-rule. He argues working-class resistance is affected by the size of plants, homogeneity of the community, hierarchies within plants, and the heterogeneity of workers (age, gender, race, and nationality) and that the degree of worker resistance constrains management. Management is pressured on the one hand to accumulate capital and on the other hand to contain labour. He argues "top managers may loosen direct control over work activity as part of a strategy for maintaining or augmenting managerial control over productive activity as a whole (Responsible Autonomy), or they may be forced to loosen direct control as part of a general shift in control over productive activity in favour of the workers" (ibid.:84–85).

Direct control strategy parallels the processes Braverman identified; indeed, the defining characteristic is the separation of work's conception and execution. *Responsible autonomy* strategy parallels, to a limited extent, the social engineering practices Braverman discussed but deemed less significant. Its essence is that managers promote loyalty among workers in order to be able to grant workers greater discretion in their tasks. Responsible autonomy may be effective with workers who have secure employment, but not when there are frequent layoffs. Thus, Friedman argues, "privileged groups — managerial, administrative and technical workers (except for the lower grades of clerical workers), male, white, skilled workers, or other workers who are particularly well organized — will be distinguished by far greater employment security, as well as higher earnings" (ibid.:84–85).

The distinction is between "central"

and "peripheral" workers. Workers are central by virtue of their skills or place in exercising managerial authority or as a result of their collective power through demonstrated resistance. These workers are most often the targets for responsible autonomy. Peripheral workers are unskilled and semiskilled machine operators considered replaceable. Also included are clerical and secretarial workers. Direct control strategies are most frequently directed toward them. Moreover, peripheral workers are most often women, Blacks, or immigrants, Friedman argues, who tend to have little solidarity with central workers and little opportunity for gaining central status.

The most significant "corrective" offered by Friedman is to introduce a more dynamic and interactive sense of the labour process. The labour process is relational in that capital and labour are combined in ways reflecting strengths and weaknesses of both parties. The labour process is a critical site where classes are reproduced, but it is also a place where gender and often ethnic inequalities are exploited and nourished. Hence, the labour process is a "frontier of control" that Richard Edwards aptly characterizes as a "contested terrain."

Edwards argues control systems are based upon three dimensions: directing work, evaluating work, and disciplining or rewarding workers. He outlines three types of control. Simple or personal control is control by supervision. Technical control "involves designing machinery and planning the flow of work to minimize the problem of transforming labour power into labour" (1979:18,112). Bureaucratic control involves job descriptions, incentives, bidding for jobs and grievance procedures in the context of offices, rules, and responsibilities (ibid.:145). A weakness of Edwards's formulation is the tendency to contrast these three "types" of control rather than see them in combination. The assembly line in a modern automobile plant, for example, involves personal control in the form of shop floor supervisors, technical control in the form of the organization of the machine-paced line, plus bureaucratic control in the form of rules and procedures set by the company and negotiated with the union. Each reinforces the other.

FUTURE WORK

Canada's labour force is undergoing radical restructuring. The cruelest effect is on the million unemployed Canadians (at least 9.5 percent of the labour force). In addition, there were 514 000 *involuntary* part-time workers in 1986, mainly young people and women unable to find full-time employment.

Where are all the jobs associated with the introduction of advanced technology? They are largely located outside the country. "Canada imports almost all of its computers, robots, microelectronic chips, and other technologies used in the workplace, so the jobs gained in supplying this equipment go mainly to other countries. In the first nine months of [1986] Canada had a trade deficit of $1.7 billion in computers and $353 million in computer chips." Overall, Canada's high technology deficit of $14 billion in 1986 (the highest of all seven economic summit countries) translates into about 140 000 jobs, mostly skilled ones (*Toronto Star*, 1987). Many factors affect this situation, but a major one is Canada's weak research and development capacity. Only 1.3 percent of Canada's gross national product is spent in this area (a quarter of Japan's rate and half that of the United States). American Telephone and Telegraph of New York and Siemans of West Germany each spend more on research annually than does Canada (*The Globe and Mail*, 1987).

So where can young people in Canada expect to find jobs in the future? The most recent Employment and Immigration Canada figures confirm the continued growth of the service sector. Table 2 lists the top ten growth occupations projected for the next ten years.

Table 2
TOP TEN EMPLOYMENT GROWTH OCCUPATIONS IN CANADA 1986–1995

Salespersons (clerks)	91 000
Food services	80 000
Bookkeepers	56 000
Secretaries and stenographers	54 000
Chefs and cooks	47 000
Cashiers and tellers	47 000
Janitors and cleaners	40 000
Truck drivers	33 000
Sales management	26 000
Barbers and hairdressers	26 000

Source: The Globe and Mail, "Report on Careers" 23 March 1987:B15.

The service sector is also the primary location for **franchise** jobs. For the most part, the list reveals the low-paid, low-skilled jobs that dominate these projected demands.

A major twist has been added to the structuring of the labour process in recent years. More and more work is organized through franchise operations that rely on a particular type of labour force. Increasingly, franchises are coming to dominate retail service and sales. Franchise sales of $50 billion for 1986 accounted for some 40 percent of all retail sales. As Robert Harris, a Toronto franchise consultant, says, "Corporations, having done a lot of cost-cutting during the recession, are now looking at their distribution networks to see what other areas can be trimmed. The way to do that is through independent ownership. The companies can reduce labour costs and employ capital in more efficient ways, in exchange for giving up part of the profits" (*Financial Post*, 1986).[9] The degree of "independence" for operators of franchises can be questioned, but at issue here is the effect on the labour process.

Let's contrast the traditional way of making a hamburger with the franchise way. Traditionally, hamburgers would be

LABOUR IN THE FAST FOOD FRANCHISES

Little research has been conducted on the labour process in franchises, but Ester Reiter's "Life in a Fast-Food Factory" is a refreshing exception. She describes what it is like to work for Burger King, outlining the managerial procedures and labour practices, where instructions are specified for every operation and innovation is not welcome. She concludes "the women and teenagers at Burger King are under the sway of a labour process that eliminates almost completely the possibility of forming a workplace culture independent of, and in opposition to, management" (1985: 124, 126–27). Indications are that this labour process is rapidly coming to typify the service industries. Labour process analysts of the future will have to study the expansion of this vehemently anti-union sector of the economy, which makes its living by marginalizing workers. The social relations of production in this latest growth sector will have significant effects on the way social classes are reproduced for the next generation.

made by short-order cooks who at least had some training and/or experience, broad familiarity with the equipment, ordering of supplies, and likely were full-time adult workers who had command over the entire process from making the patty to cooking, to garnishing, and possibly even serving. Cooks have their own styles and individuality. Franchises repress individuality; it is "no surprise" service. The process is fragmented with little training, no skill, minimum wage labour, and typically done by a part-time teenage worker. The process employs the cheapest, most available, and flexible labour force.

The effects of these changes characterized by the franchise are not evenly felt within the labour force. They disproportionately affect young people and married women who experience low training, low pay, and high turnover in dead-end jobs. As of 1983, 26 percent of employed young men and 34 percent of employed young women worked part-time. Men eventually escape this status, since 98 percent of men between twenty-five and sixty-four worked full-time, yet 25 percent of women in that age group continue to work part-time (Statistics Canada, 1985:55).

Franchising is coming to be a dominant force in creating a newly structured labour market. Characterized by contractual obligations between the franchisor and franchisee, by 1985 there were 1200 franchise systems in Canada, accounting for 50 000 outlets. They have expanded into services such as lawn care, house cleaning, and child care, with obvious strongholds in convenience stores, and are overwhelming in the fast food business, as Table 3 indicates.

Table 3

FAST FOOD FRANCHISES IN CANADA, 1985

	Units	Sales ($ Million)
McDonald's	498	880
Kentucky Fried Chicken	450	288
Burger King	160	148
Dairy Queen	393	125
A & W	265	110

Source: The Globe and Mail, "Report on Franchising," 24 July 1986: B23.

CONCLUSION

Just as Marx did for his time, contemporary analysts of the labour process must recognize emerging tendencies. In recent times these have involved changes in the participation of women in paid labour, along with major developments in domestic labour; in the area of technology, automation, and especially the impact of microchips, would seem to be most significant; in the organization of work, the dramatic rise of franchises and the use of part-time work to perform highly standardized tasks is a key area. In broader terms, the internationalization of the division of labour, whereby detailed work is performed in low-wage enclaves, especially in Asia, is of note.

While it is important to describe how a society looks and even how its members think, most basic is understanding how it works (in several senses of that term). Canada's labour force broadly resembles that of other advanced capitalist societies, yet there are important distinguishing features, especially concerning the importance resources have in the economy and the weakly developed research capacity. This chapter has outlined the broader tendencies affecting all advanced capitalist societies, while remaining sensitive to the particular expressions they have in Canada. Work needs to be understood in relation to domestic labour that makes it possible, as well as the absence of work that needs to be explained. Work and its organization is a central feature for "understanding Canadian society."

Notes

[1]See all of Chapter 7, "The Labour Process and the Process of Producing Surplus Value." *Capital* (New York: International) 1967.

[2]See Chapter 13, "The Concept of Relative Surplus Value."

[3]Based upon ibid., Chapters 12, 14, and 15. It is important to note that Marx wrote in 1867 the work this sketch is based upon. This is merely a schematic of very complex processes and relationships.

[4]For a richer understanding of these processes, see Chapter 14, "Division of Labour and Manufacture" and Chapter 15, "Machinery and Modern Industry."

[5]See also David Noble, *America by Design: Science, Technology and the Rise of Corporate Capitalism*. (New York: Knopf) 1979.

[6]See, for example, symposia in the following journals: *Monthly Review* 28:3 (July–August) 1976; *Insurgent Sociologist* 8:1 (Winter) 1978; *Alternate Routes* 2, 1978; *New Left Review* 107 (January–February) 1978; and the collection *Degradation of Work? Skill, De-skilling and the Labour Process*, ed. Stephen Wood (London: Hutchinson) 1982; Craig R. Littler and Graeme Salaman, "Bravermania and Beyond: Recent Theories of the Labour Process," *Sociology*. 16:2 (May) 1982; Tony Cutler, "The Romance of Labour," *Economy and Society* 7:1 (February) 1978; Michael Burawoy, "Toward a Marxist Theory of the Labour Process: Braverman and Beyond," *Politics and Society*. 8:3/4, 1978.

[7]See also his second edition called *The Tyranny of Work: Alienation and the Labour Process* (Toronto: Harcourt Brace Jovanovich) 1987.

[8]See also Cynthia Cockburn's *Machinery of Dominance: Women, Men and Technical Know-How* (London: Pluto Press) 1985.

[9]For a comparison with the United States, see Stan Luxenburg, *Roadside Empires: How the Chains Franchised America* (New York: Viking Penguin) 1985.

DISCUSSION QUESTIONS

1. Harry Braverman's main theme is that the drive for productivity and efficiency of capital contradicts the place of workers in the process of production, since it means a loss of control for workers over the labour process and de-skilling. Discuss Braverman's argument by evaluating it in light of some kinds of work characteristic of your own area. Think, for example, of changes in bank jobs because of automated tellers, robots in automobile factories, word processors in offices, or new equipment in resource industries.
2. Rather than being homogeneous in its impact, computerization has had an uneven set of consequences for the working class. Evaluate this statement in light of your understanding of the computer's impact for factory life, the office, and in the service sector.
3. Gender and age are two characteristics associated with part-time work in franchises. How do you think these characteristics affect the militancy of such workers and the possibilities to organize them into unions?
4. Karl Marx has been dead for well over a hundred years but his method of analysis continues to provide insights. What have been the main changes in the labour process since Marx, and

how do you think his way of thinking stands up to the test of time?

5. Take any job and trace how it has changed in skills required, training practices, and nature of supervision. Has the job been affected by changes in technology, in the social relations of production, and the recruitment of women into the paid labour force? What do you think the future is for the job you have in mind?

GLOSSARY

automation the use of computer-aided technology with predetermined patterns to set machines in motion, thus reducing direct human intervention in the continuous process of production

bureaucracy control exercised through rules, files, and a staff of officials organized by a hierarchy of command and offices

detailed division of labour the subdivision of the work process into its simplest parts so each task is routinely performed

de-skilling the separation of the conception of work from its execution, involving decreasingly qualified workers to perform it as tasks become routinized

domestic labour typically unpaid work performed in the household, most often by women, to reproduce workers both day-to-day and over generations

franchise is a contractual obligation between a franchiser and franchisee for the use of specific brands and techniques to organize sales; franchises are ways of controlling managerial labour by large corporations and tend to rely upon a part-time labour force

historical materialism an approach to the study of society that assumes the foundation for analysis is the way a society organizes the production of goods and services required for living, thus affecting the social relations people enter into

labour theory of value a commodity's worth for exchange depends on the amount of labour it contains and only labour adds value to goods

scientific management the practice of de-skilling workers by separating knowledge over the labour process and subjecting control over such information to the command of managers, thus facilitating a detailed division of labour

skill a complex combination of political, ideological, and technical factors including knowledge, experience, and ability that permit control to be exercised over training and work practices

BIBLIOGRAPHY

Armstrong, Hugh and Pat Armstrong

1984 *The Double Ghetto: Canadian Women and Their Segregated Work*, rev. ed. Toronto: McClelland and Stewart.

Blauner, Robert

1964 *Alienation and Freedom: The Factory Worker and His Industry*. Chicago: University of Chicago Press.

Braverman, Harry
1974 *Labor and Monopoly Capital: The Degradation of Work in the Twentieth Century*. New York: *Monthly Review*, 14.

Clegg, Stewart, Paul Boreham, and Geoff Dow
1986 *Class Politics and the Economy*. London: Routledge and Kegan Paul.

Clement, Wallace
1981 *Hardrock Mining: Industrial Relations and Technological Change at Inco*. Toronto: McClelland and Stewart

Cockburn, Cynthia
1985 "The Nature of Skill: The Case of the Printers." In Craig R. Littler (ed.) *The Experience of Work*. Aldershot: Gower.

——
1985 *Machinery of Dominance: Women, Men, and Technical Know-How*. London: Pluto Press.

Crompton, Rosemary and Stuart Reid
1982 "The Deskilling of Clerical Work." In *The Degredation of Work[3] Skill, Deskilling and the Labour Process*.

Edwards, Richard
1979 *Contested Terrain: The Transformation of the Workplace in the Twentieth Century*. New York: Basic.

The Financial Post
1986 "Franchising: Special Report." 23 August: 11.

Fox, Bonnie, ed.
1980 *Hidden in the Household: Women's Domestic Labour Under Capitalism*. Toronto: The Women's Press.

Friedman, Andrew
1977 *Industry and Labour: Class Struggle at Work and Monopoly Capitalism*. London: Macmillan.

Gannagé, Charlene
1986 *Double Day, Double Bind: Women Garment Workers*. Toronto: The Women's Press.

The Globe and Mail
1983 21 November: B13

——
1985 20 November: B6

——
1986 "Report on Franchising." 24 July: B23

——
1987 20 January: C3.

——
1987 "Report on Careers." 23 March: B15.

Goranzon, Bo, et al. (eds.)
1982 *Job Design and Automation in Sweden: Skills and Automation*. Stockholm: Arbetslivscentrum.

Littler, Craig
1987 *The Development of the Labour Process in Capitalist Societies: A Comparative Study of the Transformation of Work Organization in Britain, Japan and the U.S.A.* London: Heinemann.

Littler, Craig R. and Graeme Salaman
1984 *Class at Work: The Design, Allocation and Control of Jobs*. London: Batsford.

——
1986 "Mechanization, Feminization and Managerial Control in the Early 20th Century Canadian Office." In Craig Heron and Robert Storey (eds.) *On the Job: Confronting the Labour Process in Canada*. Montreal: McGill–Queen's University Press.

Lowe, Graham
1987 "Class, Jobs and Gender in the Canadian Office." *Labour/Le Travailleur* 10 (Autumn).

Luxton, Meg
1980 *More Than a Labour of Love: Three Generations of Women's Work in the Home*. Toronto: The Women's Press.

Luxton, Meg and Harriet Rosenberg
1986 *Through the Kitchen Window: The Politics of Home and Family*. Toronto: Garamond Press.

——
1967 *Capital: A Critical Analysis of Capitalist Production*, Volume 1. New York: International. Original publication 1987.

Marx, Karl
1970 *A Contribution to the Critique of Political Economy*. Moscow: Progress. Original publication 1859.

——
1973 *Grundrisse: Introduction to the Critique of Political Economy*.

Harmondsworth: Penguin. Original publication 1857.

Noble, David
1978 "Social Choice and Machine Design: The Case of Automatically Controlled Machine Tools, and a Challenge for Labour." In *Politics and Society*, 8, 3/4:315.

Ontario Ministry of Industry, Trade and Technology
1985 "Flexible Automation Equipment." Toronto: Queen's Printer for Ontario (November).

Radforth, Ian
1986 "Logging Pulpwood in Northern Ontario." In Craig Heron and Robert Storey (eds.) *On the Job: Confronting the Labour Process in Canada*. Montreal: McGill–Queen's University Press.

Reiter, Ester
1985 "Life in a Fast-Food Factory." In Craig Heron and Robert Storey (eds.) *On the Job: Confronting the Labour Process in Canada*. Montreal: McGill–Queen's University Press.

Rinehart, James
1975 *The Tyranny of Work*. Don Mills, Ont.: Longmans.

Statistics Canada
1985 *Women in Canada: A Statistical Report*. Ottawa: Supply and Services Canada, 55.

Steedman, Mercedes
1986 "Skill and Gender in the Canadian Clothing Industry, 1890–1940." In Craig Heron and Robert Storey (eds.) *On the Job: Confronting the Labour Process in Canada*. Montreal: McGill–Queen's University Press.

Strong-Boag, Veronica
1986 "Keeping House in God's Country: Canadian Women at Work in the Home." In Craig Heron and Robert Storey (eds.) *On the Job: Confronting the Labour Process in Canada*. Montreal: McGill–Queen's University Press.

Thompson, Paul
1983 *The Politics of Work: An Introduction to Debates on the Labour Process*. London: Macmillan.

Toronto Star
1987 1 February: H4

Weber, Max
1946 "Bureaucracy." In H.H. Gerth and C.W. Mills, (eds.) *From Max Weber: Essays in Sociology*. New York: Oxford University Press.

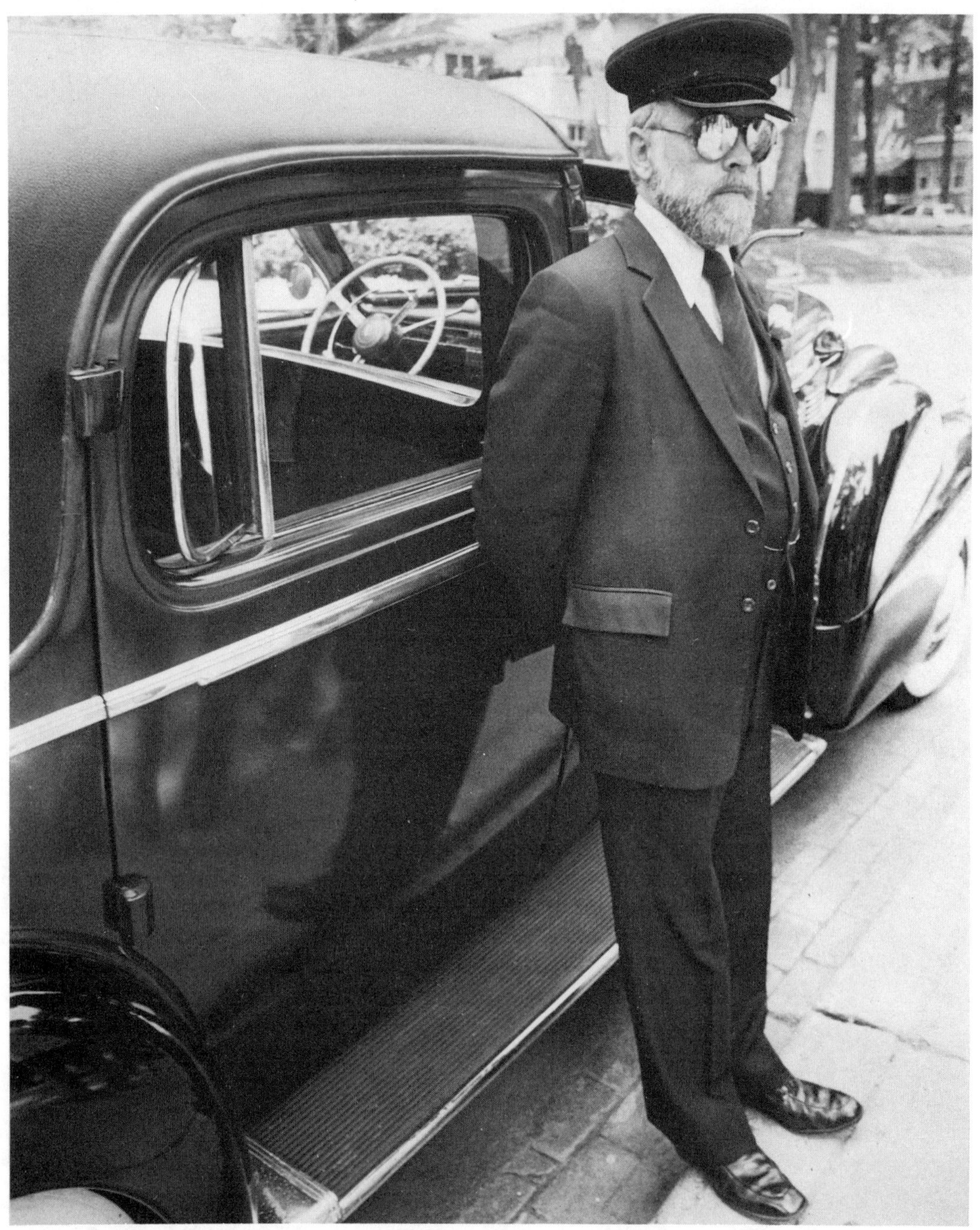

Some Canadians have chauffeurs; other Canadians cannot afford cars. *Courtesy of Dean Goodwin*

"One result of class divisions is a highly unequal distribution of income and wealth. One study shows that, in 1976, the lowest 10 percent of all family units . . . earned only 1.2 percent of all income, while the highest decile earned 26.9 percent of all income."

c h a p t e r s e v e n

Social Class and Economic Inequality

Michael Ornstein

INTRODUCTION

While expressions such as "**middle-class** tastes," "**working-class** community," and "upper-class school" are a part of our language, few Canadians could provide more than a vague description of the class structure. This ambivalence toward class is demonstrated by a national survey that found that, while only 43 percent of Canadians said they ever thought of themselves as belonging to a **social class**, 97 percent could choose which of five class categories best represented their own class position.

Social scientists are divided over how to define social classes. Following John Porter (1965:9ff), Forcese (1980:14) defines social classes as "aggregates of persons distinguished by inherited access to wealth or income, by power, and by prestige or life-style." Because wealth, income, and other measures of social class do not fall naturally into distinct categories, the "number of strata the social scientist distinguishes is arbitrary." Defined in this way, social classes are statistical categories, rather than identifiable groups in society.[1]

For Leo Johnson (1972:143) "class carries a precise definition which relates, not to the attributes of individuals, but to their external material relationships centred on those created by the productive process." In capitalist societies there are three major social classes because

> three fundamental relationships [to the means of production] exist: the **capitalist class**, or bourgeoisie, who own the means of production and purchase the **labour power** of others to operate it; the **petite bourgeoisie**, or independent commodity

producers, such as farmers and craftsmen, who both own and operate their means of production; and the proleteriat who do not own their means of production and therefore are required to sell their capacity to work—that is, their labour power—in the marketplace.

The theoretical framework of classical Marxism leaves a number of major issues unresolved in the analysis of contemporary class structure. Even determining the class position of top-level executives requires some extension of traditional class theory, since few executives of large corporations actually own their "means of production" and, like other employees, they can be fired by the corporations' owners.[2]

Rather than attempting to review the enormous theoretical and empirical literature on social class, we will address only the theoretical issues critical to the empirical analysis of the contemporary Canadian class structure. This analysis employs one of a variety of possible Marxist perspectives which conceptualize the class structure as the social expression of a capitalist economic system. Tied to class inequality are political structures that disproportionately empower the economically dominant class and a political ideology that legitimates inequality. In other words, the class structure creates and its continuation is dependent on the organization of capitalit *society*, whose institutions reflect the economic domination of capitalism. While not reducible to class differences, in capitalist society gender, racial, ethnic, and regional inequalities are to a major extent expressed in class terms. The analysis of social classes in this chapter also differs from some non-Marxist and some Marxist (particularly those in the tradition of E.P. Thompson) approaches in defining class "objectively," rather than on the basis of individuals' perceptions of their class positions or the collective action of groups.

WHY STUDY SOCIAL CLASSES?

There is a brief answer to why it is worth studying social classes, even if many Canadians do not believe classes exist, and those who do cannot agree on *which* classes exist. First, the class structure tells us a great deal about the patterns of inequality in Canadian society, about who gets what in a society, and about *why* inequalities exist. Second, an understanding of the class structure is necessary in analyzing other forms of inequality, the political structures and ideology that perpetuate inequality, and the forces that change society.

THEORETICAL PRELIMINARIES

Marxist analysis of social class begins with the "pure" form of capitalist production and the corresponding two-class system: capitalists own the factories and tools, purchase the raw materials, hire and supervise workers, and sell the commodities produced; workers sell their labour power in return for wages. While even in the early stages of capitalism, this two-class model was oversimplified, just how it should be extended to deal with contemporary capitalist societies is the subject of extensive debate.

An initial problem involves two sectors of the economy—finance and commerce—in which no commodities or services are produced,[3] although workers in these industries are paid wages for their labour power,[4] which in turn produces profits for capitalists. Because workers in the financial and commercial sectors produce no value or surplus value,[5] the question is whether they are part of the working class, part of a "middle" class, or whether they constitute a second, separate working class. The analysis below combines productive and unproductive workers in the same categories on the grounds that differences between industries may modify but do not fundamentally alter the conflicting interests of capital and labour.

In this chapter, manual and nonmanual workers are considered as separate "fractions" of the working class, because there are long-standing social and cultural differences between these groups (Giddens, 1973). Since the distinction between them is not economic, traditional Marxist theory does not differentiate manual and nonmanual workers.[6] Marxist theory is not explicit regarding divisions *within* classes, with the exception of the "labour aristocracy," who are defined as privileged workers whose political views are often more conservative than the views of other members of the working class (Bottomore, 1983:265).

Of course, in contemporary capitalist societies, commodities and services are produced by governments as well as by private corporations in the form of social programs and production by Crown corporations. Like workers in the financial and commercial sectors, government employees work for wages, but do not produce commodities (except in some Crown corporations); but unlike employees of private businesses, the labour of government employees does not directly profit capitalists. In this chapter, state employees and managers are not distinguished from their private-sector counterparts for the following reasons. Just as the emergence of large-scale, capitalist factory production in the late eighteenth century led to the growth of financial and commercial capital—and, in consequence, the employment of workers in those industries—the development of corporate capitalism in the twentieth century placed demands on the state that led to the creation of large government bureaucracies and state enterprises. Government and private-sector employees are included in the same class categories because the same evolution of the capitalist economic system and society is responsible for the creation of the class positions in both sectors of the economy. One indication of the breakdown of the traditional barriers between government and private-sector employees is the unionization of government employees. Managers and employees of Crown corporations, which produce and sell goods, are also not distinguished from their private-sector counterparts.

Contemporary capitalism has developed management hierarchies that fill a widening gap—in income and control of the work process—between capitalists and workers. The initial bipolarity of capitalist class structure, in which labourers worked under the immediate supervision by capitalists, appears to give way to a complex and graduated hierarchy. Simultaneously, the growth of joint stock companies, development of professional management training, and increased foreign ownership foster a division of labour between the owners of a corporation and its managers. The day-to-day affairs, and potentially the general direction of corporations, falls to managers who do not own the corporations.

These organizational changes suggest that the gradual displacement of "entrepreneurial" capitalism by "corporate" capitalism creates a new class consisting of people with positions in the middle of the corporate hierarchy. The levels of supervisors, managers, and some technical workers are obviously distributed along a continuum between the working and capitalist classes. But is it possible to define a distinctive middle class whose interests are intermediate between those of capital and labour, or is there some dividing point of income and authority that determines which individuals are polarized towards the working class and which towards the capitalist class? Analysis of the class position of intermediate-level supervisors and managers and of the relationship between ownership and control of large corporations is, at least partly, an empirical question. We can imagine that different historical circumstances would result in different polarizations of supervisory workers.

A final theoretical point concerns the self-employed and owners of small businesses who produce commodities and services for sale by themselves or with a few family members or employees.[7] This class, whose members are neither employees nor significant employers, is called the "petite bourgeoisie." While much reduced from the time when most agricultural and industrial production was carried out by individuals and families, substantial numbers of petit bourgeois producers remain in some industries (Ornstein, 1983; Cuneo, 1984).

Potentially, each departure from the two-class model of pure capitalist production creates a "middle"-class position which is intermediate between and combines characteristics of the capitalist and working classes. For example, like workers, supervisors are paid wages and generally enjoy little job autonomy, but supervisors perform the inherently capitalist function of making sure their subordinates work at a pace and in a manner that allows the resulting commodities to be sold at a profit. Similarly, even though public school teachers do not produce profits, like workers, most elementary and secondary school teachers are paid for their time and have little control over what they do. A major focus of our analysis must be on the large number of workers whose positions are intermediary between capital and labour.

THE CLASS STRUCTURE OF CONTEMPORARY CANADA

Table 1 describes a class structure in which the hegemony of corporate capitalism is well established. Excluding the unemployed, employers constitute just 2.7 percent of the Canadian labour force, compared to the 90.0 percent who are employees. Outside of agriculture, there are an average of 33.3 employees for each private-sector employer (in agriculture the average is 3 employees per employer). Just 6.4 percent of the labour force are "own account" workers, that is, workers who employ no one else, and 0.9 percent work without pay in family businesses. Governments supply 17.7 percent of the existing jobs.[8]

These official statistics can only be roughly translated into class terms. For example, not all the 2.7 percent of the employed labour force classified as employers are members of the capitalist class. Because the businesses they own are so small that the proprietor does much of the actual labour, some employers are in the petite bourgeoisie. Conversely, "employees" who are high-level managers occupy a class position much closer to the capitalist class than to the working class. Since unemployed people are seeking work for pay, they are not potentially employers, but rather a group more closely linked to employed workers. Table 1 also shows that women are disadvantaged in the class structure: women constitute 78.8 percent of unpaid family workers, but only 19.4 percent of employers.

Marxists have traditionally defined the class structure on the basis of the employed labour force, ignoring other groups, such as homemakers, students, retired people, and the disabled. Together, these nonlabour force participants make up 70 percent of the adult population. Each group has a different relationship to the class structure. To some extent, not-employed persons share the class position of employed family member(s), if there is one; the class position of students may be

Table 1

DISTRIBUTION OF THE LABOUR FORCE, ANNUAL AVERAGE, 1986

	Employed Labour Force			Employed and Unemployed Labour Force	All Adults	Percent Women		
	Outside Agriculture	In Agriculture	Total			Outside Agriculture	In Agriculture	Total
Employers	2.2	0.5	2.7	2.5	2.0	20.7	14.3	19.4
Own account workers	4.9	1.5	6.4	6.1	4.1	43.1	12.9	35.8
Unpaid family workers	0.3	0.6	0.9	0.8	0.5	86.7	75.4	78.8
Employees								
private sector	70.8	1.5	72.3			43.2	35.5	43.1
government	17.7	0.0	17.7					
Total	88.5	1.5	90.0	89.8	53.1			
Officially unemployed				9.6	5.2			44.2
Adults not in the force					35.1			70.0
Total	95.9	4.2	100.0	100.0	100.0			

Source: The Labour Force, December 1986, various pages. Reprinted with permission of Supply and Services Canada.

defined in terms of classes of their families of origin and/or their eventual class destinations; retired and some disabled people have class affiliations dating to when they were employed; and so on.

Still, it is important not to exaggerate the impact of social class on nonlabour force participants. The positions of female homemakers with employed husbands, for example, cannot be understood solely in relation to the social classes of their husbands. And the student activism of the 1960s cannot be easily explained in terms of the class origins or occupational aspirations of students. Similarly, the increasing political power of the aged and consequent changes in pension and other social legislation reflect a common experience that is not reducible to their class affiliations. Of course, large income differences within the aged population reflect their previous class positions.

The Canadian Capitalist Class

This analysis of the Canadian capitalist class begins with a discussion of the degree of concentration in Canadian business, foreign ownership, and regional inequality. Following this, we discuss the ownership and control of large corporations and the class and ethnic backgrounds of prominent capitalists in order to assess the "managerialist" argument that corporate capitalism has seen a shift of power from individual capitalists to professional managers, and to determine the extent to which control of major corporations is inherited. Last, we examine how the capitalist class organizes to further its interests over the interests of other classes.

Corporate Concentration, Foreign Ownership, and Regional Inequality

There is an extraordinary degree of corporate concentration in Canada. The largest twenty-five nonfinancial enterprises in Canada, which make up less than one one-hundredth of 1 percent of all enterprises, account for 23.5 percent of the sales, 34.0 percent of all assets, 33.1 percent of all equity, and 32.6 percent of all profits of Canadian corporations![9] The largest one hundred enterprises account for more than half the entire assets, equity, and profits of all corporations. This concentration reflects both the large size of the top-ranked corporations and the high degree of intercorporate ownership—the twenty-five largest enterprises control an average of twenty-three corporations each. In the financial sector, concentration is even greater. The five largest banks control more than half the assets of all financial institutions.

There is also a remarkably high degree of foreign ownership in Canada, which is disproportionately concentrated in the largest and most profitable sectors of Canadian capitalism.[10] Forty-four of the largest one hundred nonfinancial enterprises, fifty-two of the next largest one hundred enterprises, and 144 of the next three hundred are foreign-controlled. In 1983, foreign-controlled enterprises accounted for 29.6 percent of the sales, 24.3 percent of their assets, 32.9 percent of their equity, and 43.6 percent of the profits of all nonfinancial corporations. Foreign-owned corporations account for 44 percent of the sales of the largest one thousand nonfinancial enterprises, but only for 7.5 percent of the sales of enterprises smaller than the one-thousandth largest.

Corporate ownership also has a strong regional bias. Toronto is home to the head offices of thirty-nine of the largest 100, and 171 of the largest 500 Canadian nonfinancial corporations. An additional eleven of the top one hundred and eighty-six of the top 500 corporations have head offices in other parts of southern Ontario. The second largest concentration is in Montreal, which has eighty head offices of

Table 2

CHARACTERISTICS OF LEADING ENTERPRISES OUTSIDE THE FINANCIAL SECTOR, 1983*

Enterprise Characteristic	Size of Enterprise							
	Top 25	*26th to 50th*	*51st to 100th*	*101st to 200th*	*201st to 500th*	*501st to 1000th*	*All Smaller*	*Total*
Number of Enterprises								
Foreign-controlled	9	11	24	52	144	218	2,941	3,399
Canadian-private	12	13	22	45	154	281	387,238	387,765
Government	4	1	4	3	2	1	33	48
Total	25	25	50	100	300	500	390,212	381,212
Number of Corporations								
Foreign-controlled	133	80	267	271	490	508	3,490	5,239
Canadian-private	323	240	189	324	666	660	390,100	392,502
Government	129	14	23	17	4	4	33	224
Total	585	334	479	612	1,160	1,172	393,623	397,965
Financial Statistics								
			(mean, in $1,000,000)					
Sales	6,171.5	2,009.6	1,070.2	459.3	187.6	70.0	0.7	1.7
Assets	8,216.2	2,110.4	1,133.3	457.2	169.0	47.6	0.4	1.5
Equity	2,750.6	930.8	417.9	176.4	65.0	17.2	0.13	0.5
Profits	431.2	153.8	54.0	23.0	11.5	2.8	0.022	0.08
Taxable income	212.9	126.6	43.0	16.8	8.5	2.8	0.028	0.07
			(percent of total)					
Sales	23.5	7.6	8.1	7.0	8.6	5.3	39.9	100.0
Assets	34.0	8.8	9.4	7.6	8.4	3.9	27.9	100.0
Equity	33.1	11.2	10.0	8.5	9.4	4.1	23.7	100.0
Profits	32.6	11.7	8.1	7.0	10.4	4.3	25.9	100.0
Taxable income	19.7	11.7	7.9	6.3	9.4	5.2	39.8	100.0

Source: Corporations and Labour Unions Returns Act Report for 1983, Part I—Corporations: 130–1. CS61–210–1984. Reprinted with permission of Supply and Services Canada.

ON THE CONCENTRATION OF ECONOMIC POWER

Further evidence of the concentration of economic power comes from a 1977 Statistics Canada survey of families' assets and debts. This survey showed the top 2 percent of all families owned more than half of all the equity in business (including farms and professional interests) and just less than half of all stocks. The top 5 percent of families owned more than three-quarters of all equity in business and two-thirds of stocks. At the top of distribution of wealth and income are a few extraordinarily wealthy families. Shortell (1987) identifies fifty families with fortunes of $100 million or more, thirty-four with fortunes of $200 million or more, thirteen with fortunes of $500 million or more, and seven with $1 billion fortunes. All of these families own large corporations.

Reinforcing the arguments about the prevalence of family ownership is the *Financial Post's* listing of nine major groups of corporations under common ownership and control. Only two of the groups, the ones centred around Bell Canada and Canadian Pacific, are *not* family controlled. The remaining seven groups are controlled by Conrad Black, the "CEMP," Montreal-based branch of the Bronfman family, the "EDPER," Toronto-based branch of the Bronfman family, Hal Jackman, the Reichmann brothers, Paul Desmarais, the Thomson family, and the Weston family. Interestingly, the two nonfamily groups originated in government-licensed telephone and railway monopolies. In addition to the seven family-controlled groups of corporations, many individual corporations — including the Montreal-based Steinberg's grocery chain, Canadian Tire, and Eaton's department stores — are controlled by families or individual owners.

top 500 corporations (another sixteen are located elsewhere in Quebec). There are only three other major centres: Calgary has fifty-five head offices (almost entirely in the oil and gas industry); Vancouver has thirty-five; and Winnipeg has seventeen. Just one of the top 100 and seventeen of the top 500 corporations have head offices in Atlantic Canada.

The regional inequality reflected in this distribution of head offices is the result of political and social factors. While the initial development of transportation centres at strategic sites, of processing facilities near sources of raw materials and of manufacturing plants near sources of labour and/or markets was economically motivated, the present spatial distribution of head offices reflects political choices by the corporations' managements. These choices are affected by governments which pass laws, give subsidies, and provide infrastructures to attract corporations to some cities and regions and not others. In turn, head offices give some cities disproportional wealth and political influence. Not only do the highly paid executives and the planning, administrative and accounting staffs of corporate head offices add to the tax base and income of a city, but their demands for legal and other professional and technical services stimulate the local economy. The concentration of head offices in some cities affects their class structures and political climates.

Control of the Largest Corporations

According to the managerialist viewpoint of Berle and Means (1932), corporations have increasingly come under the control of managers, who replace the capitalist entrepreneurs who founded them. Correlated with and partly responsible for this shift in corporate control, stock ownership is said to have grown progressively more diffused through the population. The resulting displacement of individual and family owners by numerous, small stockholders decreases the percentage of a corporation's shares needed to exercise control to as little as 5 or 10 percent of the total, and correspondingly increases managerial power.

The managerialist arguments assume corporate ownership has become diffused among numerous stockholders. As Table 3 shows, however, no more than nine of the largest one hundred Canadian corporations are management controlled.[11] For the remaining ninety-one, an individual, family, or other corporation owns a majority or a clearly controlling block of stock. For lower ranked corporations, management control is even more unusual. The shares of only two of the corporations ranked between 101 and 200 and of seven of the corporations ranked between 201 and 500 in Canada are potentially management controlled. In total, no more than eighteen of the largest five hundred nonfinancial corporations are management controlled!

In the financial sector, the situation is different. Federal legislation prevents any single holding of more than 10 percent of the shares of a Canadian-owned bank and so effectively guarantees management control. It is possible to identify a controlling interest in every one of the larger trust companies, and a number are controlled by banks.[12]

Even eliminating the foreign-controlled and Crown corporations, less than 10 percent of the large corporations could plausibly be management controlled. Extending the analysis beyond the five

Table 3

CONTROL OF THE LARGEST CANADIAN CORPORATIONS, AS LISTED BY THE FINANCIAL POST

	Form of Control					
Sector and Size of Corporations	*Foreign*	*Individual(s) and/or Family*	*Government*	*Wide Distribution*	*Another Canadian Corporation*	*Not Given*
All nonfinancial corporations						
Largest 50	13	23	7	7	—	0
51st to 100th largest	22	25	1	2	—	0
101st to 200th largest	45	42	11	2	—	0
201st to 300th largest	50	40	4	5	—	1
301st to 400th largest	40	51	5	2	—	2
401st to 500th largest	35	59	4	0	—	2
Financial institutions						
Largest 5	0	0	0	5	0	0
6th to 10th largest	0	0	1	1	3	0
11th to 50th largest	13	3	6	1	20	0
51st to 100th largest	29	2	1	0	18	0

*Sales for nonfinancial corporations, assets for financial institutions and life insurers.

Source: The Financial Post 500, Summer 1986.

hundred largest corporations would not change the results, since smaller corporations are less likely than large ones to be publicly traded and are more likely to be under individual and/or family control.

Two factors explain the continuing influence of family capitalism in Canada. First, changes in the structure of the economy over the past decade, and particularly the rapid growth of some new industries, have allowed formerly smaller corporations to rise into the top ranks of business. These small corporations were in industries, such as food merchandising and real estate development, which have only recently become highly concentrated and in which there has been little foreign ownership, and family control remains common. Second, the wave of takeovers of the late 1970s and early 1980s allowed newcomers to the top ranks of corporations to increase their holdings rapidly. As Zeitlin's (1974) study of the large American corporations shows, there is nothing uniquely Canadian about this high degree of family control of large corporations.

Two major studies by Porter (1965) and Clement (1975) of the Canadian "corporate elite"—defined as the directors of the "dominant" Canadian corporations — as of 1951 and 1972 demonstrate that its members are disproportionately recruited from a narrow, privileged layer of society. Remarkably, there was a trend towards *less* egalitarian elite recruitment in the twenty-one years between these studies. Clement

Table 4
INDIVIDUAL CHARACTERISTIC BY CLASS CATEGORY

	Class Category						
Individual Characteristic	*Capitalists*	*Small Employers*	*Petite Bourgeoisie*	*Managers and technocrats*	*Supervisors*	*Semi-autonomous employees*	*Workers*
Percent of all employed	2.8	3.5	11.8	7.0	10.9	8.1	55.9
Percent of employees	—	—	—	8.6	13.4	9.9	68.7
Percent women	23	31	27	25	38	24	49
Percent manual workers	2	34	52	0	35	35	47
Education							
Average yrs. of attainment	14.7	12.5	11.1	14.2	12.9	14.4	11.9
Percent highschool grads	80	59	49	89	70	82	50
Percent university grads	42	21	7	29	15	30	9
Age, average years	44	40	47	42	39	37	36
Rate of pay							
Average	40.3	27.8	20.8	26.2	20.6	22.9	15.4
Average adjusted for sex, education and age	35.4	26.9	20.3	22.5	19.6	19.3	16.8
Family income							
Average	63.7	53.5	32.5	39.3	33.1	40.3	29.9
Average adjusted for sex, education and age	51.0	44.9	28.9	29.8	25.8	30.1	24.3
Home ownership (percent)	87	84	84	73	66	73	66

Source: 1981 national sample survey of the Institute for Social Research, York University.

(1975:192) found 59 percent of the Canadian-born members of the corporate elite came from "upper-class" families and 35 percent came from "middle-class" families, while only 6 percent came from working-class families. The comparable, figures from Porter (1965:292) are 50, 32, and 18 percent.[13]

A more recent study by Ornstein and Stevenson (1984) suggests that access to the capitalist class has become less exclusive in recent years: in 1981 only 39 percent of the fathers of the chief executives of the largest Canadian corporations owned businesses, and only about 15 percent owned businesses with ten or more employees. Furthermore, only 37 percent of the executives' fathers were in professional or managerial occupations. There is also evidence of increased ethnic diversity among corporate elites: for 1951 Porter reported that 92 percent of the corporate elites were of British descent and 7 percent were French — leaving only 1 percent of other backgrounds; by 1972, Clement found that the proportions were 86.2 percent British, 8.4 percent French, and 5.4 percent "other"; and Ornstein and Stevenson's 1981 sample was only 65 percent British, 9 percent French, and 26 percent of other ethnicities.

Shortell's (1987) list of the fifty greatest fortunes includes eight Jewish families (including the Reichmann family, and the two Bronfman groups, ranked second, third, and ninth in the list) and at least five families that are not British, French, or Jewish. A similar analysis of the ethnic backgrounds of wealthy families by Hunter (1986: 157) indicates that, of the 184 families with wealth of $20 million or more in 1975, 55 percent were English, 7 percent were French, and 38 percent had other origins.

While there are very large class differentials in access to the highest levels of the capitalist class, there is also recruitment from other social classes. Mobility into the highest levels of the Canadian capitalist class also appears to have increased in the last decade. More striking than the change in class backgrounds has been a remarkable increase in the fortunes of families who are of neither English nor French ethnicity, although there remains a continuing underrepresentation of French families.

A Class-Conscious Capitalist Class?

Several organizations help secure the interests of the capitalist class. At the lower level, numerous organizations — over one hundred in agriculture and over four hundred outside agriculture, according to Coleman (1986:257) — pursue goals of individual industries. In representing these industries, however, these organizations are not particularly suited to achieving and representing a more general political consensus within business. Indeed, on specific issues, such as tariffs, different industries may have conflicting goals.

More effective for pursuing the general interests of capital, such as lowering corporate taxation and limiting government regulation of safety in the workplace and environmental pollution, are more broadly based organizations, including the various Chambers of Commerce, the Canadian Manufacturers' Association, and more recently formed organizations, including the Canadian Federation of Independent Business, the Canadian Organization of Small Business, the Business Council on National Issues, and the Fraser Institute. These newer organizations represent an effort by capital to respond to a perceived loss of influence and the rapid growth of state power between the mid-1960s and early 1970s. As Useem (1984) shows, this renewed effort by the Canadian capitalist class follows similar developments in the United States and Britain.

Also mobilizing capital are the overlapping memberships of the boards of directors of the largest Canadian corporations. Studies of these "interlocking" directorates by Carroll, Fox, and Ornstein (1982) and Carroll (1986) reveal a web of connections that unites the largest Canadian corporations into a single, large network, rather than into discrete (and therefore potentially competing) groups of corporations.[14] Ornstein (1986) also shows that this network extends outward from the corporations to the boards of major universities, hospitals, and cultural and charitable organizations. These noncorporate boards provide an additional setting for relationships between prominent business executives.

In discussing the capitalist class, we have avoided the adjectives "dominant" and "ruling," which are often substituted for or used to describe the Canadian capitalist class. Understanding just how it rules is a complex problem (Block, 1978; Ornstein and Stevenson, 1984), but we have some obvious clues. First, the extreme concentration of economic power in the hands of a few corporations offers enormous organizational advantages: relatively few people have to be organized, and those people command great resources. Second, not only does the capitalist class have the capacity to become organized, it *is* organized in formal organizations through interlocking directorates. Third, the concentration of the largest corporations in certain regions in the hands for foreign owners and in certain industries produces pervasive social inequalities and large differences in the power of various elements of capital to influence government.

A final point concerns the vulnerability of big capital. Short of using force, the power of a group as small as the owners and managers of the largest Canadian corporations must rest on alliances with other groups and the support of elaborate political institutions and the exercise of ideological hegemony over other classes. Not only is the support of the fractions of the capitalist class which owns and controls medium and small-size business critical, but a large proportion of the people outside the capitalist class must at least acquiesce to capitalist domination.

The Petite Bourgeoisie

The petite bourgeoisie make their living by selling commodities or services which they produce themselves or with the assistance of family members and/or a few employees. At the boundary between the capitalist class and the petite bourgeoisie, production by individuals, with or without assistance, gives way to production by employees under the supervision of the owner of the business. While it is difficult to specify the exact dividing point between these two classes, much of the production by the petite bourgeoisie actually involves "own account workers." As of March 1986, 6.4 percent of the employed labour force were own account workers. Because precise data on the size distribution of companies is unavailable, it is not certain how many of the 2.7 percent of the employed labour force who are classified as employers should also be counted into the petite bourgeoisie.

The petite bourgeoisie is differentiated into four major fractions: retail store proprietors and independent salespeople; farmers, fishermen, hunters, and other primary producers; professional groups,[15] including lawyers, physicians, dentists, and nurses; and craft producers (many in the construction industry). There are important differences between these fractions. In terms of income, the professionals stand out from all the other groups; the primary producers (who are largely farmers) face business conditions vastly unlike those experienced by retail proprietors or small-scale craft workers; self-employed workers in the construction industry encounter a unique combination of relatively dangerous working conditions, highly cyclical demand for their labour, and generally high levels of unemployment, but relatively high wages; and so on.

In principle, all sectors of the petite bourgeoisie are under threat from capitalist producers. Clearly, the state of technology and particularly the extent of economies of scale in an industry determine the magnitude of this threat and how it changes over time.[16] Two (not mutually exclusive) strategies are available to petit bourgeois producers in competition with capitalists: producers may form co-operatives, which offer economies of scale while preserving individual ownership; or they may seek to gain a monopoly on the right to supply a good or service, thus placing a political obstacle in the way of economic forces.

Corresponding to the variation in the business conditions faced, fractions of the petite bourgeoisie have pursued varied economic and political strategies with different levels of success (Ornstein, 1983; Cuneo, 1984). Professional groups have attempted to secure monopolistic control of their standards of practice to prevent other groups from encroaching on their work and to limit the number of new practitioners to ensure a high price for their services (and limit disruptive competition). Physicians, dentists, and lawyers have been especially successful in attaining these goals, although they face continuing threats of competition from paraprofessionals and an oversupply of personnel. Pharmacists, on the other hand, or at least the continuation of the pharmacy in the petite bourgeois form of individually owned stores, are under severe attack from chain stores.

While the rhetoric of their leaders emphasizes the independence of professional groups—as a corollary to the expert judgment that their practice is said to require—like other fractions of the petite bourgeoisie, professionals have become increasingly dependent on the state, which alone can grant them monopoly powers. The risk is that, in return for state protection, professional monopolies will increasingly face state control. In health care, for example, the provincial governments are increasingly tempted to challenge professional prerogatives to save money.

In primary production, state intervention dates back to government-granted monopolies in the fur trade. In agriculture, state regulation includes granting monopolies to marketing boards that market agricultural production internationally, regulation of transportation costs, provision of research and other support, as well as direct subsidies and preferential tax treatment. Of course, there are also substantial differences between the producers of different agricultural commodities (which in turn relate to whether production is for domestic markets or for international sale, regional differences, and differences between large and small farmers). Interestingly, Canadian farmers have so far faced relatively little direct competition from large capitalist producers, presumably because increasing the scale of production beyond what is possible on family farms will not appreciably lower production costs. But low farm prices and steadily increasing productivity have steadily increased the size of a farm required to support a family.

Because they face competition from larger enterprises, small producers, retail store owners, and independent salespeople are in a different position from professionals and from farmers who are protected by marketing boards. The relative ease with which new businesses can be started contributes to the competitive pressure on small businesses. And the large number of types of businesses and their scattered locations make it more difficult for these sectors of the petite bourgeoisie to join in pressing government for protection.

Construction and similar workers, who are for the most part own account workers, are also in a unique position. They are more similar to employed workers than to other members of the petite bourgeoisie. It is not surprising that merchant sailors, labourers, and other construction tradespeople are organized into trade unions rather than into business co-operatives.

The survival of the petite bourgeoisie in the era of corporate capitalism results from economic and political factors, not from the political pressure of a single party or organization. The agrarian social movements and political parties mobilized by the petite bourgeoisie were restricted to particular regions and to just one fraction of the petite bourgeoisie. While the concentration of farmers in certain regions gives farmers a continuing advantage in articulating their concerns as a group, the alliance of farmers with labour in the New Democratic Party shows the need for farmers to ally with the working class. In contrast, professional groups are more likely to seek influence in the traditional political parties than to make common cause with other factions of the petite bourgeoisie.[17] Generally, more privileged fractions of the petite bourgeoisie are polarized toward the capitalist class and less-privileged fractions are polarized towards the working class.

The Working and Middle Classes

Ninety percent of all employed Canadians neither own nor manage the business or organization that employs them. The critical question is whether these workers constitute two or more separate social classes or whether they make up a single, large, if heterogeneous, class, potentially with two or more "fractions." Some argue that there is only a small, privileged "professional-managerial class" between capital and labour, while others think that capitalist development produces a "new middle class" that is much larger than the working class.

These questions about class structure are as much the subject of debate among Marxists (Walker, 1980) as between Marxists and non-Marxists. While agreeing that

CANADA AND TEN NATIONS COMPARED

Table 9 on page 213 presents a broader comparison of nations drawn from the *Year Book of Labour Statistics*, but is limited to information about occupations and industries, so it is necessary to make inferences about social class composition. While national differences may arise from international differences in the occupational categories, these data confirm the findings of Black and Myles. Canada and the United States with, respectively, 10.3 and 10.6 percent of all workers in the "administrative and managerial" category stand out from all other nations. Besides Australia, with 6.7 percent of the workforce in these categories, no other nation has more than 4 percent of its employed labour force in the administrative and managerial category. Canada's class structure comes closer to the American one than to the class structures of the other nations included in this table.

occupation alone cannot be equated with class, some Marxist class theorists use occupation as a class criterion — focusing particularly on occupations whose content cannot be separated from class relations. For example, Poulantzas (1975) and Carchedi (1975a, b) argue that because they work in occupations that perpetuate capitalist class ideology and enforce property rights, teachers, guards, and the police are outside the working class. Whether or not workers in these occupations are closely supervised or are paid wages by a profit-making capitalist—all traditionally understood as reflecting class position — is no longer relevant to determining their class positions. Poulantzas (1974) further restricts the working class to include only manual workers without *any* supervisory authority who produce material commodities for private firms.[18]

Wright's (1976) alternative theory[19] builds on the traditional Marxist concern with the social relations of production, and develops a class typology which allows for separation of the various elements combined in the person of the traditional capitalist. Intermediate between the capitalist and working classes are what Wright terms "contradictory locations," which combine prerogatives of the traditional capitalist, such as control over subordinates, with aspects of the working class, such as close supervision by higher managers and no control over capital or the decisions of what and how to produce for the market.

Finally, Gagliani (1981) and Lindsey (1980) distinguish *two* working classes, one being the traditional working class, whose labour is "productive" (in terms of Marxist value theory). The second working class is made up of employees in commerce and finance who do not produce commodities, but are involved in their "circulation." This separates a predominantly male working class in the "sphere of production" from a predominantly female working class in the "sphere of circulation."

A second element of the debate over the class composition of capitalist societies involves an assessment of the relative strength of two opposing trends. On one side is Braverman's (1974) view that advanced capitalism results in mass "de-skilling," as capitalists use technological advances to reduce the skill requirements of jobs. This de-skilling is said to result in "proletarianization," as declining wages and the decreased quality of work life create an increasingly large, poor, and regimented working class. Weakening and potentially reversing the proletarianization is the tendency for the most proletarianized occupations to be displaced by technology altogether, and for technological changes to produce new, skilled occupations (Derber, 1982).

A third question concerns the division, if any, between manual and mental labour. Giddens (1973 and esp. 1980: 303), Poulantzas (1975), Sohn-Rethel (1978) and Cottrell (1984) see a significant cleavage between mental and manual workers, although they differ over whether it results from the nature of the work, from differences in the working conditions, or from broader social differences. Braverman (1974), Mallet (1975), MacKenzie (1982), and Abercrombie and Urry (1983) take the opposite view that white-collar work is being "proletarianized" as practices from the industrial workplace are applied in offices.

The following empirical discussion follows Wright's approach. In interpreting the data, we make an effort to distinguish qualitative from quantitative differences. At a trivial level, one can argue that there are many different classes — each distinguishable statistically from the others in income, amount of work time devoted to different activities, and so on. Boundaries between classes and class fractions, however, should be significant enough to reflect qualitatively different interests.

Social Relations of Production

In an economy increasingly dominated by large, multi-levelled business and government organizations, each employee's class position involves two *independent* aspects of control of the workplace: control over subordinate employees, and control over her or his own work. While the owners of small businesses control their employees and their own work, supervisors who act as the front line of management in large corporations and state agencies may be as subject to authority as strict as they themselves impose on lower-level workers. Furthermore, some employees in some occupations, such as machinists, electricians, and university professors, can exert considerable control over their own work process, although they have no supervisory authority.

Wright's (1976) typology of class locations is thus based on the intersection of control over one's own work and control over the work of subordinates. Employees are divided into four groups: *workers*, who neither control their own work process (i.e., the nature and pace of their work are strongly regulated) nor control the work process of others (i.e., they have no supervisory authority); *semi-autonomous employees*, whose jobs give them a fair degree of control of their own work, but no control over other workers; *supervisors*, who control the work process of other workers but are themselves controlled by superiors; and *managers*, who control both their own work process and the work process of others. In Wright's view, the working class includes only the first four groups. Semi-autonomous employees, supervisors, and managers occupy "contradictory locations" situated *between* the three major classes of contemporary capitalism, the capitalist class, working class, and petite bourgeoisie. In this discussion, a fifth group whom Wright calls "*technocrats,*" and who plan and conduct research for management and also participate in management, are included with the managers.

This conceptual scheme raises problems. In a 1981 national survey, a startling 47 percent of all employees reported they did some supervising and 67 percent said they received supervision *less* often than two or three times a week. Only 16 percent reported the pace of their work was regulated by the speed of equipment and 24 percent were required to meet production quotas. These figures exaggerate both the degree of supervisory authority and work autonomy in the Canadian workplace, because they distinguish supervision involving the exercise of authority from work co-ordination and because no account is taken of the occupational *content* of jobs — the exercise of job autonomy involves more than the relative freedom from close supervision — the job being done must allow independent decision making. For example, while a telephone receptionist might rarely see her or his supervisor, receptionists exercise no significant control over what they do.

These complexities leave room for disagreement over how the theoretical definitions of class categories are applied. Besides measures of control over subordinates and the work process, the implementation of these class criteria requires that a boundary be established between co-ordination and supervision and between jobs that provide employees significant autonomy and jobs that do not. In the following discussion, Black and Myles's research implements a class typology identical to Wright's, while Ornstein's analysis uses his own interpretation.

On the basis of a 1982 survey, Black and Myles estimated that 17 percent of all

Table 5

VARIOUS ASPECTS OF WORK BY CLASS CATEGORY AND MANUAL/NONMANUAL DIVISION

	Class Category						
	Managers and techno-crats	*Supervisors*		*Semi-autonomous Employees*		*Workers*	
Individual Characteristic		*Nonmanual*	*Manual*	*Nonmanual*	*Manual*	*Nonmanual*	*Manual*
Percent of employees	8.5	8.7	4.7	6.4	3.5	36.7	31.5
Percent women	25	55	7	26	20	73	21
Education							
Percent highschool grads	79	79	53	90	68	72	41
Percent university grads	29	20	5	46	2	14	2
Percent experiencing any unemployment in past two years	15	22	11	12	13	28	31
Percent experiencing any layoff in past two years	4	3	9	2	14	10	25
Average rate of pay ($1,000/yr)	26	20	22	25	19	14	17
Required to produce a quota at work (percent)	15	19	35	13	23	18	34
Able to leave work to do an errand anytime (percent)	83	55	57	79	57	40	30
Supervised frequently (percent)	8	15	28	4	9	21	45

Source: 1981 national sample survey of the Institute for Social Research, York University.

employees were managers (or close advisors to managers), 12 percent were supervisors, 19 percent were semi-autonomous employees, and 52 percent were "workers." Using different criteria, Ornstein identifies 9 percent managers, 13 percent supervisors, 10 percent semi-autonomous employees, and 68 percent workers.[20] In neither scheme do the majority of the workers, who neither supervise others nor enjoy significant job autonomy, work at the kinds of manual factory jobs traditionally thought of as "working class."

Giddens (1973) uses the term "class structuration" to refer to differences in the social composition, social background, income, and lifestyles of classes and class fractions described in Table 5. Women are clearly disadvantaged in the class structure: they make up 49 percent of all workers, 38 percent of all supervisors, 31 percent of the small employers, and about 25 percent of the other class categories.[21] In other respects, the differences between these categories are only moderately large. The mean level of educational attainment, for example, ranges from 11.9 years for workers to 14.4 years for semi-autonomous employees. The age differences are quite small; the means range between thirty-six and forty-two years, which suggests individuals will not likely progress through the four categories over their lifetimes.

Most important, the range of incomes is limited. Average pay was $15,400 per year (in 1981) for workers, $20,600 for supervisors, $22,900 for semi-autonomous employees, and $26,200 for managers and technocrats. If class position helps determine wages, there should be large wage differences *after* accounting for additional factors such as sex, education, and age, which are known to affect wages. Table 5, however, indicates just the opposite: removing the effects of sex, education, and age (using the statistical technique of multiple regression) narrows the difference between the highest and lowest paid groups — the managers and workers — from $10,800 to only $5,700. Further analysis of the mean levels of *family* income (i.e., the combined income of all the members of a household) of these four class fractions reinforces these arguments. The mean household income levels range only from $29,900 per year for the working class to $39,300 per year for the managers. The rates of home ownership for the four categories vary only between 66 percent and 73 percent.

Comparing social backgrounds of the four groups (shown in Table 6) also reveals relatively small differences in parents' levels of education and fathers' class positions. Forty-six percent of the managers and technocrats came from working-class backgrounds, compared to 43 percent of supervisors, 36 percent of semi-autonomous employees, and 50 percent of workers.

Table 5 shows the results of dividing the supervisors, semi-autonomous employees, and workers (but not managers who, by definition, are considered nonmanual workers) into manual and nonmanual groups. Important differences between manual and nonmanual workers overlap and are, in some cases, larger than the differences between the class categories. These differences are a function of the particular class category involved.

Manual workers experience harsher working conditions than nonmanual workers, are more closely supervised (45 percent are checked by supervisors at least once a day compared to 20 percent of nonmanual workers), are more likely to face work quotas each day (34 versus 18 percent); are less likely to be able to leave work for errands; and are more than twice as likely to have been laid off in the previous two years (25 versus 10 percent). Only 41 percent of manual workers are

Table 6
SOCIAL BACKGROUND BY CLASS CATEGORIES

	Class Category						
Background Characteristic	*Capital-ists*	*Small Employ-ers*	*Petite Bourg-eoisie*	*Managers and techno-crats*	*Super-visors*	*Semi-auton-omous employ-ees*	*Workers*
Mother's education							
Percent highschool grads	44	34	25	27	33	36	27
Percent university grads	8	11	3	6	4	7	3
Father's education							
Percent highschool grads	52	31	18	35	30	31	26
Percent university grads	18	11	5	5	9	15	6
Father's social class				*(percentage distribution)*			
Capitalists	2	1	2	4	8	9	2
Small employers	1	21	9	6	8	10	6
Petite bourgeoisie	25	42	45	25	21	24	27
Managers and technocrats	15	2	3	5	6	9	3
Supervisors	5	7	6	9	5	6	6
Semi-autonomous employees	7	4	3	4	9	7	6
Workers	45	24	42	46	43	36	50
Total	100	100	100	100	100	100	100

Source: 1981 national sample survey of the Institute for Social Research, York University.

Table 7

INCOME DISTRIBUTION BY QUINTILES BY CHARACTERISTICS OF HOUSEHOLDS FOR 1984

	Percentage in Income Quintile			*Percent Below Poverty Line*		
Household characteristic	*Lowest Quintile*	*Second Quintile*	*Highest Quintile*	*Families*	*Unattached Individuals*	*Percent of Population*
Share of total income	4.5	10.3	43.0	14.5	37.8	—
Major source of income						
Wages and salaries	7.5	14.8	26.6	6.4	18.2	65.9
Net income from self-employment	16.9	20.1	26.1	20.6	13.7	5.0
Transfer payments	57.0	34.2	0.0	46.3	70.8	21.3
Investment income	20.5	25.6	20.5	12.8	21.5	3.9
Pensions	14.4	28.8	10.4	9.5	—	2.5
Employment status of head*						
Employee	10.5	15.4	25.9	9.2	22.3	64.4
Employer or own account	17.7	20.8	23.1	20.3	46.9	7.7
Not in labour force	42.6	30.4	5.5	27.7	58.7	27.9
Family characteristics						
Unattached individuals	8.3	43.3	4.9	—	37.8	28.7
Married couples only	8.2	28.7	22.9	8.7	—	21.2
Married couple with one child	4.0	11.5	33.5	11.6	—	36.6
Married couple with two or more children and/or other relatives	2.1	9.6	46.6	9.5	—	2.9

Lone parent family—male head	17.0	18.6	18.6	20.9	—	1.2
Lone parent family—female head	38.0	26.1	5.2	47.7	—	6.6
All other families	13.0	27.3	15.1	20.7	—	2.8
Occupation of head*						
Managerial	3.6	10.5	44.1	3.5	9.3	11.0
Professional	6.9	12.4	39.4	6.7	14.8	10.7
Clerical and sales	12.4	21.1	20.3	10.8	18.9	5.4
Service	24.0	22.4	14.8	22.3	46.6	7.2
Farming, etc.	27.4	27.0	13.7	21.2	41.3	4.8
Processing, machining, product fabrication, construction, transportation	10.0	20.1	17.5	7.9	13.9	7.1
Not in labour force	48.1	25.0	5.9	28.1	59.1	23.3

*Assumes male heads for couples.

Source: Income Distributions by Size, 1984 (Ottawa: Statistics Canada, 1986): various pages, author's calculations.

highschool graduates, compared to 72 percent of nonmanual workers; and just 2 percent of manual workers are university graduates, compared to 14 percent of nonmanual workers. Despite their lower level of education, manual workers earn an average of $3,000 *more* than their nonmanual counterparts. Wage differences between occupations and industries and gender segregation of occupations obviously prevent nonmanual workers from translating their higher levels of education into higher wages. Manual and nonmanual supervisors also differ. Supervisors of manual workers are subject to closer supervision themselves, are more likely to face production quotas, and are less well educated but better paid than their nonmanual counterparts.

The most striking difference involves semi-autonomous employees. The skilled craft workers in the manual fraction of this group have far less education and lower pay than the professional and technical workers in the nonmanual fraction of the semi-autonomous employees. Just 2 percent of the manual semi-autonomous employees are university graduates, compared to 46 percent of their nonmanual counterparts, and their average rates of pay are $19,000 and $25,000 a year, respectively. Nonmanual semi-autonomous employees also enjoy substantially better working conditions (they are much less likely to have production quotas and are less vulnerable to layoff). In level of pay, education, and job autonomy, the nonmanual semi-autonomous workers resemble the managerial group more than any of the other employee groups.

What do these data say about the Canadian class structure? First, control of the work process—the basis of Wright's theorization of social classes — is strongly related to work experience, pay, and education. The *degree* of differentiation among the various categories of employees, however, indicates class fractions rather than distinct social classes. Second, supervisory control of other workers, *unless it is accompanied by a significant degree of personal job autonomy*, is not the basis of a significant cleavage in social background, working conditions, or pay. Third, the nonsupervisory manual workers who are usually thought of as the core of the working class are distinctive. Manual workers have the least education, are most prone to layoff and unemployment, and experience the most restrictive working conditions. Fourth, to the extent there is a dichotomy among employed workers, it separates the managers *and* nonmanual semi-autonomous employees from *all* other employees. This is precisely the group identified by Barbara and John Ehrenreich (1979) as the "professional-managerial class" and by Goldthorpe, (1980), and Abercrombie and Urry (1983:118) as the "service class." Finally, while these results show important differences between manual and nonmanual workers, these only make sense in the context of class cleavages.

INCOME AND WEALTH, WORKERS AND NONWORKERS

One result of class divisions is a highly unequal distribution of income and wealth. Oja (1980:352) shows that, in 1976, the lowest 10 percent of all family units (known as the lowest "decile") earned only 1.2 percent of all income, while the highest decile earned 26.9 percent of all income. For wealth, the disproportion is still more extreme: the lowest decile owns a negligible share of all assets (less than 0.05 percent), while the top decile owns nearly half (45.6 percent). For financial assets, including real estate, automobiles, and equity in business, the top decile owned 67 percent of assets.

Studies of the distributions of income also lend themselves to analyzing the positions of groups outside the labour force who, as long as class position is defined on basis of jobs, would have no class positions. Of course, many people who are not employed are linked to the class structure by other employed members of their households. For example, homemakers may have spouses, and students often have parents in the labour force. More difficult to classify are the disabled, domestic workers, and retired people in households with no employed person. With no labour force participant in a household, income is the key determinant of a household's position in society.

While, in principle, child care, education, care of the disabled and aged, etc., could be organized as profit-making activities, contemporary capitalism leaves many forms of human activity in the hands of families and the state and largely or entirely outside the system of capitalist production. Of course, the capitalist economy indirectly affects how these societal responsibilities are addressed. That retired people receive pensions is not unique to capitalist society; but because pensions are proportional to individual's preretirement incomes, class inequalities in people's working lives are perpetuated into retirement. Similarly, the devaluation of household work and childcare is a critical aspect of the oppression of women in capitalist societies. These economic inequalities are an important, but *not* the only influence on the position of groups outside the labour force.

As Table 7 shows, households without an employed person are disproportionately poor and likely to be headed by women. Forty-six percent of the families and 71 percent of the unattached individuals whose major source of income is transfer payments are below the poverty line. Among households whose head is not employed, 34 percent are in the bottom quintile of the income distribution, and 28 percent of the families and 59 percent of the unattached individuals are below the poverty line. Because families headed by married couples often include two earners, they are disproportionately *un*likely to be in the lowest quintile of income. Single parent families, especially those (the great majority) that are headed by women, are disproportionately likely to live in poverty; almost half of all single parent families live below the poverty line.

The occupation of the household head has a powerful effect on income. Forty-four percent of all families headed by managers and 39 percent of households headed by professionals are in the *top* quintile of income. In comparison, 48 percent of the households whose head is outside the labour force, 27 percent of families headed by farmers, and 24 percent of families headed by service workers are in the lowest quintile of households.

The figures presented in this section show *all* economic classes are privileged in comparison to families with no labour force participant at all. Families that depend on transfer payments are seven times more likely to live in poverty than families relying on wages and salaries. In terms of income, even being exploited as a wage worker is a privilege.

CLASS AND POLITICAL IDEOLOGY

As classes have been defined here, individuals' beliefs that they are in the middle or in the working class, their support for a particular political party, and other aspects of their political ideology have no bearing on their class positions.[22] This is not to say individuals' class positions have no effect on their experiences and views about society. Capitalists' day-to-day experience, as owners and managers with the power to create and determine the nature of jobs, and the day-to-day experience of workers, in situations they do not control, are the context for the development of political ideas that reflect class divisions. In fact, empirical studies of ideology reveal complex and contradictory patterns of class differences, partly because many factors reduce the relationship between class and ideology. These factors include the school system, the mass media, and a political system designed to prevent the emergence of ideological conflict, and income, ethnic, and other divisions *within* social classes.

Again referring to the 1981 national sample survey, Table 8 shows the relationship between class and political ideology. There is a strong relationship between social class and class identification, but only minor class differences in whether individuals think of themselves as belonging to any social class. Just over half of all manual workers identified themselves as belonging to the working class, and only a small fraction of manual workers placed themselves in the "lower class"—a phrase more suggestive of simple hierarchy than of class stratification. In terms of "working-class" identification, manual supervisors are just behind the manual working class, which is consistent with our earlier finding that, despite their authority over lower-level workers, supervisors' work situations resemble those of the workers they supervise. About one-third of nonmanual workers, manual semi-autonomous employees, nonmanual supervisors, and the petite bourgeoisie (despite being self-employed) identify themselves as working class. Except for the working class (40 percent of whom choose this alternative) most people in each class category identify themselves as middle class. Capitalists, managers, and nonmanual semi-autonomous workers were more likely than the other groups to claim upper or upper-middle-class status.

For the questions dealing with government efforts to assist the unemployed, support the business community, and help the poor, there are rather small class differences, but assistance to the unemployed caused sharp disagreement: nearly half (44 percent) of the manual workers wanted "more" or "much more" support for the unemployed, compared to only 14 percent of the capitalists, and 16 percent of the nonmanual semi-autonomous workers. Most Canadians believe corporations *and* labour unions are too powerful for the good of society. Seventy-three percent of manual workers said that large corporations were too powerful, and an astonishing 70 percent said trade unions were too powerful. This reflects the widespread belief that the major conflict over power in Canadian society pits large institutions — corporate, union, and governmental — against individuals, small businesses, and other less powerful groups in society. Obviously, this view runs counter to a class conflict model.

There is considerable class division in opinions about strikebreaking and income distribution. Sixty-nine percent of manual workers supported a ban on strikebreaking and 62 percent favoured increasing the taxes of high earners, compared to only 18 percent and 20 percent, respectively, of the capitalists taking these positions. The remaining class groups took positions between these extremes, with small employers, nonmanual supervisors, and semi-autonomous employees generally siding with capital and nonmanual workers and manual supervisors and semi-autonomous employees siding with the manual workers.

Finally, there is moderate class division in allegiance to the federal political parties. Support for the Conservative party was strongest among capitalists, the petite bourgeoisie, and nonmanual semi-autonomous employees; support for the Liberal party revealed remarkably little class differentiation; and support for the N.D.P. was strongest among the manual supervisors and semi-autonomous employees. Only 12 percent of the manual workers and 15 percent of the nonmanual workers supported the N.D.P. Not only are class differences in party support relatively small, but the patterns are inconsistent with public attitudes on many issues. For example, manual workers' opposition to strikebreaking and support for the government's providing jobs is not matched by a high level of support for the N.D.P. which advocates these policies.

While the *direction* of the class differences in political attitudes is consistent with the structural, economic differences between social classes, the *extent* of class differences varies markedly according to the aspect of ideology being considered. The major ideological cleavage divides capitalists and small employers from all the other class categories. The manual/nonmanual division also corresponds to significant ideological differences, particularly among semi-autonomous employees and supervisors. Nonmanual semi-autonomous employees, who are in high-level white-collar occupations, are ideologically similar to managers. The similarity in the attitudes of manual workers and manual supervisors reinforces our earlier findings about working conditions and pay, which suggested the situation of manual supervisors is closer to that of the workers they supervise than to higher-level managers. Even though the petite bourgeoisie includes employers with less than five workers, on many issues the petite bourgeoisie take positions closer to those of workers than capitalists.

These patterns are more reflective of ideological class conflict than of ideological consensus or "noblesse oblige" of the privileged. If, for example, trade unions gain the right (which they have only in Quebec, at present) to prevent companies from hiring strikebreakers, it will be because workers and unions exert political pressure to obtain this and not because employers decide peaceful labour relations are in their long-term interest.

While the extent of attitudinal differences between social classes varies, on no issue is there complete polarization, and on several issues there is little class differentiation at all. This inconsistency indicates class polarization is limited in Canadian society. Even on issues directly related to the interests of social classes, substantial proportions of every class fraction give responses inconsistent with their class interest. Reasonably enough, the largest class differences are for measures of class perception, trade union rights, and income redistribution, while other issues, and particularly political party support, exhibit much smaller differences. The political party system serves to mute class differences.

COMPARING THE CANADIAN TO OTHER CLASS STRUCTURES

In discussing the Canadian class structure, we have referred to many factors that are not unique to Canada. The increasing domination of the economy by large corporations, the diffusion of authority

Table 8
POLITICAL ATTITUDES BY CLASS CATEGORY

Political Attitude	Class Category									
	Capitalists	*Small Employers*	*Petite bourgeoisie*	*Managers and technocrats*	*Supervisors*		*Semi-autonomous Employees*		*Workers*	
					Nonmanual	*Manual*	*Nonmanual*	*Manual*	*Nonmanual*	*Manual*
Sometimes think of self as belonging to a social class (percent)	37	37	38	41	40	51	45	50	46	49
Class self-identification										
upper or upper-middle class	38	20	11	26	17	3	27	10	10	4
middle class	58	67	57	61	52	54	59	59	60	40
working class	4	12	31	13	31	43	14	30	29	54
lower class	0	1	1	0	0	0	0	1	1	2
Strongly agree or agree that government should make more effort to:										
Assist the unemployed	14	23	31	30	22	24	16	28	31	44
Support the business community	45	55	45	38	44	21	28	24	32	41
Help the poor	52	48	55	65	62	49	60	65	74	64
Believe large corporations too powerful	55	80	78	73	77	68	85	78	73	73
Believe trade unions are too powerful	80	96	80	86	69	68	61	72	54	70
Strongly agree or agree that:										
Unemployment is too high because welfare is too easy to get	58	79	72	65	71	78	46	67	64	66
Government should provide jobs for those who cannot find a job	42	49	61	56	57	68	48	61	71	81
High income people should pay more taxes	20	39	54	55	61	70	36	66	55	62

During a strike, hiring of strike-breakers should be illegal	18	30	49	47	39	64	38	64	61	69
Doctors should be prohibited from charging more than is paid by medicare	42	58	69	64	66	65	60	72	73	79
Believe that government should cut back further on social programs	48	42	42	32	29	30	41	26	20	24
Federal political party identification:										
Conservative, Social Credit	37	17	39	29	27	23	39	29	28	25
Liberal	43	58	40	45	50	44	36	44	45	49
N.D.P.	1	4	7	16	9	25	12	24	15	12
Independent, other	19	21	15	11	14	6	13	3	12	14

Source: 1981 national sample survey of the Institute for Social Research, York University.

through complex chains of command, and the declining numbers of farmers, and other major trends reflect economic forces at work in every capitalist nation. That similar forces are at work, however, does not mean their relative strengths are the same—and international differences in the balance of class forces and state policies further increase international differences. For example, the domestic and international market forces that have forced many small-scale agricultural producers out of business may be offset by state programs, including price controls, subsidies, tax expenditures, and the establishment of marketing boards. Whether or not these policies are adopted depends on the political power of farmers.

Compared to other advanced capitalist nations, the Canadian economy combines a high degree of foreign control with a highly developed primary and extractive industry, relative to manufacturing. The effect of foreign, mostly American, ownership is easiest to predict: the proximity of American head offices and relatively centralized management of American multinationals suggests that the industries in which foreign ownership is high should develop a class structure that resembles that in the United States. Of course, similarities in the class structure of Canada and the United States may also reflect historical parallels in the two nations' development—such as the availability of farmland and the predominance of European immigrants.

One comparative study by Black and Myles (1986) employs consistent methods to examine Canada, the United States, and Sweden. They found a complex pattern of differences. Canada had fewer small employers (2.8 percent versus 6.0 and 4.7 percent for the United States and Sweden, respectively) but a larger petite bourgeoisie (12.3 percent of the employed labour force versus 6.8 and 5.3 percent, respectively) than the United States and Sweden. While there was relatively little variation in the proportions of managers, Canada and Sweden had distinctly more semi-autonomous employees than the

CANADA AND TEN NATIONS COMPARED

Table 9 on page 213 presents a broader comparison of nations drawn from the *Year Book of Labour Statistics*, but is limited to information about occupations and industries, so it is necessary to make inferences about social class composition. While national differences may arise from international differences in the occupational categories, these data confirm the findings of Black and Myles. Canada and the United States with, respectively, 10.3 and 10.6 percent of all workers in the "administrative and managerial" category stand out from all other nations. Besides Australia, with 6.7 percent of the workforce in these categories, no other nation has more than 4 percent of its employed labour force in the administrative and managerial category. Canada's class structure comes closer to the American one than to the class structures of the other nations included in this table.

Table 9

DISTRIBUTION OF OCCUPATIONS FOR VARIOUS NATIONS

	Percentage Distribution of Occupation							
Nation	*Professional, Technical, & Related*	*Administrative, Managerial*	*Clerical & Related*	*Sales & Related*	*Service Workers*	*Agriculture and Other Primary Production*	*Production Workers, Transport Operators, Labourers*	*Total*
Canada	16.0	10.3	16.7	9.5	13.6	5.9	27.9	100.0
U.S.A.	15.0	10.6	15.7	11.8	13.9	3.5	29.5	100.0
Australia	15.1	6.7	17.7	9.1	9.9	6.9	34.5	100.0
New Zealand	14.3	3.6	16.7	9.9	8.3	11.4	35.7	100.0
Sweden	28.2	2.4	12.3	8.2	14.2	5.1	29.6	100.0
Denmark	20.3	3.6	16.5	7.2	14.9	2.6	34.9	100.0
Germany	15.3	3.9	19.1	9.4	11.9	5.5	35.0	100.0
France	15.9	0.3	19.2	8.8	12.0	8.5	35.2	100.0
Greece	10.2	1.7	9.2	9.7	8.4	29.1	31.5	100.0
Spain	7.6	1.5	10.7	9.9	14.2	17.1	39.0	100.0
Portugal	7.5	1.4	13.6	8.4	10.8	19.7	38.7	100.0

Source: Year Book of Labour Statistics, 1985 (Geneva: International Labour Organization): various pages. Reproduced with permission of Supply and Services Canada.

United States (16.0 and 16.8 percent versus 9.4 percent for the United States). In number of supervisors, Canada is midway between the two other nations (10.0 percent, versus 12.7 percent for the United States and 7.0 percent for Sweden). Most interestingly, Black and Myles found the class distributions of *state* employees in Canada and Sweden are similar, while the class distributions of *private* employees in Canada and the United States are similar. They think these findings indicate the high degree of American ownership of Canadian industry has produced a partial "Americanization" of the Canadian class structure.

Black and Myles's results are intriguing. Theirs is the only comparison of Canadian and other national class structures that employs a common methodology and that deals with social classes in terms of ownership and control of the means of production. Unfortunately, the three-nation comparison provides a rather truncated context for comparing class structures. While there are strong theoretical reasons to include the United States and Sweden in comparisons with Canada, both these nations are highly atypical capitalist nations.

CONCLUSION

Dominating the Canadian economy are the few capitalists who control the largest corporations. In this sense, there is an extreme polarization in Canadian society, not only between the capitalists and workers as a whole, but between the people who own and control the largest of the nearly 400 000 businesses in Canada and everyone else. And the power of big capital is not the anonymous power of faceless institutions, presided over by their managers and ruled by their self-interest as organizations and by technology. For the great majority of large corporations, it is easy to identify their individual owners. The extraordinarily high level of foreign ownership in Canada further increases the polarization of economic control by adding foreign corporations to the tiny group of Canadians who controls the nation's economy.

This polarization of the economic structure and concentration of power is accompanied by the development of complex divisions within the working class. The functions of capital—planning what and how much to produce, hiring, supervising and paying workers, buying machinery and raw materials, and selling commodities—can no longer be performed by individual capitalists, and dividing of these tasks into the work of many different people creates many intermediary positions between the top level managers and the lowest level workers. Our analysis suggests that, except for top level managers (who play the role of, and should be classified with, the capitalist class) and the lower-level managers and nonmanual semi-autonomous workers, the result is the formation of a large, internally differentiated working class. There is no evidence of the formation of a large, new middle class, nor did the analysis of political ideology suggest the presence of two working classes, one engaged in productive and the other in nonproductive labour.

Important divisions within the working class are also apparent from the relationship between social class and political ideology. The polarization between capital and labour is accompanied by ideological conflict within the working class, involving both divisions between fractions of the working class, as defined on the basis of control of the labour process and the manual/nonmanual distinction, and ideological differentiation ***within*** the class fractions. Even manual workers, who are closely supervised and who have no authority over other workers, are sharply divided over fundamental political issues.

Alongside the division between capital and labour, the petite bourgeoisie fights for survival, with state intervention as the most effective means to avoid takeover by capitalists. In this struggle, some professionals and farmers are in much stronger positions than small merchants, craft workers, and primary producers.

Finally, the living standard of the half of the population who are outside the labour force is related to the class structure as well. Class privileges extend into the households of individual workers and from peoples' working lives into retirement, and households with no employed member are disproportionately poor.

This analysis of the Canadian class structure is not complete. Limitations on the length of this chapter and, often, lack of information prevented discussion of some topics. Especially lacking is information comparing Canada to other nations, which would allow us to distinguish unique features of the Canadian class structure from trends which affect all capitalist nations. The most significant limitation of this chapter has nothing, however, to do with missing information. Canadian society is a society, not just an economic system. On a larger scale, a full analysis of the class structure must examine the relations between the economic dimension of class differences and the workings of major state institutions. On a smaller scale, we need to show how social class affects the way people experience and choose to live their lives.

Notes

I thank Robert Brym and two anonymous referees for extensive and helpful comments on an earlier draft of this chapter. Tables 4, 5, 6, and 8 and the findings reported in the first paragraph of this chapter are based on a national survey of a representative sample of Canadians conducted by the Institute for Social Research of York University and funded by a grant from the Social Sciences and Humanities Research Council of Canada to Tom Atkinson, Bernard Blishen, H. Michael Stevenson, and the author. Especially, I thank Professor Stevenson for his collaboration in the design of the measures of political ideology and Professor William Johnston of the University of Western Ontario for design of the class categories.

[1]Gordon Darroch (1986) takes a similar position in an analysis of the Canadian class structure, which focuses on the concentration of capital and wealth (but makes no mention of a capitalist *class*) and on the middle class which, although it is not defined precisely, appears to include perhaps 60 percent of the entire population. Darroch characterizes middle-class "culture" by the high "value placed on meritocratic principles" (p. 392). At a time when "most Canadians no longer expect to ensure their children's futures through property inheritance or by establishing them in a craft or small business . . . they may hope to give their children *cultural capital* in the form of the credentials and social graces of the educated" (p. 392; emphasis in original). But Darroch offers no evidence that working-class values are different from those that he ascribes to the middle class.

[2]Following Carchedi (1975b), one obvious way out of the difficulty is to distinguish

ownership, conceived in a juridical sense, from possession, which involves the power to decide what the activities of a corporation are and how they are accomplished. Thus, the passive stockholder owns but does not possess the corporation, while the executive possesses but does not own it. Of course, in (mostly smaller) companies, which are more likely to be managed by their owners, this distinction does not arise.

[3]In Marxist terminology, a "commodity" is any product produced for sale at a profit. The term "service" refers to sectors of the economy, such as transportation, storage, repairs, cleaning, etc., in which a specific service is sold for profit, just like a commodity. In this framework, banking, insurance, and other financial services, and retail and wholesale trade are neither commodities nor services, since nothing is produced for sale. Often the term "service" is used differently to refer to all sectors of the economy, with the exception of manufacturing, primary production, and resource extraction.

[4]In Marxist theory, "labour power," which is the commodity that workers sell and employers purchase with wages, is distinguished from labour itself. "Labour" is the actual use of a person's skill in working. While this may seem an arcane point, from a Marxist standpoint is it important to distinguish labouring itself—which is an inherently satisfying and unalienated activity —from the experience of labour in capitalist production—which is shaped by the demand for profit and by the inequality between capitalists and workers.

[5]According to the labour theory of value developed by Marx, all value is created by workers when they manufacture commodities, transport them to where they can be used, and repair them. The expression "surplus value" refers to the difference between the value of a commodity and the total cost to the capitalist—in wages, raw material, and equipment—of making the commodity. Marx's discussion of these matters may be found in the first volume of *Capital*; for a fine discussion of theories of value, see Dobb (1973).

[6]The manual/nonmanual division is strongly related to but not identical to the difference between productive and unproductive labour. Some types of manual labour are unproductive, for example, the work of gardeners who work on the property of a municipality or an insurance company; and, conversely, some nonmanual labour is productive, for example, the work of a computer programmer employed by a private business to write a program for commercial sale.

[7]The expression "small business" is used loosely. As used to define eligibility for some government programs, it includes businesses with up to one hundred employees. In terms of Marxist theory, however, the dividing line between the petite bourgeoisie and the capitalist class corresponds to the point at which the owner of a business no longer devotes a major part of his or her time to actual production and concentrates instead on supervising employees and other aspects of management.

[8]Government spending in Canada is closer to 40 percent than 20 percent of the gross domestic product. The smaller share of total employment reflects the fact that the transfer payments require only the employment of staff to make the payments. Government purchases of goods and services from the private sector likewise contribute to government expenditures but not to government employment.

[9]An enterprise is defined by Statistics Canada as a group of corporations which, on the basis of intercorporate ownership, is determined to come under the control of a single corporation. Some enterprises control many corporations, while others consist of only a single corporation.

[10]The collection of these data is mandated by the Corporations and Labour Unions

Returns Act (known as CALURA). At the time of writing, the latest available CALURA figures referred to 1983.

[11]*The Financial Post* listing of the largest "500" nonfinancial corporations omits a few provincially chartered, private firms for which no financial data were publicly available. Most of the omitted firms are foreign-controlled and not among the largest corporations. The most notable omission is the large retail chain, Eaton's.

The number of management-controlled corporations could be less than nine, since one or more of the nine corporations whose stock is said to be "widely distributed" could be controlled through a holding of 5 or 10 percent of the stock.

[12]A number of the major insurance companies are management-controlled by virtue of their being mutual companies, which are owned (in proportion to the sizes of their policies) by their policyholders. This produces an extreme diffusion of stockholding and leaves the management in control. The other large insurance companies are (with one exception out of the largest twenty-five) either foreign-owned or controlled by other corporations.

[13]Any measurement of the precise extent of recruitment from the various social classes depends on the assumptions used to define the corporate elite and to measure its origins. In terms of defining the corporate elite, two decisions are critical: first, differentiating between "dominant" and smaller corporations; and, second, deciding which individuals associated with those corporations—usually their directors and/or top executives—qualify for inclusion in the study. Also critical is the method used to determine the social class of an individual's family of origin. For example, because university attendance was relatively unusual for working-class people at the time of Porter's and Clement's studies, both of them assumed that anyone who attended university came from a middle-class family. The difficulty with this assumption is that the highly mobile working-class people who stand any chance of entering the corporate elite are the ones who are most likely to defy the odds and attend university. Classifying all people who attended university as middle class thus biases their studies in the direction of underestimating the mobility of people from working-class origins.

[14]As Carroll (1984,1987: chap. 6) shows, at a finer level it is possible to discern "cliques" of corporations and individual directors within the larger network of corporations. Even among these cliques, however, there is a good deal of interpenetration.

[15]The traditional sociological approach to the "professions" subordinates class considerations to the study of occupational groups, which vary in their ability to organize and monopolize the practice of their occupations. In practice, the class approach distinguishes professionals who are in business for themselves from professionals employed by government or in private companies. Thus, many professional occupations are divided between two classes—for example, significant numbers of physicians are employed salary earners.

[16]"Organizational" factors are also an important determinant of when the petite bourgeoisie becomes subject to increased competition from capital. The growth of fast food chains, for example, involved the application of existing and relatively simple technology. More important was the change in the organization of stores and the use of advertising. The increasing predominance of specialized chain stores also reflects organizational, not technological changes.

[17]The Canadian Federation of Independent Business acts as a voice for small-scale capitalists rather than for the petite bourgeoisie as a whole.

[18]In this chapter, material commodities, such as automobiles, furniture, and tools, are not distinguished from nonmaterial commodities, such as computer programs. Since the production of material

commodities is more or less synonymous with production involving manual labour, Poulantzas's position implies the working class consists entirely of manual workers. Poulantzas's position is therefore similar to some neo-Weberians', particularly Giddens (1973:186ff), on the cultural and social distinctions between manual and nonmanual labour.

[19]In his later work, Wright (1985) substantially modifies this characterization of classes.

[20]There are several reasons for the discrepancy between the two figures. Ornstein limits the classification of "semi-autonomous" employees to workers in relatively skilled occupations on the grounds that only skilled occupations offer workers significant alternatives in how they go about their work; and Black and Myles define supervisory authority in terms of the supervisor's having the power to sanction employees, while Ornstein uses measures of the amount of time spent supervising and the number of people being supervised.

[21]Within these class categories, women are further disadvantaged. For example, women supervisors are paid less than men because they are subject to wage discrimination and because they tend to work in industries with lower wage rates.

[22]As Larrain (1979) argues, "ideology" is understood in a variety of ways. Interpretations of ideology may be classified into two major categories: "positive" interpretations, in which ideology is understood as the framework which a class or other group uses to interpret and respond to its situation; and "negative" interpretations, in which ideology is understood as a false view which prevents a class or group from understanding its situation and responding to it effectively. In the present discussion, ideology is understood in the positive sense as a meaningful interpretation of the situation of social classes and of their interests. This is not to say members of a class are uniform in their opinions, for there are obviously conflicts within social classes over how to further their interests.

DISCUSSION QUESTIONS

1. What is a social class? Why does it matter?
2. In what circumstances is there likely to be conflict between social classes?
3. Some day care, housework, and education is provided by businesses for profit. What, if anything, prevents a complete takeover of these activities by private business?
4. Are the various ethnic groups in Canada distributed equally in the class structure? What factors might be responsible for some ethnic groups occupying advantaged or disadvantaged class positions?
5. If industry and business policy organizations are used to further the interest of the capitalist class, what organizations represent the working class? What are the strengths and weaknesses of working-class organizations?

GLOSSARY

capitalist class owners of corporations, considered as group

labour power in Marxist theory, the commodity that workers sell and capitalists purchase with wages. Labour power is distinguished from "labour" itself, which refers to the actual use of a person's skills in working. The significance of the distinction is that which separates labour—seen as an inherently satisfying and unalienated use of a person's capacities—from the particular experience of labour in capitalist production—where the labour process is shaped by the demand for profit and by the inequality between capitalists and workers

middle class any class occupying a position intermediate between the capitalist and working class, but defined quite differently according to difference in theoretical approach. Usually distinguished from the petite bourgeoisie, as salaried employees. In non-Marxist theory, the term is generally applied to employees with levels of income and education and occupations that distinguish them from the majority of workers; in Marxist theory, the term is applied to employees whose jobs involve some mixture of the capitalist prerogatives of ownership of the means of production and control of the labour process.

petite bourgeoisie the class of own account workers and proprietors of small businesses with so few employees that the proprietor produces a significant proportion of the product or service sold

social class used variously to describe a hierarchy or functional division of society. In non-Marxist theory, the term is often used imprecisely to describe a hierarchy of income, occupational and educational groups. In the various Marxist theories, social classes are defined according to criteria usually including ownership and control of corporations and the work process.

working class employees of capitalists who sell their labour power in return for wages, considered as a group potentially organized in defence of its interests

BIBLIOGRAPHY

Abercrombie, Nicholas and John Urry
1983 *Capital, Labour and the Middle Classes*. London: George Allen and Unwin.

Bechofer, Frank and Brian Elliot
1985 "The Petite Bourgeoisie in Late Capitalism." *Annual Review of Sociology* 11:181–207.

Berle, Adolf A. and Gardiner C. Means
1932 *The Modern Corporation and Private Property*. New York: Macmillan.

Block, Fred
1978 "The ruling class does not rule: Notes on the Marxist theory of the state." *Socialist Revolution* (May–June):6–28.

Bottomore, Tom (ed.)

1983 *A Dictionary of Marxist Thought*. Cambridge, Mass: Harvard University Press.

Braverman, Harry
1974 *Labor and Monopoly Capital*. New York: Monthly Review Press.

Bruce-Biggs, B.
1979 "An Introduction to the Idea of the New Class." In B. Bruce-Biggs (ed.) *The New Class?* New Brunswick, New Jersey: Transaction Books.

Brym, Robert
1985 "The Canadian Capitalist Class, 1965–1985." In Robert Brym (ed.) *The Structure of the Canadian Capitalist Class*. Toronto: Garamond.

Carchedi, Guglielmo
1975a "On the Economic Identification of the New Middle Class." Economy and Society 4:1–86.

——
1975b "Reproduction of Social Classes at the Level of Production Relations." *Economy and Society* 4:361–417.

Carroll, William K.
1986 *Corporate Power and Canadian Capitalism*. Vancouver: University of British Columbia Press.

Carroll, William K., John Fox, and Michael Ornstein
1982 "The Network of Directorate Interlocks Among the Largest Canadian Firms." *Canadian Review of Sociology and Anthropology* 19:44–69.

Carter, Bob
1985 *Capitalism, Class Conflict and the New Middle Class*. London: Routledge and Kegan Paul.

Clement, Wallace
1975 *The Canadian Corporate Elite*. Toronto: McClelland and Stewart

Coleman, William
1986 "The Capitalist Class and the State: Changing Roles of Business Interest Associations." *Studies in Political Economy* 20:135–59.

Cottrell, Allin
1984 *Social Classes in Marxist Theory*. London: Routledge and Kegan Paul.

Crompton, Rosemary and Jon Gubbay
1977 *Economy and Class Structure*. London: Macmillan.

Cuneo, Carl
1984 "Has the traditional petite bourgeoisie persisted?" *Canadian Journal of Sociology* 10:269–301.

Darroch, A. Gordon
1986 "Class and stratification." In Lorne, Tepperman, and R. Jack Richardson (eds.) *The Social World: An Introduction to Sociology*. Toronto: McGraw-Hill Ryerson.

Derber, Charles
1982 *Professionals as Workers: Mental Labour in Advanced Capitalism*. Boston: G.K. Hall.

Ehrenreich, Barbara and John Ehrenreich
1979 "The Professional-Managerial Class." In Pat Walker (ed.) *Between Labor and Capital*. Boston: South End Press.

Financial Post
1986 *The Financial Post 500* (Summer 1986). May 24, 1986.

Forcese, Dennis P.
1980 *The Canadian Class Structure*, 2nd ed. Toronto: McGraw-Hill Ryerson.

Gagliani, J.
1981 "How Many Working Classes?" *American Journal of Sociology* 87:259–85.

Giddens, Anthony
1973 *The Class Structure of Advanced Societies*. London: Hutchinson.
1980 *The Class Structure of Advanced Societies*, 2nd ed. London: Hutchinson.

Goldthorpe, John
1980 *Social Mobility and Class Structure in Modern Britain*. Oxford: Clarendon Press.

Hall, Stuart
1977 "The 'Political' and the 'Economic' in Marx's Theory of Classes." In Alan Hunt (ed.) *Class and Class Structure*. London: Lawrence and Wishart.

Hunt, Alan, ed.
1977 *Class and Class Structure*. London: Lawrence and Wishart.

Hunter, Alfred A.
1986 *Class Tells: On Social Inequality in Canada,* 2nd ed. Toronto: Butterworths.

Jessop, Bob
1982 *The Capitalist State*. Oxford: Martin Robertson.

Larrain, Jorge
1979 *The Concept of Ideology*. London: Hutchinson.

Mallet, Serge
1975 *Essays on the New Working Class*. St. Louis: Telos Press.

MacKenzie, Gavin
1982 "Class Boundaries and the Labour Process." In Anthony Giddens and Gavin MacKenzie (eds.) *Social Class and the Division of Labour*. Cambridge: Cambridge University Press.

Meiksins, Peter
1986 "Beyond the Boundary Question." *New Left Review* 157:101–20.

Oja, Gail
1980 "Inequality of the Wealth Distribution in Canada 1970 and 1977." In *Reflections on Canadian Incomes*. Ottawa: Economic Council of Canada.

Ornstein, Michael
1983 "The Development of Class in Canada." In J. Paul Grayson (ed.) *Introduction to Sociology: An Alternate Approach*. Toronto: Gage.

Ornstein, Michael and H. Michael Stevenson
1984 "Ideology and Public Policy in Canada." *British Journal of Political Science* 14:313–34.

Porter, John
1965 *The Vertical Mosaic*. Toronto: University of Toronto Press.

Poulantzas, Nicos
1975 *Classes in Contemporary Capitalism*. London: Verso.

Scase, Richard
1982 "The Petty Bourgeoisie and Modern Capitalism: A Consideration of Recent Theories." In Anthony Giddens and Gavin MacKenzie (eds.) *Social Class and the Division of Labour*.

Shortell, Ann
1987 "Who's the Richest of Them All?" *Financial Post Moneywise Magazine*, February:22–39.

Sohn-Rethel, Alfred
1978 *Intellectual and Manual Labour: A Critique of Epistemology.* Atlantic Highlands, New Jersey: Humanities Press.

Useem, Michael
1984 *The Inner Circle: Large Corporations and the Rise of Business Political Activity in the U.S. and U.K.* New York: Oxford University Press.

Wright, Erik Olin
1976 "Class Boundaries in Advanced Capitalist Societies." *New Left Review* 98:3–41.

——
1985 *Classes.* London: Verso.

Wright, Eric Olin, D. Hacher, C. Costello, and J. Sprague
1982 "The American Class Structure." *American Sociological Review* 47:702–26.

Zeitlin, Maurice
1974 "Corporate Ownership and Control: The Large Corporation and the Capitalist Class." *American Journal of Sociology* 79: 1073–1119.

part three

Sociocultural Organization and Change

Records and revenue are no strangers to bureaucracies, as suggested by this Taxation Centre desk from the 1960s. *Courtesy* La Presse

"Over the last twenty years, the state's ability to collect revenue and spend has grown considerably. From an average of 29.8 percent of the gross national product during the years from 1960 to 1967, state spending in Canada jumped to 41.5 percent in 1984 and 45.8 percent in 1982, a remarkable 16 point increase."

c h a p t e r e i g h t

Bureaucracies in the Public and Private Sectors

Arnaud Sales

INTRODUCTION

Bureaucratic organizations in every period and society have drawn contempt, recrimination, and even revolt and subsequent reform efforts for their monetary cost; excessive centralization of power; hierarchical rigidity; narrow vision; counterproductive regulations; lengthy procedures; inflexibility; paper shuffling; and occasional corruption. Yet formal organizations possess an extraordinary ability to mobilize human energy. They therefore tend to develop in constantly changing ways, and on an ever more vast scale. General Motors, for example, currently employs nearly seven hundred thousand people worldwide. Likewise, Canada's civilian and military public administration employs, by the broadest estimate, over two million salaried employees. This figure includes military personnel, and employees of schools, colleges, hospitals, and government enterprises. In this sense, the state bureaucracy, like the differentiated bureaucracy of the large corporate enterprise, is not a seamless whole.

Although the characteristics and origins

of bureaucracies must first be identified, this chapter will not duplicate the numerous works on the subject. Instead, our analysis will concentrate on the origins of state and corporate bureaucracies, their operational boundaries within the Canadian context, and the specific qualities of each.

BUREAUCRACY AND SOCIETY

To properly understand the bureaucratic phenomenon and its social impact, the pejorative image of the inefficient and fussy paper pusher must be set aside, at least for a moment, to consider the most common analytical definitions used by social scientists when describing the growth of large organizations. Bureaucracy means both a *form of social organization* and a growing *social group* composed of individuals brought together to perform administrative duties, and whose power increasingly appears greater than that of traditional elites.

The common basis for **bureaucratization** is the need for a rational model of social administration and domination within the context of significant growth in an organization. In most mass organizations, goals are attained through a high division of labour down to the most minute detail, leading to specialization in duties.

Co-ordinating structures, regulations, and administrative procedures define each position's responsibilities and relationship to other positions. This specialization increases the need for centralized control, and therefore leads to the creation of a hierarchy that integrates each task within a chain of command. Authority, delegated within specific spheres of competence, is thereby subordinated to a final authority that defines the organization's main policies and controls its material and symbolic outputs. This final authority is more political than administrative, and at the highest levels special relationships link administrators with those who hold final authority. Nowadays, these links accentuate technocratic power, or at least blur the boundary separating the level of administration from the highest authority.

Bureaucracy follows the pyramid model. This is reflected in the flow chart, a tool unique to modern organizations. Flow chart communication tends to flow vertically rather than horizontally between individuals at the same level. And communication is indirect because information must pass through a superior to reach the highest levels of the hierarchy. Reduced interpersonal relations, while supposedly more efficient, frequently lead to communication breakdowns and "red tape," i.e., paper work.

Max Weber was the first sociologist to analyze bureaucracies (Weber, 1978; see especially vol. 2, chap. 11). He noted that

THE ORIGIN OF "BUREAUCRACY"

The word *bureaucratie* was coined in the eighteenth century by the economist Vincent de Gournay. This term combines *bure* or *bureau*, which up to the sixteenth century designated any rug covering a chest or table used for writing, with the suffix *cratie*, meaning government authority. Bureaucracy thus literally means government by *bureau*.

bureaucracies can only exist if they have access to revenue, whether in the form of profits for the corporation or taxes for the state. In fact, and this is obviously a concern for public bureaucracies, in the long run only a monetary economy provides a sufficient basis for a stable taxation system.

Weber also noted that the bureaucratization of society receives a great stimulus from growth in administrative tasks resulting from society's development. Transformations of material and social life in the areas of technology, the economy, politics, or culture made many services essential, entailing organizations capable of responding to needs which were previously unknown or provided by the local community or the family.

How can the bureaucratization and monetarization of contemporary social life be explained? The eighteenth century philosophers had called for the triumph of reason, but contrary to their hopes, rationalization led not to a world of liberty, but to one dominated by economic forces and bureaucratically organized administrations (McCarthy, 1984:xxviii). A rational inquiry increasingly challenged the authority of tradition. Ritual practice and religious symbolism lost their explanatory appeal. The ancient core of norms slowly dissolved, giving way to "the rationalization of world views, the universalization of law and morality, and accelerated processes of individuation" (Habermas, forthcoming: 74–75, as cited in McCarthy, 1984:xxii).

By becoming rationalized, the world has become receptive to modernization and new cultural forms, while simultaneously benefiting from increased economic and administrative efficiency. But links have gradually weakened between traditional normative structures (parenthood, religious belonging, social networks) on the one hand and systemic mechanisms in the economy and state power on the other. Finally, the imperatives of the economic and political subsystems have come to dominate, thereby significantly undermining social integration mechanisms. For Habermas, "the inner dynamic of capitalist growth means a continuous increase in systemic complexity, an expansion of the monetary-bureaucratic complex into ever-new areas of life" (Habermas, forthcoming:532–34, as cited in McCarthy).

Bureaucracy cannot exist without **bureaucrats**; a social group stands behind the organizational framework. Obviously, this group will be found inside any mass organization. Yet, not all the personnel in these organizations are "bureaucrats." Neither a factory worker nor a hospital nurse performs intrinsically bureaucratic work. Even if workshops and workers in today's most modern factories (IBM, for example) resemble offices and white-collar workers, respectively, nevertheless, generally "in the industrial enterprise, most workers are restricted to tasks involving only execution. Shops' layout, the number and arrangement of work positions, production rhythms, the duration and intensity of work, all this is determined by an administration operating at a distance from workshops and which to them represents a foreign and closed world" (Lefort, 1979:288–89).

In this sense, the bureaucracy as social group comprises individuals performing broadly defined administrative functions. This applies across the spectrum, from traditional office employees in mundane jobs whose prospects are being transformed by computerization, to deputy ministers in the public service, the "mandarins" feared by new ministers. As we will see, the core of the bureaucracy consists of its executives and managers, since new power circles (as Claude Lefort puts it) emerge, consolidate, and spread from there. Lefort has emphasized the dynamic nature of this group, which is defined by the institution's **administrative structure** and shapes its destiny.

STATE BUREAUCRACY

Nation-Building and Public Administration

The Federal Framework

History and geography have moulded Canadian government bureaucracies. Conversely, these bureaucracies more than any other area have been linked with the nation's major struggles, traditions, and political transformations. Colonial struggles and settlement patterns eventually led to federal institutions capable of accommodating — more or less effectively, depending on the period — the co-existence of French and British national groups. And since the nation was slowly built through the progressive incorporation of colonies, these institutions also faced the problem of administrating a vast territory. As a result, the federal administration became decentralized, while provincial governments assumed greater importance.

The federal constitutional framework has spawned several distinct public services. Complex mechanisms co-ordinate a division of tasks between them, but this does not always prevent jurisdictional conflict between the provincial and central governments, especially since state power now extends beyond traditional domains (Hodgetts, 1973:41–42). Unlike the more consolidated political institutions in other countries, those of Canada inhibit the growth of the central government's civil service, which in 1982 employed only 3 percent of the working population. If National Defence personnel (0.7 percent) and that of federal government enterprises (1.2 percent) are added, the proportion rises to 4.9 percent (Sutherland and Doern, 1986:150). On the other hand, provincial and local administrations play an important role, employing 5.1 percent of the 1982 working population (this figure excludes education, hospitals, and both provincial and local public enterprise). Even though the provincial public services' share of the working population has only grown by 0.9 percent since 1960, their importance and range of operations have expanded considerably over the past twenty-five years.

Provincial and local decentralization gave autonomy which allowed many institutions to strictly define the public service and its personnel. Civil servants are those "appointed to a position on a full-time basis and whose entry into government service has been subject to final certifica-

---

THREE ASPECTS OF GOVERNMENT BUREAUCRACY

Distinctions between types of workers in bureaucracies become clearer if pictured as three concentric circles. The largest circle represents *public* employment, and contains all categories including teachers, hospital workers, and **government enterprise** employees. A smaller second circle, standing for what Bird and Foot call *government employment*, covers municipal and provincial government employees outside the civil service. The innermost circle, taken up by the federal and provincial *civil service employment*, constitutes the "hard core" of government bureaucracy (Doern and Maslove, 1979:122).

---

tion by a central personnel agency'' (Hodgetts and Dwiwedi, 1974:180, as cited in Doern and Maslove, 1979:122). Secondary school teachers and nurses are not considered civil servants, even if the state provides their institutions with most of the budget from which employees are paid.

The Colonial Administrative Tradition and the Role of the State in Development

From the beginning, the colonial administrative tradition gave the state responsibility for the economic development of the land; not many states assumed this responsibility prior to the 1930s Depression. The problem of building a nation out of a continent-sized territory was also unique. Hodgetts emphasizes that ''Geography not only dictated the goals of the public service, it imposed the conditions which governed the ways in which the tasks themselves had to be performed'' (Hodgetts, 1973:18). Initially, the state sought, with the help of financiers and entrepreneurs, to build canals and railroads; the latter were essential to join the Atlantic with the Pacific, and thereby open up the West for settlement. For this reason, the government's first important administrative tasks after Confederation were connected to the colonization of newly opened territories: ''In essence, this preparation consisted in providing police [the R.C.M.P.], protective services, surveying and mapping the terrain [Geological Survey], and servicing the needs of the transportation facilities which were counted on to bind the new nation together'' (Hodgetts, 1973:18).

The exploitation of natural resources was also part of the state's responsibility. From the beginning, the government used state apparatuses to promote the exploitation of minerals, fisheries, lumber, and pulp and paper. The growth of state economic intervention brought the creation of bodies like the Board of Railway Commissioners, which became the Canadian Transport Commission. Later, especially during the 1960s and 1970s, the state's entrepreneurial role in industry, trade, and finance, though rarely monopolistic, was intended to strengthen specific sectors. Several Crown corporations and state agencies emerged, often organized similarly to those in the **private sector**. This is significant, since Crown corporations, including Canada Post, employ 35 percent of all federal civilian and military personnel.

The Influence of Private Sector Management Models

Finally, public administration has been influenced by management models from business. Hodgetts emphasizes the influence of Arthur Young and Company, an American consulting firm that helped reorganize the federal bureaucracy after World War I. Interestingly, the resulting system for classifying jobs (''offices'') was exceedingly complicated, a reflection of the greater variety of tasks in the public service than in private firms of equal size. Herein lies a fundamental difference between private and public sector bureaucracies. The logic and management methods of the large private firm are relatively homogeneous. Public administration differs because it operates in the general social environment, and must respond to the many demands of civil society. Over the past twenty years, this phenomenon has sharpened, with the state providing ever-increasing numbers of services in an ever more rapidly changing society.

The influence of private sector management models starts with the countless management consulting firms hired by the government to evaluate and advise ministries. It comes less directly from employees with experience in the private sector; 60 percent of Quebec civil service management and staff fall into this category

(Sales and Bélanger, 1985:259ff.). The strongest private sector influences are its steady criticism of government management methods and strong presence during royal commissions or task forces on government management. Among recent ones are the Royal Commission on the Economic Union and Development Prospects for Canada, and the Task Force on Program Review organized by former Deputy Prime Minister Erik Neilsen, which included 221 members from the private and **public sectors**.

Methods and criteria from the private sector have increasingly been used to handle public interests. Current concern with public sector financing and cost reinforces this trend. A recent Quebec study found that 61 percent of the high-level civil servants and 58 percent of the private sector executives think that the work required by their position resembles that performed by managers at the same level in the other sector (Sales, 1983). Nevertheless, certain administrative areas of the state apparatus cannot make complete use of private enterprise management methods.

THE BOUNDARIES OF PUBLIC BUREAUCRACIES

General Public Administration

The Federal Bureaucracy

One might assume that public administration falls within the departmental framework of government. But this has not been the case because such a framework could not match the marked growth of state functions. For political and organizational reasons, the multiplication of quasi-departmental agencies (commissions, councils, offices) or corporations at the federal and provincial levels occurred because the number of departments, and thus the size of the Cabinet, had to be controlled. In the case of the federal government, limits on Cabinet size stem from political tradition and concerns with efficiency. Hodgetts (1973:44–48) has argued the Canadian political tradition displays a perennial concern with relatively balanced provincial representation within Cabinet. Thus, while the number of nondepartmental organizations has multiplied, Cabinet, although now double its size at Confederation, consistently contains twenty-five or thirty ministers, depending on the government.

Two phenomena accompanied the state's greater involvement in society. First, departments assumed new, broader roles, and expanded with the creation of offices that were departments in themselves. Second, nonministerial administrative units emerged when new roles could no longer be accommodated within the departments' rigid framework. Of course, these units report to Parliament via the responsible minister. But with their own chairman, administrative staff, and technocrats, they often manage themselves. This autonomy is defended mainly on the grounds of economic efficiency, but also because it helps maintain a distance from political power. Nonministerial sectors of the state create no clear political responsibilities, and Parliament is never certain it has all the desired information about the activities of these organizations (Sutherland and Doern, 1986:39). Two departments, Energy, Mines and Resources and Transport Canada are connected to an especially high number of quasi or nondepartmental organizations. A chart of major connections illustrates these linkages. Along with growth in high-level civil servant positions this phenomenon has helped create a state technocracy.

The federal government, as defined by Statistics Canada, covers the general governments, including departments and services with special funds, and Government Enterprises (Statistics Canada, 1986a; 1986b; 1986c).

The departments form the framework

Figure 1

Excerpts from the Government of Canada's tree chart

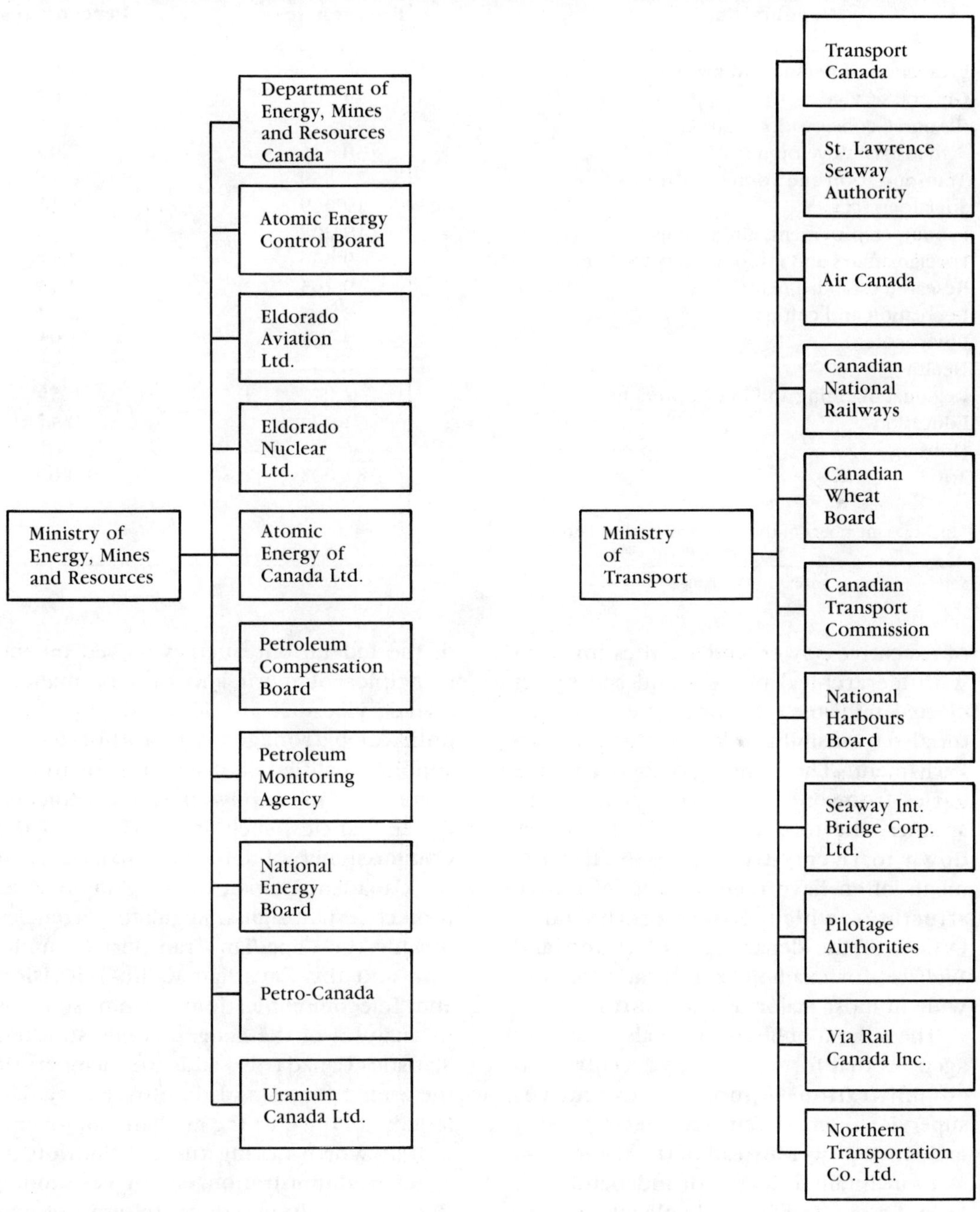

Source: Government of Canada, 1980.
Adapted by the author.

Table 1
GENERAL FEDERAL GOVERNMENT EMPLOYMENT BY FUNCTION, MARCH 1986

Function	Frequencies	Percentages
Protection of person and property*	166 926	43.81
General services	74 764	19.62
Resource conservation and industrial development	30 436	7.99
Transportation and communications	25 559	6.71
Social services	19 669	5.16
Labour, employment, and immigration	18 208	4.78
Foreign affairs and international assistance	9 556	2.51
Research establishments	9 265	2.43
Recreation and culture	8 468	2.22
Environment	7 368	1.93
Health	6 841	1.80
Regional planning and development	2 077	0.55
Education	1 774	0.47
Housing	92	0.02
Total	381 003	100.00

*Includes members of the Canadian Armed Forces.

Source: Statistics Canada, 1986a; Table 3.

of executive power, and are thus invested with hierarchical powers and run by an elected minister. The principle of ministerial responsibility closely ties them to Parliament. The number of departments varies from one federal government to another; the total of thirty in 1980 was down to twenty-five by 1986. Departments often have regional administrative structures which crisscross the land. Offices of the department of Health and Welfare, for example, are located nationwide in most major urban centres.

The federal public service also includes agencies that form a kind of decentralized administration. Appointed executives supervise them. A few agencies represent legislative power instead of the Cabinet, so as to maintain a degree of independence, even if a minister is nearly always responsible for them. Some are controlling agencies like the Public Service Commission, which play a key role in the functioning of the federal bureaucracy. Based on the principles of merit and of a permanent civil service that are designed to prevent political patronage, it is authorized to appoint qualified civil servants, or to delegate some of its powers to departments. Other agencies, such as the Office of the Commissioner of Official Languages and the Canadian Human Rights Commission, protect certain rights. Regulatory agencies include the Canadian Transport Commission and the Canadian Radio-Television and Telecommunications Commission. In its analyses of the general administration, Statistics Canada also adds the members of the armed forces and the Royal Canadian Mounted Police to the civilian employees.

It is worth noting the distribution of general administration employees among the state's main functions. In terms of employment, the protection of person and property is the most important function (primarily because of the inclusion of the armed forces and Royal Canadian Mounted Police), followed by general administrative services, natural resource conservation and industrial development, and transport and communications. Housing comes last because the Canada Mortgage and Housing Corporation is grouped with government enterprises.

In 1986, the general federal administration employed 242 399 people (Statistics Canada, 1986a:15). Adding the 32 691 employees of public agencies not under the Treasury Board, and the 87 155 military personnel of National Defence and the 18 758 members of the Royal Canadian Mounted Police, produces a grand total of 381 003. Men make up 68 percent of the total. A quarter of these employees (100 000 or 26.2 percent) work in the National Capital Region (Ottawa–Hull) while 20 000 or more are located in each of Montreal, Halifax, Toronto, and Vancouver. To cover all federal bureaucracy employment, the 206 354 employees in government enterprises (including Canada Post) must be added. The federal administration thus employed 587 357 people in March 1986.

Provincial and Local Administrations

While the general federal administration nearly doubled between 1960 and 1986, expanding to 380 000 employees from 205 000, or by 185 percent, provincial bureaucracies grew by 324 000, increasing to 486 000 employees from 162 000, a 300 percent change over a quarter century. Apart from school boards and municipal hospitals, local administration services (those of municipalities, urban communities, or regional communities) have grown less quickly, but even then their employment rose from 170 000 to 291 000, a 170 percent increase (Statistics Canada, 1986b; 1986c; Sutherland and Doern, 1986). Today, excluding government enterprises, 641 500 people work in provincial and territorial administrations, while employment in local administrations, including school boards and hospitals, totals 872 000. Thus, more than three-quarters

Figure 2
Federal government employment, March 1986

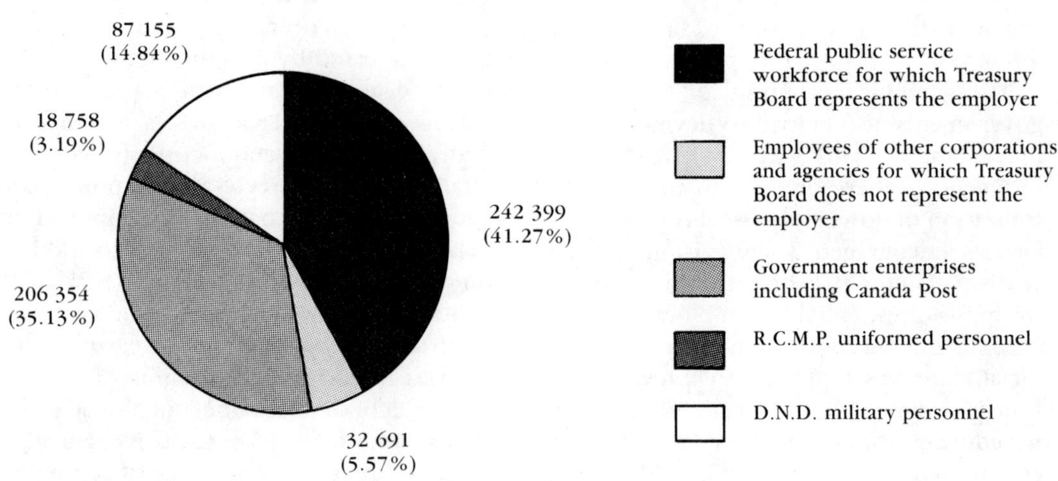

Source: Statistics Canada, 1986a:14.
Adapted by the author.

of all public sector employees work in provincial and local bureaucracies (Bird et al., 1979). What accounts for this substantial growth?

Even though Canada was already fairly industrialized and urbanized by the 1960s, many elements of a more traditional society persisted, especially in public administration. Systems of education, health, and welfare were often inadequate or nonexistent; local and provincial administrations were often rudimentary; and the Church still played a major role in Quebec.

At this point two processes intervened. Federal legislation introduced a series of innovations that the provinces were invited to participate in. But these innovations "required both funds for the beneficiaries of the services (such as grants to university students, payments to those using medical and other social services) and personnel to administer the programs and deliver the services (for example, university teachers and health professionals)" (Cameron, 1986:35). And in the end, the provinces and municipalities provided most of the personnel for implementing these policies. Furthermore, the provinces initiated their *own* programs, thereby stepping up growth in such services and the provincial state apparatuses (Cameron, 1986:35).

The growing autonomy of provincial governments also helped to develop these bureaucracies. This was particularly true in Quebec, where opposition to the centralization of power and fiscal resources in Ottawa encouraged a new vision of federalism. Under pressure for innovation (from business, an embryonic new middle class, labour federations) the Quebec provincial state was redefined in a few years. It became an economic lever and an agent for education and social policies that were comprehensive, rationalized, and suited to the modern world. The necessary resources were obtained in fierce intergovernmental battles that redefined fiscal arrangements between Ottawa and Quebec and more broadly between Ottawa and the other provinces. Linked to the movement for greater autonomy, these new arrangements were basic to provincial governments' expansion.

Government Enterprises

Federal Crown Corporations

Government enterprises, many of which are now being privatized, make up the rest of the public sector. Among those already sold are Canadair, de Havilland, Northern Transportation, and Teleglobe Canada. Many provincial state corporations have been or will be sold. For many reasons, even governments find it difficult to keep an exact count of public enterprises. Their roles vary, and subsidiaries are numerous (Canadian National, for example, has twenty-three). Furthermore, they include some mixed enterprises like the Canada Development Corporation, which is not a Crown corporation. The Comptroller General of Canada nevertheless identified up to 464 federal government corporations in 1980 (Howard and Stanbury, 1984:162). Not all of these, though, are government enterprises, that is, enterprises "created by a political authority to produce goods and services that will be sold on the market at prices which generally cover costs; conducting its everyday affairs under relatively autonomous management, or alternatively, composed of personnel who are not subject to the law on public service employment" (Bureau de la Statistique du Québec, 1985:228).

Fifteen *departmental corporations*, such as the National Museums of Canada or the Economic Council of Canada, are "entrusted with administrative, surveillance, or regulatory services of a governmental nature" (Government of Canada, 1980:710). Strictly speaking, therefore, they lack a commercial function. In contrast, *mandate corporations* such as the Royal Canadian Mint, the Canada Post Corporation, or Atomic Energy of Canada "are responsible for conducting commercial operations or services on a paracommercial basis, or conducting activities involving acquisition, construction, or disposal," which in other countries are usually undertaken by the state. Finally, the status and function of *proprietary corporations* like Air Canada, Petro-Canada, Eldorado Nuclear, or the Farm Credit Corporation come closest to those of private sector enterprises. They are "responsible for conducting lending or financing operations, or for conducting commercial or industrial operations involving production or trade in products and the provision of services to the public, and are normally expected to conduct their operations without budgetary credit" (Government of Canada, 1980). Thus, *a single continuum underlies public and private sector organizational forms*. The "purest" public organization is the ministerial department, while the "purest" private economic organization is private business enterprise. Between these two poles lie commercial Crown corporations, private, regulated public service enterprises (such as Bell Canada) and, closer yet to the private sector end of the continuum, corporations subject to various forms of regulation (see Wilson, 1981:6 for an interesting outline). This continuum becomes particularly apparent with the approximately twenty-two mixed enterprises, such as Telesat or Panarctic Oils, and private sector enterprises in strongly regulated sectors like communications. The upper managers of Crown corporations do not belong to the public service, although they may be formally considered high-ranking state employees. On the other hand, these enterprises' board directors often come from the private sector (Niosi, 1980:118–19). As in most Western nations, public enterprises therefore constitute a unique locus of interpenetration of public and private sector executives that reinforces ruling class unity. This interpenetration also shows that the logic of government enterprise is similar if not identical to that of private enterprise, except that most government enterprises cannot act fully independently because they are connected with departmental power.

Government enterprises are instruments of state policy. For this reason, since 1960 a number of government enterprises have been created to "encourage certain activities judged to be important in terms of employment or development" (Economic Council of Canada, 1986:113) (the Cape Breton Development Corporation for example). Others, tinged with economic nationalism, were created to affirm the Canadian presence or regain control in certain industrial sectors; taxpayers have often paid a stiff price for the likes of de Havilland, Telesat, or Petro-Canada. Today, we can assume the existence of 130 such federal corporations. These enterprises multiplied mainly during the 1960s and 1970s and "two-thirds of existing federal and provincial state corporations were born during the 1970s (Economic Council of Canada, 1986:8). Including the Canada Post Corporation's 86 000 employees, Statistics Canada (1986a:55) counted 206 354 federal enterprise employees in 1986.

A striking lack of coherence — what some call pragmatism — underlies the creation of Crown corporations. While Great Britain, France, or Italy have nationalized entire economic sectors, there have been no single, systematic Canadian policies. The drawn-out creation and placement of Crown corporations into sectors bear witness to this. Their establishment appears primarily intended to increase the effectiveness of government policy in specific areas, especially when private capital "will not" or "cannot" develop activities in line with goals whose national importance appears politically crucial. It may be a matter of maintaining employment, of encouraging regional development, or of saving enterprises with technological or symbolic potential. During the 1970s, many government enterprises were created to strengthen Canada's competitiveness, improve control over natural resources, or to strengthen Canadian unity and national identity, shaken by the Quebecois nationalist movement.

Provincial Crown Corporations

Provincial Crown corporations also multiplied during the 1960s and 1970s, except in the areas of electricity and to some extent telephone service, which were already developed. For example, the Hydro-Electric Power Commission of Ontario, now known as Ontario Hydro, was established at the turn of the century. In assets, Ontario Hydro's $29 billion put it just above Hydro-Québec as the largest industrial corporation in Canada today. Ontario Hydro is also a major employer, since 31 000 people work for it. Provinces have used government enterprises to enter federal jurisdictions, such as air transport. Quebec established these corporations explicitly to increase francophone control over the provincial economy. For a long time, such enterprises represented most of the few large francophone-controlled firms. But as Jorge Niosi points out, this type of state capitalism was not intended to serve large corporations ("monopolies"), but to foster the emergence and growth of a regional petite and middle bourgeoisie (Niosi, 1980:126).

By including both special agencies like the Régie de L'Assurance-automobile du Québec and de facto Crown corporations such as the Société générale de financement, the Economic Council of Canada identifies 225 provincial corporations. Their size varies enormously; only Ontario Hydro and Hydro-Québec come close to federal corporations like Petro Canada, Canadian National Railways, or the Canada Development Corporation. Of the fifteen provincial corporations among the Financial Post 500 industrials, only four have more than 5000 employees. But when it comes to regional investment, these corporations sometimes play a much larger role than federal corporations. In 1980, federal government enterprises were responsible for 4.4 percent of Quebec investment (not including maintenance), compared to 52.66 percent for provincial government enterprises, particularly Hydro-Québec. Many of these corporations are currently being privatized.

International Comparisons

According to Charles Lindblom, there are 18 000 public enterprises in the United States. However, these only account for 3 percent of employment and 2 percent of national revenue:

> Electric power is partially socialized. . . . Some railroad services and much urban transit are socialized. . . . Both federal and local governments own and rent housing; many states have socialized liquor wholesaling and retailing . . . state governments operate a variety of governmental units, own and operate warehouses, docks, conveyors, grain elevators and other transport terminal facilities, selling their services on the market (Lindblom, 1977:113–14).

Among the best-known American public enterprises are The Tennessee Valley Authority and Amtrak, a railroad company established in 1971 to continue passenger service. Furthermore, many enterprises depend on state contracts, while firms such as Chrysler have only survived because of state loans (see also Monsen and Walters, 1983).

In Canada, public enterprises have increasingly become numerous, economi-

Table 2
SCOPE OF STATE OWNERSHIP

	Posts	Tele-communi-cations	Electricity	Gas	Oil product-ion	Coal	Railways	Airlines	Motor industry	Steel	Ship-building
Australia	●	●	●	●	○	○	●	75%	○	○	NA
Austria	●	●	●	●	●	●	●	●	●	●	NA
Belgium	●	●	25%	25%	NA	○	●	●	○	50%	○
Brazil	●	●	●	●	●	●	●	25%	○	75%	○
Britain	●	●	●	●	25%	●	●	75%	50%	75%	●
Canada	●	25%	●	○	○	○	75%	75%	○	○	○
France	●	●	●	●	NA	●	●	75%	50%	75%	○
West Germany	●	●	75%	50%	25%	50%	●	●	25%	○	25%
Holland	●	●	75%	75%	NA	NA	●	75%	50%	25%	○
India	●	●	●	●	●	●	●	●	○	75%	●
Italy	●	●	75%	●	NA	NA	●	●	25%	75%	75%
Japan	●	●	○	○	NA	○	75%	25%	○	○	○
Mexico	●	●	●	●	●	●	●	50%	25%	75%	●
South Korea	●	●	75%	○	NA	25%	●	○	○	75%	○
Spain	●	50%	○	75%	NA	50%	●	●	○	50%	75%
Sweden	●	●	50%	●	NA	NA	●	50%	○	75%	75%
Switzerland	●	●	●	●	NA	NA	●	25%	○	○	NA
United States	●	○	25%	○	○	○	25%*	○	○	○	○

○ Privately owned: all or nearly all ● Publicly owned: all or nearly all 75% 50% 25%

NA — not applicable or negligible production *Including Conrail

(Adapted from a chart in *The Economist* (London). December 30, 1988 and reprinted with permission)

Source: Monsen and Walters, 1983:18–19.

cally significant, and a subject for political debate. This debate has been interpreted by some as a national trait, partly explained by geographic and demographic factors (a vast and relatively sparsely populated land), but even more by a defensive attitude taken in the face of the ever-present American threat of economic and demographic expansion. Compared to the United States, Japan, or Switzerland, Canada has a more developed public sector, but its degree of state economic intervention is not particularly high for an advanced Western economy. Table 2 offers an overview of the issue.

Compared to countries like Austria, France, Italy, the United Kingdom, or West Germany, Canada has produced a moderate public enterprise sector; employment in public enterprises is less than 5 percent of the national total.

PUBLIC AND PRIVATE BUREAUCRACIES

Public opinion associates bureaucracy with public service and the state rather than private enterprise. This is partly because in many countries the state seeks to limit public demand for its services, and therefore discourages potential users by rationing services through practices such as monetary cost, queues, spotty information, inflexibility, and inability to deal with individual problems (Lipsky, 1980:87–104). One monetary cost is the practice of applying a "deductible" to medical fees, so that users must pay part of the cost of their medical treatment. Although this should limit consumption of medical services, it particularly affects low-income groups. Similarly, "street-level bureaucracies" exact a hidden cost if they are open only during business hours, because clients who must absent themselves from work often lose part of their pay (Lipsky, 1980). Queues, which are also commonly encountered in banks and supermarkets, also broadcast the message that the organization's resources are limited. As Michael Lipsky notes: "It is dysfunctional to most street-level bureaucracies to become more responsive. Increases in clients' demands at one point will only lead to mechanisms to ration services further at another point, assuming sources remain unchanged" (1980).

These comments should be qualified, since many administrations have eliminated complicated procedures for their clients. Consider the ease with which fees for medical services are covered, thanks to compulsory premiums and health insurance cards. Obviously, the financing and management of such a program is made possible by a bureaucratic organization, which remains largely invisible to its beneficiaries. In such cases, public services are no longer criticized for inefficiency, but because they work so well, it becomes difficult to control increases in demand and costs.

The structural logic implied by public service differs from that found in the sale of manufactured goods, just as the state's political rationale differs from the economic rationality of private enterprise. Certainly, the two systems co-ordinate their policies and strategies, especially when it comes to accumulation, and they borrow management models from each other. But in capitalist societies, bureaucracy is not a unitary role that integrates economic, political, or cultural elements perfectly. On the contrary, in spite of their interconnections and interpenetrations, bureaucracies remain differentiated and heterogeneous. Claude Lefort thus argues that since the essence of the bureaucracy as social group is to crystallize into particular institutions, multicentrism tends to prevent it from achieving class unity. While this is true of capitalist societies, the socialist countries of the East should be distinguished in this regard (Lefort, 1979:304).

Of course, big business also achieves its goals by using techniques that have been rationalized, systematized, and standardized to minimize interpersonal relations. A logic of planning and calculation aimed at maximizing efficiency plays a large role in both public and private institutions. Yet, this logic applies more easily to private enterprises than to modern state apparatuses. It is therefore not surprising that Weber associated increasing bureaucratization with capitalist rationalization. Enterprises must maximize and maintain profits: this iron law imposes a need for tight calculation. Without the careful management and meticulous calculation implied by the principle of profit maximization, the private enterprise cannot avoid crises.

Yet, contrary to Weber, technical rationality of strict ends and means does not apply equally to the private and public sectors. This process appears initially, despite the many dysfunctions which have been uncovered, to apply easily to businesses. It is also useful in explaining routine state activities like the distribution of unemployment or old-age allowances. But technical rationality loses its utility, and is sometimes misleading when applied to public sector activities which cannot be reduced to simple repetition or control. The care provided by a nurse in a hospital or the teaching of English to a classful of students by a teacher are not goods with an exchange value. These roles and the tasks they imply involve a human dimension hardly reducible to calculation. For this reason, it is impossible to bureaucratically administrate, *without distortion*, schools, hospitals, government-run residences, or community service centres — that is, institutions in which services depend on social needs and political choices (Offe, 1975; Frankel, 1979).

Social and education policies in the 1960s showed little regard for the cost of services implemented because the state's coffers were full and because the long-term consequences of cost-free universal access to these services were not well understood. Nevertheless, citizen demand soon became difficult to restrict. Federal and provincial administrations tried to rationalize the delivery of social, health, and education services. Cost-benefit and cost-efficiency analysis became the major method of evaluating decisions.

The consequences proved onerous to those providing these services. There was new pressure for productivity, accompanied by performance standards and detailed formal control systems often irrelevant to the care of the sick or the qualitative improvement of teaching methods. Furthermore, a radical transformation followed in work conditions and in the professional status of the technicians providing these services (teachers, nurses . . .). They gradually lost their professional autonomy and stopped "being invested with the mission of providers of essential services exempt from any concern with profit, to become treated increasingly as variable costs to be reduced as much as possible within the context of state missions henceforth specified in terms of costs, goals, results, and performance" (Levasseur, 1980:313–14).

THE ORIGINS OF BUSINESS BUREAUCRACIES

We will not try to show one more time (see Moore, 1950; and Gouldner, 1954) why large enterprises may be considered what Weber called "unequalled models of strict bureaucratic organization." Large enterprises in industry, trade, banking, or the service sector operate with an organization based on specialization, co-ordination, hierarchy, professional management, indirect channels of communication, multiplication of committees, the appeal to rules and regulations, and the formalization and routinization of numerous tasks. But compared to public administrations, private enterprises seem to have more successfully combatted the worst consequences of increased administrative complexity; at least, this is the image they try to project. A "de-bureaucratization" trend has enhanced managerial flexibility and allows quicker decision making in a competitive environment. A recent study found 41.7 percent of Quebec public administration directors complained that they lacked freedom in performing their duties, as opposed to 17 percent of their counterparts in large enterprises (Sales and Bélanger, 1985:320). The traditional organizational hierarchy has gradually been called into question by growth in the number of specialists whose power is based on competence rather than authority. This shift to a functional hierarchy has stepped up professionalization within the enterprise. But these patterns are also elements within a larger rationalizing and systematizing process.

To understand North American business bureaucracies, then, it is essential to establish a close connection between accumulation strategies and the rationalization of top and middle management apparatuses in which techno-bureaucratic power developed and is embedded. For Alfred Chandler (1962), an historian, the evolution of large corporations has gone through four stages. The first stage focused on resource accumulation. Few businesses that were not small family concerns existed prior to 1850. At this point, enterprises were not yet bureaucracies. In the second stage, the need to maximize returns from resources led to rationalization. This, in turn, allowed further resource accumulation, followed by another rationalization phase. Strategies of growth thus regulate cycles which move back and forth between accumulation and rationalization.

The Initial Rationalization of Administrative Structures

Administrative innovations first appeared in the transport sector where operations were spread over great distances; they came to the less advanced industrial sector later. The continued expansion of canal and railroad networks provided the impetus towards new forms of organization: first came the *headquarters*, then *functional departments* which managed field units within their area of specialization (accounting, finance, maintenance, etc.). Next, the *central office* brought together department heads and the president of the firm. Rationalization continued with a formal definition of the relationships between departments and the advent of flowcharts.

In industry, however, rationalization first affected the factory and workers' tasks, rather than management. More than anything else, this occurred through the scientific organization of work and its effect on factory administration. Only in the next phase did industries adopt the railroads' organizational models. Railroads had in the meantime made it possible for urban and rural markets to expand, stimulating industrial production, promoting more intensive and complex production, and hence the establishment of a more developed administrative structure.

Rationalization of Resources and Integrated Corporations

At the end of the nineteenth century, the functions of merchant capital first become integrated with industrial enterprise, which now skipped intermediaries to deal directly with wholesalers, and sometimes even consumers. At the other end of the process, the enterprise created its own purchasing department and sought to pro-

Table 3
ENTERPRISE TYPES ACCORDING TO THE DEGREE OF DIFFERENTIATION OF THE EXECUTIVE AND MANAGERIAL HIERARCHY

Single-establishment unifunctional enterprises	Multi-establishment unifunctional enterprises	Integrated multifunctional enterprises	Integrated, diversified, and geographically dispersed enterprises
Undiffer-entiated management	Central office	Central office	Central office
Subunits with limited specialization	Management of field units	Departmental headquarters	Central offices or subsidiaries
		Management of field units	Departmental headquarters
			Management of field units

vide its own raw materials and intermediate products. Integration encouraged rapid growth and the centralization of capital, which soon led to an oligopolistic market (Chandler, 1962:26).

The power accruing from the accumulation and centralization of capital gave rise to large enterprises, but this created new organizational problems. Faced with the need for a new supervisory apparatus able to cut costs and keep track of market fluctuations, the president drew in the former department heads as vice-presidents. The distinction between executives and managers—central to the analysis of power — became formalized. Executives dealt with the long term while managers took care of day-to-day or medium-term affairs. This arrangement corresponds to the "centralized functionally departmentalized administrative structure." But in industries with rapidly changing markets or technologies, such extreme centralization type of organization constituted an organizational weakness. The solution, it was thought, was to establish a *general office*.

Continued Growth and Diversification

Confronted by market saturation and the problem of maintaining continued growth in the face of product life cycles, enterprises followed two strategies. First, the *internationalization* of the firm seeking new markets beyond its original national territory or easier access to distant countries' cheap resources gave birth to the multinational enterprise. Second, the firm *diversified* its activities, in some cases starting from a single technological base and developing a range of related products (as a manufacturer of electrical products like Westinghouse did), in other cases pulling together a number of technically unrelated activities to form a conglomerate (such as Canadian Pacific, now also a multinational). The term "conglomerate" is used when no fundamental production or marketing logic unifies the range of an enterprises's products or activities. If a certain logic underlies these, the term "diversified enterprise" applies (Government of Canada, 1978).

Multinational expansion and, according to Chandler, especially diversification led to the new division of executive and administrative tasks in the *multidivisional structure*. This fostered the decentralized management of divisions or subsidiaries, treating them as a federation of truncated enterprises.

The managerial hierarchies at the core of enterprises' bureaucracies were reinforced by these transformations, but also because productivity and profits grew and stabilized by relying on administrative co-ordination rather than market co-ordination. The resulting institutional changes help explain the striking increase in the number of executives, administrators, and professionals.

Following Chandler, it should be remembered that: (1) the modern business enterprise groups together units that could function autonomously. This has rationalized interunit transactions and allowed the implementation of administrative co-ordination; (2) the advantages of internalizing the activities of many units depends upon creating a managerial hierarchy. A group of managers can deal rationally with functions previously subject to price and market mechanisms (Chandler, 1977:6–7).

In concrete terms, this means that within enterprises unit production and distribution activities are supervised and co-ordinated by middle managers. The latter are overseen by top managers who try to control market mechanisms not only by price fixing, lobbying for tariffs, and setting up regional quota systems with competitors, but mainly by evaluating, planning, and allocating resources for future production and distribution. For example, during the 1950s, the strategies of diversification of big corporations were generally designed "to obtain the maximum return from new product as it moved through the (product) cycle from its initial commercialization to full maturity. . . . They attempted to have a number of product lines, each at a different stage of the product cycle" (Chandler, 1977:479). Among others, Lindblom (1977:5) and Chandler emphasize that these new bureaucratic enterprises have not replaced the market as the primary determinant of goods and services. But *using a strong managerial hierarchy*, they have deployed mechanisms for directing or guiding the market. Decisions concerning resource allocation and the supply of goods and services are based on estimates of immediate and long-range market demand. "What the new enterprises did do was take over from the market the co-ordination and integration of the flow of goods and services from the production of the raw materials through the several processes of production to the sale to the ultimate consumer" (Chandler, 1977:11). By the middle of the twentieth century, the salaried executives in a handful of firms "co-ordinated current flows of goods through the processes of production and distribution and allocated the resources to be used for future production and distribution in major sectors of the economy" (Chandler, 1977:11).

This is a key element in the advent of modern capitalism. In addition, the political-administrative sphere's expansion into the economic domain created new power circles. Expansion continued after the 1929 crash, especially, as the growth of the welfare state over the past thirty years has shown, in the state's apparatuses. As in all bureaucracies, the administrative hierarchy became a source of continuity, power, and sustained growth, not only for the enterprise but for itself (Chandler, 1977:8). Mechanisms for state economic regulation designed to cope with fluctuations and crises joined giant firms' internal mechanisms of politico-administrative coordination. The stabilizing market mechanisms (the self-regulating forces) defended by liberal economists early in this century proved inadequate from the moment the development of economic activities was seen to depend upon long-range decisions which were planned and executed long before reaching their goals (Gruson, 1968). As a result, the economy came increasingly to be administrated by large corporations and the state.

BUSINESS BUREAUCRACIES

To properly understand business bureaucracies, we must examine our national development. The work of Tom Naylor (1972) or Wallace Clement (1975) shows that early Canada was strongly influenced by the capitalism of merchants and bankers, with the support of transport entrepreneurs. Some firms existing at the time were Canadian Pacific, The Hudson's Bay Company, and the Bank of Montreal.

Banks

Financial institutions, especially chartered banks, remain the jewels of Canadian capitalism. The banking sector is extremely concentrated, with the five largest institutions controlling 90 percent of the country's banking assets. The Royal Bank's assets alone exceeded $96 billion in 1985. Although not the largest employers, these banks are enormous organizations; each one embraces a worldwide group of organizations linked to a nucleus, the head office. The Royal Bank employs 37 000, while the Bank of Montreal and the Imperial Bank of Commerce each have 33 000 employees. Despite extensive computerization, banks remain worlds of routine and paperwork. Consider the work involved in processing cheques and credit card vouchers.

Banks in Canada differ more than industrial enterprises from their respective American counterparts. They maintain few close connections with corporation ownership, even though they support many industrial and financial groups. Canadian banks' scale of operations also distinguishes them from American banks, which are more regionalized; the nationwide operation depends upon a regionalized multidivisional structure organized around a head office and a central computer network.

Banks' power is exercised through complex administrative structures whose size is reflected in that of the huge head office towers in Toronto or Montreal. The traditional image of a corporate executive group usually includes a chairman surrounded by a dozen vice-presidents. In fact, with, for example, over sixty vice-presidents in the Royal Bank, distinctions arise between executive or general vice-presidents, vice-presidents–general managers, division vice-presidents, senior vice-presidents, presidents of subsidiaries, etc.

Conglomerates

Canadian enterprises hold a firm grip on the transport industry, but so do Crown corporations, which possibly dominate despite the presence of Canadian Pacific. Yet, since the end of the nineteenth century, no enterprise in Canada has matched CP's size; it was the first large corporation to diversify and become a conglomerate. With a payroll of 123 000 people, CP is the largest employer, even though its assets rank below Ontario Hydro's, and

General Motors of Canada had greater 1985 sales.

Many other Canadian corporations can be considered conglomerates, although they are controlled by individuals or families, unlike CP whose shares are largely dispersed. With these groups, we switch from office sparseness to the plush drawing rooms of the Canadian Establishment, including: Conrad Black's group, formerly the Argus Corporation; Paul Desmarais's Power Corporation; the Bronfman's CEMP and EDPER, the latter of which controls Brascan, the "world's biggest landlords," the Reichmann brothers (real estate, Gulf Canada, Abitibi-Price); the Thomsons (The Bay, Simpson's, Zeller's, and newspaper chains); and, finally, the Westons (food, Holt Renfrew, etc.). These trust or holding corporations control sometimes enormous enterprises, but they rarely concern themselves with day-to-day management. This does not mean they merely watch as the money rolls in, but those who own and sometimes run these groups are much more active on boards of directors, planning long-term strategy, and selecting top executives, than in the executive and managerial structures of the enterprises they control. Furthermore, despite their financial strength, these controlling corporations are often lightly staffed; this does not make them a place for bureaucrats.

Foreign Subsidiaries

Although Canadian control grew between 1974 and 1982, foreign capital still controls 49 percent of the manufacturing sector, 45 percent of the oil and gas sector, 43 percent of the mining and refining sectors, and 26 percent of remaining industries except for agriculture and finance. Not surprisingly, therefore, the three largest manufacturers are General Motors of Canada, the Ford Motor Company of Canada, and Chrysler Canada, while in the energy sector Imperial Oil and Shell Canada lead, followed by Gulf Canada, which was recently bought by the Reichmann brothers' group. These enterprises all rank among the top ten in sales on the *Financial Post's* list of the top 500 industrials. Of the top 100 firms, thirty-three are foreign.

Many of Canada's industrial branches have thus become miniature versions of large-scale foreign oligopolies (Government of Canada, 1978:219). Under these conditions, enterprises' administrative structures are designed, and in the case of takeovers, profoundly altered by the American, British, or other parent company. Multinational corporations centralize important decision making concerning goals, strategies, and policies at the level of the firm's international executive. Interestingly, to cope with differences of language and custom, most American corporations with international subsidiaries locate foreign operations in special divisions separate from those of the United States and Canada. It is remarkable that in most cases the North American operations of Canadian and American branches have remained perfectly integrated, although Canadian branches are incorporated for legal reasons. Even as large enterprises, though, they lack the autonomy of Canadian parent companies. They are really truncated enterprises, and this affects their administrative operations. Rules and objectives originating in the foreign parent company must be followed even if they run counter to the interests of the Canadian economy. The pre-eminence of parent company/subsidiary relations over the nation's economic objectives is manifested in the monopolization of research outside the country, and even more when at the height of the oil crisis a firm such as Exxon N.Y. diverts to the United States large quantities of oil originally destined for Canada.

CORPORATE ENTERPRISE SIZE AND BUREAUCRACY

Large Canadian corporate enterprises typically operate in branches of the economy that display extreme concentration. The Royal Commission on Corporate Concentration pointed out that concentration in Canada is approximately twice that in the United States (Government of Canada, 1978:33). Yet, even though large organizations like CP or the Bell group exist, compared internationally the scale of Canadian enterprises appears fairly small. Advocates of greater concentration argue their size prevents existing Canadian firms from competing internationally. Because enterprise bureaucracies are being dealt with here, the number of employees rather than assets or value-added provides a more relevant measure of size (information on value-added is also scarcer). Certainly, the average number of employees for the top 100 American industrial enterprises exceeds eighty thousand, while for Canada the same statistic is only seventeen thousand. In addition, seventeen American industrial enterprises have above one hundred thousand employees (including among others those in their Canadian subsidiaries), compared to only two in Canada. The top one hundred Canadian enterprises employ 1.6 million people, against 8.3 million in the United States.

Table 4
NUMBER OF EMPLOYEES IN CANADA'S LARGEST FIRMS

Number of Employees (in 000's)	Industrial and Commercial Parent Companies	Financial Institutions	Life Insurers	Others*	Total
Under 2	222	79	28	41	370
2—5	101	5	10	8	124
5—10	37	0	1	1	39
10—20	26	3	0	0	29
20—50	16	6	0	0	22
50—100	5	0	0	0	5
over 100	2	0	0	0	2
Total:	409	93	39	50	591

*Fifteen investment dealers, ten real estate firms, twenty-five public accountants.

Source: Table based on figures in *The Financial Post 500* (Summer 1986). Subsidiaries and "private companies" excluded.

A relatively arbitrary size threshold frequently used to separate large firms from small and medium enterprises is five hundred employees. We were thus surprised to discover that enterprises of this size contain a minimal executive and managerial structure with at most a dozen positions (Sales and Bélanger, 1985). It appears necessary to go as far as two thousand employees before finding a complex grouping of techno-bureaucratic functions. Obviously, this type of structure grows with the size of the enterprise; a giant such as Bell Enterprises has four thousand executives and middle managers hierarchically organized so that each level contains all those below it, much like a set of wooden Russian dolls nesting one within the other. Table 4 shows only 221 Canadian firms, or 37.4 percent of the 591 largest enterprises listed in the *Financial Post 500* have two thousand or more employees. Herein lies the best chance of identifying the bureaucratized sphere.

THE GROWTH OF BUREAUCRACIES

Over the last twenty years, the state's ability to collect and spend has grown considerably. From an average of 29.8 percent of the gross national product during the years from 1960 to 1967, state spending in Canada jumped to 41.5 percent in 1981 and 45.8 percent in 1982, a remarkable 16 point increase (Government of Canada, 1985:vol. II, Table 7.30). The Canadian state spends more than those of the United States and Japan, but less than those in West Germany, France, the United Kingdom, or Italy, and certainly much less than the Swedish government, which sees 63.7 percent of the G.N.P. pass through its coffers. In salaries, services purchased, and so on, the state now spends more on itself (19.6 percent of the G.N.P. in 1980 to 1981), and it has simultaneously stepped up its redistributive role through social security programs (10.2 percent of the G.N.P.). But at the same time, a host of programs providing assistance to business has been introduced to stimulate the production of goods and services or to protect the weakest economic sectors from current structural transformations of capitalism. A task force concluded such government programs allow generous handouts to be given away under the guise of an incentive system for industry. These programs also lead to interministerial and intergovernmental overlapping, and keep 68 000 civil servants busy (Government of Canada, 1985:vol. II,41).

For reasons mentioned above, provincial administrations grew mainly during the 1960s and 1970s. Although the federal public service expanded in the early 1970s, it had previously undergone even more rapid growth (Bird and Foot, 1979:140). From 1940 to 1952 "it nearly tripled, swelling to 131 646 employees from 49 739. To date, this has been its single most significant increase in size, and yet it receives the least mention" (Morgan, 1986:1). Examination of the phenomenon thus calls for caution. At the outset, the relative contribution of the public sector to total employment must be established. The proportion changes from year to year, but usually the figures range between 18 percent and 22 percent. The Organisation for Economic Cooperation and Development (O.E.C.D.) gives a figure of 19.9 percent for 1982, compared with 19.5 percent in 1970, so the contribution of private sector employment has remained at about 80 percent. These numbers raise two questions: How does Canada compare to other countries? and, Have these proportions changed since 1960?

Canada ranks just above the average for O.E.C.D. countries: below Sweden (31.8 percent) and Denmark (31.1 percent), but above the United States (16.7 percent), France (16.1 percent), and West Germany (15.6 percent) (O.E.C.D., 1985: Table 13).

Sutherland and Doern (1986) have dealt with the issue of growth raised by the second question. They use the ratio of public sector employment to the size of the working population as an indicator. They think the working population is a measure that better reflects long-term demographic and social changes; since 1960, it has grown by 83 percent. In 1960, just under 18 percent of this population worked in the public sector. For 1984, in spite of fluctuations during the intervening years, the figure is still 18 percent. These ratios exclude military personnel in National Defence, who constituted 1.8 percent of this population in 1960, and 0.7 percent in 1980.

Can one therefore infer that the bureaucratization of society has not increased? The magnitude of figures in the original data reminds us of other realities: the multiplication of regulations which apply to society as a whole; the ever deeper penetration of finely subdivided administrations into economic relations, culture, or what were once considered private matters—training, consumption, physical and mental health, identity, social assistance, and various undertakings. Again, does the magnitude of these figures not reflect the transformation of work through rationalization within ever larger organizations?

Finally, as mentioned earlier, managerial hierarchies thrive. Much precise information is available regarding growth in the numbers of executives, managers, and professionals. Bird and Foot write "while federal employment as a whole rose by 31 percent from 1969 to the end of 1975, the number of scientific and professional employees rose 105 percent, and the small 'executive' class increased in size by 142 percent" (Bird and Foot, 1979:140; see also Lermer, 1984; and Morgan, 1986). As for the Quebec public service, the transformation from 265 executives and managers in 1960 to 2800 today gives a good idea of the group's ability to expand; while it grew elevenfold, the province's public service merely doubled. As we saw above, private enterprises have followed the same trend. We estimate 80 percent of Canada's 600 000 executives and middle managers work in the private sector, but the handful of large enterprises accounts for 35 percent of them.

Three issues concerning the social composition of managerial hierarchies remain: the participation of women, francophones, and university graduates. Has the multiplication of core positions in large public and private bureaucracies corrected long-standing female and francophone underrepresentation? Unfortunately, the answer remains negative, although significant advances have been made.

In 1986, managerial hierarchies survive as an essentially male world almost entirely closed to women. Given the magnitude of the question, here we can touch upon only a few factors which help explain this state of affairs: the forms of domination/subordination which have traditionally accompanied the complex social relations between men and women; the economic and legal (Juteau-Lee, 1981) oppression associated with these relations; attitudes towards motherhood, stereotypes within organizational cultures; hiring and promotion criteria which define traditional sectors and occupations for female workers (Kanter, 1977; Grant and Tancred-Sheriff, 1986) and relegate them to powerless positions. In a sample of business enterprises, women held no executive and only 8.8 percent of management positions (Sales and Bélanger, 1985:chap. 8). The past ten years have shown some improvement in the National Capital Region. Between 1976 and 1986, female representation climbed to 12.1 percent of top managers from 1.2 percent, and 22.5 percent of middle managers from 6.3 percent (Morgan, 1986:91, 112).

The underrepresentation of francophones in top federal government positions, so often decried by the Commissioner of Official Languages, is also well known. While francophones represent 25.6 percent of the nation's population, they hold only 20 percent of higher positions (executive category) in the public service, but are overrepresented in the administrative support category (33 percent). The same situation exists in anglo- and foreign-owned private enterprises. Progress has been made in Quebec, especially because of its language laws, but the francophone majority remains sharply underrepresented among private-sector executives and managers. While they constituted 83 percent of Quebec's population in 1982, francophones held 58.2 percent of top-level and 65.2 percent of middle-management positions in private enterprises of more than five hundred employees (Sales and Bélanger, 1985: chap. 4).

Finally, has the managerial hierarchy become a preserve for university graduates (see Porter, 1965:chap. 14; Olsen, 1980: chap. 4)? The answer is not as obvious as it might seem. Most executives and managers are well educated — six out of ten have attended university — but less than half of them hold degrees. On-the-job experience and internal promotion remain crucial, especially for positions in business management. Two comments are nevertheless in order. First, public bureaucracies have placed greater importance on university education and diplomas than large private bureaucracies. Eighty percent of top and middle managers in the Quebec civil service have studied in university, with nearly all of them obtaining a diploma. The public service's great rationalization phase of the 1970s drew a close connection between knowledge, planning, and decision-making ability. It was therefore possible to recruit graduates just when there happened to be more of them, while the graduates themselves were well aware of the opportunities offered by expanding public administrations (Morgan, 1986:chap. 3). In the private sector, the proportion of managers with some university education drops to 56 percent. Second, those without higher education have a harder time entering upper management. Even in private sector bureaucracies, 79 percent of executives have attended university, with eight out of ten obtaining a diploma. The notion of a rising technical intelligentsia seems true only at the highest levels of bureaucracy.

CONCLUSION

Arriving at the end of our occasionally somewhat rapid trip through the labyrinths of large organizations, we are struck by the impressive growth of large public and private bureaucracies. They have both created and responded to expanded social activities, as well as to profound changes in the power systems, social structure, lifestyles, and values of Canadian society. Their momentum, particularly that of state bureaucracies, has helped modernize the country and make it competitive among developed nations. The spread of political-administrative power has had the following effects:

1. A centralization of power related to organizations' consolidation
2. Market and social integration mechanisms are subject to increasingly systematic and rationalized control, or even elimination, by both public and private sector political-administrative co-ordination
3. The decision-making structure fragments into centres of authority and power which are often difficult to co-ordinate
4. Managerial positions multiply by the thousands, while the executive and managerial hierarchies to which they are linked grow larger and more complex.

New centres of bureaucratic or technocratic power lie within the state and large enterprises. Whether these forms of social organization and domination are headed towards crisis remains to be seen.

DISCUSSION QUESTIONS

1. What are the main characteristics of the bureaucracy as a form of social organization?
2. What does "bureaucrat" mean? which employee categories found in large organizations are included in this social group?
3. Comment on the following statement: The bureaucracy's core is made up of its executives and managers.
4. Explain why in state administrations nondepartmental organizations proliferated compared to the departments.
5. What are the relative employee rates of the federal, provincial, and local administrations? For greater accuracy, use the most recent versions of Statistics Canada catalogues 72007 and 72009.
6. The number of Canadian public enterprises has been estimated at 350. Can one conclude that the nation's economy is highly nationalized?
7. In your opinion, what distinguishes public sector bureaucracies from private sector bureaucracies?
8. Identify the main stages that led to the increasing administrative complexity of large corporations.
9. Comparing Canadian society in the 1960s with the situation today, would you agree that the bureaucratic form of social organization has changed significantly?

GLOSSARY

administrative structure pattern of organization through which enterprises or public services are managed. This includes both: (1) lines of authority and communication, and (2) the kinds of data and information flowing along these lines.

bureaucracy an organization with specialized functions co-ordinated through a power hierarchy, professional management, an indirect communication system, numerous committees, recourse to rules and regulations, formalization, and widespread routinization of tasks

bureaucrat considered as a social group, the term bureaucracy designates individuals engaged in the performance of administrative functions—whether office workers or the executives and salaried managers who constitute the core of bureaucracies

bureaucratization process by which a form of organization based on administrative rationality develops and spreads, typically within the context of growth in both an organization's size and the complexity of its administrative problems. Although intended to promote efficiency through forecasting and calculation, bureaucratic organization often leads to rigid management, the preservation of redundant jobs, and paper shuffling.

general government all government departments, services, special funds and organizations outside of public enterprises. Although strongly influenced by private sector management methods, administrative methods and the nature of authority are derived from the political sphere.

government enterprise capitalized enterprises in which the state holds an interest. In principle, beyond their commercial or paracommercial function, their purpose is to serve as instruments of state politics. Here, public and private sectors intersect because the administrative methods used are generally those found in private enterprises.

private sector in this case refers only to industrial, commercial, banking, and service enterprises, whose property is "private" in the sense that the state does not exercise direct control over the disposal of resources or products. This power instead rests with individuals or groups holding a share in the firm's capital, or it may be delegated to salaried executives.

public sector all federal, provincial, and local administrations and enterprises dependent upon and through which is exercised state power. Includes departments, municipalities, hospitals, as well as school boards and public enterprises.

BIBLIOGRAPHY

Alford, Robert R. and Roger Friedland
1985 *Powers of Theory: Capitalism, the State and Democracy*. Cambridge: Cambridge University Press.

Bird, Richard, et al.
1979 *The Growth of Public Employment in Canada*. Montreal: Institute for Research on Public Policy.

Bird, Richard M. and David K. Foot
1979 "Bureaucratic Growth in Canada: Myths and Realities." In G. B. Doern and A. M. Maslove (eds.) *The Public Evaluation of Government Spending*. Montreal: Institute for Research on Public Policy.

Bureau de la Statistique du Québec
1985 *Le Québec statistique,* Edition 1985–1986. Quebec: Editeur Officiel du Québec.

Cameron, David R.
1986 "The Growth of Government Spending: The Canadian Experience in Comparative Perspective." In Keith Banting (ed.) *State and Society: Canada in Comparative Perspective*. Ottawa: Minister of Supply and Services Canada.

Campbell, Colin and J. Szablowski
1979 *The Superbureaucrats: Structure and Behavior in Central Agencies*. Toronto: Macmillan.

Chandler, Alfred
1962 *Strategy and Structure*. Cambridge: M.I.T. Press.

——
1977 *The Visible Hand*. Cambridge, Mass.: Belknap Press.

Clawson, Dan
1980 *Bureaucracy and the Labor Process. The Transformation of Industry 1860–1920*. New York: Monthly Review Press.

Clement, Wallace
1975 *The Canadian Corporate Elite*. Toronto: McClelland and Stewart.

Crozier, Michel
1964 *The Bureaucratic Phenomenon*. London: Tavistock.

——
1968 "The Present Convergence of Public Administration and Large Private Enterprise and Its Consequences." *International Social Science Journal* 20(1):7–16.

Doern, G. B. and A. M. Maslove
1979 *The Public Evaluation of Government Spending*. Montreal: Institute for Research on Public Policy.

Downs, Anthony
1967 *Inside Bureaucracy*. Boston: Little Brown and Co.

Economic Council of Canada
1986 *Minding the Public's Business*. Ottawa: Minister of Supply and Services Canada.

Etzioni-Halevy, Eva
1985 *Bureaucracy and Democracy: A Political Dilemma*, (rev. ed.). Boston: Routledge and Kegan Paul.

Fainstein, Susan S. and Norman J. Fainstein
1984 Cited in "The Political Economy of American Bureaucracy." In Frank Fisher and Carmen Siriani (eds.) *Organization and Bureaucracy*. Philadelphia: Temple University Press.

Financial Post
1986 *The Financial Post 500* (Summer 1986). May 24, 1986.

Fisher, Frank and Carmen Siriani (eds.)
1984 *Organization and Bureaucracy*. Philadelphia: Temple University Press.

Frankel, Boris
1979 "On the State of the State: Marxist Theories of the State After Leninism." *Theory and Society* 7.

Gordon, Charles
1982 "Complex Organizations and Bureaucracy." In Dennis Forcese and Stephen Richer (eds.) *Sociological Views of Canada*. Scarborough, Ontario: Prentice-Hall.

Gouldner, Alvin
1954 *Patterns of Industrial Bureaucracy*. Glencoe, New York: The Free Press.

Government of Canada
1962 *Royal Commission on Government Organization*. Ottawa.

———
1978 *Report of the Royal Commission on Corporate Concentration*. Ottawa: Minister of Supply and Services Canada.

———
1980 *Organization of the Government of Canada*. Ottawa: Minister of Supply and Services Canada.

———
1985 *Report of the Royal Commission on the Economic Union and Development Prospects for Canada*, 3 vols. Ottawa: Minister of Supply and Services Canada.

———
1986 *Task Force on Program Review* (documents). Ottawa: Minister of Supply and Services Canada.

Grant, Judith and Peta Tancred-Sheriff
1986 "A Feminist Perspective on State Bureaucracy." Paper presented at the conference on *L'Etat contemporain: Au coeur de la société*, Lennoxville, Quebec, June 1986.

Gruson, Claude
1968 Origines et espoir de la Planification Française. Paris: Dunod.

Habermas, Jürgen
1984 *The Theory of Communicative Action*, vol. 1, *Reason and the Rationalization of Society*. Boston: Beacon Press.

———
1987 *The Theory of Communicative Action,* vol. 2, *Lifeworld and System: A Critique of Functionalist Reason*. Boston: Beacon Press.

Hodgetts, J. E.
1973 *The Canadian Public Service: A Physiology of Government 1867–1970*. Toronto: University of Toronto Press.

Hodgetts, J. E. and O. P. Dwiwedi
1974 *Provincial Governments as Employers*. Montreal: McGill–Queen's University Press.

Howard, John L. and W. T. Stanbury
1984 "Appendix to Measuring Leviathan: The Size, Scope, and Growth of Governments in Canada." In George Lermer (ed.) *Probing Leviathan: An Investigation of Government in the Economy*. Vancouver: The Fraser Institute.

Hummel, Ralph P.
1977 *The Bureaucratic Experience*. New York: St. Martin's Press.

Juteau-Lee, Danielle
1981 "Visions partielles, visions partiales: Visions (des) minoritaires en

sociologie.'' *Sociologie et Sociétés* 13(2):33–47

Kanter, Rosabeth Moss
1977 *Men and Women of the Corporation*. New York: Basic Books.

Kernaghan, W. D. K. and A. M. Willms
1971 *Public Administration in Canada: Selected Readings* (second edition). Toronto: Methuen.

Lefort, Claude
1979 *Eléments d'une critique de la bureaucratie*. Paris: Le Seuil.

Lermer, George (ed.)
1984 *Probing Leviathan: An Investigation of Government in the Economy*. Vancouver: The Fraser Institute.

Levasseur, Carol
1980 ''De l'Etat-Providence à l'Etat-disciplinaire.'' In Gérald Bergeron and Réjean Pelletier (eds.) *L'Etat du Québec en devenir*. Montreal: Boréal-Express.

Lindblom, Charles
1977 *Politics and Markets: The World's Political-Economic Systems*. New York: Basic Books.

Lipsky, Michael
1980 *Street Level Bureaucracy*. New York: Basic Books.

McCarthy, Thomas
1984 ''Translator's Introduction.'' In Jürgen Habermas, *The Theory of Communicative Action*, vol. 1, *Reason and the Rationalization of Society*. Boston: Beacon Press.

Mintzberg, Henry
1983 *Power in and Around Organizations*. Englewood Cliffs: Prentice-Hall.

Monsen, R. J. and K. D. Walters
1983 *Nationalized Companies: A Threat to American Business*. New York: McGraw-Hill.

Moore, Wilbert
1950 *Industrial Relations and Social Order*. New York: Macmillan.

Morgan, Nicole
1986 *Implosion: Analyse de la croissance de la fonction publique canadienne (1945–1985)*. Montreal: Institute for Research on Public Policy.

Naylor, R. T.
1972 ''The Rise and Fall of the Third Commercial Empire of the Saint Lawrence.'' In G. Teeple (ed.), *Capitalism and the National Question in Canada*. Toronto: University of Toronto Press.

Niosi, Jorge
1980 *La bourgeoisie canadienne*. Montreal: Boréal Express.

Offe, Claus
1975 ''The Theory of the Capitalist State and the Problem of Policy Formation.'' In Lindbergh et al. (eds.) *Stress and Contradiction in Modern Capitalism*. Lexington: Lexington Books.

Olsen, Dennis
1980 *The State Elite*. Toronto: McClelland and Stewart.

Organization for Economic Cooperation and Development.
1985 *OECD Economic Studies: Special Issue: The Role of the Public Sector*. Paris: O.E.C.D.

Panitch, Leo (ed.)
1977 *The Canadian State: Political Economy and Political Power*. Toronto: University of Toronto Press.

Peters, B. Guy
1984 *The Politics of Bureaucracy* (second edition). New York: Longmans.

Porter, John
1965 *The Vertical Mosaic*. Toronto: University of Toronto Press.

Sales, Arnaud
1983 ''Interventions de l'Etat et positions idéologiques des dirigeants des bureaucraties publiques et privées.'' *Sociologie et Sociétés* 15(1).

——
forthcoming
''La mobilité intersectorielle des dirigeants des secteurs publiques et privées.'' Paper presented at the 11th World Congress of Sociology, New Delhi, 18–22 August 1986.

Sales, Arnaud and Noël Bélanger
1985 *Décideurs et gestionnaires: Étude sur la direction et l'encadrement des secteurs privées et publiques.* Quebec: Editeur Officiel du Québec.

Sheriff, Peta
1976 *Sociology of Public Bureaucracies 1965–1975. Current Sociology* 24(2).

Stanbury, W. T. (ed.)
1980 *Crown Corporations: The Calculus of Instrument Choice*. Montreal: Institute for Research on Public Policy.

Statistics Canada
1986a *Federal Government Employment*, January–March. Ottawa: Minister of Supply and Services Canada.

——
1986b *Provincial and Territorial Employment*. Ottawa: Minister of Supply and Services Canada.

——
1986c *Local Government Employment*. Ottawa: Minister of Supply and Services Canada.

Suleiman, Ezra N.
1974 *Politics, Power, and Bureaucracy in France*. Princeton: Princeton University Press.

Sutherland, Sharon and G. Bruce Doern
1986 *Bureaucracy in Canada: Control and Reform*. Royal Commission on the Economic Union and Development Prospects for Canada. Ottawa: Minister of Supply and Services Canada.

Vining, A. and R. Botterel
1980 "An Overview of the Origins, Growth, Size and Functions of Provincial Crown Corporations." In W. T. Stanbury (ed.), *Crown Corporations: The Calculus of Instrument Choice*. Montreal: Institute for Research on Public Policy.

Weber, Max
1978 *Economy and Society*, 2 vols. Guenther Roth and Claus Wittich (eds.) Berkeley: University of California Press.

Wilson, V. Seymour
1981 *Canadian Public Policy and Administration: Theory and Environment*. Toronto: McGraw-Hill Ryerson.

New technology is something to learn about, and a tool for learning, in today's schools. *Courtesy of the University of Waterloo*

> *"The educational system is expected to provide individuals with the empirical knowledge and technological mastery needed for survival in the larger society, and to help them absorb values, attitudes, and interpersonal skills seen to be required for adult roles."*

c h a p t e r n i n e

Education and the Schools

Robert M. Pike

INTRODUCTION

This chapter examines the interlinkages between societies and their formal educational systems. The main focus is on educational structures and processes in Canada, but these are compared with those of several other countries — most notably the United States — that are at a similar stage of social and economic development. The comparison highlights those aspects of education in Canada that, while not necessarily "uniquely Canadian," have been strongly influenced by the historical, social and environmental experiences of the people of this country, and by the value systems that these experiences have fostered. However, because comparative educational research is often expensive, and beset by the difficulties of ensuring a reasonable compatibility of data, it is not well-developed from a sociological point of view (Boocock, 1980:277–78). Therefore, many of our comparisons are speculative, and based upon limited information.

The term "formal educational system" refers here to systems that are established and administered by public and private bodies for promoting certain skills, knowledge, and socialization experiences among the student population, which consists mainly of children, adolescents and young adults. Such promotion is mostly carried out by instruction methods (which include both direct student-teacher interaction and various modes of distance teaching) in or through schools, colleges, and universities, which are primarily devoted to teaching, learning, and pursuing knowledge. Admittedly, this definition seems to state the obvious, but we must distinguish between the activities in formal educational systems — commonly called "schooling" in North America—and other circumstances where learning may occur formally or informally. For example, some of the most difficult learning tasks for any child—notably, learning to talk—are usually achieved without recourse to formal educational methods. More debatable, the formal instruction in in-service training courses which many firms provide to their employees is not, perhaps because of the specificity of the clientele and the limited nature of the vocational goals, included in most academic discussions of formal educational systems.

In analyzing linkages between formal education and the wider society, sociologists tend to fall into one of two major theoretical camps: functionalist theorists who emphasize the role of education in contributing to social integration, cohesion, solidarity and shared norms, or conflict theorists who emphasize the role of education in maintaining social inequalities and in supporting the ideological perspectives of dominant groups. **Functionalist theory** has been criticized in recent decades for tending to accept uncritically the existing social order. For its part, early neo-Marxist **conflict theory**, which suggested education assists in the intergenerational reproduction of the social division of labour associated with the capitalist economy, has likewise been criticized for treating the school as a "figurative factory" (Curtis, 1984) in which the reproduction of commodities — students — left little room for social mobility or for the possibility of social resistance. However, as we shall see, more recent conflict perspectives, and notably those which stress cultural factors linked to social class as influences on educational opportunity, have considerable explanatory value. Furthermore, whatever their theoretical preferences, sociologists generally agree that formal education performs the following social functions, although they might disagree on how these functions should be interpreted (for further comment, see Boocock (1980:6–7).

1. The teaching of skills and subjects seen as important to a society's maintenance and future development are associated with the "instructional" and "socialization" functions of schooling: that is, the educational system is expected to provide individuals with the empirical knowledge and technological mastery needed for survival in the larger society, and to help them absorb values, attitudes, and interpersonal skills seen to be required for adult roles, including the quasi-political role of "good citizen."
2. Colleges and universities also perform a "research function," which includes building upon existing knowledge and creating new knowledge.
3. All levels of educational institutions perform a "certification function" in that they provide certificates and diplomas accepted by other educational institutions and employers as evidence that a certain level of achievement has been reached.
4. The "custodial function" requires primary and secondary schools to accept some legal responsibility for young people during their years of compulsory schooling.
5. Perhaps less obvious — but of fundamental importance to the sociologist —is the vital function that formal education plays as a sorting mechanism. This selection function, closely related to student assessment and evaluation and to credentialism, largely determines the individual's chances of

SCHOOLS AS WAREHOUSES

The custodial role of schools may involve **warehousing**. Warehousing occurs when, during periods of economic recession or a tight labour market, young people may "store" themselves for longer periods in educational institutions rather than adding to the pool of applicants for scarce jobs. Such warehousing may be encouraged by governments and potential employers.

access to subsequent educational opportunities and ultimately to particular jobs. In turn, the close linkage between the occupational structure and social stratification means the educational system plays an important role in determining an individual's ultimate social class.

The relevance of these functions will become apparent as this chapter proceeds. The chapter has three major sections. The first section explores some basic features of structure and control in Canadian education; the second section offers a sociohistorical overview of the major educational developments in Canada during the past century; the third section examines how certain basic values have influenced educational policies and processes in contemporary Canada. Throughout the chapter, the approach is macrosociological, emphasizing the relationship between education and the wider society. The strong comparative perspective is intended to demonstrate that an educational system is best understood if we recognize that the system tends to reflect the social characteristics and dominant values of the society it is in.

BASIC FEATURES OF STRUCTURE AND CONTROL

Canadian society has a weak sense of national identity and a strong sense of regional identification. Furthermore, the official definition of our national identity incorporates the doctrine of cultural pluralism as an important distinguishing characteristic (Pike and Zureik, 1975:viii–ix). To some extent, the structure and control of Canadian education mirrors these social and political orientations. The key to understanding the connection rests in section 93 of the British North America Act, which makes education a responsibility of the provincial governments by stating "In and for each province, the Legislature may exclusively make laws in relation to education" (Dibski, 1981:39). The word "exclusively" is important because it limits the overt role of the federal government in educational affairs and gives each provincial government sovereign authority over educational policy within its jurisdiction. Thus, it is difficult to speak of a "Canadian educational system" when there are thirteen systems — ten provincial, two territorial, and one federal — which show substantial variations in their educational arrangements. For example, the major direct role of the federal government in education, involving about 41 000 students, occurs through its financial support and administrative responsibility for educating such specific groups as Native people and the children of military personnel.

Public Education and Pluralism

Formal education is a large-scale enterprise in industrial societies. For example, 333 000 full-time teachers were employed in Canada from 1985 to 1986 to teach almost six million school and post-secondary students. Expenditures on education in that year were nearly $31 billion from public sources and another $2.7 billion from private sources (Statistics Canada, September 1985: tables 2, 6, 13). In fact, as shown in Table 1, Canadian governments spent a larger proportion of the Gross National Product (G.N.P.) on education than did many comparable countries, including the United States. Since Canada also has a dependent young population (that is, the age group under fifteen years, in Table 1) proportionately smaller than that of such countries as Australia and France, which spend less of their G.N.P. on public education, the Canadian government's spending on education seems generous by international standards. However, to obtain a complete comparative picture of educational funding, one would have to realize that privately funded education is more important in some countries, such as the United States and Japan, than it is in Canada.

Formal education in Canada is one of the most extensive systems of *public* education in the world. This is partly a matter of definition, because the term "public education" includes both the systems of nonsectarian public schools that exist in many provinces and those legally established Protestant and Catholic denominational schools that were given the perpetual right to public funding at the time of Confederation (Wilson, 1981:101). Indeed, to take a case in point, there is no true "nonsectarian" school sector in Quebec, since its public system of education is organized almost entirely around the two main confessions of the Christian religion. Overall, the relationship of religion to public education is complicated in Canada — one scholar has noted five different arrangements whereby the provincial governments define the legal status of established denominational schools in their jurisdictions (Wilson, op. cit.: 102)—and is not made any simpler by the varying amounts of financial support which the four western provinces and Quebec give to "private" schools. These church-affiliated and nonsectarian schools are operated and administered by private individuals and groups and did not qualify for public funding under the British North America Act. Most rely heavily on student fees, and

Table 1

NATIONAL VARIATIONS IN PERCENTAGES OF POPULATION AGED UNDER 15 AND IN PUBLIC EXPENDITURES ON EDUCATION

Country	*% Population Under 15 Years (1984)*	*Public Expenditures on Education as % of G.N.P.*
Canada	21.7	8.0 (1983)
U.S.A.	21.9	6.8 (1981)
United Kingdom	19.5	5.5 (1982)
France	21.4	5.1 (1980)
West Germany	15.6	4.6 (1982)
Australia	24.0	5.8 (1981)
Japan	22.1	5.7 (1982)

Sources: For population data: Organization for Economic Co-Operation and Development, Department of Economic Statistics, *Labour Force Statistics, 1964–1984*, O.E.C.D.: Paris, 1986, tables for individual countries. For public expenditures as a percentage of G.N.P.: U.S. Department of Commerce, Bureau of Census, *Statistical Abstract of the United States*, 1986, table 1471, p. 841.

range from well-known but exclusive "schools of privilege," through networks of Independent Christian Schools, to small individual schools run by particular ethnic groups or religious sects. At present, only 4.9 percent of primary and secondary school students are enrolled in such schools, but, as shown in Table 2, they have not suffered from the long-term drop in enrolments which the declining Canadian birth rate visited upon the public sector. On the contrary, private school enrolments are generally booming as some parents seek to attain educational and social goals, which cannot, so they believe, be attained through the public school system.

In maintaining a wholly public post-secondary sector, Canada joins many other countries — Britain and Australia, for example — that rely heavily upon government support for their universities and colleges. Furthermore, many countries provide state support for denominational and private schooling, but such support is not universal, even in Western countries. Indeed, the linking of church and state in education, which we take for granted, is quite alien to Americans. In the United States, the principle of the *separation* of church and state has been associated with the creation of a strictly secular public school system on the one hand — as one ex-American colleague described this system somewhat wryly, "It doesn't even give the chance for a moment of silence" — and a substantial number of denominational, confessional, and other private schools on the other, none of which receive public funding. Private education is not discouraged in the United States, but in the past, religious influence over education was seen as potentially socially divisive, and a nonsectarian public school

Table 2

CANADA: ELEMENTARY AND SECONDARY ENROLMENTS BY TYPE OF SCHOOL, SELECTED YEARS 1974–1975 TO 1984–1985

	Type of School			
Year	*Public*[1]	*Private*[2]	*Other*[3]	*Totals*
1974–1975	5 416.4	175.3	41.2	5 632.9
1976–1977	5 284.2	188.3	41.1	5 513.6
1978–1979	5 052.9	191.5	41.6	5 286.0
1980–1981	4 855.8	209.4	41.1	5 106.3
1982–1983	4 726.6	225.5	43.7	4 995.8
1984–1985	4 664.9	242.8	42.3	4 950.0
1985–1986	4 669.5	235.5	43.1	4 948.1
% Change				
1985–1986/1974–1975	−13.8%	+34.3%	+4.6%	−12.2%

1. Includes Protestant and Catholic separate schools operated by local education authorities according to the local school act of the province.
2. Church affiliated and nonsectarian schools operated and administered by private individuals and groups.
3. Federal schools and schools for the blind and deaf.

Source: Statistics Canada, *Education in Canada: A Statistical Review for 1978–79*, Ottawa: May 1980, table 18; Statistics Canada, *Education in Canada: A Statistical Review for 1982–83*, Ottawa: June 1984, table 20; Statistics Canada, *Education in Canada: A Statistical Review for 1985–86*, Ottawa: July 1987, table 6.

CANADIAN EDUCATION AS PUBLIC EDUCATION

Many Canadians are probably not aware that the definition of public education, including the university level, in this country is so broadly **pluralist**. Thus, many Canadian universities and their affiliated colleges have denominational origins and ties, but their reliance on governments for about 80 percent of their operating funds makes them essentially public institutions, subject to considerable government regulation. This contrasts sharply with the United States and Japan where systems of public universities and colleges exist alongside private universities funded largely through private endowments and student tuition fees. The contrast, is, however, relatively recent because Quebec and the Maritime universities, were, up to about thirty years ago, as dependent upon endowments and fees as many private universities still are in the United States (James, 1956:217). However, there was an enormous expansion of the post-secondary sector during the 1960s, and only governments were willing and able to foot the bill for this.

system as a potent factor in American nation-building. A similar attitude has been common in Canada, despite official pronouncements that unity should be achieved through diversity, and has often taken the form of attempts by provincial governments to assimilate linguistic minorities by withdrawing funding for denominational and bilingual schools. The best known attempt at assimilation was the withdrawal of public funding from tax-supported separate schools (mainly francophone) by the Manitoba government in the 1890s.

Finally, while religious pluralism has long been a formal feature of Canadian public education, so less formally has ethnic and linguistic pluralism, although often intertwined with religion. Currently, Canada espouses an official policy of bilingualism and multiculturalism. The increased scope for learning both official languages and for studying the culture and languages of other ethnic groups has, indeed, been a major educational development in recent decades. Not only young people, but increasing proportions of Canada's political, economic, and cultural elites are now fluent in both English and French.

The Locus of Authority

The management of a contemporary educational system requires both a good deal of money and substantial bureaucratic supervision and control. Indeed, in France, where most major policy decisions about education are made by the national government, the Minister of Education described his ministry in 1969 as "the largest administration in the world except for the Red Army" (Holmes, 1983:326). Such a high measure of centralized control over education at the national level contrasts with educational systems in which the locus of power and control is either divided more evenly between national, regional and, possibly, local jurisdictions or focused at the regional and local levels. Provincial government control over education places Canada firmly in this latter category. The twelve provincial and territorial governments each has overarching responsibility for teacher certification, school inspection, establishment of curriculum guidelines, and overall budgetary supervision; all of which enable them to maintain a reasonable quality and equality of educational facilities and services throughout their jurisdictions. However, the day-to-day administration of the primary and secondary schools is delegated to nonsectarian and/or denominational local school boards, which usually consist of trustees elected or appointed on a county or district basis. These boards establish and maintain schools, select qualified teachers, prepare budgets, and generally represent the public to the administration of the schools under their jurisdiction (Munroe, 1974:6). In turn, the boards delegate some decisions affecting individual schools to classroom teachers and principals.

In several other countries besides Canada, the constitutional arrangements give major authority over education to local and regional bodies. For example, education in the United States is a state responsibility in the same way it is a provincial responsibility in Canada. In addition, local school boards in the United States have traditionally wielded considerable control — probably more than in Canada — and this has led to substantial state and local variations in educational arrangements (Hurn and Burn, op. cit.:31–32). There is no particular constitutional explanation for the difference (Dibski, op. cit.:40), but the lack of an overt federal presence in Canadian education, underlined by the absence of any national Ministry concerned exclusively with educational affairs, contrasts forcefully with the real and evident presence of the U.S. government in national education through the federal Office of Education. This Office initiates and co-ordinates programs of national educational concern, and its activities are usually welcomed by state and local governments. In contrast, as one writer notes, "Canadian provinces and school boards do not welcome federal initiatives in education, holding them to be an infringement on powers granted to the provinces under the B.N.A. Act" (Dibski, op. cit.: 37–38).

The final outcome of the above situation is *not* that the Canadian federal government is unconcerned with educational matters, but that its concern is rarely expressed directly. Thus, as was noted by an international group of educational experts who reviewed Canadian educational policies for the Organization for Economic Cooperation and Development (O.E.C.D.) in 1976, the fact that no federal authority has the word "Education" in its title tends to camouflage the federal government's support for national programs in areas such as manpower training, regional development, bilingualism and multiculturalism, which are all educationally related (1976:89). Furthermore, the federal government's transfer payments to the provinces are intended to be spent mainly on post-secondary education (Johnson, 1985:passim). However, this "Do-One-Thing-As-If-It-Were-Something-Else" policy (O.E.C.D., *ibid.*) generally leaves the administration of federal programs and transfers in the hands of the provinces, and the result is often a series of unco-ordinated educational measures, rather than any nationally conceived strategems. Such a lack of co-ordination worries some people because it means this country, unlike almost all others, has no central body that formulates national policies and goals for education. Such a body would not have to be an organ of the federal government; it could be, for example, the existing Council of Ministers of Education, Canada, which is the chief medium through which the provincial governments co-operate in education at the national level. The Council is an interprovincial educational agency set up for co-ordination, liaison, and informational purposes. However, according to one commentator, it is reluctant to take on a national leadership role, being " . . . a creature of the provincial governments [which] do not, and perhaps will not, delegate to it any of the decision-making powers . . . which they so jealously guard" (Sheffield, et al., 1978:24).

Variations in Educational Arrangements and Resources

The centralization of educational control at the national level is often, as in France, the Soviet Union, and Japan, associated both with limited local input into educational decisions and substantial national uniformity in school organization, curriculum, and personnel policies (Hurn and Burn, 1982:31). In Canada, as we shall see, local input into educational decisions has often been limited because of the centralized power wielded by provincial ministries of education. On the other hand, for an observer from a country with a uniform educational structure, the interprovincial variations in basic educational arrangements in this country must seem remarkable. For example, such educational features as the length of time students must spend in school before reaching university entrance standing, the structure and content of the curriculum, the costs of university tuition, and the types of institutional structures for nonuniversity, postsecondary education all vary between provinces in an almost bewildering diversity. In a country of such huge geographical proportions and widely separated populations, there is much to be said for a substantial measure of educational diversity because of regional differences in educational priorities. However, such diversity makes it hard to conceive of Canadian schools performing the socialization function allotted to schools in other countries: that is, to act as agencies that instill all the nation's children with a common core of desired cultural traditions and values, as in France, or with a particular political ideology as in the Soviet Union. Socialization can occur within a decentralized educational system—for example, there is considerable agreement about core values in the United States and children are widely exposed to these values in the schools despite the decentralization of American education. Nonetheless, taken in conjunction with the "mosaic image" of Canadian society, and the lack of any broad consensus (not least between Quebec and the predominantly Anglophone provinces) on what our core values should be, educational diversity tends to strengthen the regional consciousness of young Canadians.

The diversity of educational arrangements in Canada also tends to be associated with provincial and regional inequalities in the provision and cost of educational facilities and services. In turn, these inequalities influence young people's educational opportunities. A broad perspective on such inequality is offered in Table 3. The table shows that in 1982 school board expenditures per enrolled student varied considerably between provinces, being considerably lower in the Atlantic provinces and higher in Quebec than elsewhere in the country. Since educational outlays as a proportion of provincial and municipal budgets are not closely linked to these variations in expenditures (see column 2 of the table), they are less a consequence of differences in government spending priorities than of provincial and regional differences in economic prosperity and in the size of the public sector. The Atlantic provinces have long been a relatively low-income region, with a limited ability to meet the costs of modern educational systems. Quebec, on the other hand, has a relatively prosperous economy, a high level of public expendi-

Table 3

TOTAL SCHOOL BOARD EXPENDITURES PER STUDENT BY PROVINCE, 1982, AND OUTLAYS ON EDUCATION AS PERCENTAGE OF TOTAL PROVINCIAL AND MUNICIPAL BUDGETS, 1981

Province	*Board Expenditures per Student (1982)**	*Education Outlays as % of Provincial and Municipal Budgets (1981)*
Newfoundland	$2,435	24.5
Prince Edward Island	2,440	21.7
Nova Scotia	2,671	23.1
New Brunswick	2,487	25.4
Quebec	4,357	25.2
Ontario	3,233	26.0
Manitoba	3,084	21.7
Saskatchewan	3,075	20.7
Alberta	3,300	17.9
British Columbia	3,502	21.1
Canada	$3,438	23.6

*Estimate

Source: Statistics Canada, *Financial Statistics of Education, 1983–84,* Ottawa: August 1987, chart 8, and Statistics Canada, *Advance Statistics of Education, 1987–88,* Ottawa: September 1987, table 12.

ture, and has obviously, at least until very recently, placed considerable priority on educational spending. However, the Quebec government recently followed the lead of many other provincial governments by introducing fiscal restraint in the educational sector.

In sum, then, in a country in which a weak national identity is accompanied by strong regional ties, the decentralized control and structure of education is a distinctive institutional characteristic. Each province has a rich and varied educational history, and each province has, often with only limited reference to the others, dealt with its educational affairs in its own way. However, all Canadian educational systems have been subjected to the same broad historical influences, and their responses to these influences have been remarkably similar. Consequently, the following historical section attempts to bring some unity out of diversity, especially with reference to the educational reforms of the past thirty years.

SOME LESSONS FROM CANADIAN EDUCATIONAL HISTORY

This brief historical overview describes how educational institutions and processes in Canada have assumed their present form. In particular, the overview points to the long-term dominance of education by certain values and attitudes that reflect our European and Loyalist roots as much as the North American pioneer experience. These values and attitudes have, however, been weakened in recent decades by strong internal and external pressures to conform to patterns of educational structure, commitments, and ideologies that draw heavily upon American precedents. Notwithstanding the differences in the educational structures and philosophies between the two countries, one must take seriously — but examine critically — the view of one O.E.C.D. expert that " . . . so much of what goes on in Canada is linked to, reflects upon, is integrated with, or deliberately separated from, the example of the United States. This is a fact of Canadian life'' (O.E.C.D., op. cit.:186).

The Rise of Popular Education

Popular education in Western societies is a product of the past 150 years. Schools for the wealthy have existed for centuries, but only during the early decades of the nineteenth century did a belief in the value of formal education for the mass of the population begin to overcome those conservative forces which saw ''educating all the brats of the neighbourhood'' (as one early Canadian opponent of public education phrased it) as an unnecessary, and possibly socially dangerous, activity (Schechter, 1977:373). The transition during this early period was marked by a move from voluntary education in which local communities and families made fundamental decisions about schooling and their participation in it—for example, the availability of schooling for most children depended largely on the willingness of communities to establish schools and the willingness of their parents to send them there—to state-supported education based upon compulsory attendance and substantial uniformity in instructional experience. Similarly, while there was little general appreciation prior to the early nineteenth century that schools and colleges did other than serve the interests of those who attended them, the central control and uniformity which accompanied mass popular education became associated with the pursuit of valued social goals (or, rather, goals which were valued by the political and social elites who decided on the structure and purposes of schooling). Some of these goals are referred to in the following discussion.

The doyen of the promoters of mass public schooling in the Canadian provinces during this early period was Egerton Ryerson, whose long reign, between 1844 and 1876, as Chief Superintendent for Schools in Upper Canada (later Ontario) witnessed the gradual extension of facilities for public elementary education in the province. By 1871, under Ryerson's guiding hand, elementary education in Ontario's nonsectarian and separate elementary schools was free, compulsory, and close to universal insofar as 85 percent of school-age children were enrolled for part of the year (Davey, 1978:224).[1] Ryerson's administrative approach, which his disciples carried to the developing school systems of Western Canada during the last three decades of the century, combined a heavy reliance on local taxes for school funding and a significant measure of control over education by the provincial government. This control was substantially greater, at least in principle, than was state control in New York State and Massachusetts, the two American states most often referred to by early Canadian school promoters (Wilson, 1978:40). It has been suggested (notably by Lawton, 1979) that such centralized administration at the provincial level reflected a paternalistic Loyalist preference for using government authority to pursue the common good. Certainly, Ryerson believed the Upper Canadian school system should promote social order and elevate the moral and economic condition of the masses. As we have suggested, pursuing these goals favoured centralization and uniformity (for example, in textbooks) rather than reliance on the varying tastes of local school boards (see Prentice and Houston, 1975:78–87).

This stress on centralized control is important for three reasons. First, even today, provincial ministries of education exert more authority over local school boards than is the case with state jurisdictions in the United States (Lawton, 1979; Anderson, 1981). So a substantial measure of provincial control stands in contrast to the decentralization of authority within the national context. Second, the development of public schooling was treated by many early "functionalist-oriented" historians as a consequence of a progressive desire to mould a more literate and knowledgeable population. However, a strong reaction to this perspective during the late 1960s and early 1970s emphasized the social control motives of the early school promoters. For example, many historians and sociologists argued that, rather than providing new opportunities, centralized authority and compulsory schooling reinforced the established order by helping to create a disciplined labour force and a politically passive working class. However, this argument has, in its turn, been criticized in recent historical research for not taking into account the limited bureaucratic resources of the early school promoters and the often successful resistance (as well as impact upon educational policy) of students, parents, and local communities. The emphasis has, therefore, shifted from social control to the historical study of "resistance": that is, the educational strategies used by students, families, and groups for maintaining their particular interests (see Wilson, 1984).

Third, centralization is important here because it provides a clue to the nature of those social values which helped mould secondary and higher education from the 1870s to the 1950s. For example, S.D. Clark argues that the considerable amount of supervision exercised over education by provincial authorities, and by the Catholic church in Quebec, indicates, along with a tradition of elitism in higher education, the dominant group's efforts to control the threats to their interests imposed by the values of American society (Clark, 1975:56). Thus, in contrast to the principles of "independence, impatience of authority, local autonomy, democracy, and egalitarianism" (ibid.) which influenced the growth of American educational institutions, highschools and universities in Canada evolved within the context of a highly conservative reverence for continuity and tradition: a reverence which, as historian Blair Neatby notes, led the highschools to reject American progressive education in favour of traditional academic curricula, and caused our universities to shudder at the prospect of teaching a wide range of professional and technical subjects, as was the early practice of public universities in the United States (Neatby, 1972:13–15). This conservative outlook, undoubtedly linked to values and attitudes imported from the Old World, was most marked in Quebec, where the Catholic church's dominance over education severely limited the opportunities for French-language secondary education until the mid-1950s. While the Church was pursuing a particular vision of French-Canadian identity and nationhood through the medium of the educational system, this vision manifested itself in the restriction of secondary schooling to a series of fee-paying classical colleges attended mainly by the children of the French-Canadian middle and upper classes. According to Neatby, "the curriculum was still based on Greek and Latin, and . . . priests still distributed prizes and punishments untroubled by the ideas of John Dewey or Sigmund Freud" (op. cit.:14). The rest of the country fared somewhat better, but still restricted highschool education mainly to an intellectual elite destined for higher education at university.

In *The Vertical Mosaic* (1965), the late John Porter subsequently argued that this elitist educational structure produced a **mobility deprivation** from which native-born Canadians suffered because they could not compete for jobs with well-educated immigrants (op. cit.: 46–47). Certainly, the Canadian population was less well-educated than the populations of many other advanced industrial countries at that time; for example, in 1956, our university enrolments (at about 8 percent of the eighteen to twenty-four age group) were equivalent to five persons per one thousand of population compared with fifteen per one thousand in the United States and nineteen in the Soviet Union (MacKenzie, 1956:191). This "mobility deprivation" is typical of restricted opportunities in educational systems which—to utilize two concepts developed by American sociologist Ralph Turner (1971) — were based on a **sponsored mobility mode** rather than a **contest mobility mode**, which has long characterized education for the White population of the United States (see Ravitch, 1983). Both modes reflect particular folk norms of a society which, in turn, define the accepted mode of upward mobility and help define the educational system. Thus, in Turner's view, under sponsored mobility, young people who ultimately fill elite positions in the society are "chosen by the established elite or their agents, and elite status is given on the basis of some criterion of supposed merit and cannot be taken by any amount of effort or strategy. Upward mobility is like entry to a private club where each candidate must be "sponsored" by one or more of the members (op. cit.: 72). In practice, such sponsorship is granted only to a few, often after gruelling tests and examinations.

On the other hand, according to Turner, contest mobility " . . . is a system in which elite status is the prize in an open contest and is taken by the aspirants' own efforts . . . since the "prize" of successful upward mobility is not in the hands of an established elite to give out; the latter cannot determine who shall attain it and who shall not" (ibid.). In practice, a contest mobility system tries to keep all children in school as long as possible, and encourages them to compete on equal terms.

In conclusion, most scholars agree that the dominant groups in Canada were effective in sponsoring their own kind. As late as the 1950s, nearly half of the small body of students who reached university were drawn from the 11 percent of all children whose fathers were highly paid professional and managerial workers (Porter, op. cit.:87). Again, Clement has shown that, in 1972, 41 percent of the Canadian economic elite compared with 20 percent of the American elite had attended top private schools during their youth: a good indication of the upper social class origins of the Canadian elite and of the important role played by "schools of privilege" in maintaining elite status from one generation to the next (Clement, 1977:240). The selection function of Canadian education at this period was, therefore, certainly characterized by a substantial element of social reproduction (that is, highly educated people tended to be of privileged social origins), although, as in all educational systems, some "humble but able" children did make it to the top. In the next subsection, we will see that "making it to the top" became a dominant motive for many young Canadians during the 1960s, a decade of unprecedented reform for Canadian education.

Educational Developments from the 1960s to the 1980s

Blair Neatby has suggested that differences between Canadian and American education during the 1930s could indicate either the emergence of a distinctive Canadian society or "that Canadians were merely lagging behind, and given time they would catch up to the progressive and **utilitarian** outlook of the United States" (op. cit.:18). Neatby opted for the former view, but the second view — that Canada was only backward — became a dominant theme in educational reform during the

1960s and early 1970s. I have argued elsewhere that during this period Canadian governments believed that more educated people meant more economic productivity: and, indeed, that high productivity levels in the United States and a generally better-educated labour force were often interpreted by policymakers as an indication that attaining American educational levels would result in American productivity levels (Pike, 1970:126; 1980:126–27). We know now this was a flawed belief; during the past fifteen years the Canadian economy has not responded with a major economic upswing to the expanded output of graduates from our colleges and universities. Nonetheless, this belief had momentous impact on education because it melded a materialistic message with the moral tenets of the liberal notion of equality of educational opportunity. Educational reforms designed to widen educational opportunities and overcome social barriers to scholastic achievement were supported because they were socially just *and* because they would lead to the more economically productive use of human resources.

The outcome of this ideological system was, as we mentioned, an unparalleled wave of educational reform. The rigid tracking systems of the highschools gave way to more flexible systems of course credit and choice. Externally administered examinations were abolished in many provinces in favour of internal evaluation by teachers (a reform that has since been sometimes reversed). At the post-secondary level, new universities opened, existing ones expanded, and community colleges were developed as alternatives to university. Also during the 1960s, major programs of financial aid for needy university students were introduced, and provincial governments began consolidating hundreds of small school boards into larger administrative units, a measure intended to facilitate the more equitable intraprovincial distribution of educational resources. These changes occurred everywhere in Canada, and were paralleled by moves in many other Western countries towards the greater democratization of secondary education and the expansion of post-secondary facilities. Internally, the greatest reform occurred in Quebec, where the "quiet revolution" caused firm intervention by the provincial government in educational affairs at the expense of the Church. Within a short time, francophone students in Quebec had access to a range of educational facilities that matched in scope and quality those of the English-Canadian provinces. That province's educational policy has subsequently demonstrated a commitment to enhancing opportunities for learning, not least through full and part-time study at the post-secondary level, which may be unrivalled elsewhere in Canada.

Two aspects of these educational reforms are particularly important for our purposes. First, they cost a good deal of money, but governments seemed — initially at least — to have a bottomless purse for educational funding. For example, in 1971 to 1972, education accounted for 22 percent of all major government expenditures at all levels compared with 14 percent in 1961; expenditures in higher education alone over the same period rose at nearly three times the rate of increase in G.N.P., from $273 million to $1,767 million (Anisef, 1982:5). This immense injection of public funding allowed schools and universities to expand and modernize their facilities and services and was an undoubted blessing to the previously underfunded educational systems. However, it was not necessarily an unmixed blessing, because in accordance with the principle that "the one who pays the piper calls the tune," it increased the already substantial supervisory authority of provincial governments at the expense of the limited autonomy of local school boards and of institutions in the post-secondary sector. Thus, 66 percent of all direct educational funding in Canada now comes from provincial and territorial governments compared with just 17 percent from municipal governments and 17 percent from other sources (Statistics Canada, September 1985:table 13). Since "the one who giveth can taketh away," such a heavy reliance on one source of money can be restrictive. And so the universities and colleges found when several provincial governments, disillusioned by the lack of the expected economic upswing and facing growing budget deficits, began the still-continuing process of cutting support for higher education in the mid-1970s.

The second important feature of these educational changes was the eagerness with which "mobility deprived" Canadians embraced the new opportunities for secondary and post-secondary education. Motivated strongly by a belief that personal investment in education would reap rich rewards in income and social status, young people stayed in school and participated in higher learning much more often between the early 1960s and the early 1970s. Approximately two-thirds of the seventeen-year-olds were still in school in 1971 to 1972, compared with just under 50 percent ten years earlier. Full-time enrolments at the post-secondary level rose from the equivalent of 10.6 percent of the eighteen to twenty-four age group in 1961 to 1962 to 18.4 percent in 1972 to 1973 (Pike, 1980:125). Such an enthusiastic response was remarkable in light of John Porter's earlier comment that Canadians undervalued education (Porter, op. cit:45). Highschools have continued to increase their "holding power" and the post-secondary institutions to expand their enrolments over the intervening years even though the large number of highly educated people seeking employment in a glutted labour market has markedly decreased prospects for intergenerational upward mobility for university graduates (Harvey, 1984:passim). Currently, students remaining to Grade 12, which is the final grade of highschool in most provinces, stands at about 85 percent compared with 70 percent in 1973 to 1974 (Anisef, 1985:Table 3.2, 56). Full-time enrolments in universities and colleges rose from 513 000 in 1972 to 1973 to 623 000 in 1979 to 1980 and 781 000 in 1985 to 1986, with an additional 316 000 students enrolled part-time in the latter year.

The tendency for more young people to continue their education has, in recent years, substantially reduced the impact of the birth rate decline on the post-secondary sector and the senior grades of highschool. This continued push for more education has been strongly influenced by two factors. First, the tight employment situation has, paradoxically, encouraged students to seek advanced educational credentials to improve their employment chances in the severe competition for appropriate jobs. There is also an element of "warehousing" here too, because universities and colleges play an important role in reducing pressures on the labour market when jobs are scarce (governments which severely cut funds for post-secondary education seem conveniently to forget this point). Second, the pursuit of advanced educational qualifications by growing numbers of Canadian women is clearly linked to their increased participation in full-time positions at higher levels of a hitherto male-dominated occupational structure. For example, of the increase in university enrolments since the early 1970s, about two-thirds is accounted for by the growing participation of women, who constituted just 37 percent of the full-time undergraduate population in 1970 to 1971 and 47 percent in 1985 to 1986. Currently, women students obtain 52 percent of all bachelor's and first professional degrees, and comprise over 40 percent of the full-time undergraduate student population in such traditional male fields as medicine, law, and commerce (Statistics Canada, July 1985: Tables 1 and 17; September 1985, Tables 7, 8, 9). Women are, however, still a minority of graduate students, obtaining 41 percent of all Master's degrees and just 25 percent of all Doctorates in 1983 (op. cit.: tables 9 and 10).

What, then, can a sociologist say of the educational developments of the past thirty years? The most important point is that public educational systems in this country have moved from a sponsored mobility mode to one based on contest mobility. In other words, rather than catering to a small intellectual elite, a combination of changing values and upward shifts in the educational requirements of the labour market have charged the highschools with the task of providing a climate where curriculum choice and scholastic assessment are relatively flexible, and where students can easily transfer into streams heading for post-secondary education (Anisef, 1982:7). The universities and colleges offer a wide range of professional and technical subjects, as well as the traditional academic disciplines, and their minimum academic standards for admission are set at levels sufficiently undemanding so that a motivated student of average (some would say mediocre) ability can go to university or college. This contest mobility pattern implies that a large proportion of students will complete highschool—which is certainly the case in Canada — and go on to post-secondary education. That Canada fits the pattern on this latter score is made clear by the data in Table 4. They show that in 1982 this country's enrolments at the third (i.e., post-secondary) level were proportionately much higher for both men and women than those of a number of other advanced industrial countries. In fact, the United States is the only Western nation with a larger proportion of its young people enrolled in university and college.

The values underlying Canadian educational philosophy and practice appear to have moved much closer to those of the United States. Thus, sociologists often describe Canada's public educational systems as having moved to a contest mobil-

Table 4

NATIONAL VARIATIONS IN SCHOOL ENROLMENT AT THE THIRD LEVEL IN RELATION TO THE 20–24 AGE GROUP OF POPULATION

	Percentages Enrolled			
Country	*Year*	*Male*	*Female*	*Total*
Canada	1982	40.6	43.7	42.1
U.S.A.	1982	53.8	59.2	56.4
United Kingdom	1982	24.1	15.8	20.1
France	1983	—	—	28.4
Sweden	1983	—	—	38.7
West Germany	1982	—	—	29.6
Australia	1983	—	—	26.3
Japan	1983	39.7	20.9	30.5

Source: Table 3.2 from UNESCO Statistical Yearbook 1985. © Unesco 1985. Reproduced by permission of Unesco.

ity pattern somewhere between the extreme contest mode of the United States and the ''controlled contest'' (or ''moderated sponsorship'') mode of Britain and other European countries (Murphy, 1979:201; Anisef, 1985:13). This description is correct insofar as most European countries have combined some educational reform with the retention of a selective secondary school sector, or stream, which is intensively academic, and which educates only a minority of students at the upper secondary level on the assumption that higher education is not appropriate for all students. Consequently, in 1980, only 40 percent of males in West Germany remained in school to the age of eighteen (the normal age for completing upper secondary schooling in Europe) and the equivalent groups for France and Britain were 39 percent and 17 percent, respectively (Clark, 1985:393). These retention rates, which compare with a U.S. high-school graduation rate in the same year of 75 percent (*ibid.*), and a typical rate of retention to Grade 12 graduation in Canada of between 60 to 70 percent, clearly relate to the national variations in post-secondary participation rates shown in Table 4. Academic selection is perhaps stricter in Canadian than in American highschools, but the closest that we come to the European model is the retention of Grade 13 as a pre-university grade in Ontario: and that grade will soon be abolished.

SOME VALUES UNDERLYING CANADIAN EDUCATIONAL POLICIES AND PRACTICES[2]

The educational developments of the past thirty years have been founded upon certain dominant values — notably, the value of equality — as philosophical bases for policy formulation. In this section, we examine the nature and effects of three sets of such values, including equality, which are strongly emphasized in contemporary Canadian education. One of the other two sets, which will be described as limited **individualism**, is a modified graft onto Canadian school policies and practices of a value deeply rooted in American society. The other — paradoxical **utilitarianism** — has strong roots in Canada and the United States, although its impact upon education has been less evident on this side of the border. These values are not exhaustive of all the values underlying Canadian education, but they are among the most important. They demonstrate also the existence of certain ''value dilemmas''—for example, equality versus excellence and individual realization versus group goals — in which some specific policy choices have either been made or are being currently debated.

The Value of Equality

Thirty years ago, Canadian historian Arthur Lower ruefully noted that Canadians were almost as dedicated to the ''great God'' Equality as Americans, and doubted this worship was compatible with maintaining academic excellence (1958:429–30). This criticism has frequently been heard in more recent times, not least in the argument that provincial governments have emphasized accessibility to post-secondary education rather than creating universities that are world-famous centres of learning (e.g., Johnson, op. cit.:20–21). Such an argument is probably correct insofar as the range of institutional quality and prestige of Canadian universities is relatively narrow compared with American institutional extremes — universities of world reputation on the one hand and colleges of dubious academic merit on the other. In actuality, university education in this country is relatively egalitarian in that there are no exclusive "Ivy League" private universities which draw their clienteles from a pool of the talented and often the wealthiest segments of the nation. Nor, as in Japan, is there a fierce nation-wide competition among students for admission to one of a few elite public universities, which are widely recognized as the "gatekeepers" for subsequent employment in that country's top corporations (Kojima, 1985:passim).

Has the "great God" provided appropriate rewards for his worshippers? The best way to answer this is to examine social patterns of access to post-secondary education. There are two reasons for this approach. First, a degree or diploma is the basic credential that allows one to compete for the better paid and more prestigious jobs in our society. Hence, it is important to know which social groups gain access to this credential. Second, one would expect the various educational measures which we have outlined to have sharply reduced those social differentials which characterized university education during the 1950s. One reduction—in gender differentials—has already been noted. We will now focus mainly on changes in the relative chances of post-secondary participation for persons of various social class origins as defined by the educational or occupational characteristics of one or both parents. There has been a good deal of research and commentary on post-secondary access in recent years (notably Pike, 1980; Anisef and Okihiro, 1982; Guppy, 1984; Anisef, 1985), and much of it focuses on social variables including class, gender, ethnicity, and place of residence which influence an individual's chances of going to university or college. We cannot here review all these findings. Suffice to note that being a member of a low-income family, having parents with a limited education, living in a rural area, and being a Native Canadian markedly reduce one's chances of post-secondary participation (see notably Alberta Advanced Education, 1984:1).

That "the massive increases in government spending on higher education and the institution of student aid programs did little to increase equality of opportunity at the university level" (Guppy, op. cit.:88) is most disturbing. However, similar findings have been reported from the United States by Hurn (1985:123) and from Australia by Anderson and Vervoorn (1983:passim). The case of the Australian universities is, in fact, particularly interesting because the abolition of all university tuition fees in Australia in 1974 did not, contrary to popular expectations, lead to any significant increase in lower-class participation. Anderson and Vervoorn think this was because financial measures could not offset the impact of "unchanging environmental conditions [which] depress scholastic achievement and keep aspirations low" (ibid.:4). Their comment offers an important key towards understanding the stubborn resilience of class differentials in Canadian university participation, as well. That lower-class children, and those from certain ethnic groups, tend to have lower educational aspirations and expectations than more advantaged classmates of similar ability is well documented in the Canadian research (notably by Porter et al.:1982) and adds to a growing international body of literature that suggests that cultural rather than material factors best explain perceived variations in educational opportunity. For example, French sociologist Pierre Bourdieu suggests that the higher the social class origins of students, the more they inherit a particular ethos and **cultural capital**—that is, a general culture, knowledge, and savoir-faire—which pays off in school (see Murphy, 1979:24). This cultural capital concept has two aspects. First, whichever schools they attend, the off-

CLASS AND EDUCATIONAL ATTAINMENT

The following statements outline the main conclusions drawn from recent Canadian research on the variable of social class.

1. The educational developments of the past few decades have substantially increased the chances of post-secondary participation for persons from all socioeconomic backgrounds. For example, in his analysis of the respondents to a large-scale national survey, sociologist Neil Guppy found persons of lower-class background (ones whose fathers had blue-collar jobs) experienced a threefold increase between the 1930s and the early 1970s in their chances of obtaining a university degree (op. cit.: Table 3). At the other end of the class scale, the chances for an individual of upper-middle-class background (one whose father was engaged in professional or managerial work) increased almost as much (Guppy, op. cit.: Table 3).
2. Notwithstanding the absolute increase in probability of university attendance, there is still a strong element of social reproduction in access to university. For example, Anisef and Okihiro have shown that in 1976 an Ontario student whose father had a university degree was about twice as likely to attend university as one whose father had a Grade 12 education (op. cit.:100–102). This disparity is similar in the other provinces, and does not appear to have been reduced significantly by the expansion of the university sector. In other words, as Guppy has shown (see above), the socioeconomic gap in probabilities of university attendance has been maintained because the increase in the attendance rates of lower-class students has been almost matched by an increase in the attendance of students from the upper social strata.
3. In contrast to the universities, the community college sector has democratized opportunities for education beyond the highschool. The relatively open admissions policies of the colleges, their vocational orientation, and their low (or no) tuition fees make them more attractive and accessible than the universities to young people of lower-class origins. Thus, community college students whose courses terminate at the college level (that is, do not lead on to university) are reasonably representative of all socioeconomic categories in the Canadian population (Pike, 1980:131).

spring of the "cultured classes" know better than the children of working-class background how to deal with the social and academic demands of the educational system, and are more aware of the long-term consequences which their program and course choices entail. Second, studies carried out in Canada and elsewhere suggest that expensive private schools provide particular educational and occupational advantages to some intellectually average and above average children from well-off families through "a carefully orchestrated program of academic and social development" (Maxwell and Maxwell, 1984:374). Thus, such schools work with these families to build upon cultural capital, and the absence of a private university system in Canada may give them a role in the maintenance, or acquisition, of upper-class status, which is greater than in countries where part of this task can be left to an elite system of private universities (ibid.).

By this point, the reader may have wondered what has happened to contest mobility. Clearly, an elite private school system is hardly compatible with its principles, but there is no incompatibility between these principles and the differences in cultural capital found in *public* educational systems based on the contest mode. This is because this mobility mode requires that a student succeed in high-school courses and also emphasizes the importance of individual motivation and interest in the choice of these course subjects — including the ones required for admission to university (Anisef, 1982:8). Ironically, therefore, contest mobility actually increases the role played in academic selection by such class-linked variables as educational aspirations and, as eminent Swedish educational scholar Torsten Husen has noted (1985), it may also increase the failure and frustration felt by the **new educational underclass**: those culturally underprivileged students who are referred to by their teachers through euphemisms — "book-tired," "nonacademically oriented," "practically oriented" (Husen:402) — and who still drop out of school before graduation. Unlike the more formal selection procedures in sponsored mobility systems, contest mobility offers these students (who would encompass many of that 30 percent of the Canadian highschool population that do not graduate at Grade 12) the same formal opportunities as their more privileged age-mates but, for that reason, the burden of their failure, and the bleak future job prospects which accompany it, rests more heavily upon their shoulders (Husen:ibid.).

As a textual footnote to the above, we should add that the danger of "blaming the victim" is very clear in such educational circumstances. It is important, therefore, to recognize that teachers' evaluations of students are sometimes strongly influenced by social stereotypes, which are acquired by the teachers in the process of their own educational and professional development. Thus, when teachers describe some students as nonacademically oriented, we should always consider the possibility that the educational difficulties confronted by these students may, on occasion, have been compounded by the teachers themselves. They are busy people, and it is very tempting for them to "write off" students who appear to conform in social origins, behaviour, and sometimes appearance, to the stereotype of a potentially low achiever and drop-out. Once this is done, there is a danger that lack of empathy and positive contact between teacher and student may actually increase the latter's chances of joining the educational underclass.

The Value of Limited Individualism

The value of individualism is associated with the development of progressive education in the United States during the 1920s and 1930s. Its acceptance in Canada was slow, and superseded an approach to education which emphasized group activities, with students learning to accept group decisions and contribute to group goals (Neatby op. cit.:13). For this reason, we have suggested that the value has been grafted onto more traditional value-orientations in Canadian education, although the graft seems to have taken firmly as an important value underlying the definition of curriculum goals and for guiding processes of course choice and assessment. Two American scholars have provided the following succinct description of the application of this value in society:

> We mean [by individualism] a belief that a society's worth depends on the extent to which individuals can achieve such personal goals as happiness or fulfillment. Such fulfillment, moreover, is not normally seen as resulting from working for collective or societal goals (as it is in the official ideology of the Soviet Union). Rather, the thrust of individualism is that roads to fulfillment or happiness cannot be socially prescribed. . . . And authority of virtually any kind, especially government authority, is seen as potentially threatening to freedom and to individual autonomy (Hurn and Burn, op. cit:19).

We have described the application of this value to education in this country as "limited" because the suspicion of government authority mentioned above is far less evident in Canada than in the United States. Opinion polls show, for example, that Canadians are less likely than Americans to see their governments as having excessive power, and more likely to accept the need for government action to promote social welfare (see, for example, Arnold, White, and Tigert, 1972). In the educational sphere, this limitation is particularly evident in the relationships between provincial and local authorities and the community. This topic will be briefly reviewed after we comment on those areas of education in which individualism is important.

Ministry of Education circulars outlining the goals of education usually refer to the desirability that students should "develop a sense of personal responsibility in society" (Ontario, 1984:3), but such a goal is often subordinate to other goals that emphasize the importance of achieving self-worth and self-reliance. By contrast, in countries that strongly value group conformity or co-operation, the dominant stress in educational philosophy and practice is not individual development, but "to awaken in the individual a sense of his participation in and relationship to a community" (Hurn and Burn:20). For example, Soviet educators place tremendous emphasis on moulding citizens who are willing to sacrifice individual interest on behalf of the **collectivity**. Russian children do not only receive political instruction in Marxism–Leninism, but are taught stories emphasizing the value of individual sacrifice for group goals. Their classroom activities also encourage co-operation between students in the same row, but competition between rows (Zadja, 1980: Chapter 3; Bronfenbrenner, 1970:passim). In Japan, likewise, fierce competition through national examinations for scarce places in prestigious secondary schools and universities does not appear to undermine the school system's success in instilling students with a strong sense of the value and desirability of social conformity (Hurn and Burn, op. cit.:28). Japanese students develop a strong sense of obligation and commitment to their school and, through it, to the wider society (ibid.).

We are not suggesting that an individualist orientation is entirely dominant in Canadian education, but in comparison with education in some countries, and, indeed, with earlier times in this country, individualism is more pivotal for educational philosophy and practice. Thus, its practical applications are evident in such post-war reforms as promotion by subject rather than grade, the maximization of student choice in highschool courses, and the assessment of graduating highschool students by their teachers rather than through uniform province-wide examinations. However, like the pursuit of equality with which individualized instruction is closely related, the effect of these child-centred reforms on academic standards has been subjected to considerable critical scrutiny.

To take a case in point, the recent report of the provincial Royal Commission on Post-Secondary Education in Nova Scotia (1985) suggests that the lack of a required core curriculum consisting of certain fundamental subjects means that many of the province's students enter university ill-prepared to cope with its demands (op. cit.: 51–53).[3] This lack of structure in the curriculum, combined with substantial school-by-school variations in teachers' marking standards, are cited as some principal causes for the high drop-out rate [about 50 percent] of Nova Scotian students who leave university before completing their degrees (op. cit.,:53). Similar complaints are common elsewhere in Canada, and have reached a crescendo in the United States where individualism in education appears, all too often, to have been equated with a lack of structure and discipline (Hurn, op. cit.: Chapter 8).

A comprehensive core curriculum of the kind referred to by the Nova Scotia Commission has been introduced in Ontario, New Brunswick, Newfoundland, and Manitoba, as well as in thirteen American states (Nova Scotia Report: 51). In addition, Quebec and Newfoundland have maintained uniform departmental examinations at the end of secondary studies, while Alberta has recently re-introduced them. These are attempts to remedy perceived weaknesses in curriculum structures and standards of student evaluation, although Canadian public education remains far more committed to child-centred learning than in most Western countries. As noted by Hurn and Burn, the amount of student choice over subjects for study has increased in most societies, but secondary school students in Britain, France, and Germany must still, as in Japan, work towards rigorous final examinations and "decisions to add new subjects [for the examinations] are made by national or central educational authorities who see themselves as guardians of educational standards and who are often acutely sensitive to the charge that any innovation means a lowering of standards" (op. cit: 22). Thus, although provincial authorities in Canada determine the structure of the school curricula, they have been more responsive than the educational authorities of many European countries to demands that these curricula be made increasingly relevant to student needs.

Finally, we return to the suggestion that individualism has only limited applicability to Canadian education. We have seen that provincial governments in this country exert greater direct control over educational policy than do their U.S. counterparts. By the same token, local school boards have less executive freedom, and this has been eroded recently by increased reliance on provincial government funding. Stephen Lawton has suggested this difference in educational administration between the two countries shows the greater willingness of Canadians to accept government authority, and he argues that it has enabled provincial ministries of education to reduce disparities in funding between school districts with their jurisdictions to a far greater extent than has happened within the American states (1979:passim). However, looking at the same theme from another angle, an interesting hypothesis emerges. The more centralized control of education in Canada may provide teachers with a greater measure of insulation against pressure by parents and local groups than is the case with the harassed teaching profession in the United States (Hurn and Burn:35). Thus, while Canadian school trustees and teachers may face irate parents and extremist community groups that wish to ban "unsuitable" books from the schools (see Dick, 1982), they seem to have a greater capacity to withstand such confrontations because it is easier for them to fall back on the provincial ministry of education as "a court of final appeal."

The Value of Paradoxical Utilitarianism

The value of utilitarianism refers to the belief that education should be useful, provide specific skills, advance careers, and enhance job prospects. In their comparative study, Hurn and Burn stressed the importance of this value in the moulding of American education (op. cit.:14–19). Its historical significance in Canada is less obvious because of the early emphasis upon a predominantly academic highschool curriculum. Nonetheless, practical and vocational studies have a long tradition in this country, and ample evidence suggests public attitudes and educational patterns in contemporary Canada reflect strong utilitarian sentiments.[4] For example, the average highschool offers far more socially useful "life-skill" electives (including courses in baby-sitting, first-aid, and community volunteer work) than would be considered appropriate in most European countries.

We shall concentrate on only one feature of utilitarianism: namely, vocational education. Vocational courses provide students with knowledge and skills that directly relate to a specific job or to a particular area of employment. In addition to the vocational orientation of the community college sectors, most provincial educational systems provide vocational and occupational education at the highschool level. This education frequently consists of short occupational programs leading to employment in the service industries or into craft apprenticeship. However, the status of these programs has become increasingly weak and ambiguous in recent decades. For example, a recent report on the school system of Prince Edward Island notes that "confusion appears to exist as to whether the highschool vocational program is designed to pursue a 'trade' or supply a personal interest . . . there is a sense that highschool students today are not counselled towards a vocational career, but rather towards courses for highschool credit" (Paquette, 1984:26–27). Likewise, in Quebec, the advisory Conseil Superieur de l'éducation has recently observed that the short vocational program in the province's secondary schools is criticized as "a dumping ground for students demoralized by earlier failure and [for] attracting only those pupils who have little aptitude for abstract intellectual pursuits" (1983:1).

This decline in the status of vocational secondary schooling points to an apparently paradoxical situation: explicitly vocational programs are in decline even though the Canadian public believes that education should provide useful skills and advance employment opportunities. How can the paradox be explained? One factor is undoubtedly the incompatibility between current concepts of educational equality and patterns of differentiated or segmented schooling which close off the avenues to post-secondary studies for some students at an early stage of their highschool careers. Another factor is the shift of vocational education upward from the highschools and into the colleges and universities. Canadian universities have not yet become adjuncts to the business community, as seems the fate of many American universities (in 1983, 24 percent of all bachelor's degrees awarded by U.S. universities were in business and management studies, compared with just 14 percent in 1971) (U.S. Department of Commerce, 1986: Table 273). However, as shown in Table 5, Canadian university education has become increasingly devoted to business and professional studies during the past fifteen years. In 1970, one-fifth of all first degrees awarded by

Table 5
CANADIAN UNIVERSITIES: BACHELORS' AND FIRST PROFESSIONAL DEGREES AWARDED BY FIELD OF STUDY, 1970–1983: PERCENTAGES

Field	*1970*	*1975*	*1980*	*1983*
Humanities	15.8	12.5	11.0	9.8
Social Sciences	15.9	17.9	17.8	17.1
Maths and Physical Sciences	6.0	5.0	5.1	6.2
Agricultural and Biological Sciences	5.4	6.2	6.3	5.4
Engineering and Applied Sciences	6.8	6.0	8.4	8.6
Commerce and Business Administration	4.9	6.6	10.0	12.7
Law	2.5	3.3	3.5	3.7
Health Sciences	5.7	6.3	6.7	6.8
Education	20.3	22.8	19.5	17.2
Fine and Applied Arts	1.4	2.7	3.1	3.2
Unclassified	15.3	10.7	8.6	9.3
	100.0	100.0	100.0	100.0
	(60 523)	(80 754)	(86 410)	(89 782)

Sources: Statistics Canada, *A Statistical Portrait of Canadian Higher Education from the 1960's to the 1980's*, Ottawa: May 1983, table 19; and Statistics Canada, *Education in Canada: A Statistical Profile for 1985–86*, Ottawa: July 1987, table 31.

Canadian universities were in business, law, engineering, and health. By 1983, almost one-third of all first degrees were awarded to students from these fields.

Canada is not alone in shifting away from secondary vocational schooling. Aaron Benevot has shown that a decline in such schooling is occurring in most Western and Third World Countries, mainly because "worldwide ideological [factors] press for systems of secondary schooling that guarantee greater formal equality for children of all social classes and serve as a means of initiating young people into their roles as citizens of the modern state" (1983:74). Despite this trend, there is not universal agreement among Canadian educationalists that it is good for all Canadian students. For example, the Quebec Conseil Superieur de l'éducation has shown hard-nosed opposition to a provincial government proposal to reduce the vocational element in schooling in favour of a longer "homogenous school experience, accessible to all young people" (op. cit.: 11). The Conseil's position is interesting because its recognition that short vocational programs may become a dumping ground for demoralized students is balanced by an affirmation that such programs can make secondary school meaningful to many "practically oriented" students (those in Husen's "new educational underclass") who fail to benefit from extended general studies (op. cit.:26).

We shall not attempt to assess the merits of this argument, except to note it highlights a value dilemma between early streaming in secondary school as a means of achieving utilitarian goals and the existence of an open contest system of schooling. More specifically, the Quebec Conseil's argument would likely be opposed by scholars who see early tracking into vocational programs as a mechanism that limits young people's educational horizons, and one that provides no answer to a job crisis caused by low demand for qualified workers (Lazerson and Dunn, 1977). But regardless of the stance one takes on the issue, there is little doubt that the fundamental need is to find ways of providing a valuable secondary school experience to highschool students who are not academically inclined and who treat extended schooling as a tedious form of custodial care (see Nelsen, 1985; Hurn, op. cit.: 273). If a solution can be found in a closer interlinkage between secondary education and the labour market, then so be it (although it is debatable whether vocational education would produce more employment at a time when job requirements are changing so rapidly). But as Husen suggests, a more effective solution might be to make highschools smaller and more socially intimate institutions: in short, places where all students can participate and develop some sense of self-worth (op. cit).

CONCLUSION

We have explored some features of education that might be considered distinctively Canadian, and some that are common to many industrial societies. We have introduced sociological concepts and theories that have helped make sense of our findings, but these concepts and theories are tools that assist in constructing our social image of Canadian education rather than blueprints that predetermine the form of that construction. Above all, our approach has been strongly comparative, emphasizing that educational systems reflect the values and traditions of the particular societies they are in. This comparative analysis has shown us that education in Canada is administratively decentralized, religiously and ethnically pluralistic, and structurally diverse. It is also remarkably "open" in that it provides substantial opportunities for advanced secondary and post-secondary education. Few other countries can claim that 40 percent of young people in the twenty to twenty-four age group have studied at the post-secondary level (Government of Canada, 1984:11).

What, therefore, are our conclusions? Here we have space for only two sets of concluding observations, one based upon the comparative analysis and the other a comment on the applicability of macro-theories to the social trends outlined in this chapter. The comparative analysis has revealed significant similarities and differences in the structure and values of education in Canada and the United States. Certainly, the two systems are more alike than education in Canada compared, say, with education in Western European nations. By the same token, the greater centralization of control over education by provincial (compared with state) governments is of considerable historical significance, as is the absence of a separation between church and state in the funding of public education in Canada. One more difference might be added: criticisms of public education in Canada—and notably that academic standards have declined in recent decades—are mild in contrast with the massive crisis of confidence which is currently shaking American public education.[5] This indicates a greater willingness (and perhaps administrative ability) among public bodies in this country to commit financial resources to the intraprovincial equalization of educational facilities and to pay adequate salaries for teachers. As a case in point, a recent report of the Council of Ministers of Education, Canada, notes that the typical Canadian school teacher is in her mid-thirties, earning roughly $29,000 to $34,000 a year, and enjoying comprehensive fringe benefits (1984:56). According to the U.S. National Commission on Excellence in Education (1983:22–23), the average salary after twelve years of teaching for an American school teacher is U.S. $17,000—a rate so low that many teachers supplement their income with summer and part-time employment. This striking contrast adds weight to the generalization that the quality of public education is probably higher in this country, and is supported by a teaching profession that enjoys a social status and material rewards which the average American teacher might envy.[6]

The above comments sound self-satisfied, and should be balanced by a critical awareness that many of the social trends outlined here are more readily explained by sociological theories that stress education's role in the struggle for status and power than by those that emphasize its positive role as an agency for social equalization. For example, take our findings on group differences in educational opportunity. Women and young people from lower-class backgrounds are now much more likely to obtain a university or college education, but the educational currency has been devalued as a means of buying admission to well-paid and satisfying work. In addition, those socioeconomic strata, which have traditionally dominated university education, have maintained their relative advantage, despite the overall expansion of the university sector. The general scenario fits in well with conflict theorist Randall Collins's view (1979) that the increasing demand for advanced educational credentials reflects a contest for power between status groups; that is, as hitherto disadvantaged groups gain more educational credentials, the privileged groups strive to maintain their educational advantages. One example of this is that the great majority of Anglophone children flooding into French immersion programs come from well-off, middle-class homes (see Olson and Burns, 1983; Olson, 1983). Fluency in both official languages is a valuable commodity in the competition for upper level management jobs.

Must we conclude, therefore, that there is little hope for a significant decrease in class inequalities in educational opportunity? As a response, let us turn to John Porter who, shortly before his death, delivered a superb lecture at York University on "Education, Equality and the Just Society" (1979). In the published introduction to that lecture, he noted that he had never doubted that equality of access to all educational institutions was and should continue to be an important objective of social reform (op. cit.:241). Porter knew that social inequalities in education were difficult to reduce in a society characterized by major inequalities in wealth and other material conditions of existence. But he kept his hope — and those of us who continue to explore the prospects for a more socially just educational system can draw inspiration from his example.

Notes

[1]Nineteenth century statistics on student enrolment imply a greater rate of attendance than actually existed. In Ontario, most rural students were still attending elementary school for one hundred days or less each year during the 1870s, while the proportion of urban students with a similar limited level of attendance was about 40 percent. Thus, for many young people, the terms "compulsory" and "universal" schooling had limited significance (see Davey, 1978:225).

[2]The idea for an exploration of the values underlying Canadian educational policies and practices is derived from the analysis of the values underlying American education by Hurn and Burn (op. cit.).

[3]The Nova Scotia report describes a highschool core curriculum as consisting

notably of English (or French for francophones), maths, sciences, social studies, the arts, and a foreign language (op. cit.: 51–52).

[4]For example, in response to an opinion survey on education carried out in Ontario in 1982, 63 percent of a representative sample of adults ranked ''job training and career preparation'' as the first or second highest priority of high school. In contrast, only 29 percent gave such priority to the ''development of creativity, imagination and critical thinking'' (see Livingstone et al., 1983: Table 5.1, 54).

[5]The body of recent literature offering criticisms of American public education is voluminous. A useful comparative critique can be found in Clark (op. cit., 1985), and a devastating attack on American academic standards is made in the report of the U.S. National Commission on Excellence in Education (op. cit., 1983).

[6]Comparing the quality of education in two countries that both show substantial regional inequalities in educational facilities and services may seem a case of ''fools rushing in.'' Nonetheless, my study of Canadian and American education convinces me that the quality of education in this country is both more even and higher overall than in the United States. This generalization does not preclude the existence of excellent school systems in some parts of the United States and less than adequate ones in some regions of Canada.

DISCUSSION QUESTIONS

1. We have seen that, unlike most Western countries, Canada has no national ministry concerned exclusively with educational affairs. Some scholars and educational administrators suggest that such a ministry is required to co-ordinate national public policy in education, but others argue that provincial and regional differences would make its tasks very difficult. What arguments do you think can be made for and against the proposal for such a national body?
2. Do you think that there is a case to be made for the complete separation of church and state which occurs in American public education? In answering this question, keep in mind that some provincial governments in Canada provide a measure of financial support to private schools, which are established to support the specific sets of values and beliefs held by particular religious and ethnic minorities. Is such support to be seen as a positive indication of our educational pluralism or the strengthening of minority interests at the expense of a sense of regional or national unity?
3. One tends to find that secondary school systems based on ''contest mobility'' are somewhat less academically selective and rigorous than those based on ''sponsored mobility,'' with the result that subsequent drop-out and failure from the universities and colleges is somewhat higher than under the sponsored mobility mode. In the light of this evidence, what social and economic arguments can be made in favour of educational systems which, like those of Canada, are based on the principles of contest mobility?
4. Since Canadian university students tend to be drawn disproportionately from the upper social strata of the

society, it is sometimes suggested that present levels of university tuition fees—which currently only cover a small proportion of the actual costs of educating a student at university—constitute a form of unfair subsidization of the upper and middle classes at the expense of the poor. This suggestion has been linked to the argument that it would be socially and economically logical to raise tuition fees to levels which approach actual costs, provided only that talented young people from lower-income families can have their fees covered by student financial aid. What do you think of this argument in the light of your knowledge of factors influencing access to higher learning?

5. What social and economic arguments would you use to support or oppose a case for increased vocational education at the highschool level?

6. Problems of discipline and vandalism are quite severe in many public schools in Canada and the United States. It is sometimes suggested that this is because, unlike the case in Japan, our schools have not been very effective in creating a sense of group solidarity and community among their students. What steps do you think might be taken to increase a sense of community and participation in Canadian schools? Utilize your own highschool experiences in formulating an answer to this question.

GLOSSARY

collectivism a term used in the context of this chapter to refer to educational philosophies and practices that place substantial emphasis upon the role of the educational system in fostering group conformity or co-operation as a means to achieving communal or national integration (see also "individualism")

conflict theories of education a substantial body of theories which emphasize the role of education in maintaining social inequalities and in supporting the ideological perspectives of dominant groups. An important distinction is usually made between Marxist and neo-Marxist theories, which tend to emphasize the role of education in the intergenerational reproduction of the social division of labour associated with the capitalist economy, and neo-Weberian theories (such as those of Randall Collins), which emphasize the role of competition between status groups in the process of increased demand for educational credentials.

contest mobility mode a particular folk norm of a society which, in turn, defines the accepted mode of upward social mobility and helps shape the educational system (see also "sponsored mobility"). Under contest mobility, elite status is like a prize in an open contest which is taken by the student's own efforts rather than granted by an established elite. In practice, an educational system based on contest mobility de-emphasizes early selection, tries to keep children in school as long as possible, and encourages them to compete on equal terms.

cultural capital the body of knowledge, general cultural patterns and capacity to deal with one's environment, which is acquired mainly through the family, and which plays an important part in helping the student to cope with the environment and expectations of the school system

educational pluralism a term that applies to systems of education which allow for the expression of a diversity of religious, ethnic, and linguistic interests in the curriculum and possibly in the administration of the schools

functionalist theories of education those theories that emphasize the functions of the educational system, notably in contributing to social integration, cohesion, solidarity, and shared norms. Functionalist theorists tend also to emphasize the role of the educational system in contributing to opportunities for upward social mobility and labour market preparation.

individualism a term used in the context of this chapter to refer to educational philosophies and practices that focus on the individual student rather than the educational system, society, or nation as the primary beneficiary of the processes of teaching and learning (see also "collectivism")

mobility deprivation limits on the opportunities for intergenerational upward mobility generated either through an educational system which restricts opportunities for advanced education to a few (see also "sponsored mobility") or through a tight labour market for qualified personnel

new educational underclass a term utilized by sociologist Torsten Husen to refer to the minority of students in countries such as Canada, Sweden, and the United States who leave school before graduation, and whose decision to do so is influenced by cultural rather than directly material disadvantages (see also "cultural capital")

sponsored mobility mode a particular folk norm of a society which, in turn, defines the accepted mode of upward social mobility and helps shape the educational system (see also "contest mobility"). Under sponsored mobility, young people who ultimately fill elite positions in the society are "sponsored" through education by members of the established elite on the basis of some criterion of supposed merit. In practice, such sponsorship is granted only to a few, often after gruelling tests and examinations.

utilitarianism a term used in the context of this chapter to refer to the belief that education should be primarily a useful activity that provides specific skills, advances careers, and enhances job prospects

warehousing a process whereby, during times of economic recession and job scarcity, young people remain longer within the formal educational system—and may be encouraged to do so—rather than adding to the pool of applicants for scarce jobs

BIBLIOGRAPHY

Alberta Advanced Education, Planning Secretariat, Participation Patterns Study
1984 *Summary Report of the Committee to Examine Participation Trends of Alberta Post-Secondary Students.* Edmonton: Government of Alberta.

Anderson, B.
1981 "Administering from a Basis in Trust." In R.G. Townsend and S.B. Lawton (eds.) *What's So Canadian About Canadian Educational Administration?* Toronto: Ontario Institute for Studies in Education.

Anderson, D.S. and A. E. Vervoorn
1983 *Access to Privilege: Patterns of Participation in Australian Post-Secondary Education*, Canberra: Australian National University Press.

Anisef, P. and Okihiro, N.
1982 *Losers and Winners*. Toronto: Butterworths.

Anisef, P.
1982 "Accessibility Barriers to Higher Education in Canada and Other Countries with Recommendations for Enhancing Accessibility in the Eighties." Paper presented at Council of Ministers of Education, Canada. Conference on *Post-Secondary Education Issues in the 1980s*, Toronto: C.M.E.C.

——
1985 *Accessibility to Post-Secondary Education in Canada: A Review of the Literature*. Ottawa: Office of the Secretary of State.

Arnold, J.S., S.J. White, and D.J. Tigert
1972 *Canadians and Americans: A Comparative Analysis*. Toronto: School of Management Science, University of Toronto.

Benevot, Arthur
1983 "The Rise and Decline of Vocational Education." In *Sociology of Education* 56, No. 2.

Boocock, S.S.
1980 *Sociology of Education: An Introduction*, 2nd ed. Boston: Houghton Mifflin

Bronfenbrenner, U.
1970 *Two Worlds of Childhood: U.S. and U.S.S.R.* New York: Basic Books.

Canada, Government of, Ministry of State (Youth)
1984 *Youth: A New Statistical Perspective on Youth in Canada*. Ottawa: Ministry of State.

Clark, B.R.
1985 "The High School and the University: What Went Wrong in America." Part I, *Phi Delta Kappa* 66, No. 6, February; and Part II, *Phi Delta Kappa* 66, No. 7, March.

Clark, S.D.
1975 "The Post Second World War Canadian Society." Canadian Review of Sociology, 12 (February): 25–32.

——
1976 *Canadian Society in Historical Perspective*. Toronto: McGraw-Hill Ryerson.

Clement, W.
1977 *Continental Corporate Power: Economic Elite Linkages Between Canada and the United States*. Toronto: McClelland and Stewart.

Collins, R.
1979 *The Credential Society*. New York: Academic Press.

Council of Ministers of Education, Canada
1984 *Teachers' Collective Agreements: A Study of Certain Aspects of Employment Concerning Canadian Public School Teachers*, C.M.E.C.

Curtis, B.
1984 "Capitalist Development and Educational Reform: Comparative Material from England, Ireland, and Upper Canada to 1850." In *Theory and Society*. 13, No. 1, January.

Davey, I.E.
1978 "The Rhythm of Work and The Rhythm of School." In N. McDonald and A. Chaiton (eds.) *Egerton Ryerson and His Times*. Toronto: Macmillan of Canada.

Dibski, D.J.
1981 "A Federal-Provincial Partnership Is Needed in Canadian Education." In

Education Canada 21, No. 1, Spring.

Dick, J.
1982 "North of 49: Schools and Controversial Books in Canada." In *Phi Delta Kappa* 63, No. 7, March.

Guppy, N.
1984 "Access to Higher Education in Canada." In *The Canadian Journal of Higher Education* XIV, No. 3.

Harvey, E.B.
1984 "The Changing Relationship Between University Education and Intergenerational Social Mobility." In *Canadian Review of Sociology and Anthropology* 21, No. 3, August.

Holmes, B. (ed.)
1983 *International Handbook of Educational Systems*, Volume 1 (Europe and Canada). Chichester: John Wiley.

Hurn, C.J.
1985 *The Limits and Possibilities of Schooling*, 2nd ed. Boston: Allyn and Bacon.

Hurn, C. and B. Burn
1982 *An Analytic Comparison of Educational Systems: Overview of Purposes, Policies, Structures and Outcomes.* Report presented to the U.S. National Commission on Excellence in Education, February.

Husen, T.
1985 "The School in the Achievement-Oriented Society: Crisis and Reform." In *Phi Delta Kappa* 66, No. 6, February.

Jaenen, C.J.
1979 "Ruthenian Schools in Western Canada." In D.C. Jones, N.M. Sheehan, and R.M. Stamp (eds.), *Shaping the Schools of the Canadian West*. Calgary: Detsilig.

James, F.C.
1956 "Comparisons and Contrasts in University Financing." In C. Bissell (ed.) *Canada's Crisis in Higher Education*. Toronto: University of Toronto Press.

Johnson , A.W.
1985 *Giving Greater Point and Purpose to the Federal Financing of Post-Secondary Education in Canada*. Ottawa: Office of the Secretary of State.

Kojima, Y.
1985 *Selection and Ideology in the Japanese Educational System*. Unpublished M.A. Thesis, Department of Sociology, Queen's University.

Lawton, S.B.
1979 "Political Values in Educational Finance in Canada and the United States." In *Journal of Education Finance* 5, Summer.

Lazerson, M. and T. Dunn
1977 "Schools and the Work Crisis: Vocationalism in Canadian Education." In H.A. Stevenson and J.D. Wilson (eds.) *Precepts, Policy and Process: Perspectives on Contemporary Canadian Education*. London: Alexander Blake Associates.

Livingstone, D.W., D.J. Hart, and L.D. McLean
1983 *Public Attitudes Toward Education in Ontario, 1982*. Toronto: Ontario Institute for Studies in Education.

Lower, R.M.
1958 *Canadians in the Making*. Toronto: Longmans, Green and Company.

MacKenzie, W.A.M.
1956 "Government Support for Canadian Universities." In C. Bissell (ed.) *Canada's Crisis in Higher Education*. Toronto: University of Toronto Press.

Magnuson, R.
1980 *A Brief History of Quebec Education*. Montreal: Harvest House.

Maxwell, M.P. and J.D. Maxwell
1984 "Women and the Elite: Education and Occupation Aspirations of Private School Females 1966/76." In *Canadian Review of Sociology and Anthropology*, Vol. 21, no. 4, No. v.

Munroe, D.
1974 *The Organization and Administration of Education in Canada*. Ottawa: Office of the Secretary of State.

Murphy, R.
1979 *Sociological Theories of Education*. Toronto: McGraw-Hill Ryerson.

National Commission on Excellence in Education.
1983 *A Nation at Risk: The Imperative for Educational Reform.* Report to the Nation and the Secretary of Education. Washington: United States Department of Education.

Neatby, H.B.
1972 *The Politics of Chaos: Canada in the Thirties*. Toronto: Macmillan of Canada.

Nelsen, R.
1985 "Books, Boredom and Behind Bars: An Explanation of Apathy and Hostility in Our Schools." In *Canadian Journal of Education* 10, No. 2.

Nova Scotia, Government of
1985 *Report of the Royal Commission on Post-Secondary Education*. Halifax: Government Printer.

Olson, P.
1983 "Inequality Remade: The Theory of Correspondence and the Context of French Immersion in Northern Ontario." In *Journal of Education* (Boston University) 165, No. 1.

Olson, P. and G. Burns
1983 "Politics, Class and Happenstance: French Immersion in a Canadian Context." In *Interchange* 14, No. 1.

Ontario, Government of, Ministry of Education
1984 *Ontario Schools, Intermediate and Senior Divisions (Grades 7–12), Programme and Diploma Requirements*. Toronto: Ontario Ministry of Education.

Organization for Economic Co-Operation and Development, Review of National Policies for Education
1976 *Canada*. Paris: O.E.C.D.

Organization for Economic Co-Operation and Development, Department of Economic Statistics
1986 *Labour Force Statistics, 1964–84*. Paris: O.E.C.D.

Paquette, W.J.
1984 *Expectations and Excellence—Meeting the Needs*. Report of the School System Review Committee, Charlottetown, Prince Edward Island.

Pike, R.M.
1970 *Who Doesn't Get to University—and Why*. Ottawa: Runge Press.

——
1980 "Education, Class and Power in Canada." In R.J. Ossenberg (ed.) *Power and Change in Canada*. Toronto: McClelland and Stewart.

Pike, R.M. and E. Zureik
1975 *Socialization and Values in Canadian Society* (2 vols). Toronto: McClelland and Stewart.

Porter, J.
1965 *The Vertical Mosaic*. Toronto: University of Toronto Press.

——
1979 *The Measure of Canadian Society*. Toronto: Gage.

Prentice, A.L. and S.E. Houston
1975 *Family, School and Society in Nineteenth Century Canada*. Toronto: Oxford University Press.

Quebec, Government of, Conseil Superieur de l'éducation
1983 *The Vocational Training of Young People: A Critical Analysis of the Ministerial Proposals and Other Food for Thought*. Quebec City: March.

Ravitch, D.
1983 *The Troubled Crusade: American Education, 1945–1980*. New York: Basic Books.

Schechter, S.
1977 "Capitalism, Class and Educational Reform in Canada." In L. Panitch (ed.) *The Canadian State: Political Economy and Political Power*. Toronto: University of Toronto.

Sheffield, E.
1978 "The National Scene." In E. Sheffield et al. *Systems of Higher Education: Canada*. New York: International Council for Educational Development.

Statistics Canada
1980 *Education in Canada: A Statistical Review for 1978–79*. Ottawa: Ministry of Supply and Services, May.

———
1983 *A Statistical Portrait of Canadian Higher Education from the 1960's to the 1980's*. Ottawa: Ministry of Supply and Services, May.

———
1984 *Financial Statistics of Canada, 1981–82*. Ottawa: Ministry of Supply and Services, December.

———
1985 *Education in Canada: A Statistical Review for 1983–84*. Ottawa: Ministry of Supply and Services, July.

———
1985 *Advance Statistics of Education, 1985–86*. Ottawa: Ministry of Supply and Services, September.

Turner, R.H.
1971 "Sponsored and Contest Mobility and the School System." In Earl Hopper (ed.) *Readings in the Theory of Educational Systems*. London: Hutchinson.

U.N.E.S.C.O.
1985 *Statistical Year Book, 1985*. Louvain: U.N.E.S.C.O.

U.S. Department of Commerce, Bureau of Census
1986 *Statistical Abstract of the United States*. Washington.

Wilson, J.D.
1978 "The Pre-Ryerson Years." In N. McDonald and A. Chaiton (eds.) *Egerton Ryerson and His Times*. Toronto: Macmillan of Canada.

———
1981 "Religion and Education: The Other Side of Pluralism." In J.D. Wilson (ed.) *Canadian Education in the 1980's*. Calgary: Detsilig.

———
1984 "Some Observations on Recent Trends in Canadian Educational History." In J.D. Wilson (ed.) *An Imperfect Past: Education and Society in Canadian Educational History*. Vancouver: Centre for the Study of Curriculum and Instruction, University of British Columbia.

Zajda, J.I.
1980 *Education in the U.S.S.R.* Oxford: Pergamon Press.

The fast pace of change in technology has markedly transformed Canadian society. *Courtesy of the University of Waterloo*

"The microelectronic revolution is . . . changing the social organization of work. . . . In the office of the future, it will be increasingly feasible for workers to remain at home, plugged into the electronic workplace through a computer terminal."

c h a p t e r t e n

Science and Technology

Edward B. Harvey

INTRODUCTION

The Enlightenment in eighteenth century Europe set the stage for a new attitude toward how knowledge could be used. A more positive attitude emerged toward the development and application of knowledge for purely secular pursuits. In this sense, these changes paved the way toward the technology-based Industrial Revolution that transformed European societies in the nineteenth century.

To this day, scientific and technological activities continue to be of central importance to the societies in which they are performed. Modern industrial societies underwrite basic research in the sciences not so much for its immediate relevance or applicability, but for its potential for future applications. Our industrial economy is driven by scientific and technological innovation, and industrial societies have socially organized and **institutionalized** science and technology. Some of the ways this has been done are examined in this chapter, including the development of universities and colleges, the role of the government in stimulating scientific and technological activity, and the protection of the rights and interests of inventors and innovators.

The interrelationships between science and technology and industrial/economic applications are highly dynamic and interactive. Clearly, technological innovation drives industrial development, but the proven payout from scientific work — through superior products or enhanced competitiveness — reflects back on the general climate, including the funding climate, for scientific and technological work.

The post-war era has witnessed significant changes in international competition and, as in the past, the established industrial societies turn increasingly toward the application of technologies to enhance industrial productivity and to regain their competitive edge. We examine some broad trends of change and discuss the implications and impacts of technology on such fundamental social structures as the **occupational system**.

We then examine in greater detail the Canadian situation as it relates to the linkages between science and technology and our overall economic and industrial situation.

Canadian society is characterized by several persistent problems that have impeded the full and effective development of our domestic scientific and technological capabilities and, ultimately, the application of these into economic development and growth.

The problems examined are often linked to our pattern of historical development as a political colony of France and England and, subsequently, as an economic dependent of the United States. The patterns that have impeded scientific and technological development and industrial applications include the persistence of strong regional differences, the branch plant syndrome, deficiencies in our technology base and our dependence on technology-oriented imports, shortages of **venture capital**, and problems relating to our supply and use of scientifically and technologically trained workers. All these problems cumulate in an overall weak performance in research and development, the zone of activity that links science and technology initiatives to industrial and broader economic applications.

We then examine future trends and actions that might be taken to improve Canada's base of science and technology and its relevance to the development of an **industrial strategy**. The issues examined include the continued development of the information economy and the implications this has. In addition, we look at some bases on which Canada could build a stronger science and technology and develop an industrial strategy. These bases include our natural resource-based economy and our highly trained human resources.

SCIENCE, TECHNOLOGY, AND INDUSTRIAL SOCIETIES

As in other industrial countries, one finds in Canada many examples of the social organization and institutionalization of science and technology. A principal example is in the system of colleges and universities that provide a framework for scientific and technologically oriented research and a venue in which the next generation of scientists and technologists is recruited and trained. The importance of recognizable and consistent standards defining the training and performance of scientists and technologists is reflected in elaborate certification procedures, including those relating to earning a degree or certificate and to the **occupational regulation** of scientific and technological employment. Engineering, for example, is a technological occupation subject to a high degree of certification and regulation.

Although universities, and to a lesser extent community colleges, have a lot of autonomy in preparing students for the conduct of scientific and technological work, governments attempt to influence scientific and technological priorities and to assure that certain fields are sufficiently attractive to students to ensure an adequate supply of trained persons. The funding mechanisms possessed by governments are the main vehicle for achieving this, for example, the types and magnitude of scholarships available through our scientific and research councils.

Governments in Canada recognize their

role in stimulating scientific and technological innovations and assisting the transition of such innovations into practical, industrial/economic applications. Where the private capital markets have proven inadequate to meet the financial requirements of research, innovation, and application, the government sector has provided some direct funding and support.

In Canada, of course, the **public sector** is a major customer for all forms of economic activity, including science and technology-based products and services. To this end, government policy has from time to time attempted to support and influence scientific and technological activities by targeting government procurement activity in selective ways. Direct subsidies are also available to specific areas of **research** through government grants and tax credits.

Research requires large amounts of time and resources, sophisticated equipment, and support facilities. The risk of failure is great. Translating scientific and technological research into industrial/economic applications is even riskier. Only a minority of new concepts are ever expressed in viable products and services, and only a minority of new services and products succeed in the marketplace. The reality of these risks is reflected in the steps governments take to protect inventors and innovators. The system of patent law represents one major institutionalized means by which scientific and technologically oriented work is encouraged and protected.

The application of technology to production processes is central to the concept of **value added**. Nations that possess sophisticated technology can produce products that earn profits in excess of the cost of the raw materials needed to produce the product. An automobile can be marketed for prices far in excess of the total costs of the raw materials required to produce it. The "know how" or technology involved in putting the product together constitutes the force of the value added, the capability that has provided the industrial world with great economic power.

In the early 1900s, for example, Great Britain, France, Germany, and the United States, with only 13 percent of the world's population, produced 74 percent of the world's manufactured products (Marsden, 1979:24–25). Value added was the secret of the great economic success of these industrial nations, and the realization of that value added in the marketplace resulted largely from the application of scientific and technological principles to industrial development and production.

The key to maintaining the system was control over colonies to ensure a regular supply of cheap raw materials and to secure international marketplaces to which the finished goods could be sold with significant profit. Indeed, World War I was largely a conflict over territory. Germany, as a result of relatively late political unification compared to Britain and France, was a latecomer to colonial acquisition and sought to militarily change the situation.

Given the enormous significance of applied science and technology to economic production, it is little wonder that these principles were jealously safeguarded and controlled historically. Insofar as the imperial powers educated the colonized, they tended to do so in institutions that ensured the objectives and values of the imperial power were inculcated. In other words, the scientific and technological knowledge — as well as other knowledge—would be in "safe hands."

All of this changed dramatically following World War II, particularly during rapid decolonization that occurred in the 1960s. As the hegemony of the traditional industrial, colonizing powers diminished, the information marketplace for science and

TECHNOLOGY CHANGES THE FACE OF NORTH AMERICAN INDUSTRY

In an automobile factory on the East Coast, a union official cannot hide the fear in his eyes and in his voice about what will happen to jobs in the plant once robots are installed. The truth is worse than he suspected. Not long after our conversation, the plant is shut down. The company says it will reopen the plant only if the work force is reduced as labour-saving machines are put in and if the union accepts wage concessions.

In a Japanese machine tool factory in Florence, Kentucky, just across the Ohio River from Cincinnati, the American sales manager explains how a fully automated flexible manufacturing system will run itself in the dark all night without the assistance of a single human being. The company is getting many expressions of interest from U.S. industry because it is in the business of selling this automated system. The firm sees gains of up to 300 percent in productivity for those who buy its automated systems. American machine tool firms tell the same story.

In a research laboratory in Pittsburgh, a bright young man describes how he is working diligently on a project that will enable a robot to see and sense an object clearly so that it can distinguish one object from another. It is only a matter of time before this robot function is fully perfected, he explains.

In a steel mill in Japan, the superintendent tells a reporter she is extremely happy with her work and happy that her company provides subsidized housing and vacation—and especially happy that her company's steel is selling so well in North America, where it is cheaper than American-made steel.

In a shoe factory in Korea, the plant manager explains that he is able to sell his shoes for export much cheaper because the wages in his factory, located in a seamy section of Seoul, are low, compared with wages in North America. Still, he says, jobs in his plant are highly desired by Korean people, as their standard and cost of living are much lower.

Along the Saudi Arabian coast, where petro-dollars that came from American and European pocketbooks are being employed to build vast new petro-chemical complexes, a group of American newspaper executives is startled to see a team of South Korean workers busy at work on a construction crew. South Korean firms have landed many important contracts here, and in North America, Saudi officials explain.

In a neat air-conditioned office in Glasgow, the economic development official shakes her head slowly at the visitor who wants to learn how to stem the tide of unemployment in old, heavy-industry cities. Three generations of men here have lived on the dole, she laments, and all they can think about is getting back the shipbuilding industry. The shipbuilding industry will never come back, and Glasgow will be lucky if its 30 percent unemployment rate doesn't get worse (Schwartz and Nelkirk, 1983:16–18).

Source: The seven examples are taken from G.G. Schwartz and W. Nelkirk, *The Work Revolution*. New York: Rawson Associates, 1983, p. 16–18.

technology "knowhow" became more fluid. As Robert Reich observes:

> Developing countries can now purchase (from international engineering and capital equipment firms) the world's most modern steel-rolling mills, paper machines, computer-controlled machine tools, or fertilizer plants. They can also get training and technical supervision to accompany the new production facilities (1983:122–23).

The post-war era has also witnessed major changes in the world marketplace, the rapid growth and diversification of the Japanese economy (see Morishima, 1982) and the emergence of new industrial countries following the Japanese model.

Table 1 compares total exports of manufactured goods of several major industrial countries from 1960 to 1981. The dramatic increase in Japanese market share is evident, while the U.S. market share has declined since 1960. Canada's share of exports increased between 1960 and 1970 and has remained constant since.

The data reflect the significant changes that have occurred in the relative standing of the major industrial economies in the post-World War II era and, in particular, the success of Japanese products, such as automobiles, in penetrating international marketplaces.

From the days of Henry Ford and the Model T to the booming post-war economy of the 1950s and 1960s, the American automotive industry seemed beyond challenge, with American manufacturers dominating the domestic and international markets. But in the 1970s, Japanese automotive products assumed a strong presence in international markets and competed strongly in the domestic U.S. market. There were several reasons for

Table 1

SHARES OF TOTAL EXPORTS OF MANUFACTURED GOODS OF DEVELOPED MARKET ECONOMIES, MAJOR INDUSTRIAL COUNTRIES 1960–81*

	1960	1970	1975	1978	1979	1980	1981
				(percent)			
Canada	3.3	4.4	3.8	4.3	4.3	4.1	4.2
Belgium and Luxembourg	5.2	5.7	5.3	5.4	5.3	5.2	—
Denmark	1.0	1.2	1.1	1.0	1.0	1.0	4.2
France	9.1	8.4	9.2	9.2	9.6	9.0	8.9
West Germany	19.0	20.4	18.4	17.9	18.3	18.1	18.5
Italy	4.1	6.4	6.7	7.6	7.8	7.0	—
Japan	5.3	10.3	12.3	13.4	12.5	14.0	14.8
Netherlands	3.8	4.2	4.5	4.2	4.4	4.3	—
Norway	1.2	1.3	1.2	1.1	1.0	0.9	0.8
Sweden	3.4	3.5	3.2	2.8	2.8	2.6	—
Switzerland	4.0	3.2	2.8	3.0	2.9	2.8	2.8
United Kingdom	14.6	9.1	8.4	7.9	7.6	7.2	—
United States	20.1	14.9	16.4	14.6	14.9	15.9	14.6

*Based on constant U.S. dollars.

Source: Calculated from data on manufactured goods exports from *Monthly Bulletin of Statistics* (New York: United Nations), various issues; and Roy A. Matthews, "Structural Change and Manufacturing Performance: Thoughts on the Argument for Industrial Policy in Canada" (Ottawa: Economic Council of Canada, 1983) Table 6. Taken from John Sargent, ed. *Canadian Industry in Transition* (Toronto, University of Toronto Press in co-operation with the Royal Commission on the Economic Union and Development Prospects for Canada and the Canadian Government Publishing Centre, Supply and Services Canada, 1986), p. 16.

this. The Japanese product was competitively priced, was often based on superior technology, and almost invariably was more economical to operate — a major consideration during times of rapidly escalating energy costs. Japanese competition in the automotive industry is simply one example. Many other new industrial countries, such as Korea and Taiwan, are making their presence felt in international marketplaces. The accelerating pace of technological change is redefining the types of industries that will succeed—and those that will not. The examples shown on page 292 illustrate the magnitude of these changes.

These changes in the occupational system are of particular importance because the occupational system in our kind of society is responsible for income distribution. Some income distribution is, of course, essential to the operation of the economy and the maintenance of social cohesion.

The forces of technological change produce new patterns of employment growth and decline. Figure 1 presents overall patterns for Canada from 1911 to 1981. In all

Figure 1
Industrial distribution of employment, 1911 to 1981

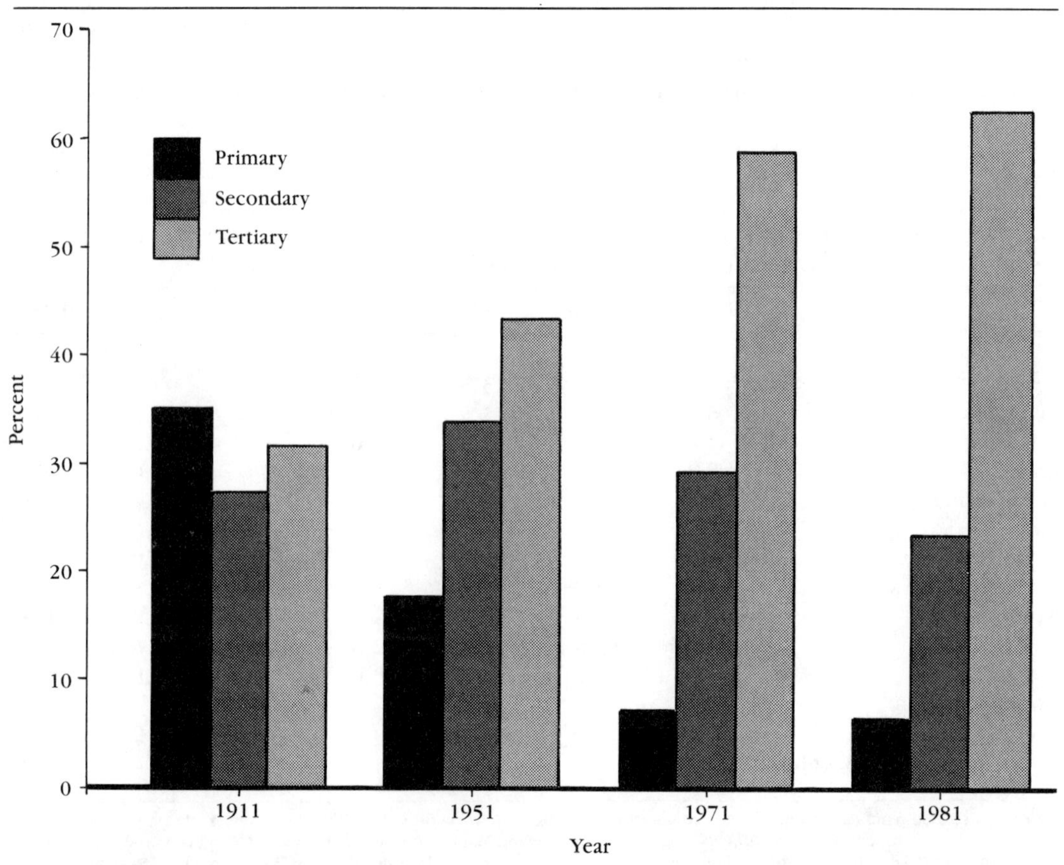

Source: Keith Newton, "Employment Effects of Technological Change: Some Implications for Education," Ottawa, Economic Council of Canada, April 1985, mimeo, p. 5.

industrial countries, the primary sector (agriculture, mining, fishing, etc.) has declined in significance over time as a provider of employment. In the natural resources and extractive industries, technology continues to replace human labour as the means for harvesting the resources. Similar trends exist in the secondary (manufacturing) sector, where an increasing number of assembly and processing functions have been automated. Most people now work in the tertiary, or service, sector, a sector that encompasses a vast range of occupations. Physicians, teachers, bus drivers, and store clerks are all in the service sector, and in this sector most of the future jobs will be created.

Service sector jobs range from low technology (e.g., fast food clerks) to high technology (e.g., computer systems analysts). High technology jobs like computer systems analysis and computer programming have fast growth rates but, because they employ relatively few people, these rates do not translate into large numbers of jobs. In fact, the occupations with the largest absolute growth over the next five years in numbers of jobs are relatively low-skilled, often low-wage, jobs in the service sector (see, for example, Levin, 1984 and Newton, 1985). Table 2 presents data for the United States on the twenty occupations with the largest absolute growth in employment from 1978 to 1990. Jobs like janitor, nurses' aide, salesclerk, cashier, and waiter lead the way. As one commentator put it, most of these are the jobs most middle-class parents hope their children

Table 2

TWENTY OCCUPATIONS WITH LARGEST ABSOLUTE GROWTH IN EMPLOYMENT IN THE U.S., 1978–1990

Occupation	**Growth in Employment (in thousands)**
Janitors and sextons	671.2
Nurses' aides and orderlies	594.0
Salesclerks	590.7
Cashiers	545.5
Waiters/waitresses	531.9
General clerks, office	529.8
Professional nurses	515.8
Food preparation and service workers, fast-food restaurants	491.9
Secretaries	487.8
Truck drivers	437.6
Kitchen helpers	300.6
Elementary school teachers	272.8
Typists	262.1
Accountants and auditors	254.2
Helpers, trades	232.5
Blue-collar worker supervisors	221.1
Bookkeepers	219.7
Licensed practical nurses	215.6
Guards and doorkeepers	209.9
Automotive mechanics	205.3

Source: H. M. Levin, "Education and Jobs in a Technological World," Information Series No. 265, The National Center for Research in Vocational Education (Ohio State University, 1984), p. 8.

will not enter. Table 3 presents similar data for Canada. As we can see, the situation is not much different.

One's occupation mainly determines one's overall social class position. Some analysts have argued technology-driven changes in the occupational system threaten the viability of the middle class. Kuttner (1983:60–72), for example, observes: "there is a good deal of evidence that job opportunities in the United States are polarizing, and that, as a result, the

Table 3

A SCENARIO[1] SHOWING OCCUPATIONS[2] CONTRIBUTING MOST TO EMPLOYMENT GROWTH, CANADA, 1983–1992

Rank	*Code*[2]	*Occupational Title*	*Projected Employment 1983 (000s)*	*Projected Employment 1992 (000s)*	*Requirements (1983–92) Total (000s)*
1	4111	Secretaries & steno	351.3	438.8	87.5
2	4131	Bookkeepers	368.2	448.5	80.3
3	9175	Truck drivers	238.0	310.0	72.0
4	1171	Financial officers	140.9	180.0	39.1
5	6191	Janitors	223.6	261.4	37.8
6	4133	Cashiers & tellers	229.6	263.8	34.2
7	8781	Carpenters	107.3	138.1	30.8
8	4197	Gen. office clerks	136.4	165.3	28.9
9	6125	Waiters	252.4	281.0	28.7
10	6115	Guards & oth. security	76.9	101.5	24.6
11	4113	Typists, clerk/typists	95.7	118.4	22.7
12	4171	Receptionists	90.4	112.0	21.6
13	1137	Sales mgmt. occs.	169.9	191.1	21.2
14	8798	Labourers: other cons.	54.2	74.9	20.7
15	3131	Nurses, grad., nonsuper.	185.5	206.1	20.6
16	8335	Welders	79.8	99.8	20.0
17	8584	Industrial farm mechanics	88.2	108.0	19.8
18	8581	Auto mechanics	140.7	160.0	19.3
19	8563	Sewing machine occs.	88.1	106.6	18.5
20	9171	Bus drivers	49.0	67.4	18.4
21	6121	Chefs & cooks	162.5	180.8	18.3
22	8780	Superv: other constr.	66.5	84.3	17.9
23	1130	Gen. managers	79.2	96.8	17.6
24	7195	Nursery workers	58.8	75.9	17.1
25	4143	E.D.P. equip. operators	71.3	88.1	16.8
26	6112	Police officers: govt.	53.8	69.3	15.5
27	4155	Stock clerks	91.5	106.6	15.1
28	2183	Systems analysts	56.8	71.9	15.1
29	4153	Shipping clerks	84.2	98.5	14.3
30	5133	Commercial traveller	95.9	109.6	13.7

1. Based on COPS reference case scenario developed by Informetrica Ltd., October 1983 and COPS' own computations. Included are all occupations which are not supervisory or residual in nature.
2. According to the *Standard Occupational Classification*, Statistics Canada, 1980.

Source: Government of Canada Consultation Paper on Training (Ottawa: Supply and Services, 1984).

country's future as a middle-class society is in jeopardy." By contrast, Samuelson (1985) contends that "the theory that middle-income jobs are slowly being destroyed, threatening the very nature of our middle-class society" is "a myth" and "intellectual rubble." This debate illustrates the complex and pervasive impacts of technological change on other social patterns and structures (see Belous, 1985).

Science and technology and their complex interactions with industrial and economic applications affect most aspects of our lives, including such fundamental features of social organization as the occupational system, so technologically driven change cannot be ignored. The alternative is deindustrialization and economic decline.

THE CANADIAN SITUATION

Canadian society requires an overall industrial strategy based on scientific excellence and sustained technological innovation. The realization of such an overall strategy has been impeded in Canada by various institutional and market problems, some of which are traced to our historical social and economic development—specifically, our beginnings as a colony and our continuing economic dependency on more highly developed industrial societies, most notably the United States. We now examine a variety of these persistent problems in greater detail.

Regional Differences

Canada has long been characterized by the persistence of pronounced regional differences and disparities (see Marsden and Harvey, 1979; Economic Council of Canada, 1977; Simeon, 1979). In particular, these regional factors have impeded the development of national industrial policies that could foster a more positive climate for science and technology.

To understand the persistence and significance of regional differences in Canada, we must examine the social and economic development that has characterized our nation. Although the Fathers of Confederation attempted to create a national economy, regional economic specialization became entrenched. Southern Ontario and Quebec dominate the production of manufactured goods, while the Western and Atlantic economies remain largely rooted in the production of natural resources and partially processed raw materials.

Diversified economies invariably weather economic changes better than natural resource economies. This was well demonstrated following Canada's lengthy economic recession during the first part of the 1980s. In the recovery period, Ontario recovered relatively quickly. The recovery of the U.S. economy provided strong demand for the diversified and technology-based industrial products that flow from Ontario. By contrast, the natural resource dependent economies of British Columbia and Alberta remain depressed.

The benefits to science and technology of Ontario's type of industrial base are reflected in the increased funding to universities and related activities that has recently occurred there. The overall climate for scientific and technological enterprise cannot be separated from the condition of the economy and the extent to which the results of scientific and technological activity help to shape and drive the industrial economy.

Regionalism in Canada has impeded the development of strong economic linkages. In fact, stronger and more extensive economic linkages exist among the countries of the European Common Market — despite their widely differing history and languages — than among the provinces of Canada.

To understand the significance of

regionalism, Canada's historical status as, first, a political colony of France and Britain and, subsequently, as an economy closely tied to, and dependent upon, the U.S. economy must be recognized. The United States, of course, has a large-scale, sophisticated and diversified economy, with enormous demands for raw materials and natural resources. At different stages of the technological development of its economy, different natural resources from Canada have been in strong demand. Since we often lacked capital to develop such natural resources, our economic progression has often been characterized by what Innis called "cyclonic development" (Neill, 1972). In broad terms, this involves a particular resource suddenly assuming an industrial importance and an attendant influx of capital, technology, and human resources to exploit the resource. The prevalence of this pattern throughout Canada's history has resulted in certain regions going through periods of intense economic development, followed by periods of decline. As Lucas (1971) has documented, the boomtown–ghost town pattern is characteristically Canadian.

The Branch Plant Syndrome

Throughout our history, the preservation of the Canadian confederation has been challenged, most recently by the referendum on Quebec sovereignty. At the time of Sir John A. Macdonald's prime ministership, the close proximity of the much more highly developed U.S. economy threatened Canadian confederation. The National Policy was formulated at that time to preserve the Canadian economy and confederation and to encourage national unity, as that generation understood it. In commenting on the National Policy, Marsden and Harvey (op. cit.:54) observe:

> The policy established tariff walls between the United States and Canada, which meant that Canadian producers were operating in more protected markets than heretofore and that American producers could not dump goods into the Canadian market, thereby lowering local prices. It had the unintended consequence of bringing about direct investment by American manufacturers in Canada (in the form of subsidiaries), thereby paving the way for the development within the Canadian economy of foreign-operated companies, in our day full-fledged multinational corporations.

Unfortunately, the "unintended consequence" of the National Policy has become a dominant fact of Canadian economic life.

ALBERTA IN THE EARLY 1980s

A recent example of the boom-bust pattern occurred in Alberta during the late 1970s and early 1980s. The great increases in oil prices, beginning in the early 1970s, made the exploitation of the Alberta oil sands—normally a very expensive means of extracting oil—economically feasible. During this period, Alberta's economy boomed, employment and income grew, and many Canadians headed west to participate in the new opportunities. In the past four years, the Alberta economy has entered a troubled period because of the economic recession of the early 1980s and the more recent softening of the world price for oil. Such **cyclical problems** are characteristic of resource-dependent economies.

Figure 2

Degree of U.S. economic control over some countries, 1970

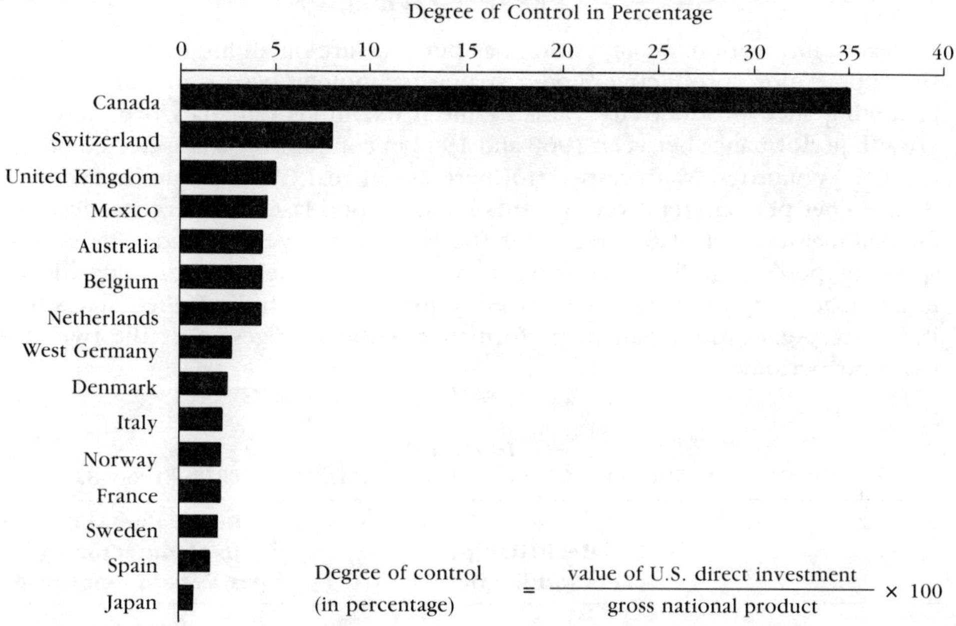

Degree of Control in Percentage

0 5 10 15 20 25 30 35 40

Canada
Switzerland
United Kingdom
Mexico
Australia
Belgium
Netherlands
West Germany
Denmark
Italy
Norway
France
Sweden
Spain
Japan

$$\text{Degree of control (in percentage)} = \frac{\text{value of U.S. direct investment}}{\text{gross national product}} \times 100$$

Source: Science Council of Canada, *Forging the Links: A Technology Policy for Canada*, Minister of Supply and Services, Ottawa, 1979, p. 38.

As the Science Council of Canada observes in a 1979 report:

> . . . Canada's dependence on foreign technology and capital (particularly American capital and technology) is on a scale unmatched by any other advanced economy. As can be seen quite clearly in Figure 2, Canada's dependence on U.S. capital in 1970 was *ten times higher* than the average of a group of thirteen member countries of the O.E.C.D. Even Mexico, a developing country, has a significantly lower level of dependence on U.S. capital (Science Council of Canada, 1979).

Being a branch plant economy has many implications. For one, branch plant countries are seldom the locations for advanced scientific and technological work in support of industry. Such work is typically done at "head office."

Dependence on Technology-Oriented Imports

Canada's natural resources — timber, minerals, agricultural products, etc. — have always been important engines of economic growth. During the post-World War II period, the massive reconstruction efforts created a strong demand for many of our natural materials. Approximately from 1945 to the end of the 1960s, the Canadian economy enjoyed a period of relatively sustained growth. Over these years, the real after-tax income of Canadians doubled, an important reflection of the economic growth and well-being that prevailed.

Consequently, government revenues also expanded, and governments made major investments in such policy areas as overall income security (pensions and

CANADA'S PRODUCTIVITY GROWTH IN COMPARATIVE PERSPECTIVE

Increased international competition has put pressure on all industrial countries to become more productive, and a strong technology base is a major key to achieving such productivity gains. Table 4 examines Canada's productivity growth performance between 1960 and 1982 in comparison with selected other O.E.C.D. countries. With respect to increases in real Gross Domestic Product (G.D.P.) per person employed, Canada ranks second last. Our percent increase on this measure was 1.6 percent for the twenty-two year period. The corresponding percentage for Japan is 6.2 percent. With respect to real value-added in manufacturing per person employed, Canada ties with the United States for last place. Again, the Japanese performance is the strongest over the twenty-two-year period.

Table 4

PRODUCTIVITY GROWTH IN SELECTED O.E.C.D. COUNTRIES, 1960–82

	Real GDP per Person Employed	**Real Value-Added in Manufacturing per Person Employed**
		(percent)
Canada	1.6	2.3
United States	1.2	2.3
Japan	6.2	8.5
West Germany	3.4	3.7
France	3.8	5.3
United Kingdom	2.2	2.6
Italy	3.9	4.9
Sweden	2.3	3.5
Australia	1.8	—

Source: O.E.C.D. *Historical Statistics 1960–82* (Paris: O.E.C.D. 1984); and J.F. Helliwell, P.H. Sturm, and G. Salon, "International Comparison of the Sources of Productivity Slowdown 1973–82," paper presented to the International Seminar on Macroeconomics, Perugia, June 24–26, 1984.

Taken from John Sargent (ed.) *Canadian Industry in Transition*, *op.cit.*, p. 48.

unemployment insurance), health care, and — most importantly for our purposes here — education, including science and technology-related activities. During the 1960s, for example, the number of universities in Ontario was significantly increased and a new system of community colleges was put into place. Between 1960 and 1970, the percentage of Canadian G.N.P. expended on education rose from 4.5 percent to 8.8 percent. Over the same period, Canadian educational institutions expanded their teaching staff from about 175 000 to nearly 320 000 (Harvey, 1976:1–27).

Despite this significant expansion, Canada still trails the United States in educational achievement. In 1980, for example, 16.3 percent of Americans aged twenty-five or older had college degrees. In Canada, in 1983, less than 10 percent of the population aged fifteen and older had college degrees (Bird, 1984).

The 1970s witnessed slower world economic growth. The rapid increases in the price of oil, which started around 1973, helped slow the economic expansion. The 1970s represented the beginning of troubled times for Canada. Economic growth slowed while inflation rose precipitously. The growth in government revenues slowed dramatically and, as a result, educational institutions—the beneficiaries of so much public investment during the 1950s and 1960s—now became targets of cutbacks. Careers in science and technology started to look less attractive.

Despite a weakened world demand for many of our natural resources and stronger competition from new suppliers, Canadians have not lost their appetite for imported goods. The problem is, of course, that every time Canadians purchase Japanese television sets or German automobiles, we export employment to these other countries and help fund the research and development activities that provide the basis for the production of sophisticated manufactured products.

Deficiencies in the Technology Base

For most industrial countries, the foundation for their productive capabilities and competitive strength is rooted in their technology base. The development of a strong technology base is an important mediating factor between the creation of productive and competitive industry and fostering a positive climate for investment into scientific research activities.

Canada's proximity to the United States, however, has resulted in a significant reliance on imported technology, which can become narrowly focused into its industrial applications. The importer of such technology has little reason or incentive to modify, improve, or expand upon the technology. When requirements change, the tendency is to turn to the original supplier and request the new technological goods or services needed. Thus, countries that are net importers of technology, like Canada, have greater difficulty creating the economic and institutional conditions that promote greater technological self-sufficiency.

The Japanese also import technology, but they tend to buy technology packages that force them to quickly come to terms with understanding the technology and developing the capacity to improve it and make modifications (Science Council of Canada, 1971). The method of acquiring technology packages outright is more costly but, in the long run, contributes to building up the type of technology base that spurs further innovation.

One example of such technology-based innovation is the development and use of robotics. Figure 3 clearly shows that we seriously lag behind other developed countries in this regard.

Figure 3

Canada's position in using automation

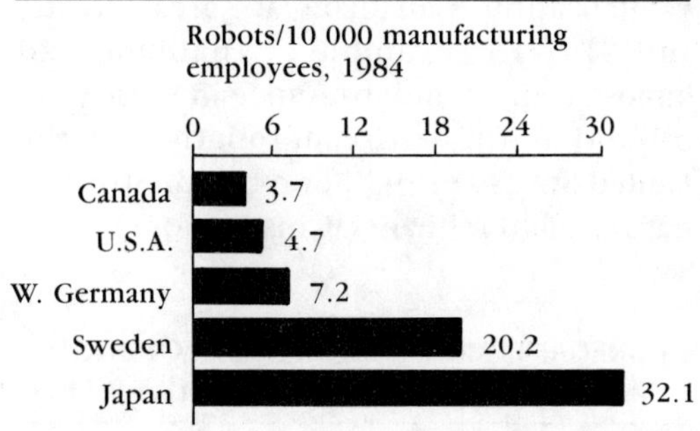

Canada has lagged in using automation to enhance productivity. In 1984, Germany, Sweden and Japan had, respectively, 2, 5 and 9 times as many robots per ten thousand manufacturing employees as did Canada.

Source: Woods Gordon; Tomorrow's Customers, 1985, p. 6.

Shortage of Venture Capital

A major deterrent to successful technological innovation in Canada has been a continuing shortage of venture capital. Unquestionably, technological innovation carries large risks. The tendency has been for investors to seek safer, more assured investments. Governments have attempted to address these problems in many ways, including getting into the venture capital business themselves, providing tax credits, and developing programs and subsidies to stimulate scientific activity.

The banking system has not been a great source of venture capitalization in Canada. In part, this must be understood in terms of the historical development of our country. As we have seen from the discussion of the National Policy, Canada's development has been as a branch plant economy, with a heavy reliance on direct foreign investment.

In this situation, the banks have developed largely as custodians of foreign capital. Such external interests have not typically placed priority on the underwriting of inevitably risky, Canadian-based technology development initiatives. Moreover, the pattern of development of Canadian financial institutions has not produced a positive setting for venture capitalization. Canadians are great savers. In 1971, for example, Canadians had almost as much life insurance in force ($94 billion) as the entire population of the United States ($159 billion) (ibid.:30). The nature of our financial institutions, however, has made it difficult to use such savings to develop venture capital resources and mechanisms.

Supply of Scientifically and Technologically Trained Workers

The availability of scientifically and technologically trained persons helps to ensure effective research and teaching in the various fields and meets the requirements of industry. A 1983 study of 217 Canadian opinion leaders from five key sectors (see Table 5) found a majority (64 percent) felt that over the next five years Canada would experience major shortages of highly skilled manpower, such as engineers and computer programmers (Hay Associates Canada, 1984).

These concerns are mirrored in a 1985 report of the Natural Sciences and Engineering Research Council of Canada, which presents supply and demand projections to 1990 for research talent in the natural sciences and engineering (Natural Sciences and Engineering Research Council of Canada, 1985). This study concludes that the forecast supply of research talent will be inadequate to meet the requirements, even with a fairly modest growth in research and development expenditures. The forecast supply will only be adequate if we have no, or slow, economic growth and no significant increase in research and development expenditures.

Persons with post-graduate degrees (M.Sc. and Ph.D.) in the natural sciences

Table 5

FORECAST: MAJOR SHORTAGES OF HIGHLY SKILLED MANPOWER, SUCH AS ENGINEERS AND COMPUTER PROGRAMMERS, WILL EXIST.

	Federal Government	Provincial Government	Industry	Researchers	Interest Groups	Total
Likely	68%	55%	69%	61%	63%	64%
Unlikely	32	45	31	39	37	36

Source: Hay Associates Canada Ltd., *Navigating Uncharted Waters: Canada's Next Ten Years*, February 1984; p. 68.

Figure 4

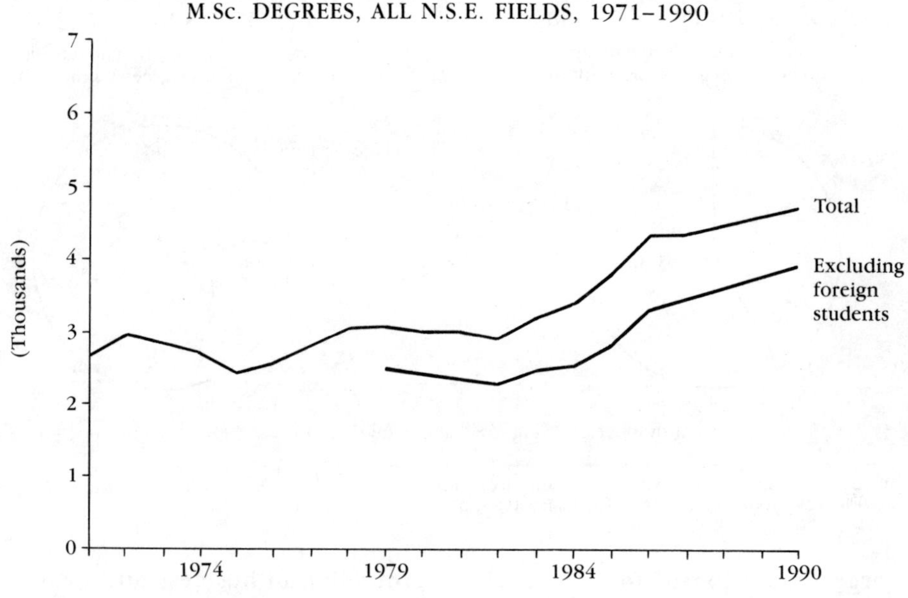

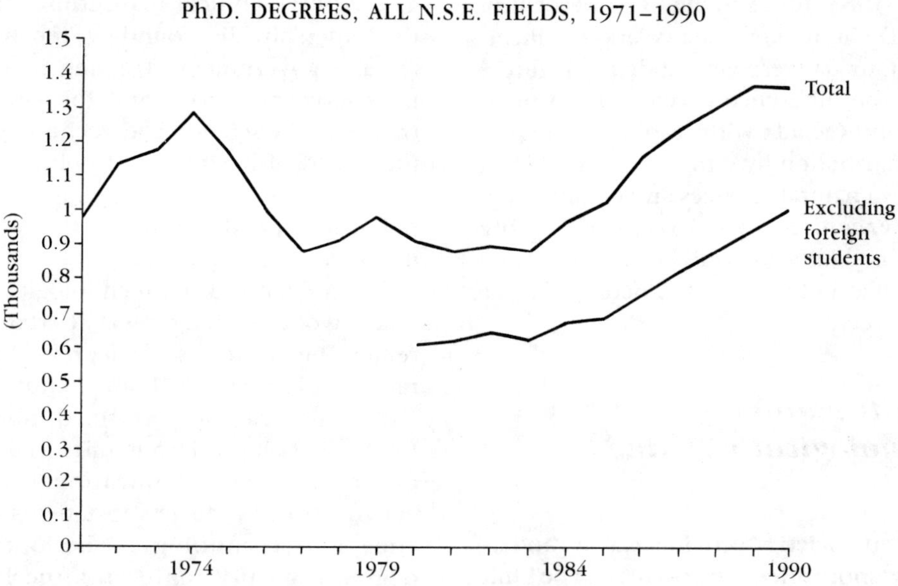

Source: Natural Sciences and Engineering Research Council of Canada; *Research Talent in the Natural Sciences and Engineering: Supply and Demand Projections to 1990*, May 1985, pp. 31–32.

and engineering represent the core of Canada's science and technology workforce. Figure 4 presents information on degrees granted (actual and projected) for master's and doctoral level degrees. Although the trend is going up, one must take account

Figure 5

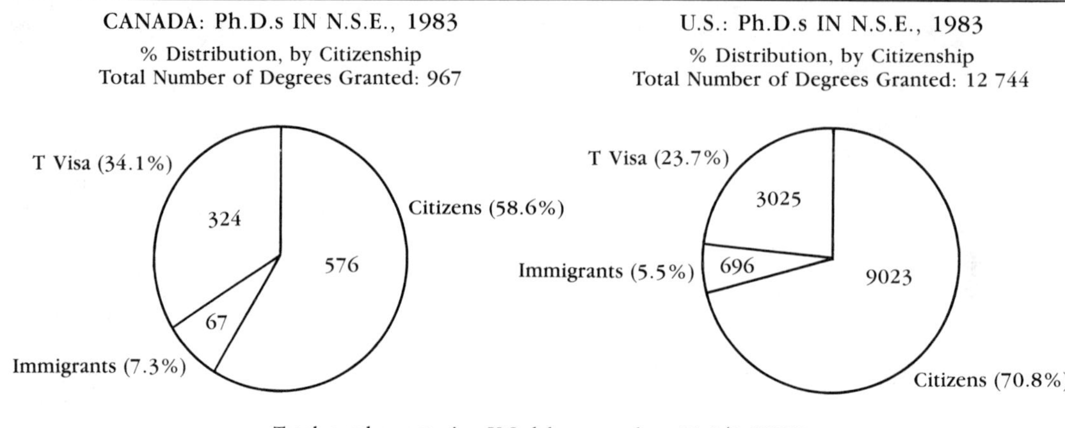

Source: Natural Sciences and Engineering Research Council of Canada; *Research Talent in the Natural Sciences and Engineering: Supply and Demand Projections to 1990*, May 1985, p. 46.

of the large proportion of foreign (visa) students who are unlikely to work in Canada. In 1983, for example, 34.1 percent of all Ph.D.s in natural science and engineering in Canada were visa students. Figure 5 shows the difference between the United States and Canada with respect to the percent distribution by citizenship in 1983 of Ph.D.s in natural sciences and engineering. The percentage of citizens receiving Ph.D.s is significantly higher in the United States than in Canada (70.8 percent versus 58.6 percent).

The Utilization of Technologically Trained People

European societies provide viable models for how more effective bridges can be built between science and technology and economic applications. France, for example, has a long and strong tradition of polytechnical education. In their elite academies, students learn not only science and technology-oriented skills, but acquire grounding in business and management, economic analysis, and political theory. These polytechnical institutions provide the leadership elite found in French industry and government. Training that facilitates movement back and forth between the fields of science and technology and the world of business and political applications is clearly advantageous. Although polytechnical education exists in Canada, it is relatively less developed.

Much scientific and technologically oriented work is hierarchical. Certain tasks require higher levels of theoretical and/or methodological skill and knowledge. Other tasks can be performed more routinely. This hierarchy is mirrored in the different levels of educational/training certification found in most fields of science and technology. The doctorate degree typically represents the highest level of certification, while technologists or technicians are further down the scale. Most of the highly industrialized European countries have a higher ratio of technologists and technicians relative to the more highly trained scientific professionals. The expanded use of technologists and technicians in support roles has increased the productivity of the more highly trained persons and has improved research and the application of research into economic and industrial uses.

Close linkages among the business, government, and science and technology sectors are undoubtedly beneficial, not only to the sectors themselves but to the larger society. Unfortunately, in Canada the linkages among these various communities often remain weak (Science Council of Canada, Report 37). The tendency of many industries to import technology, or as branch plants, receive it through their head office linkages, has resulted in a situation where the universities, and other science and technology centres, have not been the paramount suppliers of such scientific and technological know-how.

This isolation from industrial applications tends to impair the relevance and advancement of scientific and technological work in Canada. One great strength of Japanese industry has been the formation of strong partnerships among such key players as government, industry, and the education/training sector.

Table 6
INDUSTRIAL INVESTMENT IN R&D

	1967	*1977*	*1981*
	(% of domestic product of industry)		
United States	2.4	1.8	2.0
Japan	0.9	1.3	1.6
Holland	0.7	1.3	1.3
Sweden	1.3	1.9	2.3
Canada	0.7	0.6	0.8

Source: Ontario Throne Speech Background Paper, April 1986.

Table 7
SCIENTISTS AND ENGINEERS ENGAGED IN R&D

	1973	*1979*
	(per 10 000 of labour force)	
Japan	54.8	65.6
West Germany	37.4	46.1
Holland	29.7	36.9
Switzerland	30.8	36.1
France	28.4	31.6
Canada	23.2	23.3

Source: Ontario Throne Speech Background Paper, April 1986.

Weak Research and Development (R&D) Performance

Canada's R&D performance, measured as a percentage of the domestic product of industry, is compared with other industrial countries for various years in Table 6 and Figure 6. Canada ranks last. Table 7 examines the number of scientists and engineers engaged in R&D per 10 000 of labour force. In Japan in 1973, there were 54.8 scientists and engineers engaged in R&D per 10 000 of labour force. By 1979, this had risen to 65.6. The corresponding figures for Canada in 1973 and 1979 were 23.2 and 23.3, respectively.

Canada's weak R&D performance is symptomatic of the various institutional and market problems we have examined, several related to our historical development. The changes in the world economy — increased competition and rapid technological change — are creating pressures in Canada, as elsewhere, for stronger scientific and technological capabilities and the effective linkage of these capabilities to the productive economy.

Figure 6
Industrial R & D expenditures as a percent of the domestic product of industry for selected O.E.C.D. countries

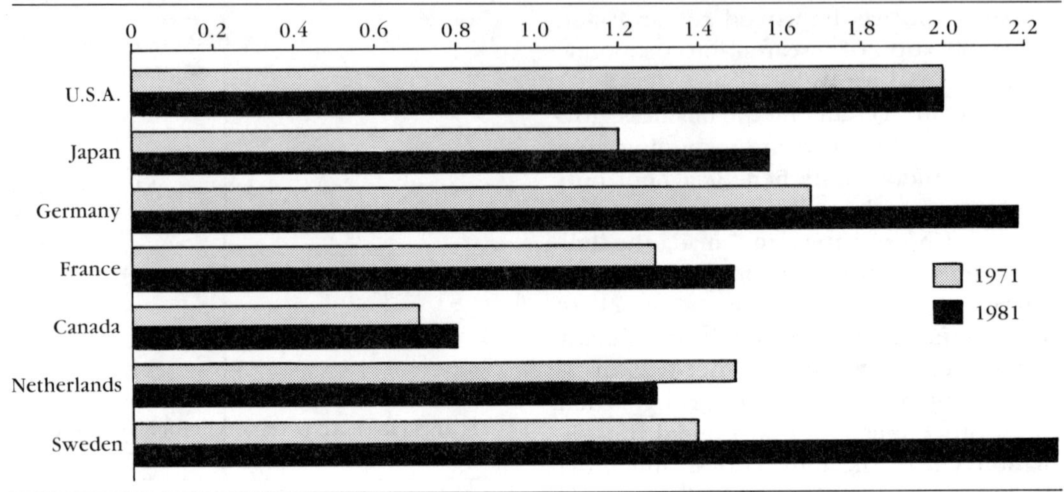

Source: Statistics Canada, *Science and Technology Indicators 1984*, Minister of Supply and Services, Ottawa, 1985, p. 94.

FUTURE DIRECTIONS

As the pace of technological change accelerates and international competition becomes more stringent, the Canadian economy faces important adaptive challenges. Science and technology will play a role in helping meet that challenge.

We need more sophisticated decision-making structures that can bring together the interests of governments, business, unions, and the education/training sector. In other countries, such as Japan, the United States, and France, one finds many more such interlocking networks, either formal or informal. Unfortunately, in Canada, the development of such co-operative structures has been impeded by the often adversarial nature of relationships among business, government, and the trade unions, and further exacerbated by strong regional differences.

Entering new technological fields and/or making competitive adaptations does not imply abandoning current forms of economic production. In fact, in many instances the key to the future development of Canada's economy rests in building upon areas where the nation already enjoys comparative economic strength (see, for example, Science Council of Canada, Study 23, 1972; and Economic Council of Canada 1977 and 1978). For example, Canada's long history as a major producer of agricultural products has resulted in some important scientific and technological innovations in that field. Similarly, the geographically dispersed nature of the country has resulted in important innovations in transportation and communication. Canada's role in developing the space arm used in the U.S. space shuttle program is a case in point.

Notwithstanding the potential gains to be realized, developing new scientific and technological processes in order to reap economic returns is a risky process. In Canada, there will be a continued role for government to play in providing venture capital, research grants, and tax incentives to stimulate such activity.

Implications for Education

Education also has a role to play in developing a more positive environment in Canada for scientific and technological activities. This is not limited to training personnel. Public awareness of the nature of scientific and technological work and its application into industry is quite limited. As David Suzuki has commented:

> . . . the collective public ignorance about science is appalling. The wide acceptance and popularity of astrology, UFOs, ESP, Uri Geller, plant communication, the Bermuda Triangle, Pyramid Power, and Chariots of the Gods attests to a failure of the scientific method to penetrate everyday life (Page, 1979).

The result is generally a lack of public political pressure to support scientific and technological work.

It is, of course, entirely possible to graduate from university and still have virtually no knowledge about scientific and technological matters. It has been argued that this situation should be addressed through the increased use of "science and society" courses in the post-secondary curriculum.

As for the persons who are, or will be, working at the very intersection of science, technology, and industrial/economic adaptations, here the requirements are also changing. As a recent report of the Science Council of Canada observes:

> In our complex, modern society, providing the managerial and technological inputs for a technology-based enterprise requires more than just having a number of trained and competent individuals. It requires that these individuals learn to function in a complementary way and as a well-coordinated team. Such a team requires a long time to build up, and once it is acquired, it represents a large investment; its value as a team far exceeds the sum of the values of its component members. Not only must the members learn to work harmoniously as a unit, but, more difficult still, they must become coupled and finely attuned to the broader outer environment in which they operate. Only in this way can they get the necessary inputs and effect the meaningful outputs that are essential to success in the world of high technology (Science Council of Canada, op. cit.).

These developments have provoked debates over appropriate directions for educational policy. We have recently seen more emphasis on making students computer literate. The job growth trends analyzed earlier in this chapter, however, suggest many future jobs will not require such skills.

There is also a major debate over the impact of technology on job content. Analysts such as Braverman (1974) see an irreversible trend toward work simplification and de-skilling. Harvey and Blakely, in a recent survey of high technology firms in Ontario (Harvey and Blakely:1–12), found that many employers identified technology-driven impacts upon job content other than de-skilling. In particular, many employers identified a need for well-trained, flexible generalists who could adapt readily to fast-paced technological change, and function well in "boundary spanning roles" that go beyond the traditional definitions of jobs and job responsibilities.

A further debate emphasizes the importance of creating more effective linkages between scientific and technological research in Canadian universities and the commercialization of such research. Although such development is desirable, it appears unlikely to be realized by educational institutions alone. New kinds of institutional linkages among governments, industry, and universities are required.

The Fast Pace of Technological Change

Canadians do not have the luxury of taking a long time to deal with the problems and challenges discussed in this chapter. Increasing international competition and rapid technological change are realities. In particular, the fast pace of change in microelectronics and computing are transforming industrial society and creating a new information economy. As Arthur J. Cordell observes:

> At the centre of the current transformation is the computer—no longer a room-sized machine radiating heat from a million vacuum tubes, but a compact, reliable piece of electronic circuitry that can be packed into a suitcase. The enormous reductions in size and cost of computers have been made possible by the development of the silicon chip—a marvel of miniaturization whose million microscopic components give today's tiny computers abilities equal to those of the largest computers of the last decade (Cordell, 1985: 3–4).

Computerization permits the storage, accessing, and utilization of vast amounts of information that would have been unmanageable in the pre-computer era. Microprocessors can now be used to project and control inventories and production systems and, of course, are at the heart of the increasing number of work activities that can be automated, ranging from word processors in the office to industrial robots in the factory.

The microelectronic revolution is also changing the social organization of work. Existing telephone lines allow for the straightforward linking of data bases and computerized communication centres, with little concern for geographical dispersion. In the office of the future, it will be increasingly feasible for workers to remain at home, plugged into the electronic workplace through a computer terminal in their residence. The proliferation and rapid flows of information will work to the disadvantage of traditional, hierarchical forms of organization. The businesses that succeed will increasingly be flexibly organized with management systems that speed, rather than impede, the flow of communication.

The management of complex processes of technological change presents challenges to industry, unions, education, and public policy generally. The formation of effective public policy is complicated by the absence of consensus on the implications and impacts of technological change. This is well illustrated by a 1981 Gallup Poll commissioned to gather public opinion on societal impacts of microelectronic technology. The poll was conducted in both the United States and Canada, using comparable samples and the same questions.

Turning to Table 8, as Marsden observes in her analysis of the poll results:

> Canadians (at least from Ontario) truly seem to be more pessimistic. Canadians are more likely to believe that microelectronics makes their jobs more boring (26 percent compared with 14 percent); more hazardous (18 percent compared with 11 percent); less challenging (31 percent compared to 21 percent) and less secure (38 percent compared to 27 percent) (Marsden, 1982).

The survey also showed, for both countries, that:

> Professional and executive people are by far much more optimistic about all job-related attributes except perhaps health hazards. . . . there is significant concern about job security, challenge of job, and interest of work among clerical, skilled labour and unskilled labour. Very few skilled labourers feel that microelectronics has increased job hazards (9.5 percent), which differs somewhat from the feeling of the others, and skilled labourers seem less concerned with stress than clerical and unskilled labour (ibid.).

Table 8
RESPONSES FROM ONTARIO AND U.S. GALLUP POLL QUESTIONS ON THE IMPACT OF ELECTRONIC TECHNOLOGY ON VARIOUS ASPECTS OF WORK BY SEX

	Ontario			**U.S.**		
	M	*F*	*Total*	*M*	*F*	*Total*
Interest						
More interesting	50.7	46.5	49.1	55.3	54.0	54.8
Same	18.2	19.6	18.8	21.5	19.5	20.7
More boring	24.0	28.6	25.7	14.4	14.5	14.4
Don't know/Not stated	7.1	5.2	6.4	8.8	12.0	10.1
Hazard to Health						
Less hazardous	37.1	31.0	34.8	43.3	39.8	41.8
Same	35.1	36.4	35.6	34.0	32.8	33.5
More hazardous	16.1	21.1	18.0	10.8	11.1	10.9
Don't know/Not stated	11.9	11.4	11.7	11.9	16.3	13.8
Stress						
Less stress	44.8	44.3	44.6	47.6	44.3	46.2
Same	23.9	18.7	22.0	20.2	21.0	20.5
More stress	22.8	30.4	25.7	22.8	23.4	23.1
Don't know/Not stated	8.5	6.6	7.7	9.3	11.4	10.2
Salary						
Higher salary	39.8	37.2	38.8	45.1	39.2	42.7
Same	31.5	37.3	33.6	31.2	32.9	31.9
Lower salary	16.0	15.8	15.9	12.7	13.3	12.9
Don't know/Not stated	12.8	9.8	11.7	11.0	14.5	12.5
Security of Job						
More job security	28.9	27.6	28.4	35.3	30.5	33.3
Same	31.3	26.1	29.3	27.3	28.4	27.8
Less job security	30.3	40.5	34.2	28.2	25.9	27.3
Don't know/Not stated	9.5	5.7	8.1	9.2	15.1	11.7
Challenge						
More challenge	43.1	49.3	45.4	48.6	47.5	48.1
Same	20.1	12.7	17.3	20.7	20.5	20.6
Less challenge	29.5	34.0	31.2	20.9	20.5	20.7
Don't know/Not stated	7.3	4.0	6.1	9.8	11.5	10.6

Sources: Gallup Ontario Omnibus conducted for Ministry of Transportation & Communication, February 1981, and *A Gallup Survey of Electronic Technology* (U.S.), March 1981.

CONCLUSION

Technology-driven change has had, and will continue to have, many and significant social impacts. Fast-paced technological change is already transforming the occupational system, a fundamental structure that gives people much of their social identity and provides the mechanism for most of the distribution and redistribution of income in society. Technological change cannot be ignored. To do so is to accept the inevitable loss of competitiveness, accelerating de-industrialization and decay in our standard of living.

Canada faces special problems and opportunities in adapting to these changes. Our political and economic history has created institutional obstacles to the pace of our industrial adaptation and development. These include the strength of regionalism in Canada, the branch plant character of our industrial development, and impediments to the adequate capitalization of new ventures. These institutional problems are reflected in several more specific patterns, such as our weak commitment to research and development, relatively poor productivity in recent years, and underdeveloped organizational arrangements and policy tools for knitting together governments, industry, and unions in collective action.

Notwithstanding these problems, Canada is rich in natural and human resources. Significant areas of "comparable advantage" exist in the economy, including the sectors of transportation and communication, agriculture and food processing, and natural resource extraction techniques. The issue for the 1980s and beyond is, in part, how to build on areas of strength, create new technological "success stories," achieve productivity gains and enhance export market shares. In the 1970s, much of the debate on these issues centred around the concept of an "industrial strategy," which often emphasized nationalistic approaches to industrial/economic development. In the 1980s, the nationalistic approach has been challenged by a call for greater integration between the Canadian and U.S. economies—as reflected in the current push for free trade. Whichever options or combinations thereof emerge as a dominant force in Canadian policy, the relationships between science, technology, and industrial development will continue to be shaped by the deeply historically rooted institutional patterns discussed in this chapter.

DISCUSSION QUESTIONS

1. How has Canada's historical pattern of development shaped its current economic situation and the industrial policies and directions of the nation?
2. What are some of the social impacts of electronic technology? Will these impacts affect different people in different ways?
3. Discuss Canada's R&D track record compared to other industrial countries.
4. What types of actions would have to be taken to provide Canada with a more effective industrial strategy? What are the major obstacles to achieving such a strategy?
5. What are the effects of regionalism on science and technology in Canadian society? Why is regionalism such an important social force in Canada?

GLOSSARY

basic research scientific research not designed for the immediate production of economic or industrial benefits

cyclical trends trends which repeat themselves in a relatively regular way—as in the business cycle of boom and recession

industrial strategy an integrated set of policies designed to guide a nation's economic development.

institutions social structures involving laws, regulations, and the commitment of resources to achieve major social objectives such as health, education, and social stability

occupational regulation control of admission standards to an occupation or regulation of how the occupation is to be practised, as in professional associations

occupational system the division of labour or network of jobs found in industrial societies

public sector that part of the economy directly supported by public revenues such as taxes; for example, education, police services, government

value added the economic value that is added to a product or industrial process by technology; the market value of automobiles and other manufactured goods is considerably in excess of the value of the raw materials required to produce them, for example

venture capital investment capital for high risk but potentially high return industrial development

BIBLIOGRAPHY

Belous, Richard J.
1985 "Middle Class Erosion and Growing Income Inequality: Fact or Fiction." Washington, D.C.: Congressional Research Service, No. 28.

Bird, Richard M.
1984 "Is Increasing Employment in 'High Tech' Industry a Sensible Policy Goal for Ontario?" *Policy Study* #84-4. Toronto, University of Toronto Institute for Policy Analysis, mimeo.

Braverman, Harry
1974 *Labor and Monopoly Capital*. New York: Monthly Review Press.

Cordell, Arthur J.
1985 *The Uneasy Eighties: The Transition to an Information Society*. Summary of Background Study 53, Ottawa.

Economic Council of Canada
1977 *Living Together: A Study of Regional Disparities*. Ottawa.

———
1978 *Proceedings.* Conference on Industrial Adaptation, June 26, 27, and 28. Ottawa: Ministry of Supply and Services Canada.

Harvey, Edward B.
1976 "Dimensions of a Decade: Canadian Higher Education in the Sixties." In G. McDiarmid (ed.) *From Quantitative to Qualitative Change in Ontario Education*. Toronto: O.I.S.E. Press.

Harvey, E.B. and J. H. Blakely
"Human Capital: New Skills for New Jobs." In *Ideas on Innovation* 1, No. 3.

Hay Associates Canada Ltd.
1984 *Navigating Uncharted Waters: Canada's Next Ten Years*. February.

Kuttner, Bob
1983 "The Declining Middle." *The Atlantic Monthly*, July.

Levin, Henry
1984 "Education and Jobs in a Technological World." The National Center for Research in Vocational Education, Ohio State University, Information Series, No. 265.

Lucas, Rex
1971 *Milltown, Minetown, Railtown*. Toronto: University of Toronto Press.

Marsden, L. R.
1982 *Social and Economic Debates on the Impact of Microelectronics in Canada*. Ottawa: A report prepared for the Task Force on Microelectronics and Employment, June.

Marsden, L. R. and E. B. Harvey
1979 *Fragile Federation: Social Change in Canada*. Toronto: McGraw-Hill Ryerson.

Morishima, Michoi
1982 *Why Has Japan "Succeeded?": Western Technology and the Japanese Ethos*. London: Cambridge University Press.

Natural Sciences and Engineering Research Council of Canada
1985 *Research Talent in the Natural Sciences and Engineering: Supply and Demand Projections to 1990*. May.

Neill, Robin
1972 *A New Theory of Value: The Canadian Economics of H. A. Innis*. Toronto: University of Toronto Press.

Newton, Keith
1985 "Employment Effects on Technological Change: Some Implications for Education." Economic Council of Canada, mimeo, April.

Page, James E.
1979 "A Canadian Context for Science Education." A discussion paper prepared for the Science Council of Canada. Ottawa: October: 45.

Reich, Robert B.
1983 *The Next American Frontier*. New York: Times Books.

Samuelson, Robert J.
1985 "Demolishing a Myth." *The Washington Post*, June 26, D1.

Schwartz, G. G. and W. Nelkirk
1983 *The Work Revolution*. New York: Rawson Associates.

Science Council of Canada
1971 *Innovation in a Cold Climate: The Dilemma of Canadian Manufacturing*. Ottawa, October: 28.

——
1972 *Innovation and the Structure of Canadian Industry*. Special Study No. 23, Ottawa.

——
1979 *Forging the Links: A Technology Policy for Canada*. Report 29. Ottawa: 28

——
Canadian Industrial Development: Some Policy Directions. Summary of Report 37. Ottawa: 9–42.

Simeon, Richard
1979 "Federalism and the Politics of a National Strategy." In *The Politics of an Industrial Strategy: A Seminar*. Science Council of Canada, January.

Watching television is the most frequent leisure time activity of Canadians, young and old.
Courtesy of S.J. Wilson

"Canadian television contains more 'nonentertainment' programming than its American counterpart, but is principally a medium for drama originating in the United States."

c h a p t e r   e l e v e n

Mass Media and the Arts

John Jackson

INTRODUCTION

Placing "the arts" and the "mass media" side by side may seem an unusual juxtaposition. In everyday thought the referents of each are quite different. "Mass media" conjures up images of television, rock videos, and the like served to an undifferentiated mass. In contrast, "the arts" bring to mind art galleries, symphony orchestras, and other more "refined" activities reserved for elite audiences. This chapter rejects this dichotomy. A soap opera, a poem, a TV advertisement, and a painting are all forms of **discourse**. Each combines selected elements of everyday experience into imaginative representations of possible worlds and each carries a certain authority. Each is a means of producing and disseminating meaning, a fundamental characteristic of human societies.

Discourse and discursive practices will be important concepts in our discussion to follow. Careful thought will also be given to the terms: mass, **culture**, art, and media, a prerequisite to sorting out the complex relations between cultural practices and social organization. This discussion will set the framework for an examination of the mass media and the arts in a socio-historical context.

To study the mass media and the arts requires drawing upon fields of study common to sociology and related fields. Considering the products of these practices (e.g., the broadcast, the novel, the painting) places one in the domain of **ideology** and requires expertise in textual analysis. To deal with the state, the private sector or capital as sponsors or promoters, and audiences takes one into the domains of politics, economics, and social class. To deal with the creators or artists places us in the domains of literary and artistic traditions and demands a consideration of networks of people with particular social and political orientations.

This chapter has two objectives: to propose a way of looking into or investigating the mass media and the arts from a sociological point of view and to provide an overall view of the issues and events related to these practices. The first part of the chapter will examine selected concepts and ways of talking about the media and the arts. The second part will review cultural production through four points of reference—the artifacts of the process or the "text," the organization of the process, the artists, and reception.

ORIENTATION TO THE INQUIRY

Words like "mass," "media," and "art" carry several, often contradictory, meanings in ordinary conversation as well as in theoretical discourse. Their meanings change according to the ideological orientation of particular theories. "Mass," and the "masses," is an interesting concept since it carries both positive and pejorative meanings. Conservatives often use it with contempt, implying a critique of democracy. Here a distinction is made between the minority elite and the masses: mass being associated with "common," "base," or "mean." In contrast, from a revolutionary perspective, especially the populist varieties, mass takes on positive connotations, referring to "the people," "the common people," or "ordinary people" as the vanguard of social and political change. An interesting twist takes place among revolutionaries who eschew populism. Here mass media, mass communications, and mass culture refer to institutions perpetrated by elites to control a population through the destruction of authentic popular culture (Williams, 1976:192–97; Rioux, 1984).

The meaning intended in this chapter is closer to the latter. We will, however, suggest a slightly different meaning for "mass media," following a consideration of "media," a less politically charged word. "Medium" has been used in English since at least the beginning of the seventeenth century to refer to an "intervening or intermediate agency or substance" between thought and its mode of expression (Williams, 1976:203).

As Williams points out, a countertrend in cultural studies takes speaking, writing, acting, and broadcasting as *primary practices* rather than as media or intermediate agencies between thought and expression (1976:203–5). We would do well to follow this direction. If we do not, we risk allocating creative activity to a secondary position, as somehow or other "not real work." It is better to refer to various *means of communication* and then examine the structures of control, creation, and reception, rather than to retain the somewhat loaded concept of "mass media."

"Art" and "the Arts" are no less problematic. Williams informs us that the specialization of these terms to a particular group of skills — painting, drawing, engraving, and culture — was not fully established in English until the early 1800s. Initially, art referred to any kind of skill. Specialization of meaning begins in the seventeenth century.

This eighteenth century usage persists. Art and the Arts, capitalized, refer to creative and imaginative work separated from other skills viewed as manual labour. Keeping in mind that the particular skills included in or excluded from the "higher" category change according to time, place, and circumstance, we must recognize that these changes in meaning are rooted in social, political, and economic changes. As Williams notes: "This complex set of historical distinctions . . . can be primarily related to changes inherent in capitalist commodity production, with its specialization and reduction of use values to exchange values" (1976:42).

In reviewing the changing meaning of "mass" and "art," one cannot help but notice the parallel development. Mass, in its pejorative sense, distinguishes between

ART AS A COMMODITY

Part of the process in which art as a "higher calling" became distinguished from manual labour involved a defensive move to protect creative and imaginative work from the commodification of all human practices. There is some irony in the fact that, as the principal form of patronage of the arts shifted toward the marketplace, art became a commodity and artists became wage or salaried workers, or independent commodity producers. A recent Government of Canada report titled *The Status of the Artist* takes this position, recommending that artists be granted a tax status similar to that of farmers and fishermen (1986a:11). The current use of the term "cultural industries" and the necessity of referring to the dollar value of cultural and artistic production in order to justify state patronage is further evidence of the influence of a marketplace discourse on our understanding of creative work.

a minority elite and the general population. Art, in its specialized meaning, distinguishes between the "finer" practices of that elite and the practices of ordinary people. Changes in the meanings of these terms carry both hidden hypotheses about reality and the very history of social and political change in particular societies.

MAJOR CONCEPTS

Culture

Referring to Williams's *Marxism and Literature*, the concept "culture" carries two major meanings: (1) as a noun referring to "inner" processes, specifying "intellectual life," and "the arts"; and (2) as a noun referring to configurations of "whole ways of life" (1977:17). Most of us use the word in both senses. In the first sense, the concept has been used and continues to imply a related concept, that of "civilization." A "cultured person" is, at once, a "civilized person." This use parallels the pejorative use of "mass" and the specialization of the meanings of "art" and "the arts." All imply a minority elite over and against "the masses."

Taking principally the second meaning, though keeping the first in mind, let us consider culture as a signifying system. For our purposes, then, culture refers to those human practices and agencies that give meaning to everyday life. To put it another way, "culture (is) the *signifying system* through which necessarily . . . a social order is communicated, reproduced, experienced and explored" (Williams, 1981:13). Meaning is necessarily created and shared at all levels of human practice and in all forms of social life. Therefore, culture, referring to the creation and sustaining of meanings, encompasses language, the arts, journalism, advertising, theatre, and broadcasting, or any practice devoted to the building of meaning systems.

A note of caution is necessary. There is a danger of including in this conceptualization the notion of cultural integration. That is, when one speaks of a national culture or the culture of any social group, there is a tendency to assume a unity of meanings within the designated group (see Sorokin, 1937:4). We are inclined to speak of "Canadian culture" or "American culture" as though there were an integrated set of signifying systems common to and shared by all members of these geopolitical units. At the same time, we refer to

"Black" and "White" cultures in the United States, and French- and English-Canadian cultures in Canada. But at whatever level of complexity and size the boundaries of a social group are drawn, there will be found variations on a main theme, as well as competing meaning systems within that group.

The relations between various meaning systems are important. Following work by George Gurvitch, these relations may be described as complementary, ambiguous, reciprocal, or polarized (1962:207). For example, the meanings assigned to the present federal government's free trade negotiations by Western and Central Canadians are neither reciprocal nor complementary; the relations between these two sets of meanings are at times ambiguous and at times polarized. The differences in meaning assigned by each region are related to different economic and sociohistorical experiences. Putting aside the concept of cultural unity, we may yet refer to central tendencies of meaning or "the mainstream culture" within particular social groups. Given the existence of different signifying systems within social groups, how do certain meanings become privileged, dominant, or mainstream? This is a question of power — what factions within a group can sustain a particular meaning system in a relatively dominant position?

Ideology

The answer to this question requires understanding the concept of ideology. Ideology refers to the processes and the forms whereby particular ways of interpreting experience assume dominance (Giddens, 1983:19). The empirical question becomes who or what faction is in a position to assume control of those institutions related to the creation and reproduction of meaning. What faction(s) in Ontario, Saskatchewan, or Nova Scotia, for example, control educational institutions? What faction(s) control the means of communication in Canada as a whole (e.g., see Clement, 1975:270–86)? As noted earlier, we must be careful not to assume an omnipresent and ubiquitous form of signification (the cultural unity concept again) common to a strand of Marxian thinking and structural-functionalists (e.g., see Abercrombie and Turner, 1980). Any social group may contain meaning systems opposing the mainstream themes, meaning created by writers, performers, or producers working outside of the mainstream.

Ideology is thus an aspect of culture, referring to the intertwining of power and systems of meaning. Insofar as it is our task to deal with those practices related to "the media" and "the arts," we are in the domain of the creation of imaginative world visions which may sustain, oppose, or provide alternatives to mainstream visions. Any product of these practices is a consequence of a skillful combination of values, beliefs, and experiences to convey a particular message. The concept of discourse provides a useful way of considering this process and its products.

Discourse

Discourse refers to the structure of an argument, to conversation, and to speaking or writing formally. It carries with it a sense of persuasion, pleading, or incitement. Discourse analysis has its roots in the ancient discipline of rhetoric and, more recently, it has been associated with the study of written and spoken languages (e.g., see van Dijk, 1985). It has been extended to refer to all forms of communication, including broadcasting productions, advertising, the visual arts, and the like. William Leiss and others justify this extension in their recent book *Social Communication in Advertising*:

> The term discourse should refer to both verbal and pictorial communicative modes. Advertisements certainly are fictions, that is, imaginative creations or artful

> representations of possible words, and they strive mightly to redescribe reality by taking familiar components of everyday life . . . and conjuring up scene after scene full of hypothetical interactions between these components and a product (1986:241).

Mikhail Bakhtin uses "discourse" as a term to refer to "a method of using words /we can include pictures and other forms of communication/ that presumes a type of authority (Holquist, 1981:427)." Insofar as the authority associated with persuasion is held by a dominant group, the extent to which ideology penetrates or is excluded from particular discourses becomes an important question in communications studies.

A SOCIOLOGY OF DISCURSIVE PRACTICES

If "the media" and "the arts" are discursive practices, the end result (the TV serial, the painting hanging in an art gallery, the novel, etc.) is but one point of reference. It is also necessary to consider the creators themselves and their social settings, the organizational framework within which the practices are pursued and the products distributed, and the reception of the products. The product itself may be at once an artifact of the practice, static in time and place, and a continuation of the practice through time as it is received by new audiences, readers, and viewers.

Disciplines like sociology tend to concentrate on the organizational and technological frameworks within which discursive practices take place and, to a lesser extent, on the social settings which locate the creators. Disciplines like literary and art criticism tend to concentrate on the artifact and the biographies of the creators. But much work crosses the boundaries, bringing two or more of the points of reference into play. Not to cross these boundaries leads to a very narrow view of cultural practices.

The Artifact

Any attempt at an overall summary of the major approaches to the analysis of discourse in cultural products would be an over-simplification. In the main, the approaches vary according to the extent to which the analysis concentrates on the artifact itself or brings other points of reference into play, and this, in turn, varies according to fundamental assumptions made about social reality. For example, and following Eagleton, a pure *phenomenological* analysis brackets "the actual historical context of the product, its author, conditions of production, and readership" (1983:59). *Reception theory*, a development from phenomenology and *hermeneutics*, "examines the readers' (in this case, the appropriate audience) role" as an element in the dynamic process of discourse creation (1983:74–77).

Structuralism and *semiotics* locate meaning in the relations between signs and the rules of combination of signs. This parallels the privileging of grammar and syntax over the spoken word in the study of language. In other words, the content of the story is put aside while "deep meaning" is located in the form. The perennial problem inherent in any form of structural analysis remains one of bracketing the world outside of the text and the creative process itself. Variations attempt to break the rigid boundaries of "hard" structuralism. Lucien Goldmann's *genetic-structuralism* introduces the time dimension, calling for a consideration of the relations of the structure of the text to its origins in social time and place (1975; see also, Nielsen and Jackson, 1984). In Lotman's semiotics, the text's relations to other texts, codes, and literary traditions is brought into play (Eagleton, 1983:103). Structuralism shifted interest from the construction of meaning as a private experience to an acknowledgement of shared systems of signification and from the privileged text of literature to all constructions of meaning. This is especially evident in the *post-structuralism* found in the works of Lacan, Foucault, and Kristeva (Eagleton 1983:134).

At this point it is appropriate to return to our central concept of discourse. Discourse analysis, as pointed out by Eagleton, ''shares with . . . structuralism and semiotics an interest in the formal devices of language.'' With reception theory it shares an interest in the effects of these devices on the ''consumer'' and, with other approaches, it shares an interest in the linkage between communication and forms of power (1983:206). Thus, in analyzing a text, a researcher examines what devices are used to plead and persuade and how are they used. Following this mode of analysis, we will examine work in the fields of broadcasting, painting, and literature.

Broadcasting

Prior to attending to broadcasting artifacts, it would be useful to know what is broadcast over the principle medium, television. The bulk of television programming is devoted to ''entertainment.'' (See Table 1.) Drama represents around a third of the entertainment programming on Canadian TV. English language TV devotes 13.1 percent less of its broadcasting time to entertainment than American TV, French language TV 9.1 percent less. These differences between Canadian and U.S. broadcasting are probably influenced by the C.B.C. and other public outlets (the U.S. data do not include public broadcasting). Furthermore, one might wonder about how much entertainment programming on Canadian TV is of U.S. and other foreign origin.

Table 2 answers this question. It is obvious that not much programming of Canadian origin is available to English-speaking Canadians. Keeping in mind that neither Table 1 nor Table 2 refer to viewing patterns but to availability, entertainment programming is largely of foreign

Table I

PERCENTAGE AIRTIME TV PROGRAMS AVAILABLE BY TYPE AND SECTOR*

Type of Program	Canada *English*	*French*		**U.S.A.**
News	11.0	6.0		9.4
Public Affairs	12.0	23.0		4.5
Instruction	11.0	6.0	Other ''Non-entertainment''	
Religion	4.0	—		12.0
Subtotal	38.0	35.0		25.9
Drama	34.0	30.0		
Sports	6.0	11.0		74.1
Other	22.0	24.0		
Subtotal	62.0	65.0		74.1
Total	100%	100%		100%

*Canadian data: 6 a.m.–2 a.m., 1984; U.S. data: 6 a.m.–12 p.m., 1978

Source: Canada, *Report of the Task Force on Broadcasting Policy*, 1986, pp. 91–92.
Source: Head & Sterling, 1982:230

origin for both English- and French-speaking Canadians. News and public affairs just about split for English-speaking Canadians, while the bulk of this type of programming is of Canadian origin for French-speaking Canadians. Some programming originates in Britain and France, but the bulk of foreign programming is of U.S. origin. Canadian television contains more "non-entertainment" programming than its American counterpart, but is principally a medium for drama originating in the United States. Nevertheless, the analysis of newscasts on Canadian TV is of importance, insofar as this type of programming is one of the major types of Canadian origin available.

A recent analysis of English language C.B.C. news coverage of the 1983 British election is an example of the kind of analysis referred to above (Knight and Taylor, 1986). News broadcasting on radio and television most certainly presents "the facts," but it does this in certain ways; that is, the news is presented within a selected frame determined by journalists, editors, and producers. These frames are built out of choices made as to what "facts" to broadcast and what "facts" to ignore; the sequence of presentation of selected "facts" and amount of time devoted to each selection; the juxtaposition of certain "facts" with others; the use of reporting by the "anchor person" only, by a journalist on the scene, or by an expert; and the scenic background for reports on a particular "fact." All of these choices structure the discourse of a newscast.

Graham Knight and Ian Taylor took these devices into account when demonstrating the ahistorical, empiricist, and consensual orientation in the C.B.C.'s reporting of the 1983 British election. They found a shift to the right politically in the coverage (1986:244). Focusing on the spoken text and "centring interpretive attention on the relationship between what is *present* in a discourse and what is *absent* from it," Knight and Taylor examined: (1) the use of reporting on opinion polls to "frame" the news; (2) how the main political parties were differentially identified and defined; and (3) how the main election issues—unemployment and the economy — were represented (1986: 233–34).

Table 2
PROPORTION OF BROADCAST TIME FOR TYPES OF CANADIAN AND FOREIGN PROGRAMMING*

Type	**English Programs** *Canadian origin*	*Foreign origin*	**French Programs** *Canadian origin*	*Foreign origin*
News	46.0	54.0	99.0	1.0
Public Affairs	52.0	48.0	78.0	22.0
Sports	68.0	32.0	92.0	8.0
Drama	2.0	98.0	10.0	90.0
Music/ Variety/ Quiz	25.0	75.0	66.0	34.0
All Programs	28.0	72.0	57.0	43.0

*6 a.m.–2 a.m., 1984.

Source: Canada, *Report of the Task Force on Broadcasting Policy*, 1986, p. 95.

Using polls to frame the newscasts cast the election as a "horse race" and, thus, as a single event divorced from the context and recent history of British political and economic life. The stress was on a two-way party race between Labour and the Conservatives, ignoring the Alliance party. This permitted an interpretation that avoided the political meaning of the loss of Labour votes to the third party. In sum, using the polls to frame a particular *interpretation* of the election directed attention away from the centre-left Alliance coalition as a principal cause of the breakdown of Labour Party loyalty. The impression was that all of Britain had turned Tory, even though the combined opposition vote was at 51 to 53 percent!

Ideology enters here not in the sense that owners of the means of communication demand the election news be broadcast in a certain way, but in the sense that the mainstream view of the electoral process permeates the everyday thought of producers, journalists, and viewers alike. Not only is the process perceived as a unique event, akin to a sports spectacular, but the perspective separates thought about governance from its sociocultural, political, and economic context. The technology and the social organization of broadcasting also lend themselves to this type of framing of "facts."

This kind of analysis gives priority to the discourse built into a text. The emphasis is on how a text is structured in order to deliver a particular message. Another, more common, type of analysis of broadcasting texts gives priority to items of content rather than to structuring. Muriel Cantor and Suzanne Pingree's (1983) study of soap operas on U.S. television is a case in point. All of the broadcasts referred to in this study were available to Canadian viewers with A.B.C., C.B.S., and N.B.C. network access. Three of the eleven available were found on the C.T.V. network and one on the C.B.C.

Content analysis enumerates categories of items (social class, family relations, gender roles, values, etc.) present in a text or set of texts. Each category, comprising sentences (or other units of analysis) in which the designated item is defined as present is assumed to be a discrete event that may be counted and added. Thus, an investigator may report on the percentage of "topics of conversation" dealing with "business-career" issues as compared to the percentage dealing with "feelings" (Cantor and Pingree, 1983:107).

Structural analyses, such as found in the report on news broadcasting, addresses the *relations* among devices or themes in a discourse. The question is: how are identifiable devices combined to achieve certain effects? The number of times an item, device, or theme appears in a text is irrelevant. However, content analysis provides a picture of the "surface" content of texts (see Jackson, 1981:232–49).

In their study of American soap operas on radio and television, Cantor and Pingree report on the results of a content analysis of "The Guiding Light," using radio and television scripts of broadcasts between 1948 and 1982. This serial, the only soap opera to successfully transfer from radio to television, began in 1937 and is still broadcast over the C.B.S. network. They found a decrease in the proportion of messages articulating general values and an increase in the proportion of those articulating concrete social relations within the family (1983:102–3). With respect to "topics of conversation," topics addressing business and careers showed a marked increase at the expense of "romance," "personality," and "feelings," to name a few of the categories used (1983:107). Of interest is the shift over time of interaction and "romance" from the home to the work setting and an increase in the number of women occupying roles in the world of work (1983:99–105).

MINORITIES AND THE MEDIA: NATIVE CANADIANS IN THE DAILY PRESS

News presents the facts, but journalists, editors, and publishers make decisions regarding what facts to present and what facts to ignore; the juxtaposition of selected news items; and the placement of news items. These decisions yield a particular discourse on the world in which we live.

This study employed a content analysis examining the frequency of stories about Native Canadians, the types of events covered, article placement, and headline wording in a large Ontario metropolitan daily between 1971 and 1975.

Finding 1: Location of Items Concerning Amerindians and Inuit

	Amerindians	Inuit
% Items 1st page	6.4	6.4
Mean page # of item	11.2	10.9
Median page # of item	8.1	8.3

Conclusion: Assuming that readers assign more importance to front page stories, the importance of Native Canadians is reduced by placing most news items around pages 8 to 11.

Finding 2: Distribution of Types of Events Reported

	Amerindians	Inuit
Gov. Land Claims	51.7%	46.2%
Conflict	28.6%	21.8%
Nonconflict	19.5%	32.0%

Conclusion: Native Canadians are represented principally as peoples seeking government assistance and involved in conflict situations, Inuit peoples slightly less so than Amerindians. The ability of readers to envision Native peoples in daily life situations is reduced.

Through the selection and placement of facts the press constructs an image of reality which, in turn, contributes to a way of thinking about native peoples.

Source: Benjamin D. Singer, "Minorities and the Media: A Content Analysis of Native Canadians in the Daily Press." *The Canadian Review of Sociology and Anthropology*, 19:3, pp. 348–359.

The authors note that soap operas *reflect* and *mirror* the life of the day. "A fictionalized representation of our social structure and social relations are presented. These. . . . provide a mirror of the world" (1983:69). This may be so, but do these serials, as part of the broader genre of romantic fiction, create rather than merely reflect a particular discourse of interpersonal relations based on the romantic ideal? To answer this question requires an analysis more in keeping with the various modes of analysis discussed above, be it structuralism, semiotics, or phenomenology. For example, the appearance of women in work roles may well have increased in soap operas, but how is this feature used as a device to structure a discourse on gender relations? Does the discourse support existing meaning systems, provide alternatives, or articulate opposition? These questions are not readily dealt with in content analysis, and it is these kinds of questions that lead the researcher to the point where ideology and discourse intersect.

A look at a discourse analysis of a radio drama broadcast in 1944 illustrates this technique. The play was a half-hour broadcast from Toronto over the C.B.C. Trans-Canada network titled "Within the Fortress." It was written by Len Peterson and produced by Andrew Allan for the Sunday evening *Stage* series. The series offered a new play every Sunday, either an original Canadian drama or an adaptation of a classical and contemporary play written for legitimate theatre. This play was broadcast during World War II at a time when Allied fortunes were beginning to improve.

The play is set on the Eastern Front when the Russians were beginning to push the German armies westward. The protagonist, Omers, an Intelligence officer in the Germany army, is called back to Berlin to review problems of troop morale. As his plane heads west, he reviews in his mind the events leading up to the war and the current fears of a German defeat. His dream-like thoughts introduce the listener to a critical discourse of the events and circumstances leading up to the opening of hostilities in 1939. In so doing, the playwright humanizes the enemy in the persons of Omers and his wife and in the unfolding of events from 1930 onwards. The German officer, his wife, and their son become persons with whom the audience can readily identify, permitting a consideration of the more general social, economic, and political causes of the war.

Through a host of voices the complexity of pre-1939 events in Germany is unravelled: poverty, worker exploitation, unemployment, the lack of opportunities, inflation, and the consequences of Germany's defeat in 1918. Communists and Jews became the scapegoats as ordinary and embittered people sought explanations. In this atmosphere, the Nazi party grew. A finger is pointed at the petite bourgeoisie and business—at capitalists—whose preoccupation with the threat of communism encouraged a fascist opposition.

This description of the play is far from a straight reading of the content of the script and the sound version. It is already a structural reading in which the play is described in terms of its themes and their interrelations. We can take the analysis a step further by identifying the discourse and noting the devices used to create it. The discourse is that of the Canadian centre-left political position on World War II. There is support for the Allied war effort as a struggle against fascism, but the war is perceived as having its roots in the clash of capitalist imperial powers. Keeping in mind that the members of the audience are steeped in war propaganda—patriotism, a hate, bordering on racism, for the enemy, and the sense of an allied victory—the playwright must first bring the audience into a frame of mind where they consider the socioeconomic causes of war, based upon a capitalist political economy. He does this with two devices. First, by placing a German officer in a family setting with a loving wife and child who can express the same fears as the audience themselves feel serves to humanize the enemy. Secondly, the defeat of the German armies is presented as imminent. This is not only consistent with the "reality" of news bulletins at the time, but also retains the enemy *qua* enemy. Having temporarily released the audience from its preoccupation with propaganda, the play may then critique war itself.

HOW CANADIANS SPEND THEIR LEISURE TIME

Canadians devote most of their leisure time to watching television. Listening to radio ranks second in interest, but is largely background to other activities. Reading books, newspapers, and magazines remains an important activity. "Home" entertainment and socializing with friends occupies considerably more time than attending movies, live performances, and spectator sports.

Selected Activities, 1976

Activities	*Participation* (in millions)	*No. of Hours Per Week* 0–3	3–7	8–14	+15
Watching television	15.7	17.7%	27.4%	25.6%	28.7%
Listening to radio	13.9	32.4%	30.1%	18.2%	18.8%
Socializing with friends/relatives	13.2	25.8%	40.2%	21.6%	12.1%
Reading newspapers & mags.	12.7	51.5%	34.3%	10.0%	3.4%
Reading books	9.4	40.0%	34.4%	16.9%	8.2%
Listening to records, tapes	9.3	49.5%	29.3%	12.3%	8.3%

Source: Statistics Canada, 1976. Catalogue 87–501, Cultural Statistics, Table 35, p. 70

The Visual Arts

In the early 1970s, B.B.C. television broadcast a series entitled "Ways of Seeing." In the text accompanying the production, John Berger stated:

> The art of any period tends to serve the ideological interests of the ruling class . . . what is being proposed is . . . that a way of seeing the world, which was ultimately determined by new attitudes to property and exchange, found its visual expression in the oil painting (1972:86–87).

In the fall of 1984, forty years after the first broadcast of "Within the Fortress," a recording of this play was presented to an introductory sociology class at Concordia University in Montreal. In the main, the class was composed of students born between 1960 and 1965. Their initial reaction was amazement; to quote one student, "How could they get away with stuff like that during the war—I thought that radio would broadcast only propaganda?" To answer this question requires a look at the C.B.C. itself and the particular writers and producers working there at that time. To this we will shortly turn.

The emphasis in Berger's analysis is on the linkage between practices in the visual arts and power, that is, ideology. The analysis takes up several themes, among them the relations between property and exchange as redefined by capitalism, and the reproduction of these relations in the imagery and marketing of oil painting, the objectification of women in painting, and the carry over of these two themes into advertising. This structural approach isolates a particular theme in one domain of social practices: property and exchange relations, for example. This is followed with a search for homologous forms in oil paintings.

Gaile McGregor's *The Wacousta Syndrome: Explorations in the Canadian Landscape* follows a similar analysis (1985). McGregor isolates the form assumed by the person/nature theme in an early Canadian novel, *Wacousta* (Richardson, 1906). She then explores the presence of this form in Canadian literature and painting. The study is especially useful because it compares the shape assumed by this theme in Canadian and American works.

Richardson's novel, published in the 1830s, expresses a negative relation between fortress and forest, between person and nature. The perspective is well recognized in Canadian literature (e.g., see Moss, 1974; Atwood, 1972; Frye, 1976:342). *Wacousta*, a "wilderness romance," is compared with a parallel genre in American writing (e.g., see Cooper's *The Last of the Mohicans*). McGregor points to Cooper's work in which:

> According to the mythic pattern, man does not merely "confront" nature, but takes a spiritual journey *through* it, enduring its gothic aspect as a kind of a "dark night of the soul" that must be traversed before reconciliation can be achieved with the sources of life and fertility that it—or "she"—may alone offer (1985:8).

In contrast, Richardson does not allow his reader to penetrate nature outside of the fortress and through to a reconciliation. Nature is "sinister and menacing," "a distortion, as McGregor notes, of the conventional pattern (1985:9)." In this form the person/nature, now self/not-self theme, is examined in Canadian painting, where it is expressed as centre/ground relations. McGregor examines the presence of this form in nineteenth century Canadian and American paintings. In Canadian paintings, centre/ground relations present nature as threatening. For example, in comparing the "panoramic" mode in landscape painting, she notes the Canadian tendency to favour domesticated (urban, semi-urban) scenes over the American preference for raw nature and, where person and raw nature are brought together, Canadians tend to draw the viewer out of and away from the border between civilization and nature. The American tendency is to draw the viewer into and through nature (1985:3–25). This conclusion is followed through to the present in painting and literature based on the hypothesis that "the characteristic Canadian response seems omnipresent in all aspects of Canadian cultural history" (1985:26). The explanation offered is rooted in a consideration of the order/change perspective as experienced and expressed by Americans and Canadians within the context of their varying colonial experiences.

Arthur Kroker has adopted an equally penetrating analysis of Canadian culture. He begins by delineating archetypical themes in the responses of Canadian thinkers to technology. These themes, in turn, are both located in cultural practices, especially via the products of electronic communications and the visual arts, and assumed as a base for a critique of technological development itself. The contrast between American and Canadian thinkers is found in the formers' celebration and the latters' critique of technology. In *Technology and the Canadian Mind*, Kroker presents three archetypical responses to technological development — humanism, dependency, and realism. These are represented, respectively, by the works of Marshall McLuhan, George Grant, and Harold Innis (1984:14–15). To summarize:

> Grant may write a tragic "lament" and McLuhan might privilege the "utopian" possibilities of technology, but Innis's ideal was always of attaining "balance and proportion" between the competing claims of empire (power) and culture (history) (1984:15).

Elaborating on these themes through an extensive study of these three thinkers, Kroker searches for parallels in various cultural practices. For example, the paintings of Alex Colville are offered as visual representations of the discourse found in the work of George Grant. Referring to the form (the placement of objects and people in relation to each other) of Colville's painting "To Prince Edward Island," Kroker states that the artist "speaks directly to the anxiety and bewilderment of an age haunted by an overwhelming sense of the loss of some good fundamental to the human spirit" (1984:23). Grant and Colville, then, share a common discourse, expressed philosophically and visually, and rooted in the Canadian lament over loss of self in the face of power and domination effected by the American empire through its control of technology.

A difficulty with McGregor's and Kroker's approaches is that both assume the presence of a unified Canadian culture presumably based on common experiences. This assumption is based on a vision of Canada as a centralized nation-state. The extent to which alternative visions (e.g., the Quebec–Canada dual nation vision or a vision based on confederation rather than federation) are allowed to enter these studies is very limited. A more recent analysis of the visual arts by Kroker and Hughes departs from this unified approach and searches for alternative and oppositional visions (1985). This article "Technologie et art emancipatoire: la vision manitobaine" analyzes the work of four Manitoba artists. Although the same three archetypical responses to technology are used, regional responses within English Canada are acknowledged. Furthermore, and more importantly, the category of technological realism is changed to technological vitalism to acknowledge a particular oppositional art form in Manitoba.

Writing

"Each and every literary fact presupposes a writer, a book, and a reader; or, in general terms, an author, a product, and a public" (Escarpit, 1971:1). A sociology of literature, no less than any other discursive practice, requires attention to these points of reference.

In sociology, analyses of the products of writing have taken one of three general approaches (see Routh and Wolff, 1977; Laurenson and Swingewood, 1971; Nielsen and Jackson, 1984). First, one might speak of "sociologically aware studies of literature." Here literature is taken as a documentary text revealing aspects of social reality. Literary works mirror society. This approach is found in the Graysons' analysis of social class in the English-Canadian novel (1978a) and in an essay by Marchak in which she claims that

> This literature, English–Canadian, may be read as sociological documentation; it displays assumptions, style, content, and concerns the shift within Canadian society from a British colony . . . to an American satellite (1978:204).

A second approach addresses the social origins of literature. Here we find such work as the Graysons' study of authors (1978b) and McDougall's essay (1971) in which the expression of social class in English-Canadian novels is considered in relation to the class origin of authors. A third approach considers literature as a social practice supporting or opposing existing mainstream meaning systems and possessing a relationship to, but maintaining a relative autonomy from, other practices.

McGregor's work is closer to this approach than the first two, as she extends her analysis from painting to literature. The first approach referred to above is inclined to content analysis, the second is properly an analysis of the creators, not the product, and the final approach will adopt any of the major theoretical orientations earlier discussed.

Analyses of Canadian literature tend to examine the way a single theme — social class, nature, isolation, survival, community, technology—is expressed in writing. Margaret Atwood's search for patterns in Canadian literature structured around the survival theme is a case in point (1972). Informed by a feminist perspective, Atwood examines Canadian literature from the perspective of her typology of "victim positions" (1972:36–39). The survival theme, and the sense of victimization associated with a preoccupation with the obstacles to survival, is derived from the often-referred-to Canadian colonial mentality. Selected Canadian poetry and novels are examined from the point of view of four victim positions: denial of the position; acknowledgment of the position, but explaining it as an act of fate; acknowledging the position, but refusing to accept it as inevitable; and "the creative nonvictim." The latter two positions have the potential for articulating alternative and oppositional or emancipatory visions.

In a similar fashion, John Moss, in *Patterns of Isolation*, selects isolation as a key theme in Canadian literature. Using a typology of garrison, frontier, colonial, and immigrant experiences, selected writings are searched for expressions of isolation (1974). Both Atwood's and Moss's work adopt a content analysis where texts are searched for the presence or absence of a particular theme, and thus accept literature as a reflection of social processes. Neither consciously adopts a theoretical orientation. McGregor's 1985 work referred to above does, as she moves her analysis from literature to painting and back with a sense of discursive practices and form. For McGregor, literature is not an autonomous reflection of society, but itself intervenes into history as a creative act.

Regardless of the approach adopted to the product, the notion of victim appears as a major theme in Canadian thought. It is articulated in McGregor's person-nature construct and Kroker's discussion of Grant's lament. It is the key to Atwood's discussion and present in Moss's discussion of isolation. What is missing to a great extent in the study of English-Canadian literature, not necessarily in the literature itself, is the search for a critique based on emancipatory practices — on Atwood's creative nonvictim position, on the articulation of alternatives and opposition. Indeed, some have noted that Canada is an absent nation, insofar as its cultural discourse is based on a negation of itself, on a constant collapse to victimization as the basic ingredient of English Canada's world view (Nielsen, 1986).

The Production Process

Contrary to the image of the lone artist working apart from all the mundane ties of everyday life, the artist is imbedded in a web of social relations that affects the creative act and the process that brings the finished piece of work to some public. In different times and in different places, varying patterns of social relations link cultural practices to a public. For example, a creative writer may be employed by a corporation or an advertising agency, may gain an income through royalties from publishers based on contracts for individual works, or may have a long-term contract with a publisher. Each arrangement relates the artist to the means of cultural production and to the public in different ways, and each will have different implications for the artist's ability to assume a sustaining, alternative, or opposing world view.

The specific organizations (broadcasting companies, publishing houses, art galleries, etc.) or agencies which, for the most part, control the means of production and distribution of creative work, are important actors in the total process. If artists are creators of discourse, then cultural agencies are the custodians of discourse. Accordingly, the question of ownership becomes important. Ownership means control, and much of the debate in Canada regarding cultural agencies revolves around the question of national identity and public or private control. We might open an inquiry along these lines with a brief look at the publishing industry.

In publishing, as in broadcasting, foreign control penetrates deeply into the English-Canadian market. Slightly over half of book sales in Canada, 52.3 percent, are through foreign-controlled publishers. And more than three-quarters, 78.1 percent, of the sales of imported titles are through foreign-controlled firms. These firms, located in Canada, are large well-established American and British publishers often owned by major multinational corporate conglomerates. As noted in Table 3, the Canadian firms, accounting for less than half the total sales, distribute most of the titles by Canadian authors—80.7 percent of the sales of large firms and over 90 percent of the sales of small and medium firms. In general, any market penetration by foreign firms results in fewer titles by Canadian writers.

The French language market presents a different pattern. Only 20.6 percent of

Table 3

PERCENTAGE ENGLISH LANGUAGE PUBLISHERS' REPORTED OWN AND IMPORTED BOOK SALES, BY ORIGIN OF CONTROLLING INTEREST AND SIZE OF FIRM, 1981

Size	**Canadian-controlled**	**Foreign-controlled**	**Total**
		(In thousands of dollars)	
Small			
Own Titles	96.8	—	96.8
Imports	3.2	—	3.2
Subtotal	($4,696.4)	—	($4,696.4)
Medium			
Own Titles	92.3	—	92.3
Imports	7.7	—	7.7
Subtotal	($11,559.6)	—	($11,559.6)
Large			
Own Titles	80.7	39.9	58.7
Imports	19.3	60.1	41.3
Subtotal	($228,450.8)	($267,856.0)	($496,306.8)
Total			
Own Titles	81.6	39.9	59.8
Imports	18.4	60.1	40.2
	($244,706.8)	(267,856.0)	($512,562.8)

Source: Statistics Canada, Catalogue 87–523; Cultural Statistics, 1978–81; "Book Publishing: A Financial Analysis" Text Table IX, p. 29. Reproduced with permission of the Minister of Supply and Services Canada. Data converted to percentages.

total sales are through foreign-controlled companies, and these companies, in turn, control only 24 percent of the sales of imported titles. Foreign-controlled firms have penetrated the French language market, but in quite a different way. First, Table 4 shows that of the total sales of foreign-controlled firms, 54.3 percent are titles by Canadian authors writing in French. Compare this to 39.9 percent in the English-Canadian market. Second, looking at only the large Canadian-controlled firms in Table 4, 44.3 percent of their sales are imported titles, compared to 19.3 percent for large firms in the English market (see Table 3). This means Canadian publishers in the French language market have much better access, as agents of foreign firms located abroad, to the lucrative market in foreign titles than do their English counterparts. Furthermore, foreign-controlled firms based in Canada but operating in the French language market are less reluctant to publish Canadian titles.

The parallel to the penetration of foreign cultural practices in the broadcasting industry as measured by availability in Tables 1 and 2 is notable. Foreign cultural agencies penetrate both the French and English language markets, but in the former case foreign penetration is less and of a different kind. Undoubtedly, there is the "language barrier," but there is also in everyday life a deeper sense of one's self and one's requirements for locally produced discourse (e.g., see Blishen, 1978).

The issue of control in French and English Canada with respect to a sense of cultural and political boundaries quickly slips

Table 4

PERCENTAGE FRENCH LANGUAGE PUBLISHERS REPORTED OWN AND IMPORTED BOOK SALES, BY ORIGIN OF CONTROLLING FIRM AND SIZE OF FIRM, 1981

Size	Canadian-controlled	Foreign-controlled	Total
		(In thousands of dollars)	
Small			
Own Titles	97.2	—	97.2
Imports	2.7	—	2.7
Subtotal	($1,224.2)	—	($1,224.2)
Medium			
Own Titles	99.6	16.5	96.8
Imports	.4	83.5	3.2
Subtotal	($10,469.2)	($361.8)	($10,831.0)
Large			
Own Titles	55.7	55.2	55.6
Imports	44.3	44.8	44.4
Subtotal	($47,272.8)	($14,904.4)	($62,195.2)
Total			
Own Titles	64.3	54.3	62.3
Imports	35.7	45.7	37.7
	($58,984.2)	($15,266.2)	($74,250.4)

Source: Statistics Canada, Catalogue 87–523; Cultural Statistics, 1978–81; "Book Publishing: A Financial Analysis" Text Table XIV, p. 35. Reproduced with permission of the Minister of Supply and Services Canada. Data converted to percentages.

into a discussion of the merits of state versus private control of cultural agencies and direct state subsidies to artists. The tension between the public and private sectors with respect to the support of artists and of cultural agencies has been present since the beginnings of the English-Canadian national project. As early as 1858, D'Arcy McGee (one of the "Fathers of Confederation") sought protection for Canadian literature through tariffs on foreign books. In 1883, the editor of the short lived *Canadian Literary Magazine* called for support from those who felt "a desire that Canada should possess a literature of its own" (Davison-Wood, 1981).

Questions of collectivity, community, and national identification cannot be articulated in a market discourse. Concepts like individualism, commodity, and commercial viability are the keywords. These concepts will more and more dominate the

PRIVATE VERSUS PUBLIC CONTROL OF CULTURAL AGENCIES?

The tension between public and private control of cultural agencies has remained at the centre of the debate over national sovereignty in English Canada. Early in 1986, the federal government approved the sale of Prentice-Hall of Canada Limited, a major publisher, to Gulf & Western Industries Inc. of New York, a multinational conglomerate with holdings in several communications firms in the United States. The arrangement with Gulf & Western was that there would be "no Canadian equity share, and no performance guarantees." Gulf & Western was required to sell 51 percent of Ginn & Company, a Toronto textbook publisher it bought in 1985, to Canadians. Simon & Schuster, a Gulf & Western-owned publisher in the United States, was required to distribute its books through a Canadian publisher and "give international exposure to (ten) 'promising' Canadian authors each year for a decade." According to a government official, as reported in *The Financial Post*, "The lobby from Gulf & Western was absolutely incredible . . . It was heavy. It was directed from the White House to the Prime Minister's Office (March 22, 1986)."

The production and distribution of discourse is almost totally a marketplace phenomenon. It is "big business" with political and economic implications and, in this light, it is interesting to note the public-private tension reflected in expressively and instrumentally oriented discourse. On the one hand, and this is a part of the current "free trade" negotiations with the United States, the protection of cultural industries in Canada is defended on the grounds of national sovereignty. On the other hand, the rationale for protection and state subsidization shifts to a market discourse, noting the impact of cultural industries on the Canadian economy. Measured by Gross Domestic Product, the direct impact of cultural agencies on the economy was 1.7 percent of the G.D.P., higher than that

> of the tobacco, the rubber and plastic, the textile, the clothing, and furniture and fixtures industries, and about the same as the metal and mines, the food and beverage, the electrical power, gas and other utilities, and the accommodation and food services industries (Statistics Canada, 1986b:10).

manner in which people see themselves. To put it another way, cultural objectives are incompatible with the marketplace. To illustrate: a recent federal report on economic growth and culture and communications recommended that the Book Publishing Development Program:

> be replaced by a new program of industry assistance focusing on profitability as opposed to the volume of sales, and that the new program be totally independent of any "cultural objectives" other than the creation of a commercially viable Canadian-owned publishing industry (Canada, 1986c:312).

We have now isolated two major axes central to English-Canadian cultural discourse: a **nationalism/continentalism axis**, centred on the national sovereignty question, and the **public/private enterprise axis**. The marketplace discourse tends to dominate at the continentalist and private poles of each axis. A community or collective orientation tends to dominate at the nationalism and public enterprise poles. There is no necessary coincidence, however. A marketplace discourse may be structured in terms of national objectives, as in the case above where Canadian-owned publishing is specified.

A third axis has to do with struggles for regional (provincial) autonomy in the cultural, economic, and political fields. This **central-decentral axis** is expressed in Western and Atlantic alienation in the face of continuing centralization of decision making and power in all fields and practices. The Quebec–federal opposition is different insofar as it is essentially a debate over the dual-nation concept of Canada, rather than regional decentralization. The regional discourse is found in the following statement by the writer George Woodcock.

> I believe that to deny regionalism is to deny the Canadian nation as it historically and geographically exists . . . this view of confederation is different from the centralizing and Joacobinical interpretation of Canadian political structures posed by . . . (the) ruling liberal party . . . it is more in accord with historical truth . . . and closer to the cultural activities of Canada where literary and artistic traditions are not homogeneous (1981:10–11).

In contrast, the *Report of The Federal Cultural Policy Review Committee* addresses the "regional question" not in terms of the heterogeneity of Canadian cultural practices, but in terms of the problem of regional markets in a centralized state, essentially a market discourse (1982:70–72). The market discourse adopted in this report is in keeping with the fact that it is much more continentalist in orientation than the earlier Massey Report on Canadian cultural issues (Canada, 1951). The trends on all three axes are obvious, the pull is toward the private, continentalist, and centralization poles. There is a certain irony in the contradictions inherent along each axis. A movement toward the nationalist pole requires the mobilization and centralization of human and fiscal resources, a move that inevitably pulls toward centralization on the regional-central axis.

The nationalization of broadcasting in Canada is a history of the interaction of Canadian cultural practices around these three axes. The story illustrates the linkages between the organization of the production of discourse, the creation of discourse, and the product itself. We will briefly examine the development of C.B.C. radio theatre.

Public broadcasting in English Canada has its roots in locally based university stations and, as early as 1923, in the use of the telegraph facilities of the Canadian National Railways (C.N.R.). The C.N.R. broadcast its first live drama from Moncton, New Brunswick in 1925. Station C.K.U.A., operated by the University of

Alberta, the Government of Alberta, and the Alberta Wheat Pool, was broadcasting locally written and produced drama over its extensive western network by 1928.

Two characteristics of these early days of broadcasting require attention. First, C.K.U.A. was locally owned and controlled and its drama productions were tied to local theatre groups. Secondly, C.N.R. broadcasting was Canada-wide and founded on an explicit nationalist mandate. The first C.N.R. president envisioned the new railway (a fusing of five bankrupt, privately owned railways into a Crown corporation in order to save private capital from debts incurred) as a device to diffuse "ideas and ideals nationally by radio" (Weir, 1965:4).

Although the railway encouraged locally developed programming, it carried with it the seeds of centralization and a mandate to promulgate a nationalist vision. The "Romance of Canada" series, dramatic presentations on early Canadian heroes, produced in and broadcast from the C.N.R.'s studios in Montreal between 1930 and 1932, was designed to promote a national identity. In the words of the railway's president, "We hope to kindle in Canadians generally a deeper interest in the romantic early history of their country" (Weir, 1965:53). A discourse built around the nationalist and centralist poles began very early in Canadian broadcasting. In contrast, broadcasting in the United States began under the supervision of the secretary of commerce explicitly for the purpose of regulating a commercial medium, while in Canada it began under the supervision of the ministry of the marine in order to preserve the airwaves of public use.

The strengthening of the centralist national position rested and continues to rest on opposition to American encroachment. Private broadcasting operated alongside the C.N.R. unit and several local public stations. These private stations, owned by newspapers, manufacturers of electrical and radio equipment, and other interests opposed the nationalization project. Private stations in Toronto and Montreal had joined the American N.B.C. and C.B.S. networks. The fear of an encroaching American discourse prompted the formation of associations to pressure the government into nationalizing radio, while associations based in the private sector opposed this move. The struggle took place mainly in English Canada, with Quebec anxiously watching on the sideline. Any move to nationalize and centralize a major communications technology would severly limit Quebec's ability to follow its own destiny.

The complex web of formations involved in this struggle set the base for the shape broadcasting was to take by 1936, and set in motion tensions still present in Canadian cultural practices. The nationalists, including prominent members of the Liberal Party of Canada, western social democrats, and various intellectuals, professionals, and artists with left to left-liberal political leanings, coalesced around the Radio League of Canada. According to the League's President, Graham Spry, the issue was Canadian identity, a case of "either the state or the United States" (Hardin, 1974:257). On the other side were corporate interests, including private broadcasting firms and the Canadian Pacific Railway. The Canadian Association of Broadcasters became their principal lobbying association.

At one level, this was a struggle over the definition of Canada as a nation. At another level, it was over the commodification of the production and distribution of discourse. It was not a struggle between dominant and subordinate social classes for control of the means of communication, but one between fractions of the dominant class, including intellectuals and artists. The positions taken and the composition of the sides remain intact today, and are most visible in the debates over public support for the arts and the fate of cultural agencies in the free trade negotiations with the United States. In any case, a 1932 compromise placed private broadcasting under the regulatory control of the Canadian Radio Broadcasting Commission (C.R.B.C.) which, in turn, operated a Canada-wide broadcasting network, assuming control of the C.N.R. network and several local public stations.

At first, this new state organization supported locally produced radio theatre. C.K.U.A. continued its work, now linked with the C.R.B.C. national network. The C.R.B.C. itself encouraged local repertory theatre—the Radio Theatre Guild of Montreal, Vancouver's Theatre of the Air, Winnipeg's Western Radio Players, and Halifax's Nova Scotia of the Air (Fink, 1981:233–34). Though local production appeared to be firmly in place, accompanied with its supporting vision of Canada as a composition of relatively autonomous cultural centres, the seeds of centralization had already germinated. The C.N.R. Vancouver drama unit was dropped by the C.R.B.C. in 1932. C.K.U.A. continued to produce plays until it too lost access to the national network. Local production centres remained, but as *regional* centres within a hierarchically controlled bureaucracy. The previously strong ties with local theatre communities slowly disappeared, with the exception of Montreal, where resistance to centralization remained for some time, and Toronto, where production control was located.

By the time the Canadian Broadcasting Corporation was formed in 1936, centralized control was firmly established. Although the move toward the C.B.C. was related to demands from the private sector for a separation of the regulatory and broadcasting functions of the state as combined in the C.R.B.C., it also had to do with complaints from English Canadians over the amount French was used on the C.R.B.C.'s national network and concerns in all provinces over their lack of control over the medium. The story continues to the present with a constant shifting from a nationalist to a continentalist position as private capital pushes to gain control, and from a regional to a centralist position as nationalists attempt to restrain the push and pull of capital. This is evident in the recent federal task force report on broadcasting, where the trend toward increasing privatization is condemned and reduced regional inputs to the system are recommended (Canada, 1986b)

Cultural Formations: The Artists

Raymond Williams uses the term "formations" to refer to "forms of organization and self-organization which seem much closer to cultural production" (1981:57). The reference is to circles of artists, and others, directly tied to cultural practices as distinct from the bureaucracy of cultural agencies. In painting, for example, the distinction is between the artists and the owners and managers of galleries. In Canadian painting, the "Group of Seven" is an excellent example of a self-organized circle or network of artists with a shared tradition. Of course, not all painters are affiliated with tightly organized circles of fellow artists, but most are part of some formation. Such networks are important collective actors in the production of discourse. They carry and sustain particular schools of thought, world visions, and production styles that may support or oppose mainstream thinking. Accordingly, the relations within formations and between formations and cultural agencies is important. One obvious question, for example, is, are radio and television writers hired by the station as employees, as is partly the case in American soap opera production, or are their scripts purchased by the broadcaster, as is the case in C.B.C. drama production? To illustrate these issues, we will continue the story of the C.B.C. and radio drama.

There were two overlapping formations prominent in the nationalization of Canadian broadcasting and the subsequent building of a national drama department. On the one hand were people and associations affiliated with the Canadian Radio League, referred to above. On the other hand was a cluster of writers, producers, and performers who gravitated toward Toronto during the early 1940s, associated with English-language radio drama. The former formation, composed of various politicians (affiliated with the Liberal and C.C.F. parties), intellectuals, educators, church people, broadcasting workers, and people affiliated with the agricultural co-operative movements in Western Canada and the Maritimes, not only pushed the Conservative government of the time toward nationalization, but also set the nationalist and social-democratic political orientation within which the new national broadcasting company was to operate.

Furthermore, this formation recruited like-minded people to manage and produce for the C.R.B.C./C.B.C. In 1943, a Vancouver-based C.B.C. producer named Andrew Allan was brought to Toronto to head the National Drama Department. He produced the new *Stage* series, which he conceived of as "Canada's national theatre of the air." Writers he had known in Vancouver and others, principally from Western Canada, were recruited through various ties to the first formation. A new formation, a circle of artists composed of young men and women who had experienced the Great Depression and World War II and who shared a western populist ideology, became the creators of C.B.C. radio drama. For a decade, their ability to produce a critical discourse through drama was sustained because of the tone set by the initial formation. By the 1950s, TV was becoming the dominant medium, and along with television arrived a new set of technocratic managers replacing the original social-democratic formation with one whose orientation was much closer to marketplace requirements. This explains the demise of critical and popular radio drama. It was not simply due to the preference of audiences for TV over radio as an entertainment medium.

Reception

Given what is available, how does the audience distribute its television viewing time? Table 5 demonstrates that almost half of the English-Canadian viewers' time in front of the set and a little over a third of the French-speakers' time is devoted to drama. News and sports rank second for both groups. English-speaking viewers devote less time to public affairs programming. Consider the information in Table 6 in relation to Table 2. The category receiving most of the viewers' time, drama, is almost totally foreign in origin — 98 percent for English Canadians, equal to the availability. French Canadians give 80 percent of their time devoted to drama to programs of foreign origin, 10 percent less

Table 5

PERCENTAGE VIEWING TIME BY PROGRAM TYPE AND LANGUAGE OF AUDIENCE*

Type of Program	English	French
News	12.0	13.0
Public Affairs	6.0	12.0
Sports	12.0	12.0
Drama	48.0	36.0
Other	22.0	27.0

*Time period: 6 hours–2 hours, 1984.

Source: Report of Task Force on Broadcasting, 1986, pp. 91–92. Reproduced with permission of the Minister of Supply and Services Canada.

Table 6
PROPORTION OF VIEWING TIME FOR TYPES OF CANADIAN AND FOREIGN PROGRAMMING BY LANGUAGE OF AUDIENCE*

Type	English		French	
	Canadian Origin	*Foreign Origin*	*Canadian Origin*	*Foreign Origin*
News	89.0	11.0	100.0	0
Public Affairs	62.0	38.0	99.0	1.0
Sports	71.0	29.0	96.0	4.0
Drama	2.0	98.0	20.0	80.0
Music/ Variety/ Quiz	18.0	82.0	87.0	13.0
All programs	28.0	71.0	68.0	32.0

*Time period: 6 a.m.–2 p.m., 1984

Source: Canada, Report of Task Force on Broadcasting, 1986, p. 95.

than the availability of such programs. Overall, English Canadians devote 72 percent of their viewing time to foreign programs, while French Canadians devote only 43 percent of their time in this direction.

The trend with respect to availability is toward an increasing amount of foreign programming. What is not known is the trend with respect to viewing time. It could be assumed, at some risk, that the more that foreign programming is made available, the more will viewers, especially English Canadians, make use of it. It is also tempting to advance the language barrier as the explanation for the shorter amount of time devoted to foreign programming by French Canadians. Whatever the explanation, data of this type simply assumes the audience is a passive recipient, rather than an active participant in the process.

The final element in the complex of discursive practices is reception. It is, of course, only final in that the receiver (the reader, the viewer, the listener) of the discourse is thought of as at the end of the process. But we must think of the process as an ongoing one in which each subject (the artist, the "text" or the product, the agencies, and the receiver) "have each other in mind" insofar as the process is interactive. Thus, the audience ceases to be the mere object of the process and becomes an active participant.

Research directed toward reception generally assumes two positions, each with its accompanying methodology. Usually the audience is thought of as object, as a "blank page," that merely reproduces the received discourse. Studies of the effects of television and print and ratings of programs according to viewer preferences assume the audience simply receives the message as constituted, like a speeding bullet from a high-powered rifle. In contrast, studies based on reception theory, which has emerged from the phenomenological and hermeneutic critical traditions, assume the audience to be an actor in the process, deconstructing and reconstructing the messages received in the codes and contexts common to their social location. The reading or viewing act is no less creative than the act of producing discourse.

Since the 1940s, research in which the audience is taken as the passive recipient has developed hand-in-hand with the increasing use of the electronic media for advertising. The major purpose is to find a market for a product through the use of print, radio, and television. Between 1982 and 1984, revenues from the sale of air time by private radio and television in Canada increased from 1.1 to 1.3 billion dollars. C.B.C. revenues in this category increased from 110.1 to 154.1 million dollars (Statistics Canada, 1985). Television and radio ratings based on viewer preferences and corresponding studies of the demographic characteristics of audience segments are designed to locate the correct market for particular products. In a very real way, the commodity sold by the electronic and print media are not the program or text, but the audience. This tradition of audience studies has taken place within the discourse of the marketplace.

Studies that deal with the effects of broadcasting and print on the recipients follow the same theoretical and methodological tradition. This model assumes the message passes from the product to a socially atomized individual, albeit one sharing certain demographic characteristics (age, income level, gender, occupational status) with others. Studies of the effects of violence, pornography, and the like following this model are anything but conclusive (Cantor and Pingree, 1983:113–46; Piepe et al., 1975:50–51).

Some studies have crossed the line to some extent. In these studies the researcher assumes members of an audience belong to social networks which, in turn, relate to kinship, social class, community, and occupation. The networks are taken as the location of the codes (not mere preferences) and contexts with and within which people "read" communications received. A study by several British social scientists on *Television and the Working Class* is a case in point (Piepe et al., 1975). The previously referred to essay on soap operas recommends a similar direction (Cantor and Pingree, 1983). Nevertheless, these studies remain within a "causal" framework; that is, interpretation is somehow caused by the background characteristics of the viewer — social class, ethnicity, gender, etc.

As Eagleton has noted, the examination of the reader's role in discursive practices is fairly new (1983:74). A book is simply black marks on a page organized in a certain way and, likewise, a television program is but coloured dots organized in a certain way. The reader or viewer makes sense of the received material. The process of reading, listening, or viewing is dynamic, and to tap this process one must examine how the recipient deconstructs and reconstructs the material received. Are the codes and context identical to those of the creator or different? In what ways?

Very little communications research has been done in this tradition. Some very promising research may be found in the work of James Heap (1977, 1985). Working in a phenomenological tradition, Heap has examined classroom learning in Ontario's public school system. The research concentrates on the receiver's role in the production of knowledge and in the act of reading. The receiver, or pupil, is viewed as an active participant in the process.

> The thing-as-read is always sensuously encountered within the world, that is, as within the course of someone's life. It is from that life that the thing-as-read draws its sense, even when it lends sense to that life (1977:104).

The work of Jacques Leenhardt in France and colleagues in Hungary provides a rare example of this kind of research outside of the school setting. A recent study was conducted in the two countries where five hundred readers from different social origins were selected to read two novels. The data allowed the researchers to construct "four systems of evaluation among the readers," which could be seen as corresponding to four autonomous systems of reading. Here, then, we do not have atomized individuals, all receiving messages in identical ways, but four totally different systems used to interpret messages received. The systems vary acordingly: one interpreted the works according to *ethical* criteria, another according to *social causality*, another according to *ideals*, and another was characterized by the lack of a critical attitude (1980–81:218–19). This kind of research locates the concept of "effects" in a quite different way from that which is generally acceptable to the market-research orientation.

CONCLUSION

This chapter has elaborated on a way of looking at "the media" and "the arts." To combine such diverse activities as television and the visual arts is not an exercise in sociological reduction. On the contrary, the combination rests on the view that all such practices are means for creating and communicating meaning, the most human of all human activities. Our perspective places creative work in a sociohistorical context in relation to other human practices and stresses process over structure.

It is, nevertheless, all too easy to assume that the points of reference provided—the artifact, the creative formations, the organization of production and dissemination, and reception—together yield a system of some sort. On the contrary, these "parts" do not form a system. A collage would be a better metaphor. The "parts" or points of reference stand in a very uneasy relation to each other; the relations are at times ambiguous, at times complementary, and at times polarized. To fully understand the process requires unravelling these dialectical relations, allowing for ambiguity, harmony, and opposition, specific to time and place, between poet, publisher, state, and market.

DISCUSSION QUESTIONS

1. In what ways is it possible to consider the output of the media (e.g., radio, television, the press) and the arts (e.g., painting, poetry, literature) as similar phenomena?
2. Does the meaning of words like "the media," "the arts," and "culture" change over time? If meanings do change, can such changes be related to changes in the ways in which societies are socially and economically organized?
3. How do certain meanings of words and concepts become privileged over others?
4. Critically discuss the proposition that art is a reflection of society.
5. If people interpret messages received according to shared codes, is it possible that television drama originating in the United States is interpreted differently by English Canadians, French Canadians, and Americans?

GLOSSARY

centralization/decentralization axis refers to the "regional question" in English-Canadian political and economic discourse. The issue revolves around the degree of autonomy possessed by the regions or provinces in relation to central Canada and/or the federal government.

culture a *signifying system* through which a social order is communicated, reproduced, experienced, and explored. Culture refers to those human practices and agencies that give meaning to everyday life.

discourse A method of using language or other means of communication that presumes a type of authority associated with persuasion, pleading, or incitement

ideology the processes and the forms whereby particular ways of interpreting experience assume dominance—the intertwining of power and culture

nationalism/continentalism axis refers to the "national question" in English-Canadian political and economic discourse. The issue centres on the question of national sovereignty in relation to the United States.

public/private enterprise axis refers to the debate on the merits of state versus private ownership and control of cultural and economic institutions

BIBLIOGRAPHY

Abercrombie, Nicholas et al.
1980 *The Dominant Ideology Thesis*. London: George Allen & Unwin

Atwood, Margaret
1972 *Survival*. Toronto: House of Anansi Press.

Audley, Paul
1983 *Canada's Cultural Industries: Broadcasting, Publishing and Film*. Toronto: James Lorimer.

Berger, John
1972 *Ways of Seeing*. London: British Broadcasting Corporation and Penguin Books.

Blishen, Bernard
1978 "Perceptions of National Identity." *Canadian Review of Sociology and Anthropology* 15:2.

Burnett, David
1983 *Colville*. Toronto: Art Gallery of Ontario and McClelland and Stewart.

Canada
1951 *The Royal Commission on National Development in the Arts, Letters and Sciences*. Ottawa: King's Printer.

—
1982 *Report of the Federal Cultural Policy Review Committee*. Ottawa: Minister of Supply and Services.

—
1986a *The Status of the Artist*. Ottawa: Minister of Supply and Services.

—
1986b *Report of the Task Force on Broadcasting Policy*. Ottawa: Minister of Supply and Services.

—
1986c *Economic Growth: Culture and Communications*. A study team report to the Task Force on Program Review. Ottawa: Minister of Supply and Services.

Cantor, Muriel G. and Suzanne Pingree
1983 *The Soap Opera*. Beverly Hills, California: Sage Publications.

Cappon, Paul
1978 *In Our Own House: Social Perspectives on Canadian Literature*. Toronto: McClelland and Stewart.

Clement, Wallace
1975 *The Canadian Corporate Elite*. Toronto: McClelland and Stewart.

Cooper, James F.
1906 *The Last of the Mohicans: A Narrative of 1757*. London: Dent.

Davison-Wood, Karen
1981 "A Philistine Culture? Literature, Painting and the Newspapers in Late Victorian Toronto." Unpublished Ph.D. Dissertation, Humanities Ph.D. Program, Concordia University, Montreal.

Eagleton, Terry
1983 *Literary Theory: An Introduction*. Oxford: Basil Blackwell Publisher Limited.

Escarpit, Robert
1971 *Sociology of Literature*. London: Frank Cass & Co. Ltd.

The Financial Post
1986 March 22, 1986.

Fink, Howard
1981 "The Sponsors v. The Nations Choice: North American Radio Drama." Peter Lewis (ed.) *Radio Drama*. New York: Longman Group.

Fournier, Marcel
1984 "Littérature et sociologie au Québec." *Etudes françaises* 19:3.

Frye, Northrop
1976 "Conclusions." Carl F. Klinck (ed.) *Literary History of Canada: Canadian Literature in English*, 2nd ed., vol. 2. Toronto: University of Toronto Press.

Giddens, Anthony
1983 "Four Theses on Ideology." *Canadian Journal of Political and Social Theory* 7:1,2.

Goldmann, Lucien
1975 *Towards a Sociology of the Novel*. London: Tavistock Publications.

Grayson, J. Paul and L.M. Grayson
1978a "Class and Ideologies of Class in the English Canadian Novel." *The Canadian Journal of Sociology and Anthropology* 15:3.

——
1978b "The Canadian Literary Elite." *Canadian Journal of Sociology* 3:3.

Gurvitch, George
1962 *Dialectique et sociologie*. Paris: Flammarion.

Hardin, Herschel
1974 *A Nation Unaware: The Canadian Economic Culture*. North Vancouver: J.J. Douglas.

Head, Sydney W. and Christopher H. Sterling
1982 *Broadcasting in America*, 4th ed. Boston: Houghton Mifflin.

Heap, James L
1977 "Toward a Phenomenology of Reading." *Journal of Phenomenological Psychology* 8, 1977–78.

——
1985 "Discourse in the Production of Classroom Knowledge." *Curriculum Inquiry* 15:3.

Holquist, Michael
1981 *The Dialogic Imagination: Four Essays by M.M. Bakhtin*. Austin: University of Texas Press.

Jackson, John D.
1981 "On the Implications of Content and Structural Analysis." In Liora Salter (ed.) *Communication Studies in Canada*. Toronto: Butterworths.

——
1984 "La sociologie de la littérature au Canada anglais." *Etudes françaises* 19:3.

Knight, Graham and Ian Taylor

——
1986 "News and Political Consensus: C.B.C. Television and the 1983 British Election." *Canadian Review of Sociology and Anthropology* 23:2.

Kroeber, A.L. and C. Kluckhohn
1952 "Culture: A Critical Review of Concepts and Definitions." *Papers of the Peabody Museum of American Archeology and Ethnology* 47:1.

Kroker, Arthur
1984 *Technology and The Canadian Mind*. Montreal: New World Perspectives.

Kroker, Arthur and Kenneth J. Hughes
1985 "Technologie et art emancipatoire: la vision manitobaine." *Sociologie et Sociétés* 17:2.

Laurenson, D.T. and A. Swingewood
1971 *The Sociology of Literature*. London: MacGibbon and Kee.

Leenhardt, Jacques
1980–81 "Introduction à la sociologie de la lecture." *Revue des sciences humaines* 49:177.

Leiss, William et al.
1986 *Social Communication in Advertising*. Toronto: Methuen Publications.

Marchak, Patricia
1978 "Given a Certain Latitude: A (Hinterland) Sociologist's View of Anglo-Canadian Literature." In Paul Cappon (ed.) *In Our House: Social Perspectives on Canadian Literature*. Toronto: McClelland and Stewart.

McDougall, Robert L.
1971 "The Dodo and the Cruising Auk: Class in Canadian Literature." In Eli Mandel (ed.) *Contexts on Canadian Criticism*. Toronto: University of Toronto Press.

McGregor, Gaile
1985 *The Wacousta Syndrome: Explorations in the Canadian Landscape*. Toronto: University of Toronto Press.

Morrow, Raymond A.
1985 "Critical Theory and Critical Sociology." *The Canadian Review of Sociology and Anthropology* 22(5).

Moss, John
1974 *Patterns of Isolation in English Canadian Fiction*. Toronto: McClelland and Stewart.

Nielsen, Greg
1986 "Le Canada dans Radio-Canada: articulation de la culture sans qualités." Paper presented to The International Conference on the Evolution of Broadcasting, Montreal, October 1.

Nielsen, Greg and John D. Jackson
1984 "Toward a Research Strategy for the Analysis of CBC English-language Radio Drama and Canadian Social Structure." *The Canadian Journal of Sociology* 9:1.

O'Neill, John
1985 "Phenomenological Sociology." *The Canadian Review of Sociology and Anthropology* 22:5.

Peterson, Len
1944 "Within the Fortress," a radio drama directed by Andrew Allan and broadcast on the *Stage* series by the C.B.C., Toronto. Script available at the Centre for Broadcasting Studies, Concordia University, Montreal. Sound version available at the Sound and Film Division, Public Archives of Canada, Ottawa.

Piepe, Anthony et al.
1975 *Television and the Working Classes*. Lexington, Mass.: Lexington Books, D.C. Heath and Co.

Reid, Dennis
1973 *A Concise History of Canadian Painting*. Toronto: Oxford University Press.

Richardson, Major John
1906 *Wacousta: A Tale of the Pontiac Conspiracy*. Toronto: Historical Publishing Company. (Originally published in 1832.)

Rioux, Marcel
1984 "Remarks on Emancipatory Practices and Industrial Societies in Crisis." *The Canadian Review of Sociology and Anthropology* 21:1.

Routh, J. and J. Wolff (eds.)
1977 *The Sociology of Literature: Theoretical Approaches*. Sociological Review Monograph, #25. Keele: University of Keele.

Singer, Benjamin
1982 "Minorities and the Media: A Content Analysis of Native Canadians in the Daily Press." *Canadian Review of Sociology & Anthropology* 19:3

Sorokin, Pitirim
1937 *Social and Cultural Dynamics*, Volume I. New York: The American Book Company.

Statistics Canada
1979 *Cultural Statistics*. Catalogue 87-501.

——
1985 "Annual Radio and Television Broadcasting, 1984." Catalogue 56–204.

——
1986a "Book Publishing: A Financial Analysis." Catalogue 87-523, *Cultural Statistics, 1978–1981*.

——
1986b "The Economic Impact of the Arts and Culture Sector." Catalogue 87-532, *Cultural Statistics*.

——
1986c *Cultural Statistics*. Catalogue 57-527.

Stewart, Sandy
1985 *From Coast to Coast*. Toronto: C.B.C. Enterprises.

Todorov, Tzvetan
1984 *Mikhail Bakhtin: The Dialogical Principle*. Minneapolis: University of Minnesota Press.

van Dijk, Teun A.
1985 *Handbook of Discourse Analysis*, Volume I. New York: Academic Press.

Weir, E.A.
1965 *The Struggle for National Broadcasting in Canada*. Toronto: McClelland and Stewart.

Williams, Raymond
1976 *Keywords: A Vocabulary of Culture and Society*. London: Fontana Paperbacks, Flamingo edition.

——
1977 *Marxism and Literature*. Oxford: Oxford University Press.

——
1981 *Culture*. London: Fontana Paperbacks.

Woodcock, George
1981 *The Meeting of Time and Space: Regionalism in Canadian Literature*. Edmonton: Newest Press.

The interior of the Cathedral of Montreal. *Courtesy of National Archives Canada/PA 29745*

"Religion . . . has a subtle but persistent influence in areas of power and over economic rewards. Beliefs, rituals, politics, and economics interpenetrate one another."

c h a p t e r t w e l v e

Religion and the Churches

John Simpson

INTRODUCTION

Few areas of social life offer more challenge to sociological analysis than religion. Both the exercise of power through political **institutions** and the creation and distribution of wealth through economic institutions seem, at first glance, to be more obvious and necessary for social life than religion. Yet religion exists in every known society. Why?

Religion is not only pervasive in human societies, it also seems unique to human societies. All forms of life must struggle to survive and reproduce. Humans, for example, must eat. Some forms of life are socially organized for survival and reproduction. Thus, both wolves and gorillas live and reproduce in groups that, like human societies, are stratified — some individual members are more powerful and dominant than others. But as far we can tell, no pack of wolves or band of gorillas uses a complex symbol system to refer to nonempirical beings. Human societies do. Why?

Systematic answers to such questions—indeed, the questions, themselves—begin to appear in Western thought in the eighteenth century. Intensified efforts to answer them occurred during the nineteenth century when political upheaval, the organization of certain production activities on the industrial model, and the emergence of modern science suggested society can be changed by human action. Sociology arose in that milieu, and without exception the most prominent founders of the discipline included religion in their analysis of social life.

Although Marx, Durkheim, Weber, and other founding figures differed in their assessments of the role of religion in society and the future of religion in modern industrial societies, each assumed religion could only be analyzed in terms of its linkages and connections with other institutions in a society. In particular, the relationships between religion and the organization of power or politics in a society and religion and a society's economy were major themes in their writings. Those themes reflect the most fundamental notion of the sociological perspective: *societies are systems of interrelated parts*. The sociological perspective on religion, then, suggests that religious beliefs, rituals, and practices may represent symbolic transformations of actions and structures from other parts of a society, while the economy or polity of a society may be driven by elements that stem from a religious source. This chapter analyzes religion in Canadian society from that point of view.

In this chapter, a population-based model is used to explore religion in Canada. This model assumes the fundamental unit of analysis is a person's religious identity. Analysis is built on the frequency and distribution of religious identities in the population.

A great many questions can be addressed using a population-based framework. Four topics are explored in this chapter. We begin by discussing the demographics or religious composition of contemporary Canadian society. The first task is describing the religious identities in a population and their distribution in geographic space. That information provides an estimate of the capacity for religious action in a population and the constraints and directions that religion can or does impose on action in a society. For example, a religiously homogeneous society usually has less capacity for religiously based conflict — all other things being equal — than a religiously diverse society.

The second section of the chapter addresses some consequences that follow from the pattern of religious identities in the Canadian population. Particular attention is paid to the impact religion has had on the formation and development of Canadian society and, especially, the configuration and use of power in the public arena.

The third section probes the relationship between religious identity and economic achievement among Canadians. Does religion affect economic action? That question has fascinated sociological analysts ever since Max Weber proposed his much disputed thesis linking Calvinistic Protestantism to the rise of capitalism in Western Europe. Are religious identities among Canadians today associated with differences in income?

Our final section discusses secularization. Changes in the religious capacity and parts of systems are usually discussed by contemporary sociologists with reference to secularization. Secularization, as we shall see, has implications not only for individuals but also for institutions, organizations, and culture, often in unrelated and diverse ways. Is Canadian society, today, more secularized than it was, say, forty years ago? The answer — in some ways definitely "Yes," in other ways, perhaps, "No"—depends on what is analyzed — individual identities, institutions, organizations, or culture.

These topics by no means exhaust the range of possibilities regarding the sociological analysis of religion in Canadian society. In any society, religion is a diverse, complex, thematically rich focus of action, and Canadian society is no exception.

THE DEMOGRAPHY OF RELIGION

National Patterns

Most North Americans today trace their ancestry to immigrants from other continents and not to indigenous peoples. Thus, when asked what religious group they identify with, most Canadians name a religious tradition that was founded elsewhere and brought to Canada.

Table 1 displays the number of persons in Canada, according to the 1981 census, identifying with major Eastern and Western religious traditions. While 90 percent of Canadians claim a Catholic, Eastern Orthodox, or Protestant identity, thus making Canada's religious composition overwhelmingly Christian, other important world religions are well represented in Canada, some in sizeable numbers. The two other religions of "people of the book" — Judaism and Islam — that originated in the Near East are present in more than token numbers. Traditions that trace their origin to the South Asian continent also have a visible presence: Hinduism, Sikhism, and Buddhism. The East Asian (Chinese) traditions of Confucianism and Taoism have relatively few adherents.

Table 2 gives percentage figures for specific denominations or denominational traditions that were cited as a religious identity by 1 percent or more of the population in the 1981 census. A large plurality of Canadians identify themselves as Roman Catholics (46.5 percent); the United Church of Canada (15.6 percent) and the Anglican Church in Canada (10.1 percent) and between them can claim a little over 25 percent of the population. In 1981, then, as in previous census years, a large majority of Canadians (72.2 percent) identified themselves with one of those three denominations. Those denominations or their organizational ancestors were established in Canada before Confederation, as were all the other Protestant traditions shown in Table 1 except the Pentecostals, who are a sect of Christianity that arose in this century.

Of special interest in Table 1 are the Jews and those of the Greek Orthodox faith. In general, Jews, like other non-Christian groups (excepting, of course, those who identify with the indigenous religions of Native peoples), trace their immigration history to the later part of the

Table 1

MAJOR WESTERN AND EASTERN RELIGIOUS IDENTITIES IN THE CANADIAN POPULATION

Identity	N
Catholic (Christian)	11 402 605
Protestant (Christian)	9 914 580
Eastern Orthodox (Christian)	361 560
Jewish	296 425
Islam	98 160
Hindu	69 500
Sikh	67 710
Buddhist	51 955
Confucianist	2 010
Taoist	765
Other Eastern Non-Christian	15 785
Para-Religious Groups	13 450
No Religious Preference	1 783 530

Source: Statistics Canada 1981 Census of Canada, Population: Religion (Catalogue 92–912, Ottawa, 1983). Reproduced with permission of the Minister of Supply and Services Canada.

Table 2

THE LARGEST RELIGIOUS IDENTITY CATEGORIES IN THE 1981 CENSUS OF CANADA (1% OR MORE OF THE POPULATION

Religious Identity	%
Roman Catholic	46.5
United Church	15.6
Anglican	10.1
No Religious Preference	7.4
Presbyterian	3.4
Lutheran	2.9
Baptist	2.9
Pentecostal	1.4
Greek Orthodox	1.3
Jewish	1.2
N = 24 083 495	

Source: Statistics Canada 1981 Census of Canada, Population: Religion (Catalogue 92–912, Ottawa, 1983). Reproduced with permission of Supply and Services Canada.

nineteenth century and the twentieth century. In a similar vein, Greek Orthodox, like most Christians in Canada who are neither Francophone Catholics nor Protestant, were not present in large numbers in Canada until after Confederation. Within the Catholic tradition itself, some ethnic groups, e.g., Italians, first appear in large numbers in Canada within the last fifty years.

The most diverse category heading in the 1981 census is "Protestant," which has fifty-four subheadings. The Eastern Orthodox category with eight subheadings is the second largest. The Protestant category, it should be noted, includes groups that are not directly related to or derived from **churches** and traditions associated with the sixteenth century revolt against the Roman Catholic Church in Europe. Thus Mormons, Jehovah's Witnesses, and Spiritualists are classified as Protestant.

While there are fifty-four Protestant categories in the 1981 census, there are only three categories under the Catholic heading: Roman Catholic, Ukrainian Catholic, and the Polish National Catholic Church. The Ukrainian Catholics are in communion with Rome, while the Polish group derives from a schism with Rome. Diversity within Protestantism in Canada as elsewhere manifests itself through the creation of new organizations or sects, while diversity within the Roman Catholic Church is expressed within a large umbrella organization.

Of some interest is the fact that "No Religious Preference" is the fourth largest category in the population (7.5 percent). However, only 0.85 percent of those who claim no religious preference classify themselves as agnostic or atheist.

Provincial Differences

Table 3 shows the numerical dominance and diversity of religious identities within each province. Only groups with 1 percent or more of the population of a province appear in Table 4. While the 1 percent figure is somewhat arbitrary, it provides a rough measure of group visibility at the provincial level, with the recognition that a small group that is well organized and presses claims, grievances, or political goals in the media and public arena may be more visible than a much larger group that is not so well organized.

Within the limitations of the measure, then, a number of interprovincial comparisons can be made. Quebec is the least religiously diverse of all of the provinces, with 88.1 percent of its populaton identifying itself as Roman Catholic. Jewish traditions, Anglicans, and the United Church of Canada each claim more than 1 percent of the population, but together they only comprise 5.7 percent of the Quebec population.

Like Quebec, Newfoundland provides an interesting contrast with many other provinces. While the "big three"—Roman Catholic, United Church of Canada, Anglican — are all strong in Newfoundland, Newfoundland is the only province where the Anglicans claim a substantial percentage (27.2 percent) of the population. Also, Newfoundland is the only province where a noticeable proportion of the population is concentrated in a few Christian **sects**. The Pentecostals and the Salvation Army together claim 14.6 percent of the population there.

Some comparability exists between Prince Edward Island and Nova Scotia, although Nova Scotia has fewer Roman Catholics than Prince Edward Island, and the Anglicans and Baptists are proportionately stronger in Nova Scotia, while the Presbyterians are somewhat stronger in Prince Edward Island. Unlike any of the other Maritime provinces, Nova Scotia enjoys a visible Lutheran community, a product of German immigration in the eighteenth century.

New Brunswick is the only other prov-

Table 3

RELIGIOUS IDENTITIES WITH 1% MORE OF A PROVINCIAL POPULATION

Identity	*Nfld.*	*P.E.I.*	*N.S.*	*N.B.*	*Quebec*	*Ont.*	*Man.*	*Sask.*	*Alta.*	*B.C.*
Roman Catholic	36.3	46.5	36.9	53.8	88.1	35.0	26.5	29.3	25.9	19.4
United Church	18.6	24.5	20.2	12.7	2.0	19.4	23.7	27.5	23.7	20.2
Anglican	27.2	5.6	15.6	9.6	2.1	13.6	10.7	8.1	9.1	13.8
Presbyterian	—	10.4	4.6	1.8	—	6.1	2.4	1.7	2.9	3.3
Lutheran	—	—	1.5	—	—	3.0	5.8	9.3	6.5	4.5
Baptist	—	5.0	12.1	12.8	—	3.4	1.9	1.8	3.0	3.0
Pentecostal	6.6	1.1	1.3	3.1	—	1.4	1.6	1.7	1.9	2.0
Greek Orthodox	—	—	—	—	—	1.6	2.0	2.2	2.1	—
Jewish	—	—	—	—	1.6	1.7	1.5	—	—	—
Ukrainian Catholic	—	—	—	—	—	—	4.9	3.1	1.8	—
Mennonite	—	—	—	—	—	—	6.3	2.7	—	1.1
Jehovah's Witnesses	—	—	—	—	—	—	—	1.0	—	1.2
Salvation Army	8.0	—	—	—	—	—	—	—	—	—
Church of Latter Day Saints	—	—	—	—	—	—	—	—	1.9	—
Sikh	—	—	—	—	—	—	—	—	—	1.5
No Religious Preference	1.0	2.7	4.1	2.9	2.1	7.2	7.5	6.3	11.7	20.9
N =	563 750	121 225	839 800	689 370	6 369 070	8 534 265	1 013 705	956 140	2 213 650	2 713 615

Source: Statistics Canada 1981 Census of Canada, Population: Religion (Catalogue 92-912, Ottawa, 1983). Adapted by author. Reprinted by permission of Ministry of Supply and Services Canada.

Table 4

PERCENTAGE OF THOSE AGE 30 TO 65 AND IN THE LABOUR FORCE (1980) EARNING $50,000 OR MORE BY RELIGIOUS IDENTITY, EDUCATION, AND SEX

Religious Identity

Amount of Education

	Sex	*Anglican*	*Presbyterian*	*United Church*	*Luthran*	*Baptist*	*Pentecostal*
Some University	M	4.5 (3259)	4.9 (1057)	5.3 (5130)	5.4 (1094)	3.5 (893)	3.5 (424)
or Less	F	0.6 (1824)	0.2 (582)	0.5 (2782)	0.7 (563)	0.4 (458)	0.0 (204)
B.A. or	M	26.5 (535)	24.4 (168)	26.0 (758)	20.0 (100)	15.5 (116)	4.8 (21)
More	F	0.0 (167)	8.7 (46)	2.1 (284)	2.6 (38)	0.0 (29)	0.0 (5)

	Sex	*Mennonite/ Hutterite*	*Roman Catholic*	*Eastern Orthodox*	*Jewish*	*Eastern Non-Christian*	*No Religion*
Some University	M	6.2 (242)	2.5 (14,442)	2.9 (556)	12.9 (303)	2.1 (332)	4.0 (2044)
or Less	F	0.0 (100)	0.2 (6893)	0.4 (250)	3.9 (181)	0.5 (182)	0.0 (767)
B.A. or	M	2.5 (40)	19.8 (1654)	14.1 (64)	37.9 (190)	11.2 (169)	16.3 (683)
More	F	10.0 (10)	1.6 (547)	3.7 (27)	1.3 (77)	1.8 (55)	3.8 (211)

Source: Adapted from Statistics Canada 1981 Census of Canada Public Use Sample Tape Household/Family File, based on a 2% sample of households/families enumerated in the 1981 census. The numbers in parentheses are cell frequencies. They are the base numbers of the percentages. A population estimate for a cell frequency can be obtained by multiplying the frequency by 50. Reproduced by permission of Minister of Supply and Services Canada.

ince besides Quebec with a majority of Roman Catholics. While Anglicans, Presbyterians, and the United Church of Canada claim proportionately fewer members in New Brunswick than in Nova Scotia, New Brunswick's profile in Table 3 tends toward the Nova Scotia pattern.

Table 3 suggests religious diversity increases beyond the Maritimes and Quebec. There are also marked increases in the proportion of those indicating no religious preference in Ontario and the provinces to the west. Ontario and Nova Scotia, however, are similar in certain respects, the main differences being a larger percentage of Baptists in Nova Scotia, and proportionately visible Jewish and Greek Orthodox communities in Ontario.

Manitoba and Saskatchewan are, in terms of the measure employed, the most religiously diverse provinces. They, together with Alberta, are remarkably similar in the distributions of the proportionately visible religious groups, especially when the Roman Catholics, United Church of Canada, and Anglicans are compared. Differences exist between these provinces, however, in terms of sectarian groups. Thus, 1.9 percent of Albertans identify themselves as Mormons (Church of Latter Day Saints).

While British Columbia is a religiously diverse province, it is also, by a large margin, the least religious province in Canada. Twenty-one percent of that province's population indicated no religious preference. Furthermore, 34 percent of Canada's declared agnostics and 36 percent of the atheists live in British Columbia according to the 1981 census. British Columbia is curious in other respects, too. It is the only province where Roman Catholics are not a plurality, that distinction belonging to the United Church of Canada. Furthermore, it is the province where the Roman Catholic Church, the United Church of Canada, and the Anglican Church most nearly resemble one another in proportionate terms with, respectively, 20.2 percent, 19.4 percent, and 13.7 percent of the population. British Columbia is also the only province where a religious tradition from Asia claims more than 1 percent of the population. Sikhs comprise 1.5 percent of the population there.

While Canada, then, is religiously diverse, it is also a country where Christian traditions with historical roots in Britain and Western Europe dominate the demography of religious identity from Newfoundland to British Columbia. In two provinces — New Brunswick and Quebec — Roman Catholics are in an absolute majority. In all provinces except British Columbia, Roman Catholics have the largest plurality. On the other hand, the United Church of Canada and the Anglicans together outnumber the Roman Catholics in Newfoundland, Manitoba, Saskatchewan, Alberta, and British Columbia. In all provinces, those who identify with either the Roman Catholic, United Church of Canada, or Anglican denominations form a majority of the population, ranging from 53.4 percent in British Columbia to 92.1 percent in Quebec (where Roman Catholics claim 88.1 percent of the population).

As the data suggest, much of the history of religion in Canada is the story of conflict, competition, and accommodation between Roman Catholics, the United Church of Canada (and its organizational ancestors), and the Anglicans. However, sectarian challenges to the mainline denominations are also part of the story, as is the increasing diversity of the religious composition of the population through immigration. Finally, all religions in Canada face competition from processes that encourage people to indicate they have no religious identity.

RELIGION AND THE CANADIAN PUBLIC ARENA

Historical Developments

It is difficult not to be impressed by the complexity of Canadian society. A major source of that complexity is the legacy of British and French colonization in North America. All of the societies in the New World are products of colonization, but only Canada has a history of two European **charter groups** intermingling and confronting one another, with no final assimilation of one group by the other.

Although the British dominated the French in North America by 1760, the foundations of Quebec society — its language and religion — were not destroyed. Even though an official policy of Anglification was proclaimed in 1763, the British never penetrated certain core institutions —schools, colleges, hospitals, orphanages, parish churches — that were founded and controlled by the Roman Catholic Church in New France and successfully preserved French-Canadian society once the tie with France was severed. The most ambitious post-conquest attempt at assimilation — the union of Canada East (Quebec) and Canada West (Ontario) in the United Provinces of Canada (1841 to 1867)—failed to bring about the intent of its architect, Lord Durham: the assimilation of French Canadians to the language and value structure of the British settlers.

Perhaps the most important consequence of Canada's historical roots is the pattern of societal authority that evolved from the accommodation of French and British peoples in North America. The executive or centralizing tendency in Canada can be traced back to both French and British sources (McRae, 1974:238–61). New France was an extension of the nation-state of Louis XIV, where the absolute monarch governed in league with a subordinate, hierarchical church. That model was transferred to the New World, but without the counterbalancing background of the older European feudal traditions, which effectively limited absolute centralizing authority. On the British side, the portion of North America remaining under British control after the American Revolution was dominated until well into the nineteenth century by imperially appointed governors without the mechanisms of responsible government that were characteristic of Britain, itself, at the time. Those centralizing tendencies have complicated the Canadian situation because they were set in the midst of the fundamental French–British duality that forestalled any permanent centralization of power in favour of one group or the other. Much different patterns prevailed in societies that are closely related to Canada historically.

Both the American and French Revolutions were socially critical movements. Stable centralized patterns of authority that were contiguous with national sovereignty were established. In the British case, a pattern of authority existed that counterpoised the centralizing tendencies of the Crown and the aristocracy, Parliament, and, eventually, Cabinet government. In Canada, however, centralizing tendencies were transplanted without effective traditions of opposition. Oppositional forces in Canada have had to invent their own logic.

In the absence of a revolution or a definitive civil war, centralizing tendencies have combined with the English–French duality to produce a history of accommodation and conflict between centralized authority and groups and regions that perceive themselves as marginalized or faced with the threat of marginalization. Thus, Canada more than many other societies is characterized by ongoing processes of complex and intricate adjustment between significant groups and regions under the tutelage of relatively fragile centralized authority.

The centralizing tendencies in the exercise of power that existed among both the British and French in 1760 guaranteed Canada would emerge from the accommodation of two absolutes. On the French side, ethnicity, language, and religion formed a seamless whole, a condition not found on the other side, where both nonconforming and established religion commanded loyalties among a population that was ethnically diverse and regionally scattered by the time of Confederation.

The salience of religion in the public domain at the time of Confederation was unchallenged: "Membership in a particular denomination ranked high as a badge of personal identity. To know a man's religious affiliation was to have an important clue to the politics he professed, the moral taboos he observed, and even the newspapers he read. Religion also played a major role in determining lines of cleavage within colonial communities. The framers of the British North America Act found it necessary to devote more space to the rights of religious than of ethnic minorities" (Grant, 1972:1). The salience of religion for public life in the immediate post-Confederation period is epitomized in the great pride Prime Minister Alexander Mackenzie expressed when he succeeded in 1873 in delicately balancing his Cabinet of federal ministers with "five Catholics, three members of the Church of England, three Presbyterians, two Methodists, one Congregationalist, and one Baptist" (Dawson, 1954:215–6).

Today, the fundamental duality of Canadian society persists, but it is no longer based on an ethno-religious distinction. The basis of the duality is ethno-linguistic, with a distinction being drawn between *Québécois* and other Francophone *Canadiens* on the one hand, and, on the other hand, the remaining elements of the Canadian population irrespective of religion. This fundamental shift is attributable, at least in part, to the diversification of the Canadian population through immigration and, especially, the immigration of large numbers of Roman Catholics of various ethnic backgrounds who diluted the uniqueness of the French Roman Catholic ethno-religious dimension.

The shift from **dualism** based on an

RELIGION IN CANADA IN THE VICTORIAN AGE

". . . Religion—not wealth and not politics—was the chief concern, the main ideal occupation of Canadians, both British and French. The Age is indeed to be comprehended only in terms of the idea of Providence, that God and His Church were very present actors in the World. The fact indeed even transcended the differences between French and English. The great gulf actually lay between Catholic and Protestant, and much of the difficulty of co-existence of British and French arose from the Protestant creeds of the former, the Catholic faith of the latter. . . . Religion was thus the chief guide of life for most Canadians; it touched all matters from personal conduct to state policy. All politics were indeed sectarian . . . the assured Old Presbyterian in Macdonald could not but dislike the thrusting Free Kirkman in Brown, the *rouge* Laurier distrust the clerical Langevin" (Morton, 1968:314).

ethno-religious distinction to dualism based on an ethno-linguistic distinction ensured the continuation of Canadian dualism. Thus, the institutional secularization of Quebec society in the Quiet Revolution of the 1950s and 1960s was matched at the end of the 1960s by a heightened interest in developing the bicultural and, especially, the bilingual base of Canadian society, arguably a clear sign that an ethno-linguistic/cultural focus was replacing the older ethno-religious distinction as the basic structural principle of Canadian society. Shortly thereafter the multiculturalism policy was evolved.

Although religion and ethnicity frequently coincide among the many groups that make up the Canadian "mosaic," e.g., most Greeks are Greek Orthodox, multiculturalism is officially based on ethnic and not ethnic-religious identity. Thus, while Ukrainians may make distinctions among themselves between those who are Ukrainian Catholic or Orthodox, multiculturalism invokes an interest only in the ethnic category "Ukrainian."

Despite the secularization of Canadian dualism and the advent of multiculturalism, the Canadian public arena is still not radically secularized in certain respects. Nowhere is this more visible than in the "school question." Both the language of instruction (French or English) and educational auspices (religious or nonreligious) have been battlegrounds for the funding of schools by the state since well before Confederation. The British North America Act of 1867 gave responsibility for education to the provinces with the proviso that the federal government would protect the educational rights of religious minorities as they existed at the time. That safeguard notwithstanding, provincial politicians have from time-to-time sought to acquire power on the basis of a school question. Thus, the Liberals came to power in New Brunswick in 1870 by promising to replace religiously oriented schools with a free public education system. An 1871 law effectively curbed separate Roman Catholic schools for francophones. Roman Catholics protested, but only secured some of their demands.

The most notorious school question in Canadian history was raised in 1890 in Manitoba. The dual separate-public system that had been guaranteed when Manitoba entered Confederation was done away with by a newly elected Liberal government and replaced with a nondenominational system without minority language instruction. Appeals to the Conservative federal government proved futile, and even the election of a sympathetic French-speaking Roman Catholic as prime minister in 1897 (Wilfrid Laurier) did not restore the terms of the Manitoba Act of 1870, the act that brought Manitoba into Confederation.

In Ontario, separate Roman Catholic schools were guaranteed by the British North America Act of 1867, but both the level and extent of funding have stirred controversy over the years. In 1886, a Liberal government roused the fury of Conservatives by enhancing the funding of the separate system. Fifty years later, Mitchell Hepburn, the newly elected Liberal premier, sponsored legislation that improved the tax assessment system in favour of the separate system. The resulting uproar led to the repeal of the law a year later. More recently, the extension of financing to separate highschools in Ontario by former premier William G. Davis was widely regarded as a major factor in the defeat of the Conservatives in the 1984 provincial election.

Contemporary Comparative Perspectives

Echoes remain in provincial politics of the influential role that religious cleavages once played in Canadian public life. Thus, in the fall of 1986, a bill was passed by the Ontario Legislature that prohibits discrimination on the basis of sexual orientation. The bill was strenuously opposed by the Cardinal Archbishop of Toronto, but supported by representatives of the United Church of Canada. At the same time, the minority Liberal government took a firm stand against the Sunday-opening of major retail stores in the wake of determined efforts across Canada by large department stores to open on Sundays. The Archdiocese of Toronto firmly opposed Sunday opening. Again, at the same time the Ontario Solicitor-General resigned his Cabinet position after being charged under the Liquor Licence Act with "consuming liquor outside a residence—in this case on an Ontario Provincial Police boat on which he was entertaining the head of Scotland Yard" (*The Globe and Mail*, December 4, 1986).

While the conjunction of those events may be circumstantial, events may have been managed to provide a positive image of the government to a variety of religious sensibilities. Religiously conservative Catholics and Protestants, offended by the anti-discrimination legislation, would be appeased by the stand of the government against Sunday-opening. Traditional Protestant elements that have long favoured tight control of liquor would be appeased by the resignation of a minister of the Crown for an infraction of a section of the Liquor Licence Act of Ontario that is, undoubtedly, frequently honoured in the breach.

Religion, then, still enters into politics at the provincial level. However, it is very unlikely today that religion would be a major issue in federal politics. Contrasting Canada with the United States in that regard underscores the point and illustrates one consequence of dualism in Canadian society.

In the United States, in recent years several issues about personal morality — homosexuality, pornography, abortion — have been successfully politicized by fundamentalist Protestants led by TV evangelists such as Jerry Falwell and Pat Robertson. Why has a so-called Moral Majority movement not arisen in Canada, given that public opinion on the issues in the two countries is very similar? About 60 percent to 70 percent of the population in both countries have conservative views on homosexuality, pornography, and abortion (Simpson and Macleod, 1985). That distribution is an important political resource in America but has not served as a basis for mass political mobilization at the national level in Canada. Why?

The population base for a politics of morality is found among Protestant sectarians and, particularly, among fundamentalist Baptists, and there are considerably fewer of them in Canada than in the United States. A large majority of Canadians — at least 90 percent — identifies with something other than a sectarian Christian tradition. It has been estimated that for every Baptist church member in Canada, there are 136 in the United States, while the ratio of the American population to Canada's is only about ten to one (Hiller, 1978). The appeal of a politics of morality, then, is limited by the demography of religion in the country.

However, even if there were more sectarian Protestants in Canada, it is unlikely that a national politics of morality could be sustained because of the limitations imposed by the "sociologic" of accommodation based on dualism. Moral Majority-type politics in the United States symbolizes the empowerment of Protestant sectarians in the national political arena and represents a serious attempt to impose their sectarian moral views on the population. The logic of Canadian dualism prohibits attempts by sectarian Protestants to impose their moral rules through political action on others. Dualism vitiates the notion that Canada as a nation should stand under the aegis of either a Protestant Evangelical god or a Roman Catholic deity. That constraint, in the final analysis, is the most important reason why Moral Majority-type national politics cannot gain a foothold in Canada.

American society is not segmented or divided into ethno-religious or ethno-linguistic groups, whose interests define the basic features of the federal political arena as in Canada. In that regard, Canada resembles certain European democracies, which are highly segmented along religious and linguistic lines. At the same time, however, federal political parties in Canada are not rigidly organized on a religiously or ethnically segmented basis as they are, say, in the Netherlands or Belgium. A federal party that aspires to form a government in Canada cannot appeal simply to Roman Catholics or French-speaking Canadians or, on the other hand, to Protestants or English-speaking Canadians. Successful federal parties must appeal to and incorporate the interests of all significant segments of Canadian society.

In the Netherlands, for example, since the end of the nineteenth century political parties have been organized in terms of the major religious and ideological divisions in the society. Furthermore, the parties coincide with institutionally complete blocs in the society and represent the interests of those blocs. Thus, there are Calvinist, Roman Catholic, and secular blocs (subdivided into socialist and liberal groups). Each bloc in addition to having its own political party tends toward institutional completeness. That is, in most cases, it has its own schools, mass media, health care organizations, and labour and economic subsector. Thus, it is possible, at least in theory, for, say, a Dutch Calvinist to live his or her life without ever coming into contact with a member of another bloc to obtain goods, services, education, health care, etc. Blocs themselves, it should be noted, are internally stratified along the class lines but the organization of political parties along bloc lines is a formidable barrier to the emergence of a strong class-based political movement in the Netherlands.

Like the Netherlands, Belgium, too, is highly segmented along religious/ideological lines with Roman Catholic, Liberal, and Socialist sectors, each with its own political party and institutions. While there are fewer religious/ideological cleavages in Belgian society than in the Netherlands (Belgium lacks a Calvinist bloc), there is a linguistic cleavage in Belgium (French–Flemish) that crosscuts the traditional sectors and has, itself, become a significant factor in Belgium's politics. Thus, language-based political parties and voluntary associations have arisen and put pressure on the older parties to incorporate language-based wings. No federal party in Canada is formally affiliated with an autonomous language or religion-based political organization.

Viewed in comparative perspective then, religion in the Canadian public arena has some features that resemble religiously segmented European societies and other features similar to those in the United States. Like the Netherlands and Belgium (and Switzerland and, in certain respects, Austria) but unlike the United States, Canadian society is segmented along an historically important religion-linguistic dimension. Like the United States and unlike the segmented democracies of Europe, however, political parties in Canada are broad-based and not organized along bloc lines. To the extent, then, that religious interests seek a role in the political arena, intraparty accommodation must occur (assuming there are opposing interests), since political parties seek the support of all segments of the population. The pressure for accommodation has its most dramatic contemporary effect as a barrier to entry into the federal political arena of a Protestant-based politics of personal morality or, for that matter, a Roman Catholic–based "right-to-life" movement opposed to abortion. Both would violate the logic of accommodation that is the mainspring of Canadian dualism and that sets Canada apart from other nations in the relationship between religion and politics.

RELIGION AND AFFLUENCE

The relationship between religion and the economic aspects of social life is a major theme in the work of the founders of sociology. Marx assumed religious ideology justifies inequalities in the distribution of wealth and that religion palliates the condition of oppressed classes by promising a better life to come. Weber wrote at length on religious values and ethics, the social contexts in which they arise, and the effects they have on everyday life. In his most famous work, *The Protestant Ethic and the Spirit of Capitalism*, Weber argued an affinity exists between the values of Calvinistic Protestantism and the development of capitalism in post-Reformation Europe.

While Marx and Weber raised important questions about the relationship between religion and economic matters in societies, few sociologists today accept all of their conclusions. In contadiction to Marx, religion can be either a force supporting the status quo or a force for change as contemporary revolutionary and social movements in many places attest: Iran, Poland, Sri Lanka, the Punjab, and the Philippines. As far as Weber is concerned, few scholars today would limit the explanation of the rise of capitalism in the west to an apprehended affinity between Calvinism and capitalism in sixteenth century Europe.

Whatever questions are asked or theoretical answers given, both Marxian and Weberian points of view still rest on a fundamental empirical question: Is there a relationship between religion and the distribution of rewards that a society has to offer? The answer to that question has implications for assessing the extent to which religion is a basis of social cleavage and conflict in a society. Furthermore, learning the relationship between religion and the distribution of social resources and rewards would add to our knowledge of the extent to which a society is secularized. If inequalities in the distribution of wealth and the means to obtain wealth are attributable to religious differences, it is difficult to argue a society is, in fact, radically secularized.

What is the relationship between religion and the distribution of resources and rewards in Canadian society? That is a conceptually simple question, but answering it is no simple matter. We shall explore the question with data from the 1981 Canada Census. Unfortunately, not all interesting and pertinent questions can be answered using census data. Furthermore, space does not permit an exhaustive analysis of the existing data.

Table 4 contains a cross-tabulation of data from the 1981 Canada Census. The figures represent the percentage of respondents in a particular cell who earned $50,000 or more in 1980, the last complete year before the 1981 census. Thus, the 4.5 percent figure in the Anglican-Some University or Less-Male cell means that 4.5 percent of the respondents with those characteristics earned $50,000 or more in 1980. To understand the table, we need to discuss the nature of the income and religion categories and the reason for including education and gender as variables in the cross-tabulation.

Our exploratory research focuses on the incomes of individuals. In particular, we are interested in whether economic success or affluence varies across religious identities. Is religious identity itself a resource or associated with something that is a resource that impedes or enhances an individual's chance of earning a high income?

Viewing religious identity as a possible resource raises the question about other resources that may influence high income attainment and could possibly explain any detected relationship between religious identity and income. In modern societies education is a significant predictor of income and, therefore, we take into account the effects of education on earnings. Suppose we find that a high proportion of Anglicans earns $50,000 or more per year. Now that finding could be explained by a high level of education among Anglicans and not by some intrinsic factor associated with being Anglican; hence, the necessity to control for the effects of education on income where the relationship between religious identity and income is under assessment.

Another resource that affects income is gender. Does gender interact with religious identity to affect economic success?

In the Census of Canada, religion refers to specific religious groups or bodies, denominations, sects, cults, or religious communities, and respondents are instructed to report a specific denomination even if they are not necessarily active members of the denomination. Hence, the information used to form the categories in Table 4 does not reflect actual membership, nor the degree of affiliation with, or commitment to, a given religious group, but rather stated identification with a specific religious group, body, sect, **cult**, community, or individual belief system.

The religion categories in Table 4 vary considerably in internal diversity and comparability. Four categories refer to distinct denominational bodies — Anglican, Presbyterian, United Church of Canada, and Roman Catholic. Lutheran, Baptist, Pentecostal, and Mennonite/Hutterite designations are not denominationally distinct since more than one denominational body could be represented within each category. This is also true of the Eastern Orthodox and Jewish categories. The Eastern–Non-Christian category is religiously diverse. Small numbers of cases in the sample prevent further breakdown of those categories into component groups.

Before discussing Table 4 in detail there is another important matter that merits attention. Over twenty years ago, the late John Porter noted the "difficulty of separating the influences of ethnic affiliation and religion on class structure" in Canadian society (1965:98). Generally speaking, separating the influences of ethnic affiliation and religion on any individual or social attribute is difficult. That is so because in many cases religion and ethnicity are highly correlated. For example, since virtually all Quebecois are Roman Catholic, sorting out the separate effects of ethno-culture and ethno-religion among the Quebecois becomes a problem. Where a religious denomination or category is ethnically diverse as the Roman Catholics are in Canada, the analyst must try to determine the extent to which religion may have different effects across ethnic groups within the same faith.

Taking into account the problem raised by Porter and other features of the religion categories in Table 4, two intelligible comparisons can be made without further controls. The six Protestant categories from Anglican to Pentecostal are reasonably comparable. Most Canadians who identify with one of those denominations or traditions trace their ancestry to Western Europe, Northern Europe, or the United Kingdom. Income diversity within the Anglican–Pentecostal range of categories, then, might be attributable at least in part to religious effects.

Two categories of particular interest are

the Jewish and Mennonite–Hutterite classifications. Most members of those groups trace their ancestory to either a Western or Eastern European source. Furthermore, both groups have a history of persecution by various European states, emigration to escape persecution, and distinct but decidedly different group survival strategies that are intertwined with religion and have implications for economic outcomes. A comparison of the Mennonite–Hutterite and Jewish categories, then, is a potentially rich source of insights into the effects of religion on economic outcomes.

Figures are reported for the Roman Catholic, Eastern Orthodox, and Eastern–Non-Christian categories but no interpretation is attempted here. The Roman Catholic category is ethnically diverse. The Eastern Orthodox category is denominationally and ethnically diverse while the Eastern–Non-Christian category is ethnically and religiously diverse and includes those identifying with Islam, Hinduism, Sikhism, Buddhism, Baha'ism, Confucianism, Taoism, and other Eastern Non-Christian traditions. All three categories, then, require further breakdown before intelligible comparisons are possible.

Turning now to Table 4, we see that expected gender and education effects are present. The proportion of successful males compared to females is higher in every case except among highly educated Mennonite–Hutterites where the affluence rate among males is 2.5 percent while the figure for females is 10.0 percent. The small number (ten) of female cases on which the 10.0 percent figure is based raises a question about the stability of the 10.0 percent figure. In any event, the data clearly indicate females within the same educational categories as males are less likely to be affluent.

The effect of education on economic success can be seen by comparing the figures within the gender and religion categories. Among males, higher levels of education result in higher rates of success in every case, with most of the differences between the percentages being substantial. Among females, on the other hand, the pattern is more equivocal. In eight of the twelve possible comparisons, highly educated women have a higher success rate than less well-educated women. However, the differences between the percentages are usually small. In three cases (Anglican, Baptist, Jewish), success rates are higher among the less well-educated women, while there is no difference between Pentecostal women at the two educational levels. Again, caution is in order because of small numbers in some instances, but the conclusion from Table 4 is clear: gender prevents women from reaping the same economic benefits from education as men.

Does religion affect economic success? Our first comparison is among the Protestants in Table 4 ranging from the Anglican to the Pentecostal categories. Anglican, Presbyterian, United Church, and Lutheran groups constitute churchly traditions that at some time were either established as a state church or aspired to become a national church. Lutherans have roots in Northern Europe; Anglicans, Presbyterians, and the United Church trace their organizational heritages to bodies in the United Kingdom. Those traditions, then, are associated with British hegemony in North America and the foundation of Canada as a unit within the British Empire.

Baptist and Pentecostals differ from Anglicans, Presbyterians, United Church persons, and Lutherans in never having been established or intimately connected with the state. With roots in the European Reformation period, the Baptist tradition predates the Pentecostal tradition which is a New World phenomenon that arose early in the twentieth century. Of the six Protestant traditions, Pentecostalism is the most sectarian in emphasis and practice.

Turning to Table 4 for the six Protestant

identities described above, there are only unpatterned negligible differences between the religion categories among both males and females with less than a university degree. Among women with a B.A. or more, being a Presbyterian appears to increase one's chances of being affluent. Among highly educated, males, there are negligible differences between the Anglican, Presbyterian, and United Church categories. Identification with one of those traditions, however, appears to somewhat increase the odds for affluence in comparison with the Lutheran category and definitely increase the odds in comparison with the Baptist and Pentecostal categories. Furthermore, there is decreasing affluence going from the Lutheran to the Baptist to the Pentecostal category.

Excepting highly educated female Presbyterians, differences in affluence between Protestant religious traditions appear only among highly educated males and, furthermore, only between churchly and sectarian traditions. For well-educated male Protestants then, identification with a churchly tradition of British origin appears to mark a boundary between the less successful and the more successful. While further research is needed to explain that pattern, it may be that mainline religious traditions of British derivation have served as a boundary marker for entry into highly paid male-dominated professions requiring considerable education. More generally, identification with those traditions may mark and maintain boundaries that preserve differences in opportunity structures.

Turning to the Mennonite–Hutterite and Jewish categories in Table 4, we note first of all that both of those traditions have more in common with Baptists and Pentecostals than with Anglicans, Presbyterians, and the United Church in terms of establishment/non-establishment. Neither the Mennonite–Hutterite or Jewish traditions were established in Europe in the sense of being a state religion. Furthermore, Jews, Mennonites, Hutterites, and Baptists suffered persecution at the hands of various states of Europe. Unlike Baptists and Pentecostals, however, both Mennonite–Hutterites and Jews evolved distinct survival strategies that are group oriented and have implications for affluence.

Among males and females with less than a university degree, Jews have higher rates of affluence than Mennonite–Hutterites. Among the highly educated, Jewish males have a very high rate of affluence in comparison with their male Mennonite–Hutterite counterparts, while for females the relationship is, apparently, reversed although the small number of highly educated female Mennonite–Hutterites in the table (ten) casts some suspicion on the 10.0 percent rate of affluence in that cell. Of some interest is the fact that there is a higher rate of affluence among the less educated Mennonite–Hutterite males (6.2 percent) than among their more educated brethren (2.5 pecent). There is also a higher rate of affluence among less educated Jewish women (3.9 percent) than among their better educated sisters (1.3 percent).

The essential difference between the Mennonite–Hutterites and the Jews is that the former chose a rural community model for survival that was not dependent upon high levels of education for success, while the Jews' strategy depended upon urbanized settlement and occupational specialization where differences in education would make for differences in success. In Canada, both groups have thrived despite being subjected to discrimination from time to time.

The role of religion in maintaining boundaries is, perhaps, the crucial question when it comes to Mennonite–Hutterites and Jews. There is a distinct secular stratum among those who claim Jewish or

JEWISH ECONOMIC SUCCESS

Why have the Jews been so economically successful in North America? (It should be noted that not all Jews are, in fact, well-off. Silberman (1985) estimates that about 15 percent of the Jews in America live in poverty or difficult economic circumstances today.)

The education level among the Jewish population is higher than among other population groups and education is positively associated with income. That is one reason for success, but to it must be added a number of other factors. Jewish immigrants to North America had higher skills levels and were more familiar with urban life than many other immigrant groups. They were not peasants or labourers. Many were the offspring of merchants or petty traders and thus were able to take advantage of the retail and wholesale trade that occurred with the industrialization and urbanization of North America in the latter part of the nineteenth century. An exceedingly high percentage of the offspring of Jewish immigrants have gone into the professions and have prospered with the expansion of the service sector of the economy.

Given their experience of persecution in Europe, Jews tended to be cautious about having fixed assets such as large tracts of arable land, although Jews in Canada have been successful farmers (Paris, 1980). The preference for keeping their capital as liquid as possible because they had to be prepared to flee at any time still shapes Jewish behaviour "even among those who have forgotten why; group memory is not easily erased. One reason Jews are so attracted to the professions is that they can carry their capital in their heads; and Jewish businessmen gravitate toward fields in which capital requirements are low and turnover rapid. The quest for liquidity is particularly strong among those who fled Hitler. Felix Rohatyn, the investment banker who played a major role in saving New York City from bankruptcy in the 1970s, vividly recalls his family's escape from France on foot across the Pyrenees. Rohatyn spent the evening before they left opening toothpaste tubes from the bottom and stuffing them with small gold coins—all that was left of the family fortune. "That experience has left me with a refugee's theory of wealth," Rohatyn has told several interviewers. "What is real to me is what I can put in the back of a toothpaste tube, or what I carry round in my head" (Silberman, 1985:134).

Mennonite identity, but it is difficult to imagine how those identities would be socially anchored in the long run if Jewish and Mennonite beliefs and religious practices were suddenly to disappear.

With no alternative reference points other than their religion, the case seems clear for the Mennonite–Hutterites: secularization would imply the disappearance or severe attenuation of the identity. The case is different for Jews because it might be possible for religious practice to disappear while the identification remained with reference to the State of Israel. Once religious practice ceases, assimilation to the surrounding culture would probably be rapid and complete given an absence of other reference points. However, as things stand now, religious identification does mark a boundary for both Mennonite–Hutterites and Jews, and that boundary is intimately connected with differing rates of affluence.

Our belief discussion suggests religious identity cannot be ruled out as a possible source for understanding affluence in Canada. Among selected comparable categories in Table 4, highly educated Protestant males are more likely to be affluent if they identify with a church-type denomination associated with British/Anglo-Canadian hegemony in North America (Anglican, Presbyterian, United Church of Canada) than if they identify with a tradition associated with the states of Northern Europe (Lutheran) or a sectarian tradition (Baptist, Pentecostal). Furthermore, those who identify with Judaism exhibit a higher rate of affluence than those with a Mennonite–Hutterite background. Those differences may exist because religious identification delimits the boundaries of occupational opportunity structures. Thus, among highly educated males religious identity might facilitate entry into highly paid occupations for Anglicans, Presbyterians, and those who identify with the United Church of Canada. It also might be the case that an Anglican, Presbyterian, or United Church of Canada identity marks a boundary defining differential access to capital and the control of capital held by the dominant charter groups.

SECULARIZATION

The concept of secularization is richer and more complex than popular culture suggests. Some years ago, Pierre Berton wrote in ***The Comfortable Pew*** that at a certain point in his life he ". . . began a slow drift away from the [Anglican] church, unmarked by any really violent, anti-religious convictions. Mine was a rebellion born of apathy. More compelling interests entered my life . . ." (1965:20). Now it is very tempting to ascribe Berton's drift, which probably describes the experience of many Canadians, to some fault within the church or to the spiritual torpor of the individual himself. However, doing so would obscure the structural reality that underlies the apathy. People frequently find themselves in a choice situation — church or X—and they gradually drift into X. But what does X represent?

Before X came along there was no choice between church and X. Church was the only possibility. So X represents a complication of the structural situation in which the individual is embedded. The complication of the structural situation arises from what sociologists call **differentiation**, in which **autonomous functionally** specialized **subsystems** are created in a society, subsystems that, typically, represent the **rationalization** of some sphere of action. When differentiation occurs, choice arises, and choice itself can be viewed as an aggregation of forces that push the individual one way or the other.

Berton's apathy cannot be simply attributed to the unattractiveness of the church or to Berton's own spiritual condition. Rather, his apathy is partly a product of the development of society itself. Berton's "secularization," then, has sources outside his own religious motivations that have little to do with the potency or efficacy of the church as a vendor of religion. This suggests we should be wary of attempts to view secularization as the product of only individual choice or organization enfeeblement.

Another thing to keep in mind is the extent to which a model of secularization is adequate for the entire range of religious traditions in Canada today. If, for example, a model of secularization focuses on the extent to which the individual holds certain beliefs, does that not miss the point with respect to, say, Judaism or Islam?

Doctrines are secondary in determining whether a Jew is secularized or not. What counts is the enactment of appropriate practice inside and outside the community. In Islam, beliefs too are secondary. The attestation to the faith is practice and beyond that there is only practice: prayer, fasting, almsgiving, and pilgrimage. For Islam, the matter is even more complicated, since Canada is not Islamic and therefore is radically secularized from a Muslim perspective.

In some world religions, it is even difficult to conceive of secularization as a possibility. Thus, if secularization involves a reduction in the impact of religion on everyday life, ancient Buddhism left no room for secularization since, as Max Weber pointed out, "There is no path leading from [ancient Buddhism's] . . . consistent pattern of world-flight to any economic ethic or to any rational social ethic" (1978:628). In other words, religion cannot withdraw or be cast out of the everyday world because it is radically absent in the first place.

Secularization, then, is a more complex matter than much popular thought about it suggests. Our exploration of secularization in Canadian society will focus on three types that are analytically independent: cultural-interpretive, organizational, and institutional secularization.

On the cultural-interpretive level, secularization involves replacing beliefs that anchor meaning in supramundane, transcendental terms with notions that they have only an historical, material, social, or scientific frame of reference. A cultural shift from the belief that God literally created the universe in seven days to a scientifically based cosmological theory of the origin and evolution of the universe that makes no reference to God is a simple example of cultural-interpretive secularization.

While it is easy to define cultural-interpretive secularization, establishing its occurrence as an empirical event is more difficult. Educational expansion may be one indicator. In industrial societies, cultural secularization tends to be correlated with the expansion of modern post-secondary education. Given the rapid expansion of post-secondary education in Canada over the past twenty-five years, Canadian culture is, undoubtedly, more secularized today than it was in the pre-World War II period.

On the organizational level, secularization involves changes in the rate of participation by a population in organized religious activity, that is, activity that derives its meaning from a supramundane, transcendental frame of reference. While precise measurement of changes in cultural secularization at the individual level is difficult, it is comparatively easy to measure long-term trends in participative or organizational secularization. The traditional measure here is church attendance, and the best available data indicate the sizeable declines have occurred since the end of World War II. According to Bibby

> . . . [a]t that time two in three Canadians were attending services weekly; today the figure has dropped to one in three. Despite the perception of Protestant prosperity in the 1950s, attendance—now about 25 percent—has in fact decreased from the late 1940s through the early 1970s, levelling off in recent years . . . [at] about 25 percent. Roman Catholic attendance, seemingly immune to secularization through the mid-1960s, has decreased dramatically during the last two decades. Standing at 85 percent in 1965, it was plummeted to a current, unprecedented low of under 45 percent" (1986:3).

These declines derive from at least four sources. Among Roman Catholics, the rapid institutional secularization of Quebec society loosened the tie between the church and the individual and contributed to a noticeable reduction in the importance of religion at the individual level there (Dumont, 1985). Also, among Roman Catholics, rates of church attendance have been affected by the liberalizing trend of the Vatican II Council and to some extent by immigration from areas of Europe where relatively low rates of church attendance are the norm, e.g., Italy. Among both Roman Catholics and Protestants, increasing societal complexity that has accompanied the social and industrial development of Canada since World War II has been a major factor in the secularization of Canadian society.

Both cultural-interpretive and organizational secularization are subject to measurement at the individual level of analysis. Institutional secularization is a different matter for it has to do with the structure of the relations between religion and other institutions in a society, most notably the economic and political systems. Institutional secularization can occur in two ways: the separation of religion from other institutional spheres or the transfer of a function from the control of religion to another institutional sphere.

The classic example in the West of secularization in institutional segregation is the separation of church and state in the United States, where the structure and activities of the state and organized religion are formally irrelevant to one another. This means, among other things, that the state has no direct fiduciary relationship or financial caretaking role with any aspect of organized religion. That, of course, is not the case in Canada where, among other things, the state is intertwined with religion in educational subsystems, e.g., support of Roman Catholic separate schools and, in some provinces, the training of clergy in Christian theological schools.

While Canada is not highly secularized in institutional segregation on the church-state dimension, there are quite a few recent examples of secularization involving a transfer of the control of functions from the church to the state. Thus, in the last twenty-five years or so some universities that were church-affiliated have come under the formal financial control of the state. Certainly, the most dramatic recent example occurred in Quebec's "Quiet Revolution" when formal control of social services, hospitals, and educational institutions passed from the hands of the church to the state.

Cultural-interpretive, organizational, and institutional secularization are, then, analytically distinct dimensions. Furthermore, they are not necessarily positively associated in a given society. In the United States, where institutional secularization is high, cultural/interpretive and organizational secularization are relatively low. Creationism competes with evolutionary theory and church attendance rates are moderately high. In Canada, on the other hand, there is considerably less institutional secularization, but organizational secularization as measured by, say, church attendance rates is roughly similar to the United States at the national level. In the United Kingdom, where institutional secularization is low, the Church of England being established, organizational secularization in terms of church participation is very high (low church attendance).

The relationship between the three dimensions of secularization, then, varies from society to society. There is, however, at least one common process underlying the three dimensions. Where social changes that result in cultural, organizational, or institutional secularization occur, they can typically be described as the result of relativization. Relativization occurs where cultural themes, organizational participation, or institutional arrangements come into contact with plausible and compelling alternatives that delegitimize absolute claims and encourage mutual adjustment. For example, the stage is set for relativization, where scientifically based cosmologies confront the belief that the Book of Genesis in the Bible describes the actual sequence of events regarding the origin of the universe, where alternatives to church attendance (Sunday shopping) exist, and where the control of functional activities, such as social services, shifts from religious to secular institutions.

Absolute religious claims can also be relativized and thereby secularized through adjustment to pluralism and religious diversity. For example, certain absolute literal claims — the Jews are God's chosen people, the Roman Catholic Church is the only true church, only Jesus saves (orthodox Protestantism) — have been substantially modified by elements and groups within each tradition under the constraints of religious pluralism in North America.

Canada, today, is undoubtedly more secularized at the cultural-interpretive and organization-participatory levels than it was at the end of World War II. Proportionately fewer people attend religious services, the secular arts flourish, and the role of organized mainline religion in shaping public opinion has diminished. Is secularization self-limiting? We have seen above that there are barriers to radical secularization at the institutional level in Canadian society. Is there any reason to believe Canadian society will not continue to become increasingly secularized in participation and beliefs?

According to Rodney Stark and William Sims Bainbridge (1985), secularization *is* a self-limiting process because it creates an opportunity structure for religious innovation and the revitalization of moribund religious structures and beliefs. Stark and Bainbridge argue, in effect, that in any population the distribution of religious needs is constant over time. The satisfaction of religious needs, however, can vary since it is dependent on the extent to which effective religious rewards or "compensators" are generated by religious organizations. Over the long run, churches tend to identify with dominant secular cultures and, hence, weaken their ability to generate effective religious rewards.

The resulting vacuum can be filled in two ways. Where churchly traditions prevail, sects may arise. Sects are religious organizations created when a group separates from a church and forms a new organization. Sects, typically, are in much higher tension with secular culture than churches, and usually represent a revival or intensification of depleted churchly traditions.

Where churchly traditions are not strong, according to Stark and Bainbridge, there is a tendency for cults to form. Cults do not represent splits from well-established churches but, rather, purvey new ideas and behaviour that may deviate radically from the beliefs and practices of churches and their sectarian offspring. Cults, like sects, exhibit more tension with dominant secular cultures.

Neither sects nor cults are strangers to Canada. Among the sects, the various Pentecostal bodies are perhaps the most prominent tradition today (see Table 3 above). The more visible cults include Scientology, the Unification Church (Moonies), est, and ISKCON (Hare Krishna). Furthermore, recruitment to sects in the past and the distribution of cults throughout Canada today seem to conform to Stark and Bainbridge's theoretical predictions. Clark (1948) and Mann (1955) document the appeal that sec-

FRONTIERS AND RELIGIOUS SECTS IN CANADIAN SOCIETY

S.D. Clark, a founder of the discipline of sociology in anglophone Canada, has written extensively on the relationship between social change and religious forms in Canadian society. "Clark's primary concern is to show how religious organization is affected by socioeconomic contextual factors. . . . He does this by making the focus of social change the frontier. . . . Clark define[s] the frontier as "new areas of economic exploitation" which makes new demands on social organization. . . . Clark argued that frontiers disturbed traditional forms of social organizations and produced considerable social disorganization. Only as the economy matures does social stability return. So he argues that the "church has grown out of the conditions of a mature society; the sect has been a product of what might be called frontier conditions of social life" . . . In other words, frontiers are inherently unstable, and sectarianism should be viewed as a temporary adaptive device to instability. Because they broke down feelings of isolation, strengthened bonds of fellowship, and created communities of saints, "the evangelical movements were essentially movements of social reorganization or social reunification." . . . He analyzes the Great Awakening in Nova Scotia (1760–1783), the Great Revival in the Maritime provinces (1783–1832), and the Great Revival in Central Canada (1783–1832), pointing out that it was the "unattached" or "footloose" frontier populations alienated from the established religious organizations who found social integration through religious reform. However, with the growth of wealth, improved social standing, and an educated clergy, for example, these sectarian efforts lost their excitement and began to denominationalize. Rural frontiers were then succeeded by new frontier populations that had recently migrated to cities, attracted by activity such as shipbuilding in the Maritimes and manufacturing in Ontario. Sectarianism arose again as poverty and unemployment developed on urban frontiers. Clark's conclusion is that sectarian religion is a product of the disorganizing effects of social change found on any frontier" (Hiller, 1977:420–21).

tarian forms of religion have had on the frontier peripheries of developing Canadian society, where churchly forms of religion were present but unable to satisfy the religious needs of many frontier inhabitants. Stark and Bainbridge (1985), themselves, present a variety of data to support their prediction that cult activity will be concentrated where conventional churches are weakest.

Perhaps the most dramatic feature of the Stark–Bainbridge data is the comparison between British Columbia and other provinces and regions in Canada. Recalling that of all of the provinces, British Columbia has by far the highest proportion of those indicating "No Religious Preference" and the lowest proportion of those identifying with a mainstream religious denomination or tradition (Table 3 above), the expectation is that British Columbia would also have the highest rate of cult activity. The Stark–Bainbridge data support that expectation. On each of five independent measures of cult rates per million population, British Columbia far exceeds the other provinces. There are, for example, over twice as many Christian Scientists per million population in British Columbia than in any other province.

CONCLUSION

This chapter will have accomplished its purpose if readers realize that Canadian society cannot be understood until the religious factor has been taken into account. That goal does not encompass a special plea for religion but, simply, the recognition that a full analysis of any society — including those that are officially atheistic—must refer to symbolic cultural elements that transcend everyday reality and rituals that generate collective solidarity.

This chapter argues that religion in Canada, today, has a subtle but persistent influence in arenas of power and over economic rewards. Beliefs, rituals, politics, and economics interpenetrate one another. For some Canadians, that interpenetration is short and direct, for example, the pious Jew who won't do business on the Sabbath or the conservative Christian who has scruples about opening her business on Sunday. For others, the impact of religion may be seemingly negligible or absent. But even they live within an institutional matrix that bears the marks of religious influence and elicits responses to structural elements in the society that are intimately linked to religion.

DISCUSSION QUESTIONS

1. Examine the "No Religious Preference" category in Table 3. Do you detect a geographic pattern in the data and, if so, how would you explain it?
2. What is meant by describing Canadian society as dualistic, and how has the dualistic nature of Canadian society changed since Confederation?
3. Using a reference such as the *Dictionary of Canadian Biography* or *The Canadian Encyclopedia*, determine the political affiliations and religious views of the public figures named in the last sentence of the quote in the box on p. 353 entitled "Religion in Canada in the Victorian Age."
4. Discuss the role of religion in the maintenance of ethnic identity for some ethnic group in Canada with which you are familiar.
5. Describe the role that religion plays in the politics of the province in which you live.

GLOSSARY

charter group a group usually defined in terms of ethnicity, language, or religion that is a founding group of a society. In Canada, the French and English would be considered charter groups.

church a religious group that accepts the social environment in which it exists

cult a deviant religious tradition with no ties to a church or sect

differentiation the development of a specialized subsystem that performs a function previously performed by a less specialized subsystem

dualism the division or segmentation of a society on a dimension of two categories, for example French–English, Protestant–Roman Catholic, Black–White

functional autonomy the claim by a social unit and recognition of the claim by other social units that the social unit has original jurisdiction over its activities and goals

institution a set of subsystems in a society that performs a major function, for example, the economy, the polity, or the educational subsystem

rationalization the deliberate choice of goals or ends by a social unit and the determination of the most effective means to achieve the goals or ends usually by analyzing costs and benefits

sect a religious group that rejects the social environment in which it exists. Sects are formed by splits from churches

subsystem any socially organized unit within a society

BIBLIOGRAPHY

Berton, Pierre
1965 *The Comfortable Pew*. Toronto: McClelland and Stewart.

Bibby, Reginald W.
1986 *Anglitrends: A Profile and Diagnosis*. Toronto: Diocese of Toronto.

Clark, S. D.
1948 *Church and Sect in Canada*. Toronto: The University of Toronto Press.

Dawson, R. M.
1954 *The Government of Canada*, 2nd ed. Toronto: The University of Toronto Press.

Dumont, Fernand
1985 "Mutations de la culture religieuse au Quebec." *Canadian Issues/Themes canadiens* 7:10–21.

The Globe and Mail.
1986 "Ontario Solicitor-General Resigns After Liquor Charge." Toronto: December 4: Al.

Grant, John Webster
1972 *The Church in the Canadian Era: The First Century of Confederation*. Toronto: McGraw-Hill Ryerson.

Hiller, Harry H.
1977 "The Contribution of S. D. Clark to the Sociology of Canadian Religion." *Sciences religieuses/Studies in Religion* 6 (4) 415–27.

——
1978 "Continentalism and the Third Force in Religion." *The Canadian Journal of Sociology* 3(2) 183–207.

Mann, W. E.
1955 *Sect, Cult and Church in Alberta*. Toronto: The University of Toronto Press.

McRae, K. D. (ed.)
1974 "Consociationalism and the Canadian Political System." In *Consociational Democracy: Political Accommodation in Segmented Societies*. Toronto: McClelland and Stewart.

Morton, W. L. (ed.)
1968 *The Shield of Achilles: Aspects of Canada in the Victorian Age*. Toronto: McClelland and Stewart.

Porter, John
1965 *The Vertical Mosaic: An Analysis of Social Class and Power in Canada*. Toronto: The University of Toronto Press.

Silberman, Charles E.
1985 *A Certain People: American Jews and Their Lives Today*. New York: Summit Books.

Simpson, John H. and Henry G. MacLeod
1985 "The Politics of Morality in Canada." pp. 221–40 in *Religious Movements: Genesis, Exodus, and Numbers* edited by Rodney Stark. New York: Paragon House.

Stark, Rodney and William Sims Bainbridge
1985 *The Future of Religion: Secularization, Revival and Cult Formation*. Berkeley: University of California Press.

Weber, Max
1978 *Economy and Society*, vol. 1, edited by Guenther Roth and Claus Wittich. Berkeley: University of California Press.

A large family has become a rarity in this country; this was much less the case in previous decades, as suggested by this Quebec family from the early forties at mealtime. *Courtesy of National Archives Canada/PA 112893*

> *"Change is a normal aspect of participating within a family.... At present, change ... seems to be going in a similar direction in all industrialized societies."*

c h a p t e r t h i r t e e n

Families: Evolving Structures

Margrit Eichler

INTRODUCTION

The family is one of the most important social institutions. This is true not only in a sociological sense, but also in a personal sense. When one asks who have been the people most important in shaping one's character, the list will likely consist primarily of family members. Whether their influence has been good or bad (it has usually been a mixture) it is likely to have been significant.

The vast majority of us are born into a family and live with family members for most of our lives. This is one of the few things that does not seem to change. For the rest, families are in a constant flux, whether we look at our own family situation or general trends concerning families within a society, or even across different societies. Paradoxically, then, one constant when looking at families is change.

In this chapter, we shall look at change first from a micro perspective, by considering the changes that go on within most families. We shall then consider the changes through which the family as an institution is going by looking at trends from a macro perspective. Of course, the two perspectives are simply different sides of the same coin.

When looking at family trends from a macro perspective, we shall see the changes occurring in Canadian families are similar to those occurring in families in other highly industrialized countries. Lastly, we shall consider some changes that are just starting — namely the new reproductive technologies and their potential impact on families.

CHANGES AT THE MICRO LEVEL

Our image of a family still conforms to a monolithic image (see Eichler, 1983). We still see families as nuclear ones that come into existence when a young man and woman marry. In due time, they are expected to have a child. Using this set of assumptions, we then construct models around this type of family which focus on particular aspects.

One such model is the developmental approach, which lists typical stages or cycles through which a family goes. There are many versions of this approach, but the one defined as most important (Hill and Rodgers, 1964:171–211, McGoldrick and Carter, 1982:168) or as one of the most important (Rodgers and Witney, 1981; Norton, 1983; McLeod and Ellis, 1983) is Duvall's. Duvall (1985:26) identifies the following typical stages:

1. Married couples (without children)
2. Childbearing families (oldest child birth—thirty months)
3. Families with preschool children (oldest child two and a half to six years)
4. Families with schoolchildren (oldest child six to thirteen years)
5. Families with teenagers (oldest child thirteen to twenty years)
6. Families launching young adults (first child gone to last child's leaving home)
7. Middle-aged parents (empty nest to retirement)
8. Aging family members (retirement to death of both spouses)

There are problems with using such a simple model of life cycles. As has been noted before (Murphy and Staples, 1979, Norton, 1980 and 1983), it is inappropriate to assume all—or even most—families follow such a model. In 1984, for instance, almost 17 percent of all Canadian women giving birth that year were not married. These women may or may not marry subsequently, and their husband may or may not be the father of their first child. Obviously, their life cycle will look different than the one just described. Further, the chances of a marriage ending in divorce in Canada are around 40 percent. Once again, the life cycle of people in divorced families differs from the one described above, especially when children are involved, and when people marry. In 1985, 30 percent of all marriages contracted in that year involved at least one previously married partner.

This does not mean the life cycle approach is useless, but it must be adapted to encompass the complexities that exist. Once we do this, the developmental approach points up the on-going change in all families. To play through this scenario, let us briefly look at the life cycle of the type of family that underlies Duvall's model, and then look at it from a change perspective.

The birth of a first child is a monumental event that affects every aspect of a young couple's life. Whether the wife keeps her job or quits it, there is now a young human being that requires care twenty-four hours a day, seven days a week. If she quits her job, the couple will feel a financial pinch exactly when they need more money because their expenses have jumped. If she keeps her job, as is the norm, the couple will have to search for affordable day care of reasonable quality that is at a convenient location.

The new baby requires a complete readjustment for the couple. Their sleeping patterns, eating patterns, time commitments, recreation, finances, and especially the interaction between them, will change drastically. They were a dyad: now they are a triad. Where before they could adjust their actions to their mutual wishes, they now have to consider the needs of a small human being who communicates only in the most rudimentary manner. The interaction between husband and wife is likely to become more sex stereotyped (LaRossa and LaRossa 1981).

When a second child is born, the adjustment required is almost as great as for the first child for the parents, since yet another timetable has to be integrated into the overall family schedule. For the first child, the second child is likely to require as great an adjustment as for the parents.

And so things continue. When children leave home, when they marry, have children, etc., predictable changes occur in many families. However, to use a life cycle approach profitably, we need to recognize that many families do not follow the pattern in the manner suggested above. Many families evolve when an unmarried woman gives birth. Others involve previously married partners, who may already have children with a previous partner. These children may or may not become a part of the new family. Adults may find themselves simultaneously at more than one life stage with respect to their children. Some adults will enter an on-going family unit (parent–child) at a later stage without having participated in the preceding stages. Conversely, a couple may share the early stages without sharing the later ones. Children may be members of more than one family simultaneously, namely, their mother's and their father's, where the two do not share the same household and where contact with the noncustodial parent has been maintained.

These patterns have implications for the people within the families and for society at large. In the next section, we shall look more systematically at some important structural changes which have occurred in families in Canada and in other highly industrialized societies.

CHANGES AT THE MACRO LEVEL

When looking at trends in families in Canada and other societies, we can once more note the persistence of change. One can observe demographic changes, in particular, changes in **fertility rates** (i.e., the number of children born to women) and **life expectancy** (i.e., how long a woman or a man of a given age can expect to live). Other changes concern the structure of the family, particularly with respect to illegitimacy rates (i.e., the proportion of children born to unmarried women as compared to married women), **divorce rates** (i.e., the proportion of marriages ending in divorce) and **remarriage rates** (i.e., the proportion of marriages that involve at least one previously married partner).

Together, these changes have important implications for all of us. To gain some overview of what is happening in families, we must also examine the division of labour between the sexes.

A different set of changes that affects families is taking place in family law and policies affecting families. These changes reveal how Canadian society looks at families.

Lastly, we shall consider some incipient changes in our collective understanding of parental relationships caused by recent medical advances in reproductive technologies and the new social arrangements surrounding them.

If we compare Canada with other highly industrialized countries, we find that by and large families seem to move in a similar direction in industrialized countries — a phenomenon explained by **convergence theory**. "Convergence" means moving from different positions toward some common point. To know that countries are alike tells us nothing about convergence. There must be movement over time toward some identified common point'' (Inkeles, 1981:14).

There is more convergence than divergence in trends concerning families in industrialized countries.

Changes in Fertility

Worldwide, women have fewer children than they used to have. Comparing 1950 to 1955 with 1975 to 1980, we find the **gross reproduction rate** (i.e., the numbers of daughters born per woman) declined from 2.44 to 1.91 (United Nations, 1985:19, t. 15). Looking only at Canada, women in the 1980s have about half the number of children they had in the 1960s. Whereas in 1960, the average woman had 3.9 children, in 1984 the average woman only has 1.7 children (computed from Eichler, 1983:37 and Statistics Canada, 1986a:9).[1]

This is a common trend in highly industrialized countries. The twenty countries with the lowest fertility rate in 1982 in ascending order are: Switzerland, the Federal Republic of Germany, Luxembourg, the Netherlands, Denmark, Sweden, Austria, Belgium, Finland, the German Democratic Republic, Japan, Norway, Singapore, Canada, France, Italy, New Zealand, the U.S.A., Great Britain, and Australia (United Nations, 1985:21).

Reasons for this decline are manifold. They include better access to birth control means and greater longevity due to, among other things, reduced infant mortality. As the chances for an infant to survive to adulthood increase (and we will see in the next section that they have increased in all countries), women have fewer children.

In addition, with increasing industrialization, countries produce fewer children. As they move away from agriculture and primary sector industries, and as mass education becomes a reality, having children brings economic penalties rather than rewards. So women have fewer children.

Changes in Life Expectancy

Life expectancy has increased significantly all across the world. Although the life expectancy in industrialized countries is much higher than in developing countries, the relative gain in life expectancy is greater in the developing regions, since they started from a lower level. Across the entire world, the average life expectancy at birth was 45.8 years for 1950 to 1955. This rose to 57.3 years from 1975 to 1980. For North America, life expectancy rose from 69.0 years from 1950 to 1955 to 73.3 years from 1975 to 1980. (United Nations, 1985:22).

In Canada, for a male born in 1931, the life expectancy was 60.0 years, and for a female born that year it was 62.1 years. By contrast, for a male born in 1986, the life expectancy is estimated at 70.2 years and for a female 78.3 years (Statistics Canada, 1979:21). In other words, between 1931 and 1986, Canadian males will, on average, have added an estimated 10.2 years to their lives, while females will have added an estimated 16.2 years.

The importance of changes in fertility rates and life expectancy for families is hard to overestimate. For the society as a whole, it means that our age pyramid is changing. A greater proportion of our population than ever before will be old rather than young. In North America, 41.9% of all people were under age fifteen in 1950. This reduced to 34 percent in 1980, and is projected to decline further to 32.2 percent in 2025. By contrast, the proportion of old people shows a great upswing. In 1950, 12.5 percent of the North American population was over sixty-five. This increased to 16.7 percent in 1980, and is estimated to increase to 27.6 percent in 2025 (United Nations, 1985: 18). Worldwide, the differential growth rates will shift the population balance further away from the more developed regions to the less developed regions (see Table 1).

In Canada, the shifting population pyramid means our kinship structure is changing. As women have fewer children, people will have fewer aunts and uncles. A single child has no brother or sister, and his or her children will therefore have no aunts or uncles on at least one side, and— if two single children marry — on both sides. The single child, in turn, will have no blood related nephews and nieces (he or she may have some through marriage). On the other hand, some people will acquire relatives through successive marriages (cf. Bohannan, 1971; Furstenberg and Spanier, 1984, Gross, 1985).

As people live longer, young children are more likely to have more grandparents who are still alive, and those grandparents are likely to have fewer grandchildren. As more people live until they have reached the "old-old stage" (usually seen as being over eighty) they will also need more care. The person most likely to provide this care is, at present, daughter or daughter-in-law, who herself is no longer young.

Women tend to marry men who are, on average, more than two years older than themselves; conversely, men marry women younger than themselves. Since men have a shorter life expectancy, this

Table 1

POPULATION SIZE AND RATE OF INCREASE FOR THE WORLD, MORE DEVELOPED REGIONS AND LESS DEVELOPED REGIONS, MEDIUM VARIANT. 1950–2025

	World		**More-developed regions**[a]		**Less-developed regions**[b]	
Year	*Population (millions)*	*Rate of increase*[c] *(percentage)*	*Population (millions)*	*Rate of increase*[c] *(percentage)*	*Population (millions)*	*Rate of increase*[c] *(percentage)*
1950	2504	–	832	–	1672	–
1955	2746	1.84	887	1.28	1859	2.11
1960	3014	1.86	945	1.27	2069	2.14
1965	3324	1.96	1003	1.19	2321	2.30
1970	3683	2.06	1047	0.87	2636	2.55
1975	4076	2.03	1095	0.89	2981	2.46
1980	4453	1.77	1136	0.74	3317	2.14
1985	4842	1.67	1173	0.64	3669	2.02
1990	5248	1.61	1209	0.60	4040	1.92
1995	5679	1.58	1243	0.56	4436	1.87
2000	6127	1.52	1276	0.52	4851	1.79
2005	6567	1.39	1304	0.45	5263	1.63
2010	6995	1.26	1330	0.39	5664	1.47
2015	7410	1.15	1354	0.36	6055	1.33
2020	7806	1.04	1376	0.32	6429	1.20
2025	8177	0.93	1397	0.29	6780	1.06

[a]Including the countries of Northern America and Europe, Australia, Japan, New Zealand and the Union of Soviet Socialist Republics.

[b]Including the countries of Africa, Latin America, East and South Asia and Oceania (excluding Australia, Japan and New Zealand).

[c]Average annual rate of increase for each five-year period since the preceding date.

Source: Eichler, 1983. Copyright, United Nations Demographic Yearbook 1959, 1965, 1969, 1975, 1981. Reproduced with permission.

results in a marked imbalance in old age: men tend to die while married, and consequently tend to be looked after by their wives until death, while women are much more likely to die as widows, and consequently tend *not* to be looked after by their husbands. In 1984, 62 percent of all men who died in that year were married, compared to only 32 percent of the women who died (computed from Statistics Canada, 1986b:50, t. 20). We thus find a great imbalance in the sex ratio of patients in nursing homes.

We find equally dramatic changes with respect to illegitimacy, divorce, and remarriage rates.

Births to Unmarried Women

In some Canadian provinces, the legal concept of illegitimacy has been abolished. In other provinces and many other countries, the concept is still used. Overall, we note a dramatic increase in the proportion of births to unmarried women in Canada since 1960.

This increase in illegitimacy rates is a trend in most highly industrialized countries with a few notable exceptions: Italy, Japan, the Netherlands, Poland, and Switzerland all had illegitimacy rates of less than 5 percent in 1980.

We shall consider the importance of this phenomenon, together with that of the divorce and remarriage rates.

Divorce Rates

Overall, divorce has increased dramatically. In Canada at the turn of the century, the annual average number of divorces for the period 1896 to 1900 was eleven (Pike: 1975:125). This compares to 61 980 divorces in 1985. Part of this increase, of course, occurred because there are more people in Canada in 1985 than there were in 1900. Nevertheless, the increase in divorce is real.

Table 2

BIRTHS TO UNMARRIED MOTHERS, CANADA, 1960–1984

Year	Numbers	Percent of Total Births
1960	20 413	4.3
1961	21 490	4.5
1962	22 443	4.8
1963	24 458	5.3
1964	26 556	5.9
1965	28 078	6.7
1966	29 391	7.6
1967	30 915	8.3
1968	32 629	9.0
1969	34 041	9.2
1970	35 588	9.6
1971	32 693	9.0
1972	31 257	9.0
1973	31 005	9.0
1974	19 183	5.9
1975	24 846	8.7
1976	25 995	10.2
1977	37 801	10.8
1978	39 508	11.4
1979	42 311	11.9
1980	46 014	12.8
1981	50 125	13.9
1982	55 625	15.3
1983	58 181	16.0
1984	61 265	16.7

Source: Computed from Eichler, 1983: 206, Statistics Canada, 1986b: 12.

The jump in divorce rates between 1968 and 1969 marks the year in which Canada's first federal divorce act was proclaimed. It is too early to state whether the decrease in the number and rate of divorces which started in 1983 is a real decline or a temporary reversal. Since the federal government was drafting new divorce legislation in this period, which eventually came into force in 1986, people may have simply delayed filing for divorce in anticipation of the new law.

Whether divorce rates increase or

THE CANADIAN DIVORCE RATES IN COMPARATIVE PERSPECTIVE

For divorce, there is a strong convergence in all industrialized countries. With the single exception of Italy, whose divorce law until recently was shaped by the Vatican, we find a great and consistent increase in the rates of all industrialized countries; (see Table 4).

slightly decrease in the future, the divorce rate is very high. Putting it into other terms, the likelihood of a marriage to end in divorce has been calculated at just under 40 percent. (McKie et al., 1983:64–70).

Table 3

INCIDENCE OF DIVORCE IN CANADA, 1921–1985

Year	Number	Rates*
1921	558	6.4
1931	700	6.8
1941	2 462	21.4
1951	5 270	37.6
1961	6 563	36.0
1962	6 768	36.4
1963	7 686	40.6
1964	8 623	44.7
1965	8 974	45.7
1966	10 239	51.2
1967	11 165	54.8
1968	11 343	54.8
1969	26 093	124.2
1970	29 775	139.8
1971	29 685	137.6
1972	32 389	148.4
1973	36 704	166.1
1974	45 019	200.6
1975	50 611	222.0
1976	54 207	235.8
1977	55 370	237.7
1978	57 155	243.4
1979	59 474	251.3
1980	62 019	259.1
1981	67 671	278.0
1982	70 436	285.9
1983	68 567	275.5
1984	65 172	259.4
1985	61 980	244.4

*Per 100 000 population.

Source: Computed from Ambert, 1980, Eichler, 1983, and Statistics Canada, 1985:16 and 1986c:16.

Table 4

CRUDE DIVORCE RATES

	1960	1970	1980
Australia	0.65	1.02	4.75
Austria	1.14	1.40	1.77
Belgium	0.50	0.66	1.47
Bulgaria	0.90	1.16	1.48
Czechoslovakia	1.12	1.74	2.21
Canada	0.39	1.37	2.59
Denmark	1.46	1.93	2.65
Finland	0.88	1.31	1.98
France	0.66	0.79	—
G.D.R.	1.42	1.61	2.68
G.F.R.	0.88	1.26	1.56
Hungary	1.66	2.21	2.59
Italy	—	—	0.21
Japan	0.74	0.93	1.21
Netherlands	0.49	0.79	—
New Zealand	0.69	1.12	—
Norway	0.66	0.88	1.62
Poland	0.50	1.06	1.12
Sweden	1.20	1.61	2.39
Switzerland	0.87	1.04	1.65
U.K.	0.51	1.18	3.01
U.S.A.	2.18	3.46	5.19
U.S.S.R.	—	2.62	3.50

Source: U.N. Demographic Yearbook 1976, 1978, 1981. Copyright, United Nations. Reproduced by permission.

Remarriage Rates

Most people remarry after a divorce, although men are more likely to do so than women. As a consequence, with a high divorce rate we also have a high remar-

Table 5

MARITAL STATUS OF BRIDES AND GROOMS, CANADA, 1967–1985

Year	Percentage single bride and groom	Percentage with at least one previously married partner
1967	87.7	12.3
1968	87.7	12.3
1969	84.9	15.1
1970	89.0	11.0
1971	83.4	16.6
1972	83.2	16.8
1973	81.9	18.1
1974	80.4	19.6
1975	78.6	21.4
1976	76.9	23.1
1977	76.1	23.9
1978	75.1	24.9
1979	74.3	25.7
1980	73.5	26.5
1981	72.5	27.5
1982	71.9	28.1
1983	70.6	29.4
1984	70.1	29.9
1985	70.3	29.7

Source: Computed from Eichler, 1983:232–34, and Statistics Canada, 1985 and 1986c.

riage rate. In fact, Canadian statistics show a constant increase in the proportion of marriages involving previously married people, as can be seen in Table 5.

The observed absolute and relative increase in the number of children born to unmarried women (20 413 in 1960, representing 4.3 percent of all births as compared to 65 265 in 1985, representing 16.7 percent of all births in that year) is *not* due to a greater likelihood of women giving birth, especially young women. On the contrary, when we consider the proportion of all teenage women who have given birth during this time, the likelihood of a teenager giving birth has decreased to less than half of what it was twenty-five years ago.

If we look at fertility rates and births to unmarried women in conjunction, we must conclude the great relative and absolute increase in the latter is due to an unwillingness to marry simply because a child is on the way, rather than to an increase in pregnancies among young women.[2]

During the past two decades, the stigma attached to an unmarried woman who gives birth to a child has greatly lessened. Whereas most children born in this way used to be given up for adoption, they are now mostly kept by their mothers. Presumably, this reduces the willingness of a woman to marry the man who made her pregnant unless the couple could anticipate an acceptable marriage relationship. As long, however, as an unmarried birth to a woman meant giving up the child, marriage might have been preferred.

A similar interpretation can be applied to the divorce statistics. It is important not to mistake divorce statistics as a perfect indicator of (a) marriage breakdown or (b) the quality of a marriage. Marriage breakdown (other than termination by death) may occur in ways other than divorce: through permanent desertion, permanent separation, migratory divorces (Pike, 1975:124) or continued cohabitation with a complete communications breakdown. McVey and Robinson (1981:361) have suggested that if we add the separated population to the divorced population at any one point we arrive at a marriage "dissolution index" at least one-and-a-half times greater than estimates based only upon the incidence of divorce.

There are highly unhappy but very stable marriages. The increase in the divorce rate, then, probably means people are less willing to tolerate an unhappy marriage and prefer divorce over remaining unhappily married. It probably does *not* mean an increase in the unhappiness of married people.

Indeed, one can argue the contrary: with the relative ease of divorce, marriage becomes more of a voluntary union than it used to be, and therefore the overall quality of marriages has probably improved rather than deteriorated.

Because of an increase in divorce, we find an increasing proportion of children and men living apart from some of their immediate family members. For them, their household and their family do not contain the same people. This is truer for men than for women, since only about 15 percent of all children are in the custody of fathers, and about 70 percent to 80 percent are in the custody of mothers (the rest are in someone else's care).

Division of Labour

The term division of labour is usually used in connection with the way an entire society divides its labour among various groups: some people extract materials from the earth, others produce goods from these materials, which are sold by yet others, other groups provide a large array of services, etc.

The term also describes the types of work women and men do in society and in the family. Until the early 1960s, women tended to be almost exclusively responsible for the work done at home, while men were commonly regarded as the breadwinners for families. Even at that time, though, there were many women in the labour force, but they tended to be single or married with children, of whom the youngest was at school. Most married women dropped out of the labour force with the birth of their first child (see Ostry, 1968:19) and often re-entered the labour force at a later stage. Until about 1980, the majority of wives were housewives.

Around 1980, Canada crossed a threshold concerning the participation of mothers and wives in the labour force. Since 1983, not only the majority of wives and mothers of school-age children, but also the majority of mothers of preschool children have been in the paid labour force.

This marks a drastic change in the way society divides its work between women and men. While until 1980 it was possible to state that men were primarily responsible for the paid work and women for the unpaid family work, this is no longer true for the majority of Canadian families.

One would expect that such a far-reaching change in the roles women play, would cause an equally dramatic shift in the roles men play within the family. This hasn't happened.

A set of studies, with data collected in 1971, found women did most of the housework and childcare. They also show that "despite the radical difference which a paid job makes in the working week of married women, their husbands' contribution to the regular necessities of the household remain small and virtually unchanged" (Meissner et al., 1975).

That was in 1971. Since then, a fair amount of change has taken place in public awareness, in the numbers and proportion of women in the labour force, in government pronouncements concerning sex equality, in commissions studying various issues regarding sex equality, etc. However, between 1971 and 1981, the workload of *employed* females at home remained almost unchanged — as did the workload of employed males at home. In Vancouver, employed females worked 3.9 hours per day on family care, compared to 1.45 hours per day for comparable males. In Halifax, the average daily load for females was 2.9 hours per day and for males 1.8 (computed from Harvey, 1983).

Overall, then, women continue to do the lioness's share of "family care" even though most of them also work in the labour force.

SUMMARY OF CHANGES WITHIN FAMILIES

Looking at the various trends in conjunction, then, we can make several observations.

Fertility has dropped considerably; women have fewer children than ever before. Both women and men live longer. The two factors together mean our population has shifted from having more young to having more old people. A higher proportion of births than ever before are to unmarried women. Divorce has increased dramatically since 1968 and can be expected to remain high. As a consequence, remarriages have become an ever-increasing proportion of our marriages. Together, these trends have produced an increasing disjunction between marital and parental roles, and an increasing portion of the population is not living together with all their biological parents/children. This phenomenon applies more to men than to women.

Further, most wives and mothers are now in the paid labour force but women continue to do most of the family work.

Some consequences of these changes include:

1. There is no longer one typical life cycle that is meaningful for all families. Instead, there are complex life cycles which may involve simultaneous membership in more than one stage and/or entry into one stage without having gone through the preceding stages.
2. Household and family membership are not identical for many children, many men, and some women.
3. In many households, the various members may have different family relationships.
4. Most wives and mothers are in the paid labour force.
5. There is an increasing diversification of family types, due to the high incidence of births to unmarried women, divorce, and remarriage.

LEGAL CHANGES

Many industrialized countries have gone through several revisions of family-related laws in the past few decades, and Canada is no exception. The two major sets of legislation (there are many others) concern divorce and family law.

Divorce Law

Canada has gone through two major shifts with respect to divorce law: in 1968, the country received its first unified divorce law. Until then, the availability of divorce varied from province to province. In Newfoundland and Quebec, for instance, the courts had no rights to grant divorce decrees. Petitioners living in those provinces could divorce only by having private Acts passed by the federal Parliament.

The Divorce Act of 1968 (which is under federal jurisdiction in contrast to the family laws, which are under provincial jurisdiction) specified divorce could occur after three years of separation on the basis of marriage breakdown, or sooner on the basis of a marital offence (adultery, physical or mental cruelty, etc.).

The second major change took place in 1986, with the coming into force of the Divorce Act, 1985. It specifies that a divorce will be granted if the spouses have been living separate and apart for at least one year preceding the petition for divorce. A divorce may also be granted at any time because of adultery or physical or mental cruelty.

The effect of this new law cannot yet be determined, since too little time has elapsed since its proclamation.

Provincial Family Laws

If the changes in divorce law have been great, changes in provincial family law are at least equally great. Space restrictions prohibit a province-by-province discussion so only the broadest trends will be summarized here.

The first family law reform act was proclaimed in 1978 in Ontario. Since then, every province and territory has changed its family law at least once. Prior to 1978, the duties and rights of spouses were generally seen as different. Men were considered responsible for the economic well-being of all family members (even beyond death and divorce, as witnessed by life insurance policies, survivors' benefits in pensions, and alimony payments), while women were responsible for housework, childcare, and generally keeping the family working. Now the rights and duties of each spouse have, in principle, been equalized (in fact, this is not the case).

With regard to property, the matrimonial home is now usually an asset that must be shared between the spouses, with the exception of Quebec. However, in spite of the many legal reforms, ex-wives and their children are likely to suffer a great drop in income upon divorce, while ex-husbands tend to enjoy an increase. One U.S. study found on average that ex-wives and their children experience a 73 percent decline in their standard of living, while ex-husbands experience a 40 percent rise in their living standards (Weitzman, 1985). While we do not have a comparably comprehensive Canadian study, all indications are that the proportions would be similar in this country.

For the purposes of maintenance (and in some provinces, also for property rights) the status of common-law spouses has been made more like that of legally married spouses.

Overall, these changes amount to a new legal conception of marriage and divorce. Where before the legal notions were based on a difference of functions of spouses, they are now based on the similarity of functions of the spouses. Sometimes such assumption of equality is inappropriate, as when a wife who has been a housewife for twenty years is supposed to become economically self-sufficient within two years, or when, in a custody dispute, the rival claims of father and mother are given equal status, irrespective of who has been the primary caretaker during the marriage. While sex equality should be a goal of jurisprudence and social policy, wrongly *assuming* its existence may be detrimental to the weaker partner.

SOCIAL POLICIES AFFECTING FAMILIES

Policies are always informed, either implicitly or explicitly, by models of soci-

Table 6
THE OLD FAMILY MODEL

Ideology	Sex-role differentiation
Economic responsibility	Husbands/fathers as breadwinners, wives secondary earners or nonearners
Economic dependency	Wives/children as dependents of husband/fathers
Household composition	Assumption of congruence between household and family membership
	The nuclear family seen as normative
	Wives equated with mothers, husbands equated with fathers
Household management	Wives/mothers as full-time or part-time homemakers with sole responsibility for household management
	Husband/fathers not responsible for household management
	Unclear distinction between spousal and parental obligations
Personal care	Mothers/wives/adult daughters(-in-law) responsible for provision of care of children and adults
	Fathers/husbands/sons(-in-law) not responsible for provision of care for children and adults

ety. Policies that affect families are implicitly based on some understanding of what the family is. In the preceding sections, we have seen families in Canada — and in industrialized countries in general — have gone through great changes in the past quarter century. This has resulted in a situation in which many public policies have become insufficient and inappropriate. If one aspect of society changes, this usually causes social strain unless parallel change occurs in other, related parts of society.

Such strain is now evident as far as families are concerned. This has led to a reawakening of interest in family policy in different countries. Before the mid-1970s the interest in such issues was remarkably low (cf. Kamerman and Kahn, 1978:9–16).

Canada is no exception. We have already seen that the structure of families and the law relating to families has changed drastically. The change in social policies has, unfortunately, not kept pace. To appreciate how policies relate to families, we will construct two hypothetical types of families; one the "old" family, and the other the "new" family.

The old family model can be summarized in Table 6 (from Eichler, 1985: 394–400).

The policies that correspond to this model can be summarized in Table 7.

Consider how appropriate such a model of the family and the policies that logically follow from it are for today. As we have seen, the law now assumes equality rather than differentiation between spouses. Regarding economic responsibility and dependency, the majority of wives earn an income. Consequently, the majority of husbands/fathers are no longer sole breadwinners. However, wives/mothers still do most of the housework and care for other family members. Just as clearly, this is ine-

Table 7
POLICIES CONGRUENT WITH THE OLD FAMILY MODEL

Ideology	Sex-role differentiation
Economy:	
labour market policy	Men seen as primary earners, women as secondary earners or nonearners.
	Preference is therefore given to men over women in employment programs, women are treated as labour force reserve
	A large wage-differential by sex
	Employers and labour law regulations treat male workers as unencumbered by family responsibilities, and female workers as encumbered or potentially encumbered
tax structure	Provides relief to male earners with dependants (i.e., wife and/or children)
other government transfers	Provide replacement income in case male breadwinner is absent or unable to earn income
	Provide replacement care in case of incapacity or absence of wife/mother
Household composition	For purposes of eligibility for benefits, household membership is equated with family membership, and eligibility is determined on basis of family need rather than individual entitlement
	Rights and obligations of non-coresidential parents are not enforced
Social services	No universal day care, no universal relief for care of adult family members in need of care, no institutionalized right to care for temporarily sick family members on the part of workers

quitous where the wife has a full-time job. For many people, household and family membership is not congruous, due to the high rates of births to unmarried women, divorce, and remarriage. The need for care for older people has expanded because of increased longevity, and for children because of the high labour force participation of mothers and fathers.

The policies appropriate for this new model of the family differ from those that are appropriate for the old model of the family. It can be summarized in Table 9.

If we compare the new model of the family with contemporary Canadian reality, the match is by no means perfect. Although Canada has repeatedly committed itself to the notion of sex equality (see Eichler, forthcoming), substantial groups of people still believe in and practise sex-role differentiation. Although the majority of wives and mothers are in the labour force, women continue to earn substantially less than men, and a strong minority of wives are housewives. In such instances, not only are the children dependants of the fathers, but wives are dependants of their husbands. There are still

Table 8
THE NEW MODEL OF THE FAMILY

Ideology	Sex equality
Economic responsibility	Husbands and wives (father and mothers) are both earners, equally responsible for their own support and that of the children
Economic dependency	Children are dependants of their mothers and fathers
Household composition	No assumption of congruence between household and family members A wide variety of family types acknowledged and accepted Wives not unquestioningly equated with mothers, nor husbands with fathers
Household management	Shared responsibility between husband and wife Clear distinction between spousal and parental obligation
Personal care	Mothers/fathers, wives/husbands, daughters/sons, daughters-in-law/sons-in-law equally responsible for provision of care for family members in need of care to the degree that this can be combined with full-time paid work

Table 9
POLICIES CONGRUENT WITH THE NEW FAMILY MODEL

Ideology	Sex equality
Economy:	Women and men seen as primary wage earners
labour market policy	All employment programs equally targetted to female and male workers No wage differential by sex Family responsibilities of male and female workers equally recognized and accepted
tax structure	Provides relief to parents
other government transfers	Provide replacement income and replacement care in case of absence or inability of one parent
Household composition	Eligibility for benefits is based on individual entitlement rather than family status. Household and family membership are not equated, unless, in fact, congruent Rights and obligations of non-coresidential parents are enforced
Social services	Wide network of social services for childcare and adults in need of care and/or wage replacement system for people caring full-time for family members

groups that take the nuclear family as a normative model that they would like to impose on all of society (see Eichler, 1985). Although legally the rights and duties of wives and husbands have been equalized, in fact women continue to bear the brunt of the burden.

On what model of the family, then, should our policies be based? during this transitional phase which is likely to continue for a while? As a society, we are moving towards the "new" family and away from the "old" family, but transition periods create problems. The appropriate policy response would be to base policies in principle on the new model of the family, but to recognize that there are substantial minorities of families that consist of adults who are middle-aged or older and who made their choices when the old model prevailed. Transitional policies should therefore not, for instance, assume that wives can be equal economic partners with their husbands if they have been full-time housewives for twenty or more years.

Among the urgent immediate needs would be an improvement of social services. In particular, day care for children is grossly insufficient (Status of Women Canada, 1986) as is the care available for the aged.

EMERGENT CHANGES

In recent years, new reproductive technologies have increasingly captured headlines in the mass media. "Test tube babies," that is, babies conceived through **in vitro fertilization (IVF)** are a reality today. By 1984, there were at least one hundred IVF clinics across the world (Corea, 1985:119). The first publicized case of what has been misleadingly called **surrogate motherhood** (involving a woman who carries a child for another couple for a fee, i.e., a preconception contract for the production and eventual purchase of a child) occurred in 1976 (Keane, 1981). Since then, many more cases have occurred, although it is impossible to state how many, since no agency or organization keeps count of them. In the United States in 1984, at least sixteen companies were selling the reproductive services of women (Raymond, 1986:5).

Nevertheless, taking all cases across the world together, we are still talking about a tiny number of people who are directly affected by either IVF or preconception contracts for the production of a child. Why, then, all the fuss?

Preconception reproductive contracts and IVF techniques have revolutionized parenthood, and unless we pass legislation controlling both, they may change the experience of parenthood for every future parent.

Let us look at IVF first. In vitro fertilization consists in extracting an egg from a woman, fertilizing it with sperm, letting the embryo develop for a certain time, and implanting it in a woman. The first baby generated in this manner, Louise Brown, was born in 1978. The procedure involved a great medical-technical innovation, but as long as the egg and the sperm of a husband-wife couple are used and the pre-embryo is implanted into the woman from whom the egg had been taken, no significant social innovation is involved.

However, it is just as possible to implant the fertilized egg into another woman. The first baby born to a woman who had received a donated egg was born in 1984 (Ontario Law Reform Commission Report, 1985). This means that we now must distinguish between three types of mothers: a genetic mother (the egg donor), a uterine mother (the woman who gives birth to the child), and a social mother (the woman who rears the child).

For men, there has always been a certain

disjunction and uncertainty with respect to fatherhood. Now we have entered a period where the same may become true for mothers. At present, no clear laws regulate the use of genetic materials. This becomes important, for instance, when a woman has a hysterectomy, and this results in what is called "harvesting of an egg." If this egg gets inseminated and implanted in another woman, the first woman may be a genetic mother without being a uterine or social mother. Who owns the egg?

For men, a somewhat parallel situation obtains in the case of **artificial insemination** by donor, in which men donate semen so that a woman can be fertilized. Unless the donor is also the husband of the woman, he will typically have no legal or social obligations toward the resulting child. Again, we have no accurate figures to assess how frequently this procedure is used, but there are certainly many thousands of such inseminations practised in Ontario alone every year (Ontario Law Reform Commission, 1985:18).

There are, however, important differences between semen and egg donation, the most important being that the latter involves a serious and dangerous operation, while the former involves a short, simple and nondangerous action—masturbation into a container (Victoria, 1983). So far, there is no evidence that sperm has ever been collected from an unwilling male, nor is there any hard *documentation* that an egg has been harvested from an unwilling woman. However, the potential for eggs to be collected against a woman's will is great and there are *suggestions* that this may have already been done without the knowledge and consent of the women involved (Corea, 1984).[3]

This new *medical* procedure, together with the new *social* arrangement in which women contract for a fee to carry a child for someone else, takes us to a stage where we are technically capable of using women as fetus carriers for others. For instance, a woman of colour could give birth to someone else's white baby for a fee. The potential for exploitation is tremendous. While Great Britain (Warnock, 1985) and Sweden have come out firmly against surrogate motherhood, several companies arrange such services in the United States (and sell some of them to Canada), and the Ontario Law Reform Commission Report has suggested that "surrogate motherhood" be legalized, so that preconception reproductive contracts would become legally enforceable. The commission has also recommended that if the contractual mother (who is usually also the genetic mother) decides she wants to keep her child, it should be taken from her by force. This is precisely what happened in March 1987 in the famous "Baby M" case, in which a contractual mother lost custody of her child in a bitter legal dispute.[4]

If such a law ever came into force in Canada, we would have legalized baby selling, no matter how the issue is put (American College, 1983). At present, all forms of baby selling are illegal in Canada, and therefore contracts concerning them are unenforceable. If reproductive preconception contracts became enforceable in Canada, we would have socially redefined the meaning of parenthood as a contractual arrangement, in which the financially stronger party has greater rights, rather than as a social-biological arrangement, in which parents have natural rights to their children, which are only lost under extraordinary circumstances.

All parents could further be affected if a minority were to use IVF and other techniques to preselect the sex of their child. In the IVF process, doctors can preselect the sex of the eventual baby. If this, and other forms of sex preselection, became

THE ISSUE OF CONTRACTUAL MOTHERS

We will consider only one more implication of the new reproductive technologies and social arrangements. With preconception contracts for the production of children, contractual mothers are obliged to engage in certain behaviours and avoid others during their pregnancy. (This is proposed in the already quoted Ontario Law Reform Commission Report, 1985, and is documented for at least one U.S. firm which arranges preconception reproductive contracts [cf. Ince, 1984:99–116]). What will happen if a husband — or a third party — sues a woman because she did not follow a doctor's orders during pregnancy? What if the woman does not agree with the prescribed treatment? What if the doctor prescribes bedrest for a woman who needs to work full-time to survive? What recourse would there be against invasive treatment for the benefit of the fetus but to the detriment of the woman? (The use of caesarian sections is a well-established example of this dilemma.)

The issue is burning, since the first case in which a third party sued a woman for taking drugs and failing to follow her doctor's order during her pregnancy is currently before the courts in the United States (*Toronto Star*, 1986). The woman gave birth to a brain-dead child, and was charged with fetal abuse. Even more important, in April 1987, a Canadian judge declared a fetus a "child in need of protection" and made it the ward of a Children's Aid Society. The danger that pregnant women will be compelled to undergo treatment that they do not wish to undergo for the sake of the fetus they carry has thus already been legally sanctioned in at least one precedent-setting Canadian case. While such developments are frightening in their own right, this becomes even more so if one segment of mothers—contractual mothers—are legally forced to follow doctor's orders no matter what their personal wishes are. This may set a legal precedent for other mothers. These issues potentially affect every woman in childbearing age, as well as every potential father.

widespread, involving, let us say, 10 percent of the population, and if it turned out that people preferred boys over girls, at least as first children, as is to be expected according to the relevant literature (e.g., Council for Science and Society, 1984:56, Hamner, 1981, Williams, 1986:22–27), we would all be fundamentally affected. We would end up with a changed sex ratio, different availability of potential spouses, and different characters for males and females, since first-born children tend to be different from later-born children in predictable ways. If a government decides that such consequences would be too undesirable, it may interfere, e.g., by taxing people who have a child of the sex that is an oversupply more heavily than those who have a child of the undersupplied sex. This is suggested as a solution to such a potential problem by two Australian writers (Singer and Wells, 1984:169–71). The result of this would be that such provisions would force all people to choose their children's sex, even if only a minority wishes to do so.

CONCLUSION

This brief overview of trends has shown families are changing. Change is a normal aspect of participating within a family. It is also a normal aspect of societies as a whole. At present, changes at the macro level seem to be going in a similar direction in all industrialized societies.

In particular, women have fewer children, people live longer, and this changes the age composition of entire societies, as well as the kinship structures of individual families.

More children are born to unmarried women, divorce is frequent, and remarriages constitute a significant proportion of all marriages. As a consequence, many people have family members in more than one household. This is particularly true for children and men, less so for women, who are more likely to have custody of their children.

Looking at illegitimacy rates, divorce and remarriage rates as a complex, what can we observe? The overall conclusion we can draw is that there is also an increasing disjunction between marriage and parenthood.

Most wives and mothers are now in the labour force in Canada, but housework and family care are still disproportionately done by women. Family and divorce law have made divorces easier to obtain, and have defined the rights and obligations of wives and husbands equally rather than differently, as was the case until the late 1970s.

Social policies have not kept pace with evolving family structures. Changes are needed here which, however, must recognize that in transitional periods no "pure" policy will do justice to all segments of society.

Finally, medical innovations in reproductive technologies coupled with social innovations in parenting arrangements have brought us to the threshold of a new era in parent-child relations. Unless legislation is passed to control this latter trend, parenting in general, and in particular pregnancies, could become regulated in a so far unimagined manner by the medical profession, the legal profession, and the state.

Notes

[1]Note that the U.N. figures refer only to daughters, while the Canadian figures refer to both daughters and sons. In order to make them comparable, the U.N. figures must be multiplied by two.

[2]Another aspect that is relevant in this context are abortion rates. Abortion rates rose until 1979 and have declined since that time. This suggests that in recent times actual *pregnancy* rates, not just fertility rates, have declined.

[3]There is also the danger of subtly or less subtly coercing women who are involved in IVF programs to "donate" eggs.

[4]This case is currently being appealed.

DISCUSSION QUESTIONS

1. Discuss why the divorce rate is not a sufficient indicator of marriage breakdown.
2. Describe and explain the division of labour between women and men in the family. Speculate on future trends.

3. Identify and describe three current transfer programs (e.g., Unemployment Insurance, Old Age Security, the Guaranteed Income Supplement, Social Assistance, the Family Allowance) and analyze whether they fit the "old" or the "new" model of the family.
4. Consider the different types of mothers now in existence: social, uterine, and genetic. What combinations are possible? Combine this with the various types of fathers in existence. What are possible parental relationships?
5. Describe the family life cycle of a woman who has given birth while unmarried, and subsequently marries a divorced man who had one child with his previous wife.

GLOSSARY

artificial insemination insemination of an egg by means other than sexual intercourse

convergence theory theory that purports that something is moving from different positions towards some common point

divorce rate the proportion of marriages ending in divorce

fertility rate the average number of children born to a woman during her lifetime

gross reproduction rate the average number of daughters born per woman

in vitro fertilization (IVF) (literally: in glass fertilization) The fertilization of a human egg by semen outside the body in a glass dish and subsequent implantation of the embryo in a woman

life expectancy the average number of years a woman or man can expect to live

remarriage rate the proportion of marriages involving a previously married bride or groom

surrogate mother descriptively inaccurate term used to describe a woman who contracts, for a fee, to be artificially inseminated, to bear a child, and to hand it over to the contracting party. A more accurate term would be "contractual mother."

BIBLIOGRAPHY

Ambert, Anne-Marie
1980 *Divorce in Canada*. Don Mills: Academic Press.

American College of Obstetricians and Gynecologists
1983 *Ethical Issues in Surrogate Motherhood*. ACOG Statement of Policy.

Bohannan, Paul
1971 "Divorce Chains, Households of Remarriage, and Multiple Divorces." In Paul Bohannan (ed.) *Divorce and After*. New York: Doubleday.

Corea, Gena.
1985 *The Mother Machine. Reproductive Technologies from Artificial*

Insemination to Artificial Wombs. New York: Harper and Row.

Corea, Genoveffa
1984 "Egg snatchers." In Rita Arditti, Renate Duelli Klein, and Shelley Minden (eds.) *Test-Tube Women: What Future for Motherhood?* London: Pandora Press.

Council for Science and Society
1984 *Human Procreation. Ethical Aspects of the New Techniques*. Report of a Working Party. New York: Oxford University Press.

Duvall, Evelyn Millis and Brent C. Miller
1985 *Marriage and Family Development*, 6th ed. New York: Harper and Row.

Eichler, Margrit
1983 *Families in Canada Today. Recent Changes and their Policy Consequences*. Toronto: Gage.

——
1984 "The familism-individualism flip-flop and its implications for economic and social welfare policies." In Australian Institute of Family Studies, International Sociological Association, and Committee on Family Research (eds.) *Social Change and Family Policies*. Twentieth international CFR seminar. Melbourne: Australian Institute of Family Studies.

——
1985 "Family Policy in Canada: From Where to Where?" In Rosalie S. Abella and Melvin L. Rothman (eds.) *Justice beyond Orwell*. Canadian Institute for the Administration of Justice. Montreal: Les éditions Yvon Blais.

——
1985 *The Pro-Family Movement: Are They For or Against Families?* Feminist Perspectives, # 4a. Ottawa: Canadian Institute for the Advancement of Women.

——
forthcoming "Social Policy Concerning Women." In Shankar Yelaja (ed.) *Canadian Social Policy*, 2nd ed.

Furstenberg, Frank F. and Graham B. Spanier
1984 *Recycling the Family*. Beverly Hills, California: Sage.

Gross, Penny
1985 *Kinship Structures in Remarriage Families*. Unpublished Ph.D. thesis, University of Toronto, Department of Sociology.

Hamner, Jalna
1981 "Sex predetermination, artificial insemination and the maintenance of male-dominated culture." In Helen Roberts (ed.) *Women, Health and Reproduction*. London: Routledge and Kegan Paul.

Harvey, Andrew S.
1983 *Time and Time Again: Explorations in Time Use*, Vol. 4. Employment and Immigration Canada: 22–26, t. 7,8,11, and 12.

Hill, Reuben and Roy H. Rodgers
1964 "The Developmental Approach." In Harold J. Christensen (ed.) *Handbook of Marriage and the Family*. Chicago: Rand McNally.

Ince, Susan
1984 "Inside the surrogate industry." In Rita Arditti, Renate Duelli Klein, and Shelley Minden (eds.) *Test-Tube Women: What Future for Motherhood?* London: Pandora Press.

Inkeles, Alex
1981 "Convergence and divergence in industrial societies." In Mustafa O. Attir, Burkhart Holzner, and Zdenek Suda (eds.) *Directions of Change: Modernization Theory, Research and Realities*. Boulder, Colorado: Westview Press.

Kamerman, Sheila B. and Alfred J. Kahn (eds.)
1978 *Family Policy: Government and Families in Fourteen Countries*. New York: Columbia University Press.

Keane, Noel with Dennis L. Breo
1981 *The Surrogate Mother*. New York: Everest House.

LaRossa, Ralph and Maureen Mulligan LaRossa
1981 *Transition to Parenthood: How Infants Change Families*. Vol. 119 of the Sage Library of Social Research. Beverly Hills: Sage Publications.

McGoldrick, Monica and Elizabeth A. Carter
1982 "The Family Life Cycle." In Froma Walsh (ed.) *Normal Family Processes.* New York: The Guilford Press.

McKie, D. C., B. Prentice, and P. Reed
1983 *Divorce: Law and the Family in Canada.* Ottawa: Statistics Canada, Cat. 89–502E.

McLeod, P. B. and J. R. Ellis
1983 "Alternative Approaches to the Family Life Cycle in the Analysis of Housing Consumption." *Journal of Marriage and the Family.* 45, # 3: 699–708.

McVey, Wayne W., Jr. and Barrie W. Robinson
1981 "Separation in Canada: New Insights Concerning Marital Dissolution." *Canadian Journal of Sociology* 6, # 3; 353–66.

Meissner, Martin et al.
1975 "No Exit for Wives: Sexual Division of Labour." *Canadian Review of Sociology and Anthropology* 12, 4: 424–39.

Murphy, Patrick E. and William A. Staples
1979 "A Modernized Family Life Cycle." *Journal of Consumer Research* 6, 1: 12–22.

Norton, Arthur J.
1980 "The Influence of Divorce on Traditional Life-Cycle Measures." *Journal of Marriage and the Family*: 63–69.

——
1983 "Family Life Cycle: 1980." *Journal of Marriage and the Family.* 45, # 2: 267–75.

Ontario Law Reform Commission
1985 *Report on Human Artificial Reproduction and Related Matters.* 2 vols. Toronto: Ministry of the Attorney General.

Ostry, Sylvia
1968 *The Female Worker in Canada.* One of a Series of Labour Force Studies in the 1961 Census Monograph Program. Ottawa: Dominion Bureau of Statistics.

Pike, R.
1975 "Legal Access and the Incidence of Divorce in Canada: A Socio-historical Analysis." *Canadian Review of Sociology and Anthropology* 12, 2: 115–33.

Raymond, Janice
1986 "Man-made reproduction." In *Choices* 6: 4–5, 7, 13, 17.

Rodgers, Roy H. and Gail Witney
1981 "The Family Cycle in Twentieth Century Canada." *Journal of Marriage and the Family* 43, # 3: 727–40.

Singer, Peter and Deane Wells
1984 *The Reproduction Revolution: New Ways of Making Babies.* Oxford: Oxford University Press.

Statistics Canada
1979 *Population Projections for Canada and the Provinces, 1976–2001.* Ottawa: Statistics Canada.

——
1986a *Family Characteristics and Labour Force Activity: Annual Averages, 1977–1984.* Cat. 71–533. Ottawa: Minister of Supply and Services.

——
1986b *Births and Deaths. Vital Statistics Vol. I. 1984.* Cat. 84–204. Ottawa: Minister of Supply and Services.

——
1986c *Marriages and Divorces. Vital Statistics Vol. II. 1985.* Cat. 84–205. Ottawa: Minister of Supply and Services.

Status of Women Canada
1986 *Report of the Task Force on Child Care.* Ottawa: Minister of Supply and Services.

Toronto Star
1986 "Mother charged with fetal abuse after drugs found in brain-dead son." Oct. 2: A3.

United Nations
1985 *World Population Prospects: Estimates and Projections as Assessed in 1982.* Population Studies # 86. New York, Dept. of International Economic and Social Affairs.

Victoria Committee to Consider the Social, Ethical and Legal Issues Arising from In Vitro Fertilization.
1983 *Report on donor gametes in IVF.* August.

Warnock, Mary
1985 *A Question of Life: The Warnock Report on Human Fertilisation and Embryology*. Oxford: Basil Blackwell.

Weitzman, Lenore J.
1985 *The Divorce Revolution: The Unexpected Social and Economic Consequences for Women and Children in America*. New York: Free Press.

Williams, Linda S.
1986 *But What Will They Mean for Women? Feminist Concerns About the New Reproductive Technologies*. Feminist perspectives # 6. Ottawa: Canadian Research Institute for the Advancement of Women.

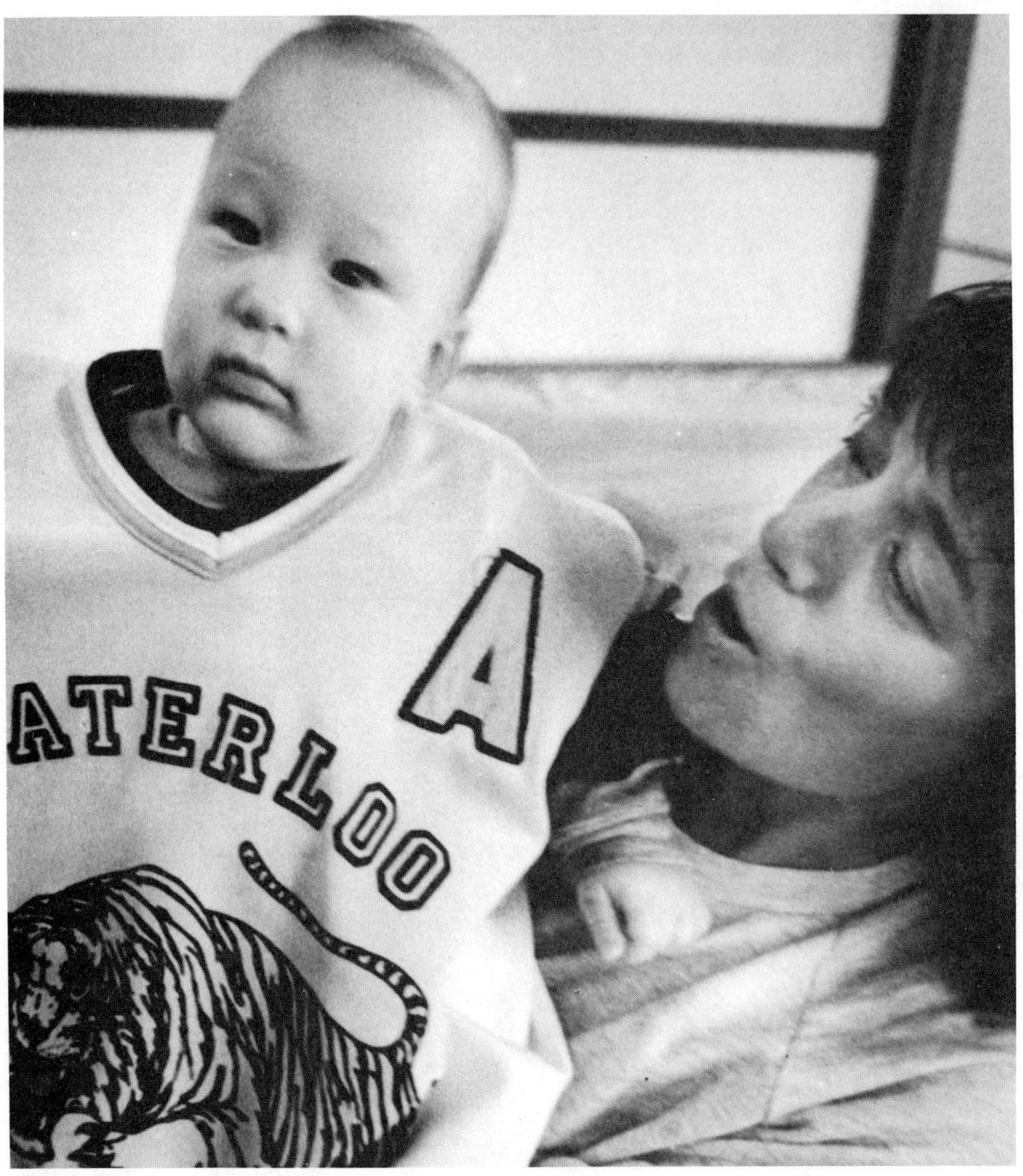

For this nine-month-old boy, socialization to an identity is already well underway.

> *"The selves people develop, their identities, their self-images, emerge over time as individuals encounter socially structured activities."*

c h a p t e r   f o u r t e e n

Socialization, Subcultures, and Identity

Nancy Mandell

INTRODUCTION

What differentiates a Canadian from an American? Is there a "typical" Canadian? Or is Canadian identity elusive? This chapter articulates a model of socialization that captures the emergence of Canadian identity. We explore how institutional practices, cultural values, and everyday relationships shape Canadian culture. In particular, we explore how Canadian identity has been shaped historically and is currently constructed by socialization processes which differ by culture, region, ethnicity, class, gender, and age.

IMAGES OF SOCIALIZATION

Socialization refers both to the ways an individual comes to act in accordance with society's rules and the ways an individual interacts with others through gestures, reflection, and interpersonal communication.

Many socialization studies focus on the *macro order*, the structural organization of a society. Analysis centres on how individuals learn norms, values, language, skills, patterns of belief, and thought essential for social living. These social elements are seen as emanating from institutions, large-scale organizations, and powerful and controlling adults. Researchers emphasize the structural situations in which socialization takes place. As agencies of socialization, institutions inculcate their rules, goals, and patterns of behaviour. Success is measured by the degree to which individuals conform.

Institutions, cultures, and societies have no independent existence, however. It is people who live, act, and change society (Garfinkel, 1967 as quoted in Robertson, 1976:119). Although social institutions influence social interaction, they are themselves the product of that interaction. It is the *micro order*, the intricate web of minute, day-to-day activities, that make up the ongoing life of society. Cumulatively, these often unnoticed and habitual events constitute socialization (Robertson, 1976: 119).

Conceptualizing socialization as the effects of institutions neglects the agency of individuals. Viewing socialization as the sum of individual actions ignores the power of structured collectivities. Yet, sociological studies tend to emphasize either institutional constraints or individual interpretations. A brief review of the parameters of each approach will familiarize the reader with the ongoing socialization debate.

Clay Moulding: The Structural Approach

Structuralists see socialization as the process by which individuals learn how to behave in a group or society. They emphasize how individuals take on behaviour that permits them to succeed in the **culture** (Zigler et al., 1982). This is not as easy as it seems, since each society has many formal and informal rules. Also, cultural rules are not applied equally to everyone. Rules vary with one's status, gender, race, and religion. For example, Canadians are likely to share beliefs in democracy, freedom, and equality of rights, but they disagree on how to actualize these.

To structuralists, socialization is the process through which the culture's rules are learned. Relevant sociocultural information is seen as emanating from institutions and is directed toward seemingly receptive individuals. The family, the educational system, the state, and the churches inculcate normatively appropriate behaviours into malleable social receptacles. Institutional agents of socialization thus ensure that Canadians, especially young ones, are subjected to and internalize similar customs, values, and beliefs. According to this model, a successful society transmits sociocultural beliefs from one generation to the next in an orderly fashion.

In this approach, social structure determines behaviour. Individuals are like blobs of clay easily moulded by social forces emanating from constraining institutions. Canadians are said, for example, to primarily endorse liberal political ideologies as a result of their almost continual exposure to liberal federal government. This "top down" image paints Canadians as empty vessels passively waiting to be filled with whatever economic, social, or political beliefs that ruling elites deem significant. Specifying these "rulers" is a requirement of structuralist socialization theories. For functionalists, following Claude Lévi-Strauss and Talcott Parsons, socialization answers the question "How is society possible?" The answer offered is that children acquire language, internalize culture, and learn social rules from powerful adults. Conflict theorists see ruling elites as the most influential socialization agents. A small elite owns the means of economic production, controls Canadian media and advertising, dictates educational and health policy, and frames family law. As John Porter revealed in *The Vertical Mosaic* (1965), the Canadian economic elite who hold interlocking directorships form a closed and powerful social group. Canadian socialization was seen as infiltrated on all levels by this pervasive economic dominance.

Whether functionalist or conflict-oriented, the theories tend to refer children's present lives to their presumed adult futures (Thorne, 1987). They also assume a division between the supposedly completed nature of the adult and the incomplete child (Jenck, 1982). As a result, structuralists have concentrated on childhood socialization. To a structuralist, childhood relentlessly unwinds from within, inevitably creating a competent adult. Society shapes this development according to prevailing images of children. Children have been portrayed as animal-like, primitive, evil forces whose irrational drives must be controlled by adults. The Canadian state acts as a benevolent patriarch, determining acceptable behaviour.

Alternatively, children are conceptualized as flower-like, sweet, innocent beings who must be carefully nurtured and protected in order to flourish. In Canadian society, women have traditionally been assigned the task of caring for small children.

In both cases, the evil and the innocent, the root image is of inevitable biological-psychological maturation. This image suggests children possess a universal human essence. Individual variation exists only within finite, organic limits. Further, maturation implies a natural, universal, and inevitable sequence of physical and cognitive development. Upon this biological bedrock, determinists superimpose cultural variation to explain group differences.

Since the clay moulding view of socialization specifies the end product of socialization, the moulding process must also be described. This is particularly evident in the educational system's definition of children. Canadian education assumes children, are, in every way, inferior to adults. Pedagogues measure children's psychological and social incompetencies and identify corrective cognitive-biological skills. Elaborate descriptions of cognitive and social stages of development are then concretely linked to adult standards of achievement and institutionalized through their inclusion in the school curriculum. Normatively appropriate definitions and measures of children's behaviour are diffused to the general population through child care manuals, doctors' admonitions, daycare workers, and school teachers. With little solicitation, Canadian women acquire a cultural definition of proper child rearing. The message from a variety of socialization sources is consistent: follow the expert's advice and successful children will emerge.

Within Canada, the prevailing ideology suggests women, men, and children have equal access to successful socialization techniques, and thus are individually responsible for their own failures and successes.

Structuralists then emphasize the macro order, the movement of organizations, institutional interrelationships, and their eventual impact upon their participants. Power, control, and dominance of socialization contexts are seen as keys to controlling the socialization message and its indoctrination.

Negotiated Order: The Interactionist Approach

Interactionists study how people create social situations. Investigation usually begins with what people are actually doing. The most basic social units of analysis are collective acts. *Collective activities* are social acts in which two or more people merge their lines of action with reference to each other and social objects. Unlike structuralist accounts of socialization, interactionists emphasize the role of individuals in continually creating their own identities. Norms and values are not reified as independent social universals which constrain behaviour. Rather, existing rules of conduct are viewed as negotiable and flexible.

Socialization is viewed as a negotiated reality, created within a socially bounded context. Within Canada, for example, different cultures place different socialization requirements on parents and children. Goals, expectations, and role definitions vary by social groups. Socialization becomes a lifelong process of learning various group expectations so that one knows how, with whom, about what, and when to negotiate.

Interactionists usually link structure and process through the concept of **negotiated order** and remind us that recurring networks of collective activity constitute *social organization* (Becker, 1982). Thus, social organization is a metaphor. As in a photograph, we often freeze and stop the flow of action (Hall, 1987). Social organizations are active, ongoing negotiated orders. Organization life is characterized by change and the development of a social order in which participants work out agreements and tacit understandings in response to everyday contingencies (Hall, 1987).

In his classic study of a hospital, Anselm Strauss et al. (1963) outlined the negotiated order approach, noting that all social order is negotiated, that specific negotiations are contingent on the structural conditions of the organization, that negotiations are patterned and yet reconstituted over time, and that the organization's structure and the micropolitics of the negotiated order are closely linked. Negotiated order reminds us that social structure is a relationship among members, produced and created by groups of people, and representative of its members' needs and desires.

Interactionists also ask how socialization is modified, constrained, and altered by culture, ideology, and biology. For example, the biological input in socialization has been debated endlessly in studies of gender and child development. Theorists assign some role to physical maturation in the development of social cognition. But our biology does not possess intrinsic meanings. Canadians have long assumed, erroneously, that male–female anatomical differences explain and justify gender role behaviour.

THE QUESTION OF NATIONAL IDENTITY

All socialization studies are fundamentally preoccupied with the question of identity formation on an individual and collective level.

On an individual level, sociologists investigate how individuals, in their daily encounters, take on the practices and mannerisms of their culture, including language, social cognitive skills, dress, and etiquette. **Identity** is defined as a perspective on oneself and others, formed and reinforced by daily interactions with others (Haas and Shaffir, 1978). The selves people develop, their identities, their self-images, their self-esteem emerge over time as individuals encounter socially structured activities (Hewitt and Hewitt, 1986).

On a collective level, sociologists investigate how socialization imports culture into the person. How does an individual take on a collective identity as a Canadian? While individuals are not passively indoctrinated by cultural messages, people's reactions are limited by the culture in which they live. Individuals create culture, but are born into an ongoing society with established traditions, goals, and ways of behaving. Ironically, the emergence of individual identity opens the door for social control. Our capacity to become objects to ourselves (Mead, 1938) to respond to and interpret cultural messages makes individuals unique, autonomous agents.

Becker, Geer et al. (1961) introduced the term **perspective** to capture the dialectic between self and social control, between individual and collective identity. *Perspectives* refer to " . . . a co-ordinated set of ideas and actions a person uses in dealing with some problematic situation, to refer to a person's ordinary way of thinking and feeling about and acting in such a situation." Through engagement with others, people construct and rebuild group meanings, which over time coalesce into ways of seeing and believing. Perspectives, like identities, can be fragile, temporal, negotiated, and constrained by those we encounter. Yet, recognizable group perspectives emerge from co-operative activities, in which people forge collective identities. Once we internalize the group perspective, it guides our future behaviour.

Our collective identity is represented in the arts, letters and popular culture, which provide "representative images" (Porter, 1967:48–56) and in our language, daily rituals, and in historical customs. A *national identity* is the collective identity of all participants in that society (Hiller, 1976:156). According to Hiller, a national identity is obtained when members of a society evolve a collective awareness of their unity and of the differentiation of the in-group from the out-group.

In the sixties and seventies, Canadian academics often lamented Canada's weak national identity (Hiller, 1976; Marsden and Harvey, 1979). Canada was portrayed as a country still searching for a national identity; as an identifiable political state containing two nations, French and English and many more regional and ethnic societies (Marsden and Harvey, 1979); and as almost culturally indistinguishable from America (Ogmundson, 1980). Canadian identity existed, but appeared diffuse, pluralistic, and closely tied to American culture.

As John Porter remarked in 1967: "To be a Canadian is not likely to evoke a set of feelings or images about belonging to a particular group with a clear beginning, a set of charter values, a history, and an imagined destiny" (1967:47). Canada's historical reliance on first Britain and then the United States was thought to weaken our sense of national identity. Marsden and Harvey (1979) have most clearly enunciated this dependency theory. Following the work of Porter (1965), Clement (1975), and Bell and Tepperman (1979), they argue that as a semi-peripheral country, all our major institutions are permeated by the influence and values of the core society, the United States. Some scholars have investigated the consequences of American economic domination for our country's economic decisions. Others have analyzed American penetration of our technology, media, education system, sports and games, and our tastes and values. In almost every aspect of our cultural life, the American presence permeates our thinking and influences the changes we are willing to make. Ogmundson (1980) maintains American penetration is so pervasive that Canada is no longer a separate social entity (cf. Carroll, 1985).

Dependency theorists conclude Canadian national identity is at best confused (Fry, 1979). Our uncertainty stems from our confusing past, hazardous future, our constantly oscillating population, our ethnic heterogeneity, and our relatively sparse population spread out over the third largest land mass in the world. No event marks the formation of a Canadian identity. Only within the last twenty years have we developed our unique flag, anthem, and Charter of Rights. Moreover, Canadian children are still not routinely exposed to educational and state socialization intended to inculcate national pride.

The dependence thesis has been criticized by Carroll (see Carroll, 1985 and his chapter in this volume), who has corrected some excessive estimation of Canada's economic subordination to the United States, and demonstrated Canada's involvement in multinational capitalism. His alternative theory does not, however, deny Canada's continued dependence on the American economy and American strength to counter Soviet pressures. Nor does he dismiss the cultural influence from the United States that continues to complicate the articulation of a distinctive Canadian identity.

CULTURE AND IDENTITY

Culture refers to the accumulated knowledge, experience, rules, values, and shared symbols and their meanings prevailing in any society or parts of society. **Cultural identities** include "designs for living" — distinctive ways of thinking, feeling, and acting. This includes shared norms about desirable behaviour and similar ideas about how social life should proceed. Cultural ideologies are emotionally charged sets of descriptive and normative beliefs and values that explain and justify how social institutions are or should be organized. Culture thus mirrors the economic, social, and political organization of social life. Culture also frames behaviour. It provides cultural meanings within which people interpret their experiences. Culture consists then of two parts: symbolic norms, rules of conduct, and values that guide behaviour; and a material and instrumental order of practical ideas about society that enable people to adapt to and manage their environment (Hewitt and Hewitt, 1986).

Canadian culture entails both the material and instrumental institutions of culture, as well as participation in the symbolic order (Breton, 1986). Groups and organizations with a specific interest, often economic, in the creation and conservation of culture form the cultural infrastructure. According to Breton (1986:27–66), the material order refers to institutional pursuit of interests through information, rules, procedures, technology, budgets, and networks of contacts. Institutions distribute economic opportunities and social role possibilities unequally according to language, ethnicity, age, and so on.

The symbolic element of culture is embedded in public institutions that create and disseminate culture. Symbolically, the media distributes culture through films, magazines, television programs, and books. Canadian culture is reflected in our national symbols and rituals, such as our flag, national anthem, national holidays, expositions, dedications, Royal Commissions, political documents, and in institutional positions symbolic of authority, such as the monarchy and the Governor-General.

All culture is an abstraction. Canadian culture is inferred from the behaviour of Canadians. Through material and symbolic participation in institutions and daily activities, culture is imported into people. Thus, identity is linked to culture. In turn, people expect a certain degree of consistency between their private identities and the symbolic contents upheld by public authorities (Breton, 1986).

While continually changing, Canadian culture has distinctive elements forged from its historical and socioeconomic patterns. Canadian cultural identity is multicultural, collectivist, and regionalist. Past discussions of Canadian identity have focused on the social and cultural cleavages — regional, ethnic, linguistic, status, religious — that impede the emergence of a distinct national identity. More recent writings (Breton, 1986; Blishen, 1986) concentrate on the historic development of a collective identity in spite of these divisions. Since World War II, cultural diversity has distinguished Canada. State

ARE CANADIANS LESS VIOLENT THAN AMERICANS?

Why is the incidence and severity of public violence relatively low in Canada? Why has the Canadian pattern of public violence differed from that of the United States?

Several factors explain this:

1. The Canadian national identity encompasses the shunning of violent protest. Canadian governments have been less tolerant of public disorder than American ones. Canada has emphasized "peace, order, and good government," upheld British traditions that distinguish proper and improper political conduct, and restricted the use of guns.
2. The Canadian middle-class myth of the peaceable kingdom arises from our lack of a revolutionary tradition. The myth restrains Canadians from violence. As well, the use of violence by Canadian governments has been careful, controlled, and legalistic in the sense of limited amounts and close legal regulations hedging the police and the military.
3. Canadians abhor the American practice of filling police and judicial posts on the basis of electoral popularity, evidence of brutality and indiscipline among American public and semi-private security forces. Canadians treat civil disturbance as a lower-class phenomenon of little significance.
4. Other explanations for Canadian peacefulness include resources available to the government as opposed to challenging groups; the political culture which supports an interventionist government stepping in to regulate conflicts; the relative peaceful nature, historically, of French–English relations; and low levels of citizen discontent, by international standards.

Violence seems to have been higher than usual in the 1880s, around the turn of the century, after World War I, during the Depression, and in the 1960s. Quebec and British Columbia have been most violent. The most affected industries have been primary resources, transport and communications, textiles and clothing.

Source: Adapted with the permission of the publisher from Judy M. Torrance, *Public Violence in Canada, 1867–1982*, McGill-Queen's University Press, Kingston and Montreal, 1986.

recognition of and support for multiculturalism has persisted through successive waves of immigration. Canadians have been encouraged to maintain their ethnic ties through our doctrine of cultural pluralism. On an individual and group level, ethnic loyalties are reinforced by our familial, religious, and linguistic allegiances. Being a White society is profoundly embedded in the Canadian collective identity, but the increase in non-White Canadians and their political articulation of grievances challenges this traditional identity (Breton, 1986). Institutions contribute to the development of a national identity by creating national symbols and institutions to disseminate Canadian culture. Examples include the C.B.C., the National Film Board, the National Gallery, the Public Archives, the National Museums. These institutions helped Canadians to feel Canadian and helped them embrace a policy of cultural pluralism.

Collectivism, in the form of state intervention, has been an essential part of Canadian identity. For example, Canadian governments from Macdonald's to Mulroney's have tried to legislate equality. Recent examples include parliamentary investigations into visible minorities, women, Native peoples, the disabled, and the handicapped.

Both multicultural and collectivist identities are, in part, reactions to the international dissemination of American popular culture. Technological innovations and multinational corporations have contributed to the cross-cultural diffusion of Western ideas. Canada has been barraged with American media, but has maintained a nonrevolutionary, collectivist response to change, a nonviolent regulation of its citizens, an elitist, but sensitive, response to minority claims, and a multicultural emphasis within a bilingual frame. Canadians are increasingly proud of their distinctive identity. As such, we feel less urgency to differentiate ourselves from Americans.

CANADA'S SUBCULTURES

Canadian culture shows tremendous variation in the acceptance of certain practices. Socialization of children, treatment of the elderly, voting patterns, employment attitudes, and religious practices vary by **subcultures**. Subcultures represent particular configurations of attitudes and behaviour. Ethnic, gender, age, class, regional, and religious subcultures are particularly distinct in Canada. The rest of this chapter will focus on some of these identity groups.

Ethnicity and Identity

Historically, immigration has expanded to meet the needs of the Canadian labour

---

EQUALITY NOW!

The committee made eighty recommendations on issues of social integration, employment, public policy, justice, media, and education, suggesting how visible minorities can be fully integrated into Canadian society. Most notable are suggestions for the establishment of a Ministry of Multiculturalism; public funding for race relations, intercultural training, public education, and immigrant women programs; make subsidies and tax incentive programs available for the hiring and training of visible minorities; increase the participation of visible minorities on federal boards, commissions, senior management of the Public Service and Crown corporations; review the Lord's Day Act to ensure that any religious observance legislation is consistent with Canada's multi-religious character; increase participation in the R.C.M.P. and other police forces; charge the C.B.C. to contribute to the development of national unity by promoting harmonious relations among ethnic and racial groups; eliminate racist reporting and advertising; establish race relations boards within the school boards; develop resource materials and teaching kits for facilitating more positive attitudes toward visible minorities; introduce affirmative action programs to increase the number of visible minorities in teaching and administrative positions.

Source: Report of the Special Committee on Visible Minorities in Canadian Society March 1984.

market and to open up and settle our vast territories. Traditionally, the majority of immigrants to Canada were from the United States and Northern Europe, especially Great Britain (Statistics Canada 1985). In 1968, Great Britain, Italy, and the United States together supplied 40 percent of Canada's immigrants. In 1977, immigration was more diverse, with 35 percent Europeans, 11 percent Americans, and 56 percent from other countries, especially Asian ones (Statistics Canada 1985). Immigration will likely continue to increase. Statistics Canada (1984) estimates our low fertility, currently at subreplacement levels (1.7 births per woman), and the consequent aging and slowdown of growth in the Canadian population will necessitate large-scale immigration in the future.

The considerable immigration between World War II and 1980 altered the ethnic diversity of the country. This new, largely non-White, working-class, urbanized group has been accommodated within the country's multicultural and collectivist traditions. The 1969 Official Languages Act followed the Royal Commission on Bilingualism and Biculturalism, which recommended how Canada could modify its public institutions — courts, schools, government offices — to better reflect the bicultural and bilingual character of Canada. Repatriation of the constitution in 1984 and its provision of a Charter of Rights guaranteed the rights of Native Indians, women, disabled, and visible minorities among others. The 1984 Special Committee of Parliament on Visible Minorities in Canadian Society constitutes another symbolic phenomenon. This committee was committed to removing discrimination in employment, in relations with the police, and with regard to educational opportunities (see box on page 402 for further discussion).

Discussion of ethnic identities has now shifted away from ethnic salience to race relations, reflecting the changing character of Canadian society. Future immigration will increase the demands ethnic groups make on public and private institutions.

ETHNIC INFLUENCES ON THE CHILD'S DEVELOPMENT OF AN IDENTITY

English-Canadian and French-Canadian parents are not all that distinctive in their approaches to child rearing. They actually end up being pretty much North American and not nearly so "English" Canadian or "French" Canadian as those ethnic suffixes imply. In fact, our results indicate that English-Canadian and French-Canadian parents of the same social class background are more similar in their child rearing values than either group is with same-ethnic parents of a different social class. Furthermore, it appears that English-Canadian and French-Canadian parents of a particular social class background are, in terms of these values, more like American, Greek, Portuguese, Italian, or Belgian parents of the same social class background. Thus, we come full circle here, and now begin to seriously wonder how much "distinctiveness" is real and how much is imaginary with adults who, in large measure, get the own-group-other-group contrasts started in the first place.

Source: From "Social Influences on the Child's Development" by Wallace Lambert. In *A Canadian Social Psychology of Ethnic Relations*, edited by Robert C. Gardner and Rudolf Kalin. Toronto: Methuen, 1981, pp. 73–74. Reproduced by permission.

Region and Identity

Recent debate has focused on how regions are defined, how regional identities are measured, to what extent class and ethnicity mediate regionalism, and the degree to which regionalism accounts for Canadian attitudes and values. Consequently, regional identity has been conceptualized as both a structural and a social psychological measure of one's sense of identification with, commitment to, and satisfaction with region as a place to live. Building on this concept, Matthews and Davis (1986:89–121) suggest that region of residence explains as much as or more variance than class, status, and ethnicity in factors having to do with government activities and federal-provincial relations.

From a structural perspective, regions are distinct geographical communities with peculiar economic, social, and cultural elements. Canada is generally seen as consisting of five regions, including the Maritimes, Quebec, Ontario, the Prairie provinces, and British Columbia. Regional economic disparities are clear-cut. Unemployment is highest in the Atlantic provinces. The per capita income is 59 percent to 68 percent that of Ontario. Employment is higher in the Prairie provinces, even though their per capita income lags 65 percent to 86 percent behind Ontario's. Presumably, one's Canadian identity will be shaped differently depending on whether one grows up in a French-speaking village in Quebec, a Newfoundland outport settlement, or on a rural Saskatchewan farm.

Brym (1986) has summarized the differences in mainstream and radical explanations for these regional differences. The mainstream approach, as exemplified by the report of the Task Force on Canadian Unity, defines underdevelopment as a set of gaps in material well-being between one region and another as measured by per capita income. It lists the following causes of disparities: geographical barriers which separate regions; historically tenuous connections between regions, uneven economic development resulting from regional differences in natural resources, and proximity to major markets; the ethnic distinctiveness of region; the federal system of government which divides rights and responsibilities between central and provincial governments; regional variation in political behaviour and culture.

Marxists define underdevelopment differently. Underdevelopment is conceptualized as an exploitative, unequal exchange between a wealthy metropolis and an impoverished hinterland. Trade, capital investment, and personnel are disproportionately siphoned off the hinterland to bolster capitalist expansion in the metropolis. For example, central Ontario businesses invest capital in the Atlantic region and transfer profits back to the metropolis. Over time, more profit is realized than capital invested in the area. To redress this imbalance and yet encourage private development, the state subsidizes dependent regions with transfer payments, economic development programs, and employment plans.

To what extent are regional allegiances central in the formation of Canadian identities? Few Canadian studies have addressed this question. Regions have been viewed as reflecting economic and class factors without significant political or ideological elements (Ornstein, 1986). As Ornstein points out, French–English ideological differences are greater than the internal cleavages within English Canada. Ornstein found relatively weak provincial differences on political and ideological issues. In general, Western Canadians, despite the presence of social democratic parties, are more conservative than Atlantic Canadians.

Considerable research has focused on the nature of Quebec's sense of identity.

According to Symons (1975), Quebec has all the attributes of a nation: "a territory, a language, a culture, institutions, a history, and most of all a collective will to live and a goal." Blishen (1978) asked random samples of Canadians whether they identify with their country or province first. The French in Quebec and the non-French in the Maritimes identify with their province first and country second. A high proportion of anglophones outside Quebec identify themselves as Canadians first, except in the Maritimes.

In a large probability sample, Atkinson and Murray (1980) demonstrate that Canadians have more similarities than regional differences. Compared with Americans, Canadians consider financial concerns to be just as important. In the United States, financial situation, work, leisure and love/marriage exert similar levels of influence over individual behaviour. In Canada, love and marriage are valued more than financial concerns. This trend reflects Canadians' collectivist orientations, meaning Canadians value social relationships more than Americans do. Americans value work experiences more than Canadians do, showing a greater value on achievement. The status and the sense of accomplishment derived from work are key to Americans. Atkinson and Murray (1980) conclude that the greater value of social relationships in Canada and of achievement in the United States reflect long-standing societal differences which will persist.

Gender and Identity

Men and women, on the basis of biological differences, take on and are subjected to profoundly different experiences throughout the life cycle. Thus, sex, a biological fact, becomes gender, a social phenomenon. Differential treatment of men and women constitutes **gender role socialization**, which includes all the processes whereby people learn to become masculine or feminine. *Gender roles or scripts*, masculine and feminine emotions, values, beliefs, and behaviours, are cultural and social constructions. They are well-defined dichotomous identities, which socialization agents, including families, peers, schools, occupational groups, and popular culture, intentionally and unintentionally thrust on people. Our self and other identities are so thoroughly genderized that most people could not act toward others without knowing their sex.

Gender stereotypes are the basis for gender roles or scripts. According to Marlene Mackie (1983:31), a *stereotype* refers to those folk beliefs about the attributes characterizing a social category on which there is substantial agreement. Gender stereotypes capture Canadian beliefs about natural differences between men and women and about how, as a result of these differences, male–female behaviour ought to differ. A substantial American literature and a growing number of Canadian studies document the existence of gender stereotypes in every socialization context. In identity formation, interest focuses on the consequences of these gender scripts for individual and collective behaviour. Mackie (1983:35) assumes stereotypes affect individuals in two ways. First, other people who subscribe to the stereotype may use it to guide their perception and treatment of an individual. Parents encourage sons to be aggressive and daughters to be docile. Secondly, an individual's self-image and behaviour may reflect stereotypical content. Women may consider themselves too irrational to understand maths and sciences. Men may feel too rational to clean toilets or change babies' diapers.

How Canadians meet their sexual needs, how they reproduce, how they inculcate social norms in new generations, how they learn gender, how it feels to be a man or

WHY BLAME MOM?

Think of any movie, book, play, or TV show in which a character—male or female—picks up the ringing phone and says "Hello, Mother."

With those two words, the audience is automatically primed and ready to laugh, says Chicago writer, teacher, and feminist Judith Arcana.

"By definition the mother is a joke," she told a standing-room-only crowd of more than 300 Thursday at the University of Toronto's Victoria College. She spoke at a conference called Don't Blame Mother, presented by the group Women & Therapy for therapists and health care professionals.

"Mothers are fools, clowns, or villains who push sons into homosexuality, daughters into dreadful marriages, and husbands into heart attacks."

Mother-blaming, she said, is a social-cultural phenomenon promoted by and within a culture ruled by men who have their own fantasies, needs and notions of what a mother should be.

"Children learn to devalue and even despise mother according to society's values," said Arcana, "and mothers learn to expect this devaluation."

Society's expectations of motherhood have been shaped by fathers, male pediatricians, male gynecologists, advertising copywriters, and others, "people who cannot know (the experience). And it is tainted with women hating," she said.

"The male fantasy is that a mother should love her children endlessly and uncritically. Because this is humanly impossible, every mother fails and therefore every mother can be blamed," she said.

Mothers are accountable for their children's actions and orientations, even after they are grown and long gone from the family nest, she added.

The police hunting the Boston strangler were looking for a man their psychologists had told them must hate his mother. They bypassed Albert Di Salvo, the strangler, because he, was genuinely attached to his mother and known to hate his father, an alcoholic, abusive man, "obviously the source of his son's behavior," Arcana comments.

Many mothers, though, accept the blame, because Arcana said, all mothers are caught in a bind.

"The bind is if we put our children's needs first, if we are martyrs to motherhood, we are considered neurotic. If we break out and work for pay we are considered unnatural and unloving, unfortunate dupes of the women's movement and pathetic dupes of the inflationary economy," Arcana said. "And *we* still feel guilty, we should still be at the door waiting for the kids to come home at 3.30 p.m. with fresh cookies because that is what a real mother does.

"And anything less or different is a cause for blame—in this case, for self-blame."

And the children learn to blame mother, as well, said Arcana, a divorced mother of a 15-year-old son and the author of *Every Mother's Son*, a book that explores the roles of mothers on boys becoming men and *Our Mothers' Daughters*, analyzing mother-daughter relationships.

"Children learn money is the measure of human work and success and that motherhood has no recompense. Boys learn mothers turn out to be nothing but a bunch of women,'' she said.

Even scholars and psychologists blame the world's griefs on society's mother-centred raising of children, she said. And the current tendency for mothers to work outside the home has not changed this perception.

Source: From "Why Blame Mom?" by Catherine Dunphy. Reprinted with permission — The Toronto Star Syndicate, May 25, 1987.

a woman, all of this socialization occurs within what Gayle Rubin (1984) labels the sex-gender system (Hartmann, 1981). Sex-gender is a neutral term that captures the ways society deals with sex, gender, and babies. The sex-gender is the set of arrangements by which a society transforms biological sexuality into human activities which satisfy these transformed sexual needs (Hartmann, 1981). Such a system could be sexually egalitarian or, as in Canada, gender stratified. In fact, Canada's sex-gender system has been labelled patriarchal, meaning that within Canada, social relations have developed among men which have a material base, and which, though hierarchical, establish and create interdependence and solidarity among men, enabling them to dominate women (Hartmann, 1981:1–34).

Gender Socializing Contexts

Gender identities, whether traditional, egalitarian, or quasi-egalitarian, are negotiated, reinforced, and constructed through involvement with others in socializing contexts. Lessons of gender are mediated by race and class.

Families are the basic socializing organizations that produce Canadians. Within this unit, infant care is gendered. From the moment of birth, parents differ in their response to their newborns, even when there are no discernible differences in the infants' size and weight (Deckard, 1983). Baby girls are described as softer, finer featured, smaller, and less attentive than baby boys, who appear to their parents as noisier, bigger, stronger, and more aggressive. Parents see what they expect to see and then treat their children differently. Mothers touch, talk to, and handle their infant daughters more than their infant sons. By thirteen months, girls are more dependent on their mothers. They tend to stay closer to them, talk and touch them more than boys. By age one, boys are independent, exploratory, noisy, and vigorous in their play (Deckard, 1983). Parents reinforce appropriate gender role behaviour so consistently that by age two regular patterns of behaviour differentiate boys from girls.

Throughout childhood, gender differences in play are noticeable. Summarizing this literature, Barrie Thorne (1986:167–84), an American feminist, notes that boys tend to interact in larger, more age-heterogeneous groups, engage in more rough and tumble play and fighting, have more competitive and hierarchical interactions, and more frequently use direct commands, insults, and challenges. In contrast, girls' worlds are less public. Girls develop smaller, more private friendship dyads shaped around keeping and telling secrets, shifting alliances, and indirect expressions of disagreement. Their play is more co-operative and turn-taking and less hierarchical. Their talk employs directives ("let's" or "we gotta"), which merge speaker and hearer.

By adolescence, boys and girls have constructed different ways of being. For boys, the range of possible experiences and opportunities appears limitless. Knowing men are the preferred sex, boys feel and act empowered. Their dominating conversational style reflects their positive self-image. Girls, however, develop a negative self-image early. They are rewarded for being passive, conformist, obedient, and deferential to men. Children award more social power to fathers, considering them smarter and more in charge. Girls experience Canadian society ambivalently as a hierarchical set of male-defined rules into which they must fit.

As children move into the school system, they discover gender stratification which is congruent with their early experiences. Teachers view boys' work as more creative, important, and boisterous, even though girls are considered superior in character, brightness, school work, home background, and language skills. Girls are rewarded for conforming to rules, being tidy and conscientious.

Classroom practices are similarly gendered. Boys receive much more attention than girls from teachers in daycare centres, preschools and throughout public school. Boys receive more critical admonitions and more direct praise and positive feedback. Classroom management devices, seating arrangements, the provision of gendered work or play activities, and the operation of communication structures constitute classroom practices mediated by gender. Finally, school rituals and ceremonial practices, such as assemblies, uniforms, and holiday celebrations, are occasions in which gender identities are symbolically represented as different.

In both these contexts, family and school, gender socialization has been discussed deterministically as an identity imposed upon children which reproduces asymmetrical relations within Canadian society.

The ideology of gender difference, produced and reproduced in families, schools, and institutions, permeates the occupational structure. The Abella report (1985) resulted from a 1983 Royal Commission which examined means of promoting employment opportunities for and eliminating systemic discrimination against women, Native people, disabled, and visible minorities. This report analyzed the unequal distribution of personnel and wages in various Canadian occupations, and concluded women are paid 63 percent of what men are paid in similar jobs. Women are segregated in traditionally low status, low-paying, dead-end job ghettos. Seventy-seven percent of employed women work in five major job categories, including secretarial, clerical, teaching, and health sectors (Wilson, 1986). This sexual division of labour is attributed to our stereotypical notions of men's and women's identities. Since women are primarily identified as mothers and wives, their wage labour is seen as temporary, secondary to their husbands, and secondary to their domestic responsibilities. Thus, women's subordination in the home reinforces their discrimination in the labour force. In turn, women's low occupational status and poor wages delegitimates their demands on spouses to share domestic labour. By internalizing their subordinate status, women accept almost total responsibility for home and children while working at full-time jobs. Family and occupational discrimination reinforce one another, so that in Canadian society men have a higher standard of living than women in luxury consumption, leisure time, and personalized services received at home.

Social Class and Identity

The significance of the class structure for Canadian identity stems from some of its consequences (Esheleman, 1985:250). Social class accounts for individual and group differences in opportunity and achievement in education and occupation.

For example, class differences in childhood socialization experiences affect almost every aspect of our life chances as adults. Values, behaviour, role expectations, and lifestyle differ between the working and middle class.

Class is usually approached from either a functionalist or a conflict perspective. Functionalists see social classes as aggregates of individuals who occupy broadly similar positions on scales of wealth, prestige, and power. Stratification studies measure the amount of income, education, or status individuals possess. Studies tend to focus on identifying class strata using quantitative indicators and on measuring intergenerational social mobility (Boyd et al., 1985). Despite our belief in meritocracy, there has been little upgrading or social mobility of the Canadian labour force. Single-step upward mobility is commonly experienced between generations, but Boyd et al., (1985:523) suspect that even if education were completely accessible, advantages would still adhere to family class membership for occupational success. Rises in the general level of education across the Canadian population reflect higher expectations of employers who particularly appreciate the normative influence education exerts on employees (Boyd et al., 1985; Hunter, 1981).

Conflict theorists, or Marxists, define class in terms of ownership of the means of production, including land, capital, and labour. In Marxist analysis, the capitalist class, or bourgeoisie, is composed of those 2.5 percent of the labour force who privately own and effectively control the main means of society's production: the raw materials, energy, land, factories and offices, machinery and equipment (Darroch, 1986). The bourgeoisie also own, control, or influence the main means of making a living of virtually everyone in society. The working class, or proletariat, includes all those who work for wages and produce the products or provide the services. Some people neither own capital or labour nor are compelled to sell their labour power. This petite bourgeoisie has changed with the development of monopoly capitalism, and now includes independent commodity producers, small business, managers, and professionals and technicians.

Within the bourgeoisie, Clement (1975) has differentiated among the *economic elite* in Canada (people holding senior executive and directorship positions within dominant corporations), the *capitalist class* (those who own, control and/or manage corporations employing others, including their families) and the *upper class* (those who work for the state's political and bureaucratic wings and in the capitalist class) (Marsden and Harvey, 1979:135). Building on the work of John Porter, Clement analyzed how these three groups, in conjunction with foreign investors, control economic and political decision making in Canada and are integrated into major policy-making institutions. Elites dominate the economy, politics, education, health systems, the military, policy, and cultural institutions. This tight political, economic, and social dominance has led Marsden and Harvey (1979) to characterize Canada sarcastically as an "open" country — open to capital, immigration, ideas, and cultural influences — a condition that precludes developing a dominating national identity and economy.

The petite bourgeoisie, which constitutes about 18.5 percent of the labour force, own or manage the means of production; have substantial control over their own conditions of work; and do not control the economy as a whole (Veltmeyer, 1986:64). Of particular significance in the socialization process is the role of this class as intellectuals, manufacturing and disseminating ideas and norms that help preserve the existing class relations (Veltmeyer, 1986:64).

The term proletariat is also difficult to define. In applying a Marxian conception of class to the American situation, Erik Wright et al. (1982) redefined classes in terms of social relations of control over investments, decision making, other people's work and one's own work. While the working class is the largest group in Canada (79 percent to 81 percent of Canadian employed are working class), almost half of all working-class locations are intermediate between the bourgeoisie and the proletariat. Factory foremen, for example, are close to the working class, but exercise some control over workers. Thus, their identification with the working class may be attentuated by their position of marginal superiority (Hewitt and Hewitt, 1986).

The consequences of the Canadian class structure for identity formation are pervasive. In Canada, in 1977, the wealthiest 10 percent of families controlled an estimated 67 percent of all financial assets (deposits, cash, bonds, stocks, mortgages), just less than 50 percent of total assets (financial assets, business equity, real estate, automobiles) and a little over 50 percent of net worth (total assets − debts) (Darroch, 1986). This concentration of economic power seems at odds with our liberal ideology of Canada as an open contest society, in which anyone with talent and drive can achieve upward mobility. In fact, income distribution between 1951 and 1981 showed no change despite political rhetoric about the government's redistribution of wealth from the upper- to the lower-middle classes and the poor through various taxation and subsidy programs. Income equalization payments, such as family allowances, old age pensions, and unemployment insurance, have not reduced the gaps in income between rich and poor families (Osberg, 1981).

Wealth is distributed more unevenly than income; since much wealth is accrued and transmitted through inheritance (Hunter, 1981). From 1948 to 1968, the highest income families increased the purchasing power of their incomes, the lowest 10 percent of income families lost 16 percent of the purchasing power of their incomes. Despite rhetoric to the contrary, poverty in Canada is widespread. One in six Canadians lived on low incomes in 1984. Six in every ten single mothers under age sixty-five raise their children on an income below the poverty line. One in five Canadian children grow up in families with low incomes (N.C.S.W., 1986). Approximately 1.2 million Canadian children grow up in families existing on very restricted incomes.

Income distribution studies show the middle class has not expanded, even though increasing proletarianization has affected the labour force. More workers have moved into white collar jobs, which entail less physical risk, shorter hours, the possibility of greater income, and a sense of increased social status (Darroch, 1986). Proletarianization has increasingly blurred traditional distinctions between the working class and the middle class, leading to the sense that Canada has become a mass, middle-class society.

The debate concerning the objective assignment of individuals to social classes will continue. Yet, it seems more crucial to assess how Canadians identify their class interests and how this perception conditions lifestyles and life choices. Surveys (Gallup) indicate most Canadians see themselves as middle class. This reflects in part the success of Canadian elites in maintaining tight economic and political control while fostering an ideology of opportunity. Marx's notion of false consciousness has been developed into the concept of *manipulative socialization* to account for the working class's acceptance of an inferior position in the social structure. Through manipulative socialization, the liberal democratic state does not seek to change values or alter the economic, social, political, and cultural concentration of power. Rather, through minor adjustments in welfare programs, social benefits, and progressive taxation, the elites deny inequality and class conflict.

Although income distribution has remained stable, the majority of Canadians cannot guarantee their children's class attainment through property or business inheritance. If the objective elements of class-property are not easily transferred from one generation to the next, how does class affect life chances? Neo-Marxists have invoked the idea of the intergenerational transmission of **cultural capital** in the form of credentials and lifestyle of the educated. In this conceptualization, class no longer is a structure, a category, or a static entity, but "something which happens in human relationships" (Thompson, 1980). Class becomes a process in which different social relations are reproduced. For example, educating children to assume their parents' class position involves articulating middle-class linguistic codes and inculcating appropriate cultural, political, and work attitudes. Much of this education is undertaken by mothers, who control their children's use of space and time, monitor their movement through the school system, supervise their peer associations, and stimulate their athletic and cultural hobbies. In all these ways, parents encourage in their children the interests and values they want them to acquire. Families thus reproduce social class by passing on cultural capital through their daily experiences and interactions.

Class consciousness is the way in which experiences are handled in cultural terms. It is embodied in traditions, value systems, ideas, and institutional forms (Darroch, 1986). The child first encounters class consciousness within the family. Adams (1980) differentiates between the middle-class and the working-class family model. The middle-class family style, as it developed during the nineteenth and early twentieth centuries, includes (a) economic and work values as central, including residential mobility in pursuit of opportunity, (b) husband-wife relations predicated on happiness, communication, and mutual gratification (c) socialization of children, emphasizing getting along, initiative, independence, and deferred gratification. The working-class family model descends directly from colonial times but has changed with urbanization. It includes (a) more rigid husband-wife role segregation (b) socialization of children, stressing order, obedience, honesty, respect for adults, and limits.

Parental socialization styles are clearly linked to class identity formation. Studies over the past fifty years have revealed the following correlations. Middle-class parents are more emotionally warm and expressive toward their children. Their parenting styles reflect more moderate control of aggressive impulses, greater encouragement of reciprocity, greater acceptance of the emotional complexity of child-rearing situations, and greater satisfaction in perceiving and meeting the child's physical needs. Middle-class fathers are more active in child rearing, discussing events and goals, helping with homework, teaching skills, and complimenting and encouraging the child. The development and use of verbal skills is emphasized. Child discipline hinges on the motives of the child rather than on the negatively defined outcomes of specific behaviour. Children's impulses, spontaneous outbursts, and their greater demand for responsible or sponsored independence are tolerated. Middle-class socialization is characterized by independence, interchange, and affection.

Lower-class children do not necessarily experience less emotional warmth. The sources of emotional warmth may be more dispersed among other family members or friends. Lower-class parents are less likely to live and work in the realm of ideas or to give substantial attention to explanation, reasoning, and understanding motives. Lack of time and verbal skills combine to increase the use of commands and physical response. Child discipline is predicated upon behavioural consequences and is more likely to involve physical punishment. Freedom or unsponsored independence is a central socialization characteristic. Lower-class socialization emphasizes both freedom and discipline.

Working-class socialization is often seen as oriented toward respectability and a concern with limits, neatness, and control. The working class is not merely a midpoint between the other two classes, but has a unique combination of attributes.

Considerable attention has focused on linking parental socialization styles with children's educational and occupational attainment. The family culture of the middle class is portrayed as meshing with the middle-class culture of the school system. Also, occupational success in Canadian society links academic achievement, leadership, and children's creative thinking positively to warm, accepting, understanding, and autonomy-granting parent–child relationships. Clearly, within the major socialization contexts — family, school, and work — social class affects socialization and identity formation.

To define class in structural terms assumes that positions in the social structure affect the development of identity. On an institutional level, class-related beliefs and attitudes are recognizable in work, recreation, politics, and the arts. Canada is populated by mostly working-class people who subscribe to a mass-produced notion of middle-class culture. Within this middle-class frame, Canadians define and interpret events, agree on what goods or ideas are desirable, choose between alternatives, and assess how people should behave. On an individual level, class is reproduced through people's daily rituals, conversations, engagements with children, and occupational activities. Class is also a process in which people construct social worlds, which in turn define and limit their choices. These are clearly broad descriptions. In Canada, class is mediated by gender and ethnicity. So family and group interaction patterns reflect ethnic variations (see Chapter 13 for further elaboration).

AGE AND IDENTITY

Despite its immediate visibility as an identity badge, age has received little direct attention from social scientists. Given the presumed significance of childhood for future behaviour, few sociology textbooks and fewer socialization studies address childhood as an age identity (Ambert, 1986). Even fewer works explore adolescence. Ironically, notions of age-appropriate behaviour underlie most theories of socialization. Many socialization theories measure social and cognitive growth against an adult model of competence. Piaget, for example, specified age ranges during which his developmental skills emerged. Similarly, life cycle theories associate the social stages of marriage, childbearing, and empty nesting with particular biological progressions. People "out of step" with the rest of society are treated as anomalies. Women having first babies at forty instead of twenty-four are a curiosity. In this section, we will outline some historical and contemporary images of Canadian children and adolescents, and discuss adult socialization as a continuing process and source of identity formation.

Historical Images of Children and Adolescents

How a society treats its children and adolescents depends on its views of what youngsters are like and what treatment is necessary to ensure the smooth functioning of society (Boocock, 1976). Canadian ideas of childhood and adolescence have fluctuated in the past century with changing socioeconomic and technological trends. These variations suggest childhood is a social and cultural product (Waksler, 1987). Historically, we tend to idealize changing definitions of children and adolescents as a linear development from forgetful maltreatment to considered egalitarianism. But Canada's treatment of its youth has always been based on ambiguous and contradictory images of childhood and adolescence. The "myth" of North American's love for children is reflected by these contradictions.

Barrie Thorne (1987) concludes that the interests and perspectives of North American adults infuse three contemporary images of children: as threats to adult society, as victims of adults, and as learners of adult culture. In the early stages of industrialization, children, especially those from working-class households, were seen as potential threats to adult society. For example, juvenile criminals and street gang members were associated with tough-minded and rough-talking working-class youth. Most Canadian and American children, during the eighteenth century in New France, were seen as not only insolent, pert, and arrogant, but also as independent and self-reliant. Children in New France appeared presumptuous and precocious compared with children in France. Moogk (1982) suggests these personality characteristics arose from the economic and social independence awarded North American children. As economic contributors, children tended gardens, animals, and small children. They collected wood, ran errands, and contributed in numerous essential ways. In the early days of industrial capitalism, working-class children laboured in shoemaking, clothing and tobacco factories, bakeries, and other enterprises (Palmer, 1983). A Canadian family in the late 1800s subsisted, not on an individual male wage, but on the combined earnings and unpaid contributions of husband, wife, and children.

In contrast to this image of worldly working-class children, middle-class and upper-class children have long been idealized as sweet, innocent, potential saviours of Canadian society. Salvation from social problems seemed to lie in the innocence of children and their amenability to education (Tiffin, 1982). The future greatness of Canadian society was and is thought to lie in its middle-class children.

Secondly, both working- and middle-class children have been seen as victims of adult neglect and abuse. Early welfare reforms and child labour laws were enacted under the guise of protecting children. More materialistic analyses interpret the extension of compulsory education in the late 1800s and the removal of children from wage labour as state responses to the failures of early capitalism to expand and to absorb a growing number of labourers. Compulsory education both removed roaming gangs of street children and inculcated skills necessary for the expansion of capitalism. More recent portrayals of children as victims have focused on their physical and sexual abuse, on the child pornography market, and on teenage prostitution (Badgley Report, 1984).

With the enforcement of education laws and with the foreclosure of the teen market, the middle-class emphasis on childhood and adolescence as a prolonged period of dependency eventually spread to the working class. Basic to the rise of middle-class domesticity favouring a full-time homemaker–mother was the image of children as precious protegées. Scientific theories of child development and mothering flooded the marketplace. Child care experts, child care manuals, child welfare professionals, and an influx of child educators mandated correct family socialization practices in feeding, play, discipline, and parent-child interaction patterns. Following G. Stanley Hall, John Watson, and Sigmund Freud, child developmentalists charted the maturing child's social, cognitive, and emotional growth. Hence, the third image of child as learner, the child as recipient of social norms and values, became rooted in popular culture and academic tradition. The expert's activities covered a broad spectrum, including proper care of the house and the promotion of middle-class child rearing practices. Ideologically, these experts justified their domestic socialization invasion as ensuring a sound citizenry. Politically, professional co-operation of child and adolescent socialization legitimated the expanding role of the state through this century.

In the past century in Canada, certain socialization patterns have emerged. Class distinctions in images of children seem to have blurred. While working-class children are still expected to contribute to the family economy by providing for their own needs, as adolescent consumption grows, middle-class children are increasingly finding part-time employment. All classes of children are viewed as dependants needing protection, and all classes of adolescents are seen as difficult. This is mostly speculation, since we have in Canada few studies on children's activities and participation in the home. We can only assume that with static income distribution levels and increasing numbers of married women in the workforce, children are being asked to contribute to domestic labour and are probably left on their own, as latch key children, for greater periods of time.

The re-emerging independence of children is part of a wider trend that Viviana Zelizer (1985) calls the growth of the emotionally priceless but economically worthless child. The expulsion of children from wage labour and their declining economic value, the exaltation of the middle-class domestic role for women, and the declining birth and mortality rate all contribute to the cultural process of "sacralization" of children's lives. Properly loved and protected children belong in a domesticated, nonproductive world of lessons, games, and token money.

Secondly, concomitant with the emergence of the priceless child is a trend toward public socialization. The state has increasingly assumed the burden of child and adolescent teaching in the past century. This movement from private to public patriarchy is evident in the growth of public education as a purveyor of social morals and cultural beliefs. For example, the American AIDS epidemic has sparked a debate on the efficacy of the school versus the family as an effective sex educator. The state argues only public institutions can effectively warn children thoroughly and naturally about contraceptive protection from this deadly virus. Similarly, a national system of subsidized day care is receiving increasing state support, as people come to accept that the care and socialization of children is a public responsibility.

Child welfare reforms, such as Canadian control of pornography, public assistance for mothers with dependent children, child support legislation, and joint custody laws, all intervene in the lives of Canadian children to ameliorate children's disadvantages and to guarantee social stability. Children are being protected both against the irresponsibilities of their parents and against economic exigencies. Thus far, the state has acted as a conservative mediator between the home and the larger society, maintaining current social and economic relationships within Canada.

Adolescent Identity

Studies of adolescent socialization document how peers, rather than parents, become the important reference figures. A *peer group* is ''an association of self-selected equals who coalesce around common interests, tastes, preferences and beliefs'' (Mackie, 1983:147). Peer groups have become increasingly powerful as socialization contexts in Canada in this century due to the age segregation of children in schools, where they are separated from their families from ages five to eighteen. Also, defining children and adolescents as a distinct group with special needs, interests, and activities further segregates them from adult society (Hewitt and Hewitt, 1986).

Gecas (1981) emphasizes the significance of peer groups for the development and elaboration of the self. Self-identity is articulated first within an authoritarian family and school structure. Egalitarian peer contexts tolerate individuals trying on various identities. While tolerant of experimentation, peers tend to have a monolithic impact upon adolescent beliefs and values. Fear of exclusion often leads to conformity to group norms and expectations, even when disagreement may exist (Hewitt and Hewitt, 1986).

Adolescence, as a distinct phase of social development, emerged in the late 1800s. With the institutionalization of formal education, children's dependency upon their parents lengthened. Today, approximately 22 percent of eighteen- to twenty-four-year-olds attend post-second-

WHAT DO ADOLESCENTS LEARN FROM PEERS?

Hewitt and Hewitt (1986) outline four things that peers provide to adolescents. First, peer groups provide an opportunity to socialize with others away from constant adult control and supervision. It is an egalitarian, rather than authoritarian, environment within which peers gain a different perspective on themselves and others. Secondly, this freedom allows children to learn information unavailable from adults. For example, sexual knowledge and lore is generally learned from peers rather than parents. Thirdly, this freedom provides an opportunity to develop and practise interpersonal skills in essentially egalitarian and voluntary associations. Friendship patterns developed in childhood and adolescence are often closely linked to gender roles and tend to be replicated in adult friendships. Men's friendships stress activity and are often formed around doing something together like boating, fishing, working or building. Male-male conversations most frequently discuss business and money (49 percent), sports or other amusements (15 percent), and other men (13 percent) (Thorne and Henley, 1975). Women's friendships stress expressiveness. Women experience and express more attachment, caring, and intimacy. Women-women talk revolves around men (22 percent), clothing or decoration (19 percent) and other women (Mackie, 1983:153).

ary educational schools (Statistics Canada, 1984). Dependency is thus maintained.

Adult Contexts of Socialization

Most adult socialization studies show how people change as they move through institutional settings (Becker, 1970:293). Howard Becker (1970), an American symbolic interactionist, outlines two major questions adult socialization studies pursue: (1) In what kinds of situations do the socializing institutions place their recruits, what kinds of responses and expectations are experienced, and how are these incorporated into the self? (2) What kinds of mechanisms produce the changes we observe in adults? As part of a socializing cohort, individuals take into account and are constrained by the actions of others. This processual approach to socialization counters the determinist notion of structures and institutions acting monolithically upon people. It also reminds us self- and national identity change as we encounter new people, situations, and problems.

Becoming an adult involves behavioural change and patterned stability. Interactionists see no "deep" personality characteristics persisting across social situations. Rather, individuals take on the characteristics required by the situations in which they participate. This *situational adjustment* (Becker, 1970:279) is a common mechanism in the development of the person in adulthood. By learning the situational expectations and appropriate behaviour for successful role performance, an individual "turns into the kind of person the situation demands" (Becker, 1970:279). For example, adult socialization studies demonstrate how situational adjustments occur collectively and within institutional settings.

While situational adjustment produces change, commitments lead to stability. One way of explaining behavioural consistency lies in articulating the process of *commitment*, in which externally unrelated interests of the person constrain future behaviour (Becker, 1970:284). In becoming an adult, one gradually acquires a variety of commitments — choosing an occupation, starting a family—which constrain one to follow a consistent pattern of behaviour in many other areas of life.

Of the lifelong commitments adults make, occupational roles are central. The late Everett Hughes, one of Canada's earliest and most prominent sociologists, suggests a person's work is one of the more important parts of one's social identity, self, indeed, of one's fate (Hughes, 1971:339). Occupational socialization involves the learning of new activities and social involvements in which people learn to act in new ways and learn new conceptions of themselves.

Within training settings and on the site, adults encounter the stratification system of their occupation and the society at large. The task expectations and the reward structure of the organization become visible to employees as they work. Studies of Canadian workers emphasize the high degree of alienation.

Workers learn how to get ahead in the bureaucracy and how to cope with failure. While Canadian society perpetuates the myth of an egalitarian and democratic meritocracy, adult workers learn to readjust their aspirations and self-conceptions and accommodate a relatively closed mobility system.

Socializing organizations (Seiber and Gordon, 1981) vary in the extent to which they set out to alter people's values and self-concepts. **Total institutions** (Goffman, 1967) like army camps, mental hospitals, prisons, and traditional boarding schools try to effect a complete change in their residents. Inmates are confined for entire periods of their lives, cut off from the rest of society, and under the absolute control of administrative authorities.

Most other organizations for adults are designed to bring about less drastic changes. Rules of speech, etiquette, dress, rituals, routines, symbolic codes of deference, and patterns of social relations are taken on by the members through their routine participation in the day-to-day activities of the organization. Rosabeth Moss Kanter (1977), in her classic study of an American white collar corpora tion, demonstrates the interactive relationship between workers and their social organizations. Individuals both produce social organizations and are acted upon by them. The corporate managers Kanter studied were remarkably similar in appearance, attitudes, manners, and background. This led to social conformity, which in turn created an atmosphere of stability, consistency, and dependability. These men "fitted in" to their jobs and hence could be "trusted" to perform them competently.

Professional socialization is usually considered extensive, since its goal is to produce people with competent technical expertise who will also espouse similar values and beliefs and behave consistently in all aspects of their life. Canadian studies of medical doctors vary in the extent to which the professional organization is seen as responsible for inculcating shared attitudes and values. Professionalization involves adopting and manipulating symbols. Chappell and Colwill (1981), in their panel study of Canadian medical students, emphasize the similarity of students at the outset of their medical training. In contrast, Haas and Shaffir (1988) describe the professional socialization of Ontario medical students as acquiring a cloak of competence.

In summary, occupational socialization provides adults with certain social and technical expertise. While in training and in the early days of new jobs, neophytes "learn the ropes" (Geer et al., 1968). This entails learning all the "do's" and "don'ts" of behaviour, including appropriating the native language or argot, making proper use of greeting and leave-taking rituals, correctly handling mistakes and problems, and carrying out daily business in routinized ways. Occupational socialization varies according to the degree of skill, expertise, and training required in a job. Yet both formal technical skills and informal social skills are acquired in schooling settings (law school, dental school) and in apprenticeships (hairdressing, food preparation). In all these ways, people change as they move through institutional settings.

CONCLUSION

How do Canadians describe Canada? They describe their country as stable, tolerant, liberal, democratic, civilized, and anti-imperialist; they feel Canada's social climate is conducive to personal fulfillment and affluence (Fry, 1984; Marchak, 1981; McCready, 1981). Many Canadians can describe class and locate their own position in it. They describe Canada as a meritocracy that justifies known inequalities (Hunter, 1981). Contrasting Canada with the United States, Canadians prefer their own country's record in health care, crime rates, social security, racial tolerance, peace promotion, and systems of education and government (Pitman, 1986). They are also aware of Canada's inferiority relative to the power and prosperity of the United States (Hiller, 1976).

Expressions of *national identity* within Canada vary with the ages, ethnicities, and regional residence of poll participants. Young Canadians and immigrants who have come to Canada since 1945 express feelings of national identity more than older and longer residing Canadians (Breton et al., 1980). Also, national interest in articulating our national identity varies according to internal and external threats to our country. The free trade issue with the United States has activated debates about whether Canada is "once again for sale."

Many factors have contributed to the growth of a distinct Canadian identity. These include greater economic determinancy, substantial cultural initiatives in creating national symbols, and public determination to evolve distinct Canadian institutions. As we move towards the turn of the century, Canada is forging its own unique sense of self.

DISCUSSION QUESTIONS

1. Compare and contrast the structuralist and the interactionist approaches to socialization.
2. To what extent is Canadian culture permeated by American influence?
3. How might regions affect Canadians' regional and national identities? Discuss.
4. Discuss how factors of class, age, and gender affect the socialization of Canadians.
5. Occupational socialization is considered a crucial encounter for Canadian adults within the workplace. Discuss.

GLOSSARY

cultural capital education, financial, and social credentials and lifestyle experiences parents pass on to their children

cultural identities include designs for living and distinctive ways of thinking, feeling, and acting. This includes shared norms and ideologies about desirable behaviour.

culture the accumulated knowledge, experience, rules, values, and shared symbols and their meanings prevailing in any society or parts of a society

gender role socialization all the processes whereby people learn to take on masculine or feminine attitudes and behaviour

identity a perspective on oneself and others, formed and reinforced by daily interactions with others

negotiated order theory presenting an interactional model involving a processural and emergent analysis of the manner in which the division of labour and work are accomplished in social organizations

perspectives a co-ordinated set of ideas and actions a person uses in dealing with some problematic situation to refer to a person's ordinary way of thinking and feeling about and acting in such a situation

socialization ways an individual comes to act in accordance with society's rules and the ways an individual interacts with others through gestures, reflection, and interpersonal communication

subcultures particular configurations of attitudes and behaviour often based on ethnicity, gender, age, class, region, or race

total institutions socializing organizations that try to effect a complete change in their residents

BIBLIOGRAPHY

Abella, Rosalie S.
1985 *Equality in Employment: A Royal Commission Report*. Ottawa: Ministry of Supply and Services.

Adams, Bert N.
1980 *The Family*, 3rd ed. Chicago: Rand McNally.

Ambert, Anne-Marie
1986 "Sociology of sociology: The place of children in North American sociology." In Peter Adler and Patricia A. Ader (eds.) *Sociology Studies of Child Development*, vol. 1. Greenwich, Connecticut: JAI Press.

Atkinson, Tom and Michael A. Murray
1980 "Values, domains and the perceived quality of life: Canada and the United States." *Institute for Behavioural Research*. Toronto: York University.

Badgley, Robin F.
1984 *Sexual Offences Against Children*. Ottawa: Ministry of Supply and Services.

Becker, Howard S.
1970 *Sociological Work: Method and Substance*. New Brunswick, New Jersey: Transaction Books.

——
1982 *Art Worlds*. Berkeley, California: University of California.

Becker, Howard S., Blanche Geer, Everett C. Hughes, and Anselm R. Strauss.
1961 *Boys in White: Student Culture in Medical School*. Chicago: University of Chicago Press.

Bell, David and Lorne Tepperman
1979 *The Roots of Disunity: A Look at Canadian Political Culture*. Toronto: McClelland and Stewart.

Blishen, Bernard
1978 "Perceptions of national identity." *Canadian Review of Sociology and Anthropology* 15, 2, 128–32.

——
1986 "Continuity and Change in Canadian Values." In Alan Cairns and Cynthia Williams (eds.) *The Politics of Gender, Ethnicity and Language in Canada*. Toronto: University of Toronto Press.

Boocock, Sarane Spence
1976 "Children in contemporary society." In Arlene Skolnick (ed.) *Rethinking Childhood*. Boston: Little, Brown and Co.

Boyd, Monica et al.
1985 *Ascription and Achievement: Studies in Mobility and Status Attainment in Canada*. Ottawa: Carleton University Press.

Breton, Raymond
1986 "Multiculturalism and Canadian Nation-Building." In Alan Cairns and Cynthia Williams (eds.) *The Politics of Gender, Ethnicity and Language in Canada*. Toronto: University of Toronto Press.

Breton, Raymond, Jeffrey G. Reitz, and Victor Valentine
1980 *Cultural boundaries and the cohesion of Canada*. Montreal: Institute for Research on Public Policy.

Brym, Robert J. (ed.)
1985 *The Structure of the Canadian Capitalist Class*. Toronto: Garamond Press.

——
1986 "An Introduction to the Regional Question in Canada." In Robert J. Brym (ed.). *Regionalism in Canada*. Toronto: Irwin Publishing Inc.

Carroll, William K.
1985 "Dependency, imperialism and the capitalist class in Canada." In Robert J. Brym (ed.) *The Structure of the Canadian Capitalist Class*. Toronto: Garamond Press.

Canadian-American Committee
1981 *Improving Bilateral Consultation on Economic Issues*. Montreal: C. D. Howe Institute.

Chappell, Mona L. and Nina L. Colwill
1981 "Medical Schools as Agents of Professional Socialization." *Canadian Review of Sociology and Anthropology* 18, 1:67–79.

Clement, Wallace
1975 *The Canadian Corporate Elite*. Toronto: McClelland and Stewart.

——
1979 "Uneven Development: Some Implications for Continental Capitalism for Canada." In John Allen Fry (ed.) *Economy, Class and Social Reality*. Toronto: Butterworths.

Darroch, Gordon
1986 "Class and Stratification." In Lorne Tepperman and R. Jack Richardson (eds.) *The Social World: An Introduction to Sociology*. Toronto: McGraw-Hill Ryerson.

Daudlin, Bob
1984 "Equality Now."*Report of the Committee on Visible Minorities*. Ottawa: House of Commons.

Deckard, Barbara Sinclair
1983 *The Women's Movement: Political, Socioeconomic and Psychological Issues*, 3rd ed. New York: Harper and Row.

Eshelman, J. Ross
1985 *The Family*. Boston: Allyn and Bacon.

Fine, Gary Alan
1984 "Negotiated orders and organizational cultures." In R. Turner and J. Short (eds.) *Annual Review of Sociology* 10 Palo Alto, California: Annual Reviews.

Fry, John A.
1984 *Contradictions in Canadian Society*. Toronto: John Wiley & Sons.

Fry, John A. (ed.)
1979 *Economy, Class and Social Reality*. Toronto: Butterworths.

Garfinkel, Harold
1967 *Studies in Ethomethodology*. Englewood Cliffs, New Jersey: Prentice-Hall.

Gecas, Viktor
1981 "Contents of Socialization." In Morris Rosenberg and Ralph Turner (eds.). *Social Psychology: Sociological Perspectives*. New York: Basic Books.

Geer, Blanche et al.
1968 "Learning the ropes: situational learning in four occupational training programs." In Irwin Deutscher and Elizabeth Thompson (eds.) *Among the People: Encounters with the Poor*. New York: Basic.

Goffman, Erving
1967 *Interaction Ritual: Essays on Face-to-Face Behaviour*. Garden City, New York: Doubleday Anchor Books.

Haas, Jack and William Shaffir
1978 Shaping Identity in Canadian Society. Scarborough, Ontario: Prentice-Hall.

——
1988 *Becoming Doctors: The Professionalization of Medical Students*. Greenwich, Connecticut: JAI Press.

Hall, Peter
1987 "Interactionism and the Study of Social Organization." *The Sociological Quarterly* 28, 1:1–22.

Hartmann, Heidi
1981 The Unhappy Marriage of Marxism and Feminism: Towards a More Progressive Union. In Lydia Sargent (ed.) *Women and Revolution*. Montreal: Black Rose Books.

Hewitt, John P. and Myrna Livingston Hewitt
1986 *Introducing Sociology: A Symbolic Interactionist Perspective*. Englewood Cliffs, New Jersey: Prentice-Hall.

Hiller, Harry H.
1976 Canadian Society: A Sociological Analysis. Toronto: Prentice-Hall.

Hughes, Everett C.
1971 *The Sociological Eye*. Chicago: Aldine.

Hunter, Alfred A.
1981 *Class Tells: On Social Inequality in Canada*. Toronto: Butterworths.

Jenks, Chris (ed.)
1982 *The Sociology of Childhood*. London:

Batsford Academic and Educational Ltd.

Kanter, Rosabeth Moss
1977 *Men and Women of the Corporation*. New York: Basic Books.

Mackie, Marlene
1983 *Exploring Gender Relations: A Canadian Perspective*. Toronto: Butterworths.

Marchak, Patricia.
1981 *Ideological Perspectives on Canada*, 2nd ed. Toronto: McGraw-Hill Ryerson.

Marsden, R. and E. Harvey
1979 *Fragile Federation: Social Change in Canada*. Toronto: McGraw-Hill Ryerson.

Matthews, Ralph and J. Campbell Davis
1986 "The Comparative Influence of Region, Status, Class and Ethnicity on Canadian Attitudes and Values." In Robert J. Brym (ed.) *Regionalism in Canada*. Toronto: Irwin.

McCready, John
1981 *Context for Canadian Social Policy*. Toronto: University of Toronto Faculty of Social Work.

Mead, George Herbert
1938 The Philosophy of the Act. Edited by Charles Morris. Chicago: The University of Chicago Press.

Moogk, Peter N.
1982 Les petits sauvages: The children of eighteenth-century New France. In Joy Parr (ed.) *Childhood and Family* in *Canadian History*, edited by Joy Parr. Toronto: McClelland and Stewart.

N.C.S.W. (National Council for Social Welfare)
1986 *1986 Poverty Lines*. Ottawa: Ministry of Supply and Services Canada.

Ogmundson, Rick
1980 "Toward a study of the endangered species known as the anglophone Canadian." *Canadian Journal of Sociology* 5, 1:1–12.

Ornstein, Michael D.
1986 "Regional politics and ideologies." In Robert J. Brym (ed.) *Regionalism in Canada*. Toronto: Irwin.

Osberg, Lars
1981 *Economic Inequality in Canada*. Toronto: Butterworths.

Palmer, Bryan D.
1983 *Working-Class Experience: The Rise and Reconstitution of Canadian Labour, 1800–1980*. Toronto: Butterworths.

Pitman, Walter G.
1986 "Public funding of the arts: A positive factor in Canada." *The Globe and Mail*. Toronto: May 6.

Pleck, Joseph.
1979 "Men's Family Work: Three Perspectives and Some New Data." *Family Coordinator*, 28:481–88.

Porter, John
1965 *The Vertical Mosaic*. Toronto: University of Toronto Press.

——
1967 "Canadian character in the twentieth century." *Annals of the American Academy of Political and Social Science* 370, March, 48–56.

Robertson, Ian
1976 *Sociology*. New York: Worth.

Rubin, Gayle
1984 "The Traffic in Women: Notes on the 'Political Economy' of Sex." In Alison M. Jaggar and Paula S. Rothenberg (eds.) *Feminist Frameworks*. Toronto: McGraw-Hill Ryerson.

Seiber, Timothy R. and Andrew J. Gordon
1981 *Children and Their Organizations*. Boston: G. K. Hall and Co.

Statistics Canada
1984 *Fertility in Canada: From Baby-Boom to Baby-Bust*. Ottawa: Ministry of Supply and Services.

——
1985 *Report on the Demographic Situation in Canada in 1983*. Ottawa: Ministry of Supply and Services.

Strauss, Anselm et al.
1963 "The Hospital and Its Negotiated Order." In Eliot Friedson *The Hospital in Modern Society*. New York: The Free Press.

Symons, T.H.B.
1975 *To know ourselves*. Ottawa: Association of Universities and Colleges of Canada.

Thompson, E. P.
1980 *The Making of the English Working Class*. Harmondsworth: Penguin.

Thorne, Barrie
1986 "Girls and boys together . . . But mostly apart: Gender arrangements in elementary schools." In Willard W. Hartup and Zick Rubin (eds.) *Relationships and Development*. New York: Lawrence Erlbaum.

———
1987 "Revisioning Women and Social Change: Where Are the Children?" *Gender and Society* 1, 1.

Thorne, Barrie, Chris Kramarae, and Nancy Henley (eds.)
1983 *Language, Gender and Society*. Rowley, Mass.: Newbury House Publishers.

Thorne, Barrie and Nancy Henley (eds.)
1975 *Language and Sex: Difference and Dominance*. Rowley, Massachusetts: Newbury House.

Tiffin, Susan
1982 *In Whose Best Interest? Child Welfare Reform in the Progressive Era*. Westport, Connecticut: Greenwood Press.

Torrance, Judy M.
1986 *Public Violence in Canada, 1867–1982*. Kingston and Montreal: McGill-Queen's University Press.

Veltmeyer, Henry
1986 Canadian Class Structure. Toronto: Garamond Press.

Waksler, Frances Chaput
1987 "Dancing when the music is over: A study of deviance in a kindergarten class." In Peter Adler and Patricia A. Adler (eds.) *Sociological Studies of Child Development*, vol. 2. Greenwich, Connecticut: JAI Press.

Wilson, S. J.
1986 *Women, the Family and the Economy*, 2nd ed. Toronto: McGraw-Hill Ryerson.

Wright, Erik Olin et al.
1982 "The American class structure." *American Sociological Review*, 47 (December): 709–26.

Zelizer, Viviana A.
1985 *Pricing the Priceless Child: The Changing Social Value of Children*. New York: Basic Books.

Zigler, Edward F., Michael E. Lamb, and Irvin R. Child
1982 *Socialization and Personality Development*, 2nd ed. New York: Oxford University Press.

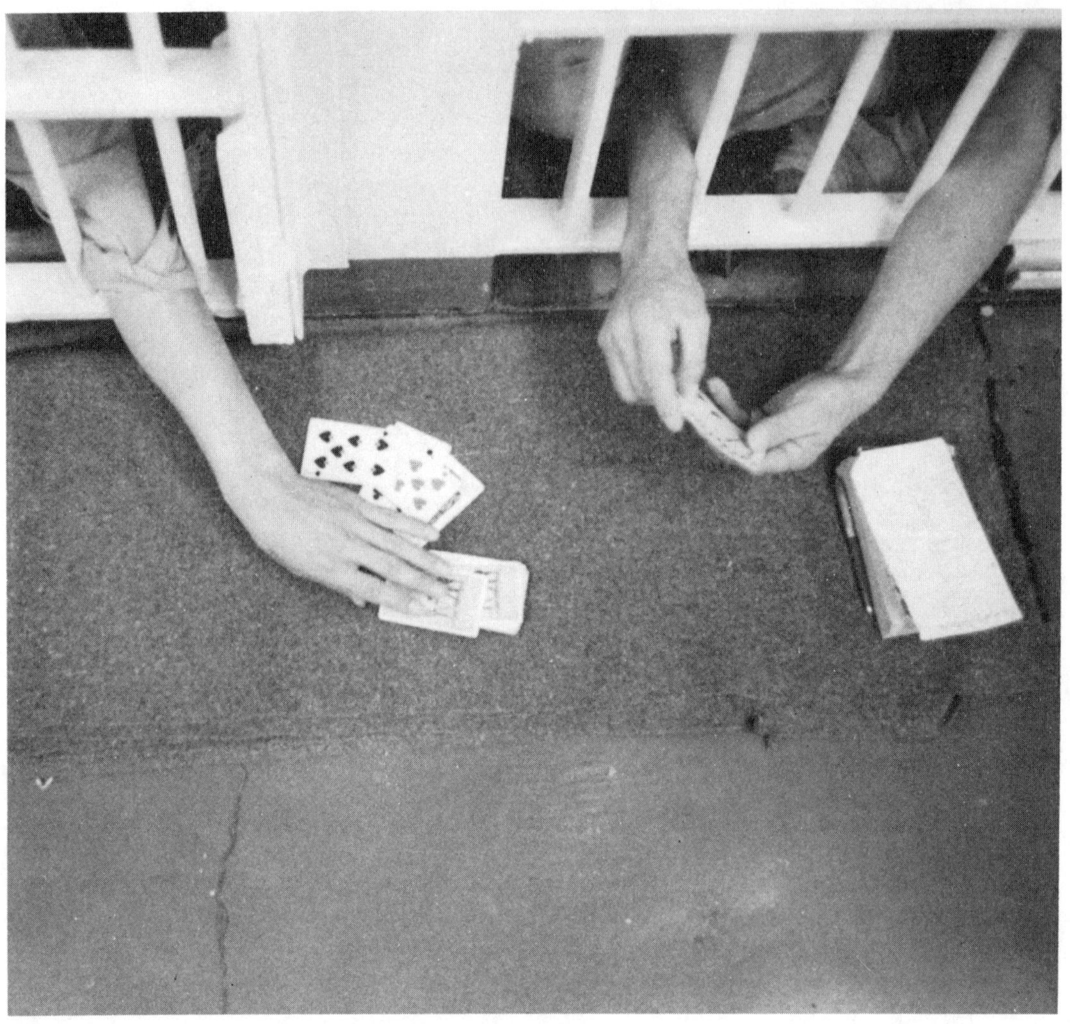

Prisoners in a cell block in Alberta. *Courtesy of National Archives Canada/PA 128104*

> *"The new Charter of Rights and Freedoms does not . . . . assure that accused prisoners will have lawyers, the right to remain silent, or the right to decline to answer questions that may incriminate them. . . . Canadians demonstrate a considerable willingness to accept laws that give social order precedence over individual rights."*

c h a p t e r   f i f t e e n

Crime, Deviance, and Legal Order

John Hagan

INTRODUCTION

Boundary maintenance is a classic sociological concept that refers to the need of social groups to clearly draw distinctions between behaviours deemed acceptable and unacceptable. However, when it comes to understanding crime and deviance in Canada, boundary maintenance's more literal meaning is also relevant. Indeed, historical disputes between Canada and the United States over territorial boundaries have influenced how crime and deviance are still experienced and controlled in Canada today. Consider the following.

As this is being written, the Canadian government has just rejected (politely, of course) a proposal by the United States to negotiate an Alaskan boundary south of the "54:40" line that establishes, at least in Canadian eyes, the site of the two countries' longest standing border dispute. In 1844, the slogan "54:40 or fight" symbolized a desire in the United States to extend that country's border north from the state of Washington to the edge of Alaska. Although this aspiration proved futile for the United States, it served as a reminder for years to come in Canada of its southern neighbour's territorial ambitions. It became important to demarcate this border in social as well as in other ways.

Today, the Canadian border-post aptly called "Boundary, Yukon" provides intriguing hints of lingering differences between Canada and the United States. A journalist, Ross Howard (1986:A7), describes this national crossing point:

> The U.S. border post on the other side of the road is a modern glass-and-fieldstone affair. Just down the U.S. road is a log cabin bar called Action Jackson's. Canada's establishment is a green-trimmed, white clapboard house. Down the road in Canada

> are a pair of green plastic-roofed public outhouses.

These hints of broader differences continue as Howard inquires about the activities of the lone woman agent working at this crossing. She reports:

> "I check the Americans for guns." Lots of Americans admit to carrying them. She sends the pistol-packing tourists back to Action Jackson's where they can check their guns at the bar for pickup when they return to the United States.

Howard adds that anyone can buy a handgun in nearby Alaskan towns, and that while they are supposed to register their handguns with the state police, "hardly anyone does."

Are these observations of continuing significance in understanding crime and deviance in Canada? Or are they simply symptoms of an outdated and misleading mythology that pervades popular conceptions of Canadian and American life? I have already suggested the former: that these differences signify variations within and between these two countries. I will now develop this argument with comparative, historical, and statistical data.

In doing so, this chapter draws on material from Canada and the United States to examine alternative North American responses to crime and deviance. The concern is with such issues as how a society's efforts to control criminal and other unwanted behaviour may be influenced by historical circumstances, structural conditions, national values, and economic constraints. The argument is that under different social conditions alternative societal strategies may be adopted to accomplish similar goals. But first, I must introduce some additional concepts that will form the background to this comparative analysis.

TWO MODELS OF THE SOCIETAL RESPONSE TO CRIME

Packer (1964) has conceptualized societal responses to crime in terms of **due process** and **crime control** models of law enforcement. These models differ most conspicuously in the rights that they accord to individuals confronted by agencies of the criminal law. The due-process model has its roots in the Enlightenment. It emphasizes the notion of John Locke and others that law can be used effectively in defence of "natural" and "inalienable rights." Accordingly, the due-process model is much concerned with exclusionary rules of evidence, the right to counsel, and other procedural safeguards thought useful in protecting accused persons from unjust applications of criminal sanctions. Where errors are to be made in law enforcement, advocates of the due-process model probably are known best for their preference that guilty persons go free before innocent persons are found guilty.

In contrast, the crime-control model receives philosophical support from the conservative reaction to Enlightenment thought. Influential here are the arguments of Edmund Burke and others that civil liberties can have meaning only in orderly societies. Thus, the crime-control model emphasizes the repression of criminal conduct, arguing that only by ensuring order can individuals in a society be guaranteed personal freedom. Advocates of crime control are less anxious to presume the innocence of accused persons and to protect such persons against sometimes dubious findings of guilt. The crime-control model does not favour the unfair treatment of individuals, but it is willing to openly tolerate some mistreatment when the measures are seen as necessary, at least symbolically, for maintaining social order. Individual "rights" here assume a discretionary status in the hands of the authoritative figures who control them.

The Anglo–American democracies with which we are most familiar tend formally more toward the due-process than the crime-control model just described. Nonetheless, the distinction between these models is one of degree. With this in mind, one Canadian social scientist notes that the "approach which is truest to our experience and most in keeping with our capabilities is that of Edmund Burke, not John Locke. Canadians — neither their judges, nor their politicians—are creatures of the Enlightenment" (Russell, 1975a:592). Similarly, in the following pages we will argue that Canada, more than the United States, tends toward a crime-control model. These alternative societal strategies derive from dissimilar societal conditions, yet are consistent with similar goals: the establishment and maintenance of legal order. We are here using the concept of "legal order" to refer to any political organization that utilizes consensual and coercive mechanisms in the form of a "legal system" to regulate hierarchical relationships between authorities and subjects (see Turk, 1969:30–51; 1977:32). We argue that for those at the top of the legal order — authorities—the consequences of the differing American and Canadian responses to crime may be much the same; however, for those at the bottom — subjects — the consequences of these alternative strategies seem to be significantly different. This chapter provides a framework within which these possibilities can be discussed.

THE UNITED STATES AND CANADA IN COMPARISON

Theories of Value Differences

We begin with some sense of the possible societal differences between the United States and Canada. Classic Canadian–American comparisons are found in the works of Clark (1942, 1962, 1976) and Lipset (1963, 1964, 1968, 1986). Both authors propose that "Whereas the American nation was a product of the revolutionary spirit, the Canadian nation grew mainly out of forces of a counter-revolutionary character" (Clark, 1962:190–91). Three factors are included among the counter-revolutionary forces that have influenced Canada: (1) the movement of British loyalists to Canada during and after the American Revolution; (2) the role played by the Church of England and the Roman Catholic Church in providing Canada with hierarchical and traditionally rooted control mechanisms; and (3) the threat posed to Canada's frontier expansion by parallel frontier activities in the United States (Lipset, 1968: chap. 2). Each factor is said to have had a conservatizing effect on the values of Canadians, as contrasted with Americans.

Thus, various authors, in different ways, have called attention to the relatively more conservative values of Canadians. Clark (1962: 191) speaks of the "forces of conservatism" that emerged in the Canadian response to its frontier experience. Naegle (1964:501) describes a "conservative mould" that makes Canada "a country of greater caution, reserve, and restraint." Vallee and Whyte (1971) speak of a Canadian "conservative syndrome" consisting of "a tendency to be guided by tradition, to accept the decision-making functions of elites . . . [and] to put a strong emphasis on the maintenance of order and predictability." On a contemporary political note, Christian and Campbell (1974:97) suggest "Like nostalgia, this disposition is by no means the prerogative of any one political party in Canada."

Porter (1967:56) links Canadian conservatism to the nation's two charter groups, noting "English and French Canadians are more alike in their conservatism, traditionalism, religiosity, authoritarianism, and elite values than the spokesmen of either group are prepared to admit." However, it is probably Lipset (1968:51) who most explicitly links these value differences to American and Canadian history: "Once these events had formed the structure of the two nations, their institutional characters were set. Subsequent events tended to enforce 'leftist' values in the south and 'rightist' ones in the north."

Lipset (1963, 1964) conceptualizes these value differences in four dichotomized variables, the first three of which are adopted from Parsons: achievement-ascription, universalism-particularism, self-orientation-collectivity-orientation,- and egalitarianism-elitism. Lipset compares four English-speaking democracies —the United States, Australia, Canada, and Great Britain — concluding that the four nations can be ordered in terms of the four polarities, and that Canada patterns itself most after Great Britain. Thus, in Lipset's terms, the Canadian value system is more ascriptive, particularistic, collectivity-oriented, and elitist than is the case in the United States. Lipset's evidence in support of these conclusions includes crime and divorce rates and levels of educational advancement. Both Lipset's evidence and conclusions have provoked significant debate.

One measure of the intensity of the response to Lipset's work is the judgment of Davis (1971:16,19) that "the Lipset concept of American . . . and Canadian Society . . . is so laced with invalid claims and ideological blind spots that it is a waste of time to refute it." Nonetheless, Davis argues that, contrary to the American values portrayed by Lipset, "the United States is a hierarchical, racist society." Davis further suggests (p. 19) that "After the First World War, the Americans quickly displaced Britain as the primary influence on Canadian society — a trend that was reinforced by the rapid decline of Britain itself to a satellite status within the American orbit." Thus, Davis argues Canada has become a "hinterland" of the American "metropolis," making Canada "a pale reflection of American stratagems and American drift." The result, according to Davis, is "not only second-class status, but also 'homogenization.' "

Similarly, Horowitz (1973, 330,346) argues that Lipset's view denies "the idea of class struggle and racial conflict in American society," and that the older British or "Imperial connection" to Canada is now replaced by a continental or "American connection" that is hemispheric in scope (see also Horowitz, 1966, 1970). Using various data, including crime statistics, Horowitz (1973:340) concludes "the differences between Canada and the United States, at the level of values, are better framed in terms of cultural lag than in terms of polarized or reified value differences" (see also Truman, 1971). According to Horowitz, American imperialism is supplanting British colonialism, and consequently the "cultural gap" is closing.

It may be instructive to briefly consider the evidence Horowitz uses in concluding (1973, 341) that "the data on criminality and homicide reveal marked tendencies toward closing the 'cultural gap.' " Canadian and American statistics on rape, robbery, breaking and entering, and theft are provided for one year only, 1966, and murder statistics are provided for Canada only, 1954 to 1970. It should be apparent that data on the same crimes from both countries and from at least two points in time are necessary to draw inferences about "closing the cultural gap." Horowitz's data, then, cannot speak properly to this issue. In a later section in this chapter, we examine the type of data required to address this issue.

Recent attempts to deal with the debate

between Lipset and his critics reveal that the issues involved are often as much semantic as empirical. Thus, according to Hiller (1976:140):

> It could be argued that the urbanization and industrialization of societies has contributed to a homogenization of values among them. If this were so, we might expect statistics of behaviour patterns to be increasingly similar. However, such a similarity might never be verified as long as structural and cultural differences (such as divorce laws, norms of family size, norms of remarriage) confound the meaning of our statistics. . . . Perhaps differences in the organization of the society (for example, forms and types of government) will help to perpetuate societal distinctions in spite of some value convergence.

This argument simultaneously seems to affirm and deny societal differences. Apparently, Hiller is arguing that values can converge, while norms, structures, and cultures remain different. Depending on how one defines these terms, this may or may not be true. As Lipset (1986:120) recently noted, "When the arguments of those identified as adhering to one or the other interpretation of the sources of Canadian–American differences (values or structure) are carefully examined, it becomes apparent that most of the distinctions really are ones of emphasis." The significant issue is which differences distinguish Canada and the United States at different points in time. Thus, as Clark notes (1976:53),

> It may be that Lipset was quite wrong in the criteria he used but, even if he were, that in no way establishes the fact that differences in the value systems of the two countries did not exist. To resolve such an issue involves an examination of the structure of the American and Canadian societies, something that Horowitz does not attempt.

The remainder of this chapter is devoted to such an examination. Our interest is in how the differences discussed by Lipset and Clark may correspond to these two societies' responses to crime and their respective efforts to establish and maintain legal order.

AN HISTORICAL OVERVIEW

It is impossible to thoroughly discuss American and Canadian history in a chapter devoted primarily to crime and legal order. Nonetheless, salient aspects of the two nations' histories can be highlighted and related to the issues confronting us. Historically, the southern part of North America contained resources that could be exploited with relatively minor governmental involvement and control (Clark, 1975:55). As well, the United States was conceived ideologically as a nation devoted to the rights and responsibilities of individuals (Lipset, 1968). One result was an ideology of individualism that, when combined with exploitable re sources, allowed and encouraged more extensive variations from the norm than was the case in the northern part of the continent (Hagan and Leon, 1978; 1980). Thus, Quinney (1970:55) notes that on the American frontier, local authorities were free to develop their own law enforcement policies or to ignore crime altogether. Similarly, Inciardi (1975:88) observes "The American frontier was Elizabethan in its quality, simple, childlike, and savage. . . . It was a land of riches where swift and easy fortunes were sought by the crude, the lawless, and the aggressive, and where written law lacked form and cohesion." Put simply, the American frontier was a criminal frontier, a model for the city life that followed. In Bell's (1953) apt phrase, "crime is an American way of life."

However, as the United States matured, the establishment of a viable legal order also became a priority. On a formal and symbolic level, the American commitment to a due-process model of law enforcement continued to increase in ideological importance. The antidote to this ideology was an equally significant national commitment and assignment of resources to police and punish deviant behaviour. Thus, although an economy of scale might be expected, the United States has spent more per capita on its police than has Canada, substantially more on its courts, and more as well on its corrections (Hagan and Leon, 1978:200). The United States has produced a legal order that combines high levels of crime with a profuse and coercive police response. Some of the historical irony of this situation is captured in Skolnick's (1975:246) description of the police as America's "asphalt cowboys."

In contrast, the Canadian approach to order was initially more firm, but also necessarily more strategic (see McNaught, 1975). In the East, law and order were handled by the military: "Thus about the fur-trading posts of New France, in the agricultural settlements of New Brunswick and Upper Canada, and in the shanty towns of Irish canal workers, the army played an important role in maintaining order . . . [and] in the isolated fishing settlements of Nova Scotia, policing was a function of the navy" (Clark, 1962:191; see also Clark, 1942). However, more efficient means were required in the West. MacLeod (1976) notes that by the 1870s the American government was spending over $20 million a year fighting the Plains Indians. At the same time, the total Canadian budget was just over $19 million. "It is not an exaggeration to say," according to MacLeod, " . . . that the only possible Canadian West was a peaceful one."

One means of realizing this possibility was to assign the North-West Mounted Police a key role in John A. Macdonald's "National Policy," giving the N.W.M.P. "power unparalleled by any other police force in a democratic country." The N.W.M.P. were to establish "peace and order." Kelly and Kelly (1976:21) contend the N.W.M.P. of the 1890s "attended to the health and welfare problems of Indians and Eskimos," whereas Brown and Brown (1973:10) write, "the N.W.M.P. were established as a semi-military force designed to keep order on the prairies and to facilitate the transfer of most of the territory of the region from the Indian tribes to the federal government with a minimum of expense and bloodshed."

Whichever account of the role of the N.W.M.P. is the more accurate, Canada's Native people were treated in a significantly different way than were Native people in the United States. America's treatment of both its Black and Native minorities was extraordinarily violent. Canada's treatment of its Native people was and may still be socially and economically poor, but it has not been nearly so violent. Meanwhile, "the winning of the Canadian west amounted to the extension of Anglo–Canadian authority in order to offset rival influences, principally United States aggrandizement, real or imagined. . . . And always in the background was American lawlessness and disorder, whether real or imagined" (Gough, 1986:194).

Clark (1962:192) summarizes the situation this way: "In the United States, the frontier bred a spirit of liberty, which often opposed efforts to maintain order. In Canada, order was maintained at the price of weakening that spirit." In more concrete terms, Canada has been able to limit its resource commitment to crime control by re-emphasizing its ideological commitment to the Burkean ideal of social order first, and individual rights second. Thus, in Canada, the police role has become preeminently symbolic, a reminder that social order ideologically precedes individual liberties. Bell and Tepperman (1979:26) note,

". . . the purpose of the Canadian state, according to the British North America Act, is to secure the blessing of 'Peace, Order and Good Government,' not liberty in the pursuit of happiness." Margaret Atwood (1972:171) observes: "Canada must be the only country in the world where a policeman is used as a national symbol."

It comes as little surprise, then, that Canadian and American traditions have differed in their efforts to prevent the arbitrary or unequal exercise of police- or court-related powers. American civil liberties, including the rights to due process and to equality before the law, are constitutionally entrenched in the American Bill of Rights. Through the American doctrine of judicial review, individuals and minorities look to judges and the courts as the guardians of their constitutionally protected liberties. In contrast, the Canadian approach has placed greater faith in the role of Parliament. Bruton (1962:108) reminds us that this faith ultimately rests on a belief in self-restraint: "Consequently, faith in parliamentary supremacy as a protection against arbitrary government becomes faith that the majority can be depended upon not to work its will in arbitrary ways . . . ." It is as yet unclear whether the Charter of Rights and Freedoms will alter this situation in significant ways.

One final indication that Canada has adopted a more restrictive approach than the United States in its response to deviance is the pattern of penal reform. Jaffary has compared the progress of penal reform in Canada, the United States, and Britain, and concludes that Canada lags behind. Penal reform really did not get under way in Canada until 1946, and only then after many years of activist support from the first woman Member of Parliament in Canada, Agnes MacPhail. Jaffary notes that the United States and England were far ahead of this pace. However, more interesting than the comparative details of these reforms is the question that Jaffary asks and attempts to answer: "Why had Canada come to the mid-century with its nineteenth-century philosophy and services virtually unchanged?" (1963:81).

Jaffary's answer is that the social and economic development of Canada posed great problems, with many of the difficulties traced to environmental factors of the type discussed by Innis, Clark, and Lipset (see also Krueger, 1982; Frye, 1982). The size of the country, the problems of communication, and the difficulties of extracting resources are all mentioned as discouraging interest in such secondary issues as penal reform. Only after settlement, industrialization, and urbanization could such changes really begin.

A persistent and significant difference in Canadian and American attitudes toward due process and crime control remains.

As Edgar Friedenberg (1980:12) writes, "These fundamentally contrasting approaches to the process of criminal justice cannot be regarded as merely alternative ways of attacking similar problems, . . . they go to the very heart of the question of national identity."

The new Charter of Rights and Freedoms does not alter this view. For example, the new rights do not assure that accused persons will have lawyers, the right to remain silent, or the right to decline to answer questions that may incriminate them (see Pye, 1982; McWhinney, 1982:55–57; Westin, 1983:27–44; McKercher, 1983, cited in Lipset, 1986:131). In contemporary and historical terms, Canadians demonstrate a considerable willingness to accept laws that give social order precedence over individual rights (Hagan and Leon, 1980). Faith in such a system depends heavily on faith in the authorities that run it. The problem is, in effect, to ensure that fair-

ON THE RIGHT TO COUNSEL

A contemporary reflection of this difference is that Canadians are more willing than Americans to forgo law reforms in favour of leaving to legal authorities the discretion to decide what accused and convicted persons require and deserve. This Canadian emphasis on ensuring fairness to the accused rather than a strict adherence to inalienable rights is illustrated in an important yet characteristically unnoticed court decision on right to counsel. Mr. Justice Martin, for the Ontario Court of Appeal, observes: "Assuming that in some circumstances the requirement of fair trial can only be met by providing counsel to assist the accused, all the relevant circumstances must be considered in deciding whether the accused in a particular case was denied a fair trial because he lacked counsel to assist him." Justice Martin then denies the appeal of the accused in this case, noting that "If, in any case, we considered that a miscarriage of justice has occurred because the accused lacked counsel, we would, of course, not hesitate to intervene" [R. v. Littlejohn and Tirabasso. (1978), Canadian Criminal Cases, 172–3].

ness results. Our reluctance to reform much Canadian criminal law suggests that this faith, rightly or wrongly, may be widely distributed (see Klein et al., 1978).

Our review of historical and contemporary evidence indicates that legal responses to crime differ in Canada and the United States. Our final concern is to determine how these differences may be reflected in national statistics on crime and deviance from the two countries. Recall that Lipset predicts an historical continuity in these statistical differences, while Horowitz has doubted their persistence. The tables presented in the following section speak to this issue.

CROSS-NATIONAL DATA ON CRIME AND DEVIANT BEHAVIOUR

By many measures, Canada is only a moderately violent nation. Table 1 and Figure 1 indicate the rates of violent crime and burglary in Canada and the United States. Although some differences exist in the collection and categorization of offences in Canada and the United States, the findings suggest a pattern: over the past ten to twenty years, and with population differences taken into account, violent offences have remained much more frequent in the United States than in Canada. For example, in spite of year-to-year fluctuations, American murder and rape rates remain about four times larger than the Canadian rates. Robbery rates have remained more than two times higher in the United States. On the other hand, the two nations' burglary rates are much more similar. By 1980, the American burglary rate was only 1.2 times the Canadian rate.

What limited data we have on self-reported juvenile delinquency confirms the impression that serious offences are more frequent in the United States than in Canada. Linden and Fillmore (1981) have compared self-report surveys conducted with adolescents during the same year in Richmond, California, and Edmonton, Alberta (see Table 3 on page 436). These indicate that as the value of property reported stolen increases, so too do the

Table 1

RATES OF MURDER, RAPE, ROBBERY, AND BURGLARY RECORDED BY POLICE PER 100 000 TOTAL POPULATION: CANADA AND THE UNITED STATES, 1960–1980*

	Murders			Rapes			Robberies			Burglaries		
Year	*Canada*[1]	*U.S.*[2]	*Ratio*	*Canada*[3]	*U.S.*[4]	*Ratio*	*Canada*[5]	*U.S.*[6]	*Ratio*	*Canada*[7]	*U.S.*[8]	*Ratio*
1960	0.9	5.1	5.7	1.4	9.6	6.9	18.1	60.1	3.3	280.4	508.6	1.8
1961	1.2	4.8	4.0	2.5	9.4	3.8	21.0	58.3	2.8	393.0	518.9	1.3
1962	1.4	4.5	3.3	3.1	9.4	3.0	26.6	59.7	2.2	441.8	535.2	1.2
1963	1.3	4.6	3.5	2.9	9.4	3.2	31.1	61.8	2.0	497.9	576.4	1.2
1964	1.3	4.9	3.8	3.9	11.2	2.9	29.4	68.2	2.3	504.0	634.7	1.3
1965	1.4	5.1	3.6	3.3	12.1	3.7	28.4	71.7	2.5	491.4	662.7	1.4
1966	1.2	5.6	4.7	3.2	13.2	4.1	28.0	80.8	2.9	500.6	721.0	1.4
1967	1.7	6.2	3.7	3.8	14.0	3.7	35.4	102.8	2.9	585.9	826.6	1.4
1968	1.8	6.9	3.8	4.3	15.9	3.7	40.5	131.8	3.3	699.9	932.3	1.3
1969	1.8	7.3	4.1	4.9	18.5	3.8	47.8	148.4	3.1	769.9	984.1	1.3
1970	2.2	7.9	3.6	5.1	18.7	3.7	54.6	172.1	3.2	834.4	1084.9	1.3
1971	2.2	8.6	3.9	5.7	20.5	3.6	52.1	188.0	3.6	873.8	1163.5	1.3
1972	2.4	9.0	3.8	5.9	22.5	3.8	54.3	180.7	3.3	875.8	1140.8	1.3
1973	2.5	9.4	3.8	7.2	24.5	3.4	59.7	183.1	3.1	898.4	1222.5	1.4
1974	2.7	9.8	3.6	8.2	26.2	3.2	75.8	209.3	2.8	1043.5	1437.7	1.4
1975	3.1	9.6	3.1	8.1	26.3	3.3	93.8	218.2	2.3	972.2	1525.9	1.6
1976	2.9	8.8	3.0	8.0	26.4	3.3	87.2	195.8	2.2	1167.0	1439.4	1.2
1977	3.0	8.8	2.9	8.1	29.1	3.6	83.8	187.1	2.2	1163.7	1410.9	1.2
1978	2.8	9.0	3.2	9.0	30.8	3.4	83.8	191.3	2.3	1186.2	1423.7	1.2
1979	2.7	9.7	3.6	9.7	34.5	3.6	88.3	212.1	2.4	1252.3	1499.1	1.2
1980	2.5	10.2	4.1	9.7	36.4	3.8	102.7	243.5	2.4	1450.3	1668.2	1.2

[1]Murder and manslaughter
[2]Murder and nonnegligent manslaughter
[3]Rape
[4]Forcible rape, attempts to commit forcible rape by force or threat of force
[5]Firearms, other offensive weapons, other robbery
[6]Use or threat to use violence to obtain property, including attempts
[7]Breaking and entering (in all kinds of buildings)
[8]Burglary

Source: The Criminal Law in Canadian Society, Ottawa: Government of Canada, 1982. Reformulated, pp. 85–88. Reprinted with permission of the Ministry of Supply and Services Canada.

national differences: rates of theft of less than two dollars are about the same in the two samples, theft from two to fifty dollars in value are about one-and-a-half times more frequent in the American sample, and thefts of more than fifty dollars in value are nearly four times more frequent in the American sample. Beyond this, the Edmonton sample shows the participants somewhat more likely to damage property, but less likely to "beat up anyone." So with minor exceptions, the pattern of American predominance prevails.

Surveys of drug use in the United States and Canada suggest another area of American predominance. Berg (1970) reviewed sixty-nine self-report studies of drug use conducted during 1969 in the United

Figure 1
Comparative indices of violent offences reported by the police in rates per 100 000 population in Canada and the United States from 1965 to 1981

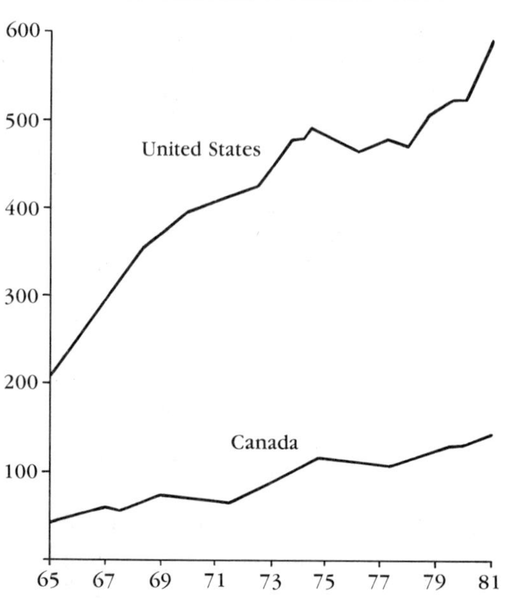

U.S. violent crimes include robbery, aggravated assault, forcible rape, and murder; Canadian violent crimes include robbery, wounding, rape, murder, attempted murder, and manslaughter.

Sources: Solicitor General Canada, *Selected Trends in Canadian Criminal Justice; Crime and Traffic Enforcement Statistics—1977–1981:* Uniform Crime Reports—1977–1981. *Selected Trends in Canadian Criminal Justice* is a publication of the Ministry of the Solicitor General of Canada.

States, while Smart and Fejer (1971) reviewed twenty-two such studies conducted from 1967 to 1970 in Canada. The studies indicate: (1) reported levels of use vary widely within each country; (2) levels of reported use changed substantially in the late 1960s; and (3) almost any basis of comparison places America ahead of Canada in the prevalence of nonmedical drug use. Table 4 on page 437 summarizes some of the information by indicating for each country the "high" reported use levels of marijuana, L.S.D., and amphetamines in college and highschool samples. Since some of the Canadian studies took place as much as one year after the American surveys, the comparison encourages a higher estimate of Canadian drug use. Yet, to the extent that these reports can be taken as valid (for a supportive Canadian test of validity, see Whitehead and Smart, 1972), the prevalence of nonmedical drug use in the United States exceeds that in Canada. Student surveys conducted in Canada from 1976 to 1982 (Addiction Research Foundation, 1982:116–17) suggest no current reason to revise this conclusion.

Turning to the most frequently abused chemical, alcohol, comparative data are available from many countries. Much of this data is built on the fact that alcoholics contribute a disproportionately large share to mortality from cirrhosis of the liver. International statistics on liver cirrhosis deaths are presented in Table 5, on page 437. This information is built into computing formulas used to estimate the prevalence of alcoholism (Popham, 1956). A resulting ranking of the estimated prevalence of alcoholism in a number of Western countries is presented in Table 6, on page 438. This ranking suggests that neither Americans nor Canadians are among the world's heaviest drinkers, but that our southern neighbours may once more exceed us.

The forms of deviance considered most serious by the public (for example, "violent crime" and "hard drug abuse") are found more commonly in the United States than in Canada. We don't know how much more deviant behaviour occurs in the United States nor whether this disparity will endure. We can, however, comment on how Canadians perceive their situation. In an opinion poll of a representative sample of Toronto households, Courtis (1970) found 28 percent of his

VIOLENCE IN CANADA AND THE UNITED STATES

The conclusion that Canada is a relatively nonviolent nation, particularly in comparison with the United States, is echoed in cross-national studies of political violence (Kirkham, Levy, and Crotty, 1970). Such studies demonstrate that despite Canada's experiences with groups like the F.L.Q., the numbers and rates of assassinations, armed attacks, demonstrations, riots, and deaths from political violence have been relatively low, and continue to be so in comparison to the United States over time (see Table 2). We are individually and collectively more violent than some, but more peaceful than most.

Table 2

POLITICAL PROTEST AND VIOLENCE IN CANADA AND THE UNITED STATES

	United States		*Canada*	
	48–67	*68–77*	*48–67*	*68–77*
Number of protest demonstrations	1179	1005	27	33
Number of riots	683	149	29	5
Deaths from political violence	320	114	8	4

Source: Taylor and Jodice (1983: 19–25, 33–36, 47–51, reproduced in Lipset (1986:129). Reproduced with permission of *Canadian Journal of Sociology* 11 (2):129.

respondents regarded crime as a very serious problem, 61 percent as only a moderately serious problem, with the remaining 12 percent largely unconcerned. This finding can be contrasted with American polls conducted during a similar period by Harris (1968) and Gallup (*Time*, 1968). These polls revealed a consensus that "crime and lawlessness" was America's most serious problem. Data reviewed here support these contrasting estimates by Canadians and Americans of recent crime problems in their respective countries.

CONCLUSION

It is possible to describe two quite different approaches used on this continent to establish and maintain legal order. We have conceptualized these two national strategies on a scale bounded at either end by the crime-control and due-process models of law enforcement. Canada comes closer to the former model, while the United States, at least formally, comes closer to the latter. We must emphasize that neither nation nor model, of course, openly encourages or eliminates abuses of the criminal process; rather, each symbolizes a different balance between individual and community interests. In this chapter, we have considered historical and contemporary correlates and consequences of the Canadian and American approaches. Historically, the southern part of this continent contained resources that could be exploited with less governmental involvement and consequently less government control. As well, the United States purportedly was conceived as a nation devoted to the rights and responsibilities

Table 3

COMPARISON OF SELF-REPORTED DELINQUENCY AMONG EDMONTON AND RICHMOND YOUTH (IN PERCENTAGES)*

	Richmond				Edmonton				
Behaviour	*Full Sample*	*Males*	*Females*	*Males/Females Ratio*	*Full Sample*	*Males*	*Females*	*Males/Females Ratio*	*Richmond/Edmonton Ratio*
Theft less than $2	45.9	52.7	30.5	1.7:1	46.5	60.1	33.3	1.8:1	0.9:1
Theft $2 to $50	15.6	19.1	7.7	2.5:1	9.8	14.1	5.6	2.5:1	1.6:1
Theft $50+	5.1	6.6	2.0	3.3:1	1.3	2.4	0.2	12:1	3.9:1
Auto Theft	8.6	10.8	3.6	3:1	3.3	5.9	0.7	8.4:1	2.6:1
Damage Property	20.3	25.5	8.6	3:1	28.0	40.3	16.0	2.5:1	0.7:1
Beat Up Anyone	33.7	41.7	15.6	2.7:1	24.4	40.9	8.1	0.5:1	1.4:1
	N = 1827	N = 1264	N = 563		N = 1154	N = 571	N = 583		

Source: Rick Linden and Cathy Fillmore, "A Comparative Study of Delinquency Involvement," ***Canadian Review of Sociology and Anthropology***, reformulated. Reprinted from the ***Canadian Review of Sociology and Anthropology***, vol. 18:3(1981).

Table 4

HIGHEST REPORTED RATES ON NONMEDICAL USE OF DRUGS IN CANADIAN AND AMERICAN SURVEYS OF COLLEGE AND HIGHSCHOOL STUDENTS

Drug	College Surveys	Percent of Drug Use U.S.	Percent of Drug Use Canada	High School Surveys	Percent of Drug Use U.S.	Percent of Drug Use Canada
Marijuana	University of Michigan	44.0%		San Mateo County, California	36.6%	
	Bishop's University		27.3%	Toronto		23.0%
LSD	*Newsweek* Survey	8.2%		San Mateo County, California	15.1%	
Amphetamines	Bishop's University		3.1%	Toronto		15.0%
	University of Michigan	24.7%		San Mateo County, California	20.8%	
	University of Western Ontario		4.1%	Niagara Counties, Ontario		9.0%

Source: Berg (1970:784) and Smart and Fejer (1971:514–17).

Table 5

INTERNATIONAL STATISTICS ON LIVER CIRRHOSIS DEATHS, 1973 TO 1979: RATES OF LIVER CIRRHOSIS DEATHS PER 100 000 POPULATION

Country	1973	1974	1975	1976	1977	1978	1979
Canada	11.4	11.6	12.0	12.1	11.9	n.a.	n.a.
United States	15.9	15.8	14.8	14.7	14.3	13.8	n.a.
Finland	4.6	5.5	6.3	5.7	5.4	n.a.	n.a.
France	34.5	32.8	33.7	32.9	31.5	n.a.	n.a.
Germany, Federal Republic	25.7	26.9	27.9	28.1	27.6	27.6	n.a.
Italy	32.3	31.9	33.3	34.2	n.a.	n.a.	n.a.
Norway	4.0	4.1	5.0	5.4	4.2	5.1	5.2
Spain	22.3	22.5	22.6	23.4	22.5	n.a.	n.a.
Sweden	10.4	10.5	12.2	12.9	12.4	12.4	12.2
Switzerland	13.8	14.8	12.8	12.8	12.9	13.3	13.6
United Kingdom	3.7	3.6	3.7	3.8	3.7	3.9	4.4

Source: Statistics on Alcohol and Drug Use in Canada and Other Countries. Toronto: Addiction Research Foundation, 1983, pp. 285–89; World Health Statistics Annual Vol. I—Vital Statistics and Causes of Deaths, 1973–76, 1977, 1979, and 1981. Geneva: World Health Organization.

Table 6

RANKING OF ESTIMATED PREVALENCE OF ALCOHOLISM IN A NUMBER OF WESTERN COUNTRIES (COUNTRIES ARE LISTED ALPHABETICALLY WITHIN CATEGORIES)

Range	Country
Extreme High	France
Upper High	Chile
	Portugal
	U.S.A.
Lower High	Australia
	Sweden
	Switzerland
	Union of South Africa
	Yugoslavia
Upper Middle	Canada
	Denmark
	Norway
	Peru
	Scotland
	Uruguay
Lower Middle	Belgium
	Czechoslovakia
	England
	Finland
	Ireland
	Italy
	New Zealand
	Wales
Upper Low	Brazil
	Netherlands
Lower Low	Argentina
	Spain

Source: Reprinted with permission of The Addiction Research Foundation of Ontario.
Source: Schmidt (1971:502)

of individuals. This "revolutionary" ideology came to be symbolized in part by constitutionally safeguarded rights to due process and to equality before the law. One result was an ideology of individualism that, combined with exploitable resources, allowed and encouraged more extensive variations from the norm than was the case in the northern part of the continent. Thus, the American frontier was also a criminal frontier, a model in some ways for the city life that followed.

However, as the United States developed as a nation, the establishment of a viable legal order also became a priority. On a formal and symbolic level, the American commitment to a due-process model of law enforcement continued to be ideologically important. The antidote to this ideology was a similar national commitment and assignment of resources to policing and punishing deviant behaviour. The United States was to have a legal order that combined higher levels of crime with an active and coercive police response.

In contrast, the Canadian approach was one of initially more firm, but also necessarily more strategic, control. Historically, the Canadian attitude placed a stronger emphasis on social order in relation to individual rights. Thus, the Canadian frontier was a closed frontier, in the sense that its development was to be closely controlled. This historical emphasis on social order is today commonly noted in the greater "respect" given by Canadians to the ideal of "law and order" (Wrong, 1955:37–38). For our purposes, it makes little difference whether this respect is identified as evidence of "hegemony," resulting from class domination, or "consensually shared values," democratically conceived and supported. It probably is both. Canada has been able to limit its resource commitment to crime control by re-emphasizing its ideological commitment to the Burkean ideal of social order first and individual rights second. Thus, in Canada, the police role is pre-eminently symbolic, a reminder that social order ideologically precedes individual freedoms. Canadian legal order is built on a broader consensus than is the American legal order—albeit a consensus that legally and historically is situated in a demonstrated willingness to apply coercion in a systematic and concerted way.

The consequences of the Canadian and American strategies of dealing with crime are essentially the same for the socially advantaged of both countries. Both nations possess a legal order that allows the safe and stable conduct of social and economic affairs. However, the consequences for the socially disadvantaged in each country can be quite different. The American situation matches a freedom to deviate for those in subordinate statuses with a heightened likelihood of criminalization. The Canadian situation discourages deviation while decreasing the likelihood of criminalization for subordinates. Which situation is "better" is less an empirical than a moral issue. But the consequences of such situations can be studied.

Canadian–American differences in the control of crime and the potentially changing character of these societal differences represent a unique opportunity for a type of comparative research that is too seldom done in North American sociology. The purpose of the comparative framework outlined in this chapter is to counter this unjustified neglect, and to promote further exploration of the differing means used to establish legal order on this continent.

DISCUSSION QUESTIONS

1. It is sometimes argued that creativity and conformity are incompatible. Does the fact that Canadian society experiences less crime than the United States mean that it is also a less creative society?
2. Are Canadians actually less criminal than Americans, or is this difference simply one of the ways in which we respond to crime in Canada?
3. Do the American and Canadian experiences with ethnic and racial diversity have anything to do with the different national experiences with crime?

GLOSSARY

boundary maintenance the practice in social groups of drawing distinctions between behaviours deemed acceptable and unacceptable

crime-control model model of law enforcement that places heavy emphasis on the repression of criminal conduct, because insuring order is seen as the only way to guarantee individual rights

due-process model model of law enforcement that emphasizes procedural safeguards thought useful in protecting accused persons from unjust applications of criminal penalties

BIBLIOGRAPHY

Addiction Research Foundation
1982 "Statistics on Alcohol and Drug Use in Canada and Other Countries." Toronto: Addiction Research Foundation.

Atwood, Margaret E.
1972 *Survival: A Thematic Guide to Canadian Literature.* Toronto: Anansi.

Bell, D.
1953 "Crime as an American Way of Life." *Antioch Review* 13:131–54.

Bell, David and Lorne Tepperman
1979 *The Roots of Disunity: A Look at Canadian Political Culture.* Toronto: McClelland and Stewart.

Berg, D. F.
1970 "The Non-Medical Use of Dangerous Drugs in the United States: A Comprehensive View." *International Journal of Addictions* 5(4):777–834.

Brown, Lorne and Caroline Brown
1973 *An Unauthorized History of the R.C.M.P.* Toronto: Lewis and Samuel.

Bruton, P. W.
1962 "The Canadian Bill of Rights: Some American Observations." *McGill Law Journal* 8:106-20.

Christian, William and Colin Campbell
1983 *Political Parties and Ideologies in Canada.* 2nd ed. Toronto: McGraw-Hill Ryerson.

Clark, S. D.
1942 *The Social Development of Canada: An Introductory Study with Select Documents.* Toronto: University of Toronto Press.

——
1962 *The Developing Canadian Community.* Toronto: University of Toronto Press.

——
1975 "The Post-Second World War Canadian Society." *Canadian Review of Sociology and Anthropology* 12:25–32.

——
1976 *Candian Society in Historical Perspective.* Toronto: McGraw-Hill Ryerson.

Courtis, M. C.
1970 "Attitudes to Crime and the Police in Toronto: A Report on Some Survey Findings." Toronto: Centre for Criminology, University of Toronto.

Davis, A. K.
1971 "Canadian Society and History as Hinterland Versus Metropolis." In R. J. Ossenberg (ed.) *Canadian Society: Pluralism, Change and Conflict.* Scarborough, Ontario: Prentice-Hall.

Friedenberg, Edgar
1980 *Deference to Authority.* White Plains, New York: M. E. Sharpe, Inc.

Frye, Northrop
1982 *Divisions on a Ground.* Toronto: Anansi.

Gough, Barry Morton
1986 "Review of Law and Justice in a New Land." *Canadian Journal of Law and Society* 1:194–95.

Hagan, John and Jeffrey Leon
1978 "The Philosophy and Sociology of Crime Control: Canadian-American Comparisons." *Sociological Inquiry* 47(3–4):181–208.

——
1980 "The Rehabilitation of Law." *The Canadian Journal of Sociology* 5(3):235–51.

Harris, L.
1968 "The Public Looks at Crime and Corrections." Washington, D.C.: Joint Commission on Correctional Manpower and Training.

Hiller, H.
1976 *Canadian Society: A Sociological Analysis.* Scarborough, Ontario: Prentice-Hall.

Horowitz, I. L.
1966 "The Birth and Meaning of America: A Discussion." *Sociological Quarterly* 7:3–20.

——
1970 (ed.) *Masses in Latin America.* New York: Oxford University Press.

———
1973 "The Hemispheric Connection: A Critique and Corrective to the Entrepreneurial Thesis of Development with Special Emphasis on the Canadian Case." *Queen's Quarterly* 80:327–59.

Howard, R.
1986 "Canada won't negotiate B.C.–Alaska border." *The Globe and Mail*, August 29, 1986:A1.

Inciardi, J. A.
1975 *Careers in Crime*. Chicago: Rand McNally.

Jaffary, S. K.
1963 *Sentencing of Adults in Canada*. Toronto: University of Toronto Press.

Kelly, W. and N. Kelly
1976 *Policing in Canada*. Toronto: Macmillan.

Kirkham, James, Sheldon Levy, and William Crotty
1970 *Assassination and Political Violence*. Washington: Government Printing Office.

Klein, J. J. Webb and J. E. DiSanto
1978 "Experience with the Police and Attitude Toward the Police." *Canadian Journal of Sociology* 3:441–56.

Krueger, R.
1982 "A Geographical Perspective: The Setting and Settlement." In W. Metcalfe (ed.) *Understanding Canada: A Multidisciplinary Introduction to Canadian Studies*. New York: New York University Press.

Linden, Rick and Cathy Fillmore
1981 "A Comparative Study of Delinquency Involvement." *The Canadian Review of Sociology and Anthropology* 18(3):343–61.

Lipset, S. M.
1963 "The Value Patterns of Democracy: A Case Study in Comparative Analysis." *American Sociological Review* 28:515–31.

———
1964 "Canada and the United States—A Comparative View." *Canadian Review of Sociology and Anthropology* 1:173–85.

———
1968 *Revolution and Counterrevolution: Change and Persistence in Social Structure*. New York: Basic Books.

———
1986 "Historical Traditions and National Characteristics: A Comparative Analysis of Canada and the United States." *Canadian Journal of Sociology* 11(2):113–55.

MacLeod, R. C.
1976 *The North-West Mounted Police and Law Enforcement 1873–1905*. Toronto: University of Toronto Press.

McKercher, William R.
1983 *The U.S. Bill of Rights and the Canadian Charter of Rights and Freedoms*. Toronto: Ontario Economic Council.

McNaught, K.
1975 "Political Trials and the Canadian Political Tradition." In M. L. Friedland (ed.) *Courts and Trials: A Multi-Disciplinary Approach*. Toronto: University of Toronto Press.

McWhinney, Edward
1982 *Canada and the Constitution, 1979–1982*. Toronto: University of Toronto Press.

Naegle, K. D.
1964 "Canadian Society: Some Reflections." In B. R. Blishen, F. E. Jones, K. D. Naegle, and J. Porter (eds.) *Canadian Society*. Toronto: Macmillan.

Packer, H.
1964 "Two Models of the Criminal Process." *University of Pennsylvania Law Review* 113:1–68.

Popham, R. E.
1956 The Jellinek Alcoholism Estimation Formula and Its Application to Canadian Data." *Quarterly Journal of Studies on Alcohol* 17:559–93.

Porter, J.
1967 "Canadian Character in the Twentieth Century" *Annals of the American Academy of Political and Social Science* 370:48–56.

Pye, A. Kenneth
1982 "The Rights of Persons Accused of Crime under the Canadian Constitution: A Comparative Perspective." *Law and Contemporary Problems* 45(Autumn):221–48.

Quinney, R.
1970 *The Social Reality of Crime*. Boston: Little, Brown.

Russell, P. H.
1975a "The Political Role of the Supreme Court of Canada in Its First Century." *The Canadian Bar Review* 53:576–93.

Skolnick, J. H.
1975 *Justice Without Trial: Law Enforcement in Democratic Society*. New York: Wiley.

Smart, R. G. and D. Fejer
1971 "The Extent of Illicit Drug Use in Canada: A Review of Current Epidemiology." In Craig Boydell, Carl Grindstaff, and Paul Whitehead (eds.) *Critical Issues in Canadian Society*. Toronto: Holt, Rinehart and Winston.

Time
1968 "The Thin Blue Line." 93(July):39.

Truman, T.
1971 "A Critique of Seymour M. Lipset's Article, 'Value Differences, Absolute or Relative: The English-Speaking Democracies.'" *Canadian Journal of Political Science* 4:497–525.

Turk, A. T.
1969 *Criminality and the Legal Order*. Chicago: Rand McNally.

____
1977 "The Problem of Legal Order in the United States and South Africa: Substantive and Analytical Considerations." *Sociological Focus* 10:31–41.

Vallee, F. G. and D. R. Whyte.
1971 "Canadian Society: Trends and Perspectives." In B. Blishen, R. E. Jones, K. D. Naegle, and J. Porter (eds.) *Canadian Society: Sociological Perspectives*. Toronto: Macmillan.

Westin, Alan
1983 "The United States Bill of Rights and the Canadian Charter: A Socio-Political Analysis." In William R. McKercher (ed.) *The U.S. Bill of Rights and the Canadian Charter of Rights and Freedoms*. Toronto: Ontario Economic Council.

Whitehead, Paul and Reginald Smart
1972 "Validity and Reliability of Self-Reported Drug Use." *Canadian Journal of Criminology and Corrections* 14(1):83–89.

Wrong, D.
1955 *American and Canadian Viewpoints*. Washington, D.C.: American Council on Education.

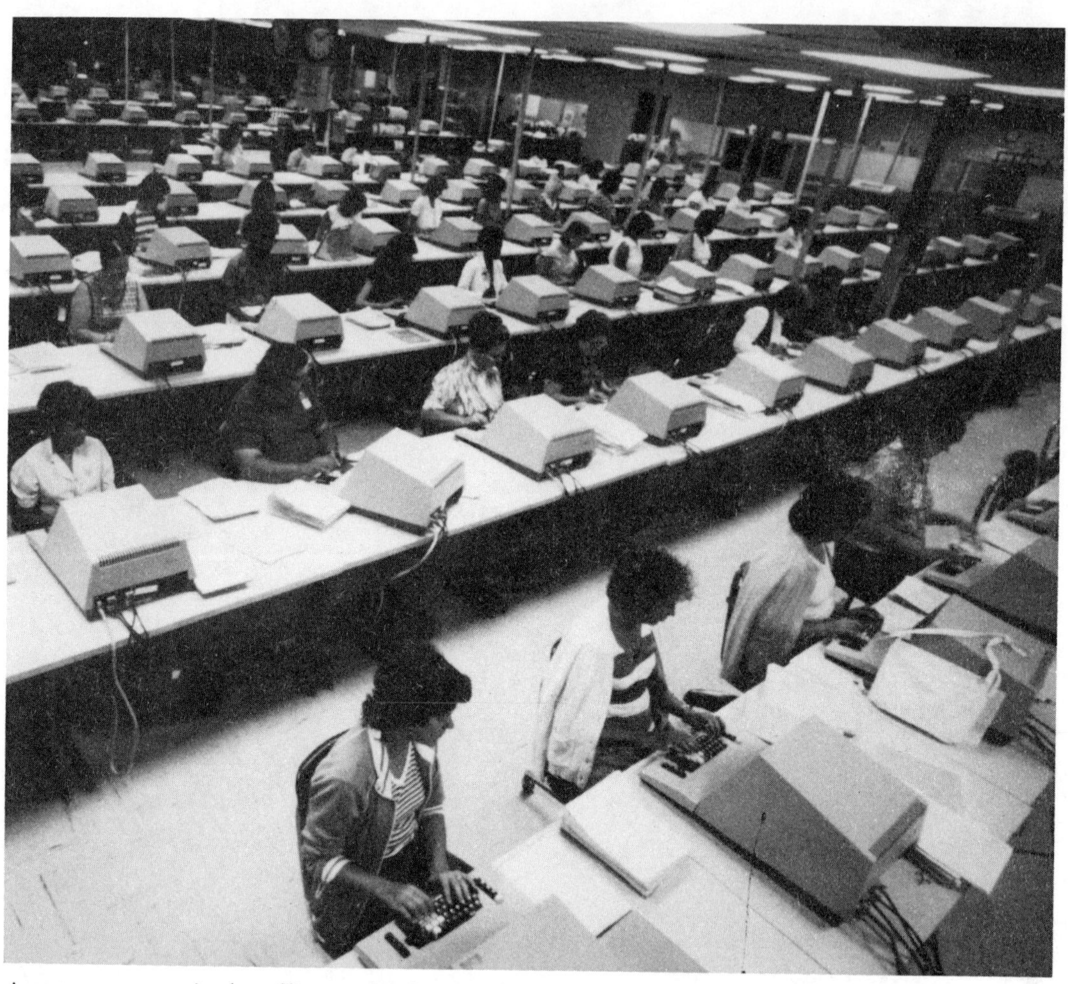

A common scene in the office work of today. *Courtesy of © Ted Wathen/Quadrant*

"Modern societies are moving ... to a service-dominated labour market, a dominant class of scientific and intellectual leaders, and an extensive use of information, as well as a labour market composed of many more women than before."

c h a p t e r   s i x t e e n

Work and Leisure

Lorna R. Marsden

INTRODUCTION

This chapter will address questions about the future of work in Canada based upon three major approaches. The first, the **post-industrial thesis**, has caused a long-standing debate in sociology. We will describe the thesis and examine how well it "fits" the Canadian situation. Second, we will examine the changing division of labour, including occupational shifts and changes in the composition of the Canadian work force, such as the recent rapid rise in the proportion of women workers. Third, we will discuss the institutional approach, which looks at the workplace and the social institutions that surround and interact with workplaces.

No one can be certain of the future. On the other hand, unless we begin to imagine the sort of future that may face us, we cannot begin to prepare young Canadians for their working lives, industries for changes in the economy and work, or state systems of planning and social insurance for the possible shocks of the future.

THE POST-INDUSTRIAL THESIS

For most of its history, sociology has been preoccupied with studying and analyzing industrial society. Since the theorists were trying to explain the rise of industrialism, capitalism, science, and rationality applied to **work** and labour, and the changes in the family and community that emerged from those changes in Northern Europe, the great contrast was between pre-industrial and industrial society. Sociologists trying to explain why industrial tasks are organized the way they are, why the nuclear family has become the accepted norm, or why a public school system arose went back to study the great transformation in the organization of labour that occurred in the eighteenth and nineteenth centuries—the period when North America was settled.

Figure 1
Industrial distribution of employment, 1911 to 1981

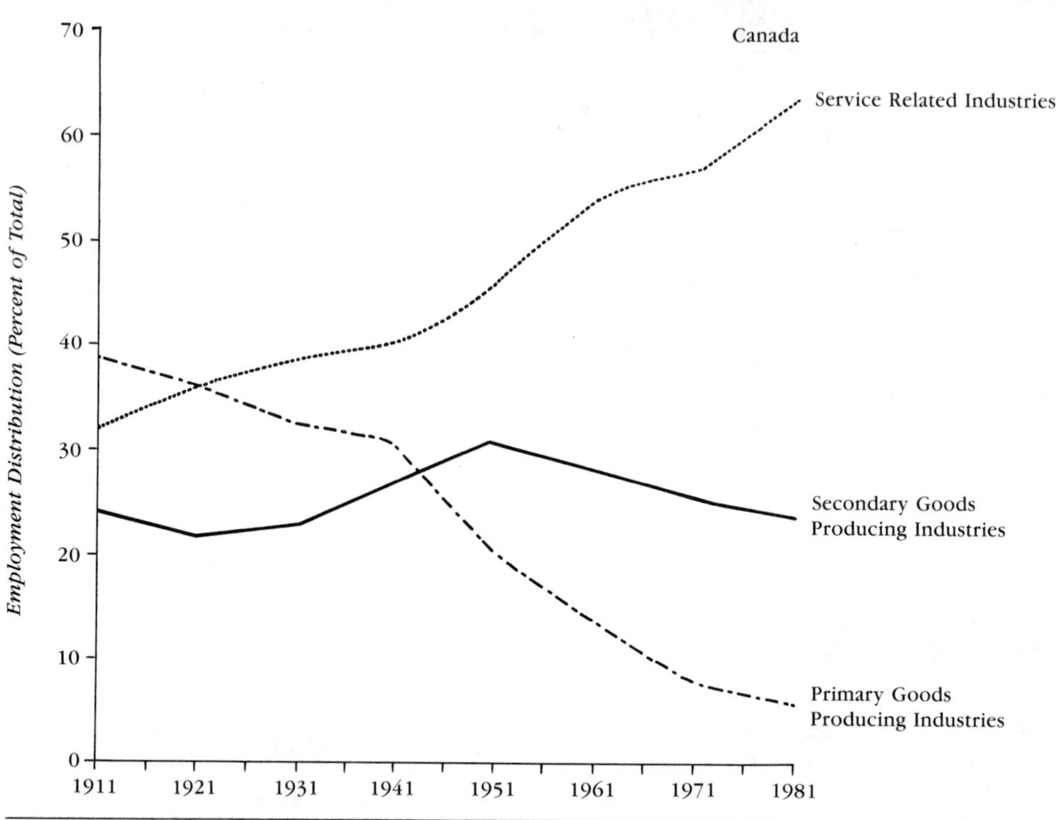

Source: Ontario Task Force on Employment and New Technology, 1985.

That settlement has been well documented, especially in French Canada, and the transition from rural to urban and from agrarian to industrial society has been studied by sociologists. For example, in the 1930s, Horace Miner wrote his famous study of St. Denis, an agrarian parish in Quebec that was apparently pre-industrial in much of its social organization. But a few years later, in 1943, Everett Hughes described an industrializing town in Quebec in *French Canada in Transition*. In the ecological tradition of research characteristic of the University of Chicago, this study described the changes in all the institutions in the community as it moved into industrial life. Meanwhile, in the tradition of political economy, sociologists and economists at McGill University and the University of Toronto were documenting the changes in Canada's staples industries. The fur trade, mining, the cod fisheries, the railways, and the technology of communications were all studied by Harold A. Innis of the University of Toronto. Both the McGill and Toronto approaches influenced the study of the frontier and the arrival of urban, industrial life (cf. S. D. Clark, *The Social Development of Canada*, 1942) and the impact of industrial work on the lives of workers and public policy (cf. Leonard Marsh, *Canadians In and Out of Work: A Survey of Economic Classes and Their Relation to the Labour Market*, 1940. Sociological studies of industrialization have continued from many perspectives (e.g., Smucker, 1980; Lucas, 1971; Rinehart, 1987; and see the important journal *Labour/Le Travailleur*).

But the industrial mode of production began to be seriously reviewed when it became apparent that the majority of workers produced not goods, but services (see Figure 1). With the application of new technology, the same number of workers could produce much more factory goods. Furthermore, management and government needed increasingly more information about work and workers in order to apply laws regulating work, pay, deductions, and compliance with regulations. One could see the increased use of personal services by workers and corporate financial services. Could we be moving out of the industrial age? How would we know if this was happening and what would it mean for workers, industries, communities, and governments?

In 1973, Daniel Bell, a U.S. sociologist, brought many of these ideas together in his book, *The Coming of Post-Industrial Society: A Venture in Social Forecasting*. His analysis rested on three characteristics of a future society no longer dominated by the industrial mode of production. The first major change would be a shift from producing goods to producing services, so that both the distribution of industries and the composition of the labour force would be profoundly changed. Second, in a post-industrial society, class relations would change, so that instead of the dominant class being the capitalist and managerial class, the "knowledge" workers in the professions and technical fields would become the elites dominating the economy. Third, and most profoundly, the resources base at the heart of industrialism—capital and its accumulation and control — would be replaced by knowledge or information. A recent **O.E.C.D.** study, *Trends in the Information Economy* (1986), illustrates the extent to which this third factor has become established in official studies.

From any theoretical perspective, the idea of a future society based on different ideas about the economy and work is intriguing. Sociologists took up the debate, and it is still underway. Indeed, the recent MacDonald Royal Commission on the Economic Union and Development Prospects for Canada published a series of volumes in 1986 of recent research in which these questions are raised. Are we still industrial? In which industries do Canadians work, and how are changes affecting these industries? All the questions are examined, largely from an economic or political viewpoint. Like sociologists, the economists and political scientists see major changes or "transitions," but toward what, exactly, is highly debatable. If Canada is changing, so is the rest of the world. Figure 2 shows manufacturing employment in six O.E.C.D. countries in the period from 1970 to 1984. Starting from a base in 1970, Canada has the highest growth in employment in manufacturing, and the United Kingdom, the greatest decline. Despite this contrast, Figure 1 shows service industries were growing rapidly. And Figure 3 shows that between 1975 and 1984 in Canada, despite a severe recession from 1981 to 1983, services to business management showed the greatest increases in employment.

But the sociological issues related to the changes in people's values about work and jobs, in the type of training and education they were undertaking, and the way work was organized on the job. In the many studies of factory production in the post-war period (e.g., Meissner, 1969 and, in the U.S.A., Blauner, 1964), the division of labour was shown to be important in the

Figure 2
Manufacturing employment in six O.E.C.D. countries

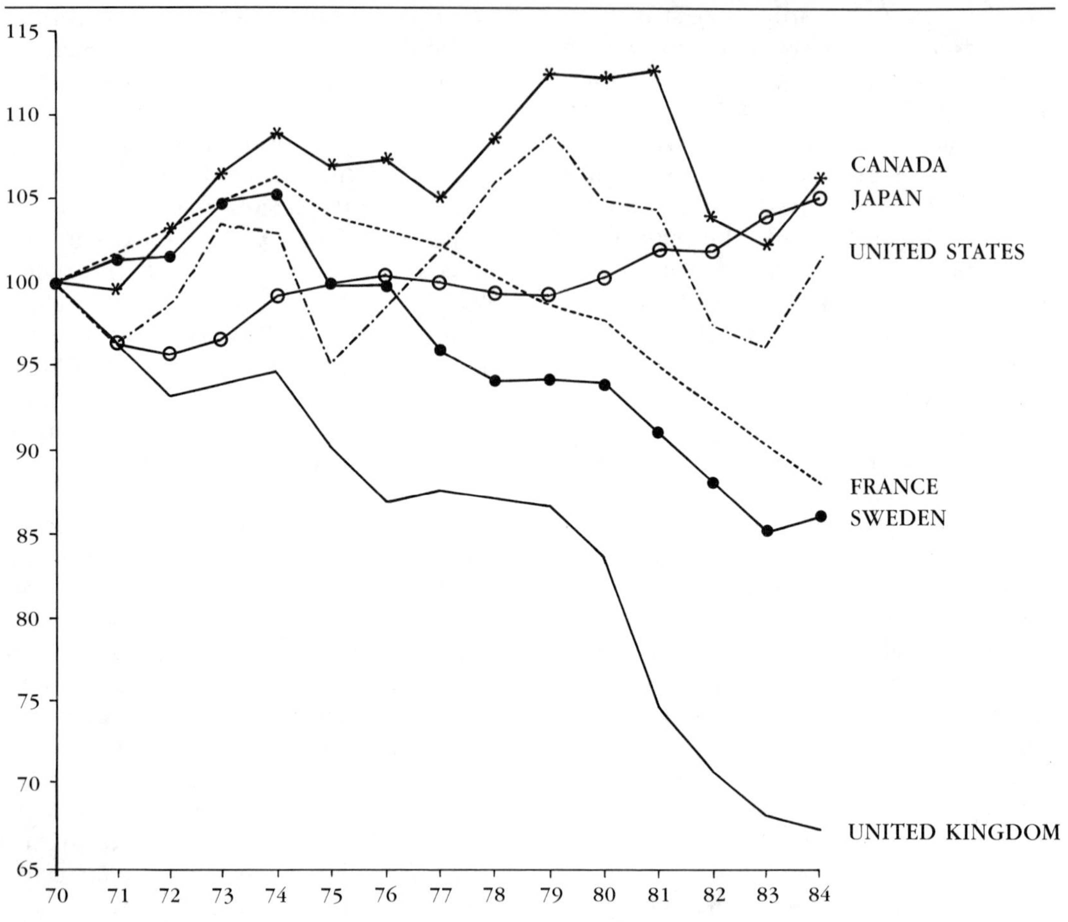

Source: O.E.C.D., *Flexibility in the Labour Market, The Current Debate*, Paris, 1986, p. 24.

organization of the workplace for the production of goods, such as automobiles or steel (e.g., Chinoy, 1955; Heron and Storey, 1986). Craft-organized tasks in which the worker made several parts or all of a machine from beginning to end had been replaced in industrial work with a very highly specialized division of labour. Not only did each worker repeatedly make some small part of the whole, but workers were organized into assembly lines to put the product together. The alienation resulting from this simple, repetitive, and often mindless work, has been studied often (Chinoy, 1955; Blauner, 1964; Rinehart, 1987). But what if instead of studying industrial problems, such as the monotony of tasks, the role of the foreman, and the nature of disputes and strikes, the work was entirely reorganized in a nonindustrial or post-industrial fashion? What questions would be suitable for study? The post-industrial theorists suggest the work ethic of industrialism, based upon the virtues of hard and highly structured work, thrift, and competition, would be replaced by a

Figure 3
Index of employment, selected industries, 1975 to 1984

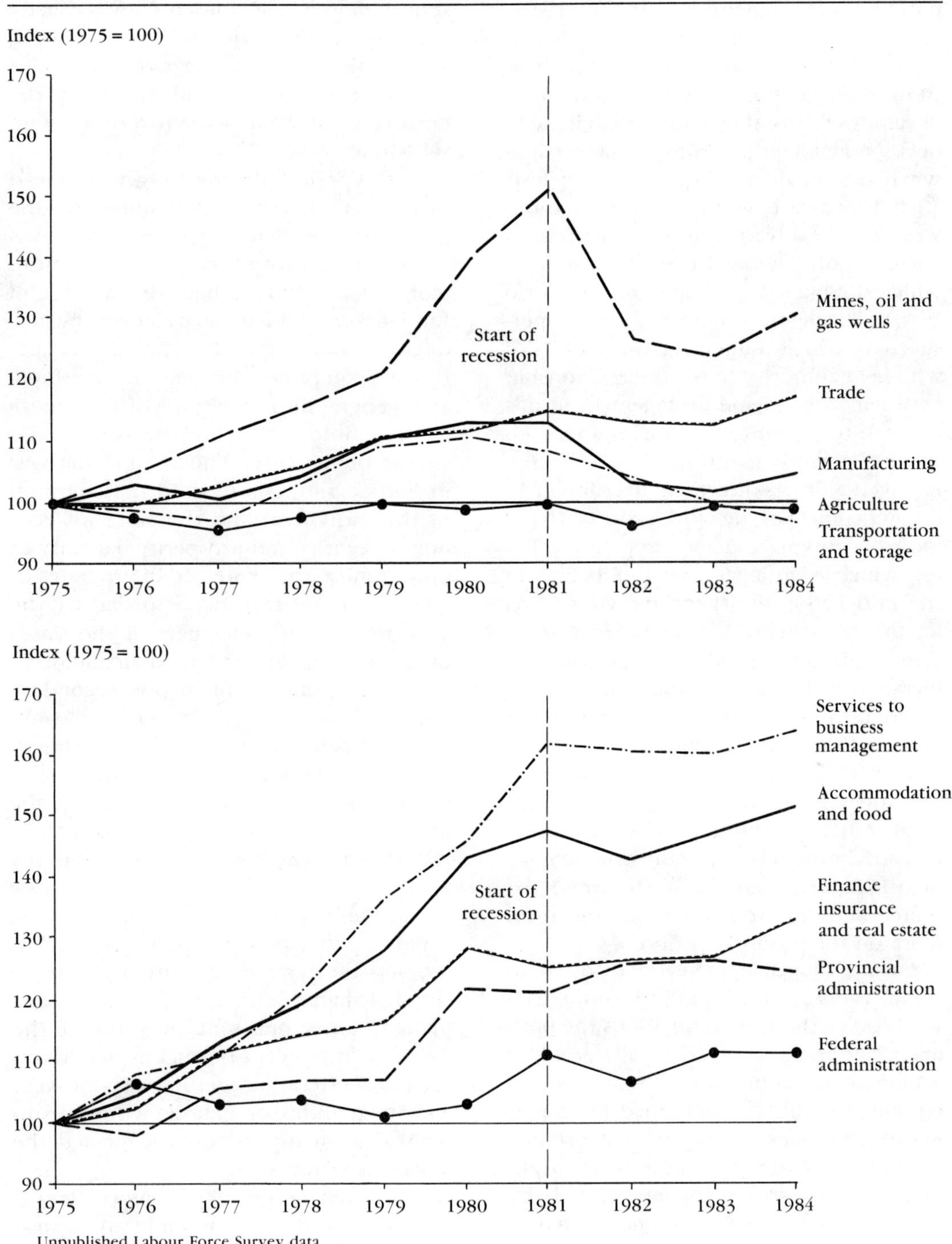

Unpublished Labour Force Survey data.

Source: W. Garnett Picot, p. 38.

different work ethic, based upon ideas about co-operation and forms of participative work behaviour (Miles, 1985; Reich, 1983). In Canada, a study by Nightingale (1982) of twenty industrial firms showed greater productivity from workers in settings where they could participate in decision making than from similar settings where they could not. Nightingale suggests attitudes toward work and values about work have evolved from the hierarchical patterns of "scientific management," which dominated until the end of World War II, through the human relations perspective, which reinterpreted the ideas of who held authority to see the relationship between workers and management in this context, to the human resources approach of the period 1960 to 1980, which involved workers directly in decision making and control of the work process, to the ideas of workplace democracy. In the latter, which Nightingale suggests begins in the mid-1960s, workers are viewed as legitimate stakeholders in the organization. Nightingale's case studies compare hierarchical industrial organizations with democratic industrial organizations in Canada. Just as comparable studies of organizations elsewhere, such as the studies of the Volvo plants in Sweden, these more democratically organized firms are making industrial products, but with what may be post-industrial values of the need for shared authority, co-operation, and team work on the production floor.

Or are they just experimenting with "improving conditions" for industrial workers? In the 1950s and 1960s the optimism about the industrial future led to a humanistic approach to workers and working conditions, described by Nightingale. The focus was on the male, skilled blue-collar worker. Wages were high, demand was strong, the post-war baby boom was underway. This meant that in most families the household consisted of one wage earner (usually the father), one homemaker (usually the mother), and some children. The household was usually without extended kin and was organized around the work of the father in indus try or office and around preparing the children for that workforce through schooling.

In this period, the idea of getting ahead through hard work was modified by the growing belief that a good education was the route to prosperity and satisfaction. More science and mathematics was useful for workers, and graduation certificates, degrees, and licensed technical occupational requirements aided occupational and geographical mobility. Those ideas existed before World War II, but the shocks of the Dirty Thirties and the war in Europe and Asia focused the attention of the individual and the state on economic security and prosperity. Equality of opportunity was expressed in programs of education and training afforded by the state to returning members of the Canadian armed forces and to their children. After 1950, enrolment in post-secondary education doubled. The engineers, the university graduates, and the formal requirements of nursing, teaching, and many other occupations tended to support the idea that a new "technocracy" of brains, rather than capital, would dominate in the future.

But these optimistic views of economic expansion, personal prosperity and mobility, and the rewards of hard work were stopped sharp by the great wave of social protest movements at the end of the 1960s, which swept through North America and Western Europe. All was not well, and inequalities of Blacks, women, students, and many minorities formed the basis of social protest.

The struggle was much more than a generational protest of children against parents. The protest was about the materialism of industrial society, the exploitation of nature by industry, the exploitation of people by employers, and the rigidity of ideas about the meaning of work and life. Counter-cultural movements, rural and urban co-operatives built upon values that had long been present in Canada. The social gospel movement early in this century in Canada had not entirely disappeared (cf. Allen, 1973), and co-operatives as an alternative to capitalist enterprise has been continuously strong (Macpherson, 1979).

For sociologists, the theory of post-industrial society had to be re-examined. While the structural shifts in industries and the types of jobs workers held continued, while the technical elite continued to grow despite university stop-outs and drop-outs and a focus on humanities and social sciences, and while the co-operative work ethic predicted for post-industrialism was much enhanced, two further components were added to the theory of the future of work.

First, technological change took a dramatic rise, not only in its form — from mechanical to computerized and from mainframe to microchip — but in its evaluation. No longer was it a simple question of ameliorating the worst conditions in the factory by better human relations, better working conditions, better pay or new machinery. Now microchips began appearing in a wide range of tools at work, allowing each worker to produce more, thus reducing employment (see Figure 4, page 452). Furthermore, unlike the earlier mainframe computers, the microchip invaded the retail sector in new types of cash registers, stocktaking, and recording machines for inventory control and worker surveillance; they invaded the office in word processors, communication links, and data-based work. Predictions of the decimation of the retail and office sectors appeared in Canada in such studies as Menzies, *Women and the Chip* (1981). Setting four possible scenarios for the impact of microtechnology to the year 2000, Menzies predicted female clerical unemployment would rise throughout the balance of the century. Figure 4 shows the changes in employment in selected Canadian industries between 1971 and 1979, distinguishing between changes due to demand for goods and services (medium dark bar) and changes due to changes in productivity and technology (darkest bar). There has been an increase in total employment (lightest bar) in every industry except agriculture, and a decline in employment due to productivity and technology in every industry except producer and consumer services. Since, as we have already seen, this is where most employment now rests and the greatest growth in employment has occurred, we are still creating jobs. But it is clear that one of the features of the new wave of technological change has been a major structural shift in employment in Canada.

And projected unemployment was not the only impact of this new technology. Further specialization in the division of labour resulted in each worker commanding a narrower range of skills in a job — a **de-skilling** process. This had already been documented in industrial and factory production, and now the debate turned to white-collar industries inspired in large part by Braverman's *Labor and Monopoly Capital* (1974).

Braverman re-examined the Marxian theories about the advance of capital and increasing control that the capitalist class would have over the factors of production. Reviewing the division of labour that accompanied industrialization and the seizure of power by management from craftsworkers, Braverman extended the ideas of "scientific management" to white-collar work. He disagreed with Bell's view of the post-industrial society. Instead of a scien-

Figure 4
Percent change in employment between 1971 and 1979, selected industries

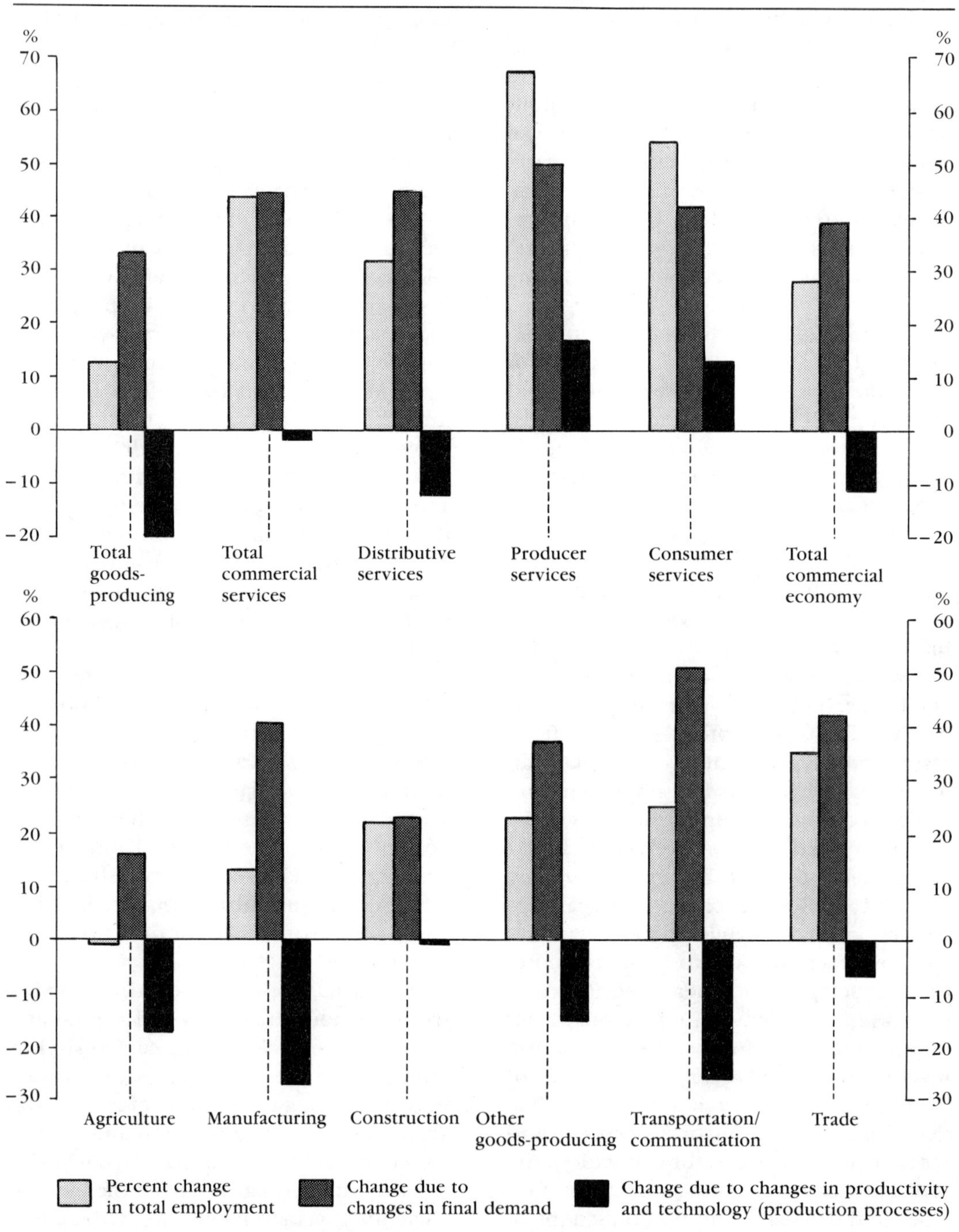

Source: Reproduced with permission of Minister of Supply and Services Canada.

tific elite, the old class of capitalists would have even more power, and in a worldwide system would squeeze more and more value from the work of each labourer by applying new technology and stronger methods of social control in the workplace. De-skilling, the proletarianization of occupations as their tasks were divided into mundane tasks under the control of management, control through computerization in numerically controlled machines, the reduction of wages, and the commoditization of everything lay ahead of us.

On the other hand, those who rejected Braverman's thesis were inclined to see the post-industrial society as enhanced by technological change. Much of the dirty and dangerous work could be handled by robots. Much of the drudgery of office work would be eliminated by the word processor and small computer. In the course of this technological change, newer and better jobs would be created. While adjustments might be painful, the economy would expand, and overall employment would increase, although working hours might decline.

By the late 1970s and early 1980s, all participants in this debate realized the composition of the paid labour force had changed, probably permanently, with the entry of a majority of women, especially married women with young children. Two incomes were not required or wanted by most families in the 1950s and early 1960s. By the 1970s, two incomes were needed by many families and in the 1980s the majority of married women both needed and wanted permanent paid employment. More attention began to be paid in the era of social protest and beyond to the situation of women, minorities, Native peoples, francophones, and disabled people in the Canadian economy. New laws to ensure greater opportunity gradually shifted from desirable, to optimal, to mandatory (Marsden, 1982 and 1985).

In addition, the post-industrial theories were amended to take into account economies other than the **formal economy**. The formal economy is accounted for in the budgets and financial records of governments. The household economy has always been excluded from such calculations, but the services performed and goods produced in the household have always been important to the Canadian economy. In her description of three generations of households in Flin Flon, Manitoba (*More Than a Labour of Love*, 1986), Luxton examines this important "informal" economy in the past, therefore allowing us to look at what might happen in the future.

For example, household composition continues to change, with children from more than one marriage blended into a single "economy" of the household. With more single parents and many more two-earner families, the variety of family and households has expanded. In addition, time constraints and increased cash flow have changed the nature of household consumption. Canadian workers spend more on prepared foods and restaurant meals. Clothes are much more likely to be bought than made at home, and home entertainment comes from a variety of machines for television, music, and games.

Canadian sociology has studied changes from the discovery of the development of industrialism in the agrarian parts of the country, such as Quebec, to typical industrial work in British Columbia, to the steady growth of the service and informations sectors. As Canadians shift their work patterns, sociologists revise the general theory of post-industrial society. To Bell's basic premises—dominance of services, the rise of the scientific elite, and the importance of information rather than capital as a resource base — have been added studies of the changed nature of social relations in the workplace from hierarchical and bureaucratic to flexible,

THE OTHER ECONOMIES

There are other "economies" where barter takes place: an exchange of neighbourhood baby-sitting services, for example, or when one person helps a neighbour build a patio and in return uses the neighbour's camper for a holiday. These, also, are traditional forms of economic exchange not accounted for in the public record. Such economic relationships go beyond neighbourhoods to the massive amounts of time donated for work in voluntary organizations from working with youth groups, to church groups, to collecting money for good causes, to organizing unions, ratepayers groups and political parties. Is this work increasing as some people have more leisure time?

This addition to the post-industrial thesis is described as the "informalization" of the future society, and implies the need for a better sociological understanding of the work people really do (Miles, 1985). Time budgeting studies have shown that shorter work weeks may not lead to more leisure. For many women, for example, a shorter working week simply substitutes household work for paid work (Meissner, 1977). The "other economies" may absorb the energies of people seeking more income. The rapid rise of part-time employment in Canada indicates time allocation is shifting, but it does not reveal the uses people make of their "unpaid" time.

co-operative, and team-based. In addition, the thesis has been expanded to account for changes brought about by the rapid impact of microchip technology. In the latter, changes in employment and the content or skill of jobs remain paramount concerns. Lastly, a new emphasis on the family's adjustments to late industrialism or post-industrialism led to the study of the informal economy.

Today, few Canadians still work in craft-based settings or on very small farms, which are almost pre-industrial in their organization of work and economic life. Certainly, some Canadian communities of Mennonities and others keep that way of life alive. A great many more Canadians work in typically industrial settings. These workers have a high division of labour into jobs with narrow, highly specialized tasks. They work in organizations that have many layers of authority arranged vertically. Work is co-ordinated and managed by supervisors who are, in turn, co-ordinated by management of increasing levels of power up to the chief executive officer. Industrial workers are usually unionized and bargain collectively about their working conditions, wages, and benefits through their unions. In the classical sense, they are often alienated from their work, what they produce, and how they produce it. It is "just a job," a way to make money to support their families, rather than a source of intrinsic satisfaction.

But many other workers are in nonindustrial jobs. They work in teams or cooperatively in units. The management structure is somewhat flat, or they are self-employed and work under contract. Much of modern work is highly automated. People work not just for pay, but also in the home and community — but all are tasks labelled as work. For many Canadians, technical supervisors are the new elite, and the heroes are not the capitalists of the past, but the engineers and financial experts of the present. People disagree about whether we now live in a post-industrial society.

Sociologists, meanwhile, examine Canada's social structure and working conditions and debate the nature of the changes in the workforce. The rise in unemployment, especially among the young, seems permanent. The presence of highly sophisticated technological tools in the office, factory, and retail outlet is widespread. And the success of television, computer hardware and software, data bases, cable communication, and electronic mail all testify to the importance of information as a resource base for work and the Canadian economy.

There is great diversity, but the trend is clear. More workers must be better trained and educated. There is no sign that this trend will decrease. More aspects of working life are information-based in banks and stores, as well as in laboratories and hospitals. The production of goods is so rationalized by machines, international markets, and transport that fewer and fewer workers produce more and more goods. The informal economy dominates in services, such as childcare and food preparation. Perhaps we have already arrived in Bell's post-industrial society, but we will not really know this except in hindsight. When we look back and recall how it was in the industrial era, we will become aware of how much has changed.

The last to change will be Canadian attitudes about work. Do young people carry the work ethic of the future? Do Canadians still believe work and the family are the most important sources of satisfaction in life? We will look at these institutions in the third section of this chapter. But first we will examine changes in the division of labour.

This can be done from the point of view of a shift in industries, from the content of the job, and from the point of view of power (e.g., Rueschemeyer, 1986). We will only indicate three major shifts which are linked closely to the post-industrial thesis: among classes; between consumer and producer; and between the genders. In each case, we will point out trends.

DIVISION OF LABOUR AND THE FUTURE

The division of labour in Canada has been slowly changing for a long time. For example, in the food retailing business, customers used to have their meat prepared by butchers while they waited. They would shop with the assistance of a clerk. Now the food is largely prepackaged and retail stores are self-service. That is, the work previously done by paid employees is transferred to consumers and to packaging workers and machines. The checkout counter is fitted with computerized scanners, resulting in faster checkouts and fewer checkout clerks. Increasingly, as private secretaries are eliminated from offices, that work is done by highly paid staff with the help of highly sophisticated telephone equipment.

So the contemporary division of labour makes the consumer of services also the provider of services, with the rented (or owned) equipment of a high technology firm or utility.

This division also moves human labour power from one part of the business to another. This is true in banking. Tellers have been displaced, in part, by automated tellers (Green Machines), but the huge expansion of banking services such as credit cards and the billing of customers for services previously not accounted for (e.g., daily interest accounts and frequent statements) have expanded the number of clerks behind the scenes. Figure 4 shows the rapid expansion of employment in producer and consumer services contributed by technology.

The great phenomena of industrial society has been the rise of the middle class. People with a good education, working in white-collar occupations as bureaucrats, managers, professionals, and technicians have been the predominant class in industrial societies. In Canada, for several generations parents have urged their children to stay on in school for a better education, which meant steady work, a salary rather than weekly wages, good working conditions, and a comfortable standard of living. Many skilled tradespeople and craftsworkers are "middle class" by socioeconomic definition. In 1981 in Canada, four in ten workers were in white-collar jobs, and one in four in professional, managerial, or administrative occupations.

Politically and socially, Canadian society is dominated by middle-class values, and most Canadians regard themselves and most of the people they know as middle class.

But some theorists argue the middle class is being eroded because the new technology is "de-skilling" the professional workers and many other skilled workers, and creating a two-class society. On one hand is a vast proletariat of workers doing largely routine, de-skilled work with no career ladders and little access to power or rewards by legitimate means. On the other hand is the new powerful class in charge of the industries, the **workplaces** and the political and social **institutions**. This includes a new technical elite of highly skilled individuals who command the economy's technological base.

These theorists see evidence in the breakdown of skills into their component parts in such jobs as machine tool operators and other skilled crafts, such as typesetting which has been replaced almost completely by computerized equipment. Computerized typesetting is done by semi-skilled workers who are paid less than typesetters and are supervised by layout specialists in the print shops. The same argument suggests doctors and lawyers are becoming highly specialized, with many of their tasks taken over by para-professional workers. They see the management process being replaced by computer programs, which instruct workers and direct tasks; secretarial work decomposing into word processing in centralized, industrialized pools; executive assistants who are more management than worker; and electronic mail and planning which may be done by managers themselves. This vision of a two-class society rests on a revised Marxian class division between a proletarianized middle class and an elite capitalist class. But as others argue (Simpson, 1985), the evidence is not yet in.

Some take the opposite view entirely. They see the new technology eliminating much of the drudgery and routine work. They argue work will become less onerous and more interesting, even in jobs that do not require much skill. In their view, the entire society will become more "middle class," with wealth being created by applying new technology to the production of goods and services.

But most observers cautiously predict little change (Kling, 1980). Status differences are long-standing among people in industrial societies, and this shows little erosion. Working tools have already changed and will change further, but human beings do not change so quickly.

Labour market theory gives us a good example of this thinking. For some time, sociologists have looked at dual labour markets: a primary labour market with good jobs requiring high levels of education, skills, and work performance, and a secondary labour market. Such jobs, which might be in any sector and be blue-collar, white-collar or pink-collar, are full-time, full-year jobs with internal career ladders and security of tenure. Workers in the primary sector are usually unionized, or have strong professional associations to shelter them. Many workers in this sector are highly educated, belong to the dominant groups in the society (i.e., men, Whites), and share the dominant values of the society.

The other labour market, the secondary labour market, has the opposite characteristics. Jobs are not long-term or high-paying. They are often part-time, part-year jobs, and the workers are not often unionized or sheltered by a worker's association. Required skills or education are low, and a highly educated worker, in this secondary labour market, would not be rewarded for it. Wages are usually hourly and have to do with the market forces more than with the attributes of the workers. Many workers in this sector are members of minority or less powerful groups (i.e., women, visible minorities, Native peoples, the disabled, or those with some difficulties in employment).

Such a theory reinforces the idea that a "dual" society may be emerging. But the dual labour market theory does not conform well to social reality. More recent theorists have discussed segmented labour markets with many different groups of workers in differing relationships with job security, unions, and wages. A group of sociologists at Dalhousie University examined labour markets there and identified a "central work world" and a "marginal work world" (Clairmont and Apostle, 1986). The segments identified in the Maritimes study are at the level of the workplace, rather than at the industry, firm, or occupational level. This conceptualization focuses on conditions in Canada's economically "dependent regions," where multinationals own the large capital enterprises and respond to a world economy and international division of labour. But being resource-based, they do not move rapidly, and powerful unions protect their workers and public sector workers. Small local firms and firms attracted by high unemployment rates, and therefore low wages, make up the secondary labour market. The Marginal Work World research shows how wages, technological change, and social and political attitudes are associated with workplace experiences, and provides a base for studying how changes will be accepted or refused, or benefit one group of Canadians or another (Clairmont and Apostle, 1986).

THE FUTURE OF WORK AND THE GENDER DIVISION OF LABOUR

Industrial society brought with it the division of labour between the household and the workplace. Eventually, the household became the main workplace of women and the factory or office for men. This division has been accepted for several generations as so common as to be "natural," and earlier sociological accounts accorded these spheres of labour concepts such as "expressive" and "instrumental" roles by gender. But the division of labour in society has continued apace. Women were drawn back into the paid labour force by demand for their skills (Oppenheimer, 1970) and a rising consciousness about the economic inequality faced by homemakers. Far from being "natural," the gender division of labour is a product of the same forces that created other divisions within the labour market.

In Canada, females constitute the fastest growing segment of the labour force, faster than youth and faster than prime age males. Married women with children under age three are recording the greatest growth in the labour force among women. Among women aged twenty-five to thirty-four, 76 percent are in the labour force and, 64 percent of those have preschool children. None of the projections of labour force growth anticipated the strength of this social trend (Ciurniak and Sims, 1980). The occupational segregation of women into certain occupational sectors has increased in Canada over the last decade, and the wage gap between women and men in similar jobs is still great (Abella, 1984). Women, including women in the paid labour force, are the largest group in poverty in Canada (National Council on Welfare, 1986). As women are advised, if they would only "choose" the better paid occupations, the wage gap would diminish. But entry into the better paid occupations is not straightforward. Of the economic and sectoral elites identified in Clement's study of the Canadian corporate elite (1975), only six were women. Women did best at powerful positions in the media.

Journalism is a quite new industry in some of its parts. Does this mean gender inequalities may be diminished in newer industries? The evidence is not in. But in the rapidly expanding field of computer operations, management, and programming, it has not proved to be the case. Indeed, as Rob Kling's data indicate, the introduction of new computer methods reinforces what already exists in management structures and designs (Kling, 1980; Kling and Iacono, 1984). In short, the future gender division of labour will depend upon political and not technological changes in the Canadian economy.

The way work is divided at any level of analysis from the work station to regional analysis of classes is an outcome of decisions made by workers and management, by husbands and wives, and by multinationals and national industries that move plants and people. The decisions are taken under the pressures of economic and social change in the world markets. We have looked briefly at three trends expected to be important in the next century.

We will examine now the changes in the social institutions in which work takes place or workers are supported, such as the family. In doing this, we will look at the values about work which Canadians hold and how these may change.

WORK, LEISURE, AND VALUES

Canadians now hold jobs in different industries than they did in the past, and while it is difficult to measure change exactly, the evidence suggests a "post-industrial" economy is emerging in our society.

Since nearly all Canadians work for a living, our family and community life are organized around our working lives. Changes in the hours of work have changed our patterns of leisure. For example, when most people worked on Saturday, family and personal leisure was confined to evenings and Sundays. But now the forty-hour work week is standard and the two-day weekend has expanded the range of leisure activities. If hours of work change again, we can expect leisure time to adjust. The number of part-time workers in Canada suggests more Canadians are using time differently (see Figure 5). Various occupations work longer shifts for fewer days. Nurses at some hospitals have bargained for such work patterns. In some industrial plants, where continuous production is required, shiftwork provides long weekends for some workers. In the service sector, nonstandard working hours are common. Airline pilots and flight attendants, childcare workers, retail workers, restaurant and entertainment workers, all adjust their working hours to the requirements of their clientele.

In two British studies, Jenkins and Sherman argued, first, that the new technology of production would reduce the amount of work available, leading to a large proportion of underemployed or unemployed

Figure 5

Part-time employment in Canada, 1953 to 1982

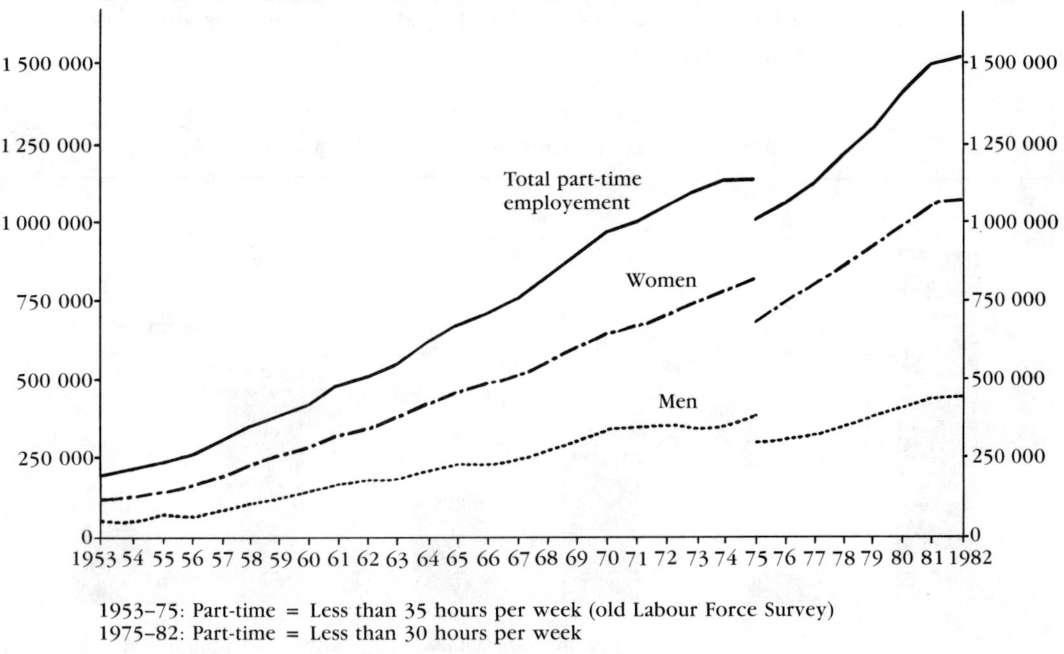

Source: Reproduced with permission of Minister of Supply and Services Canada.

people who would receive their income from state transfers (*The Collapse of Work*, 1979) and, then, in a second book, that the British people have a strong work ethic, even when they do not like their jobs, and are unprepared for long periods of leisure, especially on low incomes (*The Leisure Shock*, 1981). Work has not "collapsed" in Canada, but it is changing. Do Canadians have the strong "work ethic" that Jenkins and Sherman attribute to the British? Will the changing nature of work leave us unprepared for nonworking time?

The evidence suggests that work is important to Canadians, and that various social institutions, such as the family and the educational system, have already begun to modify our ideas about work.

In Canadian society, the Western European and Judeo-Christian values still dominate. Work is considered good not just for the material rewards, but for the sense of inner satisfaction, and for the contribution to the well-being of the community.

Our values about work—both paid and unpaid—are acted out daily in our families, in the workplace, and in the community. Our use of time in work and leisure, our self-esteem, our standing in the family and community, the lifestyle we assume, all pattern our behaviour. These social institutions reveal why work is much the same now as it has been for centuries, and how it has changed and will change further.

Social change is seldom revolutionary, dramatic, or reversible. Most changes in social patterns are incremental, occur quite slowly, and are accepted so gradually that few people are aware of change until they compare the past with the present. People tend to change their values gradu-

VIEWS OF WORK, FAMILIES, AND FRIENDS

Figure 6 shows the roles work, families and friends played in the sense of personal rewards among Canadians surveyed in the 1970s.

Figure 6
What Canadians depend on for personal rewards

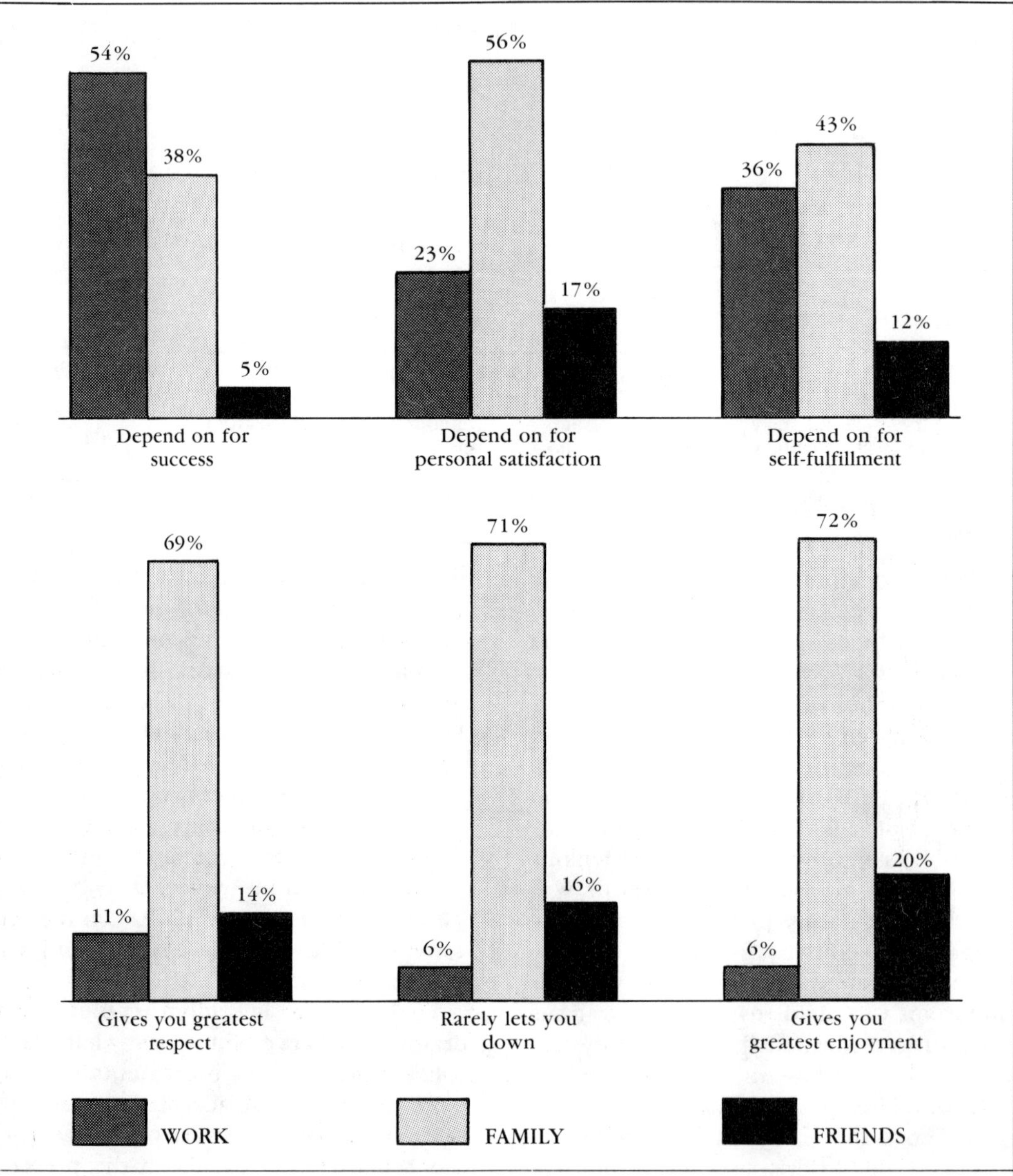

Source: M. Burnstein, N. Tienhaara, P. Hewson, and B. Warrander, *Canadian Work Values*, Ottawa, Manpower and Immigration, 1975.

The chart shows that the family is the most important source of personal rewards, but work provides Canadians with a sense of success, self-fulfillment, and personal satisfaction. In a more recent study (Atkinson and Murray, 1980), work was found to be more highly valued among the upwardly mobile and achievement-oriented. This group of Canadians are young, unmarried low-income men, high-income married men, and high-income unmarried women. Having a job in the paid labour force helps provide a personal identity and a major link between the individual, the family, and the larger community. But it is more important in some life stages than in others.

ally to meet changes in their behaviour rather than the other way around.

We can examine the lives of individuals from a "work-centred" perspective. Each person's family/household, education or training, and community all influence the workplace. What is valued highly at home will shape the values people hold at work.

Family and Household

Our first ideas and values about work and our role in the economy come from our families. This is most evident now in the attitudes and values of women. Those who grew up in households where the adult women were housewives and mothers are now adjusting to a world in which more married women with children are in the paid labour force than are at home. In 1971, one in three households had a wife at home with children, while the husband was the "breadwinner." By 1981, this was true of only one in five households, and now the proportion is even lower. In 1986, only one in ten Quebec households fits this pattern. The proportion of single-parent households rose significantly as divorce doubled between 1972 and 1984. Half of all single-parent households headed by women live below the poverty line (National Council on Welfare, 1986). Children growing up in any household now see a variety of labour force patterns in the families around them because one dominant pattern does not hold true. They will see families in which both parents work full-time or one parent full-time and one part-time. They will see one-parent families in which the adult works full-time, part-time, or not at all in the labour force. They will see families in which the mother is at home and the father in the paid labour force. Sometimes, as in the armed forces, work and family life are heavily integrated (Pinch, 1982). It is logical that young Canadians hold different ideas and values about the importance and role of work in the paid labour force from those held by their parents.

In Canada, unemployment has been the main public issue since the recession of the early 1980s. But the actual experience of unemployment falls most heavily on certain types of families. As Paul Shaw has pointed out (1985), even during the depths of the recession, the majority of Canadians either retained their jobs or suffered short-term unemployment. But some families have chronically unemployed family members (i.e., no other family income for support) and are likely to live in the Atlantic provinces or Quebec; have few skills, so even when they do have work, they earn low wages; are young, poorly educated people who live alone or live with families where others are chronically unemployed; are unemployed mothers who lead their households or who have unemployed husbands; and, finally, are Native peoples,

French Canadians, or of multiple ethnic origins. In some families, the experiences associated with the labour force are totally different from the majority of working Canadians.

Generally speaking, people who do not have jobs and are not looking for work are condemned by others. But there is a counter-culture in which work is not highly valued. To understand the importance of the family as an institution of learning about work, we must understand the variations in family values.

Those who will have to change their careers significantly in midlife also face difficulties. Many families accept this and adjust, but others do not. It requires reserves of psychological and emotional strength in marriage partners and in children, which we do not properly understand. Employers may not perceive these family problems, and both family and worklife suffer from the strains (Johnson, 1986).

In a study of young people in the O.E.C.D. countries, Coleman and Husén (1985) suggest the demand for more highly educated and trained workers and the changed household compositions are causing young people greater difficulties than before in "becoming adult." When life was divided into early childhood at home, school for ten to thirteen years, and then work or further training for work, adulthood was gained by "leaving home." With fewer jobs for beginning workers available, and a demand for more training, that point of leaving home is pushed further and further ahead, creating a dependency between the home and young people which did not previously exist. Because they do not have a job, young people are not permitted to be involved in other major family, social, or economic decisions as an "adult" would. Coleman and Husén suggest the schools should adjust to accommodate these changes. Schools may become more flexible, and already many Canadian secondary schools and universities have work-study "co-operative" programs in which students study part-time and work in the paid labour force part-time. Such programs help parents help their children find good jobs in such a changed labour market. They help teachers and schools because they motivate some students who would otherwise drop out or take inappropriate training. They help students who find school frustrating and who want the adult social role of a worker but could not otherwise find a good job (Senate, 1986, chap. 3).

Are these changed socialization experiences of young Canadians changing their values? In a national study of highschool students, Bibby and Posterski (1985) found friendship and being loved rank highest in every region of the country among young people as "terminal values," or values which are end-states that the person would like to reach. But young Canadians also gave "working hard" a high score. It is third after "honesty" and "cleanliness" as the means by which they would achieve their goals. In fact, this study's authors conclude Canadian teenagers are strongly committed to the "middle-class virtues" of cleanliness, reliability, hard work, and intelligence. This national sample of fifteen- to nineteen-year-olds in highschool place less value on family life. Only 65 percent say it is very important to them. Bibby and Posterski suggest "these findings indicate that, during these years at least, the family is failing to function as a source of happiness, compassion, and love for many Canadian young people" (ibid.:20).

This may reflect changes in family and community life, but the O.E.C.D. studies of young people in the Western industrial countries concluded the value of work and jobs remains high among young people, even those who want to work only for the money it provides to do other things (O.E.C.D., 1983).

The Redistribution of Work and Time

Industrial society separated people's days into work at the workplace and work in the household and "leisure." Most women had little leisure. The housewife was on twenty-four-hour call, and while she may have engaged in voluntary work outside the home, leisure was only possible if she could turn over the household labour to servants.

But for men, leisure was a more usual commodity. Time studies of the use made by people of their time have been referred to earlier. Clear-cut differences are found in comparative studies. American business executives and British executives show different leisure patterns. The British managers took more leisure time at home and on activities not directly linked to their jobs (Parker, 1976:67–68). Meissner's article, "The Long Arm of the Job" shows leisure patterns are closely influenced by the job among Canadians (Meissner, 1971).

The question of retirement is a separate one, even though it implies a reorganization of time and an increase in leisure activities. But leisure spent after a lifetime of work is different from leisure spent while expecting or hoping to return to paid employment.

Work-Sharing

At present, many Canadians work part-time and have few or no employee benefits. Such benefits as pensions, dental and health plans, paid vacation time, and sick leave are attached to full-time employment and are important parts of the family economy. There is an increasing demand to include part-time workers in such benefits, at least on a pro-rated basis (Wallace, 1983). But the major unions argue that instead of giving benefits to part-time employees, the average working week should be reduced. Reid (1986) notes the average full-time employee in Canada worked 40.8 hours during 1983. "Simple calculations indicate that if average working time were reduced to, say, thirty-five hours per week, and if the reduced hours were translated into additional jobs, the result would be a 17 percent increase in full-time employment" (1986:159). However, as Reid adds, there are impediments to such a straightforward solution to un employment, such as the substitutability of skills, the costs to employers, and other resistance.

It should be noted, however, as shown in Figure 5, that the definition of part-time

WORK-SHARING AND NEW JOBS

Work-sharing is an important feature of the changes occurring in the Canadian labour market, and it takes many forms. Several analysts have pointed out that many of the jobs created in Canada recently resulted from a reduction in annual working hours. This is because of a reduction in the number of working hours in a week and an increase in the number of annual statutory holidays to eleven, and an increase in paid vacation time. Peitchinis (1982) notes that people with jobs worked 476 fewer hours in 1981 than in 1951, the equivalent of 2 892 778 jobs. This work-sharing through reduced working hours created the equivalent of half the new jobs.

employment has already been reduced from working less than thirty-five hours per week to working less than thirty hours per week.

A variety of work-sharing patterns have been tried in other O.E.C.D. countries. In West Germany's flexi-year scheme, workers state how many hours they will work in a twelve-month period, but within an established minimum number of hours for full-time and for part-time employees. One department store reported that agreements were negotiated with staff and workers who could fit their working hours to their other commitments to the satisfaction of both management and workers. Job satisfaction increased, sales increased, and absenteeism dropped.

Various forms of flexible hours have been in place in Canada for some time. In a useful study of the issues in work-sharing and job-sharing, Meltz, Reid and Swartz (1981) analyzed the situation in Canada and in Ontario. They distinguish between job-sharing (two or more workers sharing a job that could be filled by one full-time worker), regular part-time employment, and work-sharing that occurs when the demand for labour is low. They use the term employment-sharing to cover all of these situations.

The authors suggest the willingness of workers to share employment is influenced by: (1) material inducements (i.e., a work-sharing employee offered a good full-time, long-term job will stop work-sharing; a worker threatened with layoffs is more likely to work-share; a part-time worker offered a high wage for more hours is likely to work-share, etc.), and (2) preferences about the use of time related to the interest of the job (the pull of family responsibilities, etc.). Key variables explaining the prospensity to work-share are worker age, gender, wage rate, and the proportion of part-time employees in the industry. Females were the group most likely to agree to work-share.

The analysis shows age and sex are importantly correlated with the desire or willingness to share employment and that demographic trends support the trend to work-sharing. The proportion of young workers is declining, and therefore the part-time worker or employment-sharing youth is replaced by a larger proportion of prime-age males. At the same time, the rate of married female labour force participation is increasing, so the demand for regular part-time employment is expected to rise.

In suggesting that the single most important policy change to support employment-sharing is to permit working employees to draw unemployment insurance benefits, Meltz, Reid, and Swartz see a permanent change coming in the labour force. "If the typical worker is employed for his preferred number of hours before work-sharing, the introduction of U.I. benefits to offset the income lost during work-sharing will cause even employees who would not have been subject to layoff to prefer to engage in some work-sharing in their own self-interest. The conclusion applies both to workers with a permanent attachment to the labour force and to those with a temporary attachment" (1981:69). However, they add that work-sharing has a limited effect on reducing unemployment even in well-developed schemes such as that of Germany.

Job-sharing, work-sharing, and employment-sharing may all be important features of a future labour market. But what difference would this make to the social organization of work and the lives of Canadians? And, second, do Canadians want this reorganization of their time?

We have discussed major shifts in the composition of the household and family. Smaller households, "blended" families, and more two-earner households mean more demands on the family. Fewer working hours will not translate directly into more leisure time. The sharing of domestic tasks and the increased demands on each family member for attention — affection, listening, caring—will require more hours in the household. Since a high value is placed on family life and on work, we must also ask whether it is preferable to have a few people working long hours with the wealth created being shared in transfer payments to those without work, or to have more people sharing the available jobs. The latter course is more compatible with current values. Thus, the work-sharing options look most attractive.

That may not be true in all occupations or for all employers, however. Many jobs require the continuous attention of a single mind. Jobs requiring theoretical knowledge in science, engineering, medicine, or research of all kinds are typical of such jobs. This may be true of many management jobs where the knowledge cannot be transferred by rules and applied by any individual. Many Canadians already work long hours of "overtime," although they are not paid for them and those jobs often enjoy the highest social prestige. They are the new technical elite of the information economy about whom Bell wrote.

But new technologies probably also reform labour in ways that dilute the effectiveness of labour. The automatically dialled telephone makes operators of us all; the work station may make clerical workers of executives; the washer-dryers in every home turn householders (or female ones anyway) into laundresses, and the relatively cheap car turns us into chauffeurs and transit drivers. One executive has told me that because his secretary is now an "administrative assistant" and cannot be asked to do mundane tasks, such as making calls and appointments, opening his mail, and bringing his coffee, he gets done in a working day only about one-third of what he did previously. (This does not mean he has less value to the company nor that it is a less efficient way of producing—his previous work may not have resulted in the same value to the firm as the reduction in clerical assistance does.) Because so many of these service tasks have to be accomplished during the business hours, to do any of the reading or sustained thinking that he did previously, he spends many more hours on his "job" during the evenings and weekends. In some occupations, then, productivity may be reduced without reducing paid work hours.

So do Canadians want to change their working time either in a week, a year, or throughout their lifetime? In the United States, workers have been asked about another approach. This redistributes work through a "cyclical life plan," replacing the current "linear life plan" (see Figure 7). In the linear life plan there is an age-graded three-phased set of activities (basically childhood, followed by work, followed by retirement). This is the pattern of North America and the rest of the industrial world. But since the amount of life time spent on work is reducing rapidly in relation to increased life expectancy, other patterns should be contemplated. Best and Stern (1976) suggest a cyclical life plan to distribute some of the education and retirement time into midlife.

The cyclical life plan is particularly attractive to people with families, since it implies parenting leave would be possible. It is also attractive to those who work in low wage, low skill, or monotonous jobs where work is not intrinsically interesting. But it is very attractive and may be highly needed by workers in highly stressful jobs in any industry. Teachers in universities have sabbatical leaves for research, but many workers require time away from highly stressful jobs, such as social work, management, and industrial production.

From the point of view of employers, however, the demand of a "flexible labour force is the demand for frequent retraining, and not all the retraining can be done on the job. No longer does a degree or cer-

Figure 7
Alternative future lifetime patterns

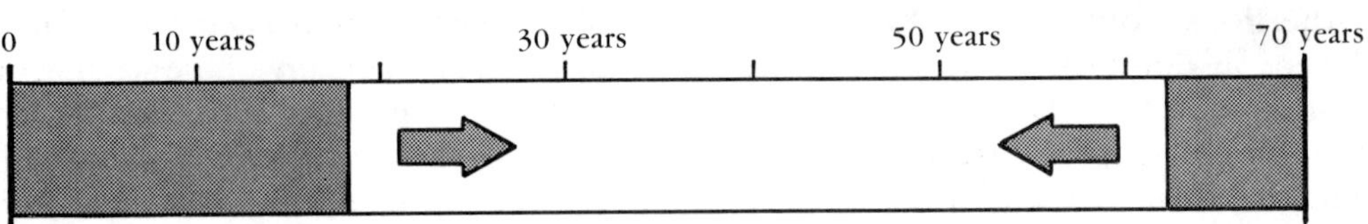

Linear Life Plan: Extended periods of nonwork during youth for education and during old age for retirement. Most work activities performed in consecutive years during midlife. Most increases in nonwork taken in reduced workweeks and expansion of time for education and retirement in youth and old age.

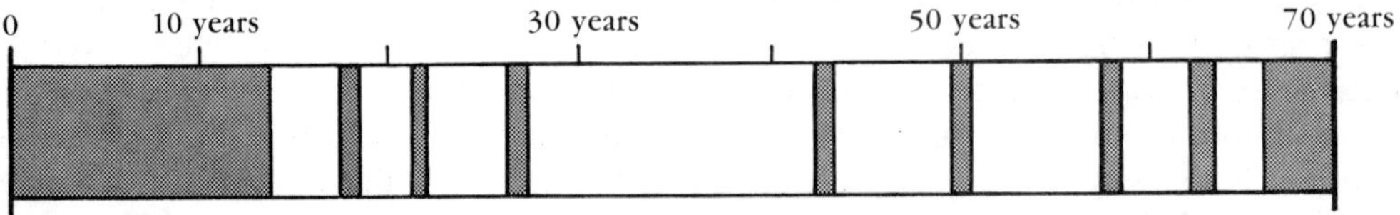

Cyclic Life Plan: Significant portions of nonwork time now spent on education during youth and retirement in old age redistributed to the middle years of life to allow extended periods of leisure or education in midlife. Most increases in nonwork time taken as extended periods away from work during midlife.

Source: Best and Stern, 1976:10.

tificate adequately prepare one for a working life. Continuing education is important to almost all professions and to many skilled and semi-skilled workers as well. In 1983, one in every five Canadians over the age of seventeen took adult education (Devereaux, 1984). This may lead to a cyclical life plan whether or not that is chosen by Canadian workers.

Best, in a 1976 review of behavioural, attitudinal, and consumer data on worker tradeoff preferences between income and free time, found that preferences shifted toward more free time but in large cumulated periods, such as an extra week of vacation (preferred over shorter work weeks).

Best and Stern point out that institutional constraints may be the major barrier to changing the lifetime patterns of U.S. workers. Work organizations fear discontinuities, loss of trained personnel with business information to competitors, and administrative costs of co-ordinating noncontinuous employees; employees fear loss of their jobs; these constitute such constraints. Best and Stern raise the question about redistribution of paid employment, leisure, and education. They suggest that the lack of public consensus on the desirability of changing the linear pattern may prevent rapid changes toward policies to implement a cyclic pattern. Fred Best's *Work Sharing: Issues, Policy Options and Prospects* (1981) incorporates the results of the work cited above. Here, Best evaluated policies on the assumption that innovation in the time aspects of labour are required to deal with structural and increasing unemployment.

He finds two successful methods. The first is the subsidized worktime reduction, discussed above in the Canadian study. Like Meltz, Reid, and Schwartz, he notes its success in mitigating unemployment in Europe and the United States. But, of course, it does not increase new employment. Best finds the other alternative, legislated reductions in the number of hours worked, to be expensive, inflationary, and a limit on the individual freedom of the worker.

A difficulty with both the Canadian and the U.S. analyses is the absence of attention of the power of various groups involved in any scheme to change work hours. **Occupations** with a labour market monopoly, such as doctors, enjoy high status and high income and control absolutely their number of working hours (unless they sell their hours to an organization that controls their time.) But the unskilled, casual workers poorly integrated into the economy may not be able to make a living wage no matter how many hours they work, even if the work is offered. Discussing the redistribution of working time requires reference not only to wages but also to occupational inequalities in shelters (unions, professional associations, industrial sectors) and the influence of economic planners.

CONCLUSION

In this chapter we have noted some current trends in the behaviour of Canadians at work and toward work at various levels. We have looked at the division of labour between women and men as an important change affecting the workplace and the domestic arrangements that support the workplace. We have looked at the values and attitudes Canadians hold about work in relation to family and personal life and at the impact of technological change on work.

These trends have been linked to the "post-industrial thesis," which suggests our Western societies are moving from a focus on industrial arrangements to something new — something only partially understood but which has several characteristics: a service-dominated labour market; a dominant class of scientific and intellectual leaders; and an extensive use of information; as well as a labour market comprising many more women than before, and an informal as well as a formal economy. All these changes are occurring in Canada and in other Western industrial societies. But the evidence is not conclusive. Work is changing, but the only way to learn the final answer is by tracking the trends, building our analysis, and living as long as possible.

DISCUSSION QUESTIONS

1. What is the validity of the post-industrial thesis in the context of Canadian society?
2. Is de-skilling primarily a result of technological changes or is it a product of management systems in the workplace?
3. To what extent is the informal economy a significant factor in the "worktime" of Canadians?
4. Does the university have dual or segmented "labour markets?"
5. Is there any evidence from your lives that people are any less interested in how they make their living (their "work values") than in previous generations? Is work less important or is it organized differently?

GLOSSARY

de-skilling a concept related to the increased division of labour during which, by dividing a job into narrower and narrower specialization, a class of workers or occupational group loses its skill and control to management

formal economy that part of the economy accounted for in the records and financial control mechanisms of government as opposed to the household economy; the barter economy or informal economy; and the black economy or illegal economy

gender division of labour emerging from the separation of the household and workplace which occurred with industrialization, male and female segregation by occupation, workplace, pay and benefits, and then training has led to gender ghettoes in the Canadian economy. There is no sign that this segregation is reduced as the economy changes. Cultural and political/legal change and action appear necessarily to reduce the inequities created by this division of labour.

labour market theory from a sociological perspective (as opposed to an economist's perspective) the interest lies in the social organization of labour into primary, secondary, or segmented markets. Barriers to movement between these markets may be a social, economic, or geographic and impede individual life chances (such as social mobility) as well as collective interests, such as unions or professional associations. In Canada, labour markets have been studied in marginal economies, single-industry towns, and on the frontier.

occupation "the social role performed by adult members of society that directly and/or indirectly yields social and financial consequences and that constitutes a major focus in the life of an adult" (Richard Hall, 1986:2)

O.E.C.D. the Organization for Economic Co-operation and Development is an agency that studies and compares data on the economies of the Western industrial capitalist nations. It includes the Western European countries, Australia, Japan, the United States, and Canada. Canada's economy has much in common with this comparison group, except that we created about one-third of our exports through commodity production (wheat, oil, fish, minerals, forest products and hydroelectric power) but only about 7 percent of Canadians work in these industries.

post-industrial thesis a theory advanced by Daniel Bell and amended by recent critics that holds that our society is changing in the following ways: the production of goods is being overtaken by the production of services; the economy is less dominated by capitalists and managers and more by knowledge workers; the major resource pool of capital is less crucial than the resource pool of information; the work ethic is shifting toward co-operation and individual initiative away from centralized control and competition; the division of labour is realigning in conjunction with the advance of microchip-based tools of production; and the informal economy is increasingly important as the labour force composition and working hours/years change

work the creation of something of value for others

work-related institutions if one takes a work-centred view of our society, the family and household, the community, and education and training institutions can be viewed as supportive of and resonating to workplace values. As modern capitalism shifts the type of work done, the type of workers in demand, and the social organization of work, these work-related institutions change to accommodate the dominant institution: work.

BIBLIOGRAPHY

Abella, Rosalie Silberman
1984 *Equality in Employment: A Royal Commission Report*. Ottawa.

Allen, Richard
1973 *The Social Passion: Religion and Social Reform in Canada*. 1914–28. Toronto: University of Toronto Press.

Anthony, P. D.
1977 *The Ideology of Work*. London: Tavistock.

Atkinson, Tom and Michael A. Murray
1982 *Values, Domains and the Perceived Quality of Life: Canada and the United States*. York University, Institute for Behavioral Research, June.

Bell, Daniel
1973 *The Coming of Post-Industrial Society: A Venture in Social Forecasting*. New York: Basic Books.

Best, Fred
1981 *Work Sharing: Issues, Policy Options and Prospects*. Kalamazoo, Michigan: W.E. Upjohn Institute for Employment Research.

Best, Fred and Barry Stern
1976 "Lifetime Distribution of Education, Work and Leisure: Research, Speculations and Policy Implications of Changing Life Patterns." *Institute for Educational Leadership, Postsecondary Education Convening Authority*, Washington, D.C., December.

Bibby, Reginald W. and Donald C. Posterski
1985 *The Emerging Generation*. Toronto: Irwin.

Blauner, Robert
1964 *Alienation and Freeedom*. Chicago: University of Chicago Press.

Bledstein, Burton
1976 *The Culture of Professionalism: The Middle Class and Development of Higher Education in America*. New York: Norton.

Braverman, Harry
1974 *Labor and Monopoly Capital*. New York: Monthly Review Press.

Burnstein, M., N. Tienhaara, P. Hewson and B. Warrander
1975 *Canadian Work Values*. Ottawa: Manpower and Immigration.

Chinoy, Eli
1955 *Automobile Workers and the American Dream*. New York: Doubleday.

Ciurniak, Dan and Harvey Sims
1980 *Participation Rates and Labour Force Growth in Canada*. Ottawa: Dept. of Finance, April.

Clairmont, Don and Richard Apostle
1986 "Work: A Segmentation Perspective." In K. Lundy and B. Warme, *Work in the Canadian Context: Continuity Despite Change*. Toronto: Butterworths.

Clark, S. D.
1942 *The Social Development of Canada*. Toronto: University of Toronto Press.

Clement, Wallace
1975 *The Canadian Corporate Elite*. Toronto: McClelland and Stewart.

Coleman, James S. and Torsten Husén
1985 *Becoming Adult in a Changing Society*. Paris: O.E.C.D.

Collins, Randall
1982 "The Nonrational Foundation of Rationality." In *Sociological Insight: An Introduction to Non-Obvious*

Sociology. New York: Oxford University Press.

Devereaux, M. S.
1984 *One in Every Fice: A Survey of Adult Education in Canada*. Ottawa: Secretary of State.

Freedman, Marcia
1976 *Labour Markets: Segments and Shelters*. Montclair, New Jersey: Allanheld, Osmun and Co.

Hall, Richard A.
1969 *Occupations and the Social Structure*. Englewood Cliffs, New Jersey: Prentice Hall.

Heron, Craig and Robert Storey
1986 "Work and Struggle in the Canadian Steel Industry, 1900–1950." In Heron and Storey (eds) *On the Job*. Toronto: McGill-Queen's University Press.

Hughes, Everett
1943 *French Canada in Transition*. Chicago: University of Chicago Press.

Jenkins, Clive and Barry Sherman
1979 *The Collapse of Work*. London: Eyre Methuen.

——
1981 *The Leisure Shock*. London: Eyre Methuen.

Johnson, Laura
1986 "Working Families: Workplace Supports for Families." A report of the Working Families Project of the Social Planning Council of Metropolitan Toronto, February.

Kling, Rob
1980 "Social analyses of computing: theoretical perspectives in recent empirical research." *Computing Surveys* 12(1):61:110.

Kling, Rob and Suzanne Iacono
1984 "Computing as an Occasion for Social Control." *Journal of Social Issues* 40(3): 77–96.

Lowe, Graham S.
1983 "The Nature of Work and the Productive Process." In J. Paul Grayson (ed.) *Introduction to Sociology: An Alternate Approach*. Toronto: Gage Publishing.

Lucas, Rex
1971 *Milltown, Minetown, Railtown: Life in Canadian Communities of Single Industry*. Toronto: University of Toronto Press.

Luxton, Meg
1980 *More Than a Labour of Love*. Toronto: Women's Press, 1980.

MacPherson, Ian
1979 *Each for All: A History of the Co-operative Movement in English Canada, 1900–1945*. Toronto: Macmillan.

Magill, Dennis
1983 "Paradigms and Social Science in English Canada." In J. Paul Grayson (ed.) *Introduction to Sociology: An Alternative Approach*. Toronto: Gage Publishing.

Marsden, Lorna
1982 "The Relationship Between the Labour Force Employment of Women and the Changing Social Organization in Canada." In Anne Holberg (ed.) *Women and the World of Work*. New York: Plenum Press.

——
1985 "The Importance of Studying Affirmative Action." *Canadian Woman Studies* 6(4) (Winter): 11–15.

Marsden, Lorna and Edward Harvey
1979 *The Fragile Federation: Social Change in Canada*. Toronto: McGraw-Hill Ryerson.

Marsh, Leonard C.
1940 *Canadians In and Out of Work*. Toronto: Oxford University Press.

Meissner, Martin
1969 *Technology and the Worker*. San Francisco: Chandler Publishing.

——
1971 "The Long Arm of the Job" *Industrial Relations* 2 (October).

——
1977 "Sexual Division of Labour and Inequality: Labour and Leisure." In Marylee Stephenson (ed.) *Women in Canada*. Don Mills: General Publishing.

Meltz, N. F. Reid, and G. S. Swartz
1981 *Sharing the Work*. Toronto: University of Toronto Press.

Menzies, Heather
1981 *Women and the Chip*. Montreal: Institute for Research on Public Policy.
Miles, Ian
1985 "The New Post-Industrial State." *Futures*, December: 588–617.
Miner, Horace
1939 *St. Denis: A French Canadian Parish*. Chicago: University of Chicago Press.
National Council on Welfare
1986 *Progress Against Poverty*. Ottawa.
Nightingale, Donald V.
1982 *Workplace Democracy*. Toronto: University of Toronto Press.
O.E.C.D.
1983 *Education and Work: One View of the Young*. Paris.
——
1986 *Flexibility in the Labour Market: The Current Debate*. Paris.
——
1986 *Trends in the Information Economy* ICCP, Paris.
Ontario Task Force on Employment and New Technology
1985 *Employment and New Technology*. Toronto: Ontario Government Publications.
Oppenheimer, Valerie Kincaid
1970 *The Female Labour Force in the United States*. Berkeley: University of California Press.
Parker, Stanley
1976 *The Sociology of Leisure*. London: George Allen and Unwin.
Peitchinis, Stephen
1982 "Microelectronic Technology and Employment: Reality and Fiction." Paper presented at Queen's University Conference.
Picot, W. Garnett
1986 *Canada's Industries: Growth in Jobs Over Three Decades, A Review of the Changing Industrial Mix of Employment, 1951–1984*. Ottawa, Statistics Canada.
Pinch, Franklin C.
1982 "Military Manpower and Social Change: Assessing the Institutional Fit." *Armed Forces and Society* 8, Summer: 575–600.
Radwanski, George
1986 *Ontario Study of the Source Sector*. Toronto: Ontario Ministry of Treasury and Economics.
Reich, Robert B.
1983 *The Next American Frontier*. Penguin.
Reid, Frank
1986 "Reductions in Work Time: An Assessment of Employment Sharing to Reduce Unemployment." In W. Craig Riddell, *Work and Pay: The Canadian Labour Market*, vol. 17. Royal Commission on the Economic Union and Development Prospects for Canada.
Rinehart, James
1987 *The Tyranny of Work*, 2nd ed. Don Mills: Longman.
Ritzer, George and David Walczak
1986 *Working, Conflict and Change*, 3rd ed. Englewood Cliffs, New Jersey: Prentice-Hall.
Rueschemeyer, Dietrich
1986 *Power and the Division of Labour*. Cambridge: Policy Press.
Senate of Canada
1986 *Youth: A Plan of Action*. Report of the Special Senate Committee on Youth, Ottawa, February.
Shaw, Paul
1985 "The Burden of Unemployment in Canada." *Canadian Public Policy* XI, 2:143–60.
Simpson, Richard L.
1985 "Social Control of Occupations and Work." *Annual Review of Sociology* 11: 415–36.
Smucker, J.
1980 *Industrialization in Canada*. Scarborough, Ontario: Prentice-Hall.
Wallace, Joan
1983 *Part-time Work in Canada: Report of the Commission of Inquiry into Part-time Work*. Ottawa: Labour Canada.
Watson, Tony J.
1980 *Sociology, Work and Industry*. London: Routledge and Kegan Paul.

part four

Social Inequality and Protest

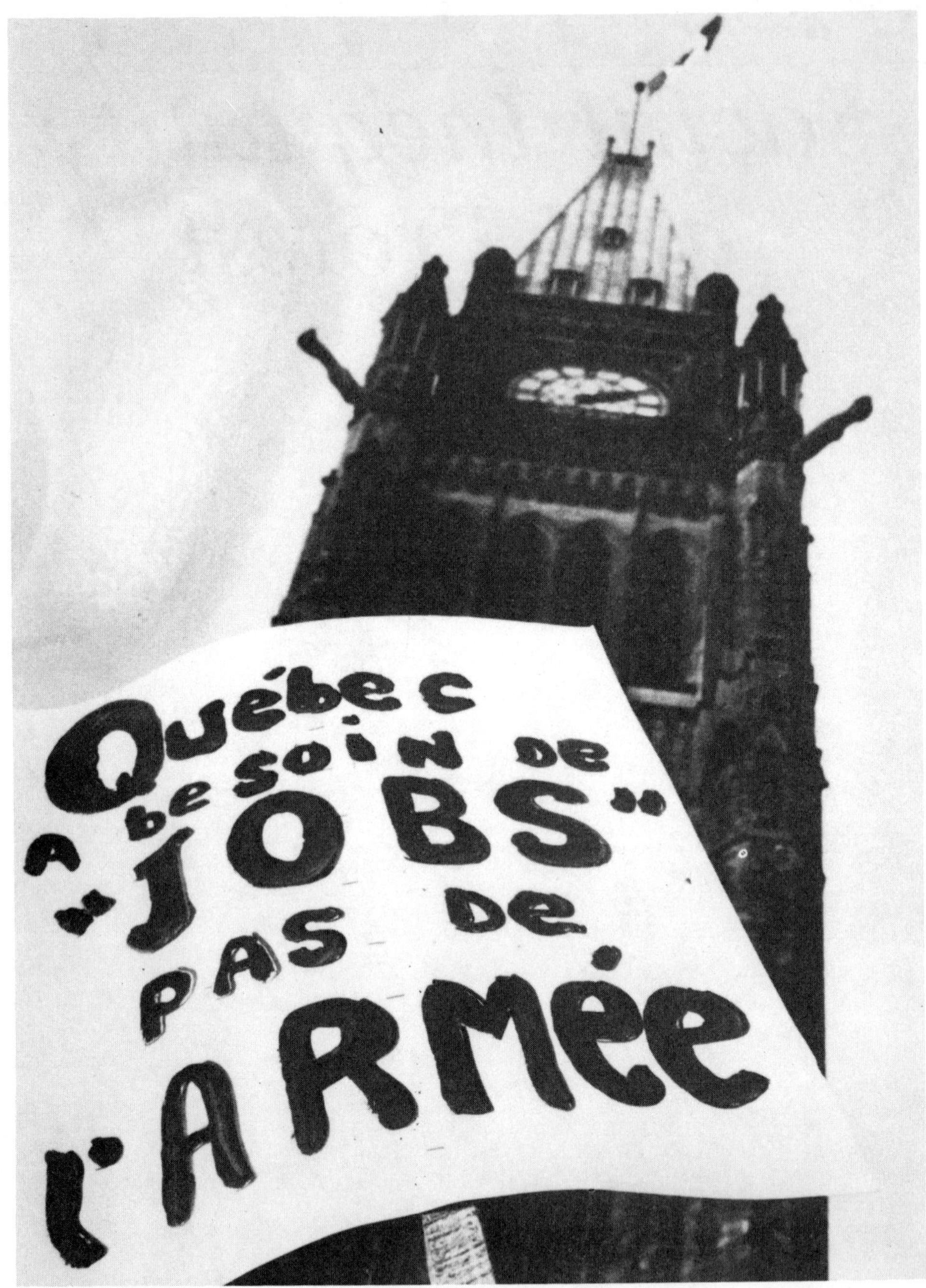

Quebec needs jobs, not the army — a protest sign on Parliament Hill, Ottawa, following the government's use of the War Measures Act in 1970. *Courtesy of National Archives Canada/PA 126347*

"All societies operate on . . . ideological bases, but not all members of the same society accept the same ideology."

c h a p t e r   s e v e n t e e n

Currents in Political Ideology

M. Patricia Marchak

INTRODUCTION

The physical sciences explain natural phenomena in terms of laws: the laws of aerodynamics, thermodynamics, relativity, gravity, and so forth. These cannot be seen by the human eye, but they explain what can be seen. The social sciences likewise explain the underlying features of social organization. But unlike the physical sciences of the 1980s (with some exceptions), the social sciences come up against enormous blockages we call **ideology**.

Ideology impedes our understanding of other features of social organization. It is also one of the most contested concepts in the social sciences. Often people use the term to refer to any curious ideas espoused by minority groups (they have ideology; we have common sense). We dismiss that usage: the ideologies that interest us, in fact, are the ideas of majorities that infuse our shared culture. We will define ideology here as shared ideas, perceptions, values, and beliefs through which members of a society interpret history and contemporary social events and that shape their expectations and wishes for the future. All societies operate on such ideological bases, but not all members of the same society fully accept the same ideology. Competing versions of social reality, history, and the future may coexist. One version may be held by a majority—in which case we can speak of a dominant ideology. Dominant ideologies normally contain core values and beliefs, and different groups in the society adopt variations of less central values in their interpretations. "Counter-ideologies" are sets of values and beliefs distinctly different from and in conflict with the dominant ideology.

Ideology, in contrast to explicit theory, is rarely consciously formulated. An outsider, the sociologist, for example, might try to decipher what people believe from how they act or how they respond to certain situations. But the believer normally assumes his/her ideas are manifestly true, that what he or she "sees" is what actually exists, and that his or her values are "normal." Therefore, a complete ideological system generally contains all kinds of contradictions. People can and do hold inconsistent beliefs and operate on values in an *ad hoc* way, without considering whether those values are congruent with their other values. Yet inconsistent as they may be, ideologies influence individual and societal behaviour.

Our personal beliefs, what sociologists call ideologies, emerge with our experience of life. This is enormously conditioned by our material existence: by our jobs, environments, homes, etc. We attend schools, are influenced by mass media, consume popular brand goods, and all of these experiences shape our versions of what the world is like.

Most of us have little influence over these conditions. But some people make decisions about the employment and income of others, the nature of the work organization and its location, how technology will be changed, and what commodities will be produced. These individuals in our society normally own or run major industrial corporations. When we study how a society develops ideological beliefs, we must question how much influence these decision makers have in shaping those beliefs. We want to consider whether their influence is embedded in the decisions and the outcomes (for example, does a certain technology tend to create certain ways of seeing the world), or whether decision makers manipulate ideas so ordinary workers believe what their "rulers" find most convenient.

We all inherit a culture, a social history, a language; these, in a sense, carry earlier belief systems. As we are exposed to schools, the mass media, neighbourhood events, family life, we begin to interpret as well as experience the world. Girls and boys may interpret what they see differently when they see the same things, depending on how their culture defines "male" and "female." In cultures with histories of animosity between religious or ethnic groups, young children may hate people whom they have never met. These and other cultural circumstances affect behaviour, the behaviour then affects material conditions (for example, creating barriers to employment for some or preferential conditions for others), and ideologies emerge as complex bundles of beliefs based on inherited culture, social positions, and material circumstances.

POLITICAL IDEOLOGIES

Ideologies are partly about the political world, and we probably find it easier to identify "political" ideologies than to link these to the more profound ideological undercurrents from which they emerge. Numerous writers and political leaders who explicitly discuss political ideas make some beliefs more public and open to scrutiny while ignoring the underlying, less articulate beliefs people hold.

Canadians separate themselves along two major political axes. One axis has to do with the emphasis placed on individual

Figure 1
Political ideologies and their positions relative to individualism and egalitarianism

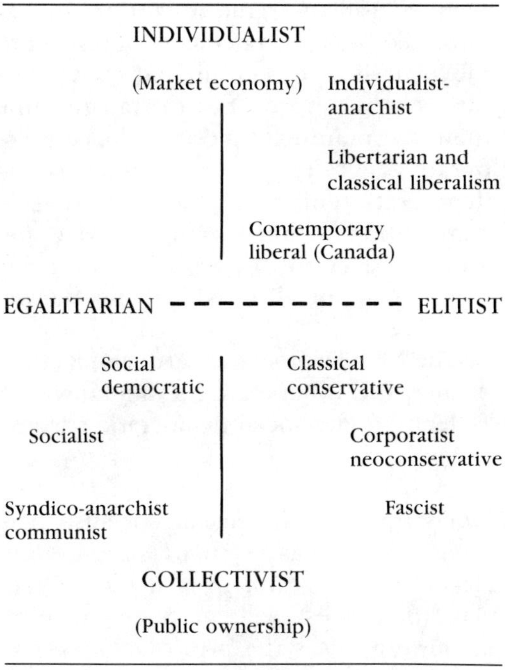

INDIVIDUALIST

(Market economy) Individualist-anarchist

Libertarian and classical liberalism

Contemporary liberal (Canada)

EGALITARIAN ---------- ELITIST

Social democratic

Classical conservative

Socialist

Corporatist neoconservative

Syndico-anarchist communist

Fascist

COLLECTIVIST

(Public ownership)

versus collective rights. Does the society have the right to channel the energies of its members, to demand certain actions and forbid others? The second has to do with the emphasis placed on equality. Are people born equal and should they continue to be equal throughout life in their opportunities, rewards for work, rights, and decision-making capacities?

Our political labels run along a continuum from extreme individualists (society has absolutely no claims on the individual, and there should be no rules, government, or constraints on individual actions) to extreme collectivists (society always has precedence over individuals, and the right to demand conformance with rules for the public good). The differences between these labelled positions are noted below, but the reader should realize that labels can mislead. Most people "lean" more toward one position or another, but few people's views fit neatly into any one category.

(Individualist) Anarchism

Anarchists argue that no government, centralized authority, nor large organizations should interfere with individual pursuits. The position has not emerged in an organized form in Canada (indeed, its nature discourages organization), but writers in the anarchist tradition may influence contemporary movements which enshrine individual rights as paramount. Note the difference between individualist anarchism and syndico-anarchism (see below).

Classical Liberalism

Liberalism as it emerged during and following the industrial revolution in Europe upheld the supremacy of the individual and the superiority of the marketplace for determining the value of human talents and production. The best government then was that which governed least. This viewpoint, adopted by contemporary libertarians, is not consistent with liberalism as it is currently expressed in Canada.

Libertarianism

Libertarians believe the individual is always supreme, individual rights are always more important than societal rights, and governments should be abolished or should only exist to protect persons and property. Democracy is harshly judged by libertarians, as is the welfare state; the first because it represents the ill-informed (ideological) preferences of the common people, the second because it reduces the rewards for initiative and entrepreneurial skills deemed essential to social survival.

Liberalism

Liberalism as expressed today in Canada combines concerns with individual rights and equality of opportunity. Equality, in this view, is largely achieved through a free educational system. The economic system, rarely called "capitalism," is perceived to be a free enterprise market, in which all sellers and buyers compete on equal terms for the attention of consumers. Labour bargains for its highest price in the labour market. Individuals improve their exchange value by increasing their "human capital," that is, by acquiring skills and knowledge. Government should regulate the marketplace and ensure that the rules are fair and equitable, but not be an economic actor in a truly free enterprise system.

Liberals rarely talk about **classes**, and class barriers are not viewed as serious impediments to individual achievements. Governments represent all sectors of the community equally, and no ruling class has inordinate power to influence government decisions. Despite stated beliefs in free enterprise, and despite the theory of *laissez-faire* liberalism as expressed in the eighteenth and nineteenth century, liberal governments in Canada have created numerous Crown corporations and, especially since 1940, intervened in all sectors of the economy. Thus, liberalism in Canada embodies a "mixed economy" approach. One party has called itself Liberal, but all major parties in Canada adopt these views in substance, and so we must be careful to recognize liberalism is not just the ideology of the Liberal party.

Social Democratic

The social democratic view criticizes capitalism but is committed to the gradual and democratic evolution of a more egalitarian and less market-oriented society. Like socialists, social democrats believe that capitalist society is organized in the interests of a class of owners, and that the majority of people — workers — are subordinated to these interests.

There are two somewhat different theoretical positions from which social democracy stems: the Marxist and the (British) Fabian traditions. Marxism has informed social democrats with respect to the analysis of capitalism and class structure, but its approaches to transforming these are more extreme than social democrats generally accept. As well, social democrats tend to see some virtues in competition within the marketplace and are less eager to dispose of all property rights than socialists within the Marxist tradition.

The New Democratic Party and its forerunner, the Co-operative Commonwealth Federation, are social democratic parties.

Socialist

By contrast with liberalism, socialists perceive capitalism as a system where a ruling class extracts wealth from a subordinate class (or classes), sells products made by labour, and uses the profits to invest in more properties and new technologies, which displace or further enslave labour. Classes exist, inequalities are built into the system, and individual freedom is highly circumscribed because labour must produce goods and services for capital. For the socialist, classes should not exist, inequalities should be minimized, and capital should not be allowed to extract value from labour. Private property should be abolished. The theoretical basis for socialism includes the writings of Marx and neo-Marxists.

Syndico-Anarchism

Syndico-anarchism is also known as socialist anarchism; these are two socialist forms of anarchism. One emerged within the European trade union movement and espoused organization of society by workers' organizations. The other form favours highly decentralized societies in which small communities (workers and others) govern themselves. Both views are hostile to capitalism and to large-scale governments of any kind. Some arguments within this framework have been incorporated into contemporary environmentalist, peace, and decentralization movements, though none of these in Canada today uses the terminology of syndico-anarchism.

Communism

Communism within Canada has been part of the international communist movement, so the positions taken by communists when affiliated with political parties are not altogether explicable in the context of Canadian society. As an ideological position, irrespective of party membership, communism is similar to socialism. Although communists anticipate that at some distant stage, centralized governments would become obsolete, they do not want to do away with government of all kinds.

Conservatism

Classical conservatism — like liberalism, not necessarily coincident with a particular political party — shares socialism's belief that there are classes, that capitalism necessarily involves inequality, and that the marketplace should not be the locus of most important social decisions. But unlike socialism, conservatism gives a high positive value to class inequalities: they are necessary because society requires leadership, and well-established leaders look after less well-established workers. Conservatism thus values a "natural" hierarchy and paternalistic relations between capital and labour. For the conservative, government should establish norms for the conduct of social life, but have a restrained role in the economy.

Corporatism

Corporatism shares conservatism's belief in a natural hierarchy of human beings, the importance of planning the economy, and the positive evaluation of social classes. It goes beyond conservatism in arguing that corporations should direct economic life. Democratic procedures typical of liberal societies are viewed as unacceptable because they allow uninformed and unpropertied individuals and groups to choose leaders and policies, and thus inhibit social progress.

Neo-Conservatism

This term refers to "the new right," though (as discussed later) the new right has more in common with libertarianism than with traditional conservatism. Unlike conservatism (the label is most confusing), it includes no concern for the poorer or weaker sections of society. It advocates giving market mechanisms absolutely free rein, that no special provisions for social welfare be built into the system, that government be reduced to protecting persons and property rights, and that political decisions be removed from democratic procedures. Like conservatism, it believes that a natural hierarchy exists and should be maintained; that a ruling class is essential for human society.

Fascism

Fascism is an extreme form of corporatism, going beyond it in accepting the necessity for force in controlling dissidents. We usually associate it with Nazi Germany, but there was a Canadian fascist party during the 1930s, and a small following has persisted throughout this century.

Some Important Distinctions

Socialism involves a version of the future that differs markedly from liberal versions. For liberals, the future is a continuum of the past and present. It sees eternal progress and the gradual elimination of imperfections in the social system. But socialism argues that only after capitalism is replaced can a more egalitarian and humane system emerge.

For liberals, capitalism is necessary reality and critiques of it are ideology. For socialists, the liberal version of capitalism is ideology. It is understood by socialists as an essential feature of the capitalist system, because it induces workers to consent to their own exploitation. They are persuaded, rather than forced (though force may on occasion be necessary) to believe that the system is fair even if it leads to extremely unequal distributions of material wealth and economic power. Part of the key to this persuasion is, say the socialists, the pretense that government is democratic and operates in the "public interest."

Socialism differs from social democracy in its approaches to democratic government and the marketplace. Social democrats believe in the gradual evolution of greater democracy and equality, and use persuasion and electoral politics to try to bring this about; socialists are more inclined to believe in the ultimate necessity for revolution (though in practice, Canadian socialists have supported electoral politics). As well, social democrats are less inclined to abolish private property and the marketplace.

The chief difference between conservatism and liberalism is in their views of the relationship between individuals and society. Traditional conservatists see society as an organic whole, within which individuals have assigned places. Liberals view society more as a collection of individuals striving for personal goals. Thus, true conservatives should be concerned with the collective moral fabric, as well as the permanence of a dominant class. Logically, liberals would be less concerned with social and moral issues, except where society infringes on individual rights.

Libertarians and "new righters" differ from liberals in their extreme focus on individual rights, and their uncompromising disdain for equality and democratic government.

All of these positions have been described as they are expressed in the Canadian context. Similar positions are part of the political spectrum in other countries, but in each case there are historical differences that slightly modify the meanings of such terms. Liberalism in the United States, for example, is closer to what Canadians recognize as social democracy; and social democracy in Canada is closer to liberalism than it is in many Western European countries.

Liberalism as Dominant Ideology

If we identify the dominant ideology as the values and beliefs held by a majority, the liberal, social democratic, and conservative positions fall within its compass.

The similarities among these three positions have greatly increased with the growth of welfare programs, more equitable taxation systems, and state interventions in the economies of most industrialized countries since the 1930s. Social democrats have become more sharply distinguished from Marxist-based socialists where they have accepted the compromise with capitalism. Conservatives have likewise accepted the compromise from the opposite position, seeing the welfare state as a means of maintaining an owning class, yet shifting the burden of care for others onto the society as a whole. Liberalism has become simply "the centre" in the political spectrum, adopting ideas from the right and the left and losing much of the emphasis on the marketplace that characterized traditional liberalism.

Political parties wearing these various labels, or political theorists espousing these points of view, make many more dis-

LIBERALS AND SOCIALISTS ON WAGES

From a liberal perspective, people's wages reflect their differing skills and education, and the higher wages are given to those who are "most important to the society" or to those whose educational qualifications are greatest.

In Canada, corporate executives, judges, and medical doctors and dentists have the highest reported incomes; architects, teachers, and nurses have much lower incomes. Critics of the liberal view point out that this distribution does not provide evidence in favour of the argument, since all of these groups may be important to the society and all may require lengthy educations.

The socialist ideology interprets these differences as evidence of differing bargaining powers of various groups, and their importance not to "the society" but rather to employers.

tinctions between the positions. It is in their interests to do so, of course, since they have to make their party seem to be the unique champion of individual rights or equal opportunity, or whatever. What interests us here is not so much the fine distinctions, but the underlying values to which the parties appeal, and which are apparently important to an electorate. Why would a large proportion of citizens in Canada believe that private property rights and certain constraints on them are legitimate, appropriate, and fair? And why do substantial numbers of Canadians move slightly more toward one pole or another in the political spectrum during times of economic change?

Rather than pursue these questions at an abstract and theoretical level, we will consider some historical and contemporary events in Canada, trying to identify the trends, changes, and groups espousing different ideologies.

HISTORY OF IDEOLOGIES

Following Canadian Confederation (1867), the government of the day established "the National Policy" (Fowke, 1957). This consisted of building railways to ship manufactured goods from Ontario to the Prairie settlers and wheat to world markets; immigration laws which encouraged settlement of the Prairies; and tariff policies which inhibited the import of manufactured goods from the United States while providing revenues to pay for the rail-

INDUSTRIAL DEVELOPMENT: HOW AND FOR WHOM?

All of these ideologies grew out of the industrial revolution, and all assume that it is appropriate for humans to "conquer" nature. Belief in progress through science and technology permeates our thinking in the twentieth century, and so one might say that the central tenet of the dominant ideology is its faith in industrial development. The difference between these positions lies in the questions: who should own industrial property, and how should the benefits be distributed?

ways. The policy remained in force until the 1930s, when the Great Depression wiped out many farms on the Prairies and unemployment rates elsewhere rose to over 20 percent.

Now consider two different ways of interpreting the National Policy and the Depression. The first, espoused by the government and businesses of the time, was that the policies were necessary for developing Canada as an independent nation. They would "open up" the Prairies, provide the conditions for population growth and expansion of agriculture, link the different parts of the sprawling country together, and create consumer markets for Canadian goods. They would retain Canada for Canadians, prevent Americans from gaining further territories in North America, and keep Canada within the British Empire. The wheat trade would help accumulate capital to establish new industries, and in time Canada would become an industrial nation. The Depression, originating elsewhere in mysterious economic forces outside Canada, unfortunately stalled this development.

The second view, espoused by many Prairie settlers over the next half century, was that the Policy pre-empted settlers from establishing independent businesses. It obliged them to purchase high-priced manufactured goods from Central Canadian (also called "Eastern") merchants and to sell their wheat at low prices to the same merchants (who then sold it at profit on the world markets). It forced them to pay railway costs for transportation links owned by investors in Central Canada. The Depression, they believed, was caused by capitalists trying to reorganize their investments around the new technologies and industries that emerged in the early twentieth century. This reorganization pushed many small businesses into bankruptcy. The beneficiaries of the reorganization were the financiers and big industrialists.

The first version predominated. It is still told in most Canadian textbooks, taught in many Canadian schools, and cited by subsequent governments and businesses in speeches. It became part of the dominant ideology of the twentieth century. But the second version was widely shared by Prairie homesteaders and their children, and it gave rise to "populist" movements between 1900 and the 1930s. These movements did not adopt a class theory of society, but a regional one, portraying Canada's dominant groups as the bankers and railroad men of Ontario; the oppressed groups as the Prairie settlers. The United Farmers of Alberta became the government of that province in 1921 while expressing this populist version of history. Co-operative movements also emerged, especially in Saskatchewan, to undermine the control of regional resources and markets held by Central Canadian businessmen (there were few businesswomen).

As wheat prices dropped and investment money moved away from Prairie agriculture, desperate people developed a much stronger version of their own exploitation. Two new major political parties were born during this period: Social Credit (blaming bankers and monetary policies for the problems, but also blaming minority groups — Jews, atheists, recent immigrants—and calling for a more paternalistic government in which the leader would make decisions for the people) (Macpherson, 1953); and the Co-operative Commonwealth Federation (C.C.F.) (blaming capitalism and the financial-industrial class, and calling for a more democratic political system, abolition of private property rights in industrial sectors, nationalization of banks, and extensive social welfare programs) (Lipset, 1950; Zakuta, 1964). The C.C.F. attracted members beyond the Prairies but was strongest in Saskatchewan.

In Quebec, Ontario, and Manitoba, fascist and corporatist groups emerged, blaming Jews, bankers, atheists, communists, and foreigners for the Depression (Betcherman, 1975). A Communist party gained new adherents despite persistent persecution, and from 1930 to 1935 the Communist League had considerable influence in the trade union movement, especially in Manitoba, British Columbia, and southern Ontario (Avakumovic, 1975; and also see Berger, 1981). In the Atlantic region, various movements emerged, some trying to establish new co-operatives among farmers and fishers; some protesting against employers and merchants (Brym and Sacouman, 1979).

Many settlers and workers in Canada did not believe the official version of the National Policy. With the onset of a Depression, these opponents were joined by many unemployed workers. They chose a wide variety of other explanations, ranging from communism to fascism. A persistent puzzle of Canadian history is why Alberta supported the Social Credit party while Saskatchewan supported the (then socialist, subsequently social democratic) C.C.F. party. Equally puzzling is why fascism had more followers in Quebec and Ontario than in the Atlantic region. The possible explanations include lack of understanding — the followers simply sought out an explanation and scapegoats for their misery, without examining the content of the ideologies. But probably more valid are explanations of differences in the kind of lives people led in different parts of Canada at that time, different experiences for immigrants from diverse countries, and the linkages between political and religious movements across the country.

In the urban centres of Ontario, Quebec, and Manitoba, the most disadvantaged population consisted of wage workers. Seeing many small businesses go bankrupt or get taken over by larger businesses, some blamed governments, financiers, and recent immigrants or visible ethnic minorities who competed with them for scarce jobs. They sought solutions that would re-establish employment, and fascism or corporatism provided one rationale in line with those frustrations and desires. Those who were both powerless and victims of this scapegoating likewise sought explanations. The Communist party at that time was supported primarily by Finnish, Ukrainian, and Russian immigrants; perhaps that was an accident of history originally, but over time it meant that other immigrants from these lands found an ethnic home within the party, and found no equivalent welcome in other parties.

On the Prairies, the rural population consisted largely of farmers. They perceived the enemies to be financiers and "eastern" merchants rather than competitive workers: both the Social Credit and C.C.F. provided rationales consistent with these perceptions. The co-operative movement in Saskatchewan may have provided a stronger base for socialism. As well, in Alberta, the governing party early in the Depression was the United Farmers, a party that had originally supported Prairie populism. Since it was unable to produce miracle cures, the Alberta population may have been more easily inclined to seek a more authoritarian and conservative form of populism than the C.C.F. provided.

The Atlantic region had suffered widespread unemployment for some time before the war; in fact, the region had begun an economic decline before the turn of the century, as its investment wealth and that of Central Canadians moved west. Its predominantly British-origin population supported the war. But Atlantic Canada spawned social movements, supported by fishers, farmers, miners, and other workers. These movements emerged, especially during the 1920s and 1930s, but failed to establish strong bases or link up with national movements, possibly because the supporters were not already established in working-class organizations. Most were small commodity producers (like the farmers of the Prairies) or even subsistence producers (growing food or catching fish sufficient only for their own livelihoods). They could not sustain long-term protest organizations.

The workers of British Columbia were mainly employed in resource industries. Mining and forestry industries had given rise to militant industrial unions (organizations of all workers in the same union, irrespective of trade). These unions had battled with the central Canadian trade unions throughout the first two decades of the century, and though the trade union movement won the battles (thus establishing Canadian unionism on a basis of separate trade, rather than industrial, organizations), B.C. workers continued to sustain modified forms of industrial unionism and were militant in pressing their claims against employers and governments. As well, during the 1930s and 1940s, communist unions were dominant in significant sectors of B.C. industry. The probable explanation for this difference between British Columbia and Central Canada is that there was not a large middle class in the "frontier" province; many wage workers in the resource industries shared geographical isolation, similar working conditions, and the social conditions suitable for organization. In many cases, the company owners were not resident, and there were few middle-level professionals or executives in resource industries.[1]

The above explanations stress the material conditions that underlay social protest movements: class differences between commodity producers, subsistence producers, wage workers; markets, shifting investments, levels of unemployment, and the like. But other conditions must be taken into account, such as religion. The Prairie population was at the centre of a "social gospel" movement throughout the 1920s and 1930s. Both the Social Credit and C.C.F. were led by religious leaders; the first by an evangelist radio broadcaster, the second by ministers of the Baptist and Methodist churches. The political movements dovetailed with religious messages, and linked up with beliefs about God, Christianity, and human destiny that were not as clearly shared by urban dwellers elsewhere in Canada. These same religious messages did not, for example, appeal to the largely Catholic French-Canadian population. In Quebec, the Catholic Church denounced both the C.C.F. and non-Catholic unions.

With the re-establishment during World War II of full employment in urban centres, and the increased demand for wheat and agricultural products for wartime allies, the "need" for explanations of unemployment and poor markets dissipated in much of the country. Fascists were designated as enemies of democracy, and democracy became the equivalent of capitalism in wartime propaganda. As soldiers were killed in the war, it became all the more important to believe that the war was just and necessary: thus preservation of whatever existed in Canada had to be worthwhile.

Other 1930s movements softened their positions as they became more entrenched in the Canadian political spectrum. The C.C.F. was elected in Saskatchewan (1944), but its stance against monopoly capitalism had already softened: it was now more intent on developing a social welfare and medical care program than in radically changing the capitalist system. In a modified form, the federal arm of the C.C.F. reached its peak of popularity shortly before the end of the war. By the mid-1940s, Alberta's Social Credit, while still in power, had given up its dedication to changing the monetary system and fiscal policies. The Communist party was banned for a period, re-emerged as the Labour Progressive Party, and elected one member to Parliament in 1943, but subsequently went into decline. Its single M.P. was convicted of espionage in 1946.

Post-War Expansion

When the war ended, there was fear that closure of war production industries and the return of soldiers would lead to increased unemployment and depression. This was avoided in North America in part by developing a welfare system and creating public-sector programs that employed workers and gave them purchasing power (known as Keynesian policies); and in greater part by the expansion of the American economy.

The United States emerged from the 1939–1945 conflict as the paramount world power. For the next twenty years, the United States effectively controlled world trade through the enormous expansion of its corporate industries, the strength of the American currency, and the back-up of its corporations by the American military forces.

The U.S. government initiated a policy of opposing what it defined as "communist aggression" after the war. It declared itself the leader of "the free world." In line with this policy, the U.S. government created a tied-aid program for the reconstruction of Europe and Japan (aid was provided in the form of goods made in the United States and Canada); a military establishment, and international agencies that would enable American businesses to invest elsewhere. In fact, the "free world" turned out to mean all capitalist countries hospitable to American capital. This did not exclude countries with military or other dictatorships, and had nothing to do with democracy.

Under the Marshall Plan, Canadian companies helped supply tied aid to European countries that were rebuilding their economies. Under the Bretton Woods Agreement, the General Agreement on Tariffs and Trade, the regulations for the new World Bank, and other international agreements, a world monetary system was established by which the American dollar became the principal exchange medium, tariffs were reduced, and entry of American corporations into other economies was facilitated.

Canada already had the highest level of foreign **direct investment** (equity shares) of all industrial countries, and by far the highest proportion of this originated in the United States. American corporations wholly or jointly owned a high proportion of the manufacturing industries of Ontario, much of the mining industry, and many of the other resource industries throughout the country. The success of American corporations elsewhere provided new markets for goods in the United States and around the globe for their subsidiaries in Canada. American military ventures abroad—especially the Korean War in the early 1950s—created a demand for Canadian resources and, under the Defence Production Sharing Agreements between Canada and the United States, markets for war-destined products made in Canadian subsidiaries. American direct investment in Canadian industries increased, and throughout most of the 1950s and 1960s the overall standard of living in Canada, as in the United States, improved steadily. Canada had, during this time, one of the highest standards of living in the world. (Government of Canada, 1972).

In this period of affluence and expansion, the ideology of individualism took firm root throughout Canada. There was general acceptance of the belief that individuals, by gaining an education and training, could move up the system to whatever positions they had the talent to occupy; there were no class barriers to upward mobility; expansion would continue indefinitely; and Canada was becoming a mature industrial society.

By the late 1950s, the C.C.F. had lost much of its support, and in 1961 it joined with organized labour under the name New Democratic Party. Although the Cold War persecution of dissidents which occurred through the 1950s in the United States did not occur in Canada to the same extent, fear of communism was widespread in Canada. Communism was no longer banned in Canada (under its name, Labour Progressive Party, it remained a political organization) but communists, and many who merely questioned Canada's continuing integration with the United States, suffered abuse in numerous ways. On the opposite flank, the Social Credit party became a mainstream organization, supporting "free enterprise."

If we consider these ideological expressions of the times, it is not difficult to link them to the economic conditions. With economic expansion, individuals could experience upward mobility. Indeed, the generation entering adulthood in the 1950s benefited from the general expansion and from the low birth rate of the previous two decades. There were many more positions in corporate hierarchies than there were people born into relatively affluent circumstances to fill them: many had to be recruited from below.

In addition to the expansion of corporations, governments became major employers. They participated in corporate expansion at home and abroad through numerous internal and international agencies, and expanded welfare and other social services designed to sustain and train the labour force. So there were many jobs, much upward mobility, almost full employment and welfare cushions for those unable to find employment. The educational system was greatly expanded, and children from lower-income families were encouraged to continue their education through universities. In short, the experiences people had during this period coincided with an ideology that emphasized individuals, individual mobility, the importance of individual freedom, acceptance of the economic power of corporations, and support for governments that enabled the growth of the corporations.

A student of ideologies would be quick to point out that linking these events to the widespread optimism and satisfaction of the period without reference to the mechanisms by which ideologies are transmitted is somewhat mechanistic. That is true, for there is not an automatic ideological response whenever the economy improves (or deteriorates). In a short chapter, however, we cannot elaborate on the precise mechanisms that push and nudge people into believing this or that. We suppose the various social media — communications media, schools, churches, political parties, and other organizations—intervene between the economic conditions and people's perceptions of them; and that other nonpolitical beliefs (such as religious beliefs) affect perceptions of reality. But our knowledge of these intervening conditions is still not adequate for a simple statement about how they affect people's ideas.

Middle-Class Movements, 1960s and Early 1970s

This relatively contented state of affairs began to unravel towards the end of the 1960s. Civil rights struggles, feminism, and opposition to the Vietnam War became organized social movements. Much opposition came from the affluent middle class, from the youth who had been nurtured in the ideology of individualism and "the free world." This large generation of "baby boomers" was notably idealistic, and had the leisure time to organize action on behalf of causes. This may be an instance where ideology itself became the important cause of group behaviour: beliefs held by many North Americans were seen to be violated by the actions of the same country that most promoted them at the government level. Alone, such ideological beliefs might have been impotent to release so much energy, but in combination with wealth, rapid communications technology, easy transportation over long distances, and a generation with the time available for organization, the beliefs could be articulated and people could be mobilized for action.

In Canada, the Vietnam War provoked new questions about Canada's complicity in American military actions. Foreign ownership became controversial. Regions developed new sources of wealth and began to reject the traditional authority of Ottawa. With new opportunities to organize provided via telecommunications, new roads, and funding for land claims research, Canadian Indians developed strong and sometimes militant associations, claiming aboriginal rights. Numerous new movements emerged: feminism, Canadianization, Quebec separatism, environmentalism, and the peace movement. They were not class-based critiques of society, and many were not easily incorporated into existing political parties. In fact all political parties of the time attempted to "capture" the sentiments behind these movements. Equal rights for women, negotiations over land rights, an accommodation with separatists, foreign ownership controls, and some pollution controls became planks in the platforms of Liberals, Conservatives, and new Democrats alike.

Slowing of the Expansion

While these events were unfolding, other, contrary, events were beginning to affect the North American economy. By the mid-1960s, European nations had successfully reconstructed their industries, and in many cases their industrial plants were technologically more advanced than the older plants of the United States. As well, the European Economic Community was established, and it resisted American competition in Europe while its companies competed with American businesses elsewhere. Japan grew into a major industrial power, penetrating the American domestic and foreign markets. The major oil-producing nations formed O.P.E.C. in the early 1960s, and were finally well enough organized to launch a major collective demand for higher oil prices in 1973. Other nations also formed collective organizations which, with varying success, inhibited further American expansion. During the late 1960s the monetary system began to break down because other nations objected to American dominance and could now put teeth into their objections.

By 1970, the Bretton Woods Agreements, which had so favoured the United States currency, could no longer be sustained, and the American government abandoned the fixed-exchange or "gold standard" rates. During this period—from about the mid-1960s onward—American companies in several industries moved the labour-intensive phases of their production to low-wage countries. They did this to reduce labour costs and to avoid the growing strength of American (and Canadian) unions. Some also moved to avoid new laws or social pressures in North America to improve women's wages, to implement pollution and environmental controls, to maintain various social programs and, generally, to take on social responsibilities as the cost of economic power.

The net result was a decline in profits for some American companies where competition undercut their markets, and increasing levels of unemployment appeared in communities from which

American corporations had fled. The impact on Canada was unevenly distributed, since residents outside southern-central Canada continued to depend mainly on resource rather than manufacturing industries. The resource industries declined by the end of the 1970s and during the early 1980s, as American industries decreased their demand for raw materials in North America.

One further change should be mentioned: the rapid introduction of computerized production systems. This technology transformed many industries, and it became itself a major industry. Several regions in North America which were boom areas in the 1950s and early 1960s were to some extent supplanted by free trade zones throughout Southeast Asia and in some other lesser developed countries. The vast range of applications of this technology introduced new products to the world market, but reduced demand for many old products and for production machinery for old products. New technologies on other fronts were developed during the 1960s and 1970s, transforming, for example, the steel and car manufacturing industries. These changes affected established communities, the labour force, and the companies of North America.

Upward mobility for those entering the labour force from the 1970s onwards began to decline, and this trend was exacerbated by the huge numbers who had reached maturity during the 1960s and early 1970s. Middle-aged parents who had experienced the boom period instilled high expectations in their children, which could not be realized in a slumping economy; individual mobility was blocked. And if the children had done what had previously "worked" for their parents—continued through school, achieved various distinctions, gained skills—and still could not find satisfactory employment, then an ideology of individual mobility became less and less credible. Women, who had been subjected to the same ideology, met with lower wages and fewer opportunities than men: they, too, had to look to social barriers rather than individual failures for an explanation. By 1980, the slump in the North American economy deepened, and official unemployment rates in Canada were above 10 percent; for the group under age twenty-five, they soared above 20 percent. In the resource regions, unemployment rates were even higher, and they continued at high levels for several years with no end in sight. The manufacturing region in south-central Canada recovered by the mid-1980s, and unemployment rates slowly declined.

At this point, the movements of the 1960s and 1970s began to wane; as organized associations, their membership began to decline. Their influence in political parties declined. New movements displaced them.

The movement with the greatest overall impact was the new right. The new right ideology mixes libertarianism, corporatism, and, within North America, evangelical religion. It was espoused in Britain by the Conservative government under Margaret Thatcher and in the United States by the Republicans under Ronald Reagan. In Canada, it was adopted by the Social Credit government in British Columbia, though aspects of the ideology and political policies of the new right were manifested throughout Canadian provinces by both the federal Liberal and Conservative parties.

This ideology argues that the welfare state and democratic processes have become unwieldy. It claims that individuals are oppressed by excessive taxes and government bureaucracies, that the poor are being maintained in poverty rather than pushed to create their own livelihoods, and that businesses (entrepreneurs in this version) cannot expand and flourish because of excessive government regulations. The new right's solution is to dismantle the welfare state, de-regulate industry, and create "incentives" for businesses to establish new industries. New right policies include "privatization" of welfare and education: closing the publicly financed institutions, and letting "the market" meet social needs.

Public opinion polls show few people adopted this ideology in its entirety. What they held, rather, were specific complaints that this ideology addressed, such as concern with the continuing weakness of the economy, suspicion that many people on welfare were cheating the system, impatience with the claims for equality and justice from minority groups, fear about the apparent disintegration of social institutions, such as the family, and anger at wage claims made by unionized workers. These complaints emerged within the context of a weak economy and declining standards of living. To the ordinary citizen, something was clearly wrong, and thus the political and economic system as it had existed for thirty years was now viewed as seriously flawed. The new right offered to turn things around.

As the new right gained strength, so, too, did left-wing ideologies gain greater electoral support in Canada. The social democratic party (N.D.P.) gradually increased its popular support base and gained power (forming the government in Manitoba, as part of a coalition with the ruling Liberal party in Ontario, as a very strong opposition party in British Columbia, as the opposition party in Alberta by the mid-1980s; and as the visible successor of the social democratic mantle formerly worn by the defeated Parti Québécois in Quebec).

Thus, in the late 1980s, we are again engaged in multiple ideologies competing with one another and influencing our political choices, as we were in the mid-1930s; and these ideologies are embedded within fairly traditional political parties. If public opinion polls are indicative, there is still a core set of values and opinions (the dominant ideology), and these continue to emphasize individualism, equality of opportunity, democracy, and the "free market." But there is a more polarized electorate in the late 1980s than in the mid-1960s. The right-wing position has become more clearly articulated and has gathered strength; the left-wing position cannot assume, as it could in the early 1970s, that the population at large favours greater equality.

Economic conditions appear to affect the probability that new beliefs, new values, opposition to the status quo, and organized resistance will find numerous supporters in a population. Certain levels of discontent and opposition probably exist at all times, but erupt with greater strength, more organization, stronger leaders, under particular conditions.

CLASS, REGION, AND IDEOLOGY

We have noted that both socialist and conservative ideologies emphasize classes, while the liberal position does not. But we have not examined ideology as a manifestation of class position. To do so moves us away from the liberal ideology. This is why it is so difficult to study ideology: even defining the term becomes ideological! This is like standing in a room full of mirrors and trying to decide which image is closest to reality.

Classes may be defined in two ways. The first is as groups ranked along a "distributional" scale in terms of their income, education, occupational status, or some combination of these and other forms of income or capital. To the extent that the dominant ideology acknowledges classes at all, it uses this definition of class. The second is as groups relative to one another in terms of power. A group that can fundamentally determine or influence the life conditions of another group is a dominant class; the other is a subordinate class. Both the conservative and socialist versions of class are of this kind and, for both, the dominant class in capitalist society consists of those who own the major production units; the subordinate class consists of those who sell their labour power in return for a wage. One may also identify various "middle" strata or classes, including farmers and other small business owners, and managers/professionals who are employed for wages but who have some delegated authority within large economic organizations. Some writers identify as well a "state class," people employed by the state rather than by private capital.

Each definition assumes that members of different classes or class fractions have different economic interests. It might be supposed, for example, that the dominant class has a much greater interest in maintaining private property rights and creating political and labour conditions conducive to continued business operations than other classes; the wage working class has more interest in the rights of organized labour; the state class, in maintaining the welfare state or advancing nationalistic policies. To some extent these "common sense" expectations are substantiated, but there is rarely a clear relationship between class membership and, for instance, voting patterns. Although support for parties emphasizing individualism over equality and free markets over government controls increases with income and occupational status, support for social democratic, socialist, or communist parties and movements, or even support for unions, is not given by a majority of wage workers. This is particularly true when a single ideology clearly predominates and, as suggested above, this occurs when the economy is expanding and the standard of living is improving.

This lack of clear linkage between beliefs and class situation puzzles many sociologists and political analysts. Some neo-Marxist scholars have argued that the dominant ideology, including the phraseology of "the free world," "free markets," "freedom of the individual," "democracy," "majority choice," and "individual rights," is deliberately advanced by a ruling class (the bourgeoisie) to mask a reality within which that class controls the economy and the political institutions. They argue that workers are taught the ideology, consume it through the media and schools, and cannot see that it is not in their class interests. Indeed, given a dominant ideology that avoids mention of classes, they are unable to identify their own class. Democratically elected governments, in this view, are instruments of the ruling class because they cannot enact legislation that seriously and over the long run conflicts with the accumulation (profit making) process. But the machinery of democracy makes government appear neutral. A chief function of such governments is to legitimate the system, while enabling it to survive and reproduce itself.

Other theorists think that ideology emerges in the everyday experiences of working people. That is, work involves a hierarchy of authority, differences in wages associated with skills and education, promotion ladders, relationships to machinery, and ultimate dependence on the sale of products in the marketplace; this experience itself leads workers to envision the world as a marketplace and the society as an aggregation of individuals loosely organized into production companies. In this view, ideology is generated from below rather than imposed from above, though in either event it supports the interests of the dominant class. Because workers are immersed in these situations, they view them as "normal" and rarely have the opportunity or incentive to consider that capitalism, rather than nature, generates these conditions. Thus, only during times of high unemployment and widespread economic insecurity would workers question whether such conditions are necessary.

Neither view explains the growth of social movements in the affluent period. Many demands made by these movements were contrary to the interests of a dominant, capitalist class. Yet at the same time, they grew out of the dominant ideology of the period, because what they demanded was consistent with the "official" beliefs in individual rights, equality of opportunity, freedom, and democracy. To capitalists, the ideology may have been too successful. Interestingly, these social movements were carried largely by middle-class young people, the beneficiaries of affluence. This may explain why the demands were not phrased in class terms: this class did not perceive itself as a class, immersed as it was in a liberal ideology of classlessness.

The "new right" ideology can more easily be understood within ruling and subordinate classes. Many new right ideas are consistent with arguments made by the Trilateral Commission in the early 1970s (Crozier, Huntington, and Watanki, 1975). The Commission was a privately sponsored association of international corporate leaders organized by the Rockefeller family in the United States. Such phrases as "an excess of democracy" and "excessive expectations" originated with their publications. They argued for less democracy and greater centralized control by governments, a position similar to corporatism. In both their view and that of the more libertarian new right movement, governments in capitalist countries should be more responsive to the interests of business, and less responsive to the numerous demands of the general population. The resurgence of class-based left-wing movements and the greater support for social democracy in Canada may be viewed as a reaction and response to the growth of the class-based and class conscious right-wing movement.

While we do not see strong relationships between class and opinions on many public opinion polls, definite ideological positions emerge and affect whole societies and regions during shifts in the nature or composition of the class structure. Of particular importance in these shifts are the various fragments of a middle class: the petite bourgeoisie (independent professionals and small commodity producers such as farmers and small business owners), the "new middle class" of managers, professionals, and state employees, and

OPPOSING VIEWS

The increasing costs of welfare, government services, and new demands, such as pollution controls and wage equity for women, were believed by some industry owners to be the cause of the downswing in their economic fortunes. The Trilateral Commission and libertarians blamed democracy for falling profits. Critics of this position blamed the expansion of American capital abroad, and the decreasing consumer power of unemployed workers at home.

DIFFERENCES OF APPROACH

Large corporations differ from small businesses in significant ways. They can plan their operations and control much more of their market. Small businesses are highly competitive for supplies as well as markets. These differences underlie their positions on government, national states, and economic planning, even when, as sometimes occurs, both groups support specific changes in the democratic system.

the upper stratum of unionized wage-workers in the private and public sectors. Consider the example of British Columbia as its central industry, forestry, went into decline in the 1980s.

British Columbia

British Columbia was one of the most affluent regions of Canada during the 1950 to 1979 years. The economy depended overwhelmingly on the export, mostly to the United States, of relatively crude forest products: dimensional (standard sizes) lumber, pulp, and newsprint. The revenues from these sales were sometimes reinvested in British Columbia, but relatively little secondary industry was established (Marchak, 1983).

In 1980, the forest products markets collapsed. High interest rates in the United States caused a sharp decrease in housing construction, and many changes around the world, including the development of new pulping technologies for different tree species which could be grown in much shorter cycles in southern climates, posed long-term problems for the industry.

The province had a highly polarized electorate throughout this period, with a Social Credit government holding power most of the time and an N.D.P. government in power from 1972 to 1975. Up to this time, the forestry unions—and particularly the International Woodworkers of America (I.W.A.)—were the major working-class organizations. Because there was so little secondary industry, and because many of the large forestry companies (and all of the large mining companies in the second largest industry) were externally owned, the "middle class" was relatively small. Most of its members resided in two cities, and were employed in the public sector.

As the depression set in (with official provincial unemployment rates at 16 percent, I.W.A. estimates for forestry regions ranging between 30 percent and 50 percent), the Social Credit government introduced a "restraint" program. This consisted of reducing the public sector, attacking welfare programs, underfunding public education and the universities, and deregulating or privatizing various industries: in short, the program of the new right. At the same time, several energy megaprojects were publicly funded, a world fair was sponsored, and tourism was touted as the next major industry for British Columbia (Magnussen et al., 1984).

How would we explain this in class terms? Supporting the government were small businesspeople, especially in the construction and tourist industries. The forest companies supported the government's restraint program, but expressed doubts about its introduction, which included persistent confrontations between government and unions, government and the educational institutions, and government and the public sector employees. But in the long run, the restraint programs promised to reduce welfare costs and the power of unionized labour. Forest companies were not averse to these effects. Emigration of workers in search of jobs elsewhere also reduced the support base for the N.D.P.

This way of analyzing the class basis of support is crude. More intriguing is the relationship between small business existence and the specific appeal of libertarianism to that sector. Small businesses compete in the marketplace. They run risks, and some of them fail. They are proud to be entrepreneurs. The new right postulates a world in which these same conditions affect everyone, so that even when the government is intervening in the economy through its megaprojects and exposition, these entrepreneurs believe that their success during a depression is due to their own efforts.

In contrast to libertarianism, which should appeal to the small business sector, corporatism is much more ideologically suited to big businesses. The big business sector is competitive on a world market, but that market is more readily controlled by the largest companies. They produce in all regions of the global economy, moving production to whichever countries offer advantages in cheap labour or tax havens. They are not entrepreneurial, and their marketplace is not properly designated "free enterprise." They require large investments of public funds in megaprojects and new infrastructures to increase profits. Some of their directors, owners, and chief officers say that democratic governments and welfare states impede corporate expansion. Thus, though libertarians (and small business) and corporatists (and large business) have significantly different interests in many respects, they have similar arguments about democracy, government regulations, public sector unions, welfare provisions, and other aspects of democratic liberal societies.

INDIVIDUALS AND IDEOLOGIES

We prefer to believe that our cherished values and ideas are distinctive; that we, and we alone, have created them out of our own intellects and hearts. But since many of these values can be predicted by outsiders who scarcely know us simply by reference to our family incomes, education, occupation, and place of residence, we have to become a little more skeptical about our ideological commitments. Each of us is part of a regional culture in which particular industries, ways of doing business, and market conditions affect our daily lives. Each of us is embedded in the class structure of our region, and our class experiences have enormous influence over

LARGE CORPORATIONS VERSUS SMALL BUSINESSES

We do not imply that every small businessperson adopts a libertarian stance, or every corporate director, a corporatist ideology. But the general economic interests of a class, subject to the general class composition and economic conditions of the region in which it resides, are manifested in tendencies toward one or another of these ideological positions. No ideologies completely embody the interests of a single class, but ideologies tend to express the most vital interests of particular classes.

what we can see and believe. The small businessperson who "hates unions on principle because they kill initiative," or the union member who "hates environmentalists because they destroy jobs"; the public sector employee who would rather see big governments than big businesses control the economy, or the big business manager who believes that governments are inherently evil, are caricatures of their class situations. So is the relatively affluent university student who believes class has no influence over who enters university.

Ideologies influence individual behaviour. This chapter has suggested that they emerge through our experiences, and these experiences are greatly conditioned by our work. Where we are wage workers, the experiences are necessarily connected to the nature of capitalist organizations, and so through the patterns of property ownership a dominant class may influence our ideological perspectives. But it is less clear whether dominant classes may influence our perceptions through manipulation of media and symbols. This seems possible only when the idealized version that they portray coincides with widespread experiences, as they did during the Cold War when the symbols of "freedom" coincided with genuine individual mobility and affluence. When "official" versions of the society are at odds with lived experience (as for Prairie homesteaders early in this century), counter-ideologies are mounted.

Ideological diversity increases during economic depressions. The dominant ideologies fail during these periods because too many people discover that the ideologies cannot explain what they experience. At such times they search for other explanations and new solutions. But a dominant ideology widely shared by a middle class can generate its own social movements during periods of affluence.

COMPARISONS BETWEEN COUNTRIES AND CULTURES

Religions, traditions, peculiar histories: these and other conditions are bound to affect our ideological perspectives. They many intensify or inhibit the effects of economic change. Feminism in India, for example, is concerned with some of the problems that concern feminists in Canada: employment conditions, unequal wages, opportunities for women, and unequal domestic responsibilities. But Indian women are embedded in joint family structures (a family consists of a man and wife, their sons and daughters-in-law, their son's dependent children, and unmarried daughters). Canadian women, typically, are linked to parental families or to nuclear families of their own. Many more Canadian women are single, divorced, and/or single parents because there are both fewer constraints on women's marital choices, and greater risk of family breakups. These different family conditions necessarily affect the way Indian and Canadian women interpret their circumstances, and what conditions they are most eager to change.

The United States and Canada appear alike in a global context that includes India, China, and many Third World cultures. But even so, there are important differences between the two, and between the various regions within each country, that affect ideological understandings. For example, public opinion polls in the United States and dramatically falling participation rates in elections suggest that a much higher proportion of Americans than Canadians are apathetic or hostile toward politics, politicians, and government. Canadians have high voting rates, suggesting we believe democratic government is satisfactory, and that governments do respond to citizens.

Another difference between the United States and Canada is the greater acceptance in Canada of traditional conservatism and social democracy through to communist political beliefs. Canada has had left-wing political parties throughout its history, though population and government acceptance of these has varied from time to time. No equivalent to the C.C.F.–N.D.P. has emerged in the United States, where the two major parties have assimilated, co-opted, or otherwise prevented the growth of political organization among left-wing groups. An ideological perspective from the left has long informed Canadians, become embedded in legislative action, influenced social policies, and affected open political debate. The same has not occurred in the United States. The left wing in Canada may be frustrated by its lack of electoral success, but it is less disenfranchised than in the United States.

A third difference between the two countries is in the extent of public ownership and government intervention in the marketplace. Canadian governments have been active in creating "Crown corporations" and taking economic initiatives that are not ideologically consonant with pure marketplace ideologies. Thus, classic liberal notions have always been tempered with more collectivist ideas. By contrast, American private capital has been much stronger, and, of course, with American expansion the ideology of "free enterprise" has had greater momentum in the United States.

CONCLUSION

In some respects, Canada is more like Western European countries than like the United States. They, too, have greater diversity of "legitimate" political parties. Several have elected social democratic or socialist governments over the post-war period, and most have developed mixed economies with private and public ownership of various industries. Unlike European countries, however, Canadian politics are not clearly class-based, nor has organized labour been able to mobilize its members to fully embrace one political party. This does not mean that class is less "real" in Canada. The problem is ideological and organizational, and its roots probably lie in the fact that North America was settled after the industrial revolution and lacks an aristocratic tradition.

These comparisons remind us that ideology at one stage affects how the economy and society develop, and thus it becomes part of the culture that conditions the further development of the society.

Notes

This article is an abbreviated discussion of material in the author's book, *Ideological Perspectives on Canada*, Toronto: McGraw-Hill Ryerson, 3rd. ed., 1987.

[1]For expansion of this argument, see Stuart M. Jamieson, *Times of Trouble: Labour Unrest and Industrial Conflict in Canada, 1900–1966*. Task Force on Labour Relations Study No. 22 (Ottawa, Information Canada), 1971.

DISCUSSION QUESTIONS

1. What is the difference between ideology and theory?
2. What are the differences and similarities between: classical and contemporary liberalism; social democracy and socialism; conservative and neo-conservative ideologies?
3. In what respects is liberalism a dominant ideology?
4. How did the ideologies prior to 1945 differ from those after World War II? Provide an explanation of these changes.
5. In what ways do class and region influence ideological perspectives? Keep in mind that different theoretical approaches would provide different answers to this question: what are the differences?
6. Taking first a liberal ideological approach, explain the employment patterns in the region where you live; then provide an explanation from a socialist perspective.

GLOSSARY

class 1. a functionalist (liberal) definition: groups ranked along a "distributional" scale in terms of income, education, occupational status, or combination of these. By this definition, there may be any number of classes, since the divisions are arbitrarily determined.

2. a Marxist definition: groups related to one another via their differing relations to the means of production, where one group owns these and others are employed for wages by that group. In this framework there are two central classes: owners (the bourgeoisie) and labour (wage workers). There may also be a class of small business owners (petite bourgeoisie) who own their own productive mechanisms but do not employ or profit from others' labour (e.g., small farm owners).

direct investment investment in a company that results in a share of ownership; in contrast to loans and portfolio investments made for purposes of gaining interest or dividends but which confer no ownership rights on the investor

ideology 1. as defined in this chapter, ideology comprises shared ideas, perceptions, values, and beliefs through which members of a society interpret history and contemporary social events and which shape their expectations and wishes for the future

2. as defined by those who take a Marxist approach, ideology consists of ideas, perceptions, values, and beliefs that support the status quo and the existing distribution of power in a capitalist system

BIBLIOGRAPHY

Avakumovic, Ivan
1975 *The Communist Party in Canada: A History*. Toronto: McClelland and Stewart.

Berger, Mr. Justice R.
1981 *Fragile Freedoms*, Chapter 5. Toronto: Clarke Irwin.

Betcherman, Lita-Rose
1975 *The Swastika and the Maple Leaf: Fascist Movements in Canada in the Thirties*. Toronto: Fitzhenry and Whiteside.

Brym, Robert J. and R. James Sacouman (eds.)
1979 *Underdevelopment and Social Movements in Atlantic Canada*. Toronto: New Hogtown Press.

Crozier, Michel J., Samuel P. Huntington, and Joji Watanki
1975 *The Crisis of Democracy: Report on the Governability of Democracies to the Trilateral Commission*. New York: New York University Press.

Fowke, Vernon
1957 *The National Policy and the Wheat Economy*. Toronto: University of Toronto Press.

Government of Canada
1972 *Foreign Direct Investment in Canada*. Ottawa: Queen's Printer.

Lipset, S. M.
1950 *Agrarian Socialism: The Co-operative Commonwealth Federation in Saskatchewan: A Study in Political Sociology*. Berkeley: University of California Press.

Macpherson, C.B.
1953 *Democracy in Alberta*. Toronto: University of Toronto Press.

Magnussen, Warren et al. (eds.)
1984 *The New Reality: The Politics of Restraint in British Columbia.* Vancouver: New Star Books.

Marchak, Patricia
1983 *Green Gold: The Forest Industry in British Columbia.* Vancouver: U.B.C. Press.

Zakuta, Leo
1964 *A Protest Movement Becalmed: A Study of Change in the CCF*. Toronto: University of Toronto Press.

White-collar workers on strike against the provincial government demonstrate outside the Legislature in St. John's.

> *"Canada typically experiences a moderate number of strikes involving a moderately large number of workers and lasting a long time. It has generally been closer to the United States than to . . . other societies, although the American data indicate decreasing militancy in contrast to an upward movement in Canada."*

c h a p t e r   e i g h t e e n

Class and Collective Protest

Peter R. Sinclair

INTRODUCTION

Ottawa: June 3, 1976. About 5000 angry dairy farmers, members of l'Union des Producteurs Agricoles (U.P.A.), demonstrated on Parliament Hill while their leaders tried to persuade the government to alter its policy of restraining quotas for milk production. When it became obvious that the negotiations had failed, the crowd grew restless. As he tried to speak to the farmers, Eugene Whelan, the Minister of Agriculture, was pelted with lumps of butter and spattered with milk; U.P.A. leaders themselves were jeered at as they tried to calm their members. During a second round of talks, a section of the crowd scuffled with R.C.M.P. officers who were protecting the building. As some burst through the cordon around Parliament, a special riot squad, wielding sticks and tear-gas guns, suddenly appeared to force back the vanguard of farmers. Shortly afterwards the crowd broke up in orderly fashion, although some set fire to their placards, park furniture, and the ornamental trees on the lawn. Back in Quebec, the protest continued by blocking highways, and on Parliament Hill there remained for a time the smell of burning and the stench of sour milk to remind politicians that their policies were bitterly opposed (*The Globe and Mail*, 6–4–76).

This incident of collective action is filled with confrontation, challenge to authority, negotiation, repression, violence, relations between leaders and followers, frustration, and perhaps some humour. How is it possible? How can it be explained? This chapter will review several explanations, but its primary focus is on the class movements in Canada, i.e., the movements of the petite bourgeoisie and the working class. Beyond brief historical summaries, the chapter concentrates on particular themes, such as the pattern of Canadian strikes in comparative perspective, the weakness of class politics in Canada, and the issue of the **institutionalization** of social movements.

WHAT IS A SOCIAL MOVEMENT?

The Quebec farmers who opened this chapter were clearly participating in collective action. Was this event part of a **social movement**? A social movement refers here to any group that attempts to change the institutional structure of society through collective action. This need not be a total reconstruction of society, but it must involve some change in how people typically behave and it should involve some concrete activity beyond just desiring change. Thus I follow Ash (1972) and Gusfield (1970), who see social movements as a combination of belief and action.

In thinking about social movements, many sociologists stress that participants are committed to the **ideology** or goals which identify the movement. Thus, Paul Wilkinson (1971:27) concludes that one of three "quintessential characteristics" is that "a social movement's commitment to change and the raison d'être of its organization are founded upon the conscious volition, normative commitment to the movement's beliefs, and active participation on the part of followers or members." Such statements seem to assume that members' beliefs and motives are indeed shared, but the evidence has tended towards the opposite conclusion: that they are in fact heterogeneous, especially as one's focus moves from the organizational core to the periphery (Stallings, 1973; Marx and Wood, 1975:382–83). Quite apart from commitment to the official goals or ideology, people may participate in a social movement for a variety of reasons, such as loyalty to friends or family, personal gain, misinterpretation, or even coercion. Therefore, it is best to think of a social movement as an attempt to bring about social change, but to recognize that the official goals of the movement will be supported more strongly by some participants than by others.

THE RESOURCE MOBILIZATION PERSPECTIVE

At the risk of oversimplification it may be stated that, until roughly 1970, most writers on social movements advocated a "discontent" or "breakdown" approach, in which the core idea is that rapid transformation of society leads to strain, discontent, or disorientation for individuals, followed by participation in essentially *irrational* collective behaviour. Those most subject to strain and deprivation were considered most likely to join social movements, unless new forms of social integration could be established to replace the traditional bonds of family, church, and community that had been eroded by rapid industrialization and urbanization.

Three problems with this approach encouraged an alternative theory called

A MODIFIED MOBILIZATION APPROACH

In line with several recent authors (Jenkins, 1983; Ferree and Miller, 1985; Klandermans, 1984; Walsh and Warland, 1983), my preference is for a theoretical framework that builds on mobilization theory but substitutes a more appropriate social psychology. It starts from the structural context, the organization of society that provides a basis for grievance, and then insists on treating people's perceptions of their situation as a valid independent factor in explaining their actions.

resource **mobilization**. First, discontent is relegated to a minor place in accounting for social movements. The new approach does not deny that such feelings exist, but holds that they are always present in a population. Thus, the central problem is to explain the articulation of this discontent. Second, socially marginal, uprooted individuals are not the most fertile ground for social movements. Indeed, in the short run, rapid social change seems to reduce overt conflict by restricting the resources available for deprived groups to mobilize. A substantial body of historical research supports an alternative theory that solidary organization, i.e., close-knit groups with much interaction, is necessary to permit the mobilization of resources for collective action (Snyder and Tilly, 1972: Shorter and Tilly, 1974; Tilly et al., 1975). Third, participation in a social movement involves a calculation of the likely returns in relation to the likely costs of action and is no less rational than other social action.

According to the mobilization perspective, social movements can be expected when resources such as money, arms, labour, and knowledge can be brought together for use by those who seek to change social institutions. This assembly and articulation of resources is the core idea of mobilization theory. Thus, Oberschall (1978:306) writes that ''Mobilization refers to the processes through which individual group members' resources are surrendered, assembled, and committed for obtaining common goals and for defending group interests.'' This process requires organization and cohesion among the deprived if they are to contribute to the movement, and often the interjection of resources from sympathetic outsiders is necessary too. It follows that social movements are more likely when potential beneficiaries of collective action are already connected through a social network. If societies are **segmented** (that is, they have rigid social divisions and their institutional structures make it difficult to express and satisfy demands through established practices), social movements are likely to emerge at some point because they are the only possible vehicle of opposition. South Africa's system of apartheid is perhaps the clearest contemporary example.

Once mobilized, a group spends some of its resources in building alliances or challenging other groups. Outcomes are determined by choice of strategy and by the distribution of resources among the contending parties. Of particular significance is the degree to which state action facilitates or represses the social movement (Tilly, 1975).

Structure

The volume and distribution of resources, the forms of group life, and the targets of a social movement are all parts of a social structure with a particular history. Social organizations are never harmonious wholes; they always contain conflicts and contradictions, which is another way of saying that they harbour in their very structure the pressure for change. Practically every account of social movements relates them in some way to strain, cleavage, conflict, or contradiction, which can always be found in the environment of any social movement, and knowledge of this structure is a necessary part of explanation. Yet, even a cursory glance at social history demonstrates that contradictions do not inevitably produce movements for change. Therefore, any explanation of social movements that only elaborates on the roots of deprivation must be incomplete. We should ask under what further circumstances does contradiction tend to produce social movements. How are actors mobilized to promote change?

Perceptions

What people think about their situation is important independent of what it looks like to an observer. To become involved in a social movement, people must deny the legitimacy of the existing structure, but this is by no means automatic for those who are deprived according to objective criteria. Often people accept the dominant culture and their place in the social order even when that place is blatantly unjust. The image of willing participants waiting only for the opportunity to act is unacceptable; often they do nothing. If they are to join a social movement, their consciousness must frequently be transformed by the actions of a committed nucleus of advocates. In this sense, the perception and interpretation of structural contradictions by social movement leaders is a vital part of social movement formation.

If people feel disadvantaged, participation in a social movement is only one of several strategies open to them. Therefore, we are forced to ask what further conditions make the appearance of a social movement as an effective political force more likely. The **relative deprivation** approach[1] accepts that feelings of frustration, whether manufactured by leaders or already widespread, are the most important links between social context and social movements. Can this view be sustained? People who feel others are receiving more rewards than they are entitled to, or that their present rewards are inadequate, or that their achievements are less than they ought to be probably would feel discontented. If, furthermore, the problem is blamed on others, a definition of the situation is created that is conducive to some protest action.

In the past, both defenders and critics of a relative deprivation approach would take general measures of welfare, such as the G.N.P. or price indices, and relate changes in these measures to the timing and volume of collective action; but they lacked any direct evidence of the attitudes and values of participants. Fortunately, several studies of contemporary movements (Useem, 1980; Walsh and Warland, 1983) have acquired appropriate data at the individual level to demonstrate that relative deprivation does affect collective action independently of structural variables. Also, Klandermans (1984) has developed a somewhat different social psychology in which (a) collective rather than individual motives are demonstrably important, and (b) people's willingness to participate in collective action depends on their evaluation of the likely success of the action in relation to its costs and benefits. Although this theory has only been tested on Dutch workers in relation to a single industrial dispute, it is a promising step towards the development of an adequate social psychology of participation to be used in conjunction with the advances of mobilization theory. Unfortunately, in research on Canadian social movements, this important information is missing, in part because it cannot be obtained reliably in historical research, in part because contemporary researchers have not considered it sufficiently important. Therefore, this analysis of Canadian movement necessarily lacks an important component of a full explanation.

Mobilization as a Career

The link between social structure and social movements is the process of mobilization. Mobilization should be treated as a career, as an ongoing process affected by the degree of success of prior social movement activity. Signs of success make it easier to draw people and their resources into the movement, while failures make mobilization more difficult. The initial formation of a social movement is favoured by the presence of leaders, a network of **solidary linkages** among prospective adherents, and a permissive environment (Clark et al., 1975). A social movement must from the beginning develop some strategy and tactics to cope with its environment, at least part of which it wants to change. How the movement itself is interpreted and reacted to is therefore of great importance. In seeking change, movements face may undergo institutionalization, a process whereby movements that challenge the social order either gradually become part of it or become concerned primarily with preserving the organization itself rather than the original objectives.

The career of a social movement should be considered as an emergent, socially conditioned response to structural contradictions. Ideally, then, a study of social movements should consider the context, how people interpret their situations, and the actual pattern of activity as the social movement unfolds. The following review of Canadian class movements makes reference to these aspects as much as the data and space will allow.

CANADIAN STRUCTURAL DIVISIONS AND SOCIAL MOVEMENTS: OVERVIEW

Given that movements are concerned with change, the starting point for analysis will be the divisions that make change desirable to some members of Canadian society. These structural sources of conflict can be used to classify social movements in a meaningful way, because they point to the object of change and to some extent to the structural location of those who take part in the action. In contrast with other recent commentators on the Canadian scene, who emphasize regionalism or centre-hinterland divisions as the source of social movements (Clark, 1982; Grayson and Grayson, 1982), the geographical dimension is relegated here to a secondary place. Instead, Canadian social movements are seen as the product of social conflicts based on:

1. Class
2. Gender
3. Culture/Ethnicity
4. Generations

This analytical specification of sources of conflict does not deny the overlap of issues when, for example, minority groups are disproportionately found in subordinate class positions.

A class refers to a group whose members share a common location in the organization of economic activity, in particular with reference to ownership and control. In so far as people recognize a shared interest and act in terms of it, class consciousness exists and classes become effective participants in social affairs, rather than merely sociological categories. The changing economy and class structure have been analyzed elsewhere in this volume. Class divisions are of paramount importance in Canadian society in that they are the sources of inequalities in power, material living conditions, and personal achievement in so many respects. Consequently, movements of subordinate classes are critical to a broad understanding of the processes of change and it is these class movements that are selected for more special attention here. Nevertheless, other divisions and other social movements are important, warranting much more attention than can be provided in this chapter.

Gender is an enduring basis of social division that has served to mobilize efforts to bring about change, notably by the suffragettes and modern feminists. Occupying a subordinate position in political and economic institutions and subject to cultural pressures that limit the sphere of action of women much more than men, Canadian women (supported by some men) have participated in a feminist movement for change, although it has been rather fragmented into numerous organizational and ideological components. Particularly when the primary focus is the labour market situation of women, gender and class issues are interconnected.

Like other societies, Canada has not rested on a broad value consensus. Differences in values are partly related to class and gender situations, but other divisions are rooted in ethnic identity, religious, and civic values. Values that are perceived not to be incorporated in dominant institutional practices become the source of movements for change in relation to the values in question. Quebec nationalism and separatism, Pro Choice and Pro Life, utopian religious movements, Native peoples, the movement against nuclear power, and the peace movement are a few examples.

Finally, divisions according to the different experience of generations should be mentioned in that the experience of age cohorts has sometimes cut across other social divisions and provided a basis for social movements. The youth/student movement of the 1960s and early 1970s is one example (see, e.g., Westhues, 1972).

Notably absent from the above list is reference to either rural–urban or regional cleavages, which I take to be a product of how the social relationships that give rise to conflict are distributed across physical space. Region in particular is not in itself socially significant, although the concentration of particular classes and ethnic groups in Canadian society has made the regional location of social movements a highly visible feature of Canada compared with most other societies.[2]

CANADIAN CLASS MOVEMENTS IN COMPARATIVE PERSPECTIVE

Populist Movements of the Petite Bourgeoisie

In line with my approach, it is important initially to describe the problem of the structural location of the petite bourgeoisie, the old middle class of small proprietors of production and distribution enterprises. They engage in trade, services (repairing appliances or running gas stations, for example), and **domestic commodity production** (D.C.P.). My focus is on the latter stratum only. D.C.P. is a form of production in which small-scale producers, who own or rent their means of production, sell commodities to maintain their households, which are also the source of labour with few exceptions. This type of commodity production is often described as independent, petty or simple, but I choose here to emphasize the domestic basis of both ownership and labour, but without implying that the household is harmonious and equal.[3]

In Canada, D.C.P. is most common in farming, fishing, and the provision of services. It is a form of production constantly threatened by a cost-price squeeze in which small producers can control neither the selling price of their products nor the costs of inputs, which are supplied by financial and industrial corporations. Unable to pass on the rising costs of production, many have been forced out of business, and ownership has become more concentrated. The petite bourgeoisie are small property holders, and as such they recoil from any suggestion that interferes with rights of personal ownership and the operation of the market. This makes them potential allies for conservatives. On the other hand, often caught between rising production costs and low prices for fish or farm products, the petite bourgeoisie is tugged in the radical direction by the structural situation in which it finds itself.

This ambiguity helps to explain two widespread characteristics of petit bourgeois movements—(1) the coexistence or alternation of both authoritarian right-wing and democratic left-wing movements; and (2) the appearance of many different, often short-lived movement organizations. What these movements have in common is a vague **populist** ideology that stresses the importance of ordinary toiling people, distrust of liberal democracy and established parties, opposition to monopolies that involves some kind of economic reform, and a virulent identification of the people's enemies, which at times can take the form of a racist attack on visible minorities (see Conway, 1978 for a comparative overview of populist ideologies).

The Southern United States has been an important centre of populism. From 1877, the Farmers' Alliance criticized the established economic and political system. A radical perspective was promoted in response to declining prices for cotton and the associated lien system whereby supplies were advanced by merchants against the security of the crop in the fields. Long before the New Deal, the Alliance advocated methods of economic control such as limiting crop acreage, withholding produce from market, fixing minimum prices, and co-operative buying and selling; indeed, the idea of a co-operative commonwealth of small producers was widespread in Alliance circles. Beginning among White small farmers in Texas, the Southern Alliance later spread to Black,

FARMERS CHALLENGE THE SOCIAL STRUCTURE

At certain times, Canadian farmers and fishermen have recognized their situation of collective dependence and have participated in social movements to defend their property and way of life in general. The largest Canadian movements followed and were influenced by late nineteenth century American populism. In response to their situation as petit bourgeois producers, both Western grain and Southern cotton farmers flocked to movements that challenged aspects of the social structure of the United States. Although the differences among movements and their internal factions cannot be considered in any detail, it will become evident that Canadian agrarian problems are not unique and that movements of broadly similar orientations have been generated elsewhere.

tenant areas and by 1892 had approximately one million members.

Mobilization theory stresses communication and organizational experience as a factor in Western agrarian social movements. A related point is that extreme destitution does not beget protest. Saskatchewan was the most depressed of Prairie provinces, but the old Liberal party was returned to office in 1935 and 1938. Furthermore, the people in the area that experienced the most severe declines in income and the worst environmental conditions (the south and southwest) were less likely to support Farmer–Labour or C.C.F. candidates than were the somewhat better off inhabitants of the parkbelt. The most deprived people may have lost hope and had no resources left to commit to a social movement, whereas those in somewhat better circumstances, but who still experienced the deprivations of the time, were able to act against the established order.

The initial approach based on economic organization did not solve the problems of most small producers and thus many looked for a political solution. There had always been advocates of direct political action, and with the collapse of the Cotton Exchange and other co-operative ventures due to undercapitalization and bitter mercantile opposition, they won over the others. Not trusting the major parties, which were considered corrupt and dominated

MOBILIZATION IN AGRARIAN MOVEMENTS

Research by Brym (1978, 1979) explicitly investigates the process of mobilization with special attention to the forms of social organization that linked participants in agrarian movements. Brym's theory of agrarian populism distinguishes between left (the Saskatchewan C.C.F.) and right populism (Social Credit), and explains the difference according to the organization of farmers and the pattern of their alliances in each case.[6] By the time these populist movements arose, a dense organizational network linked many farmers. In contrast, New Brunswick farmers were less commercially oriented, less connected with the capitalist economy that stimulated Western farmers to organize, and were disinclined to support a populist protest movement, with the exception of commercial potato growers in the St. John River valley. Brym explains the different versions of populism according to the different alliances farmers entered into. In Saskatchewan, ties to labour were stronger than to the urban petite bourgeoisie, a situation that was reversed in Alberta where Social Credit had urban roots and spread in opposition to the U.F.A./C.C.F. Brym then theorizes that Social Credit failed to dominate Saskatchewan because that province's agriculture was based more on wheat farming, which was more insecure and more associated with an egalitarian and collective spirit than was the Albertan ranching economy. Therefore, C.C.F. ideology and alliances with workers were more attractive to Saskatchewan farmers. Nevertheless, wheat farmers were actually more numerous than ranchers in Alberta and they must have supported Social Credit in large numbers. From this I conclude that the factor of political timing in relation to a crisis of legitimation of older parties was at least as important. However, no one who contemplates how people acted in those years has adequate evidence of what ordinary people thought, of how they saw their actions.

by the big corporations, an independent People's Party emerged to contest the presidential election of 1892. This party combined Western grain and Southern cotton farmers, but it lacked internal coherence because of different regional interests and understanding of what change was re quired. Palmer's (1980) study of Southern populism is particularly informative in this respect. Unity on the basis of a vague commitment to the priority of working people over elites, distrust of established parties, and the need for economic change was always threatened by differences in the amount of change desired. Some were satisfied with a policy to increase the money in circulation, and of these, the least radical were advocates of free coinage of silver at a ratio of 1:16 with gold. Others insisted on greenback legal ten der, without any real appreciation of the relationship between paper value and production. Another version was the establishment of subtreasury offices, which would advance to producers 80 percent of the value of their crop when the farmers delivered it for storage. Monopolies were attacked, especially the railroads, which some wanted put under government ownership.

Despite obtaining more than one million votes in the 1892 presidential election, the supporters of the People's Party were disappointed that more had not been attracted away from the older parties. When, in 1896, the Democrats selected as their candidate William Jennings Bryan, a free silver advocate and long a populist sympathizer, there was little hope for the new movement, which then faded from the political arena.[4]

The first Canadian farmers to threaten established powerholders in a significant way were the participants in the rebellions of 1836–1837, but during the subsequent decades of rapid expansion of the farm population, little protest was heard from central Canada's farmers. In Prince Edward Island, however, where tenancy rather than freehold ownership of land was a legacy of the island's settlement pattern, agitation for land reform was so threatening by the 1860s that troops were brought from the mainland to police the situation. In 1875, a new law, which required absentee owners to sell their land with first option to the tenants, led to a change in ownership structure and the end of the protests. It was in Western Canada that the agrarian movement became most prominent, as the settlement of the West was accomplished through the building of a wheat-exporting economy in which D.C.P. was subordinate to merchant capital and in which farm producers resented the tariff structure, which they identified with the high price of manufactured products.

As early as the 1870s, interest groups were formed in Manitoba to press for changes beneficial to farmers. By 1901, as the Prairies were undergoing a major settlement process, the Territorial Grain Growers Association was formed in southern Saskatchewan and soon won a major battle with the Canadian Pacific Railway concerning the provision of rail cars. When Saskatchewan and Alberta were created in 1905, this organization became the Saskatchewan Grain Growers Association and was soon followed by the formation of the United Farmers of Alberta. In 1903, the Manitoba Grain Growers' Association appeared. In typical populist fashion, these organizations upheld the virtue of the common farmer against the evils of grain dealers, transportation companies, and allied politicians. They attempted to gain more control over the wheat economy by displacing private capital in the key forward linkages of the industry. To defend the interests of a small property owning class, they advocated substantial changes elsewhere in the system. Thus, a farmers' grain company was established. The Manitoba government was forced to concede the introduction of publicly owned elevators by 1910 (a short-lived experiment), while co-operative elevator companies were established in the other two Prairie provinces.

Just to the south, in North Dakota, a similar wheat economy generated another American populist movement at this time (Morlan, 1955; Remele, 1981). Promoted by the American Society of Equity, co-operatives sprang up from 1906 and demands were articulated for a state-owned, terminal elevator company. As it had years before, the co-operative movement led to political action when it became apparent that demands for change were being stifled in the political system. By 1915, a Nonpartisan League (N.P.L.) had been formed with the aim of taking power by controlling the nomination process of the state Republican party. From 1917 to 1919, the N.P.L. was successful in introducing a wide range of populist reforms, including a state bank, mill, and terminal elevator. Within two years, however, charges of mismanagement and internal factional disputes brought on a recall election (itself a populist innovation) that removed some prominent N.P.L. supporters from office. The N.P.L. lost control of the legislature, but its major institutions withstood challenge.

Similarly, when Canadian farmers found that acting as a pressure group and intervening in co-operative fashion in the economy was inadequate to meet their needs, direct political action on the basis of a rural populist philosophy was advocated. In this respect, Ontario and Eastern Canada followed suit, although Quebecers remained unmobilized. The first member of Parliament elected by the United Farmers of Canada came from New Brunswick, although the prevalence of subsistence farming in much of the Maritimes and Quebec discouraged a widespread, powerful D.C.P. movement. However, the United Farmers of Ontario elected enough candidates to form a provincial government in alliance with labour in 1919.

Again, it was in the West where the impact of agrarian populism was most pronounced. The N.P.L. spread north; by 1917 there were 5000 members in Alberta and Saskatchewan, and a newspaper in each province to push the reform ideas. At the federal level, a loose coalition, formed under the free trade banner of the "New National Policy," drew on the support of disgruntled farm families to the extent that sixty-five M.P.s were elected in 1921, most from the West. Although their populist objection to conventional party organization contributed to divisive factionalism, and although the more moderate members were won back to the Liberal party, this electoral performance was a remarkable achievement for a protest movement that rested on a single occupational base. Yet the movement could not be sustained because of its limited class base and the ambivalent position of that class, which led to the formation of alliances in different political directions. In this respect, the fate of the People's Party after its defeat in 1896 is quite similar; some of its leaders were easily absorbed as reform Democrats in favour of free silver coinage, while others persisted on the radical fringes of politics, some moving in a right-wing direction. For example, Tom Watson, the famous Georgia populist and advocate of monetary reform in the 1890s, became an embittered attacker of Catholics, Jews, and Blacks.

In Alberta, the strength of the N.P.L., which favoured independent political action, forced the leadership of the United Farmers of Alberta reluctantly into politics (Morton, 1948:120). The United Farmers won the 1921 provincial election, and then governed in conservative fashion until the dramatic rise of Social Credit in 1935. Similarly, the United Farmers of Manitoba participated in several fiscally and socially conservative administrations between the world wars. Only in Saskatchewan did they stay out of politics, preferring the role of a pressure group that could not easily be ignored — until the Great Depression unfolded. In provincial politics, farm leaders showed few signs of their social movement roots, but in direct economic action change was still evident as a major marketing co-operative, the Wheat Pool, was successfully established from 1923.

The harsh experiences of drought, grasshoppers, and economic depression were followed by another surge of Prairie radicalism in the two provinces that still were primarily agrarian in their social structures. Although the United Farmers of Alberta endorsed the new Co-operative Commonwealth Federation (C.C.F.) and also showed willingness to consider the social credit theory of Major C.H. Douglas,[5] confidence in the old leadership was lacking. When William Aberhart, a well-known fundamentalist preacher, endorsed social credit and found all other parties unwilling to adopt it quickly, he led into office (1935) a new movement that combined urban and rural supporters. Aberhart could not deliver on his promises of immediate reform of the monetary system and quick prosperity, but he was able to blame the power of eastern bankers, the courts, and an intransigent federal administration for his problems. Coupled with some success in limiting foreclosures and careful husbanding of resources, Social Credit survived the wartime election of 1940 and continued to govern for the next thirty-one years while oil stimulated and transformed the Albertan economy.

In Saskatchewan, advocating a policy that included the nationalization of land (to protect farmers' occupancy), the fledgling Farmer–Labour Party was unsuccessful in the provincial election of 1932. As the C.C.F., it fared little better until, under moderate social democratic leadership, victory was achieved in 1944. The left, or democratic, populism of the C.C.F. effectively resisted encroachments from the right, or authoritarian, populism of social credit, not primarily because the social structure was different, but because Aberhart had no religious base in Saskatchewan and was unsuccessful in introducing social credit to Alberta. Furthermore, Saskatchewan farm leaders had not become discredited by their participation in a depression government and there was still political space for a left populist solution (Lipset, 1968; Richards and Pratt, 1979; Sinclair, 1975).

This interpretation is strengthened when it is realized that the failures of American democratic populism also generated a more right-wing, authoritarian variant in the 1930s. In the southern and mid-western states, movements inspired by Coughlin, Winrod, Long, and Pelly flourished briefly with their attacks against monopoly capitalism, despair of liberal democratic institutions, isolationism, preference for plebiscites, and anti-semitism. For comparative purposes the most interesting are those from the wheat states — Reverend Winrod's Defenders of the Christian Faith and Father Charles Coughlin's National Union for Social Justice. Like Aberhart, Winrod was a fundamentalist, but with more extremist views on Communists, Blacks, Jews, and Catholics. His magazine had a circulation of 100 000 during 1936–1940, mostly in Kansas, where, as Republican senate candidate in 1938, he received 22 percent of the vote (Lipset and Raab, 1970:160–62). Father Coughlin's movement was the most popular. He too advocated issuing credits as a solution to the Depression and attacked international bankers, big business, and communists.

When his presidential candidate, U.S. senator William Lemke, received only 900 000 votes in 1936, Coughlin's rhetoric became more extreme, openly advocating the corporatist state and the abolition of political parties. Opinion polls in 1938–1939 indicated his movement had the support of 15 percent to 25 percent of the population before its suppression in World War II (Lipset and Raab, 1970:161–75).

As the twentieth century progressed, Canadian farmers declined to less than 5 percent of the population and even in the Prairies they could not expect to be strong enough to form a government through their organizations. Today, the farm movement is increasingly defensive. Occasional demonstrations against low farm incomes and opposition to foreclosures and the auctioning of farm property reveal a farm movement that is even more on the defensive than in the past. Indeed, those farmers who do not survive as small capitalists are increasingly becoming proletarianized.

In coastal fisheries, the class structure is exceedingly complex, and a wide range of co-operatives, associations, and unions has emerged at various times (see Clement, 1986). My comments here will be limited to the inshore fishers who engage in D.C.P. Furthermore, only the largest of their organizations will be mentioned. Although Newfoundland's fishers had suffered for many years in an exploitative relationship with merchants, it was not until 1908 that the Fishermen's Protective Union (F.P.U.) was started. Concerned with wide-ranging economic, political, and educational reforms, the F.P.U. quickly gained support in the northeast, but not on the east and south coasts where the organizational structure was dominated by the Catholic clergy, who sided with the merchants. From its northeast base, the F.P.U. established co-operatives and elected representatives to the legislature, eventually to find its leader, William Coaker, a member of the wartime government. However, the attempt to reconstruct the relations of production in fishing failed after World War I, the F.P.U.'s co-operative trading company fell on hard times, and Coaker finally abandoned the movement. Although government initiatives from 1938 led to some co-operative development, especially in lobster selling, no social movement appeared again until 1969, when the Northern Fishermen's Union was formed among the skippers of the Port au Choix area. This group soon combined with organized plant workers into the Newfoundland Fishermen, Food and Allied Workers Union, which under the leadership of Richard Cashin became the militant spearhead for changing the conditions of labour for inshore fishers, trawlermen, and plant workers.

In the Maritimes, the extension workers from St. Francis Xavier University promoted co-operatives in the 1930s as an alternative path to development, one they hoped would avoid the evils of both capitalism and socialism. The co-operatives were successful among the inshore fishers of eastern Nova Scotia. Today, the United Maritime Co-operatives, essentially a marketing agent, is an established institution in eastern Canada; indeed, there has been considerable tension between this group and the United Maritime Fishermen, a movement organization that now militantly pursues the interests of small-scale fishers from its base in northeastern New Brunswick.

On the West Coast, the United Fishermen and Allied Workers Union represents crew and D.C.P. fishers. As Clement (1984:22) states, "Its militant practices and constant political/educational work . . . have made it a force with which to reckon." Also significant on this coast are the Native Brotherhood and the large Prince Rupert Fishermen's Cooperative, although Hayward (1984) claims that the large West Coast co-operative is a fully institutionalized business like any other, except that fishers are shareholders.

The sociological analysis of these D.C.P. movements has seldom been undertaken from a perspective based on the theory of social movements. Much of the literature describes the life history of movement organizations without necessarily providing the most relevant sociological information. It is usual, however, to find an analysis of the social structural problems that give rise to the movements, e.g., C.B. Macpherson's (1962) brilliant illumination of the contradictory position of the petite bourgeoisie in Albertan agriculture, a position that gave rise to vacillating political tendencies and that included mass support for the Social Credit movement. Another example is Sacouman's (1979) research on co-operatives. Writing on the Antigonish movement, he argues that fishers were treated as wage workers (i.e., the price of fish was controlled by the company and was the equivalent to a wage) and that their labour was exploited in a pattern of "direct underdevelopment." In contrast, impoverished subsistence farmers in the same region, who were only indirectly linked with the capitalist economy, were not mobilized by the co-operatives, which were an attempt to gain control over marketing and credit. Often, however, the jump from the structure of underdevelopment to the appearance of the social movement is too abrupt; the causal link is unclear.

Development of the Labour Movement

Members of the working class, those who sell their labour power in a capitalist economy, occupy a subordinate position relative to employers. The capitalists' power, based on the ownership of productive property, means that they control hiring, wage rates, and conditions of work. Thus, workers have had from the beginning of capitalist development an objective interest in gaining greater control over their own labour and potentially in removing employers from their position of power. The collective action of workers to achieve such objectives makes up the labour movement.

Social movements by definition challenge the existing institutional structure. In so far as improved wages and benefits mean a transfer of resources from one group to another, this enduring type of demand is consistent with the notion that movements seek change, but such demands are not part of a conscious strategy to alter the social relationships through which the economy functions. The Canadian labour movement has seldom been so radical as to challenge the basis of property ownership, but on numerous occasions workers have struggled to alter the way capital relates to labour in setting the terms of employment. In fact, the most prominent industrial disputes in Canadian labour history have focused on the recognition of effective collective bargaining rights and the desire to restrict arbitrary decisions by employers regarding the conditions of work. This applies even to the Winnipeg General Strike.

Yet the early unionists were also social radicals, as evidenced by the support of tradesmen for the patriot cause in the doomed struggles for democracy of 1836–1837. Following these major setbacks, expansion was slow for many years. Indeed, before 1872, trade unions were not legally recognized and their members were open to charges of seditious conspiracy, as occurred following a major demonstration in Toronto (1872) when workers attempted to obtain a reduction of working time to nine hours per day.

During the rapid industrialization of

Southern Ontario in the first decades of the twentieth century, strike action over wage demands and control of working conditions became frequent; indeed, 421 strikes were officially recorded from 1901 to 1914 (Heron and Palmer, 1977). Skilled workmen continued to lead these protests, as they had since the beginning of trade unionism. It was not, however, in central Canada that the most dramatic expression of the labour movement took place, but in Winnipeg, the gateway to the West. The Winnipeg General Strike of 1919 evolved out of ongoing disputes in the building and metal trades regarding cost of living wage increases and the right of workers to determine the organization of their own bargaining units. Although the actual issues of the strike were not particularly radical, it became associated with the policy of the Western Canada Labour Conference, which recommended the establishment of a single industrial labour organization (the One Big Union [O.B.U.]), a wide-ranging set of economic reforms, and even the support of revolutionary movements in Russia and Germany. Before union locals had voted on these resolutions, the strike broke out — not with any revolutionary objective, but because success in a multi-union strike in 1918 had led labour leaders to conclude that a general strike was needed to win their case. However, the atmosphere of challenge created by advocates of the O.B.U. probably contributed to the fear among capitalists, politicians, and middle-class citizens that the strike had to be defeated to quell the revolutionary potential of the Canadian workers. Only after six weeks did Winnipeg's trade unionists give in (on 26 June), their leaders having been arrested, and a peaceful demonstration attacked by special police and R.C.M.P. forces leaving one person dead and thirty injured.

The O.B.U. did not survive in Winnipeg after 1919 as a viable force, and an attempt to establish national industrial unions, federated in the All Canadian Congress of Labour, proved inadequate. For a few years, the Workers Unity League, formed in 1930 under communist control, won the support of some **industrial unions**, but it never became a major force. The successful development of industrial unionism had to await the organization of workers in the new mass production industries. Outside the more traditional Trades and Labour Congress, and supported by the Committee for Industrial Organization (C.I.O.), industrial unions rose to prominence in the thirties, highlighted by the Oshawa auto workers' strike of 1937 (Abella, 1974). Organizationally, this development was divisive, as the new industrial unions were expelled from the T.L.C. in 1938, following the C.I.O.'s expulsion from the American Federation of Labour. This schism was not healed until 1956 when the Canadian Labour Congress was established.

In the post-1945 years, many strikes have taken place in the private and public sectors. Generally, these have been defensive battles as workers have been threatened by inflation and have faced the dangers of technologically induced unemployment. It is notable, however, that English-Canadian labour leaders have not criticized capitalism as such, and their members have resisted direct political action, having failed to elect even the moderate N.D.P. in sufficient numbers to threaten the old parties at the federal level.

Meanwhile, in Quebec, the Catholic Church took the lead in organizing workers, as much to avoid external influences, such as the international unions, as to promote workers' interests, and by 1921 had assembled these moderate unions into the Canadian Confederation of Catholic Labour. Their profile remained low until 1949, partly because relatively few workers were organized (only 9 percent of paid nonagricultural workers by 1935 (Smucker 1980:223)), partly because the church discouraged aggressive tactics. By the 1940s, however, secular unions had made great inroads into the Quebec labour force, and also a more militant perspective was coming to the fore within the Catholic unions themselves. The most notable sign of change was the long, bitter fight by asbestos miners in the Eastern Townships against what they considered to be a biased arbitration procedure. The illegal strike began early in 1949, became violent at times, and brought widespread publicity and support for the workers before it was settled after almost six months.

In 1960, the link with the Catholic Church was formally abandoned with the establishment of the Confederation of National Trade Unions (C.N.T.U.), whose leaders embarked upon a radical class analysis of Quebec society and soon became an important source of support for the Parti Québecois and independence. Apart from the possible attraction of its ideology, the rapid growth of C.N.T.U. unions in the 1960s was related to the state's acceptance that unionization was permissible for public employees if they did not identify with a political party. This effectively excluded C.L.C. affiliates because they formally supported the N.D.P. By 1970, so many state employees had flocked to the unions that 46 percent of C.N.T.U. members came from the public sector (Smucker, 1980:229). The C.N.T.U. has been ideologically radical in promoting Quebec nationalism, critiquing capitalism, and advocating industrial democracy. Moreover, in industrial disputes it has been among the most militant.

UNION DENSITY: A COMPARISON WITH THE UNITED STATES

Since the nineteenth century, trade unions gradually came to represent an important segment of the nonagricultural labour force. By 1911, when the first statistics are available, only 4.9 percent had been unionized, but, by 1955, 33.7 percent were organized (Smucker, 1980:209). In recent decades, growth in absolute numbers has been tremendous (from 1.27 million in 1955 to 3.56 million in 1983), but the labour force increased almost as fast, with the consequence that only in 1983 did unionization reach 40 percent (Canada 1983:18).

Canada's level of unionization, like that of West Germany and the U.K., should now be considered of moderately high density, still well behind Australia (60 percent), Norway (60 percent), Denmark (70 percent) and, especially, Sweden (90 percent) (Bain and Price, 1980). This growth in the density of unionization in Canada has moved in the opposite direction to that of the United States, where the corresponding figures fell from 34.7 percent in 1954 to 23.6 percent in 1978, and then to as low as 19.5 percent by 1984 (Huxley et al., 1986:18). In a recent attempt to explain U.S.–Canadian differences, S.M. Lipset (1986) examines several promising answers.

First, regarding structural changes that may have weakened the ability of American unions to provide attractive benefits to prospective members, Lipset found other countries had experienced similar economic problems and changes to their occupational structures without a decline in **union density**. Indeed, by 1983, Canada had a larger tertiary sector than any other O.E.C.D. country (424). A second possibility is that a harsher legal environment in the United States, especially anti-union decisions by the federal Labor Relations Board, contributed to the relative decline. Lipset, however, shows that only since 1983 has a larger percentage of decisions gone against labour than capital. The reverse argument, that the protections afforded by the legal environment cancel the need for unions in the eyes of workers, is unacceptable when one looks to the expansion of both in Canada.[7] Third, Lipset finds no reason to believe Canadian employers are any less hostile to unions than are Americans, and thus he is unwilling to accord great significance to anti-union attitudes in the United States as an explanation of the differences.

What he finds particularly important is evidence of declining support for unions among the general public since the mid-fifties. No comparable Canadian data are presented. The theory develops along the lines that Canadians, as a result of the pattern of colonial development, are more collectivist, elitist, statist, and group-oriented than Americans (Lipset, 1986:442). Although there has been much debate over Lipset's long-standing interpretation of Canadian values, the critical literature is ignored at this point. If Canadians are indeed more favourable towards unions than are Americans (and this seems likely), the explanation probably rests in the social process whereby these values are generated. Instead of pointing to highly general and questionable value differences as the cause of specific attitudes, it would be better to concentrate on the degree to which anti-union forces influence the media and the political parties in the United States as compared with Canada. Perhaps Canadian institutions are less captives of capital than similar institutions in the United States, but more so than the social democratic countries of Europe, where levels of unionization are higher.

CANADIAN STRIKES: HOW DISTINCTIVE?

Canadian class movements have been based on what Smelser would call the structural strain of competing demands in the economy and what Marxists identify as inherent conflicts of class interest in the development of capitalism. I have argued that the explanation of these movements requires attention to the mobilization process in that consciousness of class interest cannot be assumed, nor can the transition from sense of deprivation to action. In labour movement studies, the process of mobilization has not been examined in the terms developed by resource mobilization theorists, but much relevant sociological information is nevertheless available in these reports. For example, critics of breakdown theory have clearly been correct in that it is not the most deprived and unstable elements of the working class that have formed the backbone of the labour movement. The unemployed and unskilled labourers were not the initiators of Canada's labour unions; rather it was the skilled craftsmen. Leadership has been a critical resource shaping the awareness of deprived workers that their problems lay in the nature of the economic system, and that collective action was needed to change that system to a greater or lesser extent. The most visible manifestation of that action is the strike.

A strike has many possible meanings, but any strike involves some demand for change. Strikes are not the only indicator of the existence of a labour movement or of the degree of radicalism of the movement. The strike is only part of the repertoire of possible actions that workers might take in defence of their interests.

Strike data across time and societies are difficult to compare because the definition of a strike varies and so does the method of collection. In some cases all stoppages of work that come to the attention of authorities are recorded. Sometimes only disputes at least a day long are counted or only when a minimum number of days are lost. Often "political" strikes are excluded. In some societies, this makes little difference, but in Italy, where political strikes were recorded after 1975, the strike figures increased by about 19 percent (Walsh, 1983). It is common to report the more reliable figure of employee-days lost, but this is based on the number of strikers involved and the length of strikes. Therefore, to maintain maximum information, Tables 1 to 3 report the number of disputes, the number of strikers involved, and the mean duration of disputes, but trends and comparisons should be treated only as rough guides to actual experience. The data are based on the I.L.O.'s *Yearbook of Labour Statistics*, and are presented as ratios to permit more meaningful comparison. In contrast to most other reports, which use the total labour force as the base for these ratios, only employees are included here because this group contains the potential union members. The elimination of employers and independent businessmen, as well as unpaid family workers, means that the estimates are higher than in other sources.

Tables 1 to 3 present selected data on strikes for the period 1945 to 1983 in five year averages. Even allowing for inaccurate and inconsistent measurement, sharp differences exist across societies. In tables of employee-days lost, Canada and Italy both score high, but this is based on quite different strike patterns. On this criterion, Italy, Finland, and Australia score very high, with frequent widespread, but short, strikes. Canada, on the other hand, typically experiences a moderate number of strikes involving a moderately large number of workers and lasting a long time. It has generally been closer to the United States than to any of the other societies, although the American data indicate decreasing militancy in contrast with an upward movement in Canada. The number

Table 1

NUMBER OF STRIKES PER 100 000 WORKERS, 1945–1983

Society	1945–49	1950–54	1955–59	1960–64	1965–69	1970–74	1975–79	1980–83
Canada	5.3	4.8	4.9	5.8	8.4	9.3	10.8	8.2
U.S.A.*	8.5	9.1	7.0	5.6	6.6	6.8	5.8	—
Belgium	8.8	5.0	4.0	1.7	2.1	6.1	7.3	—
Denmark	1.7	0.9	2.0	2.4	1.3	4.9	10.6	7.2
Finland	9.3	5.5	5.7	4.0	5.7	54.7	98.6	91.0
France**	10.7	15.8	15.7	14.2	12.1	21.0	20.3	15.5
Ireland	19.2	15.0	9.4	10.9	15.2	21.5	19.1	14.4
Italy	—	15.8	15.0	26.5	24.0	35.1	19.7	12.4
Netherlands	7.9	2.4	10.9	2.0	0.7	0.8	0.7	0.3
Norway	4.3	3.6	1.9	0.9	0.5	0.9	1.2	1.1
Sweden	3.7	1.2	0.6	—	0.6	2.3	2.7	2.7
U.K.	9.6	8.3	11.9	11.4	10.7	13.1	10.2	6.2
Japan	—	4.0	4.3	4.8	4.9	9.1	5.6	2.4
Australia	38.4	51.0	37.1	32.9	37.7	54.6	35.7	43.4
New Zealand	19.6	13.7	8.5	9.8	14.9	40.8	45.0	30.2

* excludes 1979
** excludes 1968

Source: Calculated from *Yearbook of Labour Statistics*, various years.

Table 2
NUMBER OF STRIKERS PER 1000 WORKERS, 1945–1983

Society	1945–49	1950–54	1955–59	1960–64	1965–69	1970–74	1975–79	1980–83
Canada	24.3	25.9	19.3	57.0	66.0	54.2	66.3	37.2
U.S.A.*	66.3	47.5	35.7	32.1	32.1	33.2	19.0	—
Austria	—	11.6	14.6	28.1	29.9	8.7	0.6	4.9
Belgium	80.5	57.9	64.9	11.2	10.7	24.7	28.2	—
Denmark	12.1	0.2	11.3	37.2	11.2	61.9	38.0	23.0
Finland	45.2	29.1	111.5	29.1	26.9	287.5	195.1	195.3
France**	265.8	118.2	108.5	146.7	194.1	127.7	84.7	24.6
Ireland	19.1	20.1	12.1	25.0	60.1	38.4	47.7	33.5
Italy	—	297.4	77.2	224.2	293.4	389.0	905.7	627.8
Netherlands	15.3	11.4	4.5	7.0	2.8	8.2	5.0	6.3
Norway	7.1	4.6	15.8	6.4	5.1	4.7	4.4	7.1
Sweden	17.2	4.4	0.6	0.7	2.6	7.2	4.6	49.9
U.K.	28.6	28.3	34.8	68.3	54.6	71.3	73.4	55.9
W. Germany	—	4.9	9.8	4.2	3.3	10.2	7.0	4.5
Japan	—	78.1	67.2	48.5	40.6	63.3	31.1	7.7
Australia	126.3	116.0	110.7	127.2	164.9	395.3	286.1	140.1
New Zealand	60.3	49.6	24.0	31.2	35.4	90.4	140.2	128.3

* excludes 1979
** excludes 1968

Source: Calculated from *Yearbook of Labour Statistics*, various years.

of strikers per one thousand workers gives a rough indication of extent of workforce participation, although some workers may be counted more than once in a year. Canadian workers are involved relatively rarely (although much more than most North and Northwest Europeans), but their strikes tend to last longer on average, with the result that Canada loses a relatively large number of employee-days due to industrial disputes.

How might the data be explained? The classic comparative study of strikes is that by Ross and Hartman (1960), who claimed that institutionalized industrial relations lead to a decrease in the importance of strikes. In so far as strikes challenge existing patterns of industrial relations, this is true by definition. Ross and Hartmann argue the theory that when the labour movement is old and membership stable, when unions and a system of collective bargaining are well established, then strikes will be less likely. Furthermore, it is argued that close links between organized labour and a political party, especially one in power, will act as a brake on union militancy, and where the state is an employer or establishes wide-ranging procedures for settling disputes, this too will reduce strikes or make them shorter. (See also Ingham, 1974.)

Without discounting all of the above, especially the political organization of labour, more recent research provides an alternative to the institutionalization model that is consistent with the mobilization perspective (Waters, 1982; Shorter

Table 3
MEAN DURATION OF STRIKES (EMPLOYEE-DAYS PER STRIKER), 1945–1983

Society	1945–49	1950–54	1955–59	1960–64	1965–69	1970–74	1975–79	1980–83
Canada	23.8	14.9	17.0	14.8	16.0	15.0	15.9	18.3
U.S.A.*	17.9	14.2	17.3	9.4	15.9	16.3	18.5	—
Austria	—	2.5	2.2	2.7	0.7	2.1	3.5	1.8
Belgium	6.1	7.0	8.6	12.4	8.6	11.8	8.4	—
Denmark	22.0	2.9	12.6	7.9	3.6	6.9	2.7	4.7
Finland	9.7	30.1	13.7	7.9	4.3	3.4	1.8	2.1
France**	3.1	3.7	1.7	1.4	1.1	1.6	2.7	4.0
Ireland	20.2	19.5	15.3	16.1	13.4	15.7	17.8	13.0
Italy***	—	1.5	5.7	4.2	4.1	3.8	1.6	1.6
Netherlands	8.0	2.1	5.6	4.8	2.1	6.4	3.4	5.2
Norway	10.9	15.1	14.4	20.4	1.8	12.8	7.4	7.3
Sweden	—	23.3	31.9	8.5	12.0	9.1	6.1	12.9
U.K.	4.4	3.3	6.2	2.1	3.2	8.9	7.3	6.6
W. Germany	—	13.6	4.8	5.5	2.0	5.3	4.2	1.0
Japan	—	5.3	6.0	4.2	3.5	2.7	2.3	2.2
Australia	5.3	3.7	2.1	1.5	1.6	1.8	2.2	9.8
New Zealand	2.3	9.8	1.9	2.4	3.4	2.3	2.6	2.6

* excludes 1979
** excludes 1968
*** excludes 1950

Source: Calculated from *Yearbook of Labour Statistics*, various years.

and Tilly, 1974; Korpi and Shalev, 1979; Korpi, 1983). Shorter and Tilly (1974), referring to the period since 1945, write:

> Where the strike rate soared, revolutionary unionism acquired new organizational resources in a drive for political representation. Where the strike rate fell, workers had been accepted into the polity, and now needed no longer to use strikes as a means for pressing political demands. Where the strike rate fluctuated, as in North America, labour had discarded the industrial work stoppage as a means of political action, turning instead to political parties (Shorter and Tilly, 1974:317).

They identify a West European pattern with many large strikes of short duration in which strikes are considered mainly as political demonstrations directed at national power centres. The U.K. is treated as a marginal member of this group, if strikes are judged as "fundamentally, localized protests over the local distribution of power" (Shorter and Tilly, 1974:327). In Northern Europe (Scandinavia, West Germany, and the Netherlands) strikes are few, relatively long, and vary considerably in size. In each, the working class has enjoyed a share of power for long periods and the state provides formal procedures for wage negotiation and dispute settlement. There has been no need to strike for political ends, and it has become superfluous in economic affairs. In North America, workers also became accepted into the polity, but the state pursued a policy of nonintervention in industrial relations, which left the strike as a necessary weapon in collective bargaining.

Unfortunately, there are problems with this account. The strike is more often used to make political statements in France and Italy, but in the absence of a well-established collective bargaining system, it is also an important part of unrest over local work and economic conditions. Local struggles are certainly political, but it is in the national context that Shorter and Tilly couch their political explanation. Belgium is a puzzle to Shorter and Tilly, and Finland is quite different from the other Scandinavian countries. Furthermore, in Norway and Sweden the state tries to keep out of industrial relations as much as possible. This may be one reason why Norwegian and Swedish strikes are much longer than others when they do break out. Also, the labour movement is well organized and has the resources to sustain long strikes. Moreover, working-class interests are not so perfectly represented in these polities that strikes have become superfluous; it is precisely the alienation from bureaucratic, centralized structures that has been presented as the root of Sweden's unofficial strike wave in 1971 (van Otter, 1975; Fulcher, 1975; Wheeler, 1975). Finally, with regard to Canada and the United States, workers do not even have representation through a strong social democratic or labour party. Organized labour is not a dominant influence in the Democratic party of the United States and, in Canada, the N.D.P., although endorsed by the Canadian Labour Congress, has struggled for years to rise from third place behind the two bourgeois parties.

Walter Korpi, like Shorter and Tilly, rejects explanations of strike patterns that emphasize the structure of collective bargaining in favour of a model that, consistent with the mobilization approach to social movements, rests on the relative capacities of capital and labour to achieve their objectives. High density of unionization, left-wing political unity, and a labour movement closely allied with a powerful political party provide the major bases of working-class strength. In conjunction with several other important intervening variables (see Figure 1), the level and shape of industrial conflict is then explained. As with Shorter and Tilly, a low level of industrial conflict does not indicate a disinterested or impotent working class, but in the case of the "low strike," North and Northwest European countries reflects the power of workers through social democratic governments to introduce favourable policies regarding distribution. "The centre of gravity of the distributive conflicts can thus be moved from the labour market into politics. As a result of the changes in distributive policies, labour disputes may decrease in extent and importance" (Korpi, 1983:170). However, only when social democratic parties are effective in pursuing a policy that favours the working class will there be a dampening effect on industrial disputes. With three exceptions, Korpi's model provided a good fit to the reported experience of industrial conflict in the twentieth century in eighteen advanced capitalist societies.[8]

Canadian workers became increasingly militant in the 1970s, and participation in industrial stoppages fell off in the depressed 1980s, which is consistent with the theory that workers feared losing their jobs in an oversupplied labour market. Rather than emphasize changes over time, however, I am interested in the consistent Canadian pattern of moderate involvement in disputes, disputes which last longer than those in most advanced capitalist societies. The key factors are: (1) the organizational resources of the Canadian labour movement, which permit long conflicts; (2) the weak political representation of labour (discussed more fully in the next

Figure 1
Schematic summary of major variables assumed to affect patterns of industrial conflict

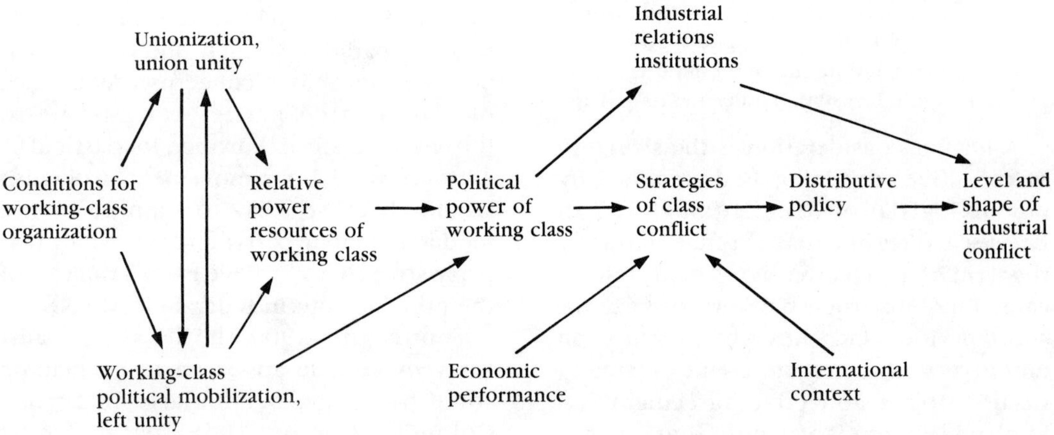

Source: From Walter Koapi, *The Democratic Class Struggle.* Routledge and Kegan Paul, 1983.

section); (3) the structure of collective bargaining in Canada, in which legal strikes cannot take place prior to the expiry of a collective agreement; and (4) the particular nature of the Canadian industrial structure.

Mobilization theory makes us aware that organization among those who experience deprivation is a precondition of action. It is certainly a precondition of the relatively long Canadian, American, and Scandinavian strikes. Canada's level of unionization is moderately high among this group of societies. However, organization does not mean the labour force will engage in strikes; indeed, the most completely organized workers, those of Norway, Sweden, Denmark, West Germany, and the Netherlands, spend relatively little time on the picket lines. We have seen how several authors explain this in terms of the institutionalization of labour relations and/or the political influence of the labour movement in these societies. Yet, Australian and British workers are fairly strike-prone despite formal associations with powerful labour parties in both instances. Thus, the political links of organized labour are not decisive factors (as Korpi has correctly observed).

Jamieson (1979) explains the high incidence of days lost in Canada for 1965 to 1975 partly in relation to the decentralized structure of the labour movement and consequently of the collective bargaining process. Canadian labour is split into different federations that exert neither political influence in Ottawa or central Canada nor authority over their member unions. Consequently, united action, such as the common front of public service unions in Quebec in 1972, is rare. The second important factor that Jamieson raises is the nature of the Canadian economy, which is dependent on unstable and capital-intensive industries concerned with the export of raw materials and semi-finished goods. Economic insecurity, associated with business cycle fluctuations, has produced numerous disputes and a militant workforce.

> Only six industries, employing less than 15 percent of all workers, accounted for 50.9 percent . . . of all man-days lost in strikes during 1965–1975. The six were:

> construction; mining, and smelting (in the broad category of manufacturing); transportation equipment (mainly automobiles); primary metals (mainly iron and steel); pulp and paper; and wood products (including the small number employed in forestry) (Jamieson, 1979:12).

A further consideration is the structure of collective bargaining as determined by labour legislation (see Huxley, 1979). Because strikes in Canada are illegal during the term of a collective agreement, unions cannot mobilize their workers to strike for short periods and thus put pressure on employers. Rather, the strike normally occurs after a collective agreement has expired, compulsory conciliation has taken place, and the two sides have found it impossible to reach another agreement. In anticipation of this possibility, companies may stockpile inventory in the hope that they can carry on business and exhaust the union.

These points demonstrate the importance of the structural context (organizational, industrial, and political) of the Canadian labour movement in the explanation of collective action. Moreover, the understanding of how Canada's organized workers have behaved is enormously aided by comparative research, which shows what factors are most decisive. It is regrettable, nevertheless, that more direct information is not available on how Canadian workers define their situation, because a full account of social movements requires knowledge of the social psychology of mobilization, as well as structural variables. It is perhaps worth noting that the increased propensity to strike in the late 1960s and 1970s compared with earlier decades is associated with a period of stagnation and inflation that threatened gains made in previous years. It is thus reasonable to suppose that the experience of relative deprivation would have contributed, in conjunction with other factors, to this strike wave.

THE WEAKNESS OF CLASS POLITICAL MOVEMENTS

In considering Canadian class movements in a comparative setting, one of the most pertinent questions concerns the absence of class-related parties comparable to those of Western Europe. In particular, why has the labour movement in English Canada been so slow to support even a moderate labour party, and why does that party struggle to achieve even a quarter of the popular vote in federal elections?

Shortly after 1900, the Marxist Socialist Party of Canada appeared to be making some headway, particularly in British Columbia (Robin, 1968). Other small social democratic and labour parties searched for support at the same time that labour unions were struggling to become established, but none could cross the threshold to become increasingly seen as a needed and viable vehicle of working-class protest. The most promising candidate by the 1930s was the C.C.F. (Co-operative Commonwealth Federation), but it was never embraced by the strongest union federations and remained a distinct outsider in the political realm. In contrast to Canada, working-class political parties developed in all major European capitalist societies, both the early industrializers like Britain and Germany and those that developed more or less at the same time as Canada, such as Sweden and Italy. Labour parties were also important from an early time in the British-settled dominions of Australia and New Zealand.

What is to account for the tardy Canadian development? Several promising structural and cultural factors will be considered here: an inadequate organizational base, a culturally fragmented population, the rejection of a political strategy by union leaders at key moments, and timely concessions by Canada's brokerage-type political parties of the establishment. None alone was decisive, but in combination they stifled the possibility of a mass socialist movement of the Canadian working class.

In considering the organizational base, it is important to recognize that compared with most industrializing societies Canada had a relatively large petit bourgeois population based primarily on freehold farming. In the first quarter of the twentieth century, a party that appealed to the sectional interests of the working class could not hope for majority support, if only because of the numerical predominance of the petite bourgeoisie. This class might side with labour when the opponent was big business and might abstractly support the interests of the "working man," but it was also divided on important issues. Whereas workers wanted to protect jobs and raise wages, farmers opposed tariffs that protected employment in central Canada and the increased costs that higher wages would mean for them, both as consumers of Canadian-made products and employers of seasonal labour. Although farmers were often battling big capital, they were far from comfortable with the idea of a state dominated by a working-class party.

The labour movement itself has exhibited a plethora of social movement organizations and internal factionalism that has inhibited united action. The politics of interest group action without supporting any particular party predominated in the craft unions and especially among the leaders of the Trades and Labour Congress through most of its history. Struggles between communists and more moderate leaders predominated in the 1930s and 1940s when united class action might have succeeded. In 1943, a public opinion poll indicated that the C.C.F. was the most popular party, which was the signal for a vicious ideological counterattack and a set of concessions to ordinary workers, from which the C.C.F. could not recover. Industrial and craft unionists could not agree. Further battles have been fought around the touchy question of national versus international unions.

An enduring factor that is widely recognized to have limited the appeal of a working-class party in Canada is cultural fragmentation. The organizational strength of the working class had been weakened by persistent cultural divisions, the most important between francophones and anglophones, who have not developed a common, national class consciousness. It is difficult for people who do not understand each other to act together, and no party with aspirations to represent workers' interests has made headway in both Quebec and English Canada.[9]

Not to be forgotten in this list is the reaction of the state and the mainline parties to socialism. On the one hand, socialists have been branded as a threat to liberty and basic democratic freedom; on the other hand, the Liberals and Conservatives have adopted enough of the specific policies advocated by labour unions and working-class parties to permit them to hold their votes. The rise of the welfare state and the federal order-in-council of 1944 to legitimize important aspects of the collective bargaining process are important aspects of this process.

INSTITUTIONALIZATION AND CANADIAN CLASS MOVEMENTS

Many pressures drive movements in the direction of institutionalization. Organization is essential to co-ordinate opposition, but those who fill organizational positions may become preoccupied with the state of the organization and their position in it, rather than with the basic objectives for which it was established. Also, as movements develop their bureaucratic structure, the distance between official leaders and ordinary members may become excessive, particularly when the movement employs professional organizers in its key positions. These are the internal forces recognized long ago by Michels in his pessimistic study of socialist parties.

The environment of the movement is also important. Concessions from opponents may cool out the less ardent supporters and conversely intransigence may discourage them. Counter-ideological campaigns may undermine the commitment of some members. Most important, radical policies usually involve uncertainty and risk, as well as constituting a challenge to established interests. This makes it hard to win over a majority of the population quickly. Thus, movements that seek power through elections are under great pressure to moderate their positions and converge towards the middle ground, where they appear increasingly like those they had originally attacked.

This process was operating at a very early stage in Saskatchewan. Important leaders of the Saskatchewan Grain Growers Association accepted offers to sit in the Liberal Cabinet in that province, while elsewhere the farmers' movements that did take office independently or in coalition with labour took few measures that distinguished them from the old parties they had attacked. In 1932, the necessity of appealing to a rural electorate committed to personal land-ownership required the C.C.F. to modify a policy to nationalize land (even though that policy was designed to protect the tenure of the smallholder). More recently, the Parti Québécois removed independence from its immediate agenda when its leaders realized they could not win a quick electoral victory on that basis. The result: election to office in 1976.

Apart from a minority of movement organizations, like the One Big Union and the C.N.T.U., the labour movement has never presented a radical critique of the capitalist system, and its energies have been directed towards establishing a more acceptable place for labour within the existing system. To this end, the labour movement accepted the legislative protection of 1946 at the cost of agreeing to abandon the right to strike within the period of a collective agreement. Particularly when one considers the conservatism

BETRAYAL OF WORKERS' INTERESTS IS NOT INEVITABLE

Although numerous cases of bureaucratic displacement of objectives may be mentioned, Canadian history shows that this is by no means inevitable. Likewise, the experience of labour movements in Europe is informative. In Sweden, where the Social Democratic Party (S.D.P.) had been in power for a long time and where the labour movement functioned with a highly centralized structure that was placed under stress by the complaints of ordinary workers in the early 1970s, the confederation of blue-collar workers responded with proposals for far-reaching change in both control of the workplace and ownership of property. The proposals, now accepted by the S.D.P., call for a proportion of profits to be set aside as workers' equity under the control of the unions, with some representation from the state. Over time, the funds would accumulate until control of many firms would pass to the workers' representatives. Thus, institutionalization in the sense of displacement of radical objectives, far from being inevitable, may sometimes be reversed.

of the early craft unionists, there has not really been a process of displacement of movement objectives on a large scale. Indeed, with the emergence of radical politics in the Quebec labour movement, the process has gone in the reverse direction.

Still, it is correct to note the failure of the Canadian labour movement as a whole to support a political party with a radical program. The C.C.F. gained little sympathy from labour when it was at its most radical, and only after its policies were thoroughly toned down in the 1956 Winnipeg declaration did the Canadian Labour Congress move towards affiliation. Yet it would be unfair to say union bureaucrats were stifling the radicalism of the members. Although the N.D.P. is a party of social democratic reform, not radical socialism, union leaders who openly support it as the party of labour have been unable to persuade their members to follow their example. One of the most recent cases in point was the failure of Richard Cashin to bring fishers and plant workers in Newfoundland to support the N.D.P. in the 1985 provincial election, even when the party fielded prominent union officials as candidates.

CONCLUSION

This chapter has shown that Canadian classes have a long history of participation in social movements to alter the conditions under which ordinary people labour. These movements have been part of an international process of capitalist development in which only the specific configuration of Canadian circumstances makes Canada unique. We hope that the value of comparison, especially with the United States, as an aid to understanding Canadian social movements has been demonstrated and also the utility of the mobilization model of social movements. As to the future, what will happen is unclear. D.C.P. will probably continue to wither away in the face of capitalist expansion, and social movements of farmers and fishers will not be able to withstand the pressure, except in the few niches where small-scale production has real advantages. Particularly in the public sector, Canada's unions are under stress at a time of fiscal scarcity for the state, and employers are militantly testing the capacity of labour in many private sector disputes. In many cases, the labour movement is struggling even to hold onto rights won in the past, and stronger ties between organized labour and the N.D.P. cannot realistically protect Canada's workers from threats to living conditions, working conditions, and the very existence of their jobs. These tasks require a vigilant, vibrant, independently organized labour force.

Notes

[1]This is a version of discontent theory best represented by Davies (1962, 1969), Gurr (1970) and Crosby (1979).

[2]The social movements of Canada's hinterland areas have been concerned with cultural issues (Quebec separatism) or class issues (Western agrarianism) and only in a few instances, as with Western Canadian separatism, has a sense of identification with the region per se generated movements for which it might be convincingly claimed that region was the prime focus.

[3]Indeed, property is usually held by male household heads and, although there is wide variation in practice, they are in a position to exploit the labour of their wives and children. This is particularly a problem when inheritance rules discriminate against daughters.

[4]This summary cannot do justice to the complex history and local variations of the populist movement. Those interested should consult the following recent sources: Goodwyn (1976), Palmer (1980) for his

analysis of ideology, and Schwartz (1976). Cherny (1981:158–59) argues that in Nebraska, populists demanded a redistribution of wealth and reordering of social values, while the Progressives who followed shared little more than regulation and reform of the political process. Shaw's (1984) study of Georgia populists, the wool hat boys, brings out the anti-Black, nativist aspects of some Southern populists and the lack of continuity in this case between areas of strong Alliance support and those that voted for populist candidates. Finally, the best single study from a sociological perspective is Barnes's (1984) work on Texas in which she examines the Alliance in terms of mobilization theory.

[5]For the best analysis of this inflationary economic theory, see Macpherson (1962).

[6]The theme that social organization promotes mobilization is also the keystone of Brym and Neis's (1978) analysis of the F.P.U. Recognition that the F.P.U. failed where organizational networks were controlled by the Catholic Church leads to the important conclusion that an organizational structure among the deprived is only a good basis for recruitment when that organization is independent of the powerholders.

[7]It is, however, important to note that recent Canadian legislation, both federal and provincial, has imposed serious restrictions on the rights of labour. See the excellent review of the trajectory of Canadian industrial relations by Panitch and Swartz (1984).

[8]In an earlier study, David Snyder (1975) compared strikes in the United States, France, and Italy, and found some support for the interpretation of French and Italian strikes in terms of political or organizational variables, whereas the assumption that strikes result from a breakdown in bargaining provided a better fit to the American data.

[9]Only by 1986 did the N.D.P. show signs of achieving significant support in Quebec.

DISCUSSION QUESTIONS

1. Contrast the resource mobilization and relative deprivation approaches to social movements.
2. Canadian populism exhibits strong national characteristics that clearly separate it from American populism. Discuss.
3. What factors account for the emergence of populist provincial governments in Western Canada?
4. Can the same model be used to explain petit bourgeois and working-class movements?
5. How can you explain the different trends in unionization in the United States and Canada?
6. In relation to other advanced industrial societies, what are the characteristics of Canadian strike patterns since 1945? How would you explain the typical Canadian pattern?

GLOSSARY

craft unions organizations of skilled workers belonging to a particular occupation, such as printing

domestic commodity production (D.C.P). small-scale production of goods and services for the market by producers who own or rent their means of production and rely on household labour

ideology in the context of social movements, a set of beliefs that legitimize collective action

industrial unions workers' organizations based on all manual occupations in a particular industry

institutionalization a process whereby movements gradually become part of the social order that they set out to challenge, or become concerned primarily with the survival of the movement organization rather than with the original objectives

mobilization a process in which resources, such as money, arms, time, and knowledge, are acquired and spent by social movements

populism a social movement, reformist rather than revolutionary, which stresses the common people rather than elites, and frequently attacks visible minorities, who are blamed for social problems

relative deprivation a social psychological theory of collective action in which priority is given to discontent that arises when people feel that their rewards are less than they ought to receive

segmented societies societies in which social groups are clearly separated in hierarchies and in which established political processes make it difficult for those in subordinate positions to represent themselves

solidary organization a close-knit group with a high rate of contact among the members

social movement any group that tries to change the institutional structure of society through collective action

union density the proportion of a specified labour force that is unionized

BIBLIOGRAPHY

Abella, Irving (ed.)
1974 *On Strike: Six Key Labour Struggles in Canada 1919–1949*. Toronto: James Lewis and Samuel.

Ash, Roberta
1972 *Social Movements in America*. Chicago: Markham.

Bain, George S. and Robert Price
1980 *Profiles of Union Growth*. Oxford: Blackwell.

Barnes, Donna A.
1984 *Farmers in rebellion: The Rise and Fall of the Southern Farmers Alliance and People's Party in Texas*. Austin: University of Texas Press.

Brym, Robert
1978 "Regional Social Structure and Agrarian Radicalism in Canada: Alberta, Saskatchewan and New Brunswick." *Canadian Review of Sociology and Anthropology* 15:339–51.

——
1979 "Political Conservatism in Atlantic Canada." In R. J. Brym and R. J. Sacouman (eds.) *Underdevelopment and Social Movements in Atlantic Canada*. Toronto: New Hogtown Press.

Brym, Robert and Barbara Neis
1978 "Regional Factors in the Formation of the Fishermen's Protective Union of Newfoundland." *Candian Journal of Sociology* 3:391–407.

Canada
1983 *Directory of Labour Organizations in Canada 1983*. Ottawa: Labour Canada.

Cherny, Robert W.
1981 *Populism, Progressivism, and the Transformation of Nebraska Politics, 1885–1915*. Lincoln: University of Nebraska Press.

Clark, Samuel
1982 "Social Movements." In James J. Teevan (ed.) *Introduction to Sociology: A Canadian Focus*. Scarborough, Ontario: Prentice-Hall.

Clark, Samuel D., J. Paul Grayson, and Linda M. Grayson (eds.)
1975 *Prophecy and Protest: Social Movements in Twentieth Century Canada*. Toronto: Gage.

Clement, Wallace
1984 "Canada's Coastal Fisheries: Formation of Unions, Cooperatives and Associations." *Journal of Canadian Studies* 19:5–33.

——
1986 *The Struggle to Organize: Resistance in Canada's Fisheries*. Toronto: McClelland and Stewart.

Conway, John
1978 "Populism in the United States, Russia and Canada: Explaining the Roots of Canada's Third Parties." *Canadian Journal of Political Science* 11:99–124.

Crosby, Faye
1979 "Relative Deprivation Revisited." *American Political Science Review* 73:103–12.

Davies, James C.
1962 "Toward a Theory of Revolution." *American Sociological Review* 27:5–19.

——
1969 "The J-Curve of Rising and Declining Satisfactions as a Cause of Some Great Revolutions and a Continued Rebellion." In H.D. Graham and T.R. Gurr (eds.) *Violence in America*, vol. 2. Washington: National Commission on the Causes and Prevention of Violence.

Ferree, Mary Marx and Frederick D. Miller
1985 "Mobilization and Meaning: Toward an Integration of Social Psychological and Resource Perspectives on Social Movements." *Sociological Inquiry* 55:38–62.

Friedmann, Harriet
1980 "Household Production and the National Economy: Concepts for the Analysis of Agrarian Formations." *Journal of Peasant Studies* 7:158–84.

Fulcher, James
1975 "Industrial Conflict in Britain and Sweden." *Sociology* 9:477–84.

Goodwyn, Lawrence
1976 *Democratic Promise: The Populist Movement in America*. New York: Oxford University Press.

Grayson, J. Paul and L.M. Grayson
1982 "Social Movements and Social Change." In R. Hagedorn (ed.) *Sociology*, 2nd ed. Toronto: Holt, Rinehart and Winston.

Gurr, T.R.
1970 *Why Men Rebel*. Princeton: Princeton University Press.

Gusfield, Joseph R. (ed.)
1970 *Protest, Reform and Revolt*. New York: Wiley.

Hayward, Brian
1984 "The Co-op Strategy" *Journal of Canadian Studies* 19:48–64.

Heron, Craig and Bryan D. Palmer
1977 "Through the Prism of the Strike: Industrial Conflict in Southern Ontario, 1901–14." *Canadian Historical Review* 58.

Huxley, Christopher
1979 "The State, Collective Bargaining and the Shape of Strikes in Canada." *Canadian Journal of Sociology* 4:223–39.

Huxley, Christopher, David Kettler, and James Struthers
1986 "Is Canada's Experience "Especially Instructive"?" In S.M. Lipset (ed.) *Unions in Transition*. San Francisco: ICS Press.

Ingham, Geoffrey K.
1974 *Strikes and Industrial Conflict: Britain and Scandinavia*. London: Macmillan.

Jamieson, S.M.
1979 "Industrial Conflict in Canada 1966–75." Discussion paper no. 142. Ottawa: Economic Council of Canada.

Jenkins, J. Craig
1983 "Resource Mobilization Theory and the Study of Social Movements." *Annual Review of Sociology* 9:527–53.

Klandermans, Bert
1984 "Mobilization and Participation: Social-Psychological Expansions of Resource Mobilization." *American Sociological Review* 49:583–600.

Korpi, Walter
1983 *The Democratic Class Struggle*: London: Routledge and Kegan Paul.

Korpi, Walter and Michael Shalev
1979 "Strikes, Industrial Relations and Class Conflict in Capitalist Societies." *British Journal of Sociology* 30:164–87.

Lipset, S.M.
1968 *Agrarian Socialism*, 2nd ed. Garden City, New York: Doubleday.

———
1986 "North American Labor Movements: A Comparative Perspective." In S.M. Lipset (ed.) *Unions in Transition*. San Francisco: ICS Press.

Lipset, S. M. and Earl Raab
1970 *The Politics of Unreason*. New York: Harper and Row.

Lipton, Charles
1968 *The Trade Union Movement of Canada, 1827–1959*, 2nd ed. Montreal: Canadian Social Publications.

Macpherson, C.B.
1962 *Democracy in Alberta*, 2nd ed. Toronto: University of Toronto Press.

Marx, Gary T. and James L. Wood
1975 "Strands of Theory and Research in Collective Behavior." *Annual Review of Sociology* 3:363–428.

Morlan, Robert L.
1955 *Political Prairie Fire: the Nonpartisan League, 1915–1922*. Minneapolis: University of Minnesota Press.

Morton, W.L.
1948 "The Social Philosophy of Henry Wise Wood, Canadian Agrarian Leader." *Agricultural History* 22:114–123.

Oberschall, Anthony
1978 "Theories of Social Conflict." *Annual Review of Sociology* 4:291–315.

Palmer, Bruce
1980 *Man Over Money: The Southern Populist Critique of American Capitalism*. Chapel Hill: University of North Carolina Press.

Panitch, Leo and Donald Swartz
1984 "Towards Permanent Exceptionalism: Coercion and Consent in Canadian Industrial Relations." *Labour* 13:133–57.

Remele, Larry
1981 "Power to the People: the Nonpartisan League." In T.W. Harvey (ed.) *The North Dakota Political Tradition*. Ames: Iowa State University Press.

Richards, John and Larry Pratt
1979 *Prairie Capitalism: Power and Influence in the New West*. Toronto: McClelland and Stewart.

Robin, Martin
1968 *Radical Politics and Canadian Labour, 1880–1930*. Kingston: Industrial Relations Centre, Queen's University.

Ross, Arthur M. and Paul T. Hartman
1960 *Changing Patterns of Industrial Conflict*. New York: Wiley.

Sacouman, R. James
1979 "Underdevelopment and the Structured Origins of Antigonish Movement Co-Operatives in Eastern Nova Scotia." In R.J. Brym and R.J. Sacouman (eds.) *Underdevelopment and Social Movements in Atlantic Canada*. Toronto: New Hogtown Press.

Schwartz, Michael
1976 *Radical Protest and Social Structure: The Southern Farmers' Alliance and Cotton Tenancy 1880–1890*. New York: Academic.

Shaw, Barton C.
1984 *The Wool-Hat Boys: Georgia's Populist Party*. Baton Rouge: Louisiana State University Press.

Shorter, Edward and Charles Tilly
1974 *Strikes in France*. London: Cambridge University Press.

Sinclair, Peter R.
1975 "Class Structure and Populist Protest: The Case of Western Canada." *Cana dian Journal of Sociology* 1:1–17.

Smucker, Joseph
1980 *Industrialization in Canada*. Scarborough, Ontario: Prentice-Hall.

Snyder, David
1975 "Institutional Setting and Industrial Conflict: Comparative Analyses of France, Italy and the United States." *American Sociological Review* 40:259–78.

Snyder, David and Charles Tilly
1972 "Hardship and Collective Violence in France, 1830 to 1960." *American Sociological Review* 37:520–32.

Stallings, R.
1973 "Patterns of Belief in Social Movements." *Sociological Quarterly* 14:465–80.

Tilly, Charles, Louise Tilly, and Richard Tilly
1975 *The Rebellious Century*. Cambridge, Mass.: Harvard University Press.

Useem, Bert
1980 "Solidarity Model, Breakdown Model, and the Boston Anti-Busing Movement." *American Sociological Review* 45:357–69.

van Otter, Casten
1975 "Sweden: Labor Reformism Reshapes the System." In S. Barkan (ed.) *Worker Militancy and its Consequences, 1965–75*. New York: Praeger.

Walsh, Edward J. and Rex H. Warland
1983 "Social Movement Involvement in the Wake of a Nuclear Accident: Activists and Free Riders in the TMI area." *American Sociological Review* 48:764–81.

Walsh, Kenneth
1983 *Strikes in Europe and the United States*. New York: St. Martin's.

Waters, Malcolm
1982 *Strikes in Australia*. North Sydney, N.S.W.: Allen and Unwin.

Westhues, Kenneth
1972 *Society's Shadows*. Toronto: McGraw-Hill Ryerson.

Wheeler, Christopher
1975 *White-Collar Power: Changing Patterns of Interest Group Behavior in Sweden*. Urbana, Illinois: University of Illinois Press.

Wilkinson, Paul
1971 *Social Movement*. London: Pall Mall Press

Engineering is one profession that was long a male preserve, but this is becoming less the case.
Courtesy of the University of Waterloo

> *"What does sexual equality mean and how does one try to create truly egalitarian relations while recognizing the biological differences . . . ? In the years ahead . . . we will each face this dilemma."*

c h a p t e r   n i n e t e e n

Gender Inequality

S. J. Wilson

INTRODUCTION

When we describe women's economic dependence on men, their disadvantage in the labour force, the unequal burden of domestic responsibilities, or the regulation of women's sexual behaviour, in this or any other society, we are referring to practices rooted in cultural tradition. In every society, members are socialized according to prescribed beliefs about a "**sexual division of labour**."[1] Consequently, most people grow up thinking that women are better suited for certain responsibilities in adulthood and men for others. Despite considerable cross-cultural variation in what men and women customarily do, a sexual division of labour is so well established that it may seem natural to some. Indeed, it is often described as such.

Sociobiologists like E.O. Wilson (1975) argue that behavioural differences between men and women are genetically determined, and thus immutable. While it may once have seemed reasonable to explain behavioural differences in terms of natural propensities, recent evidence indicates that many differences once thought innate are really the result of social conditioning. Although this remains an area of continued research, women's biology is an inappropriate justification for barriers described in this chapter. We recognize distinctive capacities and aptitudes, but these do not justify social inequality.

An important key to understanding gender inequality is to realize how social expectations shape behaviour. At each stage of life, the choices and options available to women are narrowed by the attitudes and examples of parents and other family members, the media, teachers, and employers. Young children see how their world is structured. If their babysitters and primary school teachers are women, but other professionals are men; if they encounter a traditional division of labour in their home, and the homes of their friends, and the media and educational experiences reinforce these distinctions, it is little wonder that young women envision limited options for themselves, and that young men accept this as the norm. The social importance we attach to gender differentiation both reflects and reproduces gender inequality.

Because the case for sexual equality strikes at the heart of all our social arrangements and at every social institution, there has been concerted resistance. Nevertheless, women have made inroads as religious and political leaders; have become literate and educated; and pressed for legislation to counter our disadvantage in the labour force. However, as the data in this chapter will show, the majority are still denied equitable educational access, legal protection, an adequate standard of living, and basic health and welfare services. In North America, the greatest challenge for the Women's Movement may be the conservative political climate of the 1980s, that threatens to forestall, if not reverse, the gains already made.

This chapter has three sections. The first section reviews demographic trends in women's lives and describes important changes in the structures of modern families. This is followed by a discussion of what is arguably the most important dimension of gender inequality: women's secondary position in the labour force. The final section is about political inequality, and the continuing role of the women's movement in legal, economic, social and political reform. While the focus is on Canadian data, several international comparisons place the Canadian experience in context.

DEMOGRAPHY AND WOMEN'S LIVES

In the latter half of the twentieth century, but particularly since 1970, important changes to this and other societies have challenged traditional beliefs about women. Demographic and economic changes have affected family life and the ways families sustain themselves economically. Worldwide, 47 percent of all women aged fifteen to sixty-four are in the labour force. Table 1 shows employment differences by region. Latin America has the lowest female labour force participation rates, and the U.S.S.R. has the highest. Rates are generally higher in more developed countries, although in some African countries over 80 percent of adult women are gainfully employed. The majority of

Table 1

PERCENT OF WOMEN AGED 15–64 IN THE LABOUR FORCE: WORLD REGIONS

Area	Percent
World	47
More-developed countries	59
Less-developed countries	43
Less-developed countries—excluding China	38
Africa	44
Asia	46
North America	60
Latin America	30
Europe	52
U.S.S.R.	71
Oceania	53

Source: Calculated from "The World's Women: A Profile." Population Reference Bureau Inc. Washington, D.C., 1985.

these are agricultural workers. High rates are also found in socialist countries, where the employment of women is a fundamental part of the economic strategy. Women in agricultural economies have always played active economic roles, and certain groups of women have always been gainfully employed in industrial economies. However, in the last fifteen years the unprecedented increases in labour force participation of women in Western countries have cut across social class and family structure variables.

Demographic changes, particularly in longevity and fertility, also signal important changes in women's lives. In Canada, girls born in 1981 could expect to live an average of seventy-nine years, compared to an average life expectancy of seventy-two years for boys. Women usually outlive men, but the international data shows a great variation in longevity. African countries fare worst. Ethiopian women live an average of forty-one years and men thirty-eight years (World Women Data Sheet, Population Reference Bureau, Washington, D.C., 1980). Both men and women in Japan and Iceland can expect to live almost twice as long. In China, average life expectancy has almost doubled since the 1949 revolution (Zangling, 1983).

In the West, increased longevity and decreased fertility mean that women spend less of their adult lives bearing and raising children. In Canada, the average number of children per husband–wife family was 1.3 in 1981. In 1971 it was 1.7. The corresponding figures for lone parent families were 1.8 in 1971 and 1.7 in 1981 (Statistics Canada, 1985:16). For all of the "more developed countries" of the world, the total fertility rate is at the replacement level of 2.0. Total fertility rate (the average number of children a woman will bear during her lifetime at current birth rates) is considerably higher (4.2) for "less developed countries." For most of Africa the figure is over 6. Predictably, there is a close correspondence between high fertility and high infant mortality. Low fertility is a result of improved standards of living, changing attitudes, economic constraints, increased labour force participation, and the availability of birth control. In China, low fertility has been imposed by marriage laws designed in part to reverse the bur-

VOLUNTARY CHILDLESSNESS

Recently, voluntary childlessness has increased among married couples in North America. Based on their observations of European family life, the Hunts (1982) predict an increased polarization of family-centred and career-centred lifestyles among North American families. Some couples will focus on careers and forgo children. Others will sacrifice the career of one or both partners in order to focus on family life. An important consequence of this is a widening gap in the standard of living between the two groups. As the costs of raising children climb, the decision to parent becomes as much an economic as a lifestyle consideration. While the trends are not yet dramatic, Canada's declining birth rate reflects not only smaller family size and the postponement of childbearing, but an increase in the number of childless families. Sociologists cannot describe these changes in simple cause and effect terms for there are high rates of infertility among women who marry late and continue to establish their careers before attempting to conceive.

densome population growth. The Chinese experience shows how quickly entrenched patterns can be changed if the incentive is high enough. The Chinese have reduced fertility by legislating late marriage and an obligation to practise birth control, and by rewarding one-child families.

The divorce rate in Canada has increased considerably since the 1968 Divorce Act liberalized the grounds for divorce. While lower than the United States rate, the Canadian rate doubled between 1970 and 1983. Since 1983, the divorce rate has declined slightly, but it is too soon to tell if this drop will continue. New divorce legislation came into effect in 1986. Again it will be some time before its impact is known. The slight decline in the number of divorces involving children is because there are now more childless couples. Women are far more likely to retain custody of dependent children.

Age at first marriage, divorce rates, longevity, and fertility all affect women's economic prospects. Not surprisingly, older women living alone and single mothers constitute two of the most disadvantaged groups, making up one-third of Canada's poor. Sixty percent of elderly unattached women and 45 percent of women heads of families live in poverty. Families headed by women have half as much income as male-headed families. Young single mothers with poor job prospects, and few supports for caring for young children, have difficulty breaking out of a cycle of poverty. Many older women who are widowed or divorced were never gainfully employed, and lack investment or pension income and live on social security benefits alone. In 1982, elderly Canadian women living alone had an average income of just \$10,000.[2] Even the most fortunate in both groups face a reduced standard of living when they are widowed or divorced.

ECONOMIC INEQUALITY

Labour force participation is the most important key to women's economic inde pendence even though gainful employment does not guarantee an adequate standard of living or an escape from poverty. Indeed, many employed Canadian men and women live below "the poverty line." Nevertheless, without paid work, women must rely on the support of husbands, fathers, or the state. The following paragraphs look at trends in the employment and unemployment rates of women, and the issues of part-time work, pay differentials, and labour force segregation.

Labour Force Participation

The two principal data sources on the Canadian labour force are the decennial census and the monthly labour force survey.[3] Census data shows a gradual increase in female labour force participation from 14.4 percent in 1901 to 29.3 percent in 1961. This jumped to 39.9 percent in 1971 and reached 52.9 percent in 1981. The labour force survey shows annual increases in labour force participation for women to have been approximately 1 percent per year since 1981. Compared to other O.E.C.D. (Organization for Economic Co-operation and Development) countries, these increases are dramatic. Canada now ranks close to the United States and behind only Sweden, Finland, and Norway in female labour force participation (Bakker, 1985). This is a marked change from two decades ago when Canada's rates were relatively much lower.[4]

Canada's employment patterns of *young* men and women are now similar (see Figure 1). Married women have lower participation rates than either married men or single women, although the greatest increase in participation has been for young married women. In 1931, only 3.5

Figure 1
Participation rate of women and men in the labour force by age, Canada, 1985

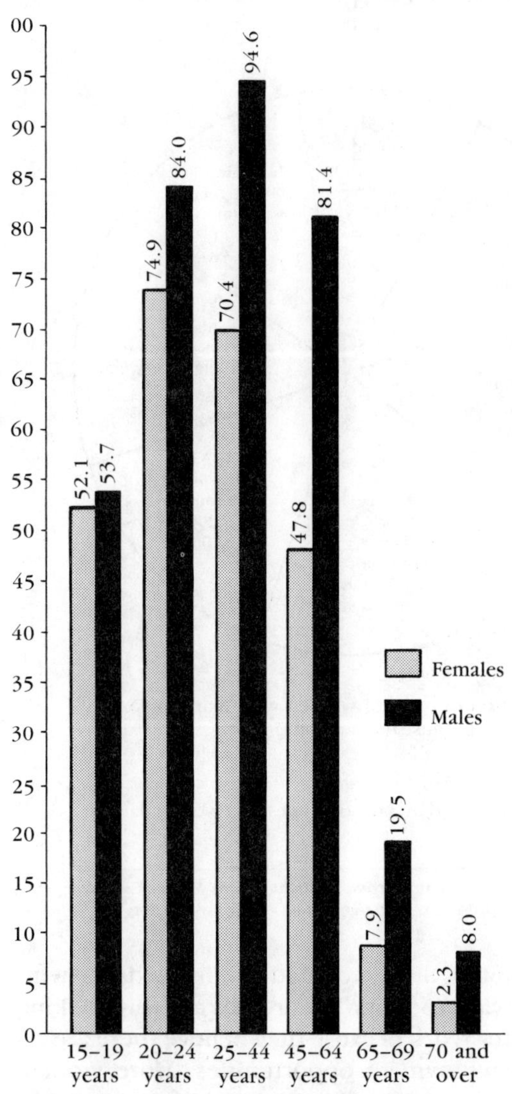

Source: Statistics Canada, Labour Force Survey Division, *The Labour Force, December 1985,* Catalogue No. 71-001.

percent of married women were in the labour force. In 1951, it was less than 8 percent. In 1981, over half of married women were gainfully employed, including 45 percent of mothers of children under three years of age. By 1984, over half of mothers with preschool children had paid jobs. As a recent Canadian study of family employment patterns shows, wives contribute an increasing share of family income. From 1971 to 1981 the proportion of wives with earnings from employment rose from 42.9 percent to 63.4 percent. In 1981, only one-sixth of all husband-wife families depended exclusively on husband's income. Wives contributed 28.1 percent of all family incomes (Pryor, 1984). Figure 2, on page 536, shows the marital status of employed women and the distribution of gainfully employed wives by husband's income.

Education is the best predictor of female labour force participation. The higher the education, the greater the likelihood of labour force participation, regardless of marital status or family size, and the lower the likelihood of unemployment. But married women in low income families also have high rates of labour force participation (National Council on Welfare, 1979).

Gerson (1983), writing about the United States, predicted that the increases in the employment of married women and mothers will persist because they stem from fundamental changes in the economy, the workplace, and private life. We predict high unemployment rates, inflation, and the instability of marriages in Canada will have a similar long-term effect.

Unemployment

Until the mid-1960s, women's unemployment rates (as officially measured) were lower than men's. From 1969 until the 1982 recession, and since 1984, proportionately more Canadian women than men have been unemployed. Unemployment is highest for young people of both sexes, but married women have higher unemployment rates than married men. It is

Figure 2
Women in the paid labour force, Canada, 1984

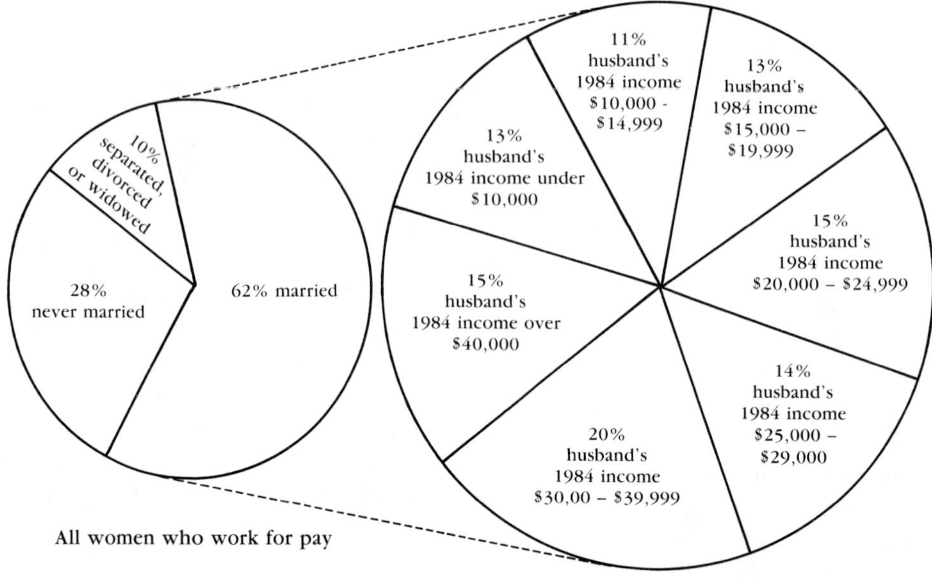

The population consists of women who reported some earned income (includes wages and salaries and/or income from self-employment) in 1984.

Source: Statistics Canada, Consumer Income and Expenditure Division, *Income Distribution by Size in Canada, 1984*. Ottawa, April 1986. Catalogue No. 13-207. Reproduced with permission of Supply and Services Canada.

impossible to measure hidden unemployment. Many women may have defined themselves as housewives rather than as actively looking for work, and these women are not counted in unemployment statistics. In 1975, the labour force survey changed the way the question concerning unemployment was worded, and this presumably uncovered some previously hidden unemployment. Rather than ask what respondents did mostly last week, the revised question read; "In the past four weeks has this person looked for another job?" Still excluded are individuals who want to work but are not actively looking for work because they believe there are no employment opportunities. More women than men are likely thereby excluded.

The Statistics Canada Report, *Women in Canada* (1985:45), attributes the dip in unemployment for women in the early 1980s to two factors. First, unemployment was higher in the goods-producing sector than in the service sector where most women work. Second, unemployment is highest for those under twenty-five, and younger men have recently suffered greater unemployment than younger women. On the other hand, women are unemployed for longer periods than men.

Part-Time Work

Compared to full-time work, part-time work is poorly paid, less secure, offers fewer benefits, and holds fewer opportunities for advancement. More than two-thirds of all part-time work is done by women and one-quarter of all working women work part time. Furthermore, an increasing number of clerical and retail sales jobs are part time. It was once assumed that part-time employment reflected a choice women made to spend time with their families. (On the other hand, approximately the same number of single and married women work part time.) Choice may have little to do with it. A recent Statistics Canada survey found that 28 percent of women working part time could not find full-time jobs. Nineteen percent worked part time because of family responsibilities (Statistics Canada, 1985:45.) Canada is woefully inadequate in meeting the child care needs of em ployed mothers. We lag behind countries such as France, Germany, and Italy, where female labour force participation rates are lower. In Canada, licensed child care spaces fill but 15 percent of the need. The rest rely on informal arrangements with relatives or unregulated childcare in private homes. Availability varies from province to province, but is generally better west of Quebec. In Manitoba in 1982, there were eighty-four licensed spaces per one thousand children under six; in Newfoundland, only nine (Statistics Canada, 1985).

Although there are more women in the labour force, women work in a limited range of jobs and earn less than their male counterparts.

Occupational Segregation

Until the 1950s, the typical female employee in Canada was young, single, childless, and worked in one of a half dozen fields. If she came from a middle-class home, or had managed to acquire sufficient formal education, she worked as a teacher, an office worker, or in retail sales. The alternatives were domestic service or factory work. Until World War II, domestic service was the most likely, although certainly not the most popular employment opportunity for Canadian women.

By mid-century, large-scale economic changes had created a demand for workers in three fields: clerical, service (especially health and education), and retail trade. Women soon held the majority of nursing, teaching, clerical, and retail sales jobs. Recent data (see Figure 3) indicates how little has changed. "In 1983, 77 percent of all female employees worked in just five occupational groups — clerical, service, sales, medicine and health, and teaching" (Statistics Canada, 1985:43). Thirty-two percent were in clerical jobs. Ninety-nine percent of stenographers and secretaries are women.

Focusing on occupations where most women worked and comparing 1971 and 1981 census data reveals the extent and stability of **occupational segregation** in Canada. Table 2 shows two measures of segregation. The first column measures **female concentration** (the number of women as a percentage of all female workers in the labour force). The second set of figures indicates what Armstrong and Armstrong (1984) called **sex typing** (the number of women as a percentage of all workers in that category). In 1981, 35.1 percent of all women worked in clerical jobs and 77.7 percent of all clerical workers were women. As the cumulative percentage columns show, there was greater female concentration in 1981 than in

Figure 3

Percentage of women in major occupational groups, Canada, 1985

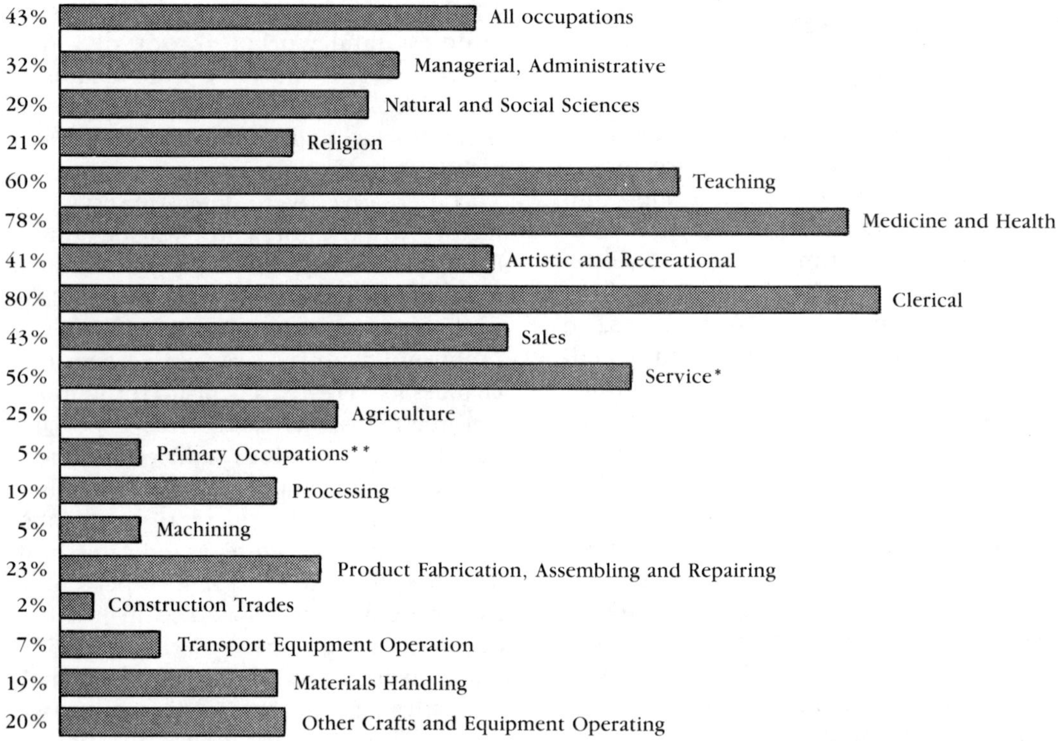

Percentage	Occupational group
43%	All occupations
32%	Managerial, Administrative
29%	Natural and Social Sciences
21%	Religion
60%	Teaching
78%	Medicine and Health
41%	Artistic and Recreational
80%	Clerical
43%	Sales
56%	Service*
25%	Agriculture
5%	Primary Occupations**
19%	Processing
5%	Machining
23%	Product Fabrication, Assembling and Repairing
2%	Construction Trades
7%	Transport Equipment Operation
19%	Materials Handling
20%	Other Crafts and Equipment Operating

*Some examples of occupations in this group are: police, firefighters, chefs, bartenders, porters, chambermaids, housekeepers, hairdressers, babysitters.

**Primary occupations includes fishing, hunting, trapping, forestry, logging, mining and quarrying.

Source: Statistics Canada, *The Labour Force, December 1985*. Catalogue No. 71-001. Reproduced with permission of Supply and Services Canada.

Table 2

FEMALE DOMINATED OCCUPATIONS 1971–1981

	Female Concentration				**Sex Typing**	
	1971		*1981*		*1971*	*1981*
Occupation	%	*cp*	%	*cp*	%	%
Clerical	31.7	31.7	35.1	35.1	68.4	77.7
Service	16.1	47.8	15.4	50.5	49.3	52.3
Sales	8.4	56.2	9.6	60.1	30.4	40.8
Health	8.1	64.3	8.3	68.3	74.3	77.6
Teaching	7.1	71.4	6.0	74.4	60.4	59.5
Fabricating	5.1	76.5	4.7	79.1	32.7	24.4

Source: Calculated from Statistics Canada, 1981 Census, Catalogue 92–920.

1971. Almost 80 percent of all employed women worked in these six fields.

Fox and Fox (1986) found a decrease in occupational segregation from 1931 to 1981. The index of dissimilarity (which measures the difference between the percentage of the male and female labour force in each occupational category) dropped from about 75 percent in 1931 to just over 60 percent in 1981. These percentages represent the number of females who would have to change occupations to eliminate the segregation. In other words, in 1981, 60 percent of all employed females would have had to change jobs to eliminate occupational segregation.

The concentration of women in clerical jobs raises fundamental concerns regarding office automation and its accompanying job displacement. The demand for workers with traditional clerical skills is being replaced by a demand for those familiar with computers. Predictably, most women employed in automated offices are data processors, and relatively few are employed in the more highly skilled and better paid jobs as technicians or programmers.

The *Report of the Royal Commission on Equality in Employment* (1984:67) summarizes occupational segregation in this way:

> In 1981, women were still largely concentrated in the clerical, sales, and service occupations. Although their representation in the administrative and professional occupations increased, they were concentrated in supportive occupations, such as those of technicians, and still constituted a small proportion of the professional occupations in the health, legal, and scientific occupations. They were equally underrepresented in the natural sciences, such as engineering, and in blue-collar occupations. In the managerial occupations, their representation was strongest in those associated with large-scale, female, white-collar unemployment, such as personnel.

Pay Differentials

On average, women working full time earn approximately 64 percent of what men earn. This wage gap has improved little over time and persists whether calculated for hourly, weekly, or annual pay. Part of

Table 3

FEMALE AVERAGE EARNINGS BY OCCUPATION AS A PERCENTAGE OF MALE AVERAGE EARNINGS, 1982

Occupation	Full-time/ Part-time workers	Full-time/ full-year workers only
	%	%
Managerial	55.6	58.2
Professional	61.8	68.0
Clerical	62.9	66.9
Sales	46.1	57.1
Service	46.7	55.5
Agriculture, etc.	47.8	56.4
Processing and machining	54.5	57.6
Product fabricating, etc.	50.2	60.8
Transportation	54.1	60.8

Source: "Equality in Employment"—*A Royal Commission Report*. Cat. No. MP 43-157/1-1984E. Reproduced with permission of the Minister of Supply and Services Canada.

the problem is that women are concentrated in low-paying service jobs. When the earnings of men and women in the same jobs are compared, pay differences are smaller. The finer the distinctions made, the lower the wage gap, and the greater the segregation. One economist (Bergman, 1974) referred to this process as "overcrowding." Wages are kept low in certain occupations because the supply of available workers exceeds the demand. There is, however, considerable variation by job sector, and professional women fare best when compared to men. (See Table 3.) However, in 1980, women university teachers earned an average salary of $26,585 compared to $35,944 for their male colleagues (Canada, 1984:74). University educated women who work full time earn only 67 percent of what male university graduates earn, and their salaries amount to only $1,600 a year more than male high school graduates (Statistics Canada, 1985:27).

EXPLAINING LABOUR FORCE INEQUALITY

Explanations of women's disadvantage in the labour force most often focus on income differences. Do wage differences reflect characteristics of individual employees, employer discrimination, or structural factors such as the organization of work and family life? These explanations imply different approaches to reducing income disparities. If the problem is one of individual differences in qualification, the issue is to ensure all individuals the same access to education and to training programs. If the problem is discrimination, the issue is to prevent discriminatory practices in hiring and promoting. If the problem is a segregated labour force, then it is necessary to make more stable and better-paid jobs equally accessible to women. In the following paragraphs, we will consider alternate ways of explaining and seeking solutions to gender inequality in the Canadian labour force.

Employee Characteristics and Education

In Canada, women with higher educational qualifications have higher rates of labour force participation, lower unemployment, and receive higher salaries relative to men than women with less education. But education does not have the same effect on occupational status for men and women. When Blishen and Carroll (1978) ranked the approximately five hundred occupations listed in the census, they created two scales: a male scale and a female scale. Both scales ranked jobs according to the educational achievements and incomes of those in the occupation. Blishen and Carroll found a close correlation ($r = 0.843$) between the male and female scales. But closer examination showed that women had higher educational certification but lower incomes than men in the same occupations.

Human capital explanations of pay differentials focus on education and training (years of experience) to account for differences in the earnings of men and women. Education and years of experience measure "human capital accumulation," and employers are assumed to reward these with higher pay. Although human capital theory has received much attention in the literature (see Denton and Hunter, 1982) it cannot account for why a large gap persists when men and women of equal education and experience are compared. Individuals simply do not have as much control over their life chances as this theory implies.

Women receive lower wages for their education and work experience. In general, women have fewer uninterrupted years of work experience than men, although the work histories of young men and women have become increasingly similar. A recent Canadian study found almost half of all women workers in a national sample reported no interruptions in work experience, but they still received lower salaries than men in the same type of work (Ornstein, 1983). Women receive lower returns for education, in part, because men and women with similar educational qualifications are recruited to different kinds of jobs. Women highschool graduates typically find work in clerical or sales jobs; university educated women are more apt to enter teaching or health-related fields. Whatever their education, men find work in a wider range of jobs. Generally, for women, the problem is not the amount of education, but the type of education they receive. Early childhood socialization, educational streaming, and lack of role models in nontraditional work have the effect of narrowing educational choices for women. While half of the university students receiving bachelor's degrees are women, the proportion of women Masters or Ph.D. students is much smaller. The numbers of women graduates in Business, Law, and Medicine has increased substantially in recent years, although most students are still men. Very few women graduate in Engineering, Math, or Science.

Affirmative Action and Employment

When pay differences are analyzed, the variance that remains unexplained when occupation, experience, and education have been held constant is understood to be the effect of discrimination. Most analysts suggest a figure between 15 and 20 percent. But as Skolnick (1982:117–18) points out, because education, occupation, and hours worked are also influenced by discrimination, the total effects of discrimination are much greater. Discrimination may be overt, as when individual employers make decisions about hiring and promoting people based on ascribed characteristics. It may also be more subtle.

SEX-ROLE STEREOTYPES IN CAREER CHOICES

Ideas about education and career alternatives seem to take root at an early age. A recent Canadian study (Ellis and Sayer, 1986) of over seven hundred elementary school children (aged six to fourteen) found pervasive sex-role stereotyping in career choices, even among the youngest children in the group. Girls felt women could enter nontraditional occupations, although they were less inclined to mention these as their own career choices. "Many of them seemed to be saying 'Yes, women can become doctors, but I expect to be a nurse,' or 'Bank managers can be women as well as men, but I am going to be a teller'" (Ellis and Sayer, 1986:55). Not surprisingly, almost all of the boys mentioned traditionally male jobs as occupational choices. Almost all of the girls expected to marry and have children, but even the oldest girls did not expect to combine motherhood and paid employment. The authors concluded: "Girls in particular need to be made aware of the realities of life for adult women so that they can plan their lives for maximum benefits to themselves, their families, and society as a whole" (ibid:57).

> The most dangerous discrimination does not result from isolated individual acts motivated by prejudice, but from assumptions and traditions which have become an intrinsic part of the employment system. Established behaviours and rules, and organizational attitudes, policies, and practices often embody a bias against dis advantaged groups that effectively excludes them from employment opportunities. This **systemic discrimination** exists even when there is no intent to discriminate (Bruce, 1985:53).

Systemic discrimination was the focus of the 1984 Commission on Equality in Employment. The Commission wanted to "explore the most efficient, effective, and equitable means of promoting equality in employment for four groups: women, Native people, disabled persons, and visible minorities" (Canada, 1984:v). Most of those with whom the commission consulted agreed that this required more government intervention. Existing legislation (requiring equal pay for work of equal value) affected only 11 percent of the labour force, since it applies only to federal employees.

The idea that women should receive equal pay for work of equal value has been an objective of the International Labour Organization since 1919. From 1977, when this became part of the Canadian Human Rights Act, individuals or groups who feel their jobs are not receiving equitable remuneration may appeal to the Commission for a ruling. Equal value (or comparable worth) is determined by comparing the skill, effort, responsibility, and working conditions of male-dominated and female-dominated jobs. Examples of jobs judged by an American study to be of comparable worth include: typing pool supervisor and painter; senior legal secretary and senior carpenter; licensed practical nurse and electrician (Canada, 1984:251). In Canada, only a handful of complaints have been registered. No doubt this principle will become more meaningfully applied as other provinces join Quebec, Manitoba, and Ontario in legislating equal pay for work of equal value.[5]

Since many felt the term affirmative action was problematic, the commission adopted a new term — **employment equity**—to describe its recommendations to eliminate systemic discrimination. Affirmative action is a term associated with American legislation. Title VII of the American Civil Rights Act prohibits discrimination in hiring, firing, employment, and benefits on the basis of race, colour, sex, or national origin. Further legislation required federal government contractors to analyze their employee profiles in terms of the underrepresentation of women and minority groups and to establish numerical goals and timetables for increasing the company's representation of these groups. In the United States, Affirmative Action is enforced by the Office of Federal Contract Compliance Programs. "The focus [of affirmative action]. is not only on equality in *treatment*, but equality in *results*. . . . Affirmative action calls for positive steps to rectify past discrimination and inequalities which have become a structured part of the system" (Cohen, 1985:23).

There is a fundamental difference between an individual's responsibility to react to discrimination and the Affirmative Action approach, which places the burden of proof on the employer to demonstrate that discrimination does *not* exist. The first case deals with isolated acts of intended discrimination; the second with the countless ways employment practices pose barriers to equal treatment. Existing Human Rights legislation in Canada deals with the first type of discrimination. The Commission recommendations were designed to deal with the latter type—systemic discrimination.

The Commission made 117 recommendations concerning the implementation of

PAY EQUITY COMES INTO LAW IN ONTARIO

Ontario's pay-equity legislation, billed by its supporters as the most progressive in North America, passed its final hurdle June 15, 1987, with unanimous approval in the Legislature. It is expected to be proclaimed into law in a few weeks.

Under the legislation, public sector employers—including the provincial government, hospitals, school boards, community colleges and municipal governments—will be required to design pay-equity plans within two years of the law being proclaimed.

Improved salaries for women as a result of the law are to start two years after proclamation, and pay equity—paying equal salaries for work of equal value to the employer—must be achieved by five years later.

In the private sector, the improved payments will have to begin after three years for employees in companies with more than 500 workers; four years later for businesses with 100 to 499 employees; five years later for operations with 50 to 99 workers; and six years later for companies with 10 to 49 workers.

. . . The delay between passage of the legislation and its proclamation will enable the Ontario Women's Directorate to prepare to deal with queries from employers about how they must go about complying with the law.

Officials at the directorate are having information kits printed for employers and have also set up a hot line to answer general questions about the law.

. . . The provincial Government is still putting together the framework of the Pay Equity Commission, which will be responsible for educating employers and workers about the law. The commission will also hear pay-related complaints from employees.

The pay-equity law aims to narrow the 36 percent wage gap between men and women resulting from discriminatory wage practices. It requires all Ontario employers with 10 or more workers to set aside 1 percent of their payroll costs to rectify gender-based wage practices.

However, employers may have to wait up to six months before officials from the Pay Equity Commission will be able to help them draft formal pay-equity plans. Such programs will be required of larger employers and are meant to advise workers about how their bosses intend to bring about equal pay for work of equal value.

Source: The Globe and Mail, June 16, 1987:1, A4.

Employment Equity, education, and training, and child care. The first recommendation was that "all federally regulated employers should be required by legislation to implement employment equity" (Canada, 1984:255). While some have criticized the Commission for the weakness of its enforcement proposals,[6] others have been impressed by its analysis of child care, education, and training as barriers to equitable opportunities in the labour force. The recommendations include a National Childcare Act to ensure universal, available, and affordable child-care for employed women.

The federal government's initial response to the recommendations was the Employment Equity Act. The act applies to all federally regulated businesses with one hundred or more employees and to companies contracting with the government (for contracts exceeding $200,000). These companies must implement employment equity by identifying discriminatory employment practices and describing their progress in eliminating these. This information is to be reported annually, beginning June 1, 1988. The Canadian Human Rights Commission will enforce the act. Because the Human Rights Commission acts on complaints, the responsibility for action rests with individuals who feel that they have been treated unfairly. This and the fact that penalties are not spelled out — there is a fine for failing to report, but not for failing to implement employment equity — renders Canadian Employment Equity far less powerful than American Affirmative Action as a tool for eliminating systemic discrimination.

Discrimination is complex and difficult to legislate against. As Bruce (1985) pointed out in the passage above, systemic discrimination exists even when there is no intent to discriminate. The discussion of discrimination raises issues concerning the structures of work organizations. Some sociologists have focused on these kinds of barriers to explain occupational segregation and income differentials.

The Structure of Labour Markets

The extent of occupational segregation found in all industrialized countries suggests that men and women work not only in different jobs, but in different labour markets. "The main segmentation argument is that inequalities and inequities which profoundly affect individual and familial life chances are in large measure a function of the way work is organized in modern society" (Clairmont, Apostle and Krickel, 1983:246).

Dual Labour Market Theory (Doeringer and Piore, 1971) was an early attempt to differentiate the labour market in this way. In this model, the **labour market** comprises two segments: **primary** and **secondary**. Because of the need for a stable labour force, jobs in the primary market are well paid, stable, and secure, have good working conditions, and opportunities for promotion. Jobs in the secondary market are less secure, have lower wages, poor working conditions, and few if any opportunities for mobility. These characteristics make mobility from the secondary to the primary sector difficult. In other words, workers in the secondary sector become locked into dead-end, poorly paid jobs. While many jobs typically done by women are in the secondary market, the split along sex lines is not as neat as some segmentation theorists originally implied.

Rubery (1978) argues that worker organizations contribute to job segmentation. Workers control the competitive effect of new supplies of labour (i.e., women) by creating barriers to certain jobs. Such barriers include unions and other worker organizations. These organizations defend against competition from less skilled supplies of labour (i.e., the secondary market) and maintain wage differences between members and nonmembers.

In Canada, 41.5 percent of male workers, but only 31.9 percent of female workers are unionized (*Women in the Canadian Labour Force, 1985–1986*, Women's Bureau, Labour Canada). Unionized women earned over three dollars an hour more than nonunionized women, and there is a smaller wage differential between unionized men and unionized women.

Marx used the concept of a *reserve army* to explain how wages are kept low in industrializing economies. The reserve army includes unemployed and migrant workers, homemakers, and workers displaced by the mechanization of industry. During economic downturns, the reserve army will grow, as more workers become unemployed. These displaced workers can work in less mechanized, expanding sectors of the economy. As Braverman (1974:384) explains: "Wage rates in these 'new' industries and occupations are held down by the continuous availability of the relative surplus population." When we consider patterns of female labour force participation in Canada, we see women have played this historical role (see Connelly, 1978). Women were available to meet the needs of capital in the expanding and labour intensive clerical, sales, and service occupations. They filled important shortages during World War II, and relinquished these jobs at the war's end. When full-time or full-year work was unavailable, or when child care was inadequate or too expensive, women took part-time jobs. They have been available to work during economic booms, or with the expansion of certain industries, and returned to the home during economic downturns. Thus, women have been the economy's "shock absorbers" (Glazer, 1980).

The dramatic increases in labour force participation of married women have not been accompanied by parallel changes in the organization of domestic labour. Child care and household maintenance remain largely women's responsibility, even when women are otherwise gainfully employed. So employed women have less discretionary time than either employed men or full-time homemakers (*Women in Canada*, 1985:5). While attitude studies indicate some men are willing to help with household tasks, responsibilities are far from equitably distributed in most homes. Several researchers have argued that women's domestic responsibilities greatly affect their labour market activities, but there have been few attempts to quantify the effect. Coverman's (1983) estimate of the impact of domestic labour on both men's and women's wages, using 1977 American data, found that time spent in domestic labour had a negative impact on wages for both sexes.

In this section we have looked at a number of explanations of gender inequality in the labour force. While the effects of education on job opportunity cannot be denied, human capital explanations of this relationship oversimplify the process. The real problem is that the type of education many women acquire does not provide the best advantage in the labour force. Although some employers may consciously discriminate against certain groups of potential employees, the major barriers to employment equity remain the countless subtle forms of systemic discrimination. Segmentation theories focus on these barriers, as well as on ways labour market structures institutionalize occupational segregation. Underlying women's disadvantage in the labour force is the dual burden of domestic and paid labour.

The following section focuses on political inequality. We begin by describing the low representation of women in national assemblies throughout the world, and then describe some important landmarks in Canadian women's struggle for political representation and the role of the women's movement in this. The first fifty years of this struggle centred on gaining the right to vote. Seven decades after achieving this goal, politics in Canada, as in other countries, remains largely a male domain. In 1979, the Feminist Party of Canada estimated that at the current rate it would take 842 years to gain equality in the House of Commons. After the 1984 election this estimate was revised to a mere 333 years (Kome, 1985:195).

POLITICAL INEQUALITY

Equality before the law, be it in labour legislation, family law, or in reproductive or sexual control, requires the formal representation of women's interests in decision-making bodies. Yet, it is a universal pattern that the greater the power of the decision-making body, the fewer women are represented. The World Women data in Table 4 indicates the proportion of women elected or appointed to national assemblies. While many Asian, African, and Latin American countries did not report this information, we can still make some interesting comparisons. Women make up 14 percent of the membership of National Assemblies throughout the world. Perhaps surprisingly, there is little difference when the more developed countries are compared to the less developed (15 percent versus 13 percent). Canada is well down the list (6 percent), as are Great Britain (5 percent), France (5 percent), and the United States (5 percent). Three hundred and twenty-seven women ran in the 1987 British election: forty-one were elected, thirteen more than had won seats in the previous election.

The range of representation summarized in the table shows how difficult it is to draw generalizations by region. Four Asian countries (Jordan, Kuwait, North Yemen, and Singapore) have no women representatives at the national level, while women make up over 20 percent of the members in Mongolia, Vietnam, and China. There is an even greater range among Latin American countries. Mexico has a record one-third representation by women. In Europe, Scandinavian and Eastern bloc countries have the highest representation of women, while the United Kingdom and France are among the lowest. Table 5 shows when women gained the right to vote in thirty-five countries. There is little correspondence between the length of time women have held the vote and their representation.

After considering the data in Tables 4 and 5, we might agree with Elise Boulding's (1980) point that the economic and political status of women in the West is hardly a model for the rest of the world. Level of economic development seems a poor predictor of political equality for women.

Table 4
WOMEN IN NATIONAL ASSEMBLIES: WORLD REGIONS

	Number of countries reporting	**Range**
Africa	21	0–14
Asia	22	0–23
North America	2	5–6
Latin America	18	1–33
Europe	24	4–31
U.S.S.R.	1	33
Oceania	4	1–10

Source: Calculated from "The World's Women: A Profile." Population Reference Bureau Inc. Washington, D.C. 1985.

Canadian Women and the Struggle for Political Representation

The concerns of the early feminists were fundamental: educational access, legal protection, improved conditions of work, health and welfare reforms. Political participation was a means to achieve these aims, but because the struggle was so lengthy, it became for many suffragettes an end in itself. Canadian women gained the federal franchise in 1918, and the right to run in federal elections a year later—after a struggle lasting over half a century.[7] Keep in mind that granting women the right to vote was not a concession to the legitimacy of their demands, but a move based on the assumption that women would support conscription. Now, seventy years

Table 5
YEARS WOMEN GAINED THE RIGHT TO VOTE

Selected Countries

New Zealand	1893	South Africa	1930
Australia	1902	Spain	1931
Finland	1906	Brazil	1932
Norway	1913	Thailand	1932
Denmark	1915	Turkey	1933
U.S.S.R.	1917	Philippines	1937
Austria	1918	France	1944
Canada	1918	Italy	1945
F.D.R.	1918	Japan	1945
Poland	1918	Yugoslavia	1945
Belgium	1919	Bulgaria	1947
Great Britain	1919	China	1947
Holland	1919	Israel	1948
Ireland	1919	Indonesia	1955
Sweden	1919	Iran	1963
U.S.A.	1920	Switzerland	1971
India	1926	Jordan	1973
Pakistan	1926		

Source: Reprint from the Spring '86 issue of the Royal Bank Reporter. Courtesy of the Royal Bank of Canada.

EXPLORING NATIONAL DIFFERENCES IN THE STATUS OF WOMEN

Using United Nations data and a sample of seventy-five countries, Stewart and Winter (1977) found two distinct dimensions of sexual equality. The first was socio-educational equality, based on measures of legal, political, and educational status; the second was economic equality. Some countries like the U.S.S.R. and Poland had high scores on both dimensions, others like Pakistan and Libya were low on both, while Zaire was high on economic equality, but low on socio-educational equality. Canada ranked twenty-third on socio-educational and thirty-second on economic equality.

Stewart and Winter next examined which of religion, education, demography, economic structure, or history best predicted the two dimensions of equality. High socio-educational equality was predicted by Christianity, high overall educational levels, socialism, and a relatively large number of children per woman. Economic status was positively related to socialism and high overall levels of education, and negatively related to Christianity, Islam, and a manufacturing economy. National wealth and high levels of technology are *not* related to the status of women.

later, women vote in roughly the same numbers as men do, but they remain largely excluded from decision-making bodies.

The first federal election in which Canadian women voted was 1921. Four women ran for office, but only one, Agnes Macphail from Grey County in Ontario, was successful. In the intervening sixty-five years sixty-seven women have been elected to federal office. Twenty-five of these were first elected since 1980. Only a handful have made it to the Cabinet, the first being Ellen Fairclough, appointed by John Diefenbaker in 1957. Judy LaMarsh became the first Liberal Cabinet minister, and the second woman Cabinet appointee, in 1963.

In October 1979, Canadian women celebrated the fiftieth anniversary of the Persons case. Prior to October 1929, according to British Common Law, "Women are persons in matters of pains and penalties, but are not persons in matters of rights and privileges." One such privilege was the right to be appointed to the senate. To reverse this situation, five women from Alberta petitioned the Supreme Court of Canada. When this failed, they appealed to the Privy Council of Great Britain, which ruled in the women's favour. Perhaps the greater strength of the suffrage movement in Great Britain influenced their decision. Cairine Wilson was appointed to the Canadian senate in 1931. But in 1985 only 11 of 102 senators were women. Three of these, including Toronto sociologist Lorna Marsden, were appointed in 1984.

Since 1970, many more women have started running for political office, although the number remains a small percentage of the total. In 1984 only 14.8 percent of the candidates in the federal election were women, and women were only 10 percent of those elected. An unprecedented six women were appointed to the Cabinet, a rate considerably higher than in previous federal elections. Brodie and Vickers (1982:35) estimated that about one in ten women candidates have been successful, compared to about one in five for men.

There are many reasons for this low success rate. The few women who have overcome the formidable barrier of the social identification of politics as a man's world will continue to be discriminated against at the recruitment level. To win the nomination in a riding where the party expects to win has been a major stumbling block. Women running for the three major parties have typically done so in ridings where their party usually loses. Typically, women have run for fringe parties, where the liklihood of being elected is slight. In the 1980 federal election, two-thirds of female candidates were Independents or fringe party candidates (Brodie and Vickers, 1982:34). In 1984, sixty-five women ran for the N.D.P. Two were elected, as were nineteen Conservatives and five Liberals. These factors interact with regional voting preferences. More women have been elected in western than in eastern provinces. Ontario has elected the most women because of the number of seats, not liberal attitudes.

It is a universal pattern that more women are elected at the local than at the regional or federal levels. In Canada, one-fifth of municipal politicians are women. The reasons for greater success at the local level are practical and political. The financial barriers are lower, and it is easier to combine local political action with childrearing and other domestic responsibilities, since travel is minimized. Municipal politics is divorced from party politics in most Canadian cities, which may explain why this is a less desirable arena for men.

The Women's Movement

In the years between gaining the vote and the beginning of the second wave of **feminism** in the 1960s, women continued to lobby for political rights (including the right of Quebec women to vote in provincial elections), health and welfare reforms (including birth control), labour force legisation, and peace. In the 1960s in all Western countries, sentiment and demography combined to create a more vigorous climate of reform. More and more, women who experienced economic and social disparities sought ways to alleviate them.

The women's movement encompasses many concerns and issues, and feminists do not always agree about priorities and tactics. Liberal feminists concentrate on changing social institutions to better serve women. An important focus is legislative reform to provide equality of opportunity in education and in the labour force, or to protect women victims of poverty or violence. Feminists influenced by Marxism, accept the need for these reforms but place greater emphasis on understanding the relationship between class and patriarchy as the twin oppressors of women. The structural constraints exposed by liberal feminists — the double day, occupational ghettos, lack of reproductive control — become central to socialist feminist arguments. Although some reforms, i.e., the right to abortion or the right to publicly supported childcare, transcend public and private domains, most liberal feminist reforms are in the public sphere. Socialist feminists argue that the personal *is* political, since private acts, such as sexual abuse and wife battering, are also political acts.

Some women's groups organize around specific issues, such as rape, to provide services to women in need. Other organizations, particularly those with regional and national networks, act as watchdogs, identifying needs and lobbying policymakers.

In the late 1960s, Laura Sabia, then president of the Canadian Federation of University Women, joined with representatives of other women's organizations to form the Committee for Women's Equality. One goal of this committee was a Royal Commission to describe the inequalities faced by Canadian women and to recommend changes. Sabia, a Progressive Conservative party member, worked closely with Liberal Cabinet member Judy LaMarsh to convince politicians of the need for the commission.

The Royal Commission Report published in 1970 analyzed sexual disadvantage in Canada, and listed 167 recommendations, which set the agenda for women's organizations for the decade. Several government agencies, including Status of Women Canada and the Canadian Advisory Council of the Status of Women (C.A.C.S.W.), were created. The National Action Committee (N.A.C.), the largest and most influential women's organization in Canada, was formed in 1972 as an umbrella for the many women's groups across the country. N.A.C. now represents more than three hundred such organizations and speaks for over three million Canadian women.

Another major battle was to entrench women's rights in the Canadian Constitution. Journalist Penney Kome documented this fight in *The Taking of Twenty-Eight: Women Challenge the Constitution* (1983). The first step was to react to the initial wording of sections of the constitution concerning "nondiscrimination rights." Members of C.A.C.S.W., N.A.C., and scores of other women wrote briefs and letters to Ottawa. While some of these suggestions were incorporated into the revised Charter, feminist lawyers believed that provisions such as those in section 15 (the major section on equal rights) could be negated by the "reasonable limits" clause in section 1 (Kome, 1985:129). Early in 1981, a new coalition of women's groups, the Ad Hoc Committee of Canadian Women on the Constitution, was formed to reinstate an override clause in section 28. Persistent lobbying and astute use of the media over the next six months had the desired effect. On November 24, 1981, section 28 was reinstated. It reads: "Notwithstanding anything in this charter, all the rights and freedoms in it are guaranteed equally to male and female persons."

In the United States, the Equal Rights Amendment, which asserts equal rights not be denied on the basis of sex, has not received legislative approval, although public opinion polls indicate majority support. This bill was defeated because of a well-organized anti-feminist lobby, and the strong anti-ERA sentiments of President Reagan. Although the American Affirmative Action program is considered exemplary by many Canadians, the defeat of the ERA indicates strong resistance to entrenching equal rights for women.

The 1984 election in Canada was a turning point for women's involvement in formal political structures. Not only did twenty-six women win seats, but for the first time women's issues were given more than passing reference. In a nationally televised debate, organized by the National Action Committee, the three leaders tried to outdo each other in voicing their understanding of the issues and in proposing changes.

Anti-Feminism

Perhaps the greatest challenge facing the women's movement in North America is **anti-feminism**. As the 1980 and 1984 U.S. elections show, the New Right is a powerful political force. Because only half of all eligible voters voted in the 1980 American election, it would be wrong to conclude that these sentiments reflect the political climate of the country as a whole. The success in mobilizing the voice of the New Right, however, cannot be denied. In the United States, the New Right is a coalition of three interests: anti-feminism, religious fundamentalism, and supply-side economics. "The New Right argument is this: welfare state expenditures have raised taxes and added to inflation, pulling the married women into the labour force and thereby destroying the fabric of the traditional patriarchal family and hence the moral order of society" (Eisenstein, 1984:46). Anti-feminists hold the women's movement responsible for the alleged breakdown of family life. In their view, the women's movement is anti-family and anti-motherhood.

In Canada, an organization called REAL (Realistic, Equal, Active for Life) Women formed in 1984. A year later it claimed a membership of twenty thousand. This group opposes abortion, and feels that the entrenchment of women's rights in the Charter of Rights will harm the traditional family. REAL Women also opposes enforced affirmative action, the principle of equal pay for work of equal value, and no-fault divorce. And they resent what they see as N.A.C.'s presumption to speak for Canadian women. REAL Women identify themselves as a pro-family organization, but Eichler (1985:27) and others think this is an inappropriate label. "The 'pro-family' movement is in fact advocating one type of family, namely the patriarchal family who can subsist on one income."

Because the social importance we attach to sex differences is established and maintained in the family, this institution *has* been a focus of feminist critique. But feminists are not anti-family. It is women's economic dependence in the patriarchal family, and the way the institution of motherhood is structured, that is problematic for feminists. Anti-feminists gloss over the structural and demographic changes that have affected family life in the post-war years. The housewife they envision represented a particular time in history. To wish for her return is, in Marshall McLuhan's terms, to view life in the rear-view mirror.

Equality, Development, and Peace

In 1975, thirteen hundred delegates from 133 countries met in Mexico to signal the beginning of the United Nations Decade on Women. A World Plan of Action developed out of this conference, which focused on three interrelated goals for women: equality, development, and peace. A conference held in Nairobi concluded the decade. Three thousand delegates representing 155 countries attended. These men and women (many countries sent only male delegates) adopted by consensus proposals covering the final fifteen years of the century. This document—*Forward-Looking Strategies for the Advancement of Women* — outlines strategies for achieving the three objectives: equality, development, and peace. In adopting this document, governments have agreed to recognize women's varied economic, political, and peace-keeping roles, and to ensure the equitable participation of women in these areas.

More exciting for women activists was the parallel nongovernmental organizations' conference — Forum '85 — held simultaneously in Nairobi. Here, thirteen thousand women from 150 countries reaffirmed their determination not to separate women's issues from global social, economic, or political inequalities. As a North American participant described it: "Despite differing ideology, geography, race, culture, colour, or age; despite their national differences that would polarize the delegates at the official conference, these women were in agreement concerning the situation of women in the world. They stood united in diversity" (Wetzel, 1986:13).

CONCLUSION

This chapter began by outlining a number of demographic trends that have had an important effect on the lives of women. Increased longevity and decreased fertility have reduced the time Western women devote to childrearing. In most countries, women's labour force participation rates continue to rise, despite little alleviation in the burden of women's responsibility for domestic maintenance. In Canada, as in other O.E.C.D. countries, women work in a limited number of jobs, for which they receive less pay than men doing the same work. Discrimination, educational streaming, labour market structures, and the assumption of domestic responsibility account for some of these inequalities. Once we understand the problems, we can begin to reduce economic inequality. One way to begin the change is to make these concerns public issues.

The number of women representatives in federal, provincial and municipal politics in Canada is very low, particularly when compared to non-Western countries. Although the women's movement has publicized women's concerns, and organizations such as N.A.C. have helped effect change, even modest legislative reforms meet resistance from anti-feminists.

While most of us accept liberal notions of individual equality, Canadians have not yet grappled with the fundamental contradiction between individual freedom and structured inequality, and so we fail to ask what Eisenstein (1984:206) calls the fundamental feminist question. "What does sexual equality mean and how does one try to create truly egalitarian relations while recognizing the biological difference constituted by women's ability to bear children?'' In the years ahead, as we carry out our familial, employment and civic responsibilities, we will each face this dilemma.

Notes

[1]In fact ''division of labour'' is a misleading term, for it implies a complimentarity of roles, and disguises the fundamental inequities that exist.

[2]Over half of this came from Old Age Security or Canada/Quebec Pension Plan programs (Statistics Canada, 1985:66). C.P.P/Q.P.P. programs are tied to labour force participation, so it is little wonder that in 1983, less than 30 percent of elderly women received these benefits.

[3]Both surveys define work as gainful employment, or working without pay in a family-owned farm or business. Both exclude housework or volunteer work. The labour force includes those working (according to the definition) or actively looking for work.

[4]Among O.E.C.D. countries, female labour force participation rates have increased in Canada, the United States, Australia, the United Kingdom and Swden; and fallen in Italy, Japan, and West Germany (Bakker, 1985). One reason for the decline in Japan and Italy is the overall decline in the agricultural sector—where many women worked.

[5]Generally, provincial legislation lags behind federal initiatives. Only Quebec, Ontario, and Manitoba have legislation to cover the public sector. Ontario has recently introduced legislation governing the private sector as well.

[6]Employers should be obliged ''to develop and maintain employment practices designed to eliminate discriminatory barriers'' to improve the participation of the four designated groups. The success of employment equity programs requires the annual filing of data to be analyzed by Statistics Canada. The commission suggested four alternate enforcement models. Three involved adding employment equity to the responsibilities of existing agencies; one proposed establishing a new independent agency.

[7]Provincial voting rights were granted in the five provinces west of Quebec in 1916 and 1917. Ontario was the last of these to elect a woman. The Eastern provinces granted provincial rights after the federal franchise was won, although not until 1940 did women in Quebec gain the right to vote, and Quebec voters did not elect a woman until 1961 (Brodie and Vickers, 1982:3).

DISCUSSION QUESTIONS

1. Describe major demographic trends influencing the status of women throughout the world. Compare First, Second, and Third World women in terms of these.
2. Elise Boulding has said that the economic and political status of women in the West is hardly a model for the rest of the world. Do you agree? Discuss.
3. Why will efforts to increase educational qualifications for young women *not* solve the problem of occupational segregation? What are other roadblocks? How might these be overcome?

4. Based on recent trends in Canadian female labour force participation, what predictions would you make about the future of work and family life?

5. What have been the major successes of the women's movement in the last two decades? Will anti-feminism forestall future gains?

GLOSSARY

anti-feminism a belief in the need to support and protect biological and social distinctions between men and women, particularly those characteristics of a traditional division of labour in the family

employment equity a term adopted by the 1984 Commission on Equality in Employment to describe measures to eliminate systemic discrimination

female concentration a measure of occupational segregation based on a ratio of the number of women in an occupation to the number of women in the labour force

feminism a belief in fundamental equality of rights for men and women based on an understanding of the social consequences of biological differences

occupational segregation the universal finding that women are employed in a narrow range of female-dominated occupations

primary labour market a term used to describe well-paid, stable, secure jobs with favourable working conditions

secondary labour market a term used to describe jobs which are less secure, have lower wages, and few opportunities for advancement

sex typing a second measure of occupational segregation based on a ratio of the number of women in an occupation to the number of workers in that occupation

sexual division of labour culturally specific attitudes governing "appropriate" behaviour for boys and girls, men and women

systemic discrimination the barriers to equal treatment imposed by a myriad of employment practices

BIBLIOGRAPHY

Armstrong, P. and H. Armstrong
1984 *The Double Ghetto*, rev. ed. Toronto: McClelland and Stewart.

Bakker, I.
1985 "The Status of Women in OECD Countries." *Employment—Research Studies*. Ottawa: Minister of Supply and Services.

Bergman, B.
1974 "Occupational Segregation, Wages, and Profits When Employers Discriminate by Race or Sex." *Eastern Economic Journal* 1 (July–August), 103–10.

Blishen, B. and W. Carroll
1978 "Sex Differences in a Socioeconomic

Index for Occupations in Canada." *The Canadian Review of Sociology and Anthropology* 15, 3:352–71

Boulding, E.
1980 *Women: The Fifth World*. Headline Series 248. New York: Foreign Policy Association Inc.

Braverman, H.
1974 *Labor and Monopoly Capital*. New York: Monthly Review Press.

Canada

Brodie, J. and J. Vickers
1982 "Canadian Women in Politics: An Overview." Canadian Research Institute for the Advancement of Women.

Bruce, M.M
1985 "Equal Opportunity, Affirmative Action, Employment Equity: One City's Experience." *Canadian Women's Studies*.

Canada
1970 *Royal Commission on the Status of Women*. Ottawa: Information Canada.

——
1984 *Report of the Royal Commission on Equality in Employment*. Ottawa: Minister of Supply and Services.

Canada, National Council on Welfare
1979 *Women and Poverty*. Ottawa: Women's Bureau, Labour Canada.

Clairmont, D., R. Apostle, and R. Krickel
1983 "The Segmentation Perspective as a Middle-Range Conceptualization in Sociology." *Canadian Journal of Sociology* 8, 3:245–72.

Cohen, M.
1985 "Employment Equity is NOT Affirmative Action." *Canadian Women's Studies*. 6, 4: 23–25.

Connelly, P.
1978 *Last Hired: First Fired*. Toronto: The Women's Press.

Coverman, S.
1983 "Gender, Domestic Labor Time, and Wage Inequality." *American Sociological Review* 48:623–37.

Denton, M. and A. Hunter
1982 *Economic Sectors and Gender Discrimination in Canada*. Ottawa: Women's Bureau, Labour Canada.

Doeringer, P. and W. Piore
1971 *Internal Labor Markets and Manpower Analysis*. Lexington, Massachusetts: Health Books.

Dubinsky, K.
1985 "Lament for a Patriarchy Lost? Anti-Feminism, Anti-abortion, and R.E.A.L. Women in Canada." Ottawa: Canadian Research Institute for the Advancement of Women.

Eichler, M.
1985 "The Pro-Family Movement: Are They For or Against Families?" Feminist Perspectives, No. 4a, Ottawa. Canadian Research Institute for the Advancement of Women.

Eisenstein, Z.
1984 *Feminism and Sexual Equality*. New York: Monthly Review Press.

Ellis, D. and L. Sayer
1986 "When I Grow Up: Career Expectations and Aspirations of Canadian Schoolchildren." Ottawa: Women's Bureau, Labour Canada.

Fox, B. and J. Fox
1986 "Women in the Labour Market, 1931–1981: Exclusion and Competition." *Canadian Journal of Sociology and Anthropology*, 23, 1:1–21.

Gerson, K.
1983 "Changing Family Structures and the Position of Women: A Review of Trends." *Journal of the American Planning Association*. 49, 2:138–48.

Glazer, N.
1980 "Everyone Needs Three Hands: Doing Unpaid and Paid Work." In S.F. Berk (ed.) *Women and Household Labor*. Beverly Hills: Sage Publications.

Hunt, J.G. and L.L. Hunt
1982 "The Dualities of Careers and Families: New Integrations or Polarizations?" *Social Problems*. 29, 5:499–510.

Kome, P.
1983 *The Taking of Twenty-Eight: Women Challenge the Constitution*. Toronto: The Women's Press.

——
1985 *Women of Influence*. Toronto: Doubleday Canada Ltd.

Ornstein, M.
1983 *Accounting for Gender Differentials in Job Income in Canada: Results from a 1981 Survey*. Ottawa: Women's Bureau, Labour Canada.

Pryor, E.
1984 "Canadian Husband-Wife Families: Labour Force Participation and Economic Trends, 1971–1981." *The Labour Force* (May). Ottawa: Statistics Canada Catalogue 71–001.

Rubery, J.
1978 "Structured Labour Markets, Worker Organization and Low Pay." *Cambridge Journal of Economics*, 2:17–36.

Skolnick, M.
1982 "Toward Some New Emphasis in Empirical Research on Women in the Canadian Labour Force." In N. Herson and D.E. Smith (eds.) *Women and the Canadian Labour Force*. Ottawa: Ministry of Supply and Services, Catalogue CR 22–9/1981E.

Statistics Canada
1985 *Women in Canada*. Ottawa: Ministry of Supply and Services.

Stewart, A.J. and D.G. Winter
1977 "The Nature and Causes of Female Suppression." *Signs*. 2, 3:531–53.

Wilson, E.O.
1975 *Sociobiology: A New Synthesis*. Cambridge, Mass.: Harvard University Press.

Wilson, S.J.
1986 *Women, the Family and the Economy*, 2nd ed. Toronto: McGraw-Hill Ryerson.

Zangling, W.
1983 "Chinese Family Problems: Research and Trends." *Journal of Marriage and the Family*. 45, 4: 943–48.

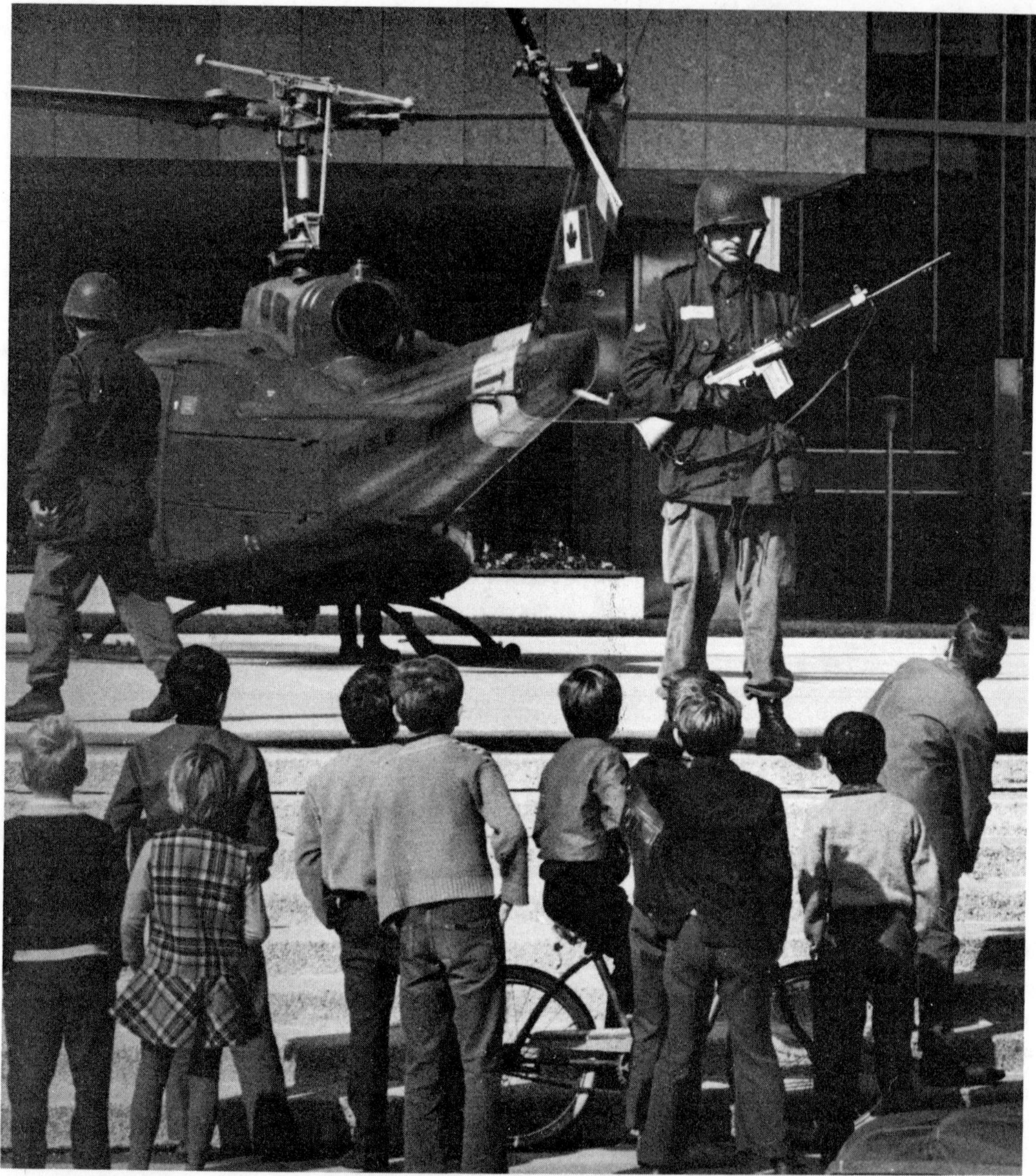

Curious youngsters watch soldiers and helicopters at Provincial Police Headquarters in Montreal during the F.L.Q. Crisis, October, 1970. *Courtesy George Bird*/Montreal Star—*National Archives of Canada/PA 129838*

"In the post-World War II period, "the most significant development . . . was the formation of the Parti Québécois . . . and its victory as a majority government in 1976. Terrorist activities, primarily by the F.L.Q., added enormously to the pressure for change."

c h a p t e r t w e n t y

French–English Relations

Raymond Breton

INTRODUCTION

The history of English–French relations in Canada is one of **competition** between two collectivities engaged in constructing and maintaining a society. Long before the 1760 conquest, the two empires were attempting to establish and expand their commercial systems. Eventually, both groups established permanent communities, with their economic, political, and social **institutions**.

In pursuing commerce and society-building, the English and French have regularly competed. Both have sought control over the resources necessary for their societal projects and, if possible, to monopolize them: to deny the other access to them; to displace the other if it was already occupying a particular resource domain; or to dominate it if this was not possible.[1]

Several categories of resources have been at stake: territory, material resources, population, political and military power, capital, access to markets, scientific and technological expertise, and alliances with surrounding collectivities. **Cultural-symbolic** resources are also required. Indeed, even though a society and its **institutions** have both an economic and technological base, they also have a symbolic dimension, a cultural character, an identity.

Competitive struggles and **conflicts** have been intermittent and limited to particular issues or institutional domains. The confrontations, sometimes coming close to civil war, have usually been resolved in some sort of **accommodation** (a treaty, a pact, a change in institutional structures or rules, an informal agreement). At times, these "accommodations" have been imposed by an external power, directly or indirectly.

This chapter reviews the history of English–French relations in Canada.[2] To facilitate the presentation, the history is divided into four phases: (1) pre-Conquest; (2) from Conquest to Confederation; (3) from Confederation to World War II; and

(4) from World War II to the present. During each period, English and French have clashed in two or more of the following arenas: (a) North America as a whole; (b) Canada (defined differently depending on the historical period); (c) Quebec; (d) Acadia; (e) Ontario; and (f) the West.

This chapter is not an essay on Quebec (or French Canada) and English Canada. Rather, it deals with the *relationship* between the two collectivities. Of course, the analysis will consider certain aspects of their respective social structure and culture. The focus, however, will be on elements that affect their relationship. Given space limitations, the analysis will necessarily be selective.

THE PRE-CONQUEST PERIOD

There were two arenas of French–English relations during this early period: Acadia and Newfoundland on the one hand and eastern North America (most of the West had not yet been explored).

In the Atlantic region, the competition was for "territorial control . . . and for domination of the valuable fisheries off its coasts" (Canadian Encyclopedia, 1985: 1037); in the Saint Lawrence, Great Lakes, and Hudson Bay areas, the competition was for control of the fur trade. Dominating access to these resources was part of the mercantile interests of the metropolitan centres and was necessary for colonization and settlement.

The French colony in Acadia had barely begun when, in 1621, the Scots also claimed the territory. They named it Nova Scotia. After several military confrontations shifted control of the territory back and forth from French to English, it was captured for good by the English, although parts of it were retained by the French (Isle Royale, or Cape Breton; Isle Saint-Jean, or Prince Edward Island; and the area corresponding to contemporary New Brunswick). This was formally established by the Treaty of Utrecht in 1713.

When contact began in the rest of the continent, a French colony already existed, but it was small (about two thousand people in 1660) and was primarily a fur trade centre. In 1670, the English established the Hudson's Bay Company. Since several important waterways flow northward into it, Hudson Bay was critical for the fur trade. Thus, the possibility that the trade could be diverted to English trading posts was soon perceived by the French as a serious threat to their trading system and to the colony that depended on it. In response, the Compagnie Française de la Baie d'Hudson (also called the Compagnie du Nord) was established "to challenge the Hudson's Bay Company on its own ground" (Canadian Encyclopedia, 1985:705). It established its own posts. Against the Hudson's Bay Company, it mounted a military offensive that failed. It went bankrupt in 1700.

In 1686, another French expedition led by Iberville occupied all the English trading posts. Not surprisingly, war soon followed. Here too, territorial control shifted back and forth between the two commercial empires. The confrontations ended with the Treaty of Utrecht (1713), whereby France ceded to England Hudson Bay and all the rivers flowing into it.

The Great Lakes and the Gulf of Mexico were other arenas of conflict. The French sought to contain the English colonies between the Allegheny Mountains and the Atlantic and established the colony of Louisiana, settlements in the Illinois country, and a garrison at Detroit. Had they succeeded, the English would have lost the fur trade in the Great Lakes region — an outcome they could not accept. Their response was to attack New France. The attack on Port-Royal was successful (1710), but the one on Quebec the following year was not.

Figure 1
Treaty areas of Canada

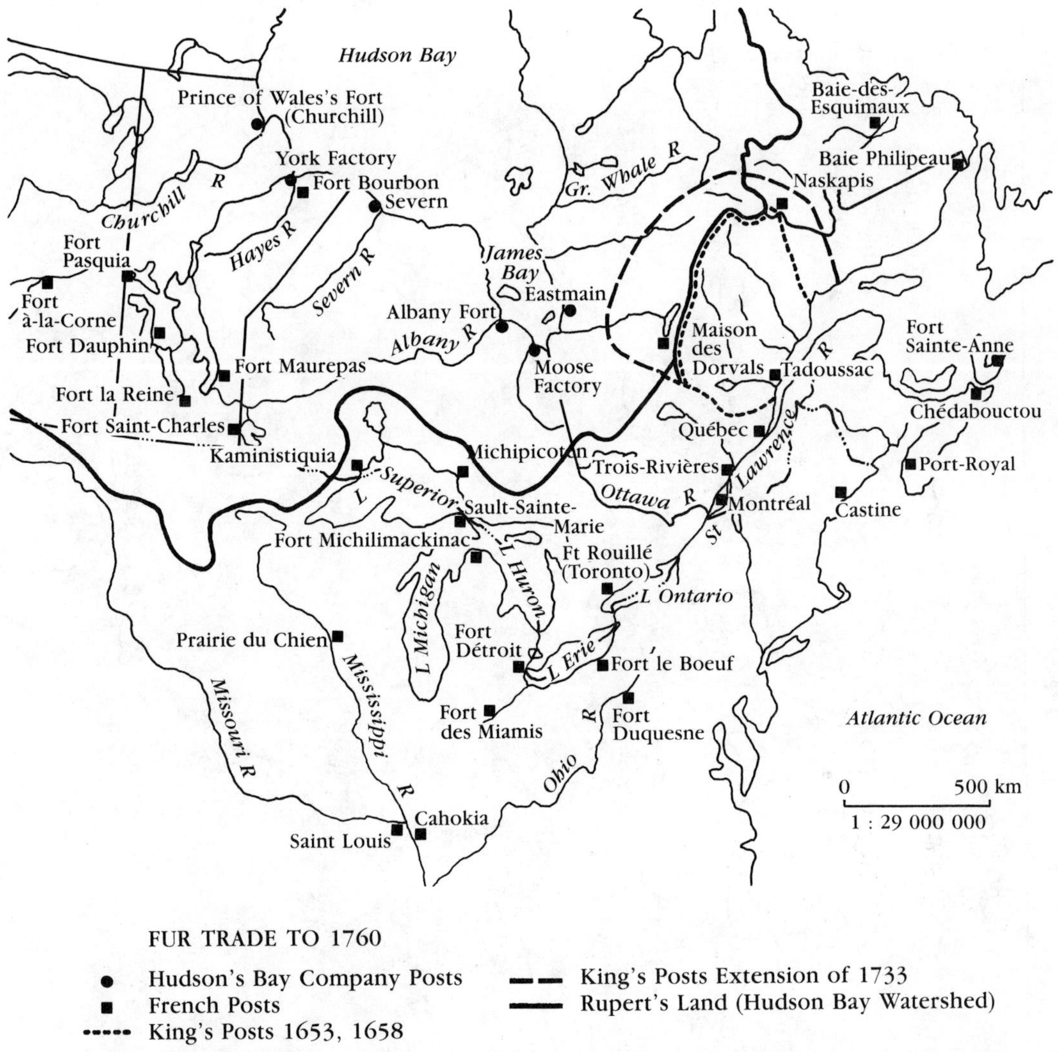

Source: Reproduced by permission of *The Canadian Encyclopedia.*

There followed thirty years of peace during which each side consolidated their internal and external situation. The 1713 Treaty had been a disaster for the French in territorial control and access to resources. To help resist an increasingly powerful English empire, the French erected Louisbourg in 1714. They also worked to consolidate what remained of their access to the Great Lakes; strengthened the Louisiana colony; and extended their fur trade routes to the West. Several measures for internal economic development and population growth were adopted. The demographic imbalance, however, was already considerably in

Figure 2

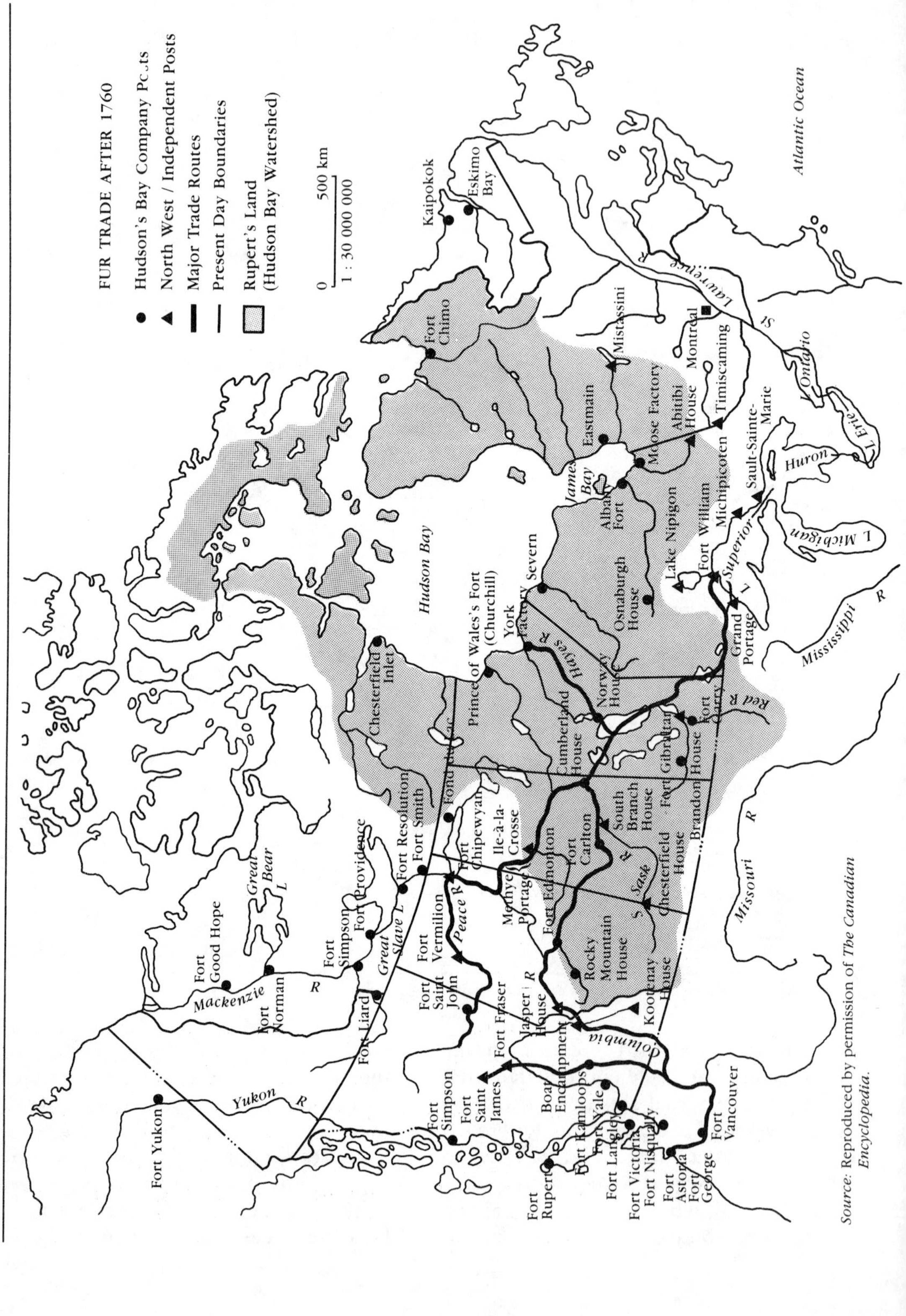

Source: Reproduced by permission of *The Canadian Encyclopedia.*

favour of the English: about three hundred thousand compared to about twenty thousand in New France.

In 1744, new confrontations began in Acadia and Newfoundland. Both sides attempted to conquer and reconquer each other's colonies and each established new settlements in the hope of containing the other's expansionary tendencies. In the middle of this conflict, the Acadians wanted to be neutral. But the English were suspicious: being French-speaking and Catholic, they were perceived as fundamentally untrustworthy. Major Lawrence's solution was twofold: first, deport them because they would always represent a threat and because they occupied valuable land that could be settled by English-speaking Protestants; second, implement a program of immigration of such settlers. Thus, between 1755 and 1763, over three-fourths of the Acadian population—some ten thousand—was deported.

A second area of confrontation was the Ohio River, an important trade route (which linked the Great Lakes and Louisiana), and Lake Ontario (which was an important link between the Saint Lawrence area and the Ohio Valley and Louisiana). A third area was Lake Champlain and the Saint Lawrence. From 1756 to 1760, the French colonies capitulated to the English: Louisbourg (in Acadia); Forts Frontenac, Dusquesne, and Niagara in the Ohio–Lake Ontario area; Forts Carillon and Saint-Frederic in the Lake Champlain area; Quebec and then Montreal in the Saint Lawrence area.

In the first phase of French–English relations, then, in the two groups tried to gain control of a vast territory and its valuable resources. Given the vastness of the territory, co-existence might have been possible. There were indeed periods of accommodation during which claims to particular areas were not challenged. But the expansion of settlement and the accompanying demand for new resources, the depletion of resources in a particular area, and, perhaps especially, the imperialistic propensities of both sides led to repeated confrontations that ended only when one side conquered the other.

FROM THE CONQUEST TO CONFEDERATION

The conquest may have ended the conflict over territory, but the competition between the two groups continued. Instead of conflicts over geographic space, collisions occurred over the control of institutions. This was inevitable as the same societal framework was to be constructed by groups with different socio-economic organization, religion, and language, and a background of antagonism and war.

Both collectivities maintained their own institutions. Thus, a plural or segmented society was formed, that is "a social structure compartmentalized into analogous, parallel, noncomplementary sets of institutions" (van den Berghe, 1969:67) and to social networks largely enclosed within ethno-linguistic boundaries.[3] In addition, institutional arrangements for incorporating the two linguistic segments had to be forged. From the outset, each group was intensely preoccupied with the effectiveness and cultural character of of its own institutions and with the possible impact of the common institutions on them.

Once the British had conquered New France, their first aspiration was to transform Quebec into a society with British institutions and an Anglo-Saxon majority. This was clearly the expectation of the Royal Proclamation in 1763. But things did not work out as planned. First, immigration was slow, so the French population remained significantly larger. Second, the French had established far-reaching connections for the fur trade, connections needed by the English-speaking merchants. Third, British administrators saw the feudal nature of the French social order as a source of support for their authority. Murray thought if the Canadians could be "indulged with a few privileges which the laws of England deny to Roman Catholics at home, (they) would soon . . . become the most faithful and useful set of men in this American empire" (quoted by McInnis, 1969:156).

Fourth, although small, French Quebec was an established, ongoing society that had to be recognized for practical reasons and because of specifications in the 1763 treaty. Finally, Quebec had a strategic military importance in relation to the American colonies and to France. Their loyalty had, therefore, to be obtained.

Thus, partly because it was impossible to do otherwise and partly because it was to their advantage to do so, British administrators tried to accommodate the French community. The English-speaking colonists, however, also had to be accommodated, especially the mercantile class whose ambitions were enormous. They frequently viewed compromises with the French with suspicion if not outright hostility.

The Quebec Act of 1774 attempted to gain French support while satisfying, or at least not antagonizing, the English colonists and merchants. "The act was a final abandonment of the efforts at a uniform system of colonial government based on English institutions" (McInnis, 1969:160). It preserved several of them, but accepted French civil law; reaffirmed freedom of Catholic worship; and reinforced the Church and seigneurial system by extending their privileges.

With the Conquest, the French society had lost its political-administrative elite and its military officers. The transfer of the commercial dependence from Paris to London prompted many French merchants to leave. Some stayed and even gained by connecting themselves with the wider British mercantile system. The clergy and most seigneurs also stayed and their positions were buttressed by the Act of 1774. Their position of social ascendancy was based, in both cases, on land ownership and on legally protected social and economic advantages (e.g., the legal right to collect tithes and rents), and on the dominance of their institutions.

This dominance was further reinforced by the virtual absence of competing elites, a phenomenon accentuated by the progressive relative decline of the French mercantile class. This decline was the result of factors opposite to those that favoured the English merchants. First, they were relatively poorly situated *vis à vis* the British market networks. Second, they were more inclined to accept the hierarchically ordered society to which they belonged by culture, language, and social ties. They responded to the opportunities it offered for social status and privileges: several used their gains from commerce to acquire seigneuries and thus gain social prominence.

The Quebec Act of 1774 rejected the idea of a "unitary" social and institutional structure and recognized that some institutional dualism was dictated by the circumstances. In its practical implementation, however, it accentuated some of the contradictions and related social tensions both within the English and French segments and between them. On the one hand, by instituting an authoritarian rule (a governor and an appointed council were to govern), it antagonized the English settlers, the merchants in particular. On the other hand, the authoritarian regime generated significant resentment in the French-speaking population — resentment against the increased power of the clergy and of the seigneurs.[4] The dualism and the feudal social structure that it strengthened was, in effect, a system of indirect rule. As the motivations of the British administrators mentioned above indicate, the idea was to obtain the support of a conquered population that had a different culture. Although a conqueror can impose its will, it is usually without moral authority. A system of indirect rule involves maintaining and even revitalizing native institutions and culture so as to be able to operate through them (Frazier, 1957:197). In the process, traditional authorities gain considerable power.

The critical precipitant of change in the institutional arrangements, however, was the arrival of the Loyalists after the American War of Independence (1775–1783). Most of the about ten thousand who came settled in what is now part of Ontario. They were followed by other migrants interested in land. Most avoided the French-speaking region, primarily because of its land holding system. "In the western country they held their farms as they had in the old colonies. Besides, the language, customs, and religion of Quebec were not theirs; and under the Quebec Act they did not find the representative system of government they had always known" (Careless, 1970:114). The appearance of this new population with "hyperloyalism to Britain, Crown, and Empire (McRae, 1964:239) changed the pattern of political demands and "rapports de force." The outcome was the division of the Old Province of Quebec into Upper and Lower Canada.

Cultural and linguistic diversity was largely managed by creating parallel geographical, social, and institutional spaces for the two collectivities. But "the merchants opposed a division of geographical area that was based on purely cultural distinctions. They were sure that in doing this, England was breaking the unity of the commercial empire of the St. Lawrence Valley to such an extent that it would become extremely difficult to work out policies that would take into consideration the needs of the economy as a whole" (Ouellet, 1967:167).

The tensions between the two collectivities were accentuated by the progressive emergence of a new group on the sociopolitical scene: a French-speaking professional class.[5] Earlier, the appearance of the Loyalists precipitated the collapse of the existing institutional arrangements. Now, a new class emerging within the French collectivity set in motion a new sequence of institutional change. The new class of professionals was well educated but relatively poor and powerless. Politics was the channel they chose to gain influence and social recognition. They organized the Parti Canadien, and the newspaper *Le Canadien*. Their mission

THE ROLE OF THE LOYALIST IN ENGLISH CANADA

To a significant degree, the loyalists were the original founders of English Canada:

> The Loyalists began to build a Canada that was not predominantly French. Modern English-speaking Canada really goes back to them, and to the Revolution that drove them out. In a sense, the American Revolution itself really answered that old problem of 1763—of how to make Canada thoroughly a part of the British Empire" (Careless, 1970:115).

was to promote the interest of the French-Canadian nation, strengthen the traditional society, and eventually attain political supremacy.

Such ambitions brought them into conflict with the merchants and capitalists who also used a political party and a newspaper to promote their interests (the Breton Party and the *Quebec Mercury*). The professional class perceived the merchants as determined to undermine French-Canadian institutions and society. "The proposals to revamp the transportation system were regarded as the logical concomitants of this general program: its only possible objective was to flood Lower Canada with English immigrants in order to achieve union of the two Canadas, and thereby to drown the French Canadians in an Anglo-Saxon sea. The aggressive attitude of the more militant-minded British simply seemed to confirm them in their convictions" (Ouellet, 1967:270). The merchant party, on its side, was attempting to counter the rising power of this group, since it opposed the realization of its economic ambitions. They were especially nervous about the Parti Canadien's demand to increase the role of the elected legislative assembly by introducing ministerial responsibility. This would make government officials accountable to a largely French legislative assembly. This organizational reform was an attempt by the new rising class to institutionalize its access to political power.

They also ran into conflict with the clergy. Their political liberalism clashed with the bishop's hierarchical conceptions of polity and society. This internal conflict is relevant because on some issues the clergy sided with the government and the merchants' party and on others with the Parti Canadien. Their stand depended on their perceptions of how particular outcomes would support or upset the social order and the dominant position that they enjoyed in it.

The Parti Patriote's demands for reform were rejected by Parliament in London in 1837. This occurred at a time of severe economic difficulties. The high level of discontent in the population was articulated by various political organizations. The result was the Revolt of 1837, a revolt easily crushed by the government.

The rebellion in Lower Canada was part of a widespread movement in the British North American colonies. They all experienced, in varying degrees, "the rule of small, tightly knit colonial oligarchies, to which Canadian history has applied the vivid but somewhat misleading term Family Compacts" (McRae, 1964:240).[6] Papineau's rebellion was accompanied by Mackenzie's in Upper Canada and by peaceful reform movements pressuring for responsible government in the Maritimes. Of course, in Lower Canada the unrest over oligarchic government had an ethnolinguistic dimension, but the split was not complete: some French supported the British party (the name the Tories in Lower Canada used to refer to themselves) and some English-speaking reformers supported French-speaking reformers (Careless, 1970:175).

Lord Durham was immediately sent from England to examine the situation. His 1839 report contained four recommendations of importance here:

1. the establishment of responsible government[7]
2. the reduction of the political power of the French Canadians by neutralizing the effect of their numerical majority in the political decision-making process—so they could not obstruct the development projects of the English-speaking business class;
3. the assimilation of French Canadians into the English culture because, left

to itself, French-Canadian society would remain static and hopelessly inferior

4. the union of Lower and Upper Canada as a step towards achieving these objectives.

The Act of Union of 1840 established "a single parliament with equal representation from each constituent section; consolidation of the debt;[8] . . . banishment of the French language from official government use; and suspension of specific French-Canadian institutions relating to education and civil law" (Canadian Encyclopedia, 1985:7). This Act's intention was quite different from the previous position taken by the British governors and administrators; their policy had been to accommodate the two cultural groups in the institutional framework. The denial of that reality almost assured the new regime would not last.

Initially, its inherent problems were hidden, partly because much of the dualism remained due to the vast territory and differences in language, civil code, judicial system, and forms of land tenure (Ormsby, 1974:271). Another reason was the economic situation (e.g., chronic unemployment and the dependence of Lower on Upper Canada for wheat), which changed attitudes toward the canal system and economic development. The large emigration of French Canadians (primarily to the United States)[9] also preoccupied the elites who saw it as detrimental to their institution-building efforts.

Finally, the political issue that dominated the period was responsible government. The new Act had not established it. This was the central issue in Nova Scotia, Prince Edward Island, and Newfoundland, as well as in the Provinces of Canada. Reformers in Canada's East and West formed a coalition that brought about the desired goal in 1848. This collaboration undoubtedly helped reduce the sting of the many negative features of the Act of Union.

But these remained and continued to erode that accommodation. Ormsby notes equal representation, as a critical aspect of the political decision-making system, contributed the most to its vulnerability:

> There were occasions when measures affecting only one-half of the province were passed or rejected by a minority from that section with the aid of a majority from the other section. . . . For more than a quarter of a century, the union managed to function as a quasi-federal system, but eventually the forces of dualism came into direct conflict with the unitary character of the constitution (272–73).

The English-speaking population grew considerably during this period: it "rose from 125 000 in 1820 to 450 000 in 1842 and then more than doubled during the remainder of the forties to reach 952 000 by 1851" (Beaujot and McQuillan, 1982:21). This growth resulted in an increased demand to abolish the provision for equal representation in the Act of Union. Now that it was a majority, the English-speaking population wanted "Representation by Population." But just as such a system was unacceptable to Upper Canadians when they were less numerous, it was not acceptable to Lower Canadians now that they were becoming the numerical minority.

These phenomena dictated a return to the federal idea that had been incorporated in the 1791 arrangement, although not in that particular institutional form. Several factors led to Confederation:

> the threat of American imperialism, the fear of the westward expansion of the United States, the necessity for improved railway communications (and) the political impasse in Canada . . . (But the fundamental problem which faced the delegates who

> met at Charlottetown and at Quebec (was) that of reconciling the conflicting interests of the two racial groups and of the conflicting principles of centralization and provincial autonomy (Stanley, 1974:276).

Federalism appeared to be the most appropriate for a situation of cultural dualism. It involves different levels of government, each with particular powers and functions. The 1867 arrangement

> gave the central government control of all matters that did not divide the two ethnic groups, on issues in which both shared a common interest. As a rule, the central power took over general services, administrative, technical and military activities. . . . Everything that dealt with social, civil, family, education, or municipal organization was allocated to the provinces. . . . They also administered public lands and forests, prisons, hospitals, and charitable institutions. The provincial jurisdiction covered municipal organization and the incorporation of companies for provincial objectives'' (Hamelin, 1961:264–65).

The negotiated arrangement permitted within the context of a common framework, the realization of the societal ambitions of *both* groups, giving each the means to construct institutions that would incorporate their own culture, language, and sociopolitical philosophy (Silver, 1982; Careless, 1970; Berger, 1970).

FROM CONFEDERATION TO WORLD WAR II

In the decades after 1867, institution-building competition in Canada was particularly intense. The outcome largely favoured English Canada.

The 1880s witnessed the rise of Canadian imperialism, a movement for the closer union of the British empire and for Canadian participation in it (Berger, 1970:3). This movement helped shape the Canadian collective identity and English–French relations. Cole points out that imperialists, as Canadians,

> did not aim at the creation of a Canadian nation. . . . They could scarcely even have conceived of a Canadian nation ethnically differentiated from its Anglo-Saxon and British forebearers. . . . (They) did, however, possess a very deep ethnic sense, a very strong consciousness of nationality. Their ethnic identity was not Canadian, but emphatically and intensely British (Cole, 1971:171).

A second significant phenomenon for defining the collective identity and the character of societal institutions was the growth of Protestant churches as powerful religious denominations[10] (Clark, 1962: 170–71). Accompanying this church building was the social promotion of Protestantism and anti-Catholicism. The Orange

CONFLICTING ORIENTATIONS

The imperialist movement began to organize Canadian branches of the Imperial Federation League. Given their ethnocultural orientation and their conception of Canada as an extension of Britain, it is not surprising that they clashed with French-Canadian nationalists, whose ethnocultural commitments were equally strong and in whose collective memory the Conquest was deeply etched. These conflicting orientations clashed frequently, especially when the Boer War began in 1899 and during the Conscription crises of the two World Wars.

Order, the Protestant Protective Association, and the Ku Klux Klan all actively defined the society as Protestant.[11] Mann (1976) observes this was one factor behind the church union movement, that

> Protestant interest in a national church was partly a reaction to the steady expansion of Roman Catholicism, especially that of French Canada. Eastern Protestants were very sensitive to Roman Catholic political power, and had organized before 1902 several specifically anti-Roman organizations which vigilantly scrutinized Roman Catholic actions and expansion (396).

In French Canada, the corresponding concern was with the Catholic character of the society. It was of special concern to the "Ultramontanes," who included the right wing of the Church, both clergy and laity. They believed in the primacy of church over state (Linteau et al., 1979: 314–21), and were anti-Protestant. As in English Canada, this period saw the institutional church grow enormously in people joining religious orders.[12]

The Protestant and Catholic movements reacted to each other's ideologies and political activities. Although the linguistic and religious cleavages coincided significantly, religious issues predominated. "Linguistic issues might arise from time to time *within* the Catholic community, but the primary line of cleavage was religious during this important formative period" (McRae, 1974:243).

Third, the elites of the two collectivities were greatly concerned with population size—both absolute and relative: absolute because society-building and expansion requires population; relative, because political power depends partly on numbers. Immigration policy was the main demographic instrument used by English-Canadian elites (Richmond, 1967); in French Canada, a natality policy was systematically pursued by the clerical elites (Henripin, 1957). Both succeeded: the two linguistic groups grew at about the same rate so that the French-origin population stayed at about 30 percent of the total population throughout the period.[13] Fourth, although the French Canadians maintained their relative numerical strength, English Canada, already larger by 1867, continually expanded during this period with the development of the West. This made the competition for political power within the federal arrangement increasingly uneven, accentuating a tendency begun when the Compact took place. Even though the arrangement was fundamentally for the political accommodation of two cultural groups,

> "the meeting . . . at Charlottetown and at Quebec introduced a new interpretation which has had a mighty impact upon the course of our later history, namely, the idea of a compact between the politico-geographic areas which go to make up Canada. . . . Once Canadians . . . began to identify provinces with specific linguistic groups, the idea of a pact between races was transformed into the idea of a pact between provinces" (Stanley, 1974: 280–81).

The addition of new provinces and their successful cultural and political appropriation by English Canadians compounded the ambiguity—an ambiguity substantially detrimental to the symbolic and political weight of the French component of Canada.

Fifth, in sp te of the failure of the 1840 arrangement, a preference for a unitary system continued on the part of the English-speaking political elite. Strong centralist tendencies were manifest in the implementation of the British North America Act.[14] There was, of course, resistance—not only from Quebec but from other provinces as well, Ontario in particular. In fact, as Fox (1969) argues, there has been since Confederation a regular "oscillation in the assertion of political power between the federal government and the provinces."

Sixth, the French were underrepresented in the federal Cabinet during most of the period: French-speaking ministers held, on the average, 22 percent of the person-years in the different governments during the 1867–1966 period. Also, their representation differed by type of ministry: policy making, 15 percent; human capital, 9 percent; support, 34 percent; co-ordinative, 34 percent; and without portfolio, 14 percent (Breton and Roseborough, 1968). Francophones were also underrepresented in the federal bureaucracy:[15] from about 36 percent before Confederation (1863), their percentage fell to about 22 percent by 1918 and to about 13 percent by 1946.

Finally, at the economic level, a shift toward the centre of the country took place. In the pre-industrialization period, wood and grain were the two main articles of commerce and the main points of development (including ship building) were along the St. Lawrence. (In the United States, they were along the Atlantic seaboard.) The substitution of steel for wood and the construction of the railroads moved the points of development to Southern Ontario in Canada (and the mid-West in the United States) Faucher and Lamontagne, 1953). This shift also contributed to the decreasing weight of French Canada in the federation.

The founding of Assiniboia as part of present day Manitoba is primarily a history of commercial and military conflict between two trading companies: the Hudson's Bay Company and the Montreal-based Northwest Company. This conflict ended when Selkirk, a Hudson's Bay Company stockholder who wanted an area to settle surplus population from Scotland and Ireland, took control of the colony in 1816 to 1817.

The settlement process really began only after this initial conflict for commercial hegemony. Institutions were established by the British, French, and Métis (of Native and French or Scottish origin). Colony building was slow: by the middle of the nineteenth century, the community had about five thousand people. But Easterners began showing an interest in the West. Businessmen saw its annexation as an opportunity for commercial expansion. Political groups, such as the Clear Grit Party of Upper Canada, saw it as additional land for settlement that would check emigration to the United States and permit more British immigration (McInnes, 1947:315). The ambition, however, was not simply colonization but to prevent the American annexation of the West and to preclude its appropriation by French speakers. Both were indeed showing an interest in making that part of the continent their own. It should be noted, however, that at that time the interested French speakers were only the Métis and those who had settled in the West. As Silver (1982) demonstrates quite convincingly, French Québécois did not see "the Northwest as a field of settlement for French Canadians." They "did not look on Rupert's Land as part of their country, (and) neither did they look on the French Catholic Métis as part of their own nationality . . . Quebec alone was the French Canadian homeland" (ibid., 74; see also Lalonde, 1982). The elite seemed primarily interested in developing the West because of its possible economic benefits for Quebec. On the other hand, many feared its annexation to Canada would tip the balance of power still further in favour of English Canada.

Events changed drastically with the annexation of the West by the Canadian government whose officials saw it "only in relation to the Hudson's Bay Company's control. . . . Not for a moment did Canada think of consulting the inhabitants of Assiniboia nor of guaranteeing them any specific rights.'' Surveyors began land division procedures without regard for the settlers already there (Hamelin, 1961: 279–80; McInnes, 1947:364). The Métis resisted. In 1869, led by Louis Riel, a group of them ''arrested the surveyors working on the registration of the Saint-Vital area, a region that the Métis considered a fief of their own'' (Hamelin, 1967:281). Attempts to stop the usurpation were made. Later the same year, the Métis seized Fort Garry and established a provisional government. The planned counterattack at Forty Garry by the Canadian party led to the capture of several of its members by the Métis and to the eventual execution of Thomas Scott. In short, a serious confrontation was underway for the control of land and institutions between French-speaking Métis and English-speaking settlers and migrants from Ontario.

These events, and especially Riel's show of force, provoked a strong reaction in Ontario where the uprising was defined as a French-Catholic attempt to overthrow British institutions:

> Ontarians were naturally struck by the prominent role which the French Catholic element played at Red River . . . many (also) looked upon the opening of the North-West not only as a great opportunity for the establishment of their own people, but as a great work of national and human progress, which would build up the wealth and population of Canada, provide homes for great numbers of people and produce food for the world's hungry. Now that work of progress was being sabotaged . . . many of them saw the uprising as a French-Canadian enterprise aimed at stopping what the *Globe* had called, in 1863, ''the wheels of Anglo-Saxon progress toward the setting sun'' (Silver, 1982:80).

Because of its lack of interest in the West as an area for French settlement, Quebec opinion defined the uprising as a part of a movement for self-determination, not a fight for French or Catholic rights. However, the definition of the situation in Ontario triggered a change in Quebec's perception of the events and of their own collective identity: the Métis came to be seen as their compatriots and the North-West as part of *their* social and geographical space. Because of Ontario's conduct—or at least Quebec's view of it—the North-West started to be seen as another French-Catholic province that could assist Quebec's struggles with English Canada (Silver, 1982:82–83).

The Manitoba Act of 1870 was the response to Riel's demands supported by Quebec's pressure on Ottawa. It incorporated most of the claims of Riel's provisional government: provincial status, official bilingualism, denominational schools, and guaranteed property rights for the inhabitants. But the question of political, economic, and cultural control was not solved. The basic issue remained: ''Would the institutions of French-speaking Roman Catholic Quebec or English-speaking Protestant Ontario prevail?'' (Lupul, 1970:273). The ambitions of groups such as Canada First, the Orange Order, the Equal Rights Association, the Protestant Protective Association, and the Canadian Imperialists were clear: it was to be British and Protestant. French-Canadian rights should be confined to Quebec. The French Catholics, on the other hand, were determined to maintain their identity and institutions. The determination of one side accentuated the resoluteness of the other.

In the end, the power distribution favoured British Protestants: in 1890 the Manitoba legislature abolished the official status of French and the dual church-controlled Board of Education. But the controversy continued. The next legislative step was the Laurier–Greenway compromise of 1896. The religious part of the

THE DEMOGRAPHIC FACTOR

The critical factor of control, however, was not the attitudes themselves, but the shift in the balance of political power that resulted from a drastic change in the composition of the population.[16] The emerging English-speaking majority had political power and used it to achieve its cultural and institutional goals. The process whereby the new majority imposed its identity and culture on the political and social (education in particular) institutions began soon after 1870 and lasted about thirty-five years (although the critical changes had been made by 1890). The use of legislative power and the resistance it generated intensified feelings and attitudes on both sides. It brought into the political conflict Ontario, Quebec, the federal government, the Supreme Court, the British Judicial Committee, and the Vatican. The intensity of the conflict was further accentuated by events such as the second Métis rebellion, Riel's trial and execution in 1885, and the Jesuit's Estates controversy (which lasted several years).[17]

agreement was accepted by the Catholic minority, following the advice of the 1897 papal encyclical. The language controversy was halted with the repeal of the bilingual clause in 1916. "The feeling against bilingualism was so strong that even the study of a second language was omitted" (Lupul, 1970:278).

> Similar developments took place in other parts of the West:
> The Territories eliminated French as a language of instruction except in the primary grades in 1892, but restored it in the upper grades for one hour per day at the end of the school day in 1901. In 1918, Saskatchewan reduced the use of French to the first year of school only, though the optional hour at the end of the school day was retained. In 1931, after continuing debates about papal influence and foreign subversion, the government . . . virtually eliminated French as a language of instruction in Saskatchewan schools. Alberta permitted only limited use of languages other than English after a crackdown on abuses of school regulations in 1913" (Friesen, 1984:260).

In New Brunswick,[18] the conflict over cultural dominance and **institutional control** also took place primarily in the field of education. The first move concerned religion, not language (in 1871, the Common Schools Act established a general public school system; public funds were provided to nonsectarian schools) (Lupul, 1970:272). The conflict between Protestants and Catholics, however, evolved into one between English and French. After a long period of isolation, poverty, and low political organization brought about by the deportation, a renewed political consciousness and mobilization emerged among Acadians in the latter part of the nineteenth century. The level of education was increasing; an elite had emerged and was growing; there were several media of public communication within the community. They were geographically concentrated and their numbers were increasing; within the Catholic component of the population, they became a majority. Thus, the Common Schools Act of 1871 occurred at a time when the Acadians' social and organizational capacity for political mobilization was increasing.

In addition, the Act would, if implemented, have important consequences for the Acadians. Most of them were Catholic and poorer than the English-speaking population. They were thus strongly affected by a legislation that eliminated government subsidies to sectarian schools. Their strong protest included a riot in 1875 in which two people died.

Predictably, the opposition to the legislation, both peaceful and violent, attracted attention in Quebec. Initially, the Quebec press saw the Act as an attack on their "co-religionists." But by 1875, newspapers were referring primarily to the *French* population of New Brunswick. Also, not surprisingly, Quebec opinion associated the events there with those in Manitoba and began defining the situation as a conspiracy against the French in the Dominion (Silver, 1982:97–100). A compromise acceptable to the Catholic hierarchy was eventually worked out. But the English–French conflict continued within the Catholic institutional system.

The hierarchy of the Church was Irish and Scottish, so an institution important to the French-speaking Catholic Acadians was largely under the control of another cultural group. The issues were not doctrinal; the confrontation was over the identity of the institution and its control. Acadians saw the Irish hierarchy as determined to prevent their own institutional development within the Catholic system and to restrict them from the high levels of the hierarchy. Considerable evidence suggests that the English-speaking hierarchy was determined to maintain its ascendancy and to impose its language and culture in the institution (Spigelman, 1975). It is with the Vatican's intervention that Acadian claims began to be recognized.

The field of education also witnessed a public conflict between the English and French in Ontario.[19] After Confederation, the existence of French schools was largely a matter of population. It is accordingly demographic changes that provoked conflicts, starting in the 1880s. First, the French-speaking population was increasing more rapidly than the English-speaking population. The French still represented only 8 percent of the population in 1911 (compared to 5 percent in 1881), but their social visibility was accentuated by their concentration in particular regions.

Also, a large Irish-Catholic population entered Canada during the second half of the nineteenth century, and those new arrivals, being Catholic, often found themselves combined with French Catholics in French and bilingual schools. The increasing English-Protestant population also often found themselves combined with francophones in traditionally French-language public schools. Objectively, those changes may not have been drastic. They were, however, perceived and interpreted in terms of the sociopolitical context of the period (described earlier) and of the societal aspirations of British-origin Ontarians. Many "feared that French in the schools in Ontario *would undermine the Anglo-Saxon character* of the province (Barber, 1969:63 emphasis added).[20] The society's cultural character was not only a public issue; it was experienced daily by parents socializing their children.

The ethnocultural majority began exercising its political power to consolidate its threatened societal project. In 1885, the study of English was made compulsory. In 1890, it became the required language of instruction except where impracticable. French was accepted as a temporary expedient (Barber, 1969:64). As in New Brunswick, these moves contributed to the politicization of the French community, prompting them to organize to maintain the institutional means they saw as necessary for achieving *their* cultural aspirations. Their increasing numbers, concentration, and cohesion based on the social organization of the traditional parish was the basis for political mobilization.

A further impetus came from the changes in collective identity in Quebec and from the emerging definition of the political situation (with regard to Confederation) associated with it. Indeed, the cause of the French minorities outside Quebec was becoming an integral part of Quebec's own societal ambitions, Quebec, however, was ambivalent. Even though a pan-Canadian collective identity was emerging, there was a lot of concern for provincial autonomy. Thus, Quebec could not pressure the federal government to intervene without risking the reduction of its own autonomy.

The controversy lasted for several years. New educational measures were introduced by the provincial government, each bringing serious reactions. The political activity of the French in turn increased the resolve of English-speaking Protestants and the pressure they applied on the government. Ironically, English-speaking Catholics sided with groups such as the Orange Order on this issue, but for different reasons. First, they perceived an educational system differentiated on linguistic lines as a threat to their hope for a religiously based separate school system[21]—a justified fear. Second, there was, as in New Brunswick, an internal conflict for the control of the Catholic Church, and the growing strength and politicization of the French was interpreted in that connection. The friction inherent in the school situation was aggravated by a perpetual church feud involving all levels of the Catholic clergy. Neither Irish nor French neglected any opportunity to strengthen their own position as they vied for control of the Catholic church in Canada. One prominent Irish Catholic of the time noted:

> Now, no one wants to do the French Canadians an injustice. The British Crown has given them what is actually an empire in the Province of Quebec, but no right or claim have they on this account, or on any other, to all the Provinces of the Dominion. They have been, with difficulty, kept out of Church control completely, in Ontario and the Maritime provinces; with difficulty driven out of that control in British Columbia. They are still in control of the Church organization in Manitoba, Alberta, and Saskatchewan. In this struggle, French Catholics were steadily building up strengths against Irish Catholics in eastern Ontario (quoted in Barber, 1969:69).

The French lost the first round: Regulation 17 in 1913 restricted French as a language of instruction to Form I (the first two years of school). But the struggle continued; in fact French resistance against Regulation 17 intensified on two fronts: political and ecclesiastical. It persisted until the Regulation was made harmless in 1927 by an arrangement allowing negotiations on a case-by-case basis (Choquette, 1975:173–220).[22] Choquette sums up the evolution of anglophones who became exhausted with the continual strife while eventually recognizing the need for an accommodation to assure the existence of the country. He also notes that an extensive change occurred among most concerned parties and, most important, the Unity League was established in Toronto. Also, organizations such as the Orange Order were in political decline.

One significant change in Quebec during this period was already discussed, namely, the political articulation of a bilingual conception of Confederation. It emerged progressively with the actions of English-Protestant groups outside Quebec:

> In 1867, French Quebeckers had seen their province alone as the home of the French-Canadian nationality, and looked to Confederation to separate it as much as possible from the others. But many were now coming to accept some notion of a Canadian nation based on equality between two races, each having guaranteed rights in *all* provinces. This view emerged from

ENGLISH CONTROL OF INDUSTRIES

Another important development was the industrialization and urbanization of the province and the impact these had on its social structure, on its sociopolitical mobilization, and on its conceptions of its place in the Canadian social and political structure. Industrialization was introduced and controlled by English speakers—a phenomenon that an extremely powerful clergy was content to accept. By defining business and industry as English, the clergy maintained their social and cultural hegemony in the society. Thus, since English and French elites each had their own institutional domains, confrontations were reduced (or postponed). At least two other factors contributed to the absence of confrontations within Quebec (as opposed to the Canada-wide scene). First, the B.N.A. Act guaranteed each group its educational system. Secondly, there was considerable emigration, primarily to the United States. The "exit" that over 800 000 people chose between 1840 and 1930 (Lavoie, 1981) probably helped contain the tensions between English and French in Quebec. But the impact of the ongoing socioeconomic changes could not be curbed indefinitely.

> events in the intervening decades. It was only *after* French Quebeckers had discovered and become concerned about French-Catholic minorities, only *after* they had tried to help the Métis, only *after* the Riel affair, the racial agitation of the late 1880s and the controversies of the 1890s—only *after* all this that the bilingual theory of Confederation could emerge (Silver, 1982:192; emphasis in original).

FROM WORLD WAR II TO THE PRESENT

In the previous period, most of the pressure and organized actions to establish or transform institutional forms were initiated by English Canadians. To a considerable extent, they gained control over public institutions and established their cultural and linguistic ascendancy. French Canadians, as French, as Catholics, or both, offered considerable resistance, attempting to protect their own institutional domains. But by and large, they had to accommodate to the anglophone societal project. In the recent period, however, the pressures for change came from the French, primarily in Quebec. English speakers generally resisted their attempts to expand their economic, political, and cultural control, but some supported these changes.

As already indicated, The Quiet Revolution of the 1960s accelerated the processes of social and political changes that began much earlier (Guindon, 1964, 1968; Behiels, 1985). These broke down what remained of the traditional social structure. The percentage of the French origin population that was urban grew from 55 percent to 71 percent between 1941 and 1961, and the rural farm population declined from 41 percent to 13 percent. Between 1950 and 1960, school attendance "more than doubled in grades nine to twelve and increased beyond grade twelve by more than 50 percent" (Brazeau, 1964:325).

In many ways, an increasingly new kind of population lived in Quebec. Its numerical expansion and power aspirations led to attempts to conquer or reconquer institutional spaces, generating confrontations with those who already controlled those spaces: the traditional French-Canadian elites, the clergy and the groups represented by the Duplessis regime; the English-speaking groups dominating the Quebec economy; the politico-bureaucratic groups controlling the federal government; and the "other ethnic groups" who had allied themselves with the Anglos and who, wittingly or not, supported their institutions.

The agenda of the new contending groups was to gain control of the means necessary for organization-building, particularly political power and capital; to displace, partly or completely, those occupying the coveted organizations and positions; to claim new ones that English speakers would, under the existing dispensation, have considered their own "turf"; and to redefine the collective identity in ways compatible with their societal aspirations. The resistance of English-speaking groups corresponded to these three lines of action: resistance to the redistribution of political and economic power; loss or potential loss of organizational domains; and transformation of the symbolic-cultural character of the Canadian society that they had struggled to establish.

Implementing this agenda led to confrontations in the Quebec, Canada-wide, and provincial arenas, although the specific claims at issue were frequently quite different from one to the other. Also, different groups of francophones pursued action in each arena. The differences—not to say contradictions — in their programs frequently brought them into conflict with one another.

In addition to a systematic change of French-Quebec society, the Quiet Revolution involved a nationalistic drive to transform its relationship with English-speaking Canada. This nationalism expressed itself in different ways, but the most important was the independentist movement. It generated an enormous pressure for change both in Quebec and in Canada. Organizationally, the movement began in the mid-1950s with the formation of several organizations covering a wide ideological spectrum. They varied in terms of general socio-political philosophy; in their nationalist program; in the strategies advocated to reach independence (e.g., through democratic procedures versus violence.[23]

The most significant development, however, was the formation of the Parti Québécois, its initial electoral accomplishments (electing six members to l'Assemblée nationale in 1970) and its victory as a majority government in 1976. Terrorist activities, primarily by the F.L.Q., added enormously to the pressure for change, culminating in 1970 with the kidnapping of James Cross and Pierre Laporte and with the latter's assassination. These events provoked the proclamation of the War Measures Act, which affirmed the power of the central state with the quasi-unanimous support of the federal Parliament (Breton, 1972).

The independentist movement was a powerful force aimed at a drastic redistribution of political power. At the cultural-symbolic level, it expressed the alienation of Québécois who could not identify with the institutions and milieu that British Canadians had created "in their own image" during the previous historical period. It expressed a sense of powerlessness with regard to institutions seen as anglophone-controlled; the sense of being at the economic and political periphery. Complete political autonomy was argued to be an essential condition for the economic and cultural vitality of Québécois society.

Several interrelated lines of action were pursued. One of the most important concerned the language of public institutions.

The changes in the linguistic rules of the game were part of the process whereby institutional control was sought. The use of state powers to impose the French language was new in Quebec. In many ways, it corresponds to the earlier use of state powers to impose English in other provinces.

As the history in English-speaking provinces shows, the process involves a long political struggle, since the outcome sought is a new dispensation in which one group assumes institutional dominance, defines the organizational rules and practices; and specifies the conditions of membership and of access to rewards. Language is crucial for gaining organizational ascendancy: one's participation in the organizational system, the centrality of one's position in it, and the rewards one can obtain depend upon one's competence in the language and linguistic practices of the controlling group.

The first comprehensive legislation "La loi sur la langue officielle" (Law 22) was adopted in 1974. It made French the official language of Quebec, making that province officially unilingual like all other provinces except New Brunswick (although its official unilingualism, like Manitoba's, is restricted by the B.N.A. Act). Law 22 contained a wide range of specifications for the language of public administration and utilities, the professions, places of work, business and education. A few years later (1977), Quebec's Assemblée nationale replaced that law with the "Charte de la langue française" (Law 101). It reasserted many of the specifications of the previous legislation, but went further by adding others, but especially by putting in place increased legal and organizational means for their implementation.

Also, since the vitality of organizational systems, public or private, depends in part on the size of the population attempts were made to direct immigrants into the French institutional system. This was especially necessary in view of the now very low birth rate among francophones. It required that control be gained over immigration (a federal prerogative), that the children of immigrants attend French schools, and that integration programs be created for immigrants. The compulsory elements of this strategy were strongly resisted by members of ethnic groups who saw their chances of upward mobility potentially threatened by a reduced competence in the dominant language. It was also resisted by anglophone institutions, particularly the schools, which were about to experience a serious reduction in the size of their clientele and, consequently, in the opportunities offered by their institutions.

Both pieces of legislation were highly controversial. This was in part because they were redefining the cultural-symbolic character of Quebec society and changing the relative sociopolitical status of the two linguistic groups. They were also controversial because they were aiming toward an increase of francophone control of the Quebec economy, an objective explicitly stated.[24] The legislation tried to open avenues of social mobility to francophones in organizations in which the English language prevailed, and acted as a barrier for many upwardly mobile francophones.

Other lines of action were also pursued. For instance, the strategy of institutional development and control also involved taking over enterprises previously owned or controlled by anglophones; establishing state agencies for the accumulation of capital; and gaining control of existing sources of capital (such as the public Pension Fund).[25]

The overall objective was to create a society that would be predominantly if not exclusively French (just like the strategy in other parts of Canada was to create a British society.) It was a return to seeing Quebec as the homeland of the French in North America — a view that, as Silver (1982) notes, prevailed at the time of Confederation. The French community did not see itself as a minority in Canada, but as a majority in its own territory. They increasingly saw themselves as Québécois, not French Canadians. Correspondingly, British-origin Quebeckers were being defined as a minority; they still had a special status, but they were nevertheless a minority.

It is not claimed that all components of the strategy were or will be successful. Gains appear to have been made, although a systematic and accurate assessment of these gains is very difficult.[26] It may even be premature to make such an assessment. Indeed, the legislation has been in place for a little over ten years only. This is a very short period of time for assessing trends and changes at the level of a society. But it seems that the **legitimacy** of French as the official and operative language in Quebec is increasing; that it is more used at work than before (Breton and Grant, 1981); that immigrants are slowly being absorbed in the francophone social and institutional networks; and that more Quebec anglophones are bilingual.

Concurrent with the separatist movement was a movement to integrate Quebec in its sociopolitical and symbolic fabric. Those pursuing this objective — the federalists — struggled to increase the presence of francophones in the federal institutions, political and administrative. The aim was to raise the power of French Canadians in defining national goals and in allocating national resources. It was also to transform the cultural-symbolic character of federal institutions so that French Canadians could identify with them and consider them their own (Breton, 1984). This federalist component of French-Canadian nationalism, continuing with the nationalism that emerged during the previous historical period, defined Canada (and not only Quebec) as the homeland of French Canadians. Supported by many English-speaking Canadians, especially in the elite, French power increased in Ottawa: more francophones were appointed as cabinet ministers and to powerful ministries; important agencies were more likely to be led by francophones than was previously the case; the proportion of francophones in the civil service increased considerably (and rapidly); and the federal institutions began changing from a primarily unilingual to a bilingual system.

The two approaches are quite different. One tries to strengthen the boundary between the two communities. It assumes that Quebec is the homeland of the French in Canada; that francophone resources and energies should be used to develop that society. This "segmentalist" view states it is unrealistic to expect the French language and culture to survive and develop elsewhere in Canada (except, perhaps, in one or two regions). In the other "pan-Canadian" approach, the francophone and anglophone communities are seen to exist in all regions of the country. Thus, it is important that in all regions, whenever numbers warrant it, services be provided for the education of children in the language and culture of the family; that other cultural facilities, such as radio and television stations, be available, and that individuals be able to use, in their own language, the services of at least the federal government — but preferably those of the other levels of government as well.

An intense opposition existed between the proponents of each of these approaches. The successes of one group were perceived as detrimental to the pursuits of the other. Some English-speaking Canadians supported the federalists because they agreed with them, although many did so because they saw them as the lesser of two evils. Many, however, did not

CLASS AND PREFERENCES FOR CHANGE IN QUEBEC

The supporters of each approach tend to come from different social groups. Independence and sovereignty-association have been endorsed primarily by intellectuals,[27] other professionals, semi-professionals and technicians, and by clerical/sales workers. In the 1980 referendum, 67 percent of intellectuals, 61 percent of other semi-professionals and technicians, and 56 percent of those in liberal professions voted yes, in contrast to 38 percent of managers and proprietors, 39 percent of farmers, and 45 percent of workers.[28] The *no* vote was a federalist vote, or rather neo-federalist, since the intention was "to set in motion negotiations for a renewed **federalism**" (Pinard and Hamilton, 1984:22–30). In short, most French Quebeckers wanted changes (only 12 percent favoured the status quo), but not necessarily the same changes.

see the opposition between the two political factions, and even sensed a sinister collusion between them to lower the status of English Canadians and erode their institutions and culture in Quebec while taking control in the rest of the country.

Parallel changes occurred outside Quebec. Modernization created new elites and a renewed organizational capacity for political action. Changing attitudes among some English Canadians, government language policies, and the independentist threat contributed to a new sense of power among francophones outside Quebec. On the other hand, the Quebec-centredness of the independentist movement incited francophones outside Quebec to think of their communities not as extensions of Quebec but as distinct sociopolitical entities. In the process, regional identities were redefined, and the provinces were perceived as the significant political environments (Juteau-Lee and Lapointe, 1979).

Thus demands for change were also articulated in provincial arenas. There were, however, considerable variations in the results. The political difficulties in giving increased official recognition and institutional services to the francophones varied. In all provinces except Quebec and New Brunswick, francophones constitute a small percentage of the total population, frequently smaller than that of other ethnic groups. Many people do not see why the French should receive special treatment. Thus institutional recognition and services are legitimated in reference to the larger pan-Canadian context, but not without meeting much resistance. Also, the high rate of assimilation of people of French origin (except perhaps in New Brunswick) weakens the political will of the provincial elites on these matters. This generates a downward spiral: the minority situation and the high rate of assimilation do not encourage governments to give recognition and services; this encourages assimilation which, in turn, reduces numerical and institutional strength.

CONCLUSION

Canada is a ***plural*** or segmented ***society*** divided along linguistic lines into two parallel institutional systems. To a large extent, the material well-being of English- and French-speaking Canadians depends on the opportunities and services provided by their linguistic subsocieties. Their individual identities are largely constructed in relation to the cultural features of their respective institutions and nourished by their symbolic activities. Their self-esteem is determined by the societal status of the linguistic group with which they identify. Thus, members of each collectivity have an interest in the vitality and growth of their own subeconomies; in the cultural character of their own subsociety; and in its public status in relation to the other. They compare their societal condition with that of the other; they constantly "watch" how well the other group is doing in different areas compared to their own.

Accordingly, both seek institutional control for the realization of their material and symbolic-cultural interests. Both want their organizational domains to expand so as to provide more opportunities as their aspirations and/or population grow. Both want institutions that embody their culture and operate in their language. The historical overview presented here shows that the history of English–French relations in Canada is characterized by recurrent power struggles for the control of the means required for society building in its economic, cultural, and linguistic dimensions.

The existence of parallel institutional systems is not the only defining feature of a plural society. These systems operate and evolve within an **overarching framework**. There exist, so to speak, two interrelated levels of societal organization. What happens at one level can have momentous implications for the other. The policies of the federal government or of national corporations can affect the economic and cultural condition of each of the linguistic subsocieties. They can affect the linguistic groups *qua* linguistic groups or because of their geographical concentration (Nielsen, 1985:143). Controlling the overarching structures of decision making and resource allocation is therefore critical. As we have seen, the English and French have competed for the control of these institutions since the Conquest.

On the other hand, what happens within each subsociety also has implications for the distribution of power at the level of the common institutions. Generally, the significant internal changes are those that have brought about new aspirations and, consequently, new demands for change, and those that have affected the relative power of the two linguistic collectivities. Three kinds of circumstantial changes that have triggered a new round of competition and conflict have been noted:

1. Changes in the extent to which one or both groups are politically mobilized either to take advantage of opportunities for further gains, or to resist or challenge the institutionalized system if they see themselves in a disadvantaged position.
2. Changes in the absolute and relative size of the two populations and the appearance on the sociopolitical scene of new categories of people or the growth of existing ones. Such changes have been the result of socioeconomic development: the rise in available resources, in education, and in organizational potential. They have accompanied the growth in state activity since World War II, especially in areas of provincial jurisdiction. Governmental expansion has meant the growth of a professional-bureaucratic class. They have been brought about by external forces such as the American War of Independence and the massive American and Anglo-Canadian investments in Quebec after World War II.
3. Contradictions or problems unresolved by previous accommodations or caused by new arrangements. Such contradictions become progressively more apparent as the arrangements are put in practice.

The overview has shown that the outcome of the conflicts has depended on the distribution of power between the two collectivities: on the moderating impact of economic and other interdependencies; and, occasionally, on the mediating influence of "third parties." The power inequality has varied from one historical period to another: the immediate post-Conquest period, the years of the American War of Independence, the second half of the nineteenth century, and the post-World War II decades have witnessed significant power shifts between French and English. Variations have also been noted between Canada-wide, Quebec, and other arenas of confrontation and accommodation (and these have differed over time as well). Given the regional character of Canadian society, and the differences in the situation of English and French in the different regions, it is misleading to speak of *the* relationship between English and French. The expression "English–French relations" refers to several relationships involving different distributions of demographic, economic, and political power. Nevertheless, there has been an underlying pattern of resource competition for societal construction and development; for the control of institutions, the opportunities they can provide, and the symbolic cultural features they embody.

Notes

[1]On the processes of mobilizing power in order to gain access to societal rewards or resources and on the resulting structure of "social closure," see Parkin (1979) and Murphy (1984).

[2]The main sources for this chapter are: The Canadian Encyclopedia (1985); Cornell, Hamelin, Ouellet, and Trudel (1967); Careless (1970); Linteau, Durocher, and Robert (1979); McInnis (1969); and Silver (1982).

[3]For a general discussion of segmentation, see also Smith (1974) and Schermerhorn (1970). For its examination in the context of Canadian society, see McRae (1974), Ossenberg (1967) and Breton (1978).

[4]About one-third are said to have supported the American troops at the time of the revolution and another third would have been ambivalent. There were also several manifestations of unrest against clergy and seigneurs (Lanctot, 1967). These findings are summarized by Ossenberg (1967:213).

[5]On the emergence of this professional class, see Ouellet (1966).

[6]"To risk a broad generalization for a fifty-year interval (the Family Compacts) included, characteristically, the heads of departments in the colonial administration, judges, most barristers, and the bishop or ranking churchman of the Church of England. But this is not all, for closely associated with this official hierarchy we find the leaders of the commercial and banking community. In the microcosm of colonial society there is no clear differentiation between the political and the economic elite" (McRae, 1964:241).

[7]"A government responsible to the representatives of the people, i.e., an executive or Cabinet collectively dependent on the votes of a majority of the elected legislature." This key principle of responsibility, whereby a government needed the confidence of Parliament, originated in established British practice. But its transfer to British North America gave the colonists control of their domestic affairs, since a governor would simply follow the advice (i.e., policies) of responsible colonial ministers, except in imperial matters" (Canadian Encyclopedia, 1985:1579).

[8]"For many years, the business groups had been struggling to procure a development in transportation, a measure they believed essential to the progress of Canada . . . Since the capitalist group had little means at their disposal, the execution of the program fell

upon the State. Large investments were needed for enterprises that would bring very little immediate return. In short, the political authorities had to realize this need for massive investments in economic development. In addition they had to consent to pool resources and credit of both provinces. . . .

. . . United Canada assumed in its entirety the debt of Upper Canada, which had been contracted with a view to defraying the cost of the Saint Lawrence canal system" (Ouellet, 1966:232).

[9]Between 1840 and 1870, about two hundred thousand left for the United States. Another seven hundred thousand left in the subsequent decades, 1870 to 1930.

[10]"The Methodist Church (Canada), the Presbyterian Church in Canada, the Church of England in Canada, and the Baptist Conference of Canada fused out of smaller and less politically effective religious bodies" (ibid:171).

[11]On this matter, see, for example, Watt (1967), Pennefather (1984), and Houston and Smyth (1980).

[12]The number of priests increased from one for 1080 persons in 1850 to one for 510 in 1890. Between 1850 and 1901, members of male religious orders increased from 243 to 1984; those of female religious orders increased from 650 to 6628 (Hamelin, 1961, and Linteau et al., 1979).

[13]While the French remained largely ethnically homogeneous, the English-speaking population became more heterogeneous: the British origin component constituted a little over 60 percent of the total in 1871 but only about 45 percent in 1971.

[14]There were many devices that could be used by the federal government to control and reduce the realm of autonomy of the provinces: "the appointment of a federal supervisor for the provinces (the lieutenant governor), the disallowance and reservation of provincial statutes, and overriding character of federal law in concurrent fields, and the assignment of all residual powers to the central regime. These statutory provisions were freely and deliberately used . . . " (Black, 1975:60). For example, Macdonald exercised the power of disallowing provincial legislation "five times during his first term of office and forty-one times from 1878 to 1891 when the provinces were beginning to assert their claims to co-ordinate status with the federal government" (Black, 1975:36).

[15]For more information on the sources of these data, see Breton and Stasiulis (1980:191–92).

[16]In 1870, approximately 82 percent of the enumerated population was Métis, the majority being French-speaking and Catholic. The proportion that was from Ontario, the British Isles, and the United States was a little less than 6 percent—a proportion that, twenty years later, had increased to 51 percent. The percentage of Roman Catholics had decreased from 44.6 percent to 13.5 percent in the same period; that of Protestants increased from 39.6 percent to 82.6 percent (Staples, 1974:290–92).

[17]The central conflictual factor was that the Quebec government asked Pope Leo XIII to arbitrate its dispute with the Jesuits. This "papist intrusion" was strongly resented by English Protestants.

[18]The discussion of the Atlantic arena of French–English relations is restricted to New Brunswick for lack of space. It is also this province in which the most significant events took place.

[19]"That (education) was the most critical and most explosive issue in French–English relations between 1880 and 1920 is beyond a doubt. Both the French-speaking and the English-speaking Canadians involved in these disputes clearly recognized that the continuing viability of the French-Canadian's identity outside the province of Quebec was dependent upon the mode and content of instruction given to French-speaking pupils. Both asserted that if that mode and content of instruction was wholly English in character, the "French fact" in Ontario, Manitoba, and in the Territories soon to become Saskatchewan and Alberta would gradually wither away.

Their point of difference was whether that could or should be allowed to happen'' (Brown, 1969:vii).

[20]''For the Orange Order, the increasing number of French Canadians in Ontario signalled danger ahead. Ontario, the stronghold of imperial loyalty and English Protestantism, was being taken over by the French'' (Barber, 1969:71).

[21]The competition for resources between the French and the Catholic institutional systems continued in subsequent decades (see Jackson, 1975).

[22]The regulation was erased from the books in 1944.

[23]See Hagy (1969) for a description of these organizations. On the independentist movement, see Pinard and Hamilton (1977, 1984); Coleman (1984) and Behiels (1985).

[24]In the White Paper published before the linguistic legislation was presented to the National Assembly.

[25]For a discussion of those strategies and an examination of their implementation, see McRoberts and Posgate (1980).

[26]The case of individuals and enterprises that would have left Quebec or that did not establish themselves there because of the language legislation is an even more difficult question. That there was an exodus seems undeniable; but its size and especially its relationship to the legislation seems impossible to establish with existing evidence. The migration of enterprises and of individuals across provincial boundaries occurs all the time. The legislation may have had an impact on the flow, but other factors were also at work. One thing is sure: the legislation did focus the attention of the media on ''the exodus,'' which, in turn, provided ammunition to interested political groups.

[27]For the purposes of their study, Pinard and Hamilton define ''intellectuals'' as ''all those who are engaged in occupational roles concerned with the creation and transmission of culture. More specifically, our notion includes first art creators and performers (novelists, painters, musicians, actors, and other artists); second, all scientists and scholars, whether in academic settings or not (biologists, chemists, economists, sociologists, etc.) . . . ; third, and by far the largest group numerically, all teachers and professors; finally, all news workers (reporters, journalists, broadcasters, etc.)'' (1984:21).

[28]The same pattern was observed over time: in the early development of the movement ''support may have been lower but was already coming from all strata, ***with the same class differentials that are still prevailing now***'' (Pinard and Hamilton 1984:44; emphasis in original).

DISCUSSION QUESTIONS

1. What are the main manifestations of dualism in the Canadian social structure?
2. What are the implications of linguistic dualism in the social structure for the organization of political, economic, or sociocultural institutions?
3. Compare the confrontations between English and French at different points of history in terms of the conditions and events that brought them about.
4. What are the similarities and differences in the issues that divided English and French at different points of history? Are there patterns common to all of them?
5. Discuss the role of demographic factors in the evolution of English–French relations over time.
6. What institutional accommodations

have been made with regard to the issues of the most recent confrontation?

7. What are likely to be the main issues of the next confrontation? What kinds of events, conditions, structural changes, or unresolved issues (of the last wave of conflict) are likely to bring it about?

GLOSSARY

accommodation the outcome of a process of adjustment between conflict groups. The concept implies a mutual adaptation, but it need not be equal on the part of each party.

conflict confrontation between individuals or groups over scarce resources. It involves a struggle aimed at weakening, harming, or even eliminating the opponent. The confrontation may or may not be violent.

competition individuals or groups compete with each other when each is attempting to possess or gain control over certain scarce resources.

cultural-symbolic as opposed to the material or instrumental dimension of institutions, the cultural-symbolic one refers to their identity, values, and traditions. It also includes their lifestyles and their linguistic and other cultural practices. Although there may be special symbols, rituals, and ceremonies to express the character or identity of an institution, the cultural-symbolic dimension is usually embedded in its material features as well.

federalism a system of government involving different levels, each with particular powers and functions (or domains of jurisdiction and responsibility). Federalism supposes co-ordination among levels, but also a degree of independence or autonomy of each level of government.

institution the concept is used here in its restricted sense to refer to a set of organizations in a functional area. A school, for example, is an organization in the educational institution. This definition does not preclude the wider concept that refers to established patterns of behaviour and normatively structured relationships in given functional areas of social activity.

institutional/organizational control the capacity to direct the use of available resources and the orientation of activity in an institution or organization and to shape its cultural-symbolic character.

legitimacy an institutional arrangement has legitimacy if it is seen as embodying the beliefs, values, and norms recognized as valid and appropriate by its relevant publics.

overarching organizational structure an organization established for the co-ordination of existing organizations and their integration into a functioning whole. Such organizations may be established in any field of activity (e.g., cultural, commercial, political, recreational).

plural or segmented society a society with "a social structure compartmentalized into analogous, parallel, noncomplementary sets of institutions" (van den Berghe, 1969) and social networks largely enclosed within ethnocultural boundaries.

BIBLIOGRAPHY

Barber, Marilyn
1969 "The Ontario Bilingual School Issue: Sources of Conflict." In D.G. Creighton et al. (eds.) *Minorities, Schools and Politics*. Toronto: University of Toronto Press.

Beaujot, Roderic and Kevin McQuillan
1982 *Growth and Dualism: The Demographic Development of Canadian Society*. Toronto: Gage Publishing.

Behiels, Michael
1985 *Prelude to Quebec's Quiet Revolution*. Montreal: McGill-Queen's University Press.

Berger, Carl
1970 *The Sense of Power: Studies in the Ideas of Canadian Imperialism, 1867–1914*. Toronto: The University of Toronto Press.

Black, Edwin R.
1975 *Divided Loyalties: Canadian Concepts of Federalism.* Montreal: McGill–Queen's University Press.

Brazeau, Jacques
1964 "Quebec's Emerging Middle Class." In Marcel Rioux and Yves Martin (eds.) *French-Canadian Society*. Toronto: McClelland and Stewart.

Breton, Raymond
1972 "The Socio-political Dynamics of the October Events." *The Canadian Review of Sociology and Anthropology* IX: 33–56.

——
1978 "Stratification and Conflict Between Ethnolinguistic Communities with Different Social Structures." *The Canadian Review of Sociology and Anthropology* 15:148–57.

——
1984 "The Production and Allocation of Symbolic Resources: An Analysis of the Linguistic and Ethnocultural Fields in Canada." *The Canadian Review of Sociology and Anthropology* 21: 123–44.

Breton, Raymond and Gail Grant
1981 *La Langue de travail au Québec*. Montreal: L'Institut de Recherches politiques.

Breton, Raymond and Howard Roseborough
1968 "Ethnic, Religious and Regional Representation in the Federal Cabinet, 1867–1966. Unpublished.

Breton, Raymond and Daiva Stasiulis
1980 "Linguistic Boundaries and the Cohesion of Canada," part 3. In Raymond Breton, Jeffrey G. Reitz and Victor Valentine (eds.) *Cultural Boundaries and the Cohesion of Canada*. Montreal: The Institute for Research on Public Policy.

Brown, Craig
1969 "Introduction." In D.G. Creighton et al. (eds.) *Minorities, Schools and Politics*. Toronto: University of Toronto Press.

The Canadian Encyclopedia.
1985 Edmonton: Hurtig Publishers.

Careless, J.M.S.
1970 *Canada: A Story of Challenge*. Toronto: Macmillan of Canada.

Choquette, Robert
1975 *Language and Religion: A History of English-French Conflict in Ontario*. Ottawa: University of Ottawa Press.

Clark, S.D.
1962 *The Developing Canadian Community*. Toronto: University of Toronto Press.

Cole, Douglas
1971 "The Problem of 'Nationalism' and 'Imperialism' in British Settlement Colonies." *The Journal of British Studies* 10: 160–82.

Coleman, William
1984 *The Independence Movement in Quebec*. Toronto: University of Toronto Press.

Cornell, P.G., J. Hamelin, F. Ouellet, and M. Trudel
1967 *Canada: Unity in Diversity*. Toronto: Holt, Rinehart and Winston.

Faucher, Albert and Maurice Lamontagne
1953 "History of Industrial Development." In Jean-Charles Falardeau (ed.) *Essais sur le Québec contemporain; Essays on Contemporary Quebec*. Québec: Les Presses de l'Université Laval.

Fox, Paul
1969 "Regionalism and Confederation." In

Mason Wade (ed.) *Regionalism in the Canadian Community, 1867–1967*. Toronto: University of Toronto Press.

Frazier, Franklin
1957 *Race and Culture Contacts in the Modern World*. New York.

Friesen, Gerald
1984 *The Canadian Prairies: A History*. Toronto: University of Toronto Press.

Guindon, Hubert
1964 "Social Unrest, Social Class, and Quebec's Bureaucratic Revolution. *Queen's Quarterly* LXX: 150–62.

——
1968 "Two Cultures: An Essay on Nationalism, Class, and Ethnic Tension." In R.H. Leach (ed.) *Contemporary Canada*. Toronto: University of Toronto Press.

Hagy, James
1969 "Quebec Separatists: The First Twelve Years." *Queen's Quartely* LXXVI: 229–38.

Hamelin, Louis-Edmond
1961 "Evolution Numerique seculaire du clerge catholique dans le Québec," *Recherches Sociographiques* 2:189–238.

Henripin, Jacques
1957 "From Acceptance of Nature to Control: The Demography of the French Canadians Since the Seventeenth Century," *Canadian Journal of Economics and Political Science* 23:10–19.

Houston, Cecil and William Smyth
1980 *The Sash Canada Wore: A Historical Geography of the Orange Order in Canada*. Toronto: University of Toronto Press.

Jackson, John
1975 *Community and Conflict: A Study of French-English Relations in Ontario*. Toronto: Holt, Rinehart and Winston.

Juteau-Lee, Danielle and Jean Lapointe
1982 "The Emergence of Franco-Ontarians. New Identities, New Boundaries." In Jean L. Elliott (ed.) *Two Nations, Many Cultures: Ethnic Groups in Canada*. Scarborough, Ontario: Prentice-Hall.

Lalonde, André
1982 "Le Patriote de l'Ouest and French Settlement on the Prairies." In Raymond Breton and Pierre Savard (eds.) *The Quebec and Acadian Diaspora in North America*. Toronto: The Multicultural History Society of Ontario.

Lanctot, Gustave
1967 *Canada and the American Revolution, 1774–1783*. Toronto.

Lavoie, Yoland
1981 *L'Emigration des Québécois aux Etats-Unis de 1840 à 1930*. Quebec: Editeur Officiel du Québec.

Linteau, Paul-Andre, Rene Durocher, and Jean-Claude Robert
1979 *Histoire du Québec contemporain: de la Confédération à la Crise*. Quebec: Boréal Express.

Lupul, Manoly
1970 "Educational Crises in the New Dominion to 1917." In J. Donald Wilson et al. (eds.) *Canadian Education: A History*. Scarborough, Ontario: Prentice-Hall.

Mann, W.E.
1976 "The Canadian Church Union, 1925." In Stewart Crysdale and L. Wheatcroft (eds.) *Religion in Canadian Society*. Toronto: Macmillan.

McInnis, Edgar
1969 *Canada: A Political and Social History*. Toronto: Holt, Rinehart and Winston

McRae, Kenneth
1964 "The Structure of Canadian History," In Louis Hartz (ed.) *The Founding of New Societies*. New York.

——
1974 "Consociationalism and the Canadian Political System." In Kenneth McRae (ed.) *Consociational Democracies: Political Accommodation in Segmented Societies*. Toronto: McClelland and Stewart.

McRoberts, Kenneth and Dale Posgate
1980 Quebec: *Social Change and Political Crisis*. Toronto: McClelland and Stewart.

Murphy, Raymond
1984 "The Structure of Closure: A Critique and Development of the Theories of Weber, Collins, and Parkin." *The British Journal of Sociology* XXXV: 547–67.

Nielsen, Francois
1985 "Toward a Theory of Ethnic Solidarity in Modern Societies." *American Sociological Review*. 50:133–49.

Ormsby, William
1974 "The Province of Canada: The Emergence of Consociational Politics." In Kenneth D. McRae (ed.): *Consociational Democracy*. Toronto: McClelland and Stewart. (Originally published in 1969).

Ossenberg, Richard
1967 "The Conquest Revisited: Another Look at Canadian Dualism." *The Canadian Review of Sociology and Anthropology* 4:201–18.

Ouellet, Fernand
1967 *Histoire économique et sociale du Québec, 1760–1850*. Montreal: Fides.

Parkin, Frank
1979 *Marxism and Class Theory: A Bourgeois Critique*. London: Tavistock.

Pennefather, R.S.
1984 *The Orange and the Black*. Orange and Black Publications.

Pinard, Maurice and Richard Hamilton
1977 "The Independence Issue and the Polarization of the Electorate: The 1973 Quebec Election." *Canadian Journal of Political Science* 10:215–59.

——
1984 "The Class Bases of the Quebec Independence Movement: Conjectures and Evidence." *Ethnic and Racial Studies*, 7:19–54.

Richmond, Anthony
1967 *Post-War Immigrants in Canada*. Toronto: University of Toronto Press.

Schermerhorn, R.A.
1970 *Comparative Ethnic Relations*. New York: Random House.

Silver, A.I.
1982 *The French-Canadian Idea of Confederation, 1864–1900*. Toronto: University of Toronto Press.

Smith, M.G.
1974 *Corporations and Society*. London: Duckworth.

Spigelman, Martin
1975 "Race et religion: Les Acadiens et la hierarchie catholique irlandaise du Nouveau-Brunswick." *Revue d'Histoire de L'Amerique Francaise* 29: 69–85.

Stanley, George
1974 "The Federal Bargain: The Contractorian Basis of Confederation," In K.D. McRae (ed.) *op. cit.* (Originally published in 1956.)

Staples, Janice
1974 "Consociationalism at Provincial Level: The Erosion of Dualism in Manitoba, 1870–1890." In K.D. McRae (ed) *op. cit.*

van den Berghe, Pierre
1969 "Pluralism and the Polity: A Theoretical Exploration." In L. Kuper and M.G. Smith (eds.) *Pluralism in Africa*. Berkeley: University of California Press.

Watt, James
1967 "Anti-Catholic Nativism in Canada: The Protestant Protective Association." *The Canadian Historical Review* XLVIII: 45–58.

Canada is multi-ethnic and multi-racial, and debate continues on whether this makes for an ethnic "melting pot" or an ethnic "mosaic." *Courtesy of Dean Goodwin*

"Prejudice and discrimination continue to restrict the opportunities faced by the non-English and non-French immigrant groups in Canada. However, these inequalities are more severe for the visible minority groups."

c h a p t e r   t w e n t y - o n e

Ethnic and Race Relations

Morton Weinfeld

INTRODUCTION

This essay focuses on the conditions of the non-English, non-French, and non-indigenous peoples in Canada. These groups are often called "immigrant groups" though most are now native-born Canadians, or "non-charter groups." The taxonomy of ethnoracial groups in Canada has always been tricky when ethnic origin data are broken down into three categories: English, French, and Other. The latter category exists often more for convenience than as a description of a meaningful social entity.

If every ethnic group had its own chapter, this book would be huge. What legitimates our grouping these diverse groups into a single analytical unit are the relatively recent nature of their migration to Canada, their relatively small size, and their distinctive constitutional status compared to the English and French. As has been amply demonstrated elsewhere in this volume. English-speaking and French-speaking Canadians and Native peoples have distinctive constitutional provisions compared to the more general provisions affecting other groups.

The 1981 Canadian census provides ethnic origin data about the Canadian population; 92.4 percent of the population selected a single ethnic origin, while 7.6 percent selected a mixed ethnic origin (e.g., French and Polish). The census lists 9.7 million of British ethnic origin, 6.4 million French, and about half a million Native peoples, including Status and non-Status Indians, Métis, and Inuit. Thus, roughly 7.4 million Canadians fall into the groups to be discussed in this section: Canadians whose ethnic origin is fully or partially of a group other than the English, the French, or Native peoples.

Table 1 shows that these groups vary in many characteristics. They differ in size, immigration history, regional and urban/rural concentration, language abilities, and economic achievements. As important are cultural differences. We have groups with backgrounds far removed from Judeo-Christian culture and values, from Western or European civilization, and from urban industrial societies. Of all these differences, the distinction between visible minorities (usually Blacks, Orientals, Indo-Pakistanis), and the others is likely to emerge as the crucial demarcation line within this classification.

This chapter has two themes. The first deals with the extent to which these immigrant groups enjoy equality of opportunity and participation in Canadian society. Are members of these groups penalized, directly or indirectly, through prejudicial attitudes or acts of **discrimination**, and with what consequences? Can they pursue educational, occupational, and income opportunities? Are there certain sectors of achievement from which they are restricted? The pursuit of equality of opportunity, or simply of nondiscrimination and fair treatment, has long preoccupied social researchers, and is a cornerstone of Canadian public policy in the latter half of the twentieth century.

The second theme deals with the degree to which these ethnic and racial groups can perpetuate their cultures and retain their autonomy and identity, if they so desire. Are they free to organize as individuals or as collectivities, to promote cultural and other group interests? Does the state help or hinder them in these efforts? This issue has likewise been the focus of extensive research and public policy efforts by federal and provincial governments.

Let the reader be warned. No simple, clear-cut answers will emerge to these questions. Indeed, differing interpretations of data will lead to conclusions about how Canada is doing in these areas. Analyses may use differing measures, evidence, theoretical orientations, and expectations. Some will describe a cup as half empty, others, as half full.

In trying to assess Canada regarding equal opportunity and tolerance of cultural pluralism, we will look at historical evolution in an implicit context of Canada as a Western, liberal-democratic state. In its treatment of ethnic minorities, particularly in the twentieth century, Canada today compares *well* with most of the world's multi-ethnic societies, particularly those of the developing world. On the other hand, Canadians hold high expectations of living up to declared ideals, and thus we are often dissatisfied with conditions that others might praise. Finally, comparisons with conditions in the United States, a society much like Canada, will help isolate points of Canadian uniqueness, or illustrates common trends.

HISTORICAL BACKGROUND

One way to begin our discussion is to analyze the dominant myths surrounding differing American and Canadian approaches to ethnic diversity. America has been described as a **melting pot**, whereas Canada has been termed a **mosaic**. According to the melting pot image of the United States, the immigrant waves were encouraged to (or depending on which historian you read, permitted to, or forced to) relinquish their Old World ties and become full and equal American citizens, sharing in the opportunities offered in American society. The term melting pot was popularized in a 1908 play by Israel Zangwill, and the metaphor implied that America was a boiling cauldron into which the various metals of Europe would be thrown, the Old World impurities boiled off, and a new entity, an American, would be created (see Gordon, 1964, chap. 5).

Canada, by contrast, was a mosaic in which immigrant groups were encouraged to (or again, permitted to, or forced to) retain their Old World attachments, cultures, and identities, without the same drive for a common inclusive Canadian citizenship and identity, and without equal opportunity. The term mosaic was popularized in the 1938 book *Canadian Mosaic* by John Murray Gibbon, which described the various Canadian ethnic groups. In 1965, the term was given added currency in John Porter's *The Vertical Mosaic*, which argued that Canada's ethnic groups were ordered in a rigid hierarchy of power and economic status, with the dominant British charter group at the top.

These metaphors did not spring from a vacuum. Aspects of history and the constitutional development of Canada and the United States helped condition their acceptance. The American pilgrims were identified as religious dissenters, committed to religious tolerance; the first pioneers in Canada were traders and colonizers, interested more in commercial gain than religious liberty. Some analysts have argued that the revolution in the United States signified more clearly a break with the Old World, with its emphasis on aristocracy and inherited status (Lipset, 1970, 1985:109–60), than did events in Canada, which have been seen as born from a counter-revolution. That English Canada never mobilized for a bloody war of independence and subsequently received as immigrants thousands of former American loyalists supposedly committed to the Crown would make Canada the more conservative society, thus less open to full acceptance of other immigrant groups. Ironically, French-Canadian society, which had been formed well before the French Revolution of 1789, likewise supported this conservative mould, particularly in the entrenched power of the Catholic Church.

Differences are also reflected in the constitutions of the two societies. The American document was more liberal, and the Bill of Rights, with its guarantees of fundamental rights for all American citizens, emphasizes commonalities rather than differences. The American Constitution is silent on particularisms like language or ethnic origin.

The British North America Act of 1867 was much less a universal document, and proclaims no majestic vision of a new society with equal rights and freedoms guaranteed for all citizens. Compare the American "life, liberty, and the pursuit of happiness" with the Canadian "peace, order, and good government." The B.N.A. Act is a contractual agreement between two founding peoples, defining a new state with four provinces. Far from a document espousing equal rights for all groups, the B.N.A. Act grants certain religious groups (Protestants and Catholics) and speakers of certain languages (English and French) special rights. The B.N.A. Act recognized collectivities as legitimate actors and emphasized group rights over those of the individual citizen.

Thus, according to these images, immigrant groups in America would tend to assimilate and begin the process of upward economic mobility. Various American symbols reinforced this image in the public consciousness: the motto *e pluribus unum* on American coins, the Statue of Liberty welcoming poor immigrants to Ellis island (still a powerful symbol, as we have recently seen), and the pledge of allegiance and English unilingualism of the public school systems.

But, apart from constitutional rhetoric and national symbols, what of the reality? John Porter (1979) argued that the life lived by immigrants and the views of dominant elites in both societies was remarkably similar, combining elements of a melting pot and mosaic position. In Amer-

CANADA–U.S. DIFFERENCES IN THE CENSUS

Another symbolic difference is the role of the census in the two societies. In the United States, the separation of church and state and the constitutional emphasis on equality and universalism has precluded questions about religious affiliation or ethnic origin; the closest approximation of the latter has been place of birth, or mother tongue, which has not been useful for third generation ethnics. The Canadian census, by contrast, has asked questions about ethnic origin (before 1951 the wording was "racial" origin), which traditionally was traced back to the first patrilineal ancestor who emigrated to Canada. These questions, as well as questions on religion and language, permit a more precise breakdown of the ethnic characteristics of Canada's population. In 1981, the Canadian census was modified to eliminate the patrilineal bias "To which ethnic or cultural group did you or your ancestors belong on first coming to this continent?" For the first time, the 1981 census accepted multiple answers on ethnic ancestry.

ica, the ethnic groups did not melt, i.e., disappear, as was discovered by American sociologists who chronicled the rediscovery — revival — of American ethnicity in the post-war period (Glazer and Moynihan, 1970; Novak, 1973). In Canada, the passing of generations has revealed substantial ethnic **assimilation**, and the fact that the mosaic is not as rigidly vertical as once believed. Moreover, despite the noble sentiments inscribed on the Statue of Liberty, American immigrants encountered substantial hostility, discrimination, and paternalism. Canadian immigrants were also quick to realize that their ancestral cultures and values were not highly valued in a society that was resolutely Anglophilic in matters cultural, social, and intellectual (Porter, 1965).

In Canada, certainly, non-British, non-French immigrants remained on the margins of mainstream society until well into the middle of the twentieth century. Canadian racism in the nineteenth and early twentieth century was an interesting mixture of scientific racism (the idea that different nationalities were racially distinct and hierarchically ordered in abilities), Anglo-Protestant elitism, class snobbery, and, a peculiar Canadian contribution, the effect of the image of the North (Berger, 1966). Briefly, Canadian elites had habitually denigrated "Southern" traits associated with the United States. Northern races were seen as superior because of their ability to withstand the rigours of the cold, and thus survive in the tough Canadian climate and terrain. Anglo-Saxons, the French, and all other Northern European races shared this trait, while Southern races, which included the Southern Mediterranean, non-Whites, and eventually Americans, were given to sloth, laziness and vice. They lacked the virtues of stability and order; American had an excess of liberty, typified by admission of large numbers of Blacks, and, of course, by the bloody Civil War.

Thus, the climatic theme is a singular Canadian contribution to a disreputable page of intellectual history, and it persisted for some time. Indeed, up until 1952, Canadian immigration policy retained a climate unsuitability clause. And Canada's Governor-General Vincent Massey could write, in 1948:

> Climate plays a great part in giving us our special character, different from that of our southern neighbours . . . it influences our mentality, produces sober temperament. Our racial composition—and this partly because of our climate—is different, too. A small percentage of our people come from central or southern Europe. The vast majority spring either from the British Isles or Northern France, and many, too, from Scandinavia and Germany, and it is in northwestern Europe that one finds the elements of human stability highly developed. Nothing is more characteristic of Canadians than the inclination to be moderate (Berger, 1966:23).

How can we assess the historical experience of these groups? Here, we must be careful of overgeneralization. Visible minorities, specifically Blacks and Orientals, fared worst. Blacks first arrived in Canada in the early 1600s and by the middle of the eighteenth century there were four thousand slaves (including some Native peoples) in Canada, along with communities of free Blacks, notably in Nova Scotia (Krauter and Davis, 1978). The Emancipation Act of the British Empire in 1833 ended slavery in Canada. Between 1850 and 1860 about twenty thousand Blacks entered Canada through the "underground railroad," though many returned home during and after the Civil War. *De jure* discrimination against Blacks persisted until well into the twentieth century; only in 1954 was the Nova Scotia Education Act amended to prohibit separate facilities for Blacks.

The Chinese experience of Canada began when seventeen thousand males were "imported" to help build the Canadian Pacific Railroad in the 1880s. With the completion of the railroad, these labourers were left with no funds to pay their way back to China, and thus became a floating pool of cheap and exploited labour. Moreover, the Chinese in Canada faced a host of discriminatory taxes, including a 1876 tax on the common pigtail worn by Chinese males. All these legal and quasi-legal restrictions were reflected in low educational and occupational status and high levels of poverty. Nevertheless, Chinese immigrants kept coming, until Canada passed a Chinese Immigration Act in 1923, keeping them out; from 1923 to 1947, only forty-four Chinese legally entered Canada.

No matter how difficult the legacy of Canada's racist past, it cannot compare with the ongoing American burden of slavery and segregation. Despite the creation of a new Black middle class, the cumulative impact of legal and institutional racism has, over generations, created a large Black American urban underclass, trapped in a tangle of welfare, unemployment, crime, and family breakdown (Wilson, 1978). The post-war legal and illegal immigration of millions of Hispanics, particularly from Mexico and Puerto Rico, has created in the American Southwest and Northeast an additional visible minority grouping struggling with poverty and prejudice (Glazer, 1985).

Blacks in Canada may comprise 1 to 2 percent of the population, compared to at least 10 to 12 percent in the United States. But since Canadian Blacks are predominantly foreign-born (largely from the Caribbean), most have been spared the generational disadvantages of the American Black population. Even in the United States, West Indian Blacks fare better economically than do American-born Blacks.

What of the early European White immigrants? Here the picture is more complex. These immigrants also encountered racism, paternalism, and blatant discrimination in employment, housing, education, etc. Their lot was hard, many working on farms or joining the new urban working class. In America, revisionist scholars have been quick to document the difficulties of upward mobility, or the racism and discrimination which immigrants faced. A typical volume was entitled *The Ordeal of Assimilation* (Feldstein and Costello, 1974). In Canada, the effect of John Porter's *The Vertical Mosaic*, including its discussion of racist sentiments in Canada, the objectively low economic status of immigrant groups throughout the first decades of this century, and their absence from elite positions even after the World War II, also has reinforced the message of the struggle and difficulties facing immigrants.

Yet these observations are insufficient to allow us to assess whether Canada provided reasonable opportunity for immigrants who arrived at the turn of the century and later. Nor does the fact that Canadians held racist attitudes towards non-White and European minorities alike resolve the issue. To paraphrase an old Jewish joke, a racist is someone who hates minorities more than is absolutely necessary. Indeed, several factors suggest that a benign interpretation of the early historical record is possible for the European immigrants.

First, as shall be documented below, the economic achievement of the children and grandchildren of these immigrants suggests that the important foundations for realizing equality were being laid. Scholars sometimes forget that many immigrants were hardly literate in any language, and disoriented by the trauma of immigration to a new and puzzling society. That many gravitated to farming or to unskilled or semi-skilled labour is thus not surprising. Moreover, that type of work was common to all Canadians of lower-class or working-class background, not only immigrants.

Second, large percentages of immigrants migrated back to the original countries, from both Canada and the United States. Estimates of this return migration are as high as one-third. For many, the original migration had been motivated by the desire to return to their homeland with sufficient money to purchase land. Some of the returnees may have been overcome by nostalgia or loneliness, and others may have found the poverty or discrimination in the new society too burdensome. (I suspect this latter group would be a minority, since poverty and occasional oppression were regular features of life in the Old World). But, in short, these immigrants were free to return; the majority of them did not (actually many Canadians may have moved to the United States). Their expectations were probably realistically tailored to the feasible. Most studies of immigrant attitudes or satisfaction, in any case, miss one key explanatory variable. What motivates many immigrants is not their own well-being, but a perception that their children and grandchildren will ultimately be better off. Semi-literate peasants arriving in the New World did not really expect to be business executives or doctors, though they held higher hopes for their descendants. And in this, of course, they were clearly right.

Third, overtly negative racism was not the only sentiment expressed by the elites. The existing xenophobia and **prejudice** was mixed with positive, if paternalistic, stereotypes (stalwart peasants in sheepskin coats), and with voluntary organizations aimed at helping immigrants adjust to their new land. One way to assess the historic record of tolerance and justice in the Canadian past is to focus on some of the worst episodes of discriminatory treatment. The severe victimization of Canada's Native peoples is described elsewhere in this volume. Earlier, we alluded briefly to the early tribulations of Blacks and Chinese workers. In the twentieth century, perhaps the two worst episodes were the deliberate exclusion of German Jewish refugees from Canada before and during World War II and the forced relocation of Canadian Japanese following Pearl Harbor.

The deliberate inaction on the part of the Canadian government, given the plight of European Jewry, has been well documented (Abella and Troper, 1983). While other factors, such as economic worries in the Depression era, played a role, anti-Semitic prejudice throughout the Canadian population, and in key federal civil servants and politicians, was important in keeping Canada's doors closed to Jewish victims of Nazi persecution.

The relocation of the Japanese is perhaps the greater tragedy, in that it involved thousands of Canadian citizens and residents (Adachi, 1976). Fuelled by a deep current of anti-Japanese (and anti-Oriental) resentment, which may have included jealousy about the prosperity of the hard-working Japanese of British Columbia and fears of an invasion of the "Yellow Peril" from the Pacific, Canada's War Measures Act was invoked. An order-in-council authorizing the evacuation of "persons of the Japanese race" was passed on February 24, 1942. (Ironically, this episode is one of the few cases where Canada acted earlier than the United States.) The Japanese were evacuated into the interior of Canada, sent to resettlement camps where movements were restricted, and had their property sold at below market prices. After the war, close to four thousand Japanese signed "voluntary" deportation orders, which sent them back to Japan.

The injustice to Japanese Canadians can be better grasped by the fact that prior to these steps, not one Japanese Canadian had been charged, let alone convicted, of sabotage. In other words, there was no objective basis of national security threats warranting such action. Equally disgraceful has been the lethargy of the Canadian government in redressing that wrong through some public apology and monetary compensation.

And yet these two terrible episodes of ethnic victimization, ironically, offer grounds for optimism. The Japanese camps were not comparable in any way to extermination camps or labour camps of the Nazis, despite the resonance of the term "concentration camps." Not one Japanese Canadian was executed or murdered by the Canadian state. Nor were there deaths by lynchings, or by bloody pogroms or massacres. These are not trivial facts. They indicate that Canada's foundation as a liberal-democratic society limited the oppression of its minorities.

Indeed, Canada has made significant strides since World War II in enhancing the human and civil rights of its minorities. Thus, Jews and Japanese Canadians, demoralized communities after the war, were by 1970 achieving economically well above the Canadian average in education, occupation, and income (see Table 2), and participating vigorously in all sectors of Canadian society.

One other major change has occurred. The role of the federal and provincial governments and courts has been dramatically transformed. As the sorry history of Blacks, Jews, Japanese, Chinese, and Native peoples reveals, government historically was the direct or indirect agency of minority misfortunes. Discrimination was either perpetrated or tolerated by the government well into the later half of the twentieth century. As Canada moves into the twenty-first century, the Canadian state has moved from active oppression and past indifference to championing the rights of minority groups. The state and its institutions are formally committed to ensuring for Canadian minority groups both equal economic opportunity and continued cultural survival.

Many factors have played a role in this transformation of the role of government. The horrors of World War II seeping into public consciousness finally prodded the Canadian (and American) governments to act vigorously against racism. Rising levels

Table 1
DEMOGRAPHIC CHARACTERISTICS OF SELECTED ETHNIC GROUPS[1] IN CANADA, 1981

	Black[2]	*Chinese*	*Czech & Slovak*	*Dutch*	*Filipino*	*German*	*Greek*	*Italian*	*Japanese*	*Jewish*	*Polish*	*Portuguese*	*Scandinavian*	*Indo-Pakistani*[9]	*Indo-Chinese*[10]	*Ukrainian*	*Yugoslavian*	*All Canada*
Size in 000's	241	300	86	408[6]	76	1100[6]	164	872	46	294	254[6]	195	283[6]	222	56	746	128	24 200
% born in Canada	20	27	58	66	21	—	43	54	75	66	41	26	83	24	10	89	41	84
Age Structure																		
% 0–14	24	24	20	20	31	15	29	24	22	20	12	29	14	—	30	23	24	23
15–24	18	19	17	21	11	20	16	20	16	14	15	19	16	—	25	19	16	19
25–44	42	35	31	30	42	30	32	20	31	30	30	31	32	—	35	28	32	29
45–64	13	16	22	21	13	25	18	20	23	18	22	17	24	14	—	20	21	19
65 +	3	7	11	7	3	10	4	6	8	15	7	3	16	3	—	10	6	10
% with Ethnic[3] Mother Tongue	—	73	49	40	46	34	75	60	46	13[8]	50	81	19	53	75	37	—	13
% with Ethnic[3] (F.B.)	—	—	22[5]	7[5]	40[5]	10[5]	57	41	23	4	21	65	2	43	72	12	—	7
Home Languages (N.B.)		31																
% able to speak[4]																		
English	91	81	98	95	98	95	89	80	95	99	90	75	95	86	68	99	—	82
French	18	4	10	6	3	5	17	22	5	30	9	16	4	7	28	5	—	32
Neither	—	19	—	1	1	1	6	—	—	1	1	20	1	—	18	—	—	1
% living in																		
Toronto	51	31	17	8	39	7	41	37	29	40	20	47	13	36	17	—	33	12
Montreal	20	6	6	1	6	2	31	19	3	32	7	12	3	7	22	—	5	12
Vancouver	3	29	8	7	14	6	4	5	27	5	5	4	20	17	7	—	8	5
All 3	74	66	31	16	59	15	76	61	59	77	32	63	36	60	46	20	46	29

% unemployed																			
Male	7.2	4.2	3.6	—	3.5	3.4	6.5[7]	4.5	3.1	4.7	—	5.3[7]	3.9	4.8	8.4	4.8[7]	6.1	6.5	7.4[7]
Female	8.5	5.4	6.4	—	4.0	5.5		7.1	5.0	6.9	—		6.0	9.8	12.2			8.7	
Occupation																			
% Mgr & Admin.	n.a.	8	10	9	—	9	7	6	10	19	—	4	—	8	5	9	6	9	
% Technical/ Scientific	6	11	12	—	7	—	—	—	12	13	—	—	—	9	9	6	6	7	
% Medicine/ Health	11	5	5	—	21	—	—	—	—	7	—	—	—	5	5	—	3	10	
Education																			
% < grade 9	11	21	18	13	9	40	31	36	11	12	25	51	20	15	20	22	23	20	
% some university	18	28	30	55	60	20	14	12	29	41	33	5	50	35	29	17	18	16	
average male income	14.9	15.1	19.2	—	15.1	—	14.6	16.2	18.7	26.4	—	14.9	—	17.6	10.5	17.1	13.7[7]	16.9	12.7[7]
average female income (in 000's)	9.2	9.0	9.5	—	11.6	—	7.6	8.0	9.4	12.0	—	7.7	—	8.6	7.0	8.6		8.4	

[1]Unless specifically indicated, data are for Canadians who indicated whole or partial ethnic identity for the specific group.

[2]Includes Caribbean. (May include some Whites and Asians as well.)
[3]"Ethnic" languages refer to languages other than English or French.
[4]Bilinguals (English–French) are included, leading to double counting and percentages greater than 100.
[5]Single figure denotes home language for both foreign-born and native (Canadian)-born combined.
[6]For those reporting single ethnic origin.
[7]Single figure denotes rate for males and females combined.
[8]Yiddish and Hebrew
[9]Includes persons who reported an origin from the Indian subcontinent such as Indian, Pakistani, Bengali, Gujarati, Punjabi, Tamil, Sinhalese, Sri Lankan, or Bangladeshi.
[10]Includes persons reporting Thai, Vietnamese, Kampuchean/Cambodian, Laotian, Malay, or Burmese origin (over 70% of the immigrants from these groups in Canada in 1981 had come within the previous three years).

Source: Socio-Economic Profiles of Selected Ethnic/Visible Minority Groups. Multiculturalism Canada, March 1986.

of education may have sapped the strength of many popular racist prejudices. Certainly, pressure from victimized groups, including militant actions, have also moved public opinion and government policy. A neo-Marxist could describe **multiculturalism** in Canada as a ploy to retain hegemony of the ruling Anglo group through a divide and rule approach, and as a means of deflecting class consciousness and obscuring economic contradictions. A cynic could put it down to a plain design by politicians to buy ethnic votes. Yet, as important as motive is the fact of this transformation, and its ongoing consequences.

DEMOGRAPHIC OVERVIEW

The immigrant groups in Canada range from large groups, such as Germans who number over one million, to a host of smaller groups who number in the hundreds, according to the 1981 census. In fact, the census found over eighty specific ethnic origin groups in Canada. Table 1, pages 594–95, describes the largest groups.

If we group Blacks, Chinese, Filipino, Japanese, Indo-Pakistani, and Indo-Chinese as visible minority groups, we note that the White European immigrant groups tend to be the "older" groups, i.e., those for whom the foundations of the community were laid long ago. Thus only 10 percent of Canada's Indo-Chinese population are born in Canada, compared to 89 percent of the Ukrainian.

Here too, we find a Canadian–American difference. In Canada, a large proportion among the Southern European immigrants (Greek, Italian, Portuguese) are foreign-born, post-1945 immigrants (see Table 1). In the United States, Americans of Southern European origin are more likely to trace their ancestry back to the turn of the century. Any cross-national comparisons of such ethnic groups (e.g., Italians) must take this difference into account. Not surprisingly, Canadian groups with a greater immigrant proportion are more likely to claim an ethnic language as their mother tongue or language of home use. Visible minority groups in Canada, compared to European immigrant groups, are more likely to have higher immigrant (and recent immigrant) proportions, come from developing as opposed to industrially developed regions, retain their ethnic languages, live in Canada's largest cities and — as we shall see — have less economic success and face greater degrees of discrimination.

No discussion of ethnicity in Canada could be complete without a digression on the Canadian census, which asks many questions pertaining to ethnic research. Apart from the ethnic origin question itself, there are questions about religion, mother tongue, language used in the home, official language knowledge, and place of birth. These data enable social scientists to put together analytical profiles not only of groups, but of subgroups within them. Thus, one can study differences between Ukrainian Catholics and Ukrainian Orthodox, or the peculiarities of Jewish (by ethnic origin) atheists, or Italian Unitarians, or patterns of interethnic or interreligious marriage. The strengths of the Canadian census are obvious: it is comprehensive, it is replicated every ten years, and it asks questions of clear interest to students of ethnic relations. But its data have important limitations.

1. Census enumerators are told to discourage respondents from selecting an ethnic origin in the New World, i.e., Canadian or American. Nevertheless, nearly seventy-six thousand hardy souls chose "Canadian" as their ethnic origin in 1981. But census procedures obviously inflate the size of ethnic groups, particularly the older European ones. A fifth generation

Canadian of Germany ancestry may be classified as German without being able to speak German, and never having read or heard of Goethe.

2. Some groups, notably Blacks, may be undercounted because the census has been poorly equipped to identify racial minorities (Winks, 1971). The census lists categories of ethnic ori gins that would be all or mainly Black: African (divided into African Black, Canadian Black, Other African, Other Black), Haitian, Caribbean. The figure of 241 000 Blacks in Table 1 is an estimate, based on several census categories and extrapolations to Canadian-born children of Caribbean-born adults.

3. Prior to 1981, the census could not adequately classify many Canadians of mixed ancestry. The patrilineal criterion was used then largely because of the importance of the father's surname. Even the 7 percent of the population in 1981 who claimed multiple ethnic origin understates the extent of mixed ethnic heritage.

4. Claims of ethnic origin can be changed by political events. When the Austro-Hungarian Empire collapsed, many Austrians in Canada disappeared, as did some German Canadians in the censi of 1921 and 1941. Some respondents, enumerators, or the computer also may be confused. Thus, the 1981 census identified almost six thousand of Canada's Native peoples as claiming Hindu, Moslem, or Sikh religion.

5. The Canadian census does not measure the subjective elements of ethnic identity, nor the range of interactions with an ethnic culture or an ethnic community. The data can measure assimilation through linguistic transfer, or loss of the ethnic language as mother tongue or as language of home use. This pattern can be seen in Table 1 where the proportions knowing or claiming the ethnic language as mother tongue are larger than those using it as the home language. This indicates linguistic assimilation. But the census does not measure second (passive) language knowledge. Many ethnic Canadians have *some* knowledge of their ethnic language, but cannot claim it as their mother tongue.

IMMIGRATION

At Confederation, Canada's population was almost exclusively of French or English origin. Over the years, the immigrant groups have increased their proportion in the Canadian population.

In 1871, the British and French comprised almost 92 percent of the Canadian population. Following the mass migrations of the late 1800s and early 1900s, the balance began shifting. By 1911, their proportion was down to 84 percent, and by 1931, to 80 percent. Immigration was curtailed in the 1930s and through World War II, only to pick up again in the 1940s. The proportions for 1951 through 1981 were 79 percent, 74 percent, 73 percent, and 72 percent. (the latter figure computed only for single origin claimants).

There has also been a continuing diversification of the sources of immigrants. Great Britain remains the major country of origin for Canadian immigrants, though some of these British immigrants may belong to other ethnic or racial groupings. But the sources of immigration have moved from Great Britain and Northern and Eastern Europe to Southern Europe (Italy, Greece, Spain, Portugal) in the postwar period, and to countries in the developing world. For example, in 1961, the ten leading sources of immigrants to Canada for any prior period were all European countries. They contributed almost 81 percent of the immigrants of theperiod, and Great Britain had contributed 30 percent. For the period 1971–81, by contrast, six of the ten leading source countries were non-European (India, Philippines, Jamaica, Vietnam, Hong Kong, and Guyana). These ten countries contributed only 57 percent of immigrants, and Great Britain only 14 percent. (See Canada's Immigrants, Statistics Canada, August, 1984, Cat. 99-936). Public perception of these changes in Canada's ethnic composition may be heightened because of the tendency of the more recent immigrant groups, both Southern European and visible minority groups, to congregate in the major Canadian cities under the glare of media and political attention.

Analysts of immigration in Canada monitor the degree of ethnic or racial exclusivity which has characterized Canadian immigration policy. Canada, like most countries, has set its immigration policy in terms of quantity and origin of immigrants to meet perceived economic needs and national self-interest. Toward the end of the nineteenth century, large numbers of European immigrants were recruited to fill the open private expanses, to create a population presence sufficient to prevent any American expansion northward, and to help unite the new Canadian state from coast to coast. Ever since, Canada has adjusted immigration to meet various manpower needs, seeking out alternatively unskilled and highly skilled manpower, the latter to meet Canada's historic lack of highly trained human capital. Even today, immigrants continue to meet economic needs, some arriving through the **points system** as highly qualified professionals. Others, often refugees, work at low level jobs many Canadians would not accept.

Throughout the twentieth century, Canada preferred European immigrants. Until 1962, geographic quotas that discriminated against non-Europeans were in effect. Beginning in the 1960s, and culminating in the 1967 Immigration Act, a new points system was introduced which was supposedly racially and ethnically neutral. Independent immigrants would receive points for universal attributes, such as knowledge of English or French, educational and occupational skills, etc. The points system, combined with provisions for family re-unification, has changed the composition of Canadian immigrants. But critics say that the system may be biased against non-White immigrants. For example, there were too few Canadian immigration offices in some Third World countries relative to the demand. Awarding points to prospective immigrants for job offers in hand might also favour Europeans, who could better make such arrangements. The immigration officer may award up to ten points at his/her discretion, an area where latent racism might surface. Even emphasizing education may penalize Third World immigrants, who may not be as likely as Europeans to have higher education, or whose educational credentials might be discounted. Ironically, by admitting highly skilled immigrants from developing nations, Canada stands accused of promoting a "brain drain" and hindering their economic development.

Canada in the 1980s has declared itself decisively committed to a two-pronged policy regarding Canada's ethnic and racial minorities. First, is the achievement of a true equality of opportunity by eliminating invidious discrimination, creating a climate of intergroup harmony. Where needed, government will act affirmatively to increase opportunities for minority groups, primarily visible minorities, often through the role of human rights commissions. Second, is the commitment to encourage minority groups to retain their cultures and promote their communal sur-

THE "MEANING" OF IMMIGRANTS

As the ethnic composition of immigrants has shifted, debates about the optimal levels of immigration to Canada are often imbued with an undertone of racial concern. Indeed, many recent Canadian public opinion polls on immigration may be simultaneously tapping attitudes about racial minorities. For many Canadians, the word immigrant may be synonymous with non-White. Increasing immigration to Canada would mean increasing the proportions of non-Whites in the country. As public expressions of overt racism fall into disfavour, they may be replaced by concerns about "excessive" immigration, or the "absorptive" capacity of Canada.

One area of ongoing debate has been in refugee policy. The tragic story of the Canadian response to the plight of European Jewry was alluded to above. A comparable challenge was placed before Canada in the late 1970s and early 1980s by Indo-Chinese "boat people," masses of refugees fleeing communism in Southeast Asia. Although there was deep evidence of Canadian reluctance (via public opinion) to mount a massive rescue effort, the Canadian government tried to facilitate the rescue and acceptance of these desperate refugees. The Canadian census of 1981 revealed fifty-six thousand Indo-Chinese living in Canada. Fully 70 percent had arrived in the previous three years, though not all had arrived as refugees. The Canadian government did not bar the door, as it had in the 1930s.

vival by guaranteeing their freedom of association and, where needed, by supporting their efforts at communal and cultural development. These two orientations define cultural pluralism in Canada today. Multicultural policies and ministries aim primarily to achieve this second objective.

EQUAL OPPORTUNITY AND MULTICULTURALISM

The first major step taken to protect human rights in Canada was the Canadian Bill of Rights, passed as an Act of Parliament in 1961. The bill addressed equality in only one clause, which maintained: "the right of the individual to equality before the law without discrimination by reason of race, national origin, colour or sex." The Bill of Rights proved ineffective as a defence of minority rights. Several provincial statutes limiting discrimination were likewise not authoritative.

Another step to protect minorities was the introduction of hate literature amendments to Canada's criminal code in 1966. These amendments prohibited the advocacy or promotion of genocide, and provided that a person "who, by communicating statements, other than in private conversation, willfully promotes hatred against any identifiable group," was guilty of an offence. This provision against group defamation knows no parallel in American legislation, where it might be construed an abridgement of free speech. For close to two decades, the hate literature amendments remained largely dormant. They were used only once, in a 1981 case involving promotions of hatred against French Canadians in Essex County, Ontario; a lower court conviction was overturned on appeal (Berger, 1981: 271). At any rate, in 1985, there were two convictions under these sections of the criminal code. The first conviction involved James Keegstra, an Alberta social studies highschool teacher who had been charged with promoting anti-Semitism in his classroom over a ten-year period. Keegstra argued that an international Jewish conspiracy lurked behind all the events of recent world history (Bercuson and Wertheimer, 1985). The second case was the Ontario conviction of Donald Andrews and Robert Smith, charged with promoting hatred against non-Whites in their white supremacist publication, *Nationalist Report*. They argued that non-Whites should be segregated from Aryans and repatriated.

These convictions and that of philo-Nazi publisher Ernst Zundel under a different section of the criminal code, raised painful questions. During the trials, courts were used as forums for the propagation of hatred. Some Canadians felt that the extensive media coverage of the trials could lead to an increase in anti-Sematic or racist sentiments, quite apart from offending the sensitivities of minorities by the factual reporting of racist messages. One study, however, found that the opposite took place: Canadians who followed media reports of the Zundel trial became more sympathetic to Jews, not less (Weimann and Winn, 1986). These trials brought into focus value conflicts between two important Canadian societal principles: opposition to racism and bigotry, and freedom of speech and expression. The Canadian courts have confirmed that the willful promotion of hatred against minority groups lies outside the protection of free speech.

The next legislative initiative on behalf of minority protection, and civil rights generally, was the passage of the Canadian Human Rights Act in 1977, and corresponding measures passed around the same time in all Canadian provinces. This Act, while also lacking constitutional entrenchment, went much further than the 1961 Bill of Rights Act, and established the Canadian Human Rights Commission as a watchdog and champion for victims of discrimination.

While these efforts to protect minorities were occurring, parallel steps were taken to enact a multicultural policy, and to assist Canadian ethnic groups in enhancing their own cultures. The idea of multiculturalism emerged from volume IV of the Report of the Commission on Bilingualism and Biculturalism in the 1960s. That volume dealt with the contribution of the "other ethnic groups" to Canada. The dualistic English and French focus of the Commission tended to make the other ethnic groups insecure, feeling they somehow would be relegated to second class status. In 1971, a multicultural policy was enunciated, which committed the Canadian government to the support of ethnic groups and their activities, and led to the setting up of a bureaucratic machinery, The Secretary of State for Multiculturalism, to channel financial support to various minority groups. In promulgating the policy, the Canadian government also endorsed the "multicultural assumption" that a positive sense of one's own ethnic identity would lead to tolerance and respect for other groups. Thus, multiculturalism, it was felt, would promote harmony. Research in Canada and elsewhere has generally not found strong support for this view. Rather, evidence suggests a kind of ethnocentric effect, so that greater preoccupation with one's own group makes one more distant from and antipathetic to others (LeVine and Campbell, 1972, Berry et al., 1977). Both the prohibition against discrimination and the commitment to multiculturalism have found their way into the new Canadian constitution and, specifically, the Canadian Charter of Rights and Freedoms.

Section 15 prohibits discrimination on certain grounds, and explicitly permits **affirmative action** programs based on preferences for disadvantaged groups:

> **15.1.** Every individual is equal before and under the law and has the right to the equal protection and equal benefit of the law without discrimination and in particular, without discrimination based on race, national or ethnic origin, colour, religion, sex, age, or mental or physical disability.
> **15.2.** Subsection (1) does not preclude any law, program or activity that has as its object the amelioration of conditions of disadvantaged individuals or groups including those that are disadvantaged because of race, national or ethnic origin, colour, religion, sex, age or mental or physical disability.

The Charter of Rights and Freedoms does not nullify the Human Rights Act of 1977, with its more detailed protections against discrimination in employment in federal agencies or Crown corporations. It is not yet clear how far these protections of section 15 will extend. This section only came into effect in 1985, as provinces were given three years from passage in 1982 to bring their provincial statutes in line with the Charter. Canadian courts have not yet developed a body of cases and decisions on the Charter that would define fully the range of protection offered, particularly regarding the acceptability of affirmative action programs which may adversely affect opportunities for majority group members. Historically, Canadian courts have not been as vigorous as American courts in interpreting or extending statutes to maximize the rights of citizens. Indeed, it is still unclear whether the protections of section 15 extend to all areas of public life or simply those under explicit federal jurisdiction.

One nagging problem is that the provinces may opt out of the requirements of section 15 by passing legislation under section 33, the "notwithstanding clause." In other words, a province could invoke section 33 and then, for a five-year period, pass and enforce a law discriminating against non-Whites, redheads, or any group. Section 1 of the Charter also provides an escape from the requirements of non-discrimination, due to "reasonable limits prescribed by law as can be demonstrably justified in a free and democratic society." These "reasonable limits" would be defined by courts on a case by case basis, if challenged.

Section 15.2 also highlights a fundamental difference in human rights in Canada and the United States, regarding affirmative action. In the United States, neither the Civil Rights Act of 1964 nor the fourteenth amendment of the constitution contain wording legitimating affirmative action. In fact, they require states to guarantee to every person equal protection of the laws, and prohibit any discrimination (along the lines of Canada's, section 15.1). The impetus for affirmative action in the United States has come from executive orders, namely, directives from the White House, which have been periodically sustained by court decisions (Benokraitis and Feagin, 1978). Thus, the constitutional basis for affirmative action is much less explicit in the United States than in Canada.

Two other sections of the Charter are important for ethnic groups. The first is sections 2 (c,d), which grant to "everyone" (not only to citizens, as for democratic rights) freedom of peaceful assembly and of association. These freedoms facilitate the creation and growth of ethnic voluntary organizations. Section 27 is a vague section whose aim is probably rhetorical; in fact, constitutional experts do not know what the clause may mean practically, or how courts might eventually interpret it

(Hogg, 1982; Tarnopolsky, 1982:345–442).

"The Charter shall be interpreted in a manner consistent with the preservation and enhancement of the multicultural heritage of Canadians." For example, if a person's multicultural heritage involves regular use of marijuana, or beating one's spouse (offences under the Criminal Code), Canadian courts would not likely accept a defence under section 27.

The broad Canadian constitutional and legal context tries to maximize individual rights and freedoms, while recognizing the role of group rights. The concern with group rights, with collectivities, such as ethnic or language groups or Native peoples, reflects a heritage of continental European political thought and experience, where history was shaped largely by intergroup clashes and emerging nationalisms. It has certainly been a dominant preoccupation of the French minority in Canada. The concern with individual rights and freedoms reflects the legacy of the British philosophy and historical experience. The liberal tradition, from John Locke to John Stuart Mill, was concerned with the relations between the individual citizen and the state; the idea of the social contact linked individuals with their ruler.

We should note that Canada's constitution remains unfinished. If amendments like those agreed to in the spring of 1987 come into effect, power may flow from the federal government to the provinces. Yet, when it comes to the issue of the protection of minority rights, some might argue that it is the federal government that has a better track record than the provinces. Changes in the federal–provincial balance of power may well have repercussions for Canada's ethnic and racial minorities.

The Canadian government faces a difficult task. In promoting equal opportunity and prohibiting discrimination on the basis of ascribed characteristics, such as ethnicity or race (section 15), Canada is positing the irrelevance of ethnic and racial origin to participation in Canadian society. The sentiment is that people should be judged as human beings, with intrinsic worth, and not prejudged by membership in a given group.

On the other hand, by enshrining in the Charter recognition of either group rights or the importance of ascriptive characteristics such as ethnic origin, and by promoting ethnic cultures and organizations through multicultural policies, Canada is stressing differences among people. From this perspective, ethnic origins and cultures are important.

Classical sociological theory suggests that it will be hard to achieve both objectives at the same time. Social theorists have suggested that as societies become more urban, modern, and industrialized, people in these societies will shed ties to the past and adopt more contemporary identities, becoming a universal "citoyen" or "tovarich." Ethnic and racial origins, like religious ties, would become less important. This suggests that when Canadian immigrant groups or group members became more fully acculturated as Canadians, they will become less, not more, committed to retaining their ancestral identities and cultures. How are immigrant groups faring in Canada today on these broad dimensions?

EQUAL OPPORTUNITY FOR ETHNIC AND RACIAL MINORITIES

There are several ways to measure the extent to which minority group members enjoy equal opportunity in general, and equal economic opportunity in particular. One could examine a group's education, occupation, and income level compared to the societal average. A second approach, popular in Canadian ethnic studies, focuses on ethnic representation in elite sectors of the society. In both approaches, we might conclude that underrepresentation is caused by prejudice and discrimination.

A third approach focuses on prejudicial attitudes held by the majority group or acts of discrimination reported by minority group members. The legal framework described earlier deals only with acts of discrimination; no governmental mechanism regulates prejudicial or stereotypic attitudes held privately by Canadians, or patterns of private, intimate behaviour.

The Mosaic: Still Vertical?

Most recent evidence suggests that the immigrant groups are more and more resembling the dominant British group in levels of socioeconomic status, as measured by education, occupation, and income. For all European immigrant groups, effective discrimination and resulting inequality have all but disappeared. This can be seen from Table 1, and from the more sophisticated analysis in Table 2. In the latter table, we can see the income gaps which remain for average minority group incomes, as deviations from the national average, controlling for sex, nativity, occupation, age, number of weeks worked, and education — all of which influence incomes. As both tables show, European ethnic groups do as well as or better than the national average. For example, consider Italian Canadians, a group which ranked poorly in Porter's original analysis in *The Vertical Mosaic*. In 1981, Italian Canadians earned just slightly below the male and female average incomes. However, as seen from Table 2, the deficit of slightly over $500 from the national average was fully explainable by the other demographic characteristics of Italian Canadians, specifically a large immigrant component and below average levels of educational attainment. Indeed, Italian incomes are even higher than we might expect, by about $150.

Comparisons between 1971 and 1981 show a reduction in the proportional disparities for various minority groups from the national mean income. This can be seen by comparing the percentage differences for 1971 with those for 1981 in Table 2 shown on page 604.

There is convergence going on. This has been found by Darroch (1979) in his study of indices of occupational dissimilarities, which have been narrowing since 1931. Other studies of generational mobility and stratification also point to the decreasing role of ethnic origin per se as a determinant of status attainment (Ornstein, 1981, Tepperman, 1975).

Yet if we focus on visible minority groups we see a mixed picture (Table 1). Some groups, like the Japanese, are doing very well. Those grouped as Indo-Pakistani likewise earn incomes above the Canadian average, due largely to an educational and occupational profile, which is well above average. This grouping may even be earning incomes lower than their credentials warrant. On the other hand, with 75 percent of the group foreign-born, problems of immigrant adjustment and integration may play a role. Indo-Chinese Canadians earn well below the Canadian average, despite high levels of educational attainment. This may reflect discrimination and the undervaluing of their educational credentials, as well as the fact that most of those responding were recent refugees from Southeast Asia.

Blacks and Chinese, as seen in Tables 1 and 2, remain substantially victimized. They earn well below what might be expected, given other background characteristics, particularly educational attainment, which is above the Canadian average for both groups. The only solace here is that Li's data for 1971 and 1981

Table 2

EFFECT OF RACIAL AND ETHNIC ORIGIN ON THE MEAN INCOME OF ETHNIC/RACIAL GROUPS IN THE EMPLOYED LABOR FORCE IN CANADA, 15 YEARS AND OVER, 1971 AND 1981

	1971[1]			1981[2]		
Ethnic groups	**Gross effect as deviation from grand mean**	**Percent(%) deviation from grand mean**	**Ethnic groups**	**Gross effect as deviation from grand mean**	**Percent (%) deviation from grand mean**	**Net effect***
1. Jewish	+3544	59.0	Jewish	+6262	44.6	+2936
2. Japanese	+ 938	15.6	Czech & Slovak	+2137	15.2	+ 63
3. Austrian	+ 744	12.4	Hungarian	+1902	13.5	+ 20
4. Russian	+ 348	5.8	Scandinavian	+1860	13.2	+1035
5. Brit. Isles	+ 294	4.9	Ukrainian	+ 795	5.7	+ 213
6. Czech	+ 105	1.7	Polish	+ 721	5.1	− 223
7. Slovak	+ 84	1.4	German	+ 652	4.6	+ 275
8. Hungarian	+ 56	.9	Croat. & Serb.	+ 459	3.2	+ 378
9. Polish	− 92	− 1.5	British	+ 356	2.5	+ 104
10. Italian	− 164	− 2.7	Dutch	+ 77	2.2	+ 77
11. Scandinavian	− 195	− 3.2	French	− 501	− 3.6	− 204
12. German	− 233	− 3.7	Italian	− 509	− 3.6	+ 149
13. Finnish	− 235	− 3.9	Other	−1113	− 7.9	− 278
14. Other	− 325	− 5.4	Chinese	−1295	− 9.2	− 931
15. Netherlands	− 384	− 6.4	Black	−1588	−11.3	−1680
16. French	− 424	− 7.1	Greek	−1894	−13.5	− 796
17. Ukrainian	− 642	−10.7	Portuguese	−2002	−14.3	+ 627
18. Negro	− 919	−15.3				
19. Chinese	−1026	−17.1				
20. West Indian	−1536	−25.6				
21. Nat. Indian	−1868	−31.1				
$\bar{x}$ = Canada	6004		Canada	14045		

*Net effect of racial and ethnic origin controlling for sex, nativity, occupation, age, number of weeks worked, and education (Li (1986)).

[1]1971 raw data from Li (1980).

[2]1981 raw data from Li (1986).

(Table 2) show the disparities seem to have decreased. In 1971, Chinese incomes and Black incomes were 17 percent and roughly 20 percent (Negro — 15 percent, West Indian, 26 percent) below the Canadian average; by 1981 these gaps were reduced to 9 percent and 11 percent, respectively.

Some indication of the persisting problems of minority groups can be seen from Table 3, which describes mean incomes of university graduates for a selection of ethnic and racial groups, for both native-born and foreign-born Canadians. With a few exceptions (Korean, Japanese, and Portuguese, for the Canadian-born, and Portuguese for the foreign-born), the European minorities earn more than do the visible

Table 3
RATES OF RETURN FOR HIGHER EDUCATION FOR SELECTED ETHNIC OR RACIAL GROUPS, CANADA, 1981

Canadian-Born			Foreign-Born		
Group	*Incomes Rank*	*Mean Incomes, University Graduates*	*Group*	*Income Rank*	*Mean Incomes, University Graduates*
Jewish	1	32 235	Czechoslavak	1	32 214
Russian	2	30 073	Jewish	2	31 106
Korean	3	28 210	Finnish	3	26 788
Japanese	4	28 202	Yugoslavic	4	25 837
Finnish	5	27 350	Russian	5	25 297
Yugoslavic	6	26 366	Ukrainian	6	24 936
Czechoslovak	7	26 074	Greek	7	24 492
Greek	8	25 670	Chinese	8	24 015
Ukrainian	9	24 936	Black	9	22 191
Indochinese	10	24 783	Indo-Pakistani	10	22 108
Chinese	11	24 370	Japanese	11	22 094
Black	12	24 085	Korean	12	20 576
Portuguese	13	22 244	Indochinese	13	20 062
Filipino	14	20 749	Portuguese	14	19 762
Indo-Pakistani	15	13 186	Filipino	15	19 332

Source: Winn (1985, p. 691). Data from 1981 Census of Canada.

minority college graduates. Part of this variation could be explained by differences in the types and extent of university education, as well as by discrimination.

Thus, in moving up the stratification system, equal opportunity exists for Canada's White immigrant groups. Visible minorities still have far to go, but there is variation in the rates of progress or achievement of differing minority groups that cannot simply be attributed to racism. For example, differences in Japanese and Chinese achievements in Canada can be explained by differences in immigrant proportion, amount and type of educational attainment, etc. (Li, 1980).

There has been a transformation of political life for immigrant groups. Through the post-war period, federal and provincial Cabinets have included increasing numbers of immigrant groups. Jews have served as premiers of provinces, as a Supreme Court Justice of Canada, and—in "Tory blue" Ontario—as a leader of the provincial Progressive Conservative party. A Black has been appointed Lieutenant-Governor of Ontario. Ed Schreyer's acceptance address for the governor-generalship was in five languages: English, French, German, Polish, and Ukrainian. These advances and appointments are not tokenism—they have real symbolic value.

In the senior Canadian civil service, long a bastion of Anglo dominance reinforced through old boy networks dating back to Mackenzie King, similar penetration has occurred. One study found noncharter representation in the state elite increased from 3 percent to 11 percent between 1953 and 1973 (Olsen, 1980). Another study of ninety-two senior bureaucrats found 20 percent of noncharter origin (Campbell and Szablowski, 1979).

IMMIGRANT GROUPS IN THE CANADIAN ELITE

What of **representation** of these groups within Canadian **elite** sectors? Porter (1965) and then Clement (1975) have documented the underrepresentation of Canadian immigrant groups, as well as francophones in Canada's corporate elite (directors of dominant Canadian corporations). In addition, Porter found Protestant Anglophones predominated in the political elite, the judicial elite, and the intellectual elite. In short, immigrants were apparently not among the "movers and shakers" in Canadian economic, political, social, and intellectual life, certainly through the 1950s and early 1960s.

Times have changed. The corporate elite of Canada is no longer as closed as it once was. Old line Anglo-Protestant dominance of the corporate elite has been challenged by new entrepreneurial successes from Western Canada, by Jewish and French firms and businesspeople. New fortunes are being made, associated with new bases of economic power (Newman, 1975, 1981). While certain sectors of corporate activity, such as the major chartered banks, remain Anglo-Protestant enclaves, other loci of economic power have emerged. Even the Board of Directors of the Royal Bank of Canada had by the early 1980s admitted a Jewish woman and a Vancouver Oriental to the ranks.

Finally, Canadian culture, whether highbrow, as measured by appointments to the Royal Society of Canada or representation as senior professors or university administrators, or popular, as measured by representation in the various media as performers, directors, or producers, has also been transformed mightily in the post-war period. The children and grandchildren of immigrants, equipped with university or other training and the requisite freedom of expressions, have exploded onto the cultural scene. Another indicator of this openness is the proliferation on campuses of chairs, programs, or courses in ethnic studies.

To be sure, the visible minorities lag far behind (Owaisi and Bangash, 1978). These groups include large numbers of recent immigrants who have not yet developed the contacts that help them "make it" in Canadian cultural or elite sectors. The corporate elite will likely be most resistant to integration by visible minorities. But within the next two or three decades, these groups will likely increase their presence in political, social, and cultural elite sectors.

Racism: Discrimination and Prejudice

Social scientists study two broad types of discrimination. **Overt discrimination** refers to specific acts of discrimination directed against specific victims by specific perpetrators. It is illegal in Canada, and its presence can be established using rules of evidence in courts of law.

More complex is discrimination called **structural, institutional or, most recently, systemic**. Here there are no overtly identifiable perpetrators caught in a specific act of discrimination. Rather, minorities are penalized because of the historic, cumulative effect of past discrimination. In addition, minorities may be excluded from old-boy networks, and face unreasonable educational or job requirements, which may screen out competent employees from possible jobs or promotions. Lower educational performances can reflect cultural biases in testing, rather than cognitive deficiencies. These barriers will not be eliminated, in the view of some analysts, by simply legislating equal opportunity. They must be attacked directly, using affirmative action programs.

Thus, in Canada as in the United States, the fight to overcome discrimination has shifted from a concern with equality of opportunity to one with equality of result. Discrimination is no longer defined by the intent or motivation of the discriminator, but by the consequences of actions, rules, or procedures on minority groups. Statistical underrepresentation of minority groups is presumed to indicate discrimination (Weinfeld, 1981a).

On the other hand, simply because a group has a high level of achievement, or individual group members are well represented in elite sectors, does *not* mean that racist sentiments — prejudice — as well as discrimination do not exist. The Bronfman family's money and power did not get patriarch Sam Bronfman into the Canadian senate. Some of the achievements of minority group members — one thinks of Jews and Japanese — may have been made despite historic and persisting racism, or even, surprisingly, because of it (Light, 1972). Even successful members of minority groups may suffer psychological distress because of persisting, if ineffectual, prejudice.

One way to measure racism is to poll majority Canadians about their attitudes or beliefs regarding immigrants. People can be queried about their personal relations with various groups, or asked to rank groups in terms of prestige.

If we look at Gallup poll data in Canada in the post-war period, we see a decline in explicitly racist attitudes, for example, on questions about approval of mixed marriages. Yet polls on immigration during this period have revealed decreasing support for higher immigration levels, as well as increasing preferences for quotas on countries of origin. Moreover, while the government's response to the boat people crisis was relatively magnanimous, public opinion data revealed less than enthusiastic support of increased refugee aid. One 1980 poll asked: if private sponsorship could be arranged, should the federal government allow the entry of more than the original target of fifty thousand refugees?; 63 percent of the respondents said no. (Of course, not all opponents of immigration are racists.)

Other studies have found Canadians perceive a prestige ranking for ethnic groups (Pineo, 1977). Not surprisingly, the English and French are ranked highest, with visible minority groups ranked well below. These rankings correspond to social distances of Canadians from minority groups. Another study found Canadians were least "aware" of visible minority groups, compared to European groups. Studies that discovered rank orders of groups, as well as existing stereotypes, did not conclude that lower ranked groups were actively disliked. "The absolute rating of all groups were quite favourable" (Berry et al., 1977: 107).

One Toronto study estimated that about one-sixth of the respondents could be classified as "very racist." One-quarter of the respondents judged West Indians, Pakistanis, and Indians as inferior (Henry, 1978). This study, done in Toronto where minorities are concentrated and friction may be greater, may be more relevant than national Gallup polls.

One indirect measure of racism is interethnic and interracial marriage. Rates of interethnic marriage in Canada are high and increasing, primarily for the European ethnic groups. Yet out-marriage seems to be increasing even for interracial unions, and rates are higher among the native-born

(Kalbach, 1970). Moreover, when minority groups intermarry, they select partners from the British (higher status) group in proportion to their weight in the population. Of course, such intermarriages can be interpreted both as acceptance by the dominant group and as loss of ethnic identity by the minority group.

Still another way to measure racism is through opinion surveys in which minority group members report their perceptions of their own conditions, or on the frequency with which they encounter discrimination. (Evidence shows some minority group members perceive more victimization for their ethnic group in general than they have themselves experienced (Weinfeld, 1980:5–15). One study of Blacks in Toronto claimed 59 percent were victimized by discrimination (Head, 1975). An unpublished survey of West Indians in Montreal found 25 percent claiming there is "very strong" prejudice, and 67 percent "some prejudice" against West Indians in Quebec. (The same survey revealed 25 percent had experienced no personal discrimination.)

A final way to gauge racism is by enumerating objectively verifiable incidents. Field studies in Toronto have found that employers clearly discriminate against non-White job applicants (Henry and Ginzberg, 1985). Another example of this approach is to tabulate the numbers of accepted complaints of discrimination of Human Rights Commissions in Canada. For example, from 1979 to 1983, the Commission investigated 531 complaints of discrimination based on national, ethnic, or racial grounds. (Investigation does not mean a finding of guilt.) The actual numbers of such complaints were 109, 94, 122, 113, and 93, certainly not a pattern of increase. Provincial Human Rights Commissions also hear complaints on these grounds.

Official statistics are notorious in underestimating the prevalence of discrimination, since most acts go unreported. But in any case, how can we interpret such numbers; do they indicate a serious problem? Are they a tip of an iceberg, depicting a society seething with deep rooted racial animosity, or are they relatively trivial? The same questions must be asked for the attitudinal survey data. What does it mean for the life of the country if 2 percent—or 20 percent—of Canadians are "racist?" But even a lowly 2 percent denotes hundreds of thousands of adult Canadian racists—more than enough to poison race relations if they were mobilized.

Racism and the fear of racism are part of the cultural climate separate from statistical trends. Consider the case of Jews in Canada. As indicated previously, Jews have done well economically and are well represented in elite sectors of Canadian society.

Yet periodically, and routinely, Jewish cemeteries, synagogues, or homes are defaced with swastikas, and Jewish defence agencies, such as the League for Human Rights of B'nai B'rith, tally such anti-Semitic incidents on a yearly basis. Perhaps, more important, racist and anti-Semitic organizations like the Western Guard publish and disseminate hate-filled material. Yet episodes such as the trials of Jim Keegstra and Ernst Zundel, and their coverage, affected members of the Jewish community, who found vile anti-Semitic canards reported daily in the media. One well-publicized act of bigotry may be more salient than a stack of poll data. The fact that diehard racist and anti-Semitic movements remain relegated to the fringes of political life in Canada may be cold comfort to minorities whose dignity is brutalized and degraded.

What can we conclude? Many observers emphasize the continuing inequalities facing visible minorities and the need for further affirmative action. This was the thrust of Judge Rosalie Abella's landmark Royal Commission Report, *Equality in Employment* (1984). The federal government accepts that affirmative action is required to overcome "systemic" discrimination, which may lead to minority underrepresentation. The Report called upon Canadian businesses and, in particular, government agencies and firms dealing with government to implement "employment equity."

Employment equity is a term which the Report proposes to replace affirmative action. It is a set of procedures aimed at improving, where necessary, "the participation of women, Native peoples, disabled persons, and specified ethnic and racial groups in the workplace." While quotas are not acceptable, it is proposed that firms will have to devise timetables for increasing minority hiring, preferably on a voluntary rather than mandatory basis. Moreover, as long as there is no legislation requiring federally and provincially regulated employers to implement employment equity, the federal government is encouraged to adopt "contract compliance" as a means to pressure firms to conform. In this approach, firms hired by the government would be required to have employment equity programs.

In the United States, the debate on affirmative action quotas and goals has been heated. Several court cases have been brought by majority males alleging reverse discrimination in these programs, and the issue has sparked debate in legal and scholarly circles.

ETHNIC SURVIVAL

Are the immigrant groups successful in retaining their ancestral cultures, identities, and communal cohesion? Or is assimilation taking place that requires old attachments with newer commitments to Canada and other cultural values?

There are several ways to measure the strength of in-group bonds. Retention of an ancestral language is one measure, and here the evidence shows a loss of the mother tongue with the passing of generations. While some knowledge of languages persists, fluency and use are down dramatically.

Another common measure deals with residential segregation, or the preference for living in a neighbourhood close to one's own group. Some of this pattern may reflect discrimination in housing or real estate markets, but for the European immigrant groups, such discrimination is probably minimal. And the evidence here too suggests that over time dispersion slowly takes place (Weinfeld, 1981b:80–100).

Social segregation refers to the preference of people to select their close friends within their own ethnic group. In a sense, this selection can be understood as preventing interethnic marriages. Both measures of friendship networks and intermarriage patterns reveal higher rates of assimilation out of the ethnic community for successive native-born generations than for immigrants.

If we focus on immigrant groups who have been here longest, have been successful economically, and are of large size, we could test the probable success of the multicultural vision in promoting group cultural survival and identity. By and large, the evidence of long-term identification is weak (Reitz, 1980). Data from a study of European ethnic groups in Toronto in the late 1970s shows systematic declines in such measures, from immigrant to second and third generation respondents (Isajiw, 1981).

Yet members of these groups do retain a sense of identity, or identification with their group. For many, the group culture may become more marginal, important only for symbolic or ceremonial occasions. Canadians may "feel" Italian, or

Polish, have pride in their ethnic heritage, and believe that multiculturalism is a good thing, yet be only minimally involved in their community or heritage (Weinfeld, 1981b).

An increasingly important dimension of ethnic life in Canada is the role of ethnic community organizations. Here, too, the evidence shows that with succeeding generations, membership and involvement in these organizations and readership of the ethnic press declines (Isajiw, 1981; Weinfeld, 1981b). Most activists are immigrants or wealthy leaders among the native-born, who may derive status or psychic gratification from leadership in ethnic communities. But one feature of middle-class ethnicity is the role of the ethnic **polity**.

In many ways, ethnic groups are organized as voluntary political units. Leaders are (s)elected more or less democratically. Financial contributions are made voluntarily (communities have no legal power of taxation) to finance community activities. Events are planned, schools are maintained, meetings are held, newspapers are published. Communities provide a myriad of recreational, social, cultural, or political services to members. In some cases, an ethnic community may also serve as an economic resource, for example, as a market for ethnic goods, as a source of capital, and as an informal network of buyers, sellers, clients, supplies, etc. (Weinfeld, 1983). Such ethnic "sub-economies" or enclaves may be important springboards for immigrants seeking their first job in a strange environment, though their relative effectiveness may be low (Reitz et al., 1981).

The business of running ethnic polities naturally falls to key ethnic organizations and leaders. Some groups have one dominant organization, others have several which compete with each other; at times these intragroup divisions may stem from old country political, ideological, or regional differences; at times they are simply battles for turf. These polities and their representative organizations perform both internal and external functions. The internal refer to cultural or social services. The external involve dealings with government or with other ethnic groups.

How meaningful or important are these organizations to ethnic Canadians? The data in Table 4 show that in Toronto in the late 1970s, most ethnic Torontonians were not informed or active members of ethnic organizations (Breton, 1981).

These figures do not necessarily measure the political efficacy of ethnic polities. After all, proportionately fewer Canadians are members, let alone active, in political parties in Canada. Ethnic communities are becoming more active in attempting to pursue their collective interests by lobbying and petitioning governments. These interests may be domestic (fighting discrimination) or international (support for the homeland).

In earlier times, such preoccupations of citizens in a Western democratic polity led to charges of dual loyalty or of ethnic groups creating a "state within a state." The strength of multicultural ideology, and its consequences of energized ethnic polities, makes such charges unlikely. Ethnic Canadians are free to petition the government through their associations, as do Canadians active in other lobbying groups, such as environmentalists, manufacturers, farmers, women, etc. Canadian politicians are slowly becoming more sensitive to the "ethnic vote," i.e., making sure that party platforms and campaigns appeal to ethnic voters in ridings where such groups are concentrated. In this sense, Canada has lagged behind the United States in recognizing the role of ethnic issues and interests in political life (Litt, 1970).

Often policy making involving minority group interests becomes emotionally charged, tinged with real or perceived rac-

Table 4

PARTICIPATION IN ETHNIC COMMUNITY ORGANIZATIONS AND ACTIVITY BY ETHNIC GROUP, TORONTO, 1978–1979

	Chinese %	German %	Italian %	Jewish %	Portuguese %	Ukrainian %	West Indian %
1. Know of any organizations or associations in the community	38	36	49	89	32	57	61
2. Was or is now a member of one or more ethnic organizations or associations	7	10	24	67	20	51	19
3. Express views about community affairs:							
– sometimes	5	6	28	42	9	40	35
– never	95	94	72	57	91	60	65
4. Informed about activities of leaders:							
– very much and somewhat	3	2	31	45	10	27	24
– not too well or not at all	25	3	36	29	27	20	22
– do not know leaders and no answer	72	95	33	26	63	53	54
N-weighted	(57)	(178)	(431)	(168)	(67)	(89)	(118)
Number of Interviews	(152)	(321)	(351)	(344)	(163)	(345)	(150)

Source: Breton (1981).

ism, and appeals for justice or human rights. Compromise on such issues of principle may be more difficult than compromises on economic policy disputes, where one can often "split the difference." Certainly, French–English relations, as well as those between the White majority and Native peoples, have been marked by such tensions. Similar problems can be seen, on a smaller scale, in other areas. One example is the ongoing debate about the size and nature of the restitution to be made by the Canadian government to Japanese Canadians, dispossessed during World War II.

CONCLUSION

Prejudice and discrimination continue to restrict the opportunities faced by the non-English and non-French immigrant groups in Canada. However, these inequalities are more severe for the visible minority groups; for White groups, the evidence shows equality of opportunity or result exists. For all groups, including visible minorities, the ethnic differentials in earned income are shrinking over time.

As immigrant groups become predominantly second and third generation, assimilation becomes more pronounced. This has happened to most of the European immigrant groups. Ethnicity may operate as a symbolic source of identity, with latent significance, but it no longer shapes daily life. Ethnic organizations, energized by multicultural policies, play an important role in ethnic communities, and in representing group interests to governments, even without an active, mass base.

Differences among the ethnic groups are pronounced. Indeed, they may not even share a common agenda. Thus, visible minority groups, composed largely of immigrants, are primarily concerned with bread and butter issues and the problem of racism; the White European groups, more established in Canada, tend to be concerned with cultural survival and national policy. Even among visible minority groups, there are important variations in the degree of economic inequalities.

The Canadian state in the twentieth century has become a declared ally of minority groups in their attempts to secure equality and to preserve their heritage and identity. Constitutionally entrenched prohibitions against discrimination, laws against the spreading of hatred, federal and provincial human rights commissions, and government supported affirmative action programs show a commitment to the former. Federal and provincial multicultural ministries, which provide financial assistance to cultural heritage projects and groups, are examples of the commitment to the latter.

Whether immigrant groups will survive as identifiable groups is now largely a matter of choice. They enjoy freedom of association, and the government provides assistance when needed. Thus, future assimilation will depend on the satisfactions or benefits which continued group identification may provide. Visible minorities, because of racial differences, will have identities reinforced. As their numbers increase, concentrated in major cities, one cannot rule out escalations of intolerance and racist behaviour.

Comparing the status of minorities in Canada today to their conditions historically, or to conditions in most parts of the world, gives one grounds for optimism. Progress has been and is being made. Nevertheless, Canada has its racists and bigots. Efforts to educate Canadian citizens about past misdeeds and human rights, and new sets of vigilant governmental institutions, may help keep their influence from spreading.

DISCUSSION QUESTIONS

1. Analyze the "Canadian mosaic" and the "American melting pot" images in terms of the legal framework and social realities of the two countries.
2. How is Canadian racism in the post-1945 period different from that which preceded it?
3. How has immigration affected the composition of Canadian ethnic and racial minorities?
4. In what ways does Canadian law, including the Constitution, protect minorities from discrimination and promote their cultural survival?
5. Do ethnic and racial minorities in Canada enjoy equal economic opportunity?
6. Discuss the evidence about cultural assimilation among ethnic and racial groups in Canada.

GLOSSARY

affirmative action a process by which employers or schools undertake to increase minority representation or progress to a degree closer to their population proportions. Also known as *employment equity* (Entrenched in section 15.2 of the Canadian Charter.)

assimilation the process whereby members of ethnic or racial groups gradually lose the elements of their group identity and cultural heritage

discrimination actions or behaviours that deprive members of minority groups of equal opportunity. *Institutional*, or *systemic*, discrimination refers to well-established selection processes that are discriminatory in their outcomes, though not necessarily in their motivation. (See section 15.1 of the Canadian Charter.)

elite representation the degree to which minority groups are represented in the major elite sectors of Canadian society

melting pot a metaphor for American society used to describe a process whereby minority groups would be encouraged, permitted, or forced to assimilate into one mainstream American culture

mosaic a metaphor for Canadian society used to describe a process whereby minority groups in Canada would be encouraged, permitted, or forced to retain their separate identities and cultures

multiculturalism the Canadian policy of encouraging ethnic groups to retain their cultures and heritages (entrenched in section 27 of the Canadian Charter of Rights and Freedoms)

points system immigrants seeking to come to Canada as independent immigrants, i.e., on their own merits, must earn over a minimum level of points. Points are awarded for attributes like age, education, language ability, skills, etc.

polity an ethnic polity refers to the voluntary ethnic community organizations, which are found within minority communities and which help structure the collective and political life of these groups

prejudice superficial or unfounded attitudes or beliefs about the negative qualities of minority groups

segregation a phenomenon, either voluntary or forced, whereby ethnic and racial groups are separated from other groups. Segregation may be residential or social.

BIBLIOGRAPHY

Abella, Irving and Harold E. Troper
1983 *None Is Too Many*. Toronto: Lester and Orpen Dennys.

Abella, Judge Rosalie
1984 *Equality in Employment*. A Royal Commission Report. Ottawa: Ministry of Supply and Services.

Adachi, Ken
1976 *The Enemy That Never Was*. Toronto: McClelland and Stewart.

Benokraitis, Nijole V. and Joe R. Feagin
1978 *Affirmative Action and Equal Opportunity: Action, Inaction, Reaction*. Boulder, Colorado: Westview Press.

Bercuson, David and Douglas Wertheimer
1985 *A Trust Betrayed: The Keegstra Affair*. Toronto: Doubleday Canada Ltd.

Berger, Carl
1966 "The True North Strong and Free." In Peter Russell (ed.) *Nationalism in Canada*. Toronto: McGraw-Hill Ryerson.

Berger, Thomas R.
1981 *Fragile Freedoms: Human Rights and Dissent in Canada* Toronto: Clarke Irwin and Co.

Berry, J.W., R. Kalin and D.M. Taylor
1977 *Multiculturalism and Ethnic Attitudes in Canada*. Ottawa: Supply and Services Canada.

Breton, Raymond
1981 "*The Ethnic Community as a Resource in Relation to Group Problems: Perceptions and Attitudes*. Toronto: University of Toronto, Centre for Urban and Community Studies. Research paper no. 122.

Campbell, Colin and George J. Szablowski
1979 *The Super-bureaucrats: Structure and Behaviour in Central Agencies*. Toronto: Macmillan of Canada.

Clement, Wallace
1975 *The Canadian Corporate Elite*. Toronto: McClelland and Stewart.

Darroch, A.G.
1979 "Another look at ethnicity, stratification and social mobility in Canada." *Canadian Journal of Sociology* 4 (1): 1–25.

Feldstein, Stanley and Lawrence Costello (eds.)
1974 *The Ordeal of Assimilation: A Documentary History of the White Working Class 1830's to the 1970's*. New York: Anchor Books.

Glazer, Nathan (ed.)
1985 *Clamor at the Gates: The New American Immigration*. San Francisco: Institute for Contemporary Studies.

Glazer, Nathan and Daniel P. Moynihan
1970 *Beyond the Melting Pot*. Cambridge: M.I.T. Press.

Gordon, Milton
1964 *Assimilation in American Life*. New York: Oxford University Press.

Head, Wilson, A.
1975 *The Black Presence in the Canadian Mosaic: A Study of Perception and the Practice of Discrimination Against Blacks in Metropolitan Toronto*. Ontario Human Rights Commission. Toronto: Queen's Printer.

Henry, F.
1978 "The Dynamics of Racism in Toronto." Toronto: York University, Department of Anthropology, mimeo.

Henry, F. and H. Ginzberg
1985 Who Gets the Work: A Test of Racial Discrimination in Employment.

Toronto: Urban Alliance on Race Relations and the Social Planning Council.

Hogg, Peter
1982 *The Canada Act, 1982*. Toronto: Carswell.

Isajiw, Wesvolod W.
1981 *Ethnic Identity Retention*. Toronto: Centre for Urban and Community Studies, University of Toronto. Research paper no. 125.

Kalbach, Warren E.
1970 *The Impact of Immigration on Canada's Population*. Ottawa: Dominion Bureau of Statistics, 1970.

Krauter, Joseph F. and Morris Davis
1978 *Minority Canadians: Ethnic Groups*. Toronto: Methuen.

LeVine, Robert A. and Donald T. Campbell
1972 Ethnocentrism: Theories of Conflict, Ethnic Attitudes, and Group Behavior. New York: John Wiley & Sons.

Li, Peter, S.
1980 "Income Achievement and Adaptive Capacity: An Empirical Comparison of Chinese and Japanese in Canada." In K. Victor Ujimoto, and Gordon Hirabayashi (eds.) *Visible Minorities and Multiculturalism: Asians in Canada*. Toronto: Butterworths.

——
1986 "Race and Ethnic Relations." In Lorne Tepperman and R. Jack Richardson (eds.), *The Social World: An Introduction to Sociology*. Toronto: McGraw-Hill Ryerson.

Light, Ivan
1972 *Ethnic Enterprise in America*. Berkeley: University of California Press.

Lipset, Seymour Martin,
1970 *Revolution and Counterrevolution*. Garden City, New York: Doubleday and Company.

——
1985 "Canada and the United States: The Cultural Dimension." In C.F. Doran and J.H. Sigler (eds.) *Canada and the United States*. Englewood Cliffs, New Jersey: Prentice-Hall Inc.

Litt, Edgar
1970 *Ethnic Politics in America: Beyond Pluralism*. Glenview: Scott, Foresman.

Newman, Peter C.
1975 *The Canadian Establishment*. Toronto: McClelland and Stewart.

——
1981 *The Aquisitors* (The Canadian Establishment, Vol. 2). Toronto: McClelland and Stewart.

Novak, Michael
1973 *The Rise of the Unmeltable Ethnics*. New York: MacMillan.

Olsen, Dennis
1980 *The State Elite*. Toronto: McClelland and Stewart.

Ornstein, Michael
1981 "The Occupational Mobility of Men in Ontario." In *Canadian Review of Sociology and Anthropology*, 18:2 May, 1981. pp. 183–215.

Owaisi, Lateef and Zafar Bahgash
1978 *Visible Minorities in Mass Media Advertising*. Ottawa: Ministry of Supply and Services.

Pineo, P.
1977 "The Social Standing of Ethnic and Racial Groupings." *Canadian Review of Sociology and Anthropology*. 14 (May), pp. 147–57.

Porter, John
1965 *The Vertical Mosaic*. Toronto: University of Toronto Press.

——
1979 "Melting Pot or Mosaic: Revolution or Reversion." In John Porter, *The Measure of Canadian Society: Education, Equality and Opportunity*. Toronto: Gage Publishers.

Reitz, Jeffrey G.
1980 *The Survival of Ethnic Groups*. Toronto: McGraw-Hill Ryerson.

Reitz, J.G., Liviana Calzavara, and Donna Dasko
1981 *Ethnic Inequality and Segregation in Jobs*. Toronto: Centre for Urban and Community Studies. University of Toronto. Research paper no. 123.

Simeon, Richard
1972 *Federal-Provincial Diplomacy: The*

Making of Recent Policy in Canada. Toronto: University of Toronto Press.

Tarnopolsky, Walters
1982 "The Equality Rights." In W.S. Tarnopolsky and G.A. Beaudoin, *The Canadian Charter of Rights and Freedoms: Commentary*. Toronto: Carswell Co.

Tepperman, L.
1975 *Social Mobility in Canada*. Toronto: McGraw-Hill Ryerson.

Weimann, Gabriel and Conrad Winn
1986 *Hate on Trial: The Zundel Affair, The Media, and the Public Opinion in Canada*. Oakville, Ontario: Mosaic Press.

Weinfeld, Morton
1980 "The Jews of Quebec: Perceived Anti-semitism, Segregation, and Emigration," in the *Jewish Journal of Sociology*, 22: 1 June.

——
1981a "The Development of Affirmative Action in Canada." *Canadian Ethnic Studies* xiii, 2:23–39.

——
1981b "Myth and Reality in the Canadian Mosaic: 'Affective Ethnicity.' " *Canadian Ethnic Studies* xiii, 3:80–100.

——
1983 "The Ethnic Sub-Economy: Explication and Analyses of a Case Study of the Jews of Montreal." *Working Papers in Migration and Ethnicity*, no. 80–6. McGill University.

Wilson, William J.
1978 *The Declining Significance of Race*. Chicago: University of Chicago Press.

Winks, Robin W.
1971 *Blacks in Canada: A History*. New Haven, Conn.: Yale University Press.

Winn, Conrad
1985 "Affirmative Action and Visible Minorities: Eight Premises in Quest of Evidence." *Canadian Public Policy* xi, 4 (December): 684–700.

Indian government in practice.

> *"Native self-government is perceived by provincial politicians as a threat. . . . Canada seems to lack the absorptive capacity . . . to withstand the relatively minor dislocation which Native self-government would entail."*

chapter twenty-two

Native Peoples

J. Rick Ponting

INTRODUCTION

Canada's Constitution lists the aboriginal peoples as Indians, Inuit, and Métis. Each category encompasses various sub-groups. Status Indians, who number close to 400 000 persons, belong to a band and fall under the jurisdiction of the Indian Act; or they have been admitted to a general register (kept by the Department of Indian Affairs and Northern Development — DIAND), but have been denied band membership.

Indians are extremely diverse ethnicly and have long thought of themselves as quite different peoples (e.g., Micmac, Cree, Haida, Dogrib, Haudenosaunee). This diversity is reinforced by ecological adaptations to different physical environments (e.g., plains Cree vs. woodland Cree vs. west coast) with resultant vast differences in symbolic and material cultures. Geographical and linguistic barriers often reinforced these differences, as did political, military or economic rivalries.

About 70 percent of status Indians live on reserves ("reservation" is the American term), while most of the remainder have migrated to cities, seeking greater opportunities.[1] Only about 57 percent of status Indians are treaty Indians, so the terms "treaty Indian" and "status Indian" are not synonymous.

Different definitions of the Métis exist today. The simplest and most comprehensive is that Métis are the offspring of a mixed (Indian–White) union who have not been accorded official status as a registered (status) Indian. The first Métis were children of marriages between Indian women

Table 1
REGISTERED INDIAN POPULATION AND INDIAN LANDS, BY REGION

	Atlantic Provinces	Quebec	Ontario	Manitoba	Sask.	Alberta	B.C.	N.W.T.	Yukon	Canada
Total Indian population, 1984[1]	13 590	34 335	77 313	52 049	54 188	43 436	61 730	8530	3638	348 809
% of total Indian population, 1984	3.9	9.8	22.2	14.9	15.5	12.5	17.7	2.5	1.0	100.0
% of total provincial/territorial population, 1984	0.6	0.5	0.9	4.9	5.4	1.9	2.2	17.2	16.5	1.4
% living off reserve, 1984[2]	28.2	14.4	31.9	26.7	34.0	24.7	35.9	7.2	24.5	28.7
Number of Indian bands, 1985	31	39	126	60	68	41	196	14	17	592
% of Indian bands, 1985	5.2	6.6	21.3	10.1	11.5	6.9	33.1	2.4	2.9	100.0
Number of reserves and settlements, 1985	67	33	185	103	142	90	1610	29	25	2284
% of reserves and settlements, 1985	2.9	1.4	8.1	4.5	6.2	3.9	70.5	1.3	1.1	100.0

[1]The official count from INAC as of December 31, 1984 is unadjusted for late-reported births and deaths (which would add about 2–3% to the population). Such an adjustment would be unlikely to alter significantly the percentages shown in this table.

Sources: INAC Program Reference Centre, *Registered Indian Population by Sex and Residence,* and *Schedule of Indian Bands, Reserves and Settlements.*

and French or Scottish fur traders. Today, Métis vary greatly in physical appearance; some are indistinguishable from Indians, others are indistinguishable from Whites. As Sealey and Lussier (1975) have demonstrated, many have a distinct Métis self-identity, built around distinctive Métis symbols, that contrasts sharply with an Indian identity.

In the 1981 census, only about 98 000 people defined themselves as Métis; but this number is hotly contested by Métis political leaders. Except for about four thousand people living in eight Métis settlements in Alberta (average land area of 156 000 acres), Métis tend to live in small rural pockets of poverty or to disperse in the larger non-Native population, in both cases without any collectively owned land base.

Some non-status Indians have lost their registered status by marriage to a non-Indian or through a process known as **enfranchisement**. Others are the offspring of such persons. Non-status Indians numbered about 75 000 in the controversial 1981 census. As members of this group opt to regain their status as registered Indians under a 1985 federal statute (**Bill C-31**), are often denied acceptance into and housing on their former reserves (especially outside British Columbia), there is much resentment between them and status Indians in some Indian communities.

The so-called "Eskimo" people comprise the Inuvialuit of the western Arctic and the Inuit of the eastern Arctic and Labrador. In the 1981 census, they numbered 25 400 people. The vast majority still live in their native communities.

The status Indian population is fragmented into almost 600 bands (administrative units formed by the government), of which about one-third are in British Columbia. There are almost 2300 reserves (70 percent in British Columbia), averaging 1100 hectares (4.3 square miles) in area. Bands range from a handful of members to the estimated 15 600 members of the Six Nations band near Brantford, Ontario. By 1996, about 25 percent of all bands (encompassing almost two-thirds of all band Indians) are projected to have one thousand or more members. Then, about 15 percent of all band Indians will live in bands of fewer than 500 members. These numbers will affect the viability of Indian self-government in future.

Ontario has the largest Indian population, over 77 000 in 1984. Altogether, Indians constitute about 1½ percent of Canada's population (5.4 percent of the Saskatchewan population, proportionately more than in any other province), while all categories of Natives in Canada constitute about 3 percent of the total Canadian population. Only in the Northwest Territories, as presently constituted, do Natives form a majority.

The falling Indian birth rate is approaching the overall Canadian rate, but is nevertheless almost twice as high (3.15 vs. 1.70 births per woman). The enormous gap in infant mortality rates—an internationally used indicator of living standards — has also narrowed drastically. There remains, however, a ten-year gap in life expectancy at birth; Indians have a lower longevity.

Indian housing has improved since the late 1970s, but remains poor (especially in rural and remote areas in Manitoba, Ontario, and Saskatchewan). According to a 1985 study, almost half of on-reserve houses fail to meet basic standards of physical condition. Overcrowding, deterioration, and a lack of basic amenities like running water have created a housing crisis for reserve Indians.

In 1980, the average annual income of the Canadian population was one and two-thirds greater than that of the status Indian population, down from three times higher in 1971. The rate at which Indians drop out of school has also decreased. As of

Figure 1

Total Fertility Rate of the Registered Indian and Total Canadian Populations, 1968–1981

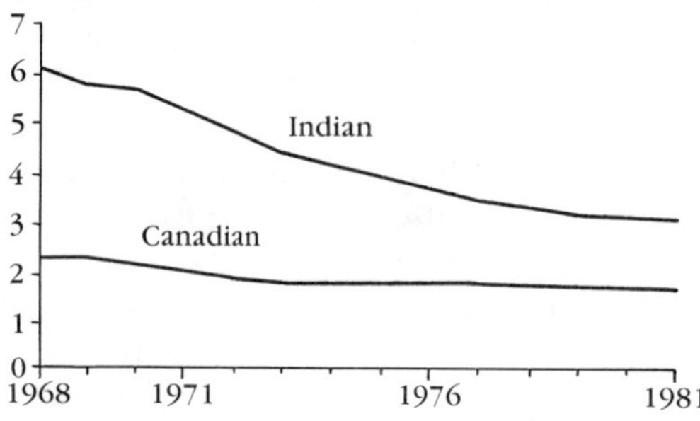

Source: B. Ram, and A. Romaniuc, *Fertility Projections of Registered Indians, 1982 to 1996*, Ottawa: INAC, 1985.

Figure 2

Infant Mortality Rate of the Registered Indian and Total Canadian Populations, 1970–1981

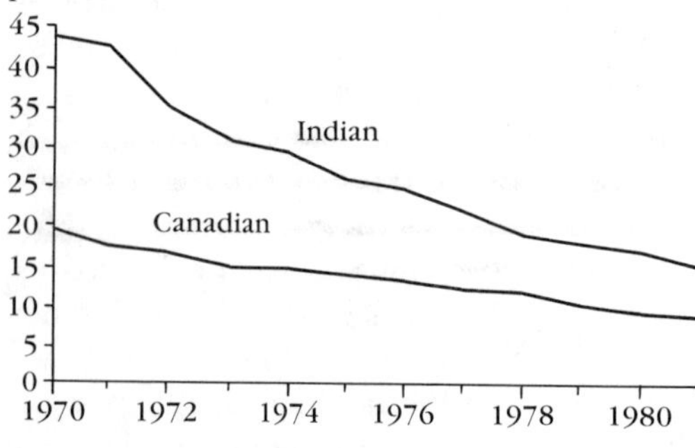

Source: G. Rowe and M.J. Norris, *Mortality Projections of Registered Indians, 1982 to 1996*, Ottawa: INAC, 1985.

1984–85, 31 percent of Indians who had entered grade 2 graduated from grade 12, compared to 18 percent nine years earlier. Major gains have also been made in the number of Indians possessing university degrees (over 2600 in the 1981 census).

However, Natives are still overrepresented in prisons: they constitute about 10 percent of the federal inmate population (serious crimes), but only about 3 percent of the overall Canadian population. In provincial and territorial prisons and jails (less serious crimes), Natives are also very heavily overrepresented.

In order to put the Native peoples' situation (and our society's treatment of them) in perspective, we need a point of reference: namely, White–Aborigine relations in Australia.

Although passing reference will sometimes be made to the situation in other countries, little attention is devoted to the situation in the United States. Various factors limit its comparability to Canada including a policy that broke up reservation lands by allotting their ownership to individuals who could then sell to non-Indians; the U.S. courts' recognition of the internal sovereignty of Indians as "domestic dependent nations"; and the proliferation of statutes dealing with Indians or Inuit peoples (over 4000 in the United States in contrast to the mere handful in Canada). Australia, on the other hand, shares with Canada a parliamentary political system, a British heritage, a widely dispersed aboriginal population, and a comparable system of reserves. Particular attention will be paid to aboriginal rights and land, relationships with the governments of the dominant society, self-government, and public opinion on Native issues.

First, though, an overview of the social, demographic, and economic situation of the aboriginal peoples in both countries will be presented, along with a cursory sketch of the history of aboriginal-White relations in Australia.

ABORIGINES IN CANADA AND AUSTRALIA COMPARED

Sociodemographic Profiles

Australia was originally a British penal colony whose commanding officer was ordered to treat the Natives with the fairness and respect due all British subjects.[2]

However, with increasing encroachment on tribal lands and watering holes by freed convicts and other ranchers, relations with the Aborigines deteriorated.

Frontier massacres and vigilantism became commonplace in the absence of any counterpart to Canada's North-West Mounted Police. Stone reports that the British were virtually certain to escape punishment for killing Natives found in or near their settlements. Powerful settlers (pastoralists), intent on maximizing their grazing lands, were particularly inclined to ignore the formally established protectorate over the Aborigines. Settlers debated the relative merits of extermination, assimilation, and segregation. Finally, Aborigines were collected and confined on reserves, frequently in the territory of a traditional enemy. Not surprisingly, tribal wars and revenge killings among the Aborigines increased.

In a manner also without parallel in Canada, Australia's settlers embraced Charles Darwin's *On the Origin of the Species* (1859), and firmly believed (until well into the twentieth century) that Aborigines were sub-human, occupied the lowest rung of Darwin's "scale of civilization," and were doomed to extinction by "natural law." This view was used to justify murder, neglect, and the failure to enter into treaties with them. In contrast to the Canadian situation, Australian Aborigines were exploited for their cheap labour, once having been reduced to a semi-starved and dependent position. The killing of Aborigines and of some Whites continued until the 1930s. The Aborigine as a British subject equal before the law became a forgotten concept.

With the increase in part-Aborigines (persons of mixed ancestry), more attention was given to educating this population and isolating them from their darker-skinned relatives. By 1937, assimilation policies had become dominant, and in 1961 all aboriginal adults were given the right to vote. In the decades that followed, Australians, like Canadians, became conscious of their image abroad on human rights issues; then, legalized discrimination against Aborigines was ended.

A social, economic, and demographic portrait strikingly similar to that for Canadian Natives could be sketched for the Australian aboriginal population. It too is ethnicly diverse. The approximately 15 000 (1981 census) Torres Strait Islanders[3] are as different from other Aborigines as Inuit are from Indians in Canada. Originally some five hundred different tribes of Australian Aborigines spoke hundreds of different languages.

Aborigines constitute about 1 percent of the total population of the country,[4] but are somewhat more evenly distributed across the country than are Canadian Natives. Like Canadian Indians, about 30 percent of Australian Aborigines live in urban areas. Canada, though, has no direct counterpart to the ghetto-like concentrations of Aborigines on the fringes of some Australian towns and cities. However, in both countries the geographic distribution of Natives reflects marginal status in society. Other direct parallels include their low level of educational attainment[5] high unemployment, severely overcrowded and deteriorated housing, high but declining infant mortality rates, and lower life expectancy than their non-aboriginal compatriots (Altman and Nieuwenhuysen, 1979).

A noteworthy difference is the virtual absence[6] in Canada of any counterpart to the "out-station movement." This is the migration of Aborigines out of White-controlled settlements and cattle stations (ranches) back to their traditional homelands in remote rural Australia, where they pursue their traditional lifestyle in "decentralized communities" largely away from daily contact with Whites.[7]

Legal Definition

Another important difference between the two countries is legal and definitional. In Canada, all members of Indian bands are registered Indians; but for some, entitlement to membership in an Indian band is a divisive and legally formalized matter.

For generations (prior to the granting of the right to vote in federal elections in 1960), the federal government stripped an Indian of his/her legal status as an Indian if (s)he acquired the federal vote or, until 1985, married a non-Indian man. Since passage of Bill C-31 in 1985, people thus stripped of their legal status, and their children, have been permitted to apply for legal reinstatement as Indians and as members of their former band. Under this controversial legislation,[8] bands without a membership code have one imposed by DIAND. Many Indians view this as a violation of their aboriginal right to determine their own group membership. Applicants for reinstatement who do not meet the requirements of membership in a given band become "general list" Indians. They do not share in the rights and wealth held by the members of the band into which they had sought admission, usually their ancestral band.

In contrast to this legalistic approach, the Australian constitutional definition of Aborigine uses three criteria: (1) self-definition as an Aborigine; (2) some aboriginal ancestry; and (3) acceptance as an Aborigine in the eyes of the aboriginal community. Though people of mixed ancestry in Canada could be legally excluded from Indian band membership, in Australia it is much less likely that such a person would be denied aboriginal status.[9]

In Australia, a stratification hierarchy based on skin colour has emerged: lighter skinned Aborigines are accorded more prestige than the darker skinned (black) ones. Such invidious, colour-based distinctions among a subordinant group usually reflect the values and practices of the dominant group. No similar differentiation has developed in Canada.

ABORIGINAL RIGHTS AND LAND

Land is at the heart of the conflict between aboriginal people and colonizing populations. To most aboriginal people, land is not merely real estate to be bought and sold like any other commodity. Nor is it merely a source of natural resource revenue. Rather, in aboriginals' world view, the land is a *spiritual* entity and the basis of the culture, lifestyle, and identity of the people. Many aboriginal cultures view the world in *holistic* terms, that is, as one large whole (or a large extended family), consisting of numerous interdependent parts. Hence, the cosmos, the land, the waters, the people, animals, and "things" which inhabit them are all viewed as spiritual beings which have wishes, rights, and obligations towards each other.

Canadian Native organizations and the federal and provincial governments spent over four years unsuccessfully trying to agree on the fundamental principles encompassed by the term "existing aboriginal rights" in that clause (section 35.1) of the Constitution Act (1982), which now recognizes and protects those rights. "Rights" are sociopolitical-legal constructions with a foundation in the moral order of society; because societal conceptions of morality change, the concept of aboriginal rights also changes.

Aboriginal rights are held by the descendants of the original people of Canada, by virtue of their ancestors' prior occupancy of the land. In Canada, those rights can be traced back historically to such crucial documents as the Royal Proclamation of 1763[10] and to the fact that most Canadian Native peoples have never explicitly given up their **sovereignty** or

AN ABORIGINAL WORLD VIEW

Canadian Indian lawyer and academic Leroy Little Bear has expressed this holistic world view, as it pertains to land, as follows:

> Land is communally owned; ownership rests not in any one individual, but rather belongs to the tribe as a whole, as an entity. The members of a tribe have an undivided interest in the land; everybody, as a whole, owns the whole. Furthermore, the land belongs not only to people presently living, but also to past generations and future generations, who are considered to be as much a part of the tribal entity as the present generation. In addition, the land belongs not only to human beings, but also to other living things (the plants and animals and sometimes even the rocks); they, too, have an interest (Little Bear, 1986: 243–59).

title to land through conquests, annexation, or treaty. Nevertheless, Canadian courts and politicians tended to practically dismiss the notion of aboriginal rights until 1973, when three of seven Supreme Court of Canada judges, hearing the land claim of the Nishga Indians of British Columbia, said the Nishgas do possess aboriginal rights to the land in dispute.[11]

Aboriginal political organizations in Canada use the term ''aboriginal rights'' more broadly, referring to the rights to (1) retain one's aboriginal identity and culture (rather than being subjected to forced assimilation); (2) choose between an aboriginal and a non-aboriginal way of life; (3) enjoy a land base or revenues from a land base, and (4) have adequately financed self-governing aboriginal institutions that provide at least as much self-determination for aboriginal peoples as other Canadians enjoy. These latter two forms of aboriginal rights, land base and self-government, cause grave concern to several provincial premiers. They fear the expense of aboriginal self-government, the loss of provincial Crown lands and revenues from them, and the loss of provincial powers to aboriginal governments. On the basis of these concerns and their professed lack of knowledge of what is meant by ''self-government,'' they blocked a proposed 1987 constitutional amendment which would have recognized Natives' inherent right to self-government.

In Canada, Natives have claimed vast tracts of land in the Arctic, Yukon, the Northwest Territories, British Columbia, and northwestern Ontario under the federal government's ''comprehensive claims'' policy. Claims of this sort have been settled with the Cree and Inuit of the James Bay and northern Quebec area (1975), and with the Inuvialuit of the Western Arctic. These modern treaties have provided Natives with a form of local or regional government; a small land (and water) base; land use privileges (e.g., hunting rights) in a larger geographical area; substantial financial compensation spread over many years; and a voice in (but not voting control over) various newly created state bodies governing such matters as land use, management of renewable resources, and environmental protection. These agreements also include economic development programs and/or corporations and mechanisms to enhance aboriginal culture and ensure aboriginal control over the education of aboriginal children.

In return, the Natives relinquished their previously unextinguished aboriginal title to vast areas of land. This latter provision raises two central issues—whether aboriginal title to the land should be extinguished (most Native leaders are adamant that it should not) and whether such large compensation payments should be made.

Claims negotiations have proceeded at a snail's pace. In an effort to speed up proceedings, a federal task force has recommended that the compensation payments in future settlements be drastically reduced and that aboriginal title not be extinguished. Under the regime proposed by this task force, Natives would have a greater role in governing the lands in dispute and would derive revenues from resource extraction by any non-Native corporations exploiting those lands.

Both the existing and proposed Canadian approaches differ markedly from contemporary land claims legislation in the United States or Australia. Admittedly, the Alaska Native Claims Settlement Act (1971) did extinguish aboriginal rights in return for almost one billion dollars in compensation payments. However, it granted ownership over large tracts of land to Native corporations. Shares in these are held now by Natives, but after 1991 they can be freely transferred to non-Natives, thereby diminishing or eliminating the aboriginal land base for future generations. Unlike Canada's James Bay and Northern Quebec Agreement, the Alaska legislation establishes no reserves and no permanent, ethnicly defined institutions, rights, privileges, or obligations. It is a clear manifestation of a **termination policy** and of an unbridled American faith in private enterprise. In Canada, both are very muted and are not found in post-1973 land claims policy.

In Australia, aboriginal lands fall into three categories.[12] The Crown-owned reserves amount to about 214 000 square kilometres. Unlike Canada, Australia has no requirement of aboriginal consent prior to alienation of aboriginal lands. As a result, huge amounts of aboriginal reserve lands have been taken from the Aborigines without their approval and sometimes without their knowledge, with devastating sociocultural consequences. The Australian courts, however, have refused to recognize an aboriginal right to the title to the lands. The second category of aboriginal lands is mission land (691 square kilometres) granted by the Crown to religious organizations to establish settlements of Aborigines. The aboriginal residents, with no recognized legal interests in these mission lands, have been evicted at the pleasure of religious organizations when some missions have closed.

Because of Aborigines' dissatisfaction with the administration of the reserves and missions (e.g., the requirement for an aboriginal to obtain a permit in order to visit another reserve, and other features akin to those found in an earlier era in Canada), in 1966 a third category of aboriginal lands[13] was established—namely, provincial-level Aboriginal Lands Trusts. Under aboriginal control but only partly independent from provincial governments, these trusts hold the title to the land and lease the land to aboriginals (individuals, companies, groups, or communities), develop it for economic purposes, and acquire new lands. However, inadequate funding has limited acquisitions.

Because Australia lacks the legal foundations for Aborigines' claims to their traditional lands, the courts have been less active on this matter than in Canada, and the churches, press, and legislatures have been more active. The Labour government of Gough Whitlam was instrumental in changing the terms of public debate from *whether* aboriginal land rights should be created/recognized in legislation, to *how much* land should be transferred and on

AN ADEQUATE LAND BASE?

A major issue for all aboriginal peoples is the adequacy of the land base to support the present and future aboriginal population. This is particularly important for the Métis, non-status Indians, and Indians on the numerous small reserves in British Columbia. Whereas in Canada the state has dragged its feet on this matter, in Australia much progress has been achieved. For instance, the Aboriginal Development Commission, with an annual budget of about $60 million, buys land on the open market for transfer to aboriginal communities and to house aboriginal legal services, medical services, housing associations, co-ops, and social centres.

what terms. Federal legislation was passed in 1976 granting aboriginal land rights in the Northern Territory, while major provincial land rights legislation was passed in the early 1980s in South Australia and New South Wales. The other provinces have also begun to legislate on this matter.

Only one example of such legislation can be discussed here: the relatively liberal federal statute pertaining to the Northern Territory. It establishes a land claims process that entitles Aborigines who "have common spiritual affiliations to a site on the land" to lay claim to Crown land. If the Aboriginal Land Commissioner rules in favour of the claimants, he recommends to the Minister and Cabinet that the land (excluding subsurface mineral rights) be turned over to one or more Aboriginal Lands Councils. If Cabinet accepts the recommendation, the land is transferred and cannot be sold to non-aborigines. As in some Canadian settlements, the aboriginal owners obtain leverage for economic gain and environmental protection by virtue of their right to veto any proposed mining of their lands.

Under this Australian statute, 40 percent of any such resource revenue goes to the Local Land Council, while the remainder can be given or loaned by the Minister for purposes that benefit other Aborigines in the Northern Territory.[14] This provision is important and contentious because such funds could enable the government to shirk its financial obligations to Aborigines. However, as a result of this statute and other mechanisms, over 30 percent of the land area of the Northern Territory is now under aboriginal control. Complementary legislation by the government of the Northern Territory preserves sacred sites, guarantees equal aboriginal participation in decision making, and **entrenches** aboriginal hunting/fishing/gathering rights on these lands. Quite different approaches have been taken, though, in the Australian provinces. About 10.5 percent of Australia's land mass is dedicated to exclusive aboriginal use.

RELATIONS BETWEEN NATIVES AND THE STATE

Historical Background

The state in Canada and Australia consists of the Cabinet, two Houses of Parliament, civil service bureaucracy, judiciary, police and army, Crown corporations, regulatory agencies, and prisons. In federal political systems the state exists at the level of the federal (or in Australia the commonwealth) government and the provincial (or in Australia, the state) government, although the provincial level does not duplicate all institutions of the federal level state.

A central feature of Canadian society is the activist or interventionist role the state plays in the lives of individuals, especially since World War II. This role has been particularly salient for status Indians for over a century. It is less pronounced in Inuit communities and less still among most Métis and non-status Indians in their capacity as Natives. In this section, we examine some issues and dimensions of this post-World War II relationship between the state and Indians, and compare Canada with Australia.

Contemporary relations between aboriginal peoples and the state can be understood only if we bear in mind the historical context: namely, (i) longstanding state policies of assimilation; (ii) the constitutional division of responsibilities between the federal and provincial governments; and in Canada (iii) the treaties; and (iv) the legal trust relationship between Indians and the Crown.

Both countries attempted to force the Natives to abandon their nomadic ways and settle down to an agricultural way of life, as farmers in Canada and as ranch hands in Australia. In addition, the state in both countries co-opted the churches, who were all too willing to "civilize" the Natives while seeking converts to their brand of Christianity. These efforts were part of a long line of attempts at social control.

The Constitution Act, 1867 (formerly known as the British North America Act, 1867) contains a provision—section 91.24—which gives the Canadian federal government jurisdiction over "Indians and lands reserved for the Indians." A later court ruling included the Inuit as Indians under section 91.24, although it exempted them from coverage under the Indian Act. This constitutional assignment of Indians and Inuit to federal jurisdiction results in a degree of legal uniformity that is absent in Australia, where the commonwealth and "provincial" levels of governments have shared jurisdiction over Aborigines since the referendum and constitutional amendment of 1967. In Canada, virtually all status Indians are administered under the Indian Act. In Australia, numerous provincial statutes produce considerable disparities, such as those between the repressive apartheid-like regime in Queensland and the liberal regime in South Australia. Disparities among Canadian Natives tend not to be rooted in the constitutional division of powers.

In Australia, no treaties were signed with the Aborigines, whereas in Canada numerous treaties were signed. In the maritimes, these were of the peace and friendship variety, while in northwestern Ontario, the Northwest Territories, and the prairie provinces, the written treaties contained clauses explicitly surrendering the land to the Whites. The circumstances surrounding the signing of many of these treaties call into question the integrity of the state. Major discrepancies have emerged between the state's written record of the transactions and provisions, on the one hand, and the testimony of Indian elders whose parents attended the signing, on the other hand (see, e.g., Cycon, 1984).

Written versions of the numbered treaties shown on the accompanying map generally included the following provisions: an agreement of peace and amity, the cession of land, initial payments to Indians, small annual payments in cash and/or goods, the designation of chiefs and councillors to negotiate and administer the treaty, guarantee of land reserved for Indians and/or right to use unoccupied territory in its natural state, and promises of government services, such as education and health care.

Figure 3

TREATY AREAS OF CANADA

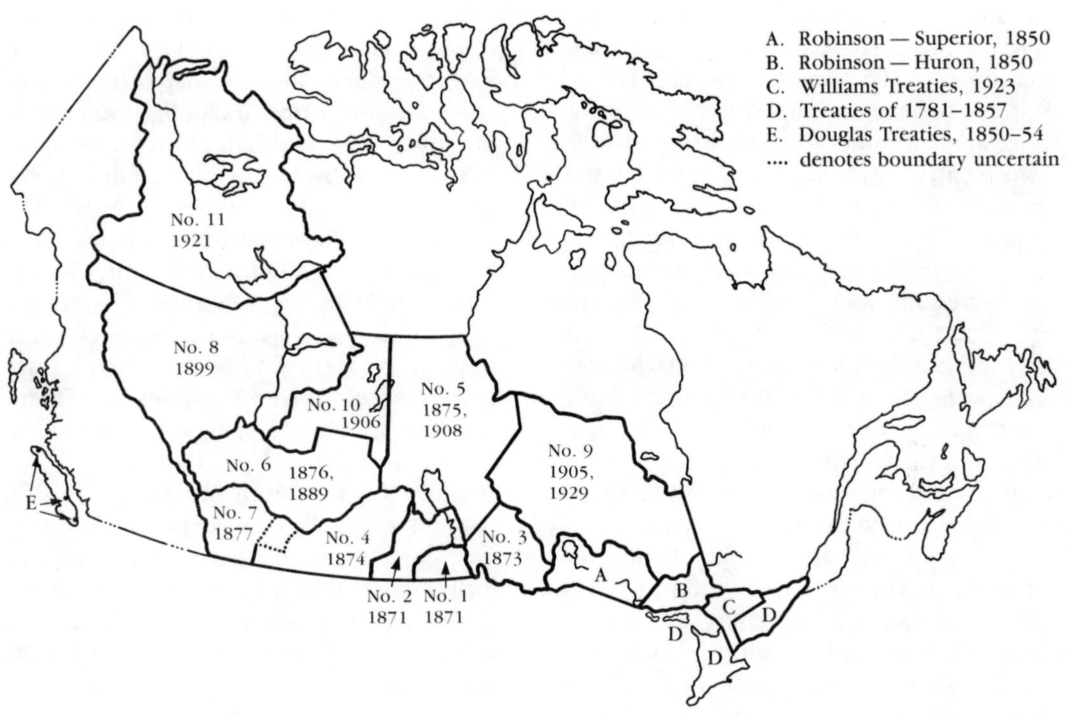

Source: Reproduced by permission of Indian and Northern Affairs Canada (revised October, 1977). Reproduced with permission of the Minister of Supply and Services Canada.

The federal state has since extended these services to that 43 percent of the Indian population not covered by treaty. In many respects, this extension has been to the advantage of the Indians involved. However, it has also extended the tentacles of the welfare state into Indian communities in detrimental ways (e.g., the creation of welfare dependency).

The treaties are also important because they provide a legal basis (rather than merely a moral basis) to some Indians' claims to government services, and because they have formed the basis of disunity among Indians in their dealings with the state. This disunity was exploited by the Alberta and Saskatchewan governments in their successful efforts to block a constitutional amendment on aboriginal rights at the First Ministers' and Aboriginal Leaders' Constitutional Conferences of the 1980s.

To treaty Indians, treaties are not relics of an earlier era without contemporary relevance, but solemn, mutual commitments which endure in perpetuity. Furthermore, treaties prove that the Indian nations were treated as sovereign nations at the time of early contact with Europeans. Treaty Indians feel they have never given up that sovereignty. This is why the Assembly of First Nations refused to compromise at the 1987 constitutional reform negotiations with the First Ministers.

Also very important to Indians is the federal government's trustee role, which legally obligates the state to act in the best interests of Indians when acting on their behalf. This complex and multi-faceted relationship is rooted in the Royal Proclamation of 1763, in various treaties and statutes from before and after confederation, and in moral and political considerations now and at the time of early contact.[15] The trustee relationship has meant different things in different historical eras and has been interpreted narrowly by some and broadly by others. The Supreme Court of Canada upheld the federal government's trustee obligations to Indians in the 1985 Musqueam decision, causing DIAND to be cautious in its dealings with and on behalf of Indians. The decision has also led other Indian bands to sue the federal government for alleged mismanagement of Indians' affairs in specific property transactions down through the years. Successful litigation could force the state to pay scores of millions of dollars in compensation. In Australia, nothing like the Canadian trustee relationship exists.

Natives as Individuals or Collectivities

Several sociological and political issues arise in Natives' relations with the state in Canada and Australia. The first is whether Aborigines are to be incorporated into society directly as individuals (**uniform incorporation**) or indirectly through intermediary organizations which attempt to represent the interests of Aborigines as a collectivity (**equivalent incorporation**), or some combination of both.

Canada's dominant ideology places much value on individual rights and shies away from collective rights, except where the interests of French Canadians or Roman Catholics are at stake. In Australia, the ethos of rugged individualism, along with past adherance to the notion of the survival of the fittest, also militates against the establishment of collective rights

Nevertheless, in both countries, legal provisions have now been made for collective rights and for a degree of equivalent incorporation. In Canada, these have taken several forms, including the protection of existing aboriginal and treaty rights in the constitution and the establishment of ethnicly based governments for the Cree and Naskapi Indians of Quebec, the Inuit of Northern Quebec, and the Sechelt Indians on British Columbia's southern coast, and others. Ironically, some of these statutes create a small-scale Native state apparatus in Native societies that were stateless prior to the arrival of Europeans.

In Australia, as in Canada, earlier attempted assimilation involved imposing the uniform mode of incorporation. But in Australia the recent departures from uniform incorporation have mainly taken the form of protecting aboriginal lands and sacred sites, not establishing self-government.

Representivity

A second major issue in Natives' relations with the state is the issue of ***representivity***. This refers to: (i) the accuracy or reliability with which the Native leadership conveys the needs, views, and aspirations of its constituents to outsiders; (2) the extent to which leaders' social characteristics mirror those of their constituents; and (iii) the responsiveness and accountability of the leaders to their constituents. As political anthropologist Sally Weaver (1985) points out, representivity in these three senses taken together constitutes an ideal—indeed, one of the paramount values—in the dominant political culture of both Canada and Australia.

Weaver found in both countries that acknowledgment of an aboriginal organization's representivity is conferred upon that organization, or withdrawn from it, as it suits the interests of the state at the time. Thus, representivity is constantly in a state of flux — constantly being assessed, acknowledged, withdrawn, and disputed. For instance, in both countries the federal/commonwealth state desperately needed Natives' advice to shape policies which would silence intense public criticism about the government's paternalism and insensitivity to the needs of Natives. Under that pressure, both governments set aside their earlier concerns about the representativeness of Native leaders and accepted the leadership of the day.

Over the longer term, the need for sound information in which both government and Native leaders have confidence has led to a three-stage evolutionary process which Weaver sees as similar in both countries. First, governments promote their own advisory committees; then governments fund Native organizations (the National Indian Brotherhood and others in Canada and the National Aboriginal Consultative Committee in Australia) to form their own lobby groups; and finally, these lobby groups are drastically restructured by government (Australia) or by the Natives themselves (Canada). Significantly, in the second stage the lobby groups encountered the insurmountable challenge of reconciling regional differences in the needs and aspirations of their extremely heterogeneous constituency, and when they failed at this, state officials challenged their representivity and, therefore, their legitimacy.

Social Control

A third issue in Natives' relations with the state concerns social control, or the imposition of sanctions (positive for conformity, negative for deviance), and the channelling of behaviour by restricting the actions of an individual or collectivity. The Australian state's refusal to provide adequate resources (e.g., for a policy research unit) to the National Aboriginal Conference (N.A.C.) (successor to the N.A.C.C.) sustained its passivity and removed N.A.C. as a significant political threat. By contrast, bureaucratic competition among Canadian government departments (specifically, DIAND and the Secretary of State) seeking to expand their **domain** resulted in substantial funding to N.I.B. (and its successor, The Assembly of First Nations) and to various other organizations.

The social control exerted by the state in Canada has usually taken place instead at the level of provincial Native organizations or individual bands.

The Indian Act of Canada has long been both a dominant feature of the state's relations with Indians and an instrument of pervasive social control over Indians. There is no direct counterpart in the lives of Australian Aborigines or Canadian Métis and Inuit, probably because the protectionist ethos out of which it emerged was not as fully developed in the dominant societies' view toward these latter three. The social control function of the Act is well illustrated by the power of the Minister to disallow band by-laws and by such amendments as those in 1927 (later repealed) that prohibited political organizing and the collection of funds for pursuing land claims.

Australia has had no single comprehensive statute like the Indian Act, but legislatively entrenched social control has been extensive. Indeed, legalized discrimination against Aborigines, especially in the late nineteenth and early twentieth centuries, was so extensive as to lead Australian social scientist C.D. Rowley to use the metaphor of Soviet novelist Alexander Solzhenitsyn's ''gulag archipelago'' to describe the ''islands'' of aboriginals scattered in isolation throughout the harsh Australian outback (Rowley, 1978: 14–15).

In both Canada and Australia, aboriginal peoples have had little voice in planning or operating the state bureaucracies in whose jurisdictions they fall. This is beginning to change significantly in both countries in the realm of education. Native leaders realize the futility of trying to achieve meaningful social, economic, and legal changes, while the aboriginal consciousness and identity are controlled by educational practices that reflect the values and priorities of the larger society. Hence, in Canada the N.I.B.'s policy of Indian control of Indian education is being implemented in an ever-increasing number of bands (219 by 1985).[16] In Australia, aboriginal control of aboriginal education has been slower because the National Aboriginal Education Committee and its provincial-level counterparts are merely advisory, rather than power-wielding bodies.

In both Canada and Australia, aboriginal peoples have been highly dependent upon the state due to their low socioeconomic status and their powerlessness. This dependency has led to the emerging desire for more self-determination or control over their own lives. In Canada, self-assertion has taken the form of demands for constitutional recognition of Natives' *inherent* right to self-government. We turn now to issues surrounding those demands, including issues pertaining to Natives' relations with the present **state apparatus**.

NATIVE SELF-GOVERNMENT AND PUBLIC OPINION

In 1969, a seminal event in Canadian Native affairs occurred when the federal state issued its **White Paper** proposal for changing the relationship between Indians and the larger Canadian society. Inspired by the high value that the **liberal philosophy** places upon equality among individuals, the report proposed a relationship which was one of uniform incorporation (as discussed above). Indian groups vehemently rejected this proposal, however, because it was fundamentally assimilationist. Indians embarked on a political renaissance that was to take them on an arduous journey toward self-government (equivalent incorporation). Other Native organizations followed suit.

Thus, in the 1980s the pivotal political issue in aboriginal affairs in Canada is aboriginal self-government. All other issues were largely held in abeyance while most national-level Native organizations sought a constitutional breakthrough which would recognize Natives' **inherent right to self-government**. Similarly, at the local or regional level, Natives increasingly took over other governments' responsibilities for administering — and sometimes designing—services for Natives. The proposals advanced by Natives ranged from the municipality-like status acquired by the Sechelt Band of British Columbia (and roundly denounced by many Indian politicians) to the Inuit proposal to divide the Northwest Territories in two and establish Nunavut (meaning "Our Land")—a new eastern Arctic territory under the control of the Inuit majority there.

Throughout most of the 1980s, the premiers of British Columbia, Alberta, and Saskatchewan blocked progress on constitutional reform in this area because, they claimed, they did not know what "self-government" meant.[17] Native leaders, on the other hand, pointed out that because of the enormous diversity among Natives, self-government would mean different things (involve different powers) in different local-level communities, and therefore could not be defined in precise legal terminology. Natives argued for a "top-down" approach, whereby the right to self-government would be enshrined in the constitution first and then variously defined through negotiations at the local or district level. However, the three most westerly provincial governments (joined in 1987 by Newfoundland) argued for a "bottom- up" approach, whereby agreements would be negotiated first at the local or district level and then enshrined in the constitution.[18]

The resulting impasse illustrates three features of Canadian society in this modern era: (1) Natives' extreme distrust of the Canadian state, formed on the basis of past and recent history; (2) the considerable power of the provincial-level state in Canadian society; and (3) the extreme reluctance of non-Native politicians toward alterations in the political institutions and constitutional division of powers.

The depth of the distrust is reflected in the fact that by 1988 self-government had come to be viewed by Indians as merely a vehicle being used by the federal government to shirk its financial obligations to Indians after transferring legal responsibilities to Indian governments.

Native self-government raises numerous social, political, and legal issues for Canadian society. Before addressing some of them, let us consider what self-government is in general terms, under most groups' definitions. It comprises up to six main components. The first is political institutions, which probably incorporate some aspects of local decision making from the traditional culture. These institutions must be accountable to the aboriginal people. The second component is control over group membership, which gives the group in question the ability to maintain social boundaries between itself and other groups or the larger society. The third component is fiscal support from economic development, from the federal government, and, for the Métis, probably from provincial governments. Self-government without an adequate financial base is a sham. The fourth component is a division of powers and responsibilities between the federal, provincial, and aboriginal governments.[19] This will vary greatly depending upon: the size and geographic location (rural, remote, or urban) of the Native population, the abundance or scarcity of natural resources, the priorities of the local-level Native community, the actual and potential management capacity of the Native population involved, economies of scale, and other factors.[20] The fifth component is a land base (e.g., Métis settlements, existing or expanded Indian reserves, or the eastern Arctic for the Inuit), without which the scope of the powers of Native governments would be narrow (e.g., Métis governments in a large city might have jurisdiction over little other than Métis education and some aspects of economic development). Finally, some Native governments might involve an "external reach," or a right to limited participation in certain aspects of Canada's foreign policy making, such as the provincial premiers enjoyed in the 1986–1987 "free trade" negotiations between Canada and the U.S.A. (see Gibbins and Ponting, 1986). Aboriginal self-government, thus conceived, is clearly not a national-independence form of separatism, contrary to what some mass media reports would have us believe.

Another conceptual approach to Native self-government highlights other issues (see Hawkes, 1985). The first is whether the government will be based on territoriality or ethnicity. In other words, will everyone in a particular geographic area come under the jurisdiction of the Native government there, or, conversely, will those of non-Native ethnicity (such as White teachers on a reserve) be excluded from the rights (e.g., voting rights) and obligations (e.g., obedience to the orders

SHOULD NATIVES HAVE SOVEREIGN OR DELEGATED POWERS?

One central issue in Native self-government is whether a Native government exercises sovereign or **delegated powers**. Natives argue for the former, the Canadian state argues for the latter. The main difference is that if powers are merely delegated to a Native government by the provincial or federal government, those powers can be taken away at a later time by that "senior" government, whereas powers recognized as being within the sovereign rights of a Native government could not be revoked by any other government. A major difference between Canada and the United States is that the activist U.S. Supreme Court long ago enunciated and recently confirmed "the doctrine of retained sovereignty," which means that Indian tribes are deemed to have never relinquished their sovereignty. They are treated as domestic dependent nations, and Native self-government is viewed as deriving from a source outside the United States' constitution. The position, which is taken by so-called "radicals" in Canada, is entirely consistent with this tenet of American jurisprudence. The "radicals" argue Indians should not seek the inclusion of the right to aboriginal self-government in the Canadian constitution because it is inconceivable that a sovereign Indian nation would be drawn into the constitution of another sovereign nation (Canada) and have its rights subjected to that nation's amending formula.

of the Native courts) associated with that Native government? Secondly, what is to be the geographical scope of the Native government — will it operate at the national level, at a regional or district level (possibly spanning provincial boundaries), or at the level of local communities? Thirdly, how autonomous will any Native government be — will it have merely administrative powers, or the power to make enforceable laws in a few fields, or will it have the power to make enforceable laws in numerous fields (some of which might be shared with another level of government)? It is likely that many of the different combinations (2 × 3 × 3) will be found eventually among aboriginal people in Canada.

Some observers have suggested that the adoption of forms of self-government acceptable to non-Native politicians would undermine the distinctiveness of traditional Native institutions of government, and would create a form of institutional assimilation where prior attempts at cultural assimilation failed. This concern is particularly acute with regard to forms of self-government that treat Native governments much like the governments of non-Native munipalities (e.g., the Sechelt model).

Perhaps the most fundamental concern about Native self-government is whether it will have a significant benefit at the grassroots level of Native communities. There are sound sociological reasons to expect that even when Native self-governments are only mildly successful, the net sociological impact on Native individuals would be profoundly positive. Elsewhere (Gibbins and Ponting, 1986) I have explained why I expect self-government to lead to a strengthening of the family unit, decreased truancy and drop-out rates in the schools, an increased sense of pride and positive identity, less alienation, a reclamation of some of the lost leadership potential in Native communities, and other benefits.

Although the financial cost of these benefits is likely to be high in the short term, over the longer term those costs will be largely offset by other savings (e.g., in welfare payments to Natives).

Aboriginal self-government now exists only to a very limited extent in this country. It is found mostly in the educational sphere, where hundreds of Indian bands have taken over full or partial control of on-reserve schooling. It is also found among the Cree, Inuit, and Naskapi peoples of northern Quebec, and the Inuvialuit of the western Arctic. However, it is of limited scope and, in the case of the Cree, has been plagued by implementation problems arising from the non-co-operation and abrogation of responsibilities of the Quebec and federal states. Elements of self-government are also found among diverse bands that have unilaterally, bilaterally, or trilaterally (with the federal and provincial governments) extended somewhat the jurisdiction of certain institutions of band government (e.g., child welfare agencies, on-reserve policing, Native courts). In the sense of control over membership, self-government also exists among those bands which have developed their own membership codes. Also, in the sense of moving out from under some of the provisions of the paternalistic Indian Act, self-government exists among the Sechlet Indians of British Columbia. The two extremes of aboriginal self-government in Canada are the Métis, for whom self-government is virtually absent, and the Northwest Territories, where at time of writing Natives occupy a bare majority of the twenty-five seats in the Territorial Assembly, and a Native person is the government leader. Attempts at self-government by the Inuit in the eastern Arctic have been stymied because of a lack of consensus with the Dene of the Northwest Territories concerning Nunavut's geographical borders. The Meech Lake accord also poses what is probably an insurmountable barrier to provincehood for Nunavut, the Northwest Territories, and Yukon.

In the United States and Australia the situation is quite different. Whereas the Indian Act of Canada focuses largely on regulating life internal to the reserve, legislation in the United States has been much more concerned with the external relations of tribes. For instance, U.S. legislation has no parallel to the sections of Canada's Indian Act pertaining to the powers of band councils. For example, tribal courts, which are common and active in the United States, have a wider ranging civil jurisdiction (e.g., marriage, divorce, child welfare, taxation, estates, licensing, commercial transactions, and real property) than those few Native courts which exist in Canada. Indeed, under the federal Indian Child Welfare Act (1978) in the United States, when an Indian child comes before a non-Native court, the latter must notify the relevant tribal court and withdraw from the case if the tribal court chooses to exercise jurisdiction.

Another major difference between Canada and the United States is in membership in the aboriginal group. Whereas in Canada, the federal government has interfered extensively, in the United States the courts have consistently recognized that one of a tribe's most basic powers is authority to determine its own membership.

The internal sovereignty of Indian tribes has been recognized for over a century and a half in the United States. Yet, the poverty of Indians there demonstrates that mere recognition of aboriginal government is no guaranteed solution to the problems of aboriginal peoples. Legal recognition must be accompanied by some political power in the larger society, and by adequate funding from the larger society or from economic development. Indians in the United States have usually had neither, for Indian issues are more marginal in U.S. political life than in Canadian political life. Thus, swings in United States policy (like defunding by the Ronald Reagan regime) have occurred without effective political opposition. U.S. laws pertaining to Indians have been more volatile and have exhibited dramatic reversals (Saunders, 1985).

In Australia, as in Canada, an extraordinary event around the early 1970s galvanized the aboriginal people's political consciousness. On the grounds of Parliament House, aboriginal people established an "aboriginal embassy"—an untidy scatter of dark tents set against the white backdrop of the Parliament buildings. This defiant civil disobedience not only caused White Australians to take notice of Aborigines and their grievances, but also became a symbolic rallying point for Aborigines, especially after clashes between demonstrators and police.

Yet, even since the aboriginal embassy incident, the Australian courts have sidestepped the issue of the sovereignty of aboriginal governments. There has been no recognition of sovereignty from the non-Native politicians.[21] The limited progress made towards self-determination, albeit not self-government, has been on four fronts: (1) symbolic recognition of the legitimacy of Aborigines' grievances and aspirations; (2) a fostering of aboriginal cultures and protection of sacred sites; (3) the recognition of land rights; and (4) economic development. Each will be addressed briefly below.

Three noteworthy steps of mainly symbolic value have been taken in the Aborigines' favour. The first is a resolution unanimously adopted by the Senate in 1975. It urged the government to acknowledge the Aborigines' prior ownership of the Australian land mass and to compensate them for the dispossession of their land. The second is a lengthy resolution passed by the House of Representatives in 1983. This speaks of "discharging a national responsibility to the Aboriginal and Torres Strait Islander people," acknowledges their prior ownership and occupancy of the land and the fact that their rights were "totally disregarded," and acknowledges the need for further measures "to ensure real equality and advancement." The resolution calls for various measures including land and compensation, programs for equality of opportunity, economic development programs, respect for (and application of) aboriginal customary law, protection of aboriginal cultural identity, and others. The third symbolic move has been the government's willingness to negotiate a "Makarrata," or compact, to redefine the relationship between Aborigines and the larger Australian society.

In recent years, one manifestation of the fostering of aboriginal cultures has been in the area of aboriginal traditional law. This is a marked departure from the pre-1960s judicial view of Aborigines as sub-humans, lacking a legal system. The departure has been facilitated by the voluminous work of Australian anthropologists and the Australian Law Reform Commission. Although some non-aboriginal courts have adopted the Canadian approach of applying tradition aboriginal family law in their interpretation of general legislation, the more common approach has been to give great weight to aboriginal law in the exercise of judicial discretion when sentencing aboriginal offenders. Aboriginal law is also recognized in various social security and social welfare schemes and at least eight statutes are aimed at protecting aboriginal sites and relics.

Although the land rights legislation has created new entities (e.g., Lands Councils) with more powers than the old Aboriginal Lands Trusts, most of those new entities lack legislative and judicial powers, or have legislative powers as meagre as those held by band councils under the Indian Act of Canada. On these aboriginal lands, a few aboriginal police forces and courts do exist, but, as in Canada, their jurisdiction is usually confined to minor crimes.

Finally, certain economic development initiatives have provided a modest step in the direction of self-determination. For instance, legislation in Queensland establishes Industries Boards as catalysts for economic development in aboriginal communities. These agencies carry on businesses themselves, or finance such businesses. They can also conduct market analyses and train Aborigines in business practices. These boards are far more independent from non-aboriginal influence than is their closest Canadian counterpart, the Native Economic Development Program.

As Morse concludes, Canada could benefit from adopting certain Australian practices. For instance, whereas the Canadian state has followed the narrow legislative approach of living up to only its "lawful obligations," Australia has recently been more concerned with fundamental issues of morality, fairness, and justice. Canada could also benefit from examining Australia's legal service programs, health organizations, hostels, community colleges, and national research institute for aboriginal studies. Australia's systems of transferring title to Aborigines for aboriginal lands, its recognition of traditional aboriginal law, and its protection of aboriginal sites are also worth examining in Morse's view.

In both Australia and Canada, public opinion impedes progress toward more self-government. Both countries are Western-style democracies, in which the majority rules and in which the aboriginal population forms a tiny minority. In the mid-1980s, the governing federal Labour Party in Australia abandoned planned national land rights legislation when faced with stiff opposition from provincial governments, which feared being voted out of office if they implemented sweeping land rights laws. Adopting a stance remarkably similar to that of the multinational oil companies seeking to build the Mackenzie Valley pipeline a decade earlier in Canada, the mining industry in Australia launched an advertising campaign that contended that all Australians' prosperity would suffer if Aborigines gained control of lands where mining was planned. A public opinion poll taken around that time found that only 18 percent of non-Aborigines supported aboriginal land rights, and 61 percent believed such new land rights would discriminate against Whites. Subsequently, Australian Prime Minister Bob Hawke suggested it would be counter-productive for the federal government to move "miles in front" of public opinion.

Public opinion in Canada, although uninformed, is more permissive than in Australia. In a comprehensive, nationwide survey of Canadian public opinion conducted in the fall of 1986, the author found that, compared to Australians, Canadians are much more receptive to aboriginal peoples' needs and rights on land-use matters. With regard to self-government for Natives, Canadians are slightly more supportive (44 percent) than antagonistic (37 percent), although this varies greatly from one region to another. However, Canadians' strong belief in equality leads them to resoundingly reject most notions of special status for Natives.[22] We seem not to realize that, for real equality to be attained by Natives, it is necessary that special arrangements and institutions be established.

CONCLUSION

It is useful to step back from the details of the Canadian and Australian cases to gain a broader picture of some dominant features of Canadian society which have emerged above.

Two dominant institutions in most societies are the economy and the state. Natives in Canada were largely relegated to the fringe of the Canadian economy even before multinational corporations became so prominent in our economy. Thus, the multinational corporation has not been a major factor in Native affairs in Canada, except for that minority of Natives living on the resource exploration frontier. Yet, even there the effect has been mixed, and many Natives now welcome resource development if measures to mitigate its most detrimental effects can be negotiated.

The state has played a central role in Natives' lives. The activist nature of the Canadian state stands out. At times the state has exploited Native people, as in the flooding of the lands of the James Bay Cree by a corporation (Hydro Québec) of the Quebec state. At times, it has intervened as a buffer between Natives and powerful corporations, as in the case of the historic Mackenzie Valley Pipeline Inquiry by state appointee Mr. Justice Thomas Berger. At times, as in the case of the Lubicon Indians of Alberta or the 1969 White Paper, the state has either stood by idly and allowed corporate interests to trample roughshod over Native interests, or has blindly pursued potentially destructive assimilationist policies. The state, acting in blissful ignorance and with the best of intentions, has also repeatedly meddled in Natives' internal affairs and triggered scenarios of misery and alienation. The Indian Act and the relocation of Inuit communities in the north are earlier examples of this, while the membership provisions of Bill C-31 is a contemporary example.

The activist character of the contemporary Canadian state is vividly demonstrated by two developments. The first is the extension of the welfare state into the Native population in the 1960s. The second is the competition between state bureaucracies to expand their domains in the early 1970s. The first development heightened the dependency mentality that the Department of Indian Affairs had already inculcated in numerous Indian communities, and exacerbated problems of alienation and alcohol abuse. Meanwhile, competition between state bureaucracies resulted in the funding of scores of Native organizations, many of which have been instrumental in the surprisingly rapid attainment of gains in self-determination.

Certain sectors of the state wield enormous power. For instance, the Department of Indian Affairs has been strong and pervasive; only within the last generation has it been effectively challenged by Indians and by other state agencies such as Treasury Board, the Department of Justice, and the Department of the Secretary of State. Similarly, the provincial-level states have amassed considerable expertise and other resources to build a strong power base for themselves. In the face of a fairly innocuous threat from Native governments, several provincial governments have jealously guarded the powers allotted to them in the Constitution Act of 1867. Their leaders have been unwilling to consider reform that involves some of the precepts that have long been in use in Australia or the United States. This suggests that they view our federation as extremely fragile.

Indeed, Canadian society in many respects *is* sociologically fragile, for our society is not based on commonality of culture, of ethnicity, or of ideology. Nor is Canada based on a shared economic interest or natural geographic boundaries and lines of trade and communication. Instead, Canada is a sociologically artificial creation. Canada's continued existence defies the sociological, economic, and geographical forces that shape the identity and cohesiveness of many other societies. In particular, the strain between French Canada and the rest of Canada — a strain underscored by Quebec's refusal to consent to the Constitution Act in 1982 — is like an exposed raw nerve in the body politic of Canada. Moreover, for a long time, that vulnerability has stood in the way of Natives. Non-Native politicians who refused to grant special status to Quebec found it logically and politically inconsistent to "grant" it to Natives, due to parallels between the situation of Natives and that of Quebec. To change metaphors, it is as if the Canadian body politic is allergic to the very medication that is needed to cure its ailment. However, the signing of the Meech Lake accord reveals that political leaders are quite willing to live with the opposite inconsistency (meaningful special status for Quebec but not for Natives).

On the one hand, Canadians fervently believe in equality. On the other hand, we practise a subtle form of racism, which is usually aversive rather than proactive. It manifests itself in our attitudes toward Third World immigrants and refugees and, for about 10 percent or less of the population, in attitudes toward Indians. Although Canada was founded upon diversity, when confronted with diversity by Native peoples or immigrants, we seem to feel insecure or threatened or affronted—to the point where we hesitate to develop the special institutions and constitutional provisions needed to accommodate that diversity. Instead, we seek to deny diversity in practice, while recognizing it mainly symbolically.

In building the provincial-level state as a powerful player in Canadian society, provincial politicians have conditioned us to distrust the national government. They have assiduously cultivated a sense of regional grievance. This also may have conditioned Canadians to look upon the special needs of Natives as privilege-seeking by Natives. Such "privileges," by definition, would leave others "disadvantaged" (even if only symbolically), and that may offend people. These same emotions are involved when provincial politicians and news media dismiss Natives' aspirations for self-government as "separatist" or as a "threat to national unity," as happened during the crucial 1987 First Ministers' and Aboriginal Leaders' Constitutional Conference, and in the month preceding it. Although effective as a means of manipulating public opinion, such behaviour obstructs progress toward the establishment of arrangements that would produce the real equality that the dominant ideology in Canada espouses.

Native self-government is perceived by provincial politicians as a threat. Unlike the United States, which recognized the internal sovereignty of Indian tribes, Canada seems to lack the absorptive capacity, the resilience, to withstand the relatively minor dislocations which Native self-government would entail. The Australian case, where the ideological and policy reorientation have had to be more extreme than in Canada, suggests those perceptions by Canadian provincial politicians are unduly alarmist.

As we look ahead through the 1990s and into the twenty-first century, we can probably form predictions as to the course of Native affairs by resorting to two truisms. The first truism is that in the final analysis power speaks louder than words or sentiment. The fact is that Natives (especially Métis) have very little power in Canadian society, while the state has very much power. However, Natives can embarrass Canadian politicans and citizens in international forums by calling international attention to the contradictions between the ideals we espouse and the reality of Natives' lives. Hence, we should anticipate that Natives will turn more to the court of international (particularly European) public opinion and to the United Nations to press their case for greater self-determination. To a limited extent also, Natives can ride the crest of other waves of political change, as they did in getting aboriginal rights included at all in the constitution. However, their ability to command resources and to force change is very limited.

Indian issues are greeted with moderate sympathy in some regions and with moderate antagonism in others, but in no province are they important enough in the public mind for that public opinion to constitute a power resource for Natives. Furthermore, the fact that public opinion at the overall national level is more supportive than antagonistic is of little consequence when the system of shared federal–provincial power enables certain provincial states to obstruct the larger national will. Thus, we can anticipate that in the absence of civil disobedience or violence, Natives will experience great difficulty in keeping Native issues on governments' agenda in the coming years.

Finally, we must also bear in mind that the state is not monolithic, but has many loci of power within it. Therefore, we must anticipate that even if Natives succeed in winning significant concessions from the elected non-Native politicians, Natives may have their aspirations frustrated by the power of an unco-operative state bureaucracy (federal and/or provincial) which perceives its own interests as being threatened.

A society cannot easily escape its history. In the past we took certain forks in the road, which closed certain options for relating to Natives. Certain approaches, such as paternalism and the intrusion of welfare, acquired considerable momentum and have had numerous vested interests — non-Native *and* Native — attached to them with the tenacity of barnacles on a ship. Over the last two centuries, we have created a mess and a maze in Native affairs. There are no perfect solutions, and we should not await their magical appearance. There are only partially flawed solutions. If they are to be attained, Canada's non-Native leaders must be more open to experimentation, based on the ideas and experiences of aboriginal peoples at home and abroad. Non-Native leaders must take a leap of faith and risk making new mistakes. Otherwise only small gains in self-determination and socioeconomic amelioration will be made in scattered Native communities. Whether the long-suffering patience of Natives will persist in the face of such gradualism is doubtful. Rather, we should anticipate a resort to more coercive strategies and tactics, such as civil disobedience, international embarrassment, and a selective use of the courts, as Natives seek to rechannel the course of Canadian history.

Notes

[1]Sociodemographic–economic data on Canadian Natives are taken from Sigger (1986).

[2]This and most of the history outlined below is from Stone (1974).

[3]The Torres Strait Islanders are a fishing people who occupy the islands of the straits, which separate northeastern Australia from Papua New Guinea. Their origins and culture are dramatically different from the aboriginals of continental Australia, as they are closer in language and culture to their Papua New Guinean neighbours.

[4]Altman's and Nieuwenhuysen's (1979) best estimate of the 1976 Aborigine population is about 121 500 or 0.87 percent of the total Australian population. In the 1981 Australian census, about 160 000 persons identified themselves as Aborigines or Torres Strait Islanders.

[5]Morse reports 1981 census data showing only three hundred Aborigines have any kind of post-secondary degree (Morse, 1984:9).

[6]The Smallboy colony in Alberta is an exception to the Canadian trend.

[7]For a discussion of the outstation movement,

see Altman and Nieuwenhuysen (1979:76–82).

[8]See Kathleen Jamieson's postscript to her chapter on "Sex Discrimination and the Indian Act" (1986) for a discussion of the controversial aspects of Bill C-31.

[9]However, various other statuses in Australia use other definitions of "aboriginal." (See Morse, 1984:16–18.)

[10]The Royal Proclamation of 1763 recognized Indian tribes as nations and required that land could be purchased from Indians only at special public meetings convened with them for that purpose.

[11]This sentence oversimplifies a complex issue. For a more detailed introduction to aboriginal rights, see Little Bear (1986), Asch (1984) or Boldt and Long (1986).

[12]The discussion of land in Australia is taken from Morse (1984).

[13]To avoid confusion, the term "province" is used in this chapter to refer to the states of Australia, which are analogous to Canadian provinces.

[14]This income redistribution feature is quite unlike any provisions in law in Canada. Here, a handful of Indian bands have acquired enormous resource revenues amounting to hundreds of millions of dollars, while the vast majority of bands remain poor.

[15]For a detailed treatment of the trustee relationship, see Nahwegahbow et al. (1983).

[16]For a useful discussion of Canada in comparative perspective, see Jordon (1986).

[17]Significantly, now knowing what the pivotal term "distinct society" means when applied to Quebec in the 1987 Meech Lake constitutional accord did not prevent those same premiers from adopting that accord.

[18]One of the reasons why this was unacceptable to Natives is that such a project would be subject to the constitutional amending formula which would enable, say, the three western provinces to block the constitutional entrenchment of an agreement reached between the Micmacs and the federal and Nova Scotia governments.

[19]In our complex, contemporary, Canadian society with its activist state at both the provincial and federal level, relations between governments are extremely important to the smooth operation of the economic and social (e.g., education, health care) life of the society. This is particularly important in areas of shared jurisdiction. Therefore, in the crucial sphere of intergovernmental relations, it might become necessary for Natives to form over-arching national-level governments if their interests are to be effectively represented. However, maintaining the cohesion of a body representing such heterogeneous Native interests would be a herculean task.

[20]A longer list is provided in Cowie (1987).

[21]This and the material below is drawn from Morse (1984).

[22]On three different questions where respondents were presented with a choice between a particular type of special status for Natives or no special status for Natives, a consistent 63 to 65 percent favoured the no special status option. Striking similarities emerged in the 1984 National Social Science Survey of urban Australians. When asked whether they thought Aborigines should get special benefits from the governments or should be treated no differently than anyone else, 71 percent chose the latter and 20 percent chose the former.

DISCUSSION QUESTIONS

1. Put yourself in the shoes of a provincial premier who himself is favourable to Native self-government on moral grounds, but whose province's electorate is not. What is your proper role as a political *leader* in a democracy—to try to lead public opinion or to follow public opinion?

Does your answer change at all when you take into account the political fate of two political leaders who played a leadership role in trying to change public opinion — Brian Mulroney on capital punishment and Ed Broadbent on pulling Canada out of the North Atlantic Treaty Organization (NATO)?

2. What potential conflicts do you see between individual rights (as defined in the Charter of Rights and Freedoms) and collective rights, where aboriginal self-government is implemented?
3. What are the advantages that accrue to aboriginal people from a policy of aboriginal control of aboriginal education?
4. Why have assimilationist policies aimed at Indians failed? That is, what sociological realities do such policies contradict?
5. Sociologically, politically, and from a human rights perspective, what are the fatal flaws in the suggestion that Indians should be put on one vast reservation in northern Canada and left alone to "do their own thing?"
6. What are the essential differences between Natives' situation in Canada and the apartheid system in South Africa? Consider a recent controversy in Native affairs in Canada in terms of the ways in which it involves movement closer to or away from an apartheid model?

GLOSSARY

activist state a state whose institutions intervene extensively in the economic and social life of the society through regulatory agencies, Crown corporations, and the provision of programs, incentives, and services

Bill C-31 a 1985 federal statute which amended the Indian Act in an attempt to remove the sex discrimination in the Act's band membership provisions. In practice, this controversial legislation has enabled the reinstatement to registered Indian status of tens of thousands of Indian women and their children, but has also merely displaced the sex discrimination onto later generations.

delegated powers powers transferred by one level of the state to either another level of the state or to some other organization. This delegation of powers can usually be rescinded unilaterally.

domain (organizational) the field of involvement of an organization, including its functions, clients, and mandate

economies of scale the per unit cost savings that can be attained by producing a product or service (e.g., a government service) for a large market rather than for a small market

enfranchisement literally, the act of acquiring the right to vote. However, in the Native affairs realm, the term refers to an Indian giving up his/her status as a registered Indian, voluntarily or involuntarily. Prior to 1960, Indians could obtain federal voting rights only by giving up their Indian status, but since then the right to vote in federal elections has been held by all Indians. Prior to the passage of Bill C-31 (an act to amend the Indian Act) in 1985, a common form of enfranchisement was that of an Indian woman who married a non-Indian.

equivalent incorporation a means of incorporating individuals into participation in the political, social, and economic rights of the society. This involves making those rights contingent upon one's membership in a legislatively recognized group, organization, or category within the society

entrenchment protection of a right or principle by placing it in the constitution or in some other statute that will be difficult to revoke

inherent right to self-government Native leaders' view that aboriginal people not only possess the right to self-government, but that it comes to them from some higher authority than the laws or constitution of non-Native governments. This higher authority is often specified as The Creator (The Great Spirit).

liberal philosophy a world view which places high value on individual rights and rejects the notion of group rights, especially in the sense of special rights granted on the basis of racial or ethnic criteria. To the liberal, government (the state) is first and foremost an instrument for maintaining law and order, achieving economic and social progress, and creating the conditions of individual liberty.

sovereignty the right and ultimate authority to make decisions and take actions affecting a certain people and/or a certain territory. The history of the doctrine of sovereignty is the history of competing and often conflicting claims to the legitimate exercise of authority. Historically, Indians granted their customs and traditions—not their chiefs or elders—the authority to guide their behaviour.

the state the various branches and levels of government, including the Cabinet, legislative bodies, the civil service bureaucracy, the judiciary, police and army, Crown corporations, regulatory agencies, and prisons. The state frequently contains competing or conflicting interests either across levels (e.g., federal vs. provincial) or within a single level (e.g., two federal departments competing for the same clientele).

state apparatus the non-elected components of the state

termination policy a government policy designed to eliminate the special rights or privileges of Natives or the special legislative provisions for Natives, such that Natives will be treated like any other members of the society. An assimilationist policy.

uniform incorporation a means of incorporating individuals into participation in the political, social, and economic rights of the society as co-equal individuals, without any intermediary role being played by any membership in a racial or ethnic category or organization. It is inherently assimilative.

welfare state a society in which governments make available to citizens a wide range of payments and/or social services for the purpose of providing a basic minimal standard of health and general living conditions to be enjoyed by all. The hallmark of the welfare state is that governments, rather than private corporations, usually deliver these payments and services.

White Paper a formal document which presents specific new policy directions that a government intends to take in a particular policy field such as national defence, transportation, or Native affairs.

Bibliography

Altman, Jon C. and Hohn Nieuwenhuysen
1979 *The Economic Status of Australian Aborigines*. London: Cambridge University Press.

Asch, Michael
1984 *Home and Native Land*. Toronto: Methuen.

Boldt, Menno and J. Anthony Long (eds.)
1985 *The Quest for Justice: Aboriginal Peoples and Aboriginal Rights*. Toronto: University of Toronto Press.

Cowie, Ian B.
1987 *Future Issues in Jurisdiction and Coordination between Aboriginal and Non-Aboriginal Governments.* Kingston, Ontario: Institute for Intergovernmental Relations, Queen's University.

Cycon, Dean et al.
1984 *Treaty Six (1876) Hearing–October 1983: Hearings, Findings and Conclusions*, mimeo.

Gibbins, Roger and J. Rick Ponting
1986 "An Assessment of the Possible Impact of Aboriginal Self-Governments in Canada." Pp. 171–245 in Alan Cairns and Cynthia Williams (eds.) *The Politics of Gender, Ethnicity and Language in Canada*. Toronto: University of Toronto Press.

Hawkes, David C.
1985 *Aboriginal Self-Government: What Does It Mean?* Kingston, Ontario: Institute of Intergovernmental Relations, Queen's University.

Jamieson, Kathleen
1986 "Sex Discrimination and the Indian Act." Pp. 112–36 in J. Rick Ponting (ed.) *Arduous Journey: Canadian Indians and Decolonization*. Toronto: McClelland and Stewart.

Jordon, Dierdre F.
1986 "Education and the Reclaiming of Identity: Rights and Claims of Canadian Indians, Norwegian Sami, and Australian Aborigines". Pp. 260–283 in J. Rick Ponting (ed.) *Arduous Journey: Canadian Indians and Decolonization*. Toronto: McClelland and Stewart.

Little Bear, Leroy
1986 "Aboriginal Rights and the Canadian 'Grundnorm.' " Pp. 243–59 in J. Rick Ponting (ed.) *Arduous Journey: Canadian Indians and Decolonization*. Toronto: McClelland and Stewart.

Morse, Bradford W.
1984 *Aboriginal Self-Government in Australia and Canada*. Kingston, Ontario: Institute of Intergovernmental Relations, Queen's University.

Nahwegahbow, David C. et al.
1983 *The First Nations and the Crown: A Study of Trust Relationships*. Ottawa: Research Report Prepared for the Special Parliamentary Committee on Indian Self-Government.

Rowley, C.D.
1978 *A Matter of Justice*. Canberra: Australian National University Press.

Sanders, Douglas
1985 *Aboriginal Self-Government in the United States*. Kingston, Ontario: Institute of Intergovernmental Relations, Queen's University.

Sealey, D. Bruce and Antoine S. Lussier
1975 *The Métis: Canada's Forgotten People*. Winnipeg: Manitoba Métis Foundation Press.

Siggner, Andrew J.
1986 "The Socio-demographic Conditions of Registered Indians." Pp. 57–83 in J. Rick Ponting (ed.) *Arduous Journey: Canadian Indians and Decolonization*. Toronto: McClelland and Stewart.

Stone, Sharman, N. (ed.)
1974 *Aborigines in White Australia: A Documentary History of the Attitudes Affecting Official Policy and the Australian Aborigine, 1697–1973*. London: Heineman Educational Books.

i n d e x